Lecture Notes in Computer Science 14771

Founding Editors

Gerhard Goos
Juris Hartmanis

Editorial Board Members

The series Lecture Notes in Computer Science (LNCS), including its subseries Lecture Notes in Artificial Intelligence (LNAI) and Lecture Notes in Bioinformatics (LNBI), has established itself as a medium for the publication of new developments in computer science and information technology research, teaching, and education.

LNCS enjoys close cooperation with the computer science R & D community, the series counts many renowned academics among its volume editors and paper authors, and collaborates with prestigious societies. Its mission is to serve this international community by providing an invaluable service, mainly focused on the publication of conference and workshop proceedings and postproceedings. LNCS commenced publication in 1973.

Markku-Juhani Saarinen · Daniel Smith-Tone
Editors

Post-Quantum Cryptography

15th International Workshop, PQCrypto 2024
Oxford, UK, June 12–14, 2024
Proceedings, Part I

Editors
Markku-Juhani Saarinen
Tampere University
Tampere, Finland

Daniel Smith-Tone
University of Louisville
Louisville, KY, USA

National Institute of Standards
and Technology
Gaithersburg, MD, USA

ISSN 0302-9743 ISSN 1611-3349 (electronic)
Lecture Notes in Computer Science
ISBN 978-3-031-62742-2 ISBN 978-3-031-62743-9 (eBook)
https://doi.org/10.1007/978-3-031-62743-9

This Springer imprint is published by the registered company Springer Nature Switzerland AG
The registered company address is: Gewerbestrasse 11, 6330 Cham, Switzerland

If disposing of this product, please recycle the paper.

Preface

PQCrypto 2024, the 15th International Conference on Post-Quantum Cryptography, was held at the Mathematical Institute, University of Oxford, United Kingdom on June 12–14, 2024. The PQCrypto conference series provides a venue for the communication of research results on cryptography under the assumption that large-scale quantum computers are available to adversaries. Since its inception, the conference focus has grown to serve not only academic and theoretical work in post-quantum cryptography but also applied and technical work, further developing the science and advancing the practical aspects of implementation and deployment of post-quantum cryptographic schemes.

PQCrypto 2024 utilized a double-blind review model. Submissions were required to be anonymized for review. 76 papers by 225 authors from 23 countries fulfilled the technical criteria and were accepted for peer review. Each one of these papers was reviewed by at least three members of the program committee. The PQCrypto 2024 program committee consisted of 44 members and additionally 28 subreviewers conducted 31 reviews. The committee then engaged in an intensive discussion phase, conducted online. Through this process, the Program Committee selected a total of 28 papers for inclusion in the technical program and for publication in these proceedings.

The diverse array of accepted articles found in these proceedings discuss multiple research arenas within the scope of the conference, including code-based cryptography, group-action-based cryptography, isogeny-based cryptography, lattice-based cryptography, multivariate cryptography, quantum algorithms, and applications.

The success of this iteration of PQCrypto was due to the efforts of many individuals and organizations. We are indebted to everyone who contributed to making PQCrypto 2024 a success. We owe thanks to the many scientists, engineers, and authors who submitted their work (of notably high average quality) to our conference. We would like to thank all members of the Program Committee and the external reviewers whose commitment and labor-intensive efforts in evaluating and discussing the submissions allowed us to compile a technical program of such high quality.

We thank our hosts, the Mathematical Institute, University of Oxford for excellent conference facilities and support. Our General Chairs Federico Pintore and Ali El Kaafarani created the event, and additionally we would like to thank Elvira Carasol and others at PQShield for local organization. We also wish to express our gratitude to Springer for handling the publication of these conference proceedings.

June 2024

Markku-Juhani Saarinen
Daniel Smith-Tone

Organization

General Chairs

Ali El Kaafarani   PQShield and University of Oxford, UK
Federico Pintore   University of Trento, Italy

Program Committee Chairs

Markku-Juhani O. Saarinen   Tampere University, Finland and PQShield, UK
Daniel Smith-Tone   National Institute of Standards and Technology,
                                        USA and University of Louisville, USA

Program Committee

Magali Bardet   University of Rouen Normandie, France
Daniel J. Bernstein   UIC, USA/RUB, Germany/Academia Sinica,
                                        Taiwan
Ward Beullens   IBM, Switzerland
Olivier Blazy   École Polytechnique, France
Katharina Boudgoust   CNRS, Univ Montpellier, LIRMM, France
Daniel Cabarcas   Universidad Nacional de Colombia sede
                                        Medellín, Colombia
Ryann Cartor   Clemson University, USA
Sanjit Chatterjee   Indian Institute of Science, India
Anupam Chattopadhyay   Nanyang Technological University, Singapore
Chen-Mou Cheng   BTQ Technologies Corp, Japan
Jung Hee Cheon   Seoul National University, Republic of Korea
Thomas Decru   Université libre de Bruxelles, Belgium
Martin Ekerå   KTH Royal Institute of Technology and Swedish
                                        NCSA, Sweden
Thibauld Feneuil   CryptoExperts, France
Scott Fluhrer   Cisco Systems, USA
Philippe Gaborit   University of Limoges, France
Tommaso Gagliardoni   Kudelski Security, Switzerland
Qian Guo   Lund University, Sweden
Michael Hamburg   Rambus Cryptography Research, USA

David Jao	University of Waterloo, Canada
Thomas Johansson	Lund University, Canada
Shuichi Katsumata	PQShield and AIST, Japan
John Kelsey	NIST, USA and KU Leuven, Belgium
Jon-Lark Kim	Sogang University, Republic of Korea
Elena Kirshanova	Technology Innovation Institute, UAE
Dustin Moody	NIST, USA
Ray Perlner	NIST, USA
Edoardo Persichetti	FAU, USA and Sapienza University, Italy
Thomas Pöppelmann	Infineon, Germany
Thomas Prest	PQShield, France
Angela Robinson	NIST, USA
Mélissa Rossi	ANSSI, France
Palash Sarkar	Indian Statistical Institute, India
Nicolas Sendrier	Inria, France
Benjamin Smith	Inria, France
Damien Stehlé	ENS Lyon, France
Rainer Steinwandt	University of Alabama in Huntsville, USA
Tsuyoshi Takagi	University of Tokyo, Japan
Atsushi Takayasu	University of Tokyo, Japan
Jean-Pierre Tillich	Inria, France
Yang Yu	Tsinghua University, China
Yu Yu	Shanghai Jiao Tong University, China
Aaram Yun	Ewha Womans University, Republic of Korea
Rina Zeitoun	IDEMIA, France

Additional Reviewers

Abel Laval	Jonas Meers
Adrien Vinçotte	Karan Khathuria
Alexander Karenin	Keewoo Lee
Andre Esser	Matthieu Rivain
Changmin Lee	Minki Hhan
Charles Meyer-Hilfiger	Minsik Kang
Denis Nabokov	Nicolas Aragon
Erik Mårtensson	Olivier Ruatta
Giulia Gaggero	Peter Pessl
Huiwen Jia	Takanori Yasuda
Hyeongmin Choe	Thom Wiggers
Jesse Elliott	Yasuhiko Ikematsu
Joel Gärtner	Youcef Mokrani
Johan Håstad	Yu Sasaki

Contents – Part I

Lattice-Based Cryptography

Contents – Part II

Quantum Algorithms

Transforms and Proofs

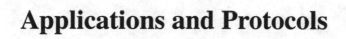

Applications and Protocols

Post-quantum Secure ZRTP

Loïc Ferreira[1]([✉])[iD] and Johan Pascal[2]

[1] Orange Innovation, Applied Crypto Group, Caen, France
loic.ferreira@orange.com
[2] Belledonne Communications, Grenoble, France
johan.pascal@linphone.org

Abstract. ZRTP is an authenticated key exchange protocol for establishing secure communications for Voice over IP applications. In this paper, we devise a post-quantum variant of ZRTP that achieves mutual authentication, session key privacy and forward secrecy against a post-quantum attacker. We correct the original ZRTP protocol to thwart a reflection attack against authentication (when the latter relies upon signatures) and avoid misbinding issues that could potentially lead to unknown key-share attacks. We prove the security of our post-quantum ZRTP protocol in a strong security model. Finally, we provide a fully functional and efficient open-source code of the corresponding application.

Keywords: Authenticated key exchange · Post-quantum cryptography · Security model · ZRTP · VoIP

1 Introduction

1.1 Context

The development of quantum computing threatens the security of most of the cryptographic mechanisms implemented and used in their devices by billions of users on a daily basis. The algorithm devised by Peter Shor [68,69] breaks the main public-key algorithms that are the very foundation of our digital life. In order to replace the current, quantum-unsafe public-key algorithms, new encryption and signature algorithms are proposed. This process received a lot of impetus with the post-quantum "competition" launched by NIST in 2016 and still ongoing.[1] This initiative was followed by other internal processes (e.g., China[2], Korea[3]).

Devising quantum-resistant public-key algorithms is a necessary but preliminary step. Indeed, these algorithms are involved in more complex cryptographic mechanisms: the security protocols. In real-life, the data exchanged every day

---

[1] https://csrc.nist.gov/Projects/post-quantum-cryptography.
[2] https://www.cacrnet.org.cn/site/content/854.html.
[3] https://kpqc.or.kr/.

© The Author(s), under exclusive license to Springer Nature Switzerland AG 2024
M.-J. Saarinen and D. Smith-Tone (Eds.): PQCrypto 2024, LNCS 14771, pp. 3–36, 2024.
https://doi.org/10.1007/978-3-031-62743-9_1

through the communication networks are protected by these security protocols. Accordingly, in parallel to the NIST process, numerous standardisation bodies (e.g., IETF, ISO/IEC, ETSI, ITU, ENISA, GSMA) inventory the technical standards vulnerable to the Shor's algorithm, and adapt these protocols to achieve a post-quantum security level. One of the next steps, in order to provide the users with the tools and resources they need to withstand quantum attacks, is to deliver efficient, quantum-resistant and fully functional communication applications. In line with this set of works, we propose a post-quantum variant of the ZRTP protocol used to secure VoIP communications, accompanied by a functional and efficient open-source code.

1.2   Related Work

Post-quantum Key Exchange Protocols. The advent of quantum computing is followed in parallel by the development of variants of key exchange protocols that aim at achieving post-quantum security. These works affect mainly popular cryptographic mechanisms used to establish secure tunnels: TLS 1.2 [22,29], TLS 1.3 [73,77], KEMTLS [32,66,67], IKEv2 [41,42,75], SSH [54], WireGuard [52,56], Noise [5]. These proposals are, for some of them, supported by implementations and benchmark results [31,36,45,47,50,64,74].

Post-quantum Signal. Regarding more specifically the authenticated key exchange protocols used in secure communication applications, Signal [71] and its X3DH [62] key exchange sub-protocol are one of the rare to be subject to post-quantum variants.

Brendel, Fischlin, Günther, Janson, Stebila [27] try to map the concept of DH-based protocol used in Signal into a Key Encapsulation Mechanism (KEM)-based one, and propose the notion of "split KEM" to retain the reusability of DH-based protocols when a (post-quantum) KEM is implemented instead. This means that the sender's static public key must be sent to the receiver in order for the latter to encapsulate a secret value. This implies an additional message flow and also breaks the asynchronicity of the Signal protocol. A limitation of this proposal is that it works for specific instantiations of the split KEM scheme and the proposed candidates become insecure when keys are reused. Also, the proposal does not take into account that one of the public keys in the genuine X3DH protocol is in fact used both as DH share (to provide implicit authentication) and signature key (to reinforce forward secrecy [71, Section 4.5]). In Brendel et al.'s proposal this would translate into yet another public key to retrieve and to deal with.

Hashimoto, Katsumata, Kwiatkowski and Prest [48,49] take a different approach with respect to the various X3DH public keys while retaining the same security properties. They define a security model (based on Canetti-Krawczyk type of models [30,58]) to formally enlighten the security properties guaranteed by the X3DH protocol. They propose a generic construction of the X3DH protocol based on standard cryptographic primitives that can be based on post-quantum assumptions, resulting in the first post-quantum secure replacement of the protocol. In addition, their protocol provides enhancements in some security aspects (impersonation) and is more limited in others (deniability, depending on the signature type), compared to the genuine X3DH protocol. Further, they deliver an open-source implementation of their protocol (based on PQClean[4] and LibTomCrypt[5]).

Cremers, Fontaine and Jacomme [35] use formal methods to provide mechanized proofs of the post-quantum computational security of Hashimoto et al.'s proposal.

In a concurrent work, Brendel, Fiedler, Günther, Janson, Stebila [26] propose a generic construction of a deniable Signal-like AKE protocol based on a designated verifier signature [53] and a KEM. When the designated verifier signature is instantiated with a ring signature, Brendel et al.'s proposal becomes very close to the scheme described by Hashimoto et al. [49].

The previous works propose post-quantum only variants of X3DH. The Signal designers adopt a different strategy and describe a hybrid key exchange protocol that they call PQXDH [57]. The latter is obtained from X3DH with the addition of a (ephemeral) post-quantum public key to the initial receiver's DH public keys. When Alice wants to send a message to Bob, she computes a first shared secret from the same various DH secrets (as in a X3DH run) augmented with the secret output by the KEM encapsulation she does with Bob's post-quantum public key. The authentication of parties remains classical.

ZRTP. The ZRTP protocol has been subject to a very small amount of analysis. Bresciani and Butterfield [28] use formal methods with ProVerif to prove that ZRTP is a secure protocol. That is, an adversary cannot learn the session key. Their analysis is done in the Dolev-Yao [39] model and assumes in particular that no attack against the authentication occurs.

Bhargavan, Brzuska, Fournet, Green, Kohlweiss, Zanella-Béguelin [15] present two attacks against ZRTP. The first one enables to modify one of the protocol message (initiator's Hello) without the change being detected, because the message is in fact independent of any further computations done during the protocol run. The adversary can leverage this flaw to change the cryptographic algorithms indicated in the Hello message and influence on the final ciphersuites choice. Although such a scenario is undesirable, its consequences are in fact minor since there are no "weak" ciphersuites in ZRTP. The second scenario presents a cross-protocol attack. ZRTP provides different key exchange modes: one is based on an ephemeral Diffie-Hellman exchange, another on a preshared symmetric key. Moreover, mutual authentication and person-in-the-middle detection can be done by comparing aloud a small substring of the main session secret (the so-called "Short Authentication String" (SAS)), instead of using signatures. Bhargavan et al. show how to interleave the DH and preshared key modes to make two honest parties compute the same SAS although the adversary sits in between the two parties (i.e., the adversary computes a dif-

---

[4] https://github.com/PQClean/PQClean.
[5] https://github.com/libtom/libtomcrypt.

ferent fresh session key with each honest party). That is, this attack breaks at the same time the authentication (when based on the SAS) and the key secrecy in ZRTP. However, Bhargavan et al. conclude that the preshared key mode is not widely implemented, and when it is, then the SAS-based authentication is unlikely proposed.

1.3 Contributions

Our contributions are the following:

- We devise a quantum-resistant authenticated key exchange protocol based on the (classical) ZRTP protocol (we do not consider the preshared key mode but only the ephemeral DH-based key exchange mode), that provides in particular mutual authentication, session key privacy and forward secrecy.
- We enhance the resulting protocol with several modifications that enable to save bandwidth, thwart a reflection attack against authentication (when the latter relies upon signatures) and avoid misbinding issues that could potentially lead to unknown key-share attacks.
- We formally prove the security of our post-quantum ZRTP protocol in a strong security model.
- We implement, test and deliver a fully functional and efficient open-source code of our post-quantum ZRTP protocol.[6]

2 Security Model

2.1 Execution Environment

In this section, we present the used security model for authenticated key exchange (AKE) protocols [37]. The corresponding security experiment is depicted by Fig. 1.

We say that an adversary is *classical* if it has access to a classical (not quantum) computing power. A *post-quantum* adversary has access to a quantum computing power (in addition to a classical one). The (classical or post-quantum) adversary interacts with the system using only classical queries.

The (post-quantum) adversary that we consider is active, controls all communication and can forward, alter, drop any message exchanged by honest parties, or insert new messages. It is also able to corrupt long-term public keys and reveal session keys. The goal of the adversary is to break any of the security properties presented in Sect. 2.2.

---

[6] The current version of this source code makes use of "Short Authentication Strings" (SAS) in order for the communicating parties to authenticate. Mutual authentication by means of signatures is deferred to a future version. Yet, the protocol we describe and analyse in this paper relies upon signatures for the authentication.

Parties. A two-party protocol is carried out by a set of parties. Each party u has an associated pair of long-term public and private keys (spk_u, ssk_u). The algorithm Keygen generates a new pair of long-term keys. The public keys spk_u are registered in a list $list_{spk}$. When the long-term private key ssk_u of party u is corrupted at time time, then $corr_u$ is set to time.

Instance. Each party can take part in multiple parallel executions of the protocol. Each run of the protocol is called a session. To each session of a party u, an instance π_u^i is associated which embodies this session's execution of the protocol and maintains the following state specific to the session:

- role $\in \{\bot, \mathtt{init}, \mathtt{resp}\}$: the role of the instance in the protocol execution, being either the initiator or the responder.
- parent: the party u which an instance π_u^i is associated to.
- pid: the identity of the intended communication partner party of the instance, initialised to $\bot$.
- sid: the identifier of the session, initialised to $\bot$.
- status $\in \{\bot, \mathtt{running}, \mathtt{accepted}, \mathtt{rejected}\}$: the status of the instance, initialised to $\bot$.
- t_{acc}: the time time when the instance accepts.
- sk: the session key computed by the instance.
- revealed $\in \{\mathtt{false}, \mathtt{true}\}$: indicates whether the session key is revealed, initialised to $\mathtt{false}$.
- tested $\in \{\mathtt{false}, \mathtt{true}\}$: indicates whether the instance is tested, initialised to $\mathtt{false}$.

We say that an instance is *honest* if it is controlled by the security game, which reflects that its behaviour is determined honestly by the game (and not the adversary). The long-term key of an honest instance can still be disclosed (the instance is then corrupted) and its session key revealed. A new instance is generated with the algorithm Activate (which definition depends on the analysed protocol). The algorithm Run delivers the next incoming protocol message, resulting in particular in an updated instance and a response message.

2.2 Security Properties

In this section, we present the security properties that define a (post-quantum) secure AKE protocol. First, we define the notion of partnership.

Partnership. The notion of partnership between two instances is based on the session identifier sid. Two instances are partnered if they share the same sid.

The three following predicates reflect the security properties captured by our model, and are also used to determine if the adversary wins the AKE security experiment (defined below).

Soundness. The *soundness* predicate Sound is used to guarantee that no three session identifiers are equal, and that two instances ending in accepting state which share the same session identifier, mutually agree on their partner's identity, and have opposite roles, do compute the same session key.

$G_{\Pi,\mathcal{A}}^{\mathsf{AKE}}$

INITIALISE
time $\leftarrow 0$
$n \leftarrow 0$
$\mathcal{T} \leftarrow \emptyset$
$b_{\mathsf{key}} \xleftarrow{\$} \{0,1\}$

NEWPARTY
$n \leftarrow n+1$
$(spk_n, ssk_n) \leftarrow \mathsf{Keygen}()$
$\mathsf{corr}_n \leftarrow +\infty$
$list_{spk}[n] \leftarrow spk_n$
return spk_n

SEND(u,i,m)
if $\pi_u^i = \bot$ then
$\quad role \leftarrow m$
$\quad (\pi_u^i, m') \xleftarrow{\$} \mathsf{Activate}(u, role)$
$\quad \pi_u^i.\mathsf{t}_{\mathsf{acc}} \leftarrow 0$
else
$\quad (\pi_u^i, m') \xleftarrow{\$} \mathsf{Run}(u, ssk_u, \pi_u^i, list_{spk}, m)$
if $\pi_u^i.\mathsf{status} = \mathsf{accepted}$ then
$\quad$ time $\leftarrow$ time $+1$
$\quad \pi_u^i.\mathsf{t}_{\mathsf{acc}} \leftarrow$ time
return m'

CORRUPT(u)
time $\leftarrow$ time $+1$
$\mathsf{corr}_u \leftarrow$ time
return ssk_u

REVEALKEY(u,i)
if $(\pi_u^i = \bot \lor \pi_u^i.\mathsf{status} \neq \mathsf{accepted})$ then
$\quad$ return $\bot$
$\pi_u^i.\mathsf{revealed} \leftarrow \mathsf{true}$
return $\pi_u^i.\mathsf{sk}$

ExplicitAuth
return $[[\forall \pi_u^i \ (\pi_u^i.\mathsf{status} = \mathsf{accepted} \land$
$\qquad\qquad \pi_u^i.\mathsf{t}_{\mathsf{acc}} < \mathsf{corr}_{\pi_u^i.\mathsf{pid}})$
$\Rightarrow \exists \pi_v^j \mid (\pi_u^i.\mathsf{pid} = v \land$
$\qquad \pi_u^i.\mathsf{sid} = \pi_v^j.\mathsf{sid} \land$
$\qquad \pi_u^i.\mathsf{role} \neq \pi_v^j.\mathsf{role} \land$
$\qquad (\pi_v^j.\mathsf{status} = \mathsf{accepted}$
$\qquad \Rightarrow \pi_v^j.\mathsf{pid} = u))]]$

TEST(u,i)
if $(\pi_u^i = \bot \lor$
$\qquad \pi_u^i.\mathsf{status} \neq \mathsf{accepted} \lor$
$\qquad \pi_u^i.\mathsf{tested})$ then
$\quad$ return $\bot$
$\pi_u^i.\mathsf{tested} \leftarrow \mathsf{true}$
$\mathcal{T} \leftarrow \mathcal{T} \cup \{\pi_u^i\}$
$k_0 \leftarrow \pi_u^i.\mathsf{sk}$
$k_1 \xleftarrow{\$} \{0,1\}^{|k_0|}$
return $k_{b_{\mathsf{key}}}$

FreshKey
$\forall \pi_u^i \in \mathcal{T}$
$\quad$ if $\pi_u^i.\mathsf{revealed}$ then
$\qquad$ return false
$\quad$ if $\exists \pi_v^j \neq \pi_u^i \mid (\pi_v^j.\mathsf{sid} = \pi_u^i.\mathsf{sid} \land$
$\qquad\qquad (\pi_v^j.\mathsf{tested} \lor \pi_v^j.\mathsf{revealed}))$ then
$\qquad$ return false
$\quad$ if $\mathsf{corr}_{\pi_u^i.\mathsf{pid}} < \pi_u^i.\mathsf{t}_{\mathsf{acc}}$ then
$\qquad$ return false
return true

Sound
if $\exists$ distinct $\pi_u^i, \pi_v^j, \pi_w^k \mid$
$\qquad \pi_u^i.\mathsf{sid} = \pi_v^j.\mathsf{sid} = \pi_w^k.\mathsf{sid} \neq \bot$ then
$\quad$ return false
if $\exists \pi_u^i, \pi_v^j \mid (\pi_u^i.\mathsf{status} = \pi_v^j.\mathsf{status}$
$\qquad\qquad\qquad\qquad = \mathsf{accepted} \land$
$\qquad \pi_u^i.\mathsf{sid} = \pi_v^j.\mathsf{sid} \land$
$\qquad \pi_u^i.\mathsf{pid} = v \land$
$\qquad \pi_v^j.\mathsf{pid} = u \land$
$\qquad \pi_u^i.\mathsf{role} \neq \pi_v^j.\mathsf{role})$ then
$\quad$ if $\pi_u^i.\mathsf{sk} \neq \pi_v^j.\mathsf{sk}$ then
$\qquad$ return false
return true

Fig. 1. Security experiment for the AKE protocol

Explicit Authentication. When the *explicit authentication* predicate ExplicitAuth is true, then all instances accepting with an uncorrupted peer, are partnered (i.e., share the same session identifier as another instance), such that the instance and its partner have opposite role, and they mutually agree on their partner's identity (upon acceptance). Our model captures also *key-compromise impersonation* attacks [18] by allowing the parent party of the tested instance to be corrupted at any point in time.

Key Freshness. The key freshness predicate FreshKey aims at excluding trivial attacks during the session key indistinguishability experiment (defined below). More specifically, if a session key is revealed or a party is corrupted (hence its private key is disclosed), then the adversary can straightforwardly win the experiment. Likewise, if, among two partnered instances, one is tested, then the adversary can correctly answer the TEST-challenge ($\mathcal{T}$ is the set of all tested instances).

Moreover, we only exclude the reveal of session keys for the tested instance and its partner instance. This captures *key independence.* That is, if the revealed keys are different from the tested instance's key, then such keys must not enable computing the session key.

The *forward secrecy* property is incorporated by allowing the adversary to corrupt any party as long as all tested sessions accept prior to corrupting their respective intended peer.

Note also that, following Cohn-Gordon, Cremers, Gjøsteen, Jacobsen and Jager [33], the security model we use allows the adversary to make many TEST-queries, which are answered (with a real or uniformly random session key) based on the same random bit b_{key}.

An *authenticated key exchange protocol* (AKE) is a two-party protocol where the security is defined in terms of an AKE experiment played between a challenger and a (post-quantum) polynomial time adversary. This experiment uses the execution environment described above. The adversary can win the AKE experiment in one of three ways: (i) by making an instance accept maliciously, (ii) by guessing the secret bit b_{key}, or (iii) by breaking the soundness of the protocol.

Definition 1 (Explicit Authentication). *An instance π_u^i of a protocol Π is said to have accepted maliciously in the AKE security experiment, if the predicate* ExplicitAuth *is false. That is,*

$$
\exists\, \pi_u^i \mid
\begin{cases}
(\pi_u^i.\text{status} = \texttt{accepted} \ \land\ \pi_u^i.t_{\text{acc}} < \text{corr}_{\pi_u^i.\text{pid}}) \\
\land \\
\forall\, \pi_v^j \ (\pi_u^i.\text{pid} \neq v \ \lor \\
\qquad \pi_u^i.\text{sid} \neq \pi_v^j.\text{sid} \ \lor \\
\qquad \pi_u^i.\text{role} = \pi_v^j.\text{role} \ \lor \\
\qquad (\pi_v^j.\text{status} = \texttt{accepted} \ \land\ \pi_v^j.\text{pid} \neq u))
\end{cases}
$$

The adversary's advantage is defined as its winning probability:

$$
\text{adv}_\Pi^{\text{auth}}(\mathcal{A}) = \Pr\left[\text{ExplicitAuth} = \texttt{false}\right].
$$

Definition 2 (Key Indistinguishability). *An adversary $\mathcal{A}$ against a protocol Π, that issues its* TEST*-query to instance π_u^i during the AKE security experiment, answers the* TEST*-challenge correctly if it terminates with output b^*, such that*

(a) the predicate FreshKey *is true, and*
(b) $b_{key} = b^*$.

The adversary's advantage is defined as

$$\mathsf{adv}_\Pi^{key\text{-}ind}(\mathcal{A}) = \Pr\left[b_{key} = b^* \mid \mathsf{FreshKey} = \mathtt{true}\right] - \frac{1}{2}.$$

Definition 3 (Soundness). *An adversary $\mathcal{A}$ against a protocol Π breaks the soundness of Π if the predicate* Sound *is false. The adversary's advantage is defined as its winning probability:*

$$\mathsf{adv}_\Pi^{sound}(\mathcal{A}) = \Pr\left[\mathsf{Sound} = \mathtt{false}\right].$$

Definition 4 (AKE Security). *We say that a two-party protocol Π is a secure AKE protocol if for all (post-quantum) polynomial time adversary $\mathcal{A}$, $\mathsf{adv}_\Pi^{auth}(\mathcal{A})$, $\mathsf{adv}_\Pi^{key\text{-}ind}(\mathcal{A})$ and $\mathsf{adv}_\Pi^{sound}(\mathcal{A})$ are a negligible function of the security parameter.*

3 Building Blocks and Assumptions

In this section, we recall the building blocks and assumptions that we will use in the security proofs of our post-quantum AKE protocol.

3.1 Chosen Ciphertext Attacks of Key Encapsulation Mechanisms

We recall the definition of a key encapsulation mechanism and the standard notion of indistinguishability under chosen-ciphertext attack.

Definition 5 (Key Encapsulation Mechanism). *A key encapsulation mechanism (KEM)* KEM = (Keygen, Encaps, Decaps) *consists of three efficient algorithms defined as follows:*

- Keygen() $\xrightarrow{\$}$ (pk, sk). *This probabilistic algorithm generates a public encapsulation key pk and a private decapsulation key sk.*
- Encaps(pk) $\xrightarrow{\$}$ (ss, ct). *On input a public key pk, this probabilistic algorithm outputs a key $ss \in \mathcal{K}$ and a ciphertext ct.*
- Decaps$(ct, sk) \rightarrow r \in \{ss, \bot\}$. *On input a ciphertext ct and a decapsulation key sk, this deterministic algorithm outputs either a key ss or a special symbol $\bot$ indicating rejection.*

The KEM KEM *is δ-correct if*

$$\Pr\Big[\mathsf{KEM.Decaps}(ct, sk) \neq ss \mid (pk, sk) \xleftarrow{\$} \mathsf{KEM.Keygen}() \wedge$$
$$(ss, ct) \xleftarrow{\$} \mathsf{KEM.Encaps}(pk)\Big] \leq \delta.$$

Definition 6 (KEM IND-CCA security). *Let* KEM *be a KEM and* $G_{\mathsf{KEM},\mathcal{A}}^{\mathsf{IND\text{-}CCA}}$ *be the experiment for indistinguishability under chosen-ciphertext attack of KEMs described by Fig. 2. For an adversary* $\mathcal{A}$ *we define*

$$\mathsf{adv}_{\mathsf{KEM}}^{\mathsf{ind\text{-}cca}}(\mathcal{A}) = \Pr\left[G_{\mathsf{KEM},\mathcal{A}}^{\mathsf{IND\text{-}CCA}} \Rightarrow 1\right] - \frac{1}{2}$$

where $\mathcal{A}$ *runs in time at most* t *and makes at most* q_{Dc} *queries to the* DECAPS *oracle.*

$G_{\mathsf{KEM},\mathcal{A}}^{\mathsf{IND\text{-}CCA}}$

INITIALISE	DECAPS(c)	FINALISE(b^*)
$b \xleftarrow{\$} \{0,1\}$	if $c = ct$ then	return $[[b = b^*]]$
$(pk, sk) \xleftarrow{\$} \mathsf{Keygen}()$	$\quad$ return $\perp$	
$(ss_0, ct) \xleftarrow{\$} \mathsf{Encaps}(pk)$	$r \leftarrow \mathsf{Decaps}(c, sk)$	
$ss_1 \xleftarrow{\$} \mathcal{K}$	return r	
return pk, ct, ss_b		

Fig. 2. Indistinguishability under chosen-ciphertext attack (IND-CCA) of KEMs.

3.2 Unforgeability of Signatures

We recall the definition of a signature scheme and existential unforgeability chosen-message attack [46].

Definition 7 (Signature scheme). *A signature scheme* Sig = (Keygen, Sign, Verify) *consists of three efficient algorithms defined as follows:*

- Keygen() $\xrightarrow{\$}$ (pk, sk). *This probabilistic algorithm generates a public verification key* pk *and a private signing key* sk.
- Sign(sk, m) $\xrightarrow{\$}$ σ. *On input a signing key* sk *and a message* m, *this (possibly) probabilistic algorithm outputs a signature* σ.
- Verify(pk, m, σ) $\rightarrow$ d. *On input a verification key* pk, *a message* m, *and a signature* σ, *this deterministic algorithm outputs a decision bit* $d \in \{\mathtt{true}, \mathtt{false}\}$ *(where* $d = \mathtt{true}$ *indicates validity of the signature).*

Definition 8 (Signature EUF-CMA security). *Let* Sig *be a signature scheme and* $G_{\mathsf{Sig},\mathcal{A}}^{\mathsf{EUF\text{-}CMA}}$ *be the experiment for signature existential unforgeability under chosen-message attack described by Fig. 3. For an adversary* $\mathcal{A}$ *we define*

$$\mathsf{adv}_{\mathsf{Sig}}^{\mathsf{euf\text{-}cma}}(\mathcal{A}) = \Pr\left[G_{\mathsf{Sig},\mathcal{A}}^{\mathsf{EUF\text{-}CMA}} \Rightarrow 1\right]$$

where $\mathcal{A}$ *runs in time at most* t *and makes at most* q_{SG} *queries to the* SIGN *oracle.*

$G_{\text{Sig},\mathcal{A}}^{\text{EUF-CMA}}$

INITIALISE	SIGN(m)	FINALISE(m^*, σ^*)
$(pk, sk) \xleftarrow{\$} \text{Keygen}()$	$\sigma \xleftarrow{\$} \text{Sign}(sk, m)$	$d^* \leftarrow \text{Verify}(pk, m^*, \sigma^*)$
$\mathcal{Q} \leftarrow \emptyset$	$\mathcal{Q} \leftarrow \mathcal{Q} \cup \{m\}$	return $[[d^* = \textbf{true} \ \wedge$
return pk	return σ	$m^* \notin \mathcal{Q}]]$

Fig. 3. Existential unforgeability (EUF-CMA) of signature schemes.

3.3 Unforgeability of MAC Schemes

We recall the definition of a MAC scheme and existential unforgeability chosen-message attack.

Definition 9 (MAC scheme). *A MAC scheme* MAC = (Keygen, Tag, Verify) *consists of three efficient algorithms defined as follows:*

- Keygen() $\xrightarrow{\$} K$. *This probabilistic algorithm generates a key K.*
- Tag(K, m) $\xrightarrow{\$} \tau$. *On input a key K and a message m, this (possibly) probabilistic algorithm outputs a MAC tag τ.*
- Verify(K, m, τ) $\rightarrow d$. *On input a key K, a message m, and a MAC tag τ, this deterministic algorithm outputs a decision bit $d \in \{\textbf{true}, \textbf{false}\}$ (where $d = \textbf{true}$ indicates validity of the tag).*

Definition 10 (MAC EUF-CMA security). *Let* MAC *be a MAC scheme and* $G_{\text{MAC},\mathcal{A}}^{\text{EUF-CMA}}$ *be the experiment for MAC existential unforgeability under chosen-message attack described by Fig. 4. For an adversary $\mathcal{A}$ we define*

$$\text{adv}_{\text{MAC}}^{\text{euf-cma}}(\mathcal{A}) = \Pr\left[G_{\text{MAC},\mathcal{A}}^{\text{EUF-CMA}} \Rightarrow 1\right]$$

where $\mathcal{A}$ runs in time at most t and makes at most q_{TG} and q_{VF} queries respectively to the TAG *and* VERIFY *oracles.*

$G_{\text{MAC},\mathcal{A}}^{\text{EUF-CMA}}$

INITIALISE	TAG(m)	VERIFY(m, τ)	FINALISE(m^*, τ^*)
$K \xleftarrow{\$} \text{Keygen}()$	$\tau \xleftarrow{\$} \text{Tag}(K, m)$	$d \leftarrow \text{Verify}(K, m, \tau)$	$d^* \leftarrow \text{Verify}(K, m^*, \tau^*)$
$\mathcal{Q} \leftarrow \emptyset$	$\mathcal{Q} \leftarrow \mathcal{Q} \cup \{m\}$	return d	return $[[d^* = \textbf{true} \ \wedge$
	return τ		$m^* \notin \mathcal{Q}]]$

Fig. 4. Existential unforgeability (EUF-CMA) of MAC schemes.

3.4 PRF Security

We recall the security notion for pseudo-random functions [12].

Definition 11 (PRF security). *Let* $F : \{0,1\}^k \times \{0,1\}^m \to \{0,1\}^n$, $k, n \in \mathbb{N}$, $m \in \mathbb{N} \cup \{*\}$, *be a function, and* $G_{F,\mathcal{A}}^{PRF}$ *be the PRF security experiment described by Fig. 5. For an adversary* $\mathcal{A}$ *we define*

$$\mathsf{adv}_F^{prf}(\mathcal{A}) = \Pr\left[G_{F,\mathcal{A}}^{PRF} \Rightarrow 1\right] - \frac{1}{2}$$

where $\mathcal{A}$ *runs in time at most* t *and makes at most* q_{FC} *queries to the* FUNC *oracle.*

$G_{F,\mathcal{A}}^{PRF}$

INITIALISE	FUNC(x)	FINALISE(b*)
$b \xleftarrow{\$} \{0,1\}$	return $f(x)$	return $[\![b = b^*]\!]$
if $b = 1$ then		
$\quad K \xleftarrow{\$} \{0,1\}^k$		
$\quad f \leftarrow F(K, \cdot)$		
else		
$\quad f \xleftarrow{\$} \mathcal{F}$		

Fig. 5. PRF security experiment. $\mathcal{F}$ is the space of all functions $\{0,1\}^m \to \{0,1\}^n$.

3.5 Hash Function Collision Resistance

We define collision resistance of hash functions as follows.

Definition 12 (Hash function collision resistance). *Let* $H : \{0,1\}^* \to \{0,1\}^\ell$, $\ell \in \mathbb{N}$, *be a function. For an adversary* $\mathcal{A}$ *we define*

$$\mathsf{adv}_H^{cr}(\mathcal{A}) = \Pr\left[(m, m') \xleftarrow{\$} \mathcal{A} \mid m \neq m' \wedge H(m) = H(m')\right].$$

3.6 Decisional and Strong Diffie-Hellman Assumptions

The decisional Diffie-Hellman assumption [21] states that, when only observing the two Diffie-Hellman shares g^x, g^y, the resulting secret g^{xy} is indistinguishable from a random group element.

Definition 13 (Decisional Diffie-Hellman (DDH) problem). *Let* $\mathbb{G} = \langle g \rangle$
be a cyclic group of prime order p. We define

$$\mathsf{adv}_{\mathbb{G}}^{\mathsf{ddh}}(\mathcal{A}) = \left| \Pr\left[\mathcal{A}(\mathbb{G}, g, g^x, g^y, g^{xy}) \Rightarrow 1 \mid x, y \overset{\$}{\leftarrow} (\mathbb{Z}/p\mathbb{Z})^* \right] - \right.$$
$$\left. \Pr\left[\mathcal{A}(\mathbb{G}, g, g^x, g^y, g^z) \Rightarrow 1 \mid x, y, z \overset{\$}{\leftarrow} (\mathbb{Z}/p\mathbb{Z})^* \right] \right|$$

where $\mathcal{A}$ runs in time at most t.

The Strong Diffie-Hellman assumption [1] states that solving the computational Diffie-Hellman problem given a restricted decisional Diffie-Hellman oracle is hard.

Definition 14 (Strong Diffie-Hellman (SDH) problem). *Let* $\mathbb{G} = \langle g \rangle$ *be a cyclic group of prime order p. Let* $\mathsf{DDH}(X, Y, Z) = [[X^{\log_g(Y)} = Z]]$ *be a decisional Diffie-Hellman oracle. We define*

$$\mathsf{adv}_{\mathbb{G}}^{\mathsf{sdh}}(\mathcal{A}) = \Pr\left[\mathcal{A}^{\mathsf{DDH}(g^x, \cdot, \cdot)}(\mathbb{G}, g, g^x, g^y) = g^{xy} \mid x, y \overset{\$}{\leftarrow} (\mathbb{Z}/p\mathbb{Z})^* \right]$$

where $\mathcal{A}$ runs in time at most t and makes at most q_{SDH} queries to its DDH *oracle.*

4   Original ZRTP Protocol

The ZRTP protocol [78] is a two-party protocol that aims at mutually authenticating the communicating parties and at computing a fresh key material that will in turn protect voice communication over IP. With the fresh key material, the application data is protected into Secure Real-time Transport Protocol [9] (SRTP) packets.

Protocol Flow. A new ZRTP run starts with the exchange of Hello messages that indicate the ciphersuites supported by each party (see Fig. 6). The party sending the next message (Commit) becomes the initiator.[7] This message transports the selected ciphersuite and other parameters. The Diffie-Hellman key exchange is done with the DHPart1 and DHPart2 messages, sent by the responder and the initiator respectively.

Identifiers. ZID_I and ZID_R are static identifiers of the initiator and responder party respectively. These parameters are pseudo-randomly chosen when the application is installed onto the device. The real identity of a given party is sent (encrypted) in the Confirm message only if authentication is done by means of a signature (see below).

---

[7] If both instances send a Commit message, a rule based on the value of the message parameters allows defining the initiator instance. The other Commit message is then discarded.

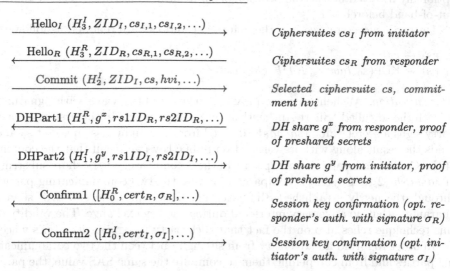

Fig. 6. Simplified view of a ZRTP protocol run

Session Keys. A fresh main session secret (s_0) is computed from (i) the newly shared DH secret, (ii) previous secret values ($rs1$, $rs2$) computed during the last protocol run and locally stored by each communicating parties, and (iii) a transcript of the messages exchanged so far during the current protocol run. Independent session keys are derived from s_0. A first set of session keys (that we call *handshake session keys*) is used to protect (confidentiality and integrity) the two last messages (Confirm1 and Confirm2). A second set (the *application session keys*) is used to protect the application SRTP packets.

Prehsared Secrets. The previous secrets $rs1$, $rs2$ involved in the computation of the fresh key material provide a form of "key continuity" between protocol runs done by the same two parties. This hinders an adversary trying to sit in between the two communicating parties (the adversary must get these past shared secrets in addition to bypassing the new DH exchange) and provides also a form of implicit mutual authentication. Note that, this is not entirely true because if two parties do not share the same $rs1$, $rs2$ values, then the latter are merely discarded from the subsequent computations done during the current protocol run [78, Section 4.3]. In particular, they are not involved in the computation of the fresh session keys. The initiator and the responder mutually verify that they share the same values $rs1$, $rs2$ by means of MAC tags (respectively $rs1ID_I$, $rs2ID_I$, and $rs1ID_R$, $rs2ID_R$) computed from the latter and transmitted in the DHPart1 and DHPart2 messages. The value that is preshared ($rs1$ or $rs2$) by the two parties is called s_1 in the session keys computation (if neither $rs1$ nor $rs2$ is shared, then s_1 is set to null). Additional secret values (s_2, s_3) are optionally involved in the computation of s_0. In such a case, they must be shared out-of-band beforehand.

During a successful session, the values $rs1$ and $rs2$ are renewed as follows:

1. $rs2 \leftarrow rs1$
2. $rs1 \leftarrow \mathsf{KDF}(s_0, label_{rs}, KDF\_Context, \ell_{rs})$

Authentication. Authentication is provided in either of two ways: with signatures or with the so-called "Short Authentication String" (SAS). In the first case, each party signs a secret value ($sashash$) derived from the main session secret s_0 and sends the result along with its verification public key (we recall that the content of the Confirm messages is encrypted). In the second case, a very short substring of $sashash$ (2 to 4 bytes) is compared aloud by the two communicating parties through the newly established SRTP tunnel. Equality of the two SAS strings guarantees that no adversary interfered during the key exchange. The validity of this technique relies also on the fact that each party recognises its peer's voice.

In order to forbid an adversary from sitting in between the two communicating parties and from compelling them to compute the same SAS value, the party that sends the last of the two DH messages must commit to this message in the form of a hash value hvi transported in the Commit message. Consequently, if the adversary is supposed to send the last message, it computes the latter before receiving the first DH message. If the adversary sends the first DH message, it sends it before knowing the second DH message. In both cases, this removes the degree of freedom that the adversary could leverage in order to make the two honest parties compute the same SAS. The two honest parties can then rely on a short string, easily manageable by humans, and the adversary is left with a probability equal to 2^{-k} to get two k-bit SAS collide (with $k \in \{16, 32\}$).

The purpose of such a technique is to avoid the burden of using signatures and the associated infrastructure (PKI). Now, it becomes rather questionable regarding a communication involving two parties that never spoke together [76].

Message Integrity. All the protocol messages from Hello up to DHPart2 are protected with a MAC tag. The MAC keys belong to a hash chain computed as follows: $H_{i+1} = \mathsf{H}(H_i)$, $i \in \{0, 1, 2\}$ (where H is a predefined hash function). A hash of the MAC key (H_{i+1}) is included in each message, and the MAC key (H_i) that enables to verify the message's tag is sent in the next message. The root value H_0, pseudo-randomly chosen, is sent (encrypted) in the Confirm messages. The intent of this mechanism is to provide a cheap and fast way to detect any message modification done by an adversary (without waiting for the Confirm messages).

5   Post-quantum ZRTP

In this section, we present the protocol obtained by modifying ZRTP in order to attain post-quantum security. Our goal is to get a quantum-resistant protocol while modifying as least as possible the current ZRTP protocol. The purpose here is to show that such a security level can be reached without need to disrupt in depth the current technical features of the protocol. We call "Post-quantum ZRTP" or "PQ-ZRTP" for short the resulting protocol, depicted by Fig. 7.

5.1   Changes with ZRTP

The main changes done to the original ZRTP protocol in order to bring it to the post-quantum security level are the following.

Key Exchange. The DH key exchange is replaced with a key encapsulation mechanism (KEM). To maintain forward secrecy, ephemeral KEM keys are computed during each protocol run. The public key is sent by the initiator in the Commit message. The corresponding ciphertext is sent by the responder in the KEMPart1 message (which takes place of the former ZRTP DHPart1 message). The reason why the public key and ciphertext are transported in the Commit and KEMPart1 messages (instead of KEMPart1 and KEMPart2) is explained next.

In practice, we will use a *hybrid* KEM (in order to thwart the so-called "harvest now, decrypt later" attacks) result of the combination of a quantum-resistant KEM (instantiated with Kyber [23] or HQC [2] in our implementation) and a classical KEM (instantiated with DHKEM [8]).

Session Keys. During the computation of the session keys the shared DH secret (in ZRTP) is replaced with the shared secret output by the KEM. Moreover the parameter *total_hash* (hash of transcript of exchanged messages) is augmented with the initiator's Hello message, that is $total\_hash = H'(Hello_I\|Hello_R\|Commit\|KEMPart1\|KEMPart2)$ (this change appears also in the unachieved proposal by Zimmerman, Johnston, Callas, Cross [79]). This thwarts one of the attacks described by Bhargavan et al. [15].

Authentication. ZRTP provides two different techniques for the parties to authenticate. The first one relies upon signatures. The second one (SAS) aims at avoiding the burden of public-key certificate management implied by the previous method, and relies upon voice recognition. Firstly, we do think that public certificates can be managed and used in a smooth and efficient way nowadays, compared to the beginning of ZRTP, including in smartphones. Secondly, relying upon (quantum-resistant) signatures enables to use arguments belonging to the realm of provable security. Therefore, our security proofs leverage this choice.

We slightly change the way signatures are computed. Indeed, in ZRTP, the signature computed by the initiator and the responder covers the same string (*sashash*). This means that an adversary, behaving as initiator, can make a whole key exchange with a victim and then merely send back the signature it receives to be correctly authenticated (and to impersonate the victim to itself). Although, it is unlikely that this theoretical attack be possible in real-life, in PQ-ZRTP we slightly change the signature computation and prepend the *sashash* value to be signed with distinct labels depending on the party's role (initiator or responder). We add a second change by including the verification public key among the signed data. Indeed, in the original ZRTP protocol, the signature is sent together with the verification key *"or a link to the key"* [78, Sections 5.7, 7.2] (without making explicit what the form of such a link could be). It may happen that such a reference do not uniquely identify the key, although the ZRTP specification do not explicitly present the latter possibility. Therefore, the purpose of this change is to prevent misbinding issues (e.g., based on the ability for an adversary to create a public key under which an (honestly generated) message-signature pair verifies) that could potentially lead to unknown key-share attacks [19,65]. Pornin and Stern [65] show that unambiguous inclusion of the verification key in the signature is enough to thwart such kind of attacks (provided there are no weak signature keys).

Even though authentication formally relies upon signatures in PQ-ZRTP, we do not forbid the possibility to use the SAS to authenticate. Indeed, in real-life, such a technique may still be desirable to a lot of users and practitioners.[8] Consequently, we adapt the way the commitment hvi is managed. In order to compute and send this parameter in the Commit message, the last message of the key exchange phase (KEMPart2) must be defined beforehand. If the KEM public key and the ciphertext are sent in the KEMPart1 and KEMPart2 messages respectively, then it is not possible to compute hvi from KEMPart2 since the ciphertext depends on the public key and the latter would be still unknown at the time hvi needs to be computed. Therefore, we reverse the computations: the public key and the ciphertext are sent in the Commit and KEMPart1 messages respectively. We include a nonce value (ni) in KEMPart2, that we involve also in the computation of the main session secret s_0. The hash commitment transported in the Commit message is then computed from KEMPart2, hence depends on ni.

Message Size. Compared to ZRTP, an important feature that is kept in PQ-ZRTP is the protocol flow which remains the same. In particular, an execution of PQ-ZRTP corresponds to the same number of messages as in ZRTP. Yet, the size of several messages (KEMPart, Confirm) is bigger since (i) our choice is to instantiate the key exchange and authentication schemes with an hybrid scheme, and (ii) the parameters (public key, ciphertext, signature) of the current post-quantum algorithms are notably larger compared to classical algorithms.

Preshared Secrets. In our protocol we do not use the optional secret values s_2 and s_3. That is, s_2 and s_3 are set to null, as envisaged by the original ZRTP specification [78, Section 4.3]. We only use s_1 which corresponds to a value ($rs1$ or $rs2$) computed during the previous protocol run between the same two communicating parties (or s_1 is set to null). Moreover, we consider that the preshared secret values $rs1$, $rs2$ (which can be understood as preshared keys), hence s_1, are uniformly sampled at random since, in practice, they are established in prior protocol runs (similar to analyses of TLS PSK [38,43]).

---

[8] The current version of the PQ-ZRTP source code relies upon SAS for the mutual authentication.

Hash Chain. We maintain the use of the hash chain $H_0, \ldots, H_3$ and the corresponding MAC tags although our protocol does not rely on the latter tags but on the integrity protection eventually provided by the Confirm messages computed with the handshake session keys. However, we conveniently use the hash chain to guarantee the uniqueness of the session identifier (which characterises the partnership between two instances) in our security proofs.

5.2   More Details

In this section, we describe more precisely the PQ-ZRTP protocol.

PQ-ZRTP corresponds essentially to the original specification of ZRTP [78]. We slightly modify the latter based on the (unachieved) proposal by Zimmerman et al. [79]. From this proposal, we keep the computation of the Confirm's IV with KDF instead of pseudo-randomly generating the parameters (this saves also bandwidth since the IVs are then not transmitted anymore). Finally, we enhance the security of the resulting protocol with the changes described in Sect. 5.1.

The computations done with symmetric-key functions (e.g., encryption and MAC tags of protocol messages) and the definition of the latter (e.g., derivation of session parameters with KDF) are the same as what is defined in ZRTP.

The session keys are made of the *handshake session keys* used to protect the Confirm messages, and the *application session keys* used to protect the application data (SRTP packets). The handshake session keys are ke_I, km_I and ke_R, km_R. The application session values are made of four parameters: a symmetric key and a salt for the SRTP messages sent by the initiator (mk_I, $salt_I$) and the responder (mk_R, $salt_R$). They are computed as in ZRTP:

$$mk_I = \mathsf{KDF}(s_0, label_{I,mk}, KDF\_Context, \ell_e)$$
$$salt_I = \mathsf{KDF}(s_0, label_{I,sl}, KDF\_Context, \ell_s)$$
$$mk_R = \mathsf{KDF}(s_0, label_{R,mk}, KDF\_Context, \ell_e)$$
$$salt_R = \mathsf{KDF}(s_0, label_{R,sl}, KDF\_Context, \ell_s)$$

where ℓ_e and ℓ_s are the bit length of the negotiated encryption cipher key and salt, and $label_*$ are fixed labels.

$KDF\_Context$ is equal to $ZID_I \| ZID_R \| total\_hash$ and $\mathsf{KDF}(K, label_{kdf}, ctx, \ell)$ is defined as $\mathsf{HMAC}(K, \texttt{0x000001} \| label_{kdf} \| \texttt{0x00} \| ctx \| \ell)$ where HMAC is built upon the negotiated hash function H' and ℓ is the expected output size ($\ell \in \{\ell_b, \ell_m, \ell_e, \ell_s\}$ where ℓ_b and ℓ_m indicate the bit length of the negotiated encryption cipher block and the negotiated MAC key respectively).

To define the partnering between two communicating instances, we use a session identifier sid set to $\mathrm{Hello}_I \| \mathrm{Hello}_R \| \mathrm{Commit} \| \mathrm{KEMPart1} \| \mathrm{KEMPart2}$.

All messages correspond to a distinct type (e.g., Hello, Commit, KEMPart) that defines also a role (initiator or responder) in some cases. The messages KEMPart and Confirm correspond both to a message type and a role (e.g., KEMPart1 vs. KEMPart2). The messages Hello and Commit correspond to a message type only. Let m.type be the flag associated to the message m that indicates m's type.

Initiator (spk_I, ssk_I) Responder (spk_R, ssk_R)

$$H_0^{\langle X \rangle} \xleftarrow{\$} \{0,1\}^{\ell_H}$$
$$H_{i+1}^{\langle X \rangle} \leftarrow \mathsf{H}(H_i^{\langle X \rangle}), i \in \{0,1,2\}$$

$\underline{\mathsf{InitHello}(\hat{I}, \pi_I)}$

$\mathsf{Hello}_I \leftarrow (H_3^I, ZID_I, cs_{I,1}, \ldots, cs_{I,n})$ $\xrightarrow{\quad \mathsf{Hello}_I \quad}$ $\underline{\mathsf{RespHello}(\hat{R}, \pi_R, m = \mathsf{Hello}_I)}$

$\mathsf{Hello}_R \leftarrow (H_3^R, ZID_R, cs_{R,1}, \ldots, cs_{R,n})$

$$rs1ID_{\langle X \rangle} \leftarrow \mathsf{MAC}'(rs1, label_{\langle X \rangle})$$
$$rs2ID_{\langle X \rangle} \leftarrow \mathsf{MAC}'(rs2, label_{\langle X \rangle})$$

$\underline{\mathsf{InitCommit}(\hat{I}, \pi_I, m = \mathsf{Hello}_R)}$ $\xleftarrow{\quad \mathsf{Hello}_R \quad}$

$ni \xleftarrow{\$} \{0,1\}^{\ell_n}$
$\mathsf{KEMPart2} \leftarrow (H_1^I, rs1ID_I, rs2ID_I, ni)$
$hvi \leftarrow \mathsf{H}'(\mathsf{KEMPart2} \| \mathsf{Hello}_R)$
$epk_I, esk_I \leftarrow \mathsf{KEM.Keygen}()$

$\mathsf{Commit} \leftarrow (H_2^I, ZID_I, cs_j, hvi, epk_I)$ $\xrightarrow{\quad \mathsf{Commit} \quad}$ $\underline{\mathsf{RespKEMPart1}(\hat{R}, \pi_R, m = \mathsf{Commit})}$

$(ss, ct_R) \leftarrow \mathsf{KEM.Encaps}(epk_I)$
$\mathsf{KEMPart1} \leftarrow (H_1^R, rs1ID_R, rs2ID_R, ct_R)$

$\underline{\mathsf{InitKEMPart2}(\hat{I}, \pi_I, m = \mathsf{KEMPart1})}$ $\xleftarrow{\quad \mathsf{KEMPart1} \quad}$

Verify $rs1ID_R, rs2ID_R$
$ss \leftarrow \mathsf{KEM.Decaps}(ct_R, esk_I)$

If $ss = \perp$ then abort. $\xrightarrow{\quad \mathsf{KEMPart2} \quad}$

$\underline{\mathsf{RespConfirm1}(\hat{R}, ssk_R, \pi_R, list_{spk}, m = \mathsf{KEMPart2})}$

Verify $rs1ID_I, rs2ID_I$

$$sid \leftarrow \mathsf{Hello}_I \| \mathsf{Hello}_R \| \mathsf{Commit} \| \mathsf{KEMPart1} \| \mathsf{KEMPart2}$$
$$\text{Compute } s_1 \in \{\mathsf{null}, rs1, rs2\}, s_2 = \mathsf{null}, s_3 = \mathsf{null}$$
$$total\_hash \leftarrow \mathsf{H}'(sid)$$
$$s_0 \leftarrow \mathsf{H}'(0\mathtt{x}000001 \| ss \| label_{s_0} \| ZID_I \| ZID_R \| total\_hash \| \ell_{s_1} \| s_1 \| \ell_{s_2} \| s_2 \| \ell_{s_3} \| s_3)$$
$$KDF\_Context \leftarrow ZID_I \| ZID_R \| total\_hash$$
$$sashash \leftarrow \mathsf{KDF}(s_0, label_{sas}, KDF\_Context, \ell_{sh})$$
$$\sigma_{\langle X \rangle} \leftarrow \mathsf{Sig.Sign}(ssk_{\langle X \rangle}, label_{\langle X \rangle} \| spk_{\langle X \rangle} \| sashash)$$
$$iv_{\langle X \rangle} \leftarrow \mathsf{KDF}(s_0, label_{\langle X \rangle, iv}, KDF\_Context, \ell_b)$$
$$km_{\langle X \rangle} \leftarrow \mathsf{KDF}(s_0, label_{\langle X \rangle, km}, KDF\_Context, \ell_m)$$
$$ke_{\langle X \rangle} \leftarrow \mathsf{KDF}(s_0, label_{\langle X \rangle, ke}, KDF\_Context, \ell_e)$$
$$c_{\langle X \rangle} \leftarrow \mathsf{ENC}'(ke_{\langle X \rangle}, iv_{\langle X \rangle}, H_0^{\langle X \rangle} \| cert_{\langle X \rangle} \| \sigma_{\langle X \rangle})$$
$$\tau_{\langle X \rangle} \leftarrow \mathsf{MAC}'.\mathsf{Tag}(km_{\langle X \rangle}, c_{\langle X \rangle})$$

$\xleftarrow{\quad \mathsf{Confirm1} \quad}$ $\mathsf{Confirm1} \leftarrow (c_R, \tau_R)$

$\underline{\mathsf{InitConfirm2}(\hat{I}, ssk_I, \pi_I, list_{spk}, m = \mathsf{Confirm1})}$

If $\mathsf{MAC}'.\mathsf{Verify}(km_R, c_R, \tau_R) = \mathtt{false}$ then abort.
$H_0^R \| cert_R \| \sigma_R \leftarrow \mathsf{DEC}'(ke_R, iv_R, c_R)$
If $\mathsf{Sig.Verify}(spk_R, label_R \| spk_R \| sashash, \sigma_R) = \mathtt{false}$ then abort.
$pid \leftarrow \hat{R}$
$status \leftarrow \mathtt{accepted}$

$\mathsf{Confirm2} \leftarrow (c_I, \tau_I)$ $\xrightarrow{\quad \mathsf{Confirm2} \quad}$

$\underline{\mathsf{RespFinal}(\hat{R}, \pi_R, list_{spk}, m = \mathsf{Confirm2})}$

If $\mathsf{MAC}'.\mathsf{Verify}(km_I, c_I, \tau_I) = \mathtt{false}$ then abort.
$H_0^I \| cert_I \| \sigma_I \leftarrow \mathsf{DEC}'(ke_I, iv_I, c_I)$
If $\mathsf{Sig.Verify}(spk_I, label_I \| spk_I \| sashash, \sigma_I) = \mathtt{false}$ then abort.
$pid \leftarrow \hat{I}$
$status \leftarrow \mathtt{accepted}$

Fig. 7. Post-quantum ZRTP protocol. $\langle X \rangle = I$ (resp. R) for the initiator (resp. responder). The MAC tags depending on the hash chain values are not represented.

Activate($id, role$)
π.sid $\leftarrow \perp$
π.recv $\leftarrow \emptyset$
π.role $\leftarrow role$
π.status $\leftarrow$ **running**
if $role = $ **init** then
    $(\pi', m') \leftarrow$ InitHello(id, π)
else
    $(\pi', m') \leftarrow (\pi, \perp)$
return (π', mi)

Run($id, ssk, \pi, list_{spk}, m$)
if π.status $\neq$ **running** then
    return $\perp$
if π.role $=$ **init** then
    if m.type $=$ **hello** then
        $(\pi', m') \leftarrow$ InitCommit(id, π, m)
        π.recv $\leftarrow \pi$.recv $\cup \{m.\text{type}\}$
    else if m.type $=$ **kempart1** then
        if (m.type $\notin \pi$.recv $\wedge$
        hello $\in \pi$.recv) then
            $(\pi', m') \leftarrow$ InitKEMPart2(id, π, m)
            π.recv $\leftarrow \pi$.recv $\cup \{m.\text{type}\}$
    else if m.type $=$ **confirm1** then
        if (m.type $\notin \pi$.recv $\wedge$
        kempart1 $\in \pi$.recv) then
            $(\pi', m') \leftarrow$ InitConfirm2(id, ssk, π)
                        $list_{spk}, m)$
            π.recv $\leftarrow \pi$.recv $\cup \{m.\text{type}\}$

else   // π.role $=$ **resp**
    if m.type $=$ **hello** then
        $(\pi', m') \leftarrow$ RespHello(id, π, m)
        π.recv $\leftarrow \pi$.recv $\cup \{m.\text{type}\}$
    else if m.type $=$ **commit** then
        if (m.type $\notin \pi$.recv $\wedge$
        hello $\in \pi$.recv) then
            $(\pi', m') \leftarrow$ RespKEMPart1(id, π, m)
            π.recv $\leftarrow \pi$.recv $\cup \{m.\text{type}\}$
    else if m.type $=$ **kempart2** then
        if (m.type $\notin \pi$.recv $\wedge$
        commit $\in \pi$.recv) then
            $(\pi', m') \leftarrow$ RespConfirm1$(id, ssk, \pi,$
                        $list_{spk}, m)$
            π.recv $\leftarrow \pi$.recv $\cup \{m.\text{type}\}$
    else if m.type $=$ **confirm2** then
        if (m.type $\notin \pi$.recv $\wedge$
        kempart2 $\in \pi$.recv) then
            $(\pi', m') \leftarrow$ RespFinal$(id, \pi, list_{spk}, m)$
            π.recv $\leftarrow \pi$.recv $\cup \{m.\text{type}\}$
return (π', m')

Fig. 8. Definition of the Activate and Run algorithms in PQ-ZRTP

The instantiation of the algorithms Activate and Run in PQ-ZRTP is given by Fig. 8. In order to define these algorithms in the case of PQ-ZRTP, the flag recv is added to the state maintained by each instance, in addition to the other flags described in Sect. 2.1. The flag recv records the type of the protocol messages received during the session.

MAC', ENC' and H' are respectively the MAC, encryption and hash function negotiated during the protocol run with the Hello messages (i.e., ciphersuites).

6 Security Proofs

In this section we first prove that the PQ-ZRTP protocol is a post-quantum secure AKE protocol according to Definition 4 (Sect. 6.2). Moreover, we consider the case (in particular in our practical implementation of PQ-ZRTP) where the KEM KEM used to make the key exchange is an hybrid KEM built upon two KEMs KEM1 and KEM2. In Sect. 6.3, we show that this hybrid KEM is IND-CCA-secure and can hence securely instantiate PQ-ZRTP. First, we start with the main theorem regarding the security of protocol PQ-ZRTP.

6.1   Main Theorem

Theorem 1 (Security of PQ-ZRTP). *Let PQ-ZRTP be the protocol described by Figs. 7 and 8. PQ-ZRTP is a secure AKE protocol according to Definition 4. More specifically, for any (post-quantum) polynomial time ((PQ)PT) adversary $\mathcal{A}$ playing the game $G^{\mathsf{AKE}}_{PQ\text{-}ZRTP,\mathcal{A}}$ described by Fig. 1 with at most n_P parties that establish in total at most n_S sessions, we have that*

$$
\mathsf{adv}^{\mathsf{sound}}_{\mathsf{PQ\text{-}ZRTP}}(\mathcal{A}) \leq n_S^2 \left(\frac{1}{2^{\ell_H + 1}} + \frac{4}{2^{\ell_{rsid}}} \right) + n_S \cdot \delta_{\mathsf{KEM}} + \mathsf{adv}^{\mathsf{cr}}_{\mathsf{H}}(\mathcal{B}_0)
$$
$$
+ 4n_S^2 \cdot \mathsf{adv}^{\mathsf{prf}}_{\mathsf{MAC}'}(\mathcal{B}_6)
$$

$$
\mathsf{adv}^{\mathsf{auth}}_{\mathsf{PQ\text{-}ZRTP}}(\mathcal{A}) \leq n_S \cdot \delta_{\mathsf{KEM}} + n_S^2 \left(\frac{1}{2^{\ell_H + 1}} + 1 - \left(1 - 2^{-\ell_{sh}} \right)^{n_S} + \frac{q_{\mathsf{H}'}}{2^{\ell_{ss} + \ell_{s_1}}} \right)
$$
$$
+ \mathsf{adv}^{\mathsf{cr}}_{\mathsf{H}}(\mathcal{B}_0) + \mathsf{adv}^{\mathsf{cr}}_{\mathsf{H}'}(\mathcal{B}_1) + n_S n_P \cdot \mathsf{adv}^{\mathsf{euf\text{-}cma}}_{\mathsf{Sig}}(\mathcal{B}_2)
$$
$$
+ n_S^2 \left(2 \cdot \mathsf{adv}^{\mathsf{ind\text{-}cca}}_{\mathsf{KEM}}(\mathcal{B}_3) + 2 \cdot \mathsf{adv}^{\mathsf{prf}}_{\mathsf{KDF}}(\mathcal{B}_4) + \mathsf{adv}^{\mathsf{euf\text{-}cma}}_{\mathsf{MAC}'}(\mathcal{B}_5) \right)
$$

$$
\mathsf{adv}^{\mathsf{key\text{-}ind}}_{\mathsf{PQ\text{-}ZRTP}}(\mathcal{A}) \leq 2n_S \cdot \delta_{\mathsf{KEM}} + n_S^2 \left(\frac{1}{2^{\ell_H + 1}} + 1 - \left(1 - 2^{-\ell_{sh}} \right)^{n_S} + \frac{2q_{\mathsf{H}'}}{2^{\ell_{ss} + \ell_{s_1}}} \right)
$$
$$
+ \mathsf{adv}^{\mathsf{cr}}_{\mathsf{H}}(\mathcal{B}_0) + \mathsf{adv}^{\mathsf{cr}}_{\mathsf{H}'}(\mathcal{B}_1) + n_S n_P \cdot \mathsf{adv}^{\mathsf{euf\text{-}cma}}_{\mathsf{Sig}}(\mathcal{B}_2)
$$
$$
+ n_S^2 \left(4 \cdot \mathsf{adv}^{\mathsf{ind\text{-}cca}}_{\mathsf{KEM}}(\mathcal{B}_3) + 4 \cdot \mathsf{adv}^{\mathsf{prf}}_{\mathsf{KDF}}(\mathcal{B}_4) + \mathsf{adv}^{\mathsf{euf\text{-}cma}}_{\mathsf{MAC}'}(\mathcal{B}_5) \right)
$$

where $\mathcal{B}_0$, $\mathcal{B}_1$, $\mathcal{B}_2$, $\mathcal{B}_3$, $\mathcal{B}_4$, $\mathcal{B}_5$, $\mathcal{B}_6$ are (PQ)PT adversaries against respectively the collision resistance of the hash function H, the collision resistance of the hash function H', the EUF-CMA-security of the signature scheme Sig, the IND-CCA-security of the key encapsulation mechanism KEM, the PRF-security of function KDF, the EUF-CMA-security of the MAC function MAC', and the PRF-security of the MAC function MAC', ℓ_{ss}, ℓ_{s_1} and ℓ_{sh} are the bit length of respectively the shared secret output by KEM, the preshared secret s_1 and sashash, and $q_{\mathsf{H}'}$ is the number of queries to H' (modelled as a random oracle) done by $\mathcal{A}$. The running time of $\mathcal{B}_0$, $\mathcal{B}_1$, $\mathcal{B}_2$, $\mathcal{B}_3$, $\mathcal{B}_4$, $\mathcal{B}_5$ and $\mathcal{B}_6$ is roughly the same as that of $\mathcal{A}$.

Theorem 1 states that PQ-ZRTP is a secure AKE protocol against post-quantum adversaries when the underlying cryptographic primitives are instantiated with quantum-resistant functions. It also states that the protocol is secure against classical adversaries when instantiated with pre-quantum functions, i.e., with a classical signature scheme and a DH-based KEM for the key exchange, such as DHKEM [8] for instance.

6.2 Security Proofs for PQ-ZRTP

In this section, we give a sketch of proofs for PQ-ZRTP (the full proofs are given in the extended version of this paper). We proceed through a sequence of games [13,70] between a challenger and an adversary $\mathcal{A}$ that aims at breaking the considered security property.

Soundness. *Game* 0. This game corresponds to the soundness security experiment described in Sect. 2.1 applied to PQ-ZRTP.

Game 1. The challenger aborts the experiment if two honest instances choose the same ℓ_H-bit long value H_0. Taking into account the maximum number of sessions n_S, this implies a collision term at most $n_S^2/2^{\ell_H+1}$.

Game 2. The challenger aborts if a collision occurs with H's outputs. This reduces to the collision resistance of H. Hence a loss equal to $\mathsf{adv}_H^{\mathsf{cr}}$.

Game 3. The challenger aborts if a decapsulation failure occurs with KEM. This implies a loss equal to $n_S \cdot \delta_{\mathsf{KEM}}$.

Game 4. The challenger proceeds only if it succeeds in guessing which partnered instances are targeted by the adversary. Hence the loss is a factor $1/n_S^2$.

Game 5. The challenger replaces MAC′ keyed $rs1$ and $rs2$, used by the two partnered instances to compute $rs1ID_I, rs2ID_I, rs1ID_R, rs2ID_R$, with random functions. Since the two instances may not used the same pair $(rs1, rs2)$, this implies a loss equal to $4 \cdot \mathsf{adv}_{\mathsf{MAC}'}^{\mathsf{prf}}$.

Game 6. The challenger aborts the experiment if different random functions yield the same output in the computation of $rs1ID_I, rs2ID_I, rs1ID_R, rs2ID_R$. Hence a loss equal to $4/2^{\ell_{rsid}}$.

The Sound predicate is false if (i) three honest instances share the same session identifier sid, or (ii) two partnered instances compute different session keys.

Regarding the first point, no two values H_3 can be equal since, all values H_0 are distinct (by Game 1) and collisions in H are excluded (by Game 2). Therefore, a sid can be shared by two instances at most.

Regarding the second point, the session identifier includes two out of three parameters that together determine the secret value s_0 (in particular *total_hash* based on sid and ss embedded into ct_R) and the other inputs used to compute the session keys (but the constant labels). Therefore, agreeing on sid (i.e., being partnered) implies sharing these two parameters, unless a failure occurs during the decapsulation, which is excluded by Game 3. Hence, agreeing on sid implies in particular that the two partnered instances share the same value ss.

Moreover, a valid test done with $rs1ID_I, rs2ID_I, rs1ID_R, rs2ID_R$ implies that both instances use the same s_1 value (which is then set to $rs1$ or $rs2$), unless a collision occurs in the computation of $rs1ID_I, rs2ID_I, rs1ID_R, rs2ID_R$. But the latter is excluded by Game 6. Such collisions being excluded, either the two partnered instances do share $rs1$ or $rs2$ (hence s_1), or they are aware they do not. In the latter case, s_1 is set to null by both instances. To that point, in either case, the two partnered instances do use the same value s_1.

Therefore, the two partnered instances use as input the same values ss, s_1 and $total\_hash$ to compute s_0. This implies that they do compute the same value s_0, and consequently the same session keys.

Consequently, Sound is true in Game 6 and the adversary's advantage is 0.

Explicit Authentication. *Game 0.* This game corresponds to the explicit authentication security experiment described in Sect. 2.1 applied to PQ-ZRTP.

Games 1-3. We reproduce the first three games from the soundness proof. Hence a loss equal to $n_S^2/2^{\ell_H+1} + n_S \cdot \delta_{\mathsf{KEM}} + \mathsf{adv}_\mathsf{H}^\mathsf{cr}$.

Game 4. The challenger aborts if a collision occurs with H''s outputs. This implies a loss equal to $\mathsf{adv}_{\mathsf{H}'}^\mathsf{cr}$.

Game 5. The challenger proceeds only if it succeeds in guessing which instance π_u^i is targeted by the adversary. Taking into account the maximum number of sessions n_S, this reduces the advantage of the adversary by a factor $1/n_S$.

Game 6. The challenger aborts if π_u^i receives a valid signature under an uncorrupted key for a message which was not produced by an honest instance. This reduces to the EUF-CMA-security of the signature scheme. Taking into account the maximum number of parties n_P, this implies a loss equal to $n_P \cdot \mathsf{adv}_\mathsf{Sig}^\mathsf{euf\text{-}cma}$.

Game 7. The challenger proceeds only if it succeeds in guessing which instance π_v^j has sent the valid signature. This reduces the advantage of the adversary by a factor $1/n_S$.

Game 8. The challenger replaces the shared secret ss output by KEM with a uniformly random value $\tilde{ss}$. This reduces to the IND-CCA-security of KEM. Hence a loss equal to $2 \cdot \mathsf{adv}_\mathsf{KEM}^\mathsf{ind\text{-}cca}$, where the factor 2 is due to the transition from the prediction-based IND-CCA experiment with a random challenge bit b to an indistinguishability-based comparison between fixed games here.

Game 9. The challenger replaces the value s_0 output by H' (modelled as a random oracle) on inputs $\tilde{ss}$ and the uniformly random (or null) s_1 with a value $\tilde{s_0}$ uniformly chosen at random. The change is not detected by $\mathcal{A}$ unless it queries H' with the "real" values $\tilde{ss}$ and s_1, respectively ℓ_{ss}- and ℓ_{s_1}-bit long. Taking into account the maximum number of queries to H', this implies a loss equal to $q_{\mathsf{H}'}/(2^{\ell_{ss}+\ell_{s_1}})$.

Game 10. The challenger replaces KDF keyed with $\tilde{s_0}$ with a random function. This reduces to the PRF-security of KDF. Hence a loss equal to $2 \cdot \mathsf{adv}_\mathsf{KDF}^\mathsf{prf}$.

Game 11. The challenger aborts if the ℓ_{sh}-bit long $sashash$ computed by π_u^i is equal to any other such value computed in another session. Hence a loss equal to $1 - (1 - 2^{-\ell_{sh}})^{n_S} \simeq n_S/2^{\ell_{sh}}$. To that point, the two instances π_u^i and π_v^j share the same values sid and s_1.

Games 12-13. The challenger aborts if π_u^i receives a valid Confirm message but no honest instance has computed its MAC tag. This reduces to the EUF-CMA-security of MAC'. Hence a loss equal to $\mathsf{adv}_{\mathsf{MAC}'}^\mathsf{euf\text{-}cma}$.

To that point, the signature received by π_u^i in a Confirm message incorporates a label ($label_R$ or $label_I$) corresponding to a role different from π_u^i.role. This signature protects the genuine signed data since no honest instance is corrupted to that point (by assumption) and since signature forgeries are excluded (due to Game 6). This signature incorporates the *sashash* value. The latter is distinct from any other such value computed in other sessions (due to Game 11). In addition, *total_hash* values are unique (since collisions on H' are excluded due to Game 4, and agreeing on sid implies agreeing on *total_hash* by construction). Therefore the signature incorporates unambiguously the session identifier sid = $\text{Hello}_I \| \cdots \| \text{KEMPart2}$. Due to Game 11, π_u^i shares the same *sashash* as the sending instance, which party is identified by the verification public key included in the signed data. Hence this proves that π_u^i shares the same sid as the instance that has computed the data sent in the received Confirm message.

Moreover, when the instance (let us call it π_v^j) that sent the Confirm message accepts, it has received a valid Confirm message (i.e., with a valid MAC tag since forgeries are excluded by Game 13) that carries an identity (embedded into a certificate). This Confirm message is computed by an instance that shares in particular the same sid as π_v^j because it carries a valid signature (by Game 6) that protects *sashash*, which implies that π_v^j shares the same sid as the sending instance (by Game 11). But the session identifiers are unique because the values H_3 are also distinct (due to Games 1-2). Therefore, the instance that has computed the Confirm message received by π_v^j is π_u^i. Consequently, π_v^j sets pid accordingly.

Therefore ExplicitAuth is true in Game 13 and the adversary's advantage is 0.

Key Indistinguishability. *Game* 0. This game corresponds to the key indistinguishability security experiment described in Sect. 2.1 applied to PQ-ZRTP.

Game 1. The challenger aborts if there exists an instance that breaks the ExplicitAuth predicate. Hence a loss equal to $\text{adv}_{\text{PQ-ZRTP}}^{\text{auth}}$.

Game 2. The challenger aborts if a decapsulation failure occurs with KEM. This implies a loss equal to $n_S \cdot \delta_{\text{KEM}}$.

Game 3. The challenger proceeds only if it succeeds in guessing the instance π_u^i targeted by the adversary and its partner π_v^j. Taking into account the maximum number of sessions n_S, this reduces the advantage of the adversary by a factor $1/n_S^2$.

Game 4-6. Similar to Games 8-10 of the explicit authentication proof. Hence a loss equal to $2 \cdot \text{adv}_{\text{KEM}}^{\text{ind-cca}} + q_{\text{H}'}/(2^{\ell_{ss}+\ell_{s_1}}) + 2 \cdot \text{adv}_{\text{KDF}}^{\text{prf}}$.

To that point, the session keys mk_I, mk_R are indistinguishable from values uniformly chosen at random.

ExplicitAuth is true by Game 1. Therefore π_u^i has an instance partner π_v^j. Moreover, this partner shares the same sid and s_1 as π_u^i, as well as the same session keys (cf. the proof of explicit authentication).

If FreshKey is true, then π_v^j is corrupted (if ever) only once π_u^i accepts. Moreover the same predicate guarantees that the partnered instance π_v^j (which shares the same session keys as π_u^i) has not been tested nor revealed. When querying the TEST oracle, the values k_0 and k_1 are then uniformly (and identically) distributed. The last game is therefore independent of the security bit b_{key}. Consequently, the probability for $\mathcal{A}$ to choose b^* equal to b_{key} is $\frac{1}{2}$. That is, its advantage is 0.

6.3   Security Proof of the Hybrid KEM

Generic Construction of the Hybrid KEM. One possible instantiation for KEM is to use an hybrid construction from two KEMs KEM1 and KEM2. The reason of such a construction is to retain the best of the two worlds, post-quantum and classical, in terms of security. The classical KEM (KEM2) benefits from long-standing and thorough analyses, hence from a high confidence, but is not able to provide any security in the post-quantum era. On the contrary, the post-quantum KEM (KEM1) is expected to withstand attacks from an adversary that can leverage a local quantum computing power, but still lacks from maturity. Therefore the purpose of using such a hybrid KEM is not to degrade the security level that one can expect from a classical scheme (when used during the pre-quantum era), with the hope that it remains secure during the post-quantum era. Moreover, the hybrid KEM protects against the so-called "harvest now, decrypt later" attacks where an adversary collects and stores data encrypted with a key derived from a classical key exchange scheme (such as DH) and waits for the advent of an efficient quantum processor in order to retroactively decrypt the data.

The security of the hybrid KEM KEM that we implement in our practical instantiation of PQ-ZRTP is studied by Bindel, Brendel, Fischlin, Goncalves and Stebila [16]. They show that the security of KEM (built upon KEM1 and KEM2) depends crucially on the function (Combiner defined by Algorithm 1) used to combine the two shared secrets output by the two underlying KEMs. In turn, this function is built upon a dual PRF (dPRF) and two PRFs (F, Extract). Let $F : (k, m) \mapsto F(k, m)$ be a function taking as first input a key k, and as second input a message m. F is a dual PRF if (i) F is a PRF, and (ii) F', defined as $F'(k, m) = F(m, k)$, is a PRF (i.e., when F takes a key as *second* input and a message as first input). Bindel et al. show that KEM is IND-CCA-secure in the post-quantum setting if dPRF is a post-quantum secure dual PRF, F and Extract are post-quantum secure PRFs, and at least one of the two underlying KEMs is post-quantum IND-CCA-secure (see Theorem 2).

Algorithm 1. Combiner

Input: shared secrets ss_1, ss_2, ciphertexts ct_1, ct_1
Output: combined shared secret ss
  1: $k_0 = \mathsf{Extract}(0, ss_2)$
  2: $k_1 = \mathsf{dPRF}(k_0, ss_1)$
  3: $ss = \mathsf{F}(k_1, ct_1 \| ct_2)$
  4: **return** ss

This means that KEM can be securely used both in the pre-quantum era and in the post-quantum era (when the adversary can request its decapsulation oracle with classical queries and leverage at the same time its local quantum computing power), even though the classical KEM (KEM2) provides then no security. This means also that data output by the hybrid KEM during the pre-quantum era and stored by an adversary cannot be successfully leveraged in the post-quantum era when a quantum computing power becomes available (i.e., KEM is not susceptible to "harvest now, decrypt later" attacks).

The hybrid KEM KEM is defined as follows. KEM.Keygen outputs a private key $sk = (sk_1, sk_2)$ and a public key $pk = (pk_1, pk_2)$ where (sk_1, pk_1) and (sk_2, pk_2) are output by KEM1.Keygen and KEM2.Keygen respectively. On input pk, KEM.Encaps outputs $ss = \text{Combiner}(ss_1, ss_2, ct_1, ct_2)$ where (ss_1, ct_1) and (ss_2, ct_2) are output by KEM1.Encaps (on input pk_1) and KEM2.Encaps (on input pk_2) respectively. On input $ct = (ct_1, ct_2)$ and sk, KEM.Decaps outputs ss.

Theorem 2 (Hybrid KEM IND-CCA security [16, Theorem 3 adapted]). *Let KEM1 be a post-quantum IND-CCA-secure KEM, KEM2 a classical IND-CCA-secure KEM, dPRF : $\mathcal{K}_0 \times \{0,1\}^* \to \mathcal{K}_1$ a post-quantum secure dual PRF, F : $\mathcal{K}_1 \times \{0,1\}^* \to \mathcal{K}'$ and Extract : $\{0,1\}^* \times \mathcal{K} \to \mathcal{K}_0$ post-quantum secure PRFs. Then the hybrid KEM KEM built upon KEM1, KEM2 and Combiner, described by Algorithm 1, is post-quantum IND-CCA-secure. More precisely, for any post-quantum IND-CCA adversary $\mathcal{A}$ against KEM, one can derive efficient post-quantum adversaries $\mathcal{B}_0, \mathcal{B}_1, \mathcal{B}_2, \mathcal{B}_3$ and $\mathcal{B}_4$ such that*

$$\text{adv}_{\text{KEM}}^{\text{ind-cca}}(\mathcal{A}) \le 2 \cdot \min \left(\text{adv}_{\text{KEM1}}^{\text{ind-cca}}(\mathcal{B}_0), \text{adv}_{\text{KEM2}}^{\text{ind-cca}}(\mathcal{B}_1) \right) + 2 \cdot \text{adv}_{\text{dPRF}}^{\text{dual-prf}}(\mathcal{B}_2)$$

$$+ 2 \cdot \text{adv}_{\text{F}}^{\text{prf}}(\mathcal{B}_3) + 2 \cdot \text{adv}_{\text{Extract}}^{\text{prf}}(\mathcal{B}_4)$$

Instantiation of the Hybrid KEM. In our practical implementation, we instantiate the underlying functions that define the hybrid KEM as follows:

- KEM1: Kyber [23] or HQC [2].
- KEM2: DHKEM [8, Section 4.1].
- Extract, dPRF, F: HMAC [11].

Bellare [10] prove that HMAC is a classical secure PRF under the assumption that the underlying compression function is a PRF. Bellare considers the case when the key is b-bit long with b the block size of the underlying compression function. Song and Yun [72] show that HMAC is a quantum secure PRF under the standard assumption that the underlying compression function is a quantum PRF. Hosoyamada and Iwata [51] confirm the statement and provide tighter bounds in the quantum random oracle model (i.e., the compression function is modelled as a quantum random oracle). The two latter works consider also a fixed key length.

Backendal, Bellare, Günther, and Scarlata [7] prove that (i) HMAC is a (variable key-length) PRF and (ii) HMAC (when keyed by its (variable length) second input) is also a PRF if either the first inputs of HMAC are all ℓ-bit long with $\ell \le b$ or they are all of any size more than b bits, where b is the block size of the underlying compression function. These results hold with additional assumptions on the underlying compression function (which must be in particular collision resistant, a dual PRF, and, when keyed by its second input, a PRF under related-key attacks).

In the computation of k_1 with dPRF, k_0 has fixed length equal to the output size of the underlying hash function (see Algorithm 1). In the computation of k_0 with Extract, we define "0" as a string of zero bytes of fixed length of the hash output. Consequently, we can safely rely upon the fact that Extract (keyed by its second input) is a PRF and dPRF is a dual PRF. Likewise, thanks to Backendal et al.'s results, F is a PRF. Moreover, we assume that HMAC when keyed by its first or (variable length) second input, is a post-quantum secure PRF. Hence, in the post-quantum setting, F and Extract (keyed by its second input) are PRFs, and dPRF is a dual PRF.

Bos, Ducas, Kiltz, Lepoint, Lyubashevsky, Schanck, Schwabe, Seiler, Stehlé [23] and Maram and Xagawa [61] prove that Kyber is a post-quantum IND-CCA-secure KEM assuming the hardness of the Module-LWE problem [24,59] in the classical and quantum random oracle models. Kyber (a slight variant of it) is selected as future NIST standard [63] and is very efficient in terms of parameters size (compared to other post-quantum schemes) and computation time.

HQC is a code-based KEM (like Classic McEliece [3] and BIKE [6]) and its security relies upon a different problem than Kyber. Aguilar-Melchor, Blazy, Deneuville, Gaborit and Zémor [2] prove that HQC is secure assuming the hardness of a decision version of the problem of decoding random families of quasi-cyclic codes for the hamming metrics (QCSD). HQC is more competitive in terms of parameter size compared to Classic McEliece and more efficient in terms of computation than BIKE. HQC is selected for round 4 of NIST PQC.[9]

Finally, we prove below that DHKEM is a classical IND-CCA-secure KEM.

Overall, this shows that our instantiation of the hybrid KEM yields an IND-CCA secure KEM.

Algorithm 2. KEM2.Keygen: key generation

Output: private key sk, public key pk

1: $x \xleftarrow{\$} (\mathbb{Z}/p\mathbb{Z})^*$
2: $y = g^x$
3: **return** (x, y)

Security of DHKEM. DHKEM is defined in [8, Section 4.1] and described by the Algorithms 2–5. DHKEM is a KEM based on the DH protocol built on a cyclic group $\mathbb{G} = \langle g \rangle$ of prime order p. DHKEM is classical IND-CCA-secure according to Definition 6 under the Strong DH assumption and modelling HKDF-Extract as a random oracle (see Theorem 3; the full proof is given in

---

[9] https://csrc.nist.gov/Projects/post-quantum-cryptography/round-4-submissions.

Algorithm 3. KEM2.Encaps: encapsulation

Input: public key pk
Output: shared secret ss', ciphertext ct

1: $(sk', pk') = $ KEM2.Keygen()
2: $ss = pk^{sk'}$
3: $ss' = $ KDF$'(ss, pk' \| pk, |ss|)$
4: **return** (ss', pk')

Algorithm 4. KEM2.Decaps: decapsulation

Input: ciphertext ct, private key sk
Output: shared secret ss'

1: $ss = ct^{sk}$
2: $pk = g^{sk}$
3: $ss' = $ KDF$'(ss, ct \| pk, |ss|)$
4: **return** ss'

---

the extended version of this paper). Note that a security proof of HPKE [8, Section 4.1], based on an authenticated variant of DHKEM, is provided by Alwen, Blanchet, Hauck, Kiltz, Lipp, Riepel [4] (using the automated theorem proving tool CryptoVerif [20]).

Theorem 3 (Security of DHKEM). *Let DHKEM be the algorithm described by Algorithms 2–5. DHKEM is an* IND-CCA*-secure KEM according to Definition 6. More precisely, for any polynomial time adversary $\mathcal{A}$ playing the game $G_{\text{KEM},\mathcal{A}}^{\text{IND-CCA}}$ defined by Fig. 2, and making at most q_{Dc} queries to its* DECAPS *oracle and q_{RO} queries to* HKDF-Extract *(modelled as a random oracle), we have that*

$$\text{adv}_{\text{DHKEM}}^{\text{ind-cca}}(\mathcal{A}) \leq \text{adv}_{\text{G}}^{\text{sdh}}(\mathcal{B}_0) + 2 \cdot \text{adv}_{\text{HKDF-Expand}}^{\text{prf}}(\mathcal{B}_1)$$

where $\mathcal{B}_0$ et $\mathcal{B}_1$ are polynomial time adversaries against respectively the SDH *problem and the* PRF*-security of function* HKDF-Expand*, and $\mathcal{B}_0$ makes at most $q_{\text{Dc}} \times q_{\text{RO}}$ queries to its* DDH *oracle. The running time of $\mathcal{B}_0$ is $t' \simeq O(q_{\text{Dc}} \times q_{\text{RO}})$ when the running time of $\mathcal{A}$ is $t \simeq O(q_{\text{Dc}} + q_{\text{RO}})$.*

6.4 Authentication

Mutual authentication in PQ-ZRTP is (provably) ensured through signatures. The latter can be of different types providing in turn different levels of security. If a classical signature scheme is solely implemented, then PQ-ZRTP can be deployed only during the pre-quantum era, while a post-quantum signature scheme forbids an adversary from impersonating a legitimate user after the advent of an efficient quantum processor. A last option consists in implementing a hybrid signature scheme, obtained by using simultaneously a classical and a post-quantum signature scheme [17,44]. A way to compute the hybrid signature is to concatenate the classical and the post-quantum signature. Such a hybrid

---

Algorithm 5. KDF$'$

Input: key ikm, context ctx, output size ℓ
Output: key K

1: $ikm' = label_{zrtp}\|ECHId\|label_{ext}\|ikm$
2: $prk = $ HKDF-Extract($``"$, ikm')
3: $info = \ell\|label_{zrtp}\|ECHId\|label_{exp}\|ctx$
4: $K = $ HKDF-Expand(prk, $info$, ℓ)
5: **return** K

---

signature is valid if and only if the two signatures (classical and post-quantum) are both valid (note however that such a construction does not guarantee non-separability). In that case, PQ-ZRTP provides security (regarding authentication) both in the classical and post-quantum era (without need to update the protocol).

To instantiate the signature scheme we select Dilithium [40] and EdDSA [14]. Dilithium is based on the hardness of finding short vectors in lattices. This scheme is SUF-CMA-secure [40] (a stronger notion than EUF-CMA) in the classical and quantum random oracle models based on the hardness of Module-LWE [24,59], Module-SIS [40,60] (MSIS) and SelfTargetMSIS [55] problems. Moreover Dilithium is also S-UEO-secure [34] (i.e., it is resistant against "exclusive ownership" attacks [19,65] where an adversary creates a public key under which an (honestly generated) message-signature pair verifies). Ed25519 is proved to be SUF-CMA-secure and S-UEO-secure [25] against a classical adversary. We assume that the EdDSA variant Ed448 provides the same security properties as Ed25519.

7 Open-source Code

The PQ-ZRTP source code corresponds essentially to the protocol described in Sect. 5. The main difference is related to the authentication mechanism. The current version of the source code makes use of SAS to guarantee mutual authentication. Indeed, in real life, such a technique is still desirable to a lot of users and practitioners. Moreover, while a pressing concern affects classical asymmetric encryption schemes due to the "harvest now, decrypt later" attacks, the same does not hold regarding signature mechanisms before the actual advent of an efficient quantum computer.

The other differences are that the Confirm's IVs are pseudo-randomly generated (and transmitted) instead of being output by KDF, and the $total\_hash$ parameter does not include the initiator's Hello message. These changes are deferred to a future version of the source code.

The source code is based on the Open Quantum Safe project (liboqs 0.9.1)[10] for the post-quantum public-key algorithms (Kyber, HQC in NIST PQC round 3 version), libdecaf (version 1.0.2)[11] for the elliptic curve operations (X25519,

---

[10] https://openquantumsafe.org/liboqs/.
[11] https://sourceforge.net/projects/ed448goldilocks/.

Table 1. Mean time of a full PQ-ZRTP execution with reference and optimised implementations for liboqs (the rest of the code uses AVX2 vector instructions in both cases).

Hybrid KEM	Public key (byte)	Ciphertext (byte)	Mean time (ms)	
			Ref.	AVX2
K25519-Kyber512	832	800	0.65	0.50
K25519-HQC-128	2,281	4,513	1.89	1.01
K448-Kyber1024	1,624	1,624	1.36	1.02
K448-HQC-256	7,301	14,525	6.90	2.99

X448), and Mbed TLS (version 3.4.0)[12] for the symmetric-key algorithms (including hash functions). The PQ-ZRTP source code is freely available at https://gitlab.linphone.org/BC/public/bzrtp.

Tests are done on Intel Core i5-6600T with 4 CPUs, cadenced at 2.7 GHz with 32 GB RAM, and the code is compiled with gcc 13.2. Table 1 gives the mean execution time of a full protocol run, corresponding to different combinations for the hybrid key exchange. We consider NIST security level 1 (equivalent to AES 128) and 5 (equivalent to AES 256) with Kyber512 (or HQC-128) and Kyber1024 (or HQC-256) respectively. K25519 and K448 indicate DHKEM instantiated with X25519 and X448 respectively.

We recall that signature operations are not included in the calculations.

The tests, done on a single laptop, do not incorporate the network interferences. However the figures presented in Table 1 illustrate clearly the efficiency of the protocol when the hybrid KEM is executed.

8   Conclusion

In this paper, we devise a quantum-resistant authentication key exchange protocol based on the (classical) ZRTP protocol that we call PQ-ZRTP. As the original ZRTP, this post-quantum variant enables to establish secure communications for VoIP. The security properties guaranteed by PQ-ZRTP hold in the pre- and post-quantum eras.

We correct the original ZRTP protocol to thwart a reflection attack against authentication (when the latter relies upon signatures) and avoid misbinding issues that could potentially lead to unknown key-share attacks. This mitigation is also incorporated into PQ-ZRTP.

We use a strong security model in the post-quantum setting that captures mutual authentication, session key privacy and forward secrecy. The security proofs that we present show that PQ-ZRTP guarantees all these security properties.

---

[12] https://github.com/Mbed-TLS/mbedtls.

Finally, we provide a fully functional open-source code of the corresponding application that illustrates the practicality and efficiency of PQ-ZRTP.

A promising avenue of improvement would be to adapt PQ-ZRTP in order to forbid an adversary from tracking a user (based on the parameter that are or may remain static, such as the ZID identifiers and the $rs1ID$, $rs2ID$ parameters). Finding the proper trade-off between the ability, on the one hand, to hide the latter parameters and, on the other hand, to deal with possible desynchronisations (in terms of $rs1$, $rs2$ secret values) would then result in a functional privacy-preserving protocol.

Acknowledgements. The authors thank the reviewers for their valuable remarks. The first author was partly supported by the French ANR MobiS5 project (ANR18-CE-39-0019-02).

References

1. Abdalla, M., Bellare, M., Rogaway, P.: The oracle diffie-hellman assumptions and an analysis of DHIES. In: Naccache, D. (ed.) CT-RSA 2001. LNCS, vol. 2020, pp. 143–158. Springer, Heidelberg (2001). https://doi.org/10.1007/3-540-45353-9_12
2. Aguilar-Melchor, C., Blazy, O., Deneuville, J.C., Gaborit, P., Zémor, G.: Efficient encryption from random quasi-cyclic codes. IEEE Trans. Inf. Theory **64**(5), 3927–3943 (2018)
3. Albrecht, M.R., et al.: Classic McEliece: conservative code-based cryptography: cryptosystem specification (2023)
4. Alwen, J., Blanchet, B., Hauck, E., Kiltz, E., Lipp, B., Riepel, D.: Analysing the HPKE standard. In: Canteaut, A., Standaert, F.-X. (eds.) EUROCRYPT 2021. LNCS, vol. 12696, pp. 87–116. Springer, Cham (2021). https://doi.org/10.1007/978-3-030-77870-5_4
5. Angel, Y., Dowling, B., Hülsing, A., Schwabe, P., Weber, F.J.: Post quantum noise. In: Yin, H., Stavrou, A., Cremers, C., Shi, E. (eds.) ACM CCS 2022, pp. 97–109. ACM Press (2022)
6. Aragon, N., et al.: BIKE: bit flipping key encapsulation (2022)
7. Backendal, M., Bellare, M., Günther, F., Scarlata, M.: When messages are keys: Is HMAC a dual-PRF? In: Handschuh, H., Lysyanskaya, A. (eds.) CRYPTO 2023, Part III. LNCS, vol. 14083, pp. 661–693. Springer, Heidelberg (2023). https://doi.org/10.1007/978-3-031-38548-3_22
8. Barnes, R., Bhargavan, K., Lipp, B., Wood, C.: Hybrid Public Key Encryption. RFC 9180 (2022)
9. Baugher, M., McGrew, D., Naslund, M., Carrara, E., Norrman, K.: The Secure Real-time Transport Protocol (SRTP). RFC 3711 (2004)
10. Bellare, M.: New proofs for NMAC and HMAC: security without collision resistance. J. Cryptol. **28**(4), 844–878 (2015)
11. Bellare, M., Canetti, R., Krawczyk, H.: Keying hash functions for message authentication. In: Koblitz, N. (ed.) CRYPTO 1996. LNCS, vol. 1109, pp. 1–15. Springer, Heidelberg (1996). https://doi.org/10.1007/3-540-68697-5_1
12. Bellare, M., Desai, A., Jokipii, E., Rogaway, P.: A concrete security treatment of symmetric encryption. In: 38th FOCS, pp. 394–403. IEEE Computer Society Press (1997)

13. Bellare, M., Rogaway, P.: The security of triple encryption and a framework for code-based game-playing proofs. In: Vaudenay, S. (ed.) EUROCRYPT 2006. LNCS, vol. 4004, pp. 409–426. Springer, Heidelberg (2006). https://doi.org/10.1007/11761679_25

14. Bernstein, D.J., Duif, N., Lange, T., Schwabe, P., Yang, B.Y.: High-speed high-security signatures. J. Cryptogr. Eng. **2**(2), 77–89 (2012)

15. Bhargavan, K., Brzuska, C., Fournet, C., Green, M., Kohlweiss, M., Zanella-Béguelin, S.: Downgrade resilience in key-exchange protocols. In: 2016 IEEE Symposium on Security and Privacy, pp. 506–525. IEEE Computer Society Press (2016)

16. Bindel, N., Brendel, J., Fischlin, M., Goncalves, B., Stebila, D.: Hybrid key encapsulation mechanisms and authenticated key exchange. In: Ding, J., Steinwandt, R. (eds.) PQCrypto 2019. LNCS, vol. 11505, pp. 206–226. Springer, Cham (2019). https://doi.org/10.1007/978-3-030-25510-7_12

17. Bindel, N., Herath, U., McKague, M., Stebila, D.: Transitioning to a quantum-resistant public key infrastructure. In: Lange, T., Takagi, T. (eds.) PQCrypto 2017. LNCS, vol. 10346, pp. 384–405. Springer, Cham (2017). https://doi.org/10.1007/978-3-319-59879-6_22

18. Blake-Wilson, S., Johnson, D., Menezes, A.: Key agreement protocols and their security analysis. In: Darnell, M. (ed.) Cryptography and Coding 1997. LNCS, vol. 1355, pp. 30–45. Springer, Heidelberg (1997). https://doi.org/10.1007/BFb0024447

19. Blake-Wilson, S., Menezes, A.: Unknown key-share attacks on the station-to-station (STS) protocol. In: Imai, H., Zheng, Y. (eds.) PKC 1999. LNCS, vol. 1560, pp. 154–170. Springer, Heidelberg (1999). https://doi.org/10.1007/3-540-49162-7_12

20. Blanchet, B.: A computationally sound mechanized prover for security protocols. IEEE Trans. Depend. Secur. Comput. **5**(4), 193–207 (2008)

21. Boneh, D.: The decision Diffie-Hellman problem. In: Buhler, J.P. (ed.) ANTS 1998. LNCS, vol. 1423, pp. 48–63. Springer, Heidelberg (1998). https://doi.org/10.1007/BFb0054851

22. Bos, J.W., Costello, C., Naehrig, M., Stebila, D.: Post-quantum key exchange for the TLS protocol from the ring learning with errors problem. In: 2015 IEEE Symposium on Security and Privacy, pp. 553–570. IEEE Computer Society Press (2015)

23. Bos, J.Wet al.: CRYSTALS - kyber: a cca-secure module-lattice-based KEM. In: 2018 IEEE European Symposium on Security and Privacy, (EuroS&P), pp. 353–367. IEEE (2018)

24. Brakerski, Z., Gentry, C., Vaikuntanathan, V.: (Leveled) fully homomorphic encryption without bootstrapping. In: Proceedings of the 3rd Innovations in Theoretical Computer Science Conference, ITCS 2012, pp. 309–325. ACM (2012)

25. Brendel, J., Cremers, C., Jackson, D., Zhao, M.: The provable security of Ed25519: theory and practice. In: 2021 IEEE Symposium on Security and Privacy, pp. 1659–1676. IEEE Computer Society Press (2021)

26. Brendel, J., Fiedler, R., Günther, F., Janson, C., Stebila, D.: Post-quantum asynchronous deniable key exchange and the Signal handshake. In: Hanaoka, G., Shikata, J., Watanabe, Y. (eds.) PKC 2022, Part II. LNCS, vol. 13178, pp. 3–34. Springer, Heidelberg (2022). https://doi.org/10.1007/978-3-030-97131-1_1

27. Brendel, J., Fischlin, M., Günther, F., Janson, C., Stebila, D.: Towards post-quantum security for signal's X3DH handshake. In: Dunkelman, O., Jacobson, Jr., M.J., O'Flynn, C. (eds.) SAC 2020. LNCS, vol. 12804, pp. 404–430. Springer, Cham (2021). https://doi.org/10.1007/978-3-030-81652-0_16

28. Bresciani, R., Butterfield, A.: A formal security proof for the ZRTP Protocol. In: 2009 International Conference for Internet Technology and Secured Transactions, (ICITST), pp. 1–6 (2009)
29. Campagna, M., Crockett, E.: Hybrid Post-Quantum Key Encapsulation Methods (PQ KEM) for Transport Layer Security 1.2 (TLS) (2021)
30. Canetti, R., Krawczyk, H.: Analysis of key-exchange protocols and their use for building secure channels. In: Pfitzmann, B. (ed.) EUROCRYPT 2001. LNCS, vol. 2045, pp. 453–474. Springer, Heidelberg (2001). https://doi.org/10.1007/3-540-44987-6_28
31. Celi, S., Faz-Hernández, A., Sullivan, N., Tamvada, G., Valenta, L., Wiggers, T., Westerbaan, B., Wood, C.A.: Implementing and measuring KEMTLS. In: Longa, P., Ràfols, C. (eds.) LATINCRYPT 2021. LNCS, vol. 12912, pp. 88–107. Springer, Cham (2021). https://doi.org/10.1007/978-3-030-88238-9_5
32. Celi, S., Hoyland, J., Stebila, D., Wiggers, T.: A tale of two models: formal verification of KEMTLS via Tamarin. In: Atluri, V., Di Pietro, R., Jensen, C.D., Meng, W. (eds.) ESORICS 2022, Part III. LNCS, vol. 13556, pp. 63–83. Springer, Heidelberg (2022). https://doi.org/10.1007/978-3-031-17143-7_4
33. Cohn-Gordon, K., Cremers, C., Gjøsteen, K., Jacobsen, H., Jager, T.: Highly efficient key exchange protocols with optimal tightness. In: Boldyreva, A., Micciancio, D. (eds.) CRYPTO 2019. LNCS, vol. 11694, pp. 767–797. Springer, Cham (2019). https://doi.org/10.1007/978-3-030-26954-8_25
34. Cremers, C., Düzlü, S., Fiedler, R., Fischlin, M., Janson, C.: BUFFing signature schemes beyond unforgeability and the case of post-quantum signatures. In: 2021 IEEE Symposium on Security and Privacy, pp. 1696–1714. IEEE Computer Society Press (2021)
35. Cremers, C., Fontaine, C., Jacomme, C.: A logic and an interactive prover for the computational post-quantum security of protocols. In: 2022 IEEE Symposium on Security and Privacy, pp. 125–141. IEEE Computer Society Press (2022)
36. Crockett, E., Paquin, C., Stebila, D.: Prototyping post-quantum and hybrid key exchange and authentication in TLS and SSH. Cryptology ePrint Archive, Report 2019/858 (2019). https://eprint.iacr.org/2019/858
37. Davis, H., Günther, F.: Tighter proofs for the SIGMA and TLS 1.3 key exchange protocols. In: Sako, K., Tippenhauer, N.O. (eds.) ACNS 2021. LNCS, vol. 12727, pp. 448–479. Springer, Cham (2021). https://doi.org/10.1007/978-3-030-78375-4_18
38. Davis, H., Diemert, D., Günther, F., Jager, T.: On the concrete security of TLS 1.3 PSK mode. In: Dunkelman, O., Dziembowski, S. (eds.) EUROCRYPT 2022, Part II. LNCS, vol. 13276, pp. 876–906. Springer, Heidelberg (2022). https://doi.org/10.1007/978-3-031-07085-3_30
39. Dolev, D., Yao, A.: On the security of public key protocols. IEEE Trans. Inf. Theory 29(2), 198–208 (1983)
40. Ducas, L., et al.: CRYSTALS-Dilithium: a lattice-based digital signature scheme. IACR TCHES 2018(1), 238–268 (2018). https://tches.iacr.org/index.php/TCHES/article/view/839
41. Fluhrer, S., Kampanakis, P., McGrew, D., Smyslov, V.: Mixing Preshared Keys in the Internet Key Exchange Protocol Version 2 (IKEv2) for Post-quantum Security. RFC 8784 (2020)
42. Gazdag, S., Grundner-Culemann, S., Guggemos, T., Heider, T., Loebenberger, D.: A formal analysis of IKEv2's post-quantum extension. In: ACSAC 2021: Annual Computer Security Applications Conference, pp. 91–105. ACM (2021)
43. Gellert, K., Handirk, T.: A formal security analysis of session resumption across hostnames. In: Bertino, E., Shulman, H., Waidner, M. (eds.) ESORICS 2021. LNCS, vol. 12972, pp. 44–64. Springer, Cham (2021). https://doi.org/10.1007/978-3-030-88418-5_3

44. Ghinea, D., et al.: Hybrid post-quantum signatures in hardware security keys. In: Applied Cryptography and Network Security Workshops: ACNS 2023 Satellite Workshops, ADSC, AIBlock, AIHWS, AIoTS, CIMSS, Cloud S&P, SCI, SecMT, SiMLA, pp. 480–499. Springer, Heidelberg (2023). https://doi.org/10.1007/978-3-031-41181-6_26

45. Giron, A.A., do Nascimento, J.P.A., Custódio, R., Perin, L.P., Mateu, V.: Post-quantum Hybrid KEMTLS performance in simulated and real network environments. In: Aly, A., Tibouchi, M. (eds.) Progress in Cryptology – LATINCRYPT 2023, pp. 293–312. Springer, Heidelberg (2023). https://doi.org/10.1007/978-3-031-44469-2_15

46. Goldwasser, S., Micali, S., Rivest, R.L.: A digital signature scheme secure against adaptive chosen-message attacks. SIAM J. Comput. **17**(2), 281–308 (1988)

47. Gonzalez, R., Wiggers, T.: KEMTLS vs. post-quantum TLS: performance on Embedded Systems. In: Batina, L., Picek, S., Mondal, M. (eds.) Security, Privacy, and Applied Cryptography Engineering, pp. 99–117. Springer, Heidelberg (2022). https://doi.org/10.1007/978-3-031-22829-2_6

48. Hashimoto, K., Katsumata, S., Kwiatkowski, K., Prest, T.: An efficient and generic construction for Signal's handshake (X3DH): post-quantum, state leakage secure, and deniable. In: Garay, J. (ed.) PKC 2021, Part II. LNCS, vol. 12711, pp. 410–440. Springer, Heidelberg (2021). https://doi.org/10.1007/s00145-022-09427-1

49. Hashimoto, K., Katsumata, S., Kwiatkowski, K., Prest, T.: An efficient and generic construction for Signal's handshake (X3DH): post-quantum, state leakage secure, and deniable. J. Cryptol. **35**(3), 17 (2022)

50. Herzinger, D., Gazdag, S.L., Loebenberger, D.: Real-world quantum-resistant IPsec. In: 2021 14th International Conference on Security of Information and Networks (SIN), vol. 1, pp. 1–8 (2021)

51. Hosoyamada, A., Iwata, T.: On tight quantum security of HMAC and NMAC in the quantum random oracle model. In: Malkin, T., Peikert, C. (eds.) CRYPTO 2021. LNCS, vol. 12825, pp. 585–615. Springer, Cham (2021). https://doi.org/10.1007/978-3-030-84242-0_21

52. Hülsing, A., Ning, K.C., Schwabe, P., Weber, F.J., Zimmermann, P.R.: Post-quantum WireGuard. In: 2021 IEEE Symposium on Security and Privacy, pp. 304–321. IEEE Computer Society Press (2021)

53. Jakobsson, M., Sako, K., Impagliazzo, R.: Designated verifier proofs and their applications. In: Maurer, U. (ed.) EUROCRYPT 1996. LNCS, vol. 1070, pp. 143–154. Springer, Heidelberg (1996). https://doi.org/10.1007/3-540-68339-9_13

54. Kampanakis, P., Stebila, D., Hansen, T.: Post-quantum Hybrid Key Exchange in SSH (2023)

55. Kiltz, E., Lyubashevsky, V., Schaffner, C.: A concrete treatment of fiat-shamir signatures in the quantum random-oracle model. In: Nielsen, J.B., Rijmen, V. (eds.) EUROCRYPT 2018. LNCS, vol. 10822, pp. 552–586. Springer, Cham (2018). https://doi.org/10.1007/978-3-319-78372-7_18

56. Kniep, Q.M., Müller, W., Redlich, J.-P.: Post-Quantum cryptography in wireguard VPN. In: Park, N., Sun, K., Foresti, S., Butler, K., Saxena, N. (eds.) SecureComm 2020. LNICST, vol. 336, pp. 261–267. Springer, Cham (2020). https://doi.org/10.1007/978-3-030-63095-9_16

57. Kret, E., Schmidt, R.: The PQXDH key agreement protocol (2023)

58. LaMacchia, B., Lauter, K., Mityagin, A.: Stronger security of authenticated key exchange. In: Susilo, W., Liu, J.K., Mu, Y. (eds.) ProvSec 2007. LNCS, vol. 4784, pp. 1–16. Springer, Heidelberg (2007). https://doi.org/10.1007/978-3-540-75670-5_1

59. Langlois, A., Stehlé, D.: Worst-case to average-case reductions for module lattices. Des. Codes Cryptogr. **75**(3), 565–599 (2015)
60. Lyubashevsky, V.: Lattice signatures without trapdoors. In: Pointcheval, D., Johansson, T. (eds.) EUROCRYPT 2012. LNCS, vol. 7237, pp. 738–755. Springer, Heidelberg (2012). https://doi.org/10.1007/978-3-642-29011-4_43
61. Maram, V., Xagawa, K.: Post-quantum anonymity of Kyber. In: Boldyreva, A., Kolesnikov, V. (eds.) PKC 2023, Part I. LNCS, vol. 13940, pp. 3–35. Springer, Heidelberg (2023). https://doi.org/10.1007/978-3-031-31368-4_1
62. Marlinspike, M., Perrin, T.: The X3DH key agreement protocol (2016)
63. NIST: module-lattice-based key-encapsulation mechanism standard (2023)
64. Paquin, C., Stebila, D., Tamvada, G.: Benchmarking post-quantum cryptography in TLS. In: Ding, J., Tillich, J.-P. (eds.) PQCrypto 2020. LNCS, vol. 12100, pp. 72–91. Springer, Cham (2020). https://doi.org/10.1007/978-3-030-44223-1_5
65. Pornin, T., Stern, J.P.: Digital signatures do not guarantee exclusive ownership. In: Ioannidis, J., Keromytis, A., Yung, M. (eds.) ACNS 2005. LNCS, vol. 3531, pp. 138–150. Springer, Heidelberg (2005). https://doi.org/10.1007/11496137_10
66. Schwabe, P., Stebila, D., Wiggers, T.: Post-quantum TLS without handshake signatures. In: Ligatti, J., Ou, X., Katz, J., Vigna, G. (eds.) ACM CCS 2020, pp. 1461–1480. ACM Press (2020)
67. Schwabe, P., Stebila, D., Wiggers, T.: More efficient post-quantum KEMTLS with pre-distributed public keys. In: Bertino, E., Shulman, H., Waidner, M. (eds.) ESORICS 2021. LNCS, vol. 12972, pp. 3–22. Springer, Cham (2021). https://doi.org/10.1007/978-3-030-88418-5_1
68. Shor, P.W.: Algorithms for quantum computation: discrete logarithms and factoring. In: 35th FOCS, pp. 124–134. IEEE Computer Society Press (1994)
69. Shor, P.W.: Polynomial-time algorithms for prime factorization and discrete logarithms on a quantum computer. SIAM J. Comput. **26**(5), 1484–1509 (1997)
70. Shoup, V.: Sequences of games: a tool for taming complexity in security proofs. Cryptology ePrint Archive, Report 2004/332 (2004). https://eprint.iacr.org/2004/332
71. Signal: Technical information (2016)
72. Song, F., Yun, A.: Quantum security of NMAC and related constructions. In: Katz, J., Shacham, H. (eds.) CRYPTO 2017. LNCS, vol. 10402, pp. 283–309. Springer, Cham (2017). https://doi.org/10.1007/978-3-319-63715-0_10
73. Stebila, D., Fluhrer, S., Gueron, S.: Hybrid key exchange in TLS 1.3 (2023)
74. Tasopoulos, G., Li, J., Fournaris, A.P., Zhao, R.K., Sakzad, A., Steinfeld, R.: Performance evaluation of post-quantum TLS 1.3 on resource-constrained embedded systems. In: Su, C., Gritzalis, D., Piuri, V. (eds.) ISPEC 2022. LNCS, vol. 13620, pp. 432–451. Springer, Heidelberg (2022). DOI: https://doi.org/10.1007/978-3-031-21280-2_24
75. Tjhai, C.J., et al.: Multiple Key Exchanges in the Internet Key Exchange Protocol Version 2 (IKEv2). RFC 9370 (2023)
76. Unger, N., Dechand, S., Bonneau, J., Fahl, S., Perl, H., Goldberg, I., Smith, M.: SoK: secure messaging. In: 2015 IEEE Symposium on Security and Privacy, pp. 232–249. IEEE Computer Society Press (2015)
77. Wiggers, T., Celi, S., Schwabe, P., Stebila, D., Sullivan, N.: KEM-based Authentication for TLS 1.3 (2023)
78. Zimmermann, P., Johnston, A., Callas, J.: ZRTP: media path key agreement for unicast secure RTP. RFC 6189 (2011)
79. Zimmermann, P., Johnston, A., Callas, J., Cross, T.: ZRTP: media path key agreement for unicast secure RTP (2012)

A New Hash-Based Enhanced Privacy ID Signature Scheme

Liqun Chen[1]($\boxtimes$)(iD), Changyu Dong[2](iD), Nada El Kassem[1](iD),
Christopher J. P. Newton[1](iD), and Yalan Wang[1](iD)

[1] University of Surrey, Guildford, UK
liqun.chen@surrey.ac.uk
[2] Guangzhou University, Guangzhou, China

Abstract. The elliptic curve-based Enhanced Privacy ID (EPID) signature scheme is broadly used for hardware enclave attestation by many platforms that implement Intel Software Guard Extensions (SGX) and other devices. This scheme has also been included in the Trusted Platform Module (TPM) specifications and ISO/IEC standards. However, it is insecure against quantum attackers. While research into quantum-resistant EPID has resulted in several lattice-based schemes, Boneh *et al.* have initiated the study of EPID signature schemes built only from symmetric primitives. We observe that for this line of research, there is still room for improvement. In this paper, we propose a new hash-based EPID scheme, which includes a novel and efficient signature revocation scheme. In addition, our scheme can handle a large group size (up to 2^{60} group members), which meets the requirements of rapidly developing hardware enclave attestation applications. The security of our scheme is proved under the Universal Composability (UC) model. Finally, we have implemented our EPID scheme, which, to our best knowledge, is the first implementation of EPID from symmetric primitives.

Keywords: Hash-based signatures · Enhanced Privacy ID · Signature-based revocation

1 Introduction

The Concept of Enhanced Privacy ID (EPID). Like group signatures [19] and Direct Anonymous Attestation (DAA) signatures [11], EPID is a type of anonymous signature scheme, which allows users in a group to sign messages such that the signatures can be verified using a group public key, and the actual signers' identities are not revealed to the verifier (beyond the fact that they belong to the group). The difference between these three types of signatures is the methods that they handle traceability and revocation. A group signature is traceable, meaning that given a signature, an authorised entity, namely a group tracer, can find the actual signer. However, to avoid the tracer being a privacy bottleneck, both DAA and EPID do not support traceability.

M.-J. Saarinen and D. Smith-Tone (Eds.): PQCrypto 2024, LNCS 14771, pp. 37–71, 2024.
https://doi.org/10.1007/978-3-031-62743-9_2

Revocation is defined as "the withdrawal of the power of a signing key that has been granted". A typical revocation method is using a revocation list. Different types of revocation lists are considered in anonymous signatures. When a group public key is on the revocation list, the entire group can be revoked. Group signatures, DAA, and EPID all support this type of revocation. When a certain group member's key material is on the revocation list, this member can be revoked. Some group signature schemes put a part of the membership credential on the revocation list, e.g. [9]. Both DAA and EPID can use a private key revocation list, such that if a signer's private key is revealed, this signer is revoked. This is not a powerful revocation since a signer's private key is known only by the signer and there is no way to force a malicious signer to revoke itself. To avoid this weakness, both DAA and EPID further have signature-based revocation. In DAA, this is through linkability, i.e., two DAA signatures signed by the same signer are linked if they use the same basename. For example, to access a digital service, signers are required to use a given basename from the service provider, who based on the user's behaviour can build a local signature revocation list. In EPID, a signature can directly be put on the revocation list, and an EPID signature includes an extra Non-Interactive Zero-Knowledge Proof (NIZKP) to demonstrate that none of the signatures in the list was signed using the current signing key, while it does not leak any extra information about a signer who has not been revoked. This is a unique and powerful feature of EPID. The challenge is to make the cost of the NIZKP as low as possible.

Related Work. The idea and first scheme of EPID were proposed by Brickell and Li [12,15]. They aim to build a new DAA scheme with enhanced revocation capabilities. Their security notion of EPID is a modification of the security model of the original DAA scheme [11] by replacing linkability with signature-based revocation. The security of their scheme is based on the strong RSA and the decisional Diffie-Hellman assumptions. Shortly after that, Brickell and Li [13,14] proposed a more efficient EPID scheme using bilinear pairings, and its security is based on the strong Diffie-Hellman and the decisional Diffie-Hellman assumptions. The computational and communicational costs of both proof generation and verification are linear to the size of the signature revocation list. The authors expected that the revocation list would be rather small. Later, Dall et al. [25] identified that the Intel SGX EPID implementation leaks sensitive key information via a cache side channel. Based on our understanding, this side-channel attack does not show any design flaw in EPID schemes. Recently, Faonio et al. [29] introduced a subversion resilient EPID (SR-EPID) scheme, which provides the same functionality and security guarantees of the original EPID, despite potentially subverted hardware. Their scheme uses also bilinear pairings. The security of their scheme is based on the External Diffie-Hellman assumption, i.e., both pairing input groups hold the decisional Diffie-Hellman assumption. As for security analysis, Muhammad et al. worked on the formal method-based security analysis of EPID-based remote attestation [46]. They made use of a fully automated formal approach using a popular automatic symbolic protocol verifier, ProVerif [7], to specify and verify the EPID-based attestation process in the Intel SGX. El Kassem *et al.* [28] presented a new security model for EPID in the Universal Composability (UC) framework.

The pairing-based EPID scheme [14] is used for hardware enclave attestation by many platforms that equip Intel Software Guard Extensions (SGX). This scheme is included in ISO/IEC standards [35]. A TPM implementation of EPID is included in the TPM 2.0 library specifications [47]. All these standard EPID schemes make use of elliptic curves and their security is based on Diffie-Hellman-related problems, so they are not quantum-safe. Designing a post-quantum EPID scheme has drawn the cryptographic community's attention. Solutions based on lattices or hash functions have appeared in the literature.

In 2019, El Kassem *et al.* [28] proposed the first EPID scheme based on lattices. The security of their scheme relies on the ring Short Integer Solution (SIS) and Learning With Error (LWE) hard problems. Their scheme is proven secure under the UC framework. In 2023, Biswas *et al.* [6] proposed another lattice-based EPID scheme. The security of their scheme relies on the hardness of the standard SIS problem. They adopted an updatable Merkle tree accumulator to ensure that any group member can join or be revoked dynamically at any time. Again in 2023, Chen *et al.* [20] proposed a new lattice-based Secure Device Onboard EPID (SDO-LEPID) scheme, their construction is based on the lattice-based DAA protocol in [23]. They implemented both the lattice-based EPID scheme [27] and their proposed scheme and claimed that their new EPID scheme is more efficient. However, we observe that the performance of their protocol can be further improved by relying on more efficient and compact lattice-based zero-knowledge proofs such as in [10,40].

Boneh *et al.* [8] initiated the study of EPID from symmetric primitives and proposed two EPID schemes. Their schemes rely on hash functions, pseudorandom functions (PRFs), and Non-Interactive Zero-Knowledge Proofs (NIZKPs) only. There is no known quantum attack on these primitives, so their schemes are quantum-resistant. More specifically, the first scheme makes use of an NIZKP of PRFs and the NIZKP is instantiated by MPC-in-the-Head (MPCitH); considering a real-world use case of remote hardware attestation, the second scheme uses a Merkle-tree-based accumulator to arrange group credentials, that allows to reduce the signature size by moving many heavy verification steps outside of the NIZKP. It is claimed that the maximum group size can reach 2^{40} theoretically. They have not implemented their schemes although discussed key sizes and signature sizes for different sizes of a group.

Our Contributions. The focus of this paper is to improve the existing work on EPID from symmetric primitives. We observe that the following aspects have not yet been completed: (1) find an efficient method to prove an unrevealed signature key has not been used to create any signatures in a signature revocation list; (2) let a symmetric-based EPID scheme handle a large group size, aiming to 2^{60}; (3) prove the security of a symmetric-based EPID scheme under the Universal Composability (UC) model; and (4) implement a symmetric-based EPID scheme and check their performance precisely. The contribution of this paper is to complete these aspects. We propose a new hash-based EPID scheme, which includes a novel and efficient signature revocation scheme. Our scheme can handle a large group size (up to 2^{60} group members), which meets the requirements of rapidly developing hardware enclave attestation applications. The security of our scheme is proved under the UC model. Finally, we have implemented our EPID scheme, which, to our best knowledge, is the first implementation of EPID from symmetric primitives.

Outline of the Paper. The remaining part of this paper is arranged as follows: Sect. 2 describes relevant preliminaries, Sect. 3 presents the proposed EPID construction, Sect. 4 and 5 provide security notions and proofs, Sect. 6 discusses our implementation result and compares it with the existing post-quantum EPID implementation results, and Sect. 7 concludes this paper. For the sake of completion, we provide the security analysis of a group membership credential scheme in Appendix A.

2   Preliminaries

2.1   Hash-Based Signatures

In a hash-based signature scheme, a private key is composed of a series of randomly generated strings, while the corresponding public key is obtained by applying hash functions to the private key. Early hash-based signature schemes, such as the Lamport scheme [39] and the Winternitz scheme [41], were one-time signatures (OTS), meaning that each key pair can only be used to sign a single message. The Merkle signature scheme [41] is the first hash-based few-time signatures (FTS). It generates several OTS key pairs and aggregates their public keys using a Merkle tree. The root of the tree serves as the overall public key. Every signature uses one OTS private key, and it is comprised of the corresponding OTS and the Merkle tree authentication path for the OTS public key. The verifier can verify multiple signatures using only the Merkle tree root.

These signature schemes are characterized as stateful, as the signer is required to maintain a state containing information such as the number of signed messages and the keys utilized. In comparison, more recent FTS schemes, such as FORS [4], is stateless as they utilize a large set of secret random strings that can be obtained from a pseudorandom function applied to the private key. Signatures are then generated by selecting elements from the set based on the message to be signed. While each signature discloses some secret strings in the set, the set size is large, and the number of signatures can be controlled to make it infeasible to forge a signature by mixing and matching secret strings from previously generated signatures. Building on the top of FORS, SPHINCS+ [4] is a more powerful stateless hash-based signature scheme. It employs a hyper-tree, i.e., a tree of trees, to organize OTS and FTS key pairs. Each SPHINCS+ signature constitutes a chain of signatures, with the initial signature Σ_0 being generated from the message, and each subsequent signature Σ_i being a signature of the public key that verifies the preceding signature Σ_{i-1}. By using the root public key, the authenticity of the signature chain can be verified. Although SPHINCS+ also has an upper limit on the number of signatures that can be generated per key pair, it can be set to an extremely large value (up to 2^{64}), making it highly unlikely to reach this limit in practical scenarios. SPHINCS+ has been chosen as one of the three digital signature schemes by the National Institute of Standards and Technology (NIST) to become a part of its post-quantum cryptographic standard [43].

2.2 MPC-in-the-Head Based Signatures

Ishai et. al. [33] introduced the idea of Zero-Knowledge Proofs (ZKP) based on "Multi-Party Communication in the Head" (MPCitH). Given a public value x, the prover proves knowing a witness w such that $f(w) = x$. To do so, the prover simulates, by itself, an MPC protocol between m parties that realizes f, in which w is secretly shared as an input to the parties, and commits to the views and internal state of each party. Next, the verifier challenges the prover to open a subset of these commitments, checks them, and decides whether to accept or not. If the MPC realizes f properly, this protocol is complete, meaning a valid statement will always be accepted. The protocol is also zero-knowledgeable because only the views and internal states of a subset of the parties are available to the verifier, and by the privacy guarantee of the underlying MPC protocol, no information about w can be leaked. For soundness, if the prover tries to prove a false statement, then the joint views of some of the parties must be inconsistent, and with some probability, the verifier can detect that. The soundness error of a single MPC run can be high, but by repeating this process independently enough times, the soundness error can be made negligible. The interactive zero-knowledge proofs can be made Non-Interactive Zero-Knowledge Proofs (NIZKP) through techniques such as the Fiat-Shamir transformation.

There are many solutions for constructing MPCitH NIZKPs, e.g., IKOS [33], ZKBoo [32], ZKB++ [18], KKW [37], Ligero++ [5], Limbo [45], BBQ [44], Banquet [2], BN++ [36], Rainer [26], AIM [38], Aurora [3], VOLE-in-the-Head [1] and Polaris [31]. They follow the same paradigm but are different in the underlying MPC protocols and have different concrete/asymptotic efficiency. In this paper, to describe our scheme, we do not need to touch the low-level details, hence we will use MPCitH (for Boolean circuits) in an abstract way. We will use the following syntax to describe a NIZKP:

$$\pi = \mathcal{P}\{(\texttt{public params}); (\texttt{witness})|\texttt{relation to be proved}\}$$

For example, to prove the same key sk is used in two different instantiations of a pseudorandom function F with different data inputs, we write:

$$\pi = \mathcal{P}\{(C_1, P_1), (C_2, P_2)); (sk)|C_1 = F(sk, P_1) \wedge C_2 = F(sk, P_2)\}$$

MPCitH has been used to generate signature schemes from a symmetric key setting. The first scheme is Picnic [18,48,49], in which the secret signing key is k and the public verification key is a pair (c,p), and the key pair satisfy the equation $c = E(k,p)$ where E is a block cipher, k is a secret key, and p and c are respectively a plaintext and ciphertext block. To enhance security and improve performance, more MPCitH-based signature schemes have been developed, e.g., Banquet [2], Rainer [26], FAEST [1], AIM [38] and Peron [24].

Our EPID scheme makes use of this type of signature scheme, and any scheme that holds the Existential Unforgeability under a Chosen Message Attack (EUF-CMA) can be used. More specifically, we create a public and private key pair from a keyed pseudo-random function written as $y = F(sk,x)$, where sk is a secret signing key and the corresponding public verification key is $pk = (x,y)$. Signing a message m essentially is to generate a non-interactive MPCitH proof of knowing sk:

$$\pi = \mathcal{P}\{(x,y); (sk)|y = F(sk,x)\}(m)$$

2.3 M-FORS and F-SPHINCS+ Signatures

To construct an EPID scheme from symmetric primitives, we need to select symmetric setting-based group membership credentials. A credential is a signature on a group member's key generated by the issuer. Following the research on hash-based group signatures [22] and hash-based DAA [21], we choose an F-SPHINCS+ signature as a group credential. The F-SPHINCS+ signature scheme is a modification of the SPHINCS+ signature scheme [4]. As a result, F-SPHINCS+ signatures are more MPCitH friendly than SPHINCS+ signatures. As depicted in Fig. 1, F-SPHINCS+ signatures make use of a hyper-tree that is a tree of M-FORS trees. We now recall the description of M-FORS and F-SPHINCS+ from [21,22].

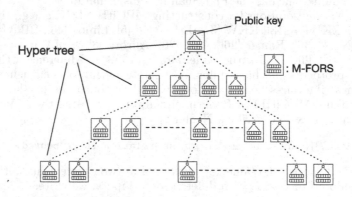

Fig. 1. F-SPHINCS+ signatures.

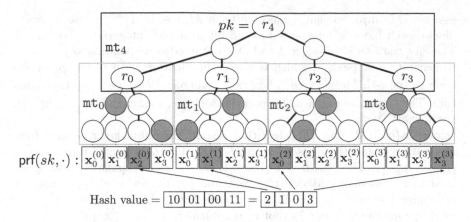

Fig. 2. M-FORS signatures.

M-FORS. The M-FORS signature scheme, as depicted in Fig. 2, is a modification of FORS used in SPHINCS+ [4]. As mentioned before, FORS is a few-time signature scheme such that each key pair can be used to sign up to q signatures. M-FORS, short for Merkle FORS, differs from FORS in that, the public key is generated as the root of a Merkle tree. The purpose of this modification is to allow a partial proof in MPCitH, which will significantly imrove the performance (see M-FORS partial proof later for a more detailed discussion). With M-FORS, the hyper-tree in F-SPHINCS+ is a q-ary tree such that the public key in a child node is signed by the signing key in the parent node, and the signing key in the leaf node signs the actual message hash. An F-SPHINCS+ signature then contains a list of $h+1$ signatures, where h is the height of the hyper-tree. The benefit of M-FORS over XMSS that is used in the original SPHINCS+ scheme is the lower verification cost. To verify a message hash that is k blocks of d-bit string, the cost is $d{\cdot}k+k-1$ hash operations. This is much less than the $(2^d-1){\cdot}k$ hashes for verifying a WOTS+ signature. On the other hand, the signing time is more than that of WOTS+. However, this is a lesser concern because in our case signing will be done in the clear (while verification needs to be done with zero knowledge). M-FORS consists of the algorithms below.

- keyGen($\mathsf{seed}, n, d, k, \mathsf{aux}$): it takes as input a random seed seed, a security parameter n, two positive integers d and k, and aux that is either an empty string or some optional data. If seed is an empty string, an n-bit random string will be chosen and assigned to it. Then a pseudorandom function prf is used to expand seed into k lists $(\mathbf{x}^{(0)}, \cdots, \mathbf{x}^{(k-1)})$, where each $\mathbf{x}^{(i)}$ contains 2^d distinct n-bit pseudorandom strings. Then $k+1$ Merkle trees $\mathbf{T} = (\mathsf{mt}_0, \cdots, \mathsf{mt}_k)$ are built. In particular, each of $\mathsf{mt}_0, \cdots, \mathsf{mt}_{k-1}$ has 2^d leaf nodes. The jth leaf node in mt_i is the hash of $\mathbf{x}_j^{(i)}$. The leaf nodes of mt_k are $r_0, \cdots, r_{k-1}$ that are the roots of $(\mathsf{mt}_0, \cdots, \mathsf{mt}_{k-1})$. keyGen outputs $(pk, sk, param)$, such that the public key $pk = r_k$ where r_k is the root of mt_k, the private key $sk = \mathsf{seed}$, and the public parameters $mp = (n, d, k, \mathsf{aux})$.

- sign(sk, MD, mp): to sign a message hash $MD \in \{0,1\}^{k \cdot d}$, parse it into k blocks, each block is interpreted as a d-bit unsigned integers $(p_0, \cdots, p_{k-1})$. Then for the i-th block p_i, $\mathbf{x}^{(i)}$ and $\mathtt{mt}_i$ (obtained by expanding sk) are used to generate $\mathtt{authpath}^{(i)}$, which is the authentication path of the p_i-th leaf node in the i-th Merkle tree. Then $(\mathbf{x}_{p_i}^{(i)}, \mathtt{authpath}^{(i)})$ is put into the signature. The signature is a list of k pairs $\boldsymbol{\sigma} = \{(\mathbf{x}_{p_0}^{(0)}, \mathtt{authpath}^{(0)}), \cdots, (\mathbf{x}_{p_{k-1}}^{(k-1)}, \mathtt{authpath}^{(k-1)})\}$.
- recoverPK(σ, MD, mp): This algorithm outputs the public key recovered from a signature σ and the message hash MD. First MD is parsed into k blocks $(p'_0, \cdots, p'_{k-1})$. Then for $0 \leq i \leq k-1$, $\boldsymbol{\sigma}_i = (x_i, \mathtt{authpath}^{(i)})$ and p'_i are used to re-generate a Merkle tree root and get the value r'_i (p'_i is used to determine the order of the siblings at each layer). Finally, $r'_0, \cdots, r'_{k-1}$ are used to compute $\mathtt{mt}'_k$ and its root r'_k is returned.
- verify(σ, pk, MD, mp): to verify a signature, call recoverPK(σ, MD, mp). If the recovered public key is the same as pk, accept the signature, otherwise reject.

F-SPHINCS+. The hyper-tree nodes in F-SPHINCS+ are addressed by a pair (a, b) where a is its layer and b is its index within the layer. The root node is at layer 0, and the layer number of all other nodes is the layer number of its parent plus 1. All nodes within a layer are viewed as an ordered list, and index each node in the list from left to right, starting from 0. F-SPHINCS+ consists of the following algorithms:

- keyGen(n, q, h): This algorithm outputs (sk, pk, fp). It takes as input a security parameter n, the degree of non-leaf nodes in the hyper-tree q, and the height of the hyper-tree h. Then it chooses d, k that are the parameters for the underlying M-FORS signature scheme. The public parameters are $fp = (n, q, h, d, k)$. It also chooses an n-bit random string as the private key sk. It generates the M-FORS key pair for the root node by calling genNode($(0, 0), sk, fp$), and set the public key pk to be the M-FORS public key $pk_{0,0}$.
- genNode($nodeAdr, sk, fp$): This algorithm generates a node in the hyper-tree given the address $nodeAdr = (a, b)$. With the private key sk used as a *seed*, the algorithm first generates a subseed with a pseudorandom function $\mathtt{seed}_{a,b} = \mathsf{prf}(seed, a\|b)$, then it calls M-FORS key generation algorithm M-FORS.keyGen ($\mathtt{seed}_{a,b}, n, d, k, a\|b$). The output $(pk_{a,b}, sk_{a,b}, mp_{a,b})$ is the content of the node at (a, b).
- mHash(msg, gr): This algorithm produces message hash and the leaf node index used in generating the F-SPHINCS+ signature. The input msg is the message to be signed, gr is a random string. The algorithm produces $MD\|idx \leftarrow H_3(msg\|gr)$, where $H_3 : \{0,1\}^* \to \{0,1\}^{d \cdot k + (\log_2 q) \cdot h}$ is a public hash function, MD is $d \cdot k$ bit long and idx is interpreted as an $(\log_2 q) \cdot h$ bit long unsigned integer.
- sign(msg, sk, fp): This algorithm produces the F-SPHINCS+ signature as a chain of M-FORS signature along the path from a leaf node to the root

node of the hyper-tree. It chooses an n-bit random string gr. Then obtain $MD\|idx \leftarrow$ mHash(msg, gr). A leaf node at (h, idx) is then generated by calling genNode$((h, idx), sk, fp)$. The M-FORS signing key $sk_{h,idx}$ is used to sign MD and generate σ_0. The parent node of (h, idx) is then generated by calling genNode$((h-1, b), sk, fp)$ where $(h-1, b)$ is the address of the parent node. Then the parent secret key $sk_{h-1,b}$ is used to sign the child public key $pk_{h,idx}$, and the signature is σ_1. Repeat the signing process until obtaining σ_h that is signed by $sk_{0,0}$ on $pk_{1,b'}$ for some b'. The F-SPHINCS+ signature is then $(gr, \mathbf{S} = (\sigma_0, \cdots, \sigma_h))$.

- verify$(msg, gr, \mathbf{S}, pk, fp)$: This algorithm verifies every M-FORS signature that is chained up in $\mathbf{S}$. Given $\mathbf{S} = (\sigma_0, \cdots, \sigma_h)$, first compute $MD\|idx \leftarrow H_3(msg\|gr)$. Then obtain $pk_0 \leftarrow$ recoverPK(σ_0, MD, mp_0), $pk_1 \leftarrow$ recoverPK (σ_1, pk_0, mp_1), repeat until $pk_h \leftarrow$ recoverPK$(\sigma_h, pk_{h-1}, mp_h)$. If $pk = pk_h$, accept the signature, otherwise reject.

Remark 1. In M-FORS algorithms, we use two tweakable hash functions [4] $H_1 : \{0,1\}^* \rightarrow \{0,1\}^n$ and $H_2 : \{0,1\}^* \rightarrow \{0,1\}^{d \cdot k}$. Almost all hash operations are done using H_1. H_2 is only used to map the k-th Merkle tree to the $k \cdot d$-bit M-FORS public key, so that when used in F-SPHINCS+ the public key is of the right size to be signed by the parent node. If M-FORS is to be used as a stand-alone signature scheme, these two hash functions can be the same.

Remark 2. The tweakable hash functions follow Construction 7 for tweakable hash functions in [4]. Namely, the hash of an input M is produced by calling a hash function with additional input as $H(\mathsf{P}\|\mathsf{ADD}\|M)$, where P is a public hash key and ADD acts as the tweak. The tweak is the address where the hash operation takes place within the hyper-tree, and it is a five part string $a_1\|b_1\|v\|a_2\|b_2$:

- (a_1, b_1), where $0 \leq a_1 \leq h, 0 \leq b_1 \leq 2^{a_1} - 1$, is the address of an hyper-tree node. Within the node, an M-FORS key pair that is based on $k + 1$ Merkle trees are stored.
- $0 \leq v \leq k$ is the index of a Merkle tree in the M-FORS key pair stored in the hyper-tree node (a_1, b_1). When $0 \leq v \leq k - 1$, the Merkle tree (of height d) is used to sign the v-th block of the message; when $v = k$, the Merkle tree (of height $\lceil \log_2 k \rceil$) is used to accumulated the roots of all the previous Merkle trees into the public key.
- (a_2, b_2) is the address of an Merkle tree node. When $0 \leq v \leq k-1, 0 \leq a_2 \leq d$ and $0 \leq b_2 \leq 2^{a_2} - 1$; When $v = k, 0 \leq a_2 \leq \lceil \log_2 k \rceil - 1$ and $0 \leq b_2 \leq 2^{a_2} - 1$.

The security analysis of F-SPHINCS+ is given in Appendix A.

M-FORS Partial Proof. The challenge for implementing a NIZKP of F-SPHINCS+ signature with MPCitH comes from the cost of $h + 1$ M-FORS signature verifications. Following the description of M-FORS, to verify a single M-FORS signature, $k \cdot (d+1) + (k-1) = kd + 2k - 1$ hashes are needed, which is in the order of 100 for a practical setting (with an extra factor of 2 if implementing with MPC_F, as a part of our EPID scheme, which will be described in Sect. 3).

The $h+1$ factor means that if implemented naively, the MPC would need to call thousands of times the sub-procedure that implements the hash function, and the size of the circuit for the whole MPC can go easily above a million-gates. Even worse, to reduce the soundness error, the same circuit needs to be executed tens to hundreds of times in an MPCitH proof. Thus, a naive implementation of a NIZKP of F-SPHINCS+ signature will result in a very large signature size and a high computational cost.

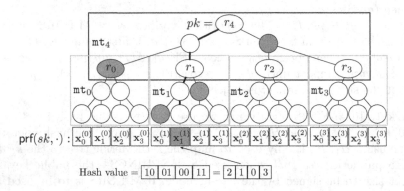

Fig. 3. M-FORS Patial Verification.

As suggested in [21,22], in an efficient MPCitH proof, rather than repeating t times an MPC procedure in which the M-FORS signatures are fully verified, we run $t' \geq k$ MPC procedures in which the M-FORS signatures are partially verified, one block in each run (see the example of partial verification in Fig. 3). More precisely, we extend the M-FORS with the following algorithms:

- partialSig(σ, MD, i, mp): to extract a partial signature of the i-th block of MD from $\sigma = \{(x_0, \mathbf{authpath}^{(0)}), \cdots, (x_{k-1}, \mathbf{authpath}^{(k-1)})\}$. The Merkle tree $\mathtt{mt}_k$ can be recomputed from σ. The partial signature is $\partial_{\sigma,i} = (x_i, \mathbf{authpath}^{(i)}, \mathbf{authpath}^{(k,i)})$ where $(x_i, \mathbf{authpath}^{(i)})$ is a copy of the i-th pair in σ, and $\mathbf{authpath}^{(k,i)}$ is the authentication path of r_i (the root of the i-th Merkle tree) in $\mathtt{mt}_k$.
- partialRec($\partial_{\sigma,i}, p_i, i, mp$): This algorithm recovers the public key from $\partial_{\sigma,i}$ and p_i. Given $\partial_{\sigma,i} = (x, \mathbf{authpath}, \mathbf{authpath}')$, first compute the Merkle tree root r_i from $(x, \mathbf{authpath}, p_i)$, then compute the Merkle tree root pk from $(r_i, \mathbf{authpath}', i)$. Output pk.

With partial-rec, only one path is used to recover the M-FORS public key instead of k paths. Why does this approach make sense? In an MPCitH proof, the same procedure is run multiple times. Each run has a soundness ϵ that a cheating prover can get away without being detected. Thus t runs are needed so that ϵ^t is negligibly small. In our case, the main cost of the MPC procedure comes from verifying all the M-FORS signatures. The full verification requires every block of the message digest or the child public key to be verified. Our observation is that if a prover has to cheat, then it has to cheat in more than 1 blocks with a high probability. If the prover has to cheat in n out of k blocks, then using partial verification with t', such that $t' \cdot n/k \geq t$, ensures that the prover has to cheat in more than t runs, and hence with a negligible success probability. As we analysed, an implementation with full signature verification requires $t \cdot (h+1) \cdot (k \cdot d + 2k - 1)$ calls to the MPC hash procedure. The partial verification based implementation, on the other hand, requires only $t' \cdot (h + 1) \cdot (d + 1 + \lceil \log k \rceil)$ MPC hash calls. The improvement is roughly $\frac{tk}{t'}$ times.

3   The Proposed EPID Scheme

3.1   Syntax

Players. The EPID scheme involves the following players:

- **An issuer** owns a group public and private key pair and manages the group membership, decides who can be a group member, and issues a group membership credential to each group member. Each group has one issuer and the issuer is also called the group manager.
- **A group member** generates a public and private key pair, receives a membership credential from the issuer for this key pair, and uses the key and credential to create EPID signatures. A group member is also called an EPID signer. Each group has many members.
- **A verifier** verifies EPID signatures by using the issuer's group public key. Each group can have an arbitrary number of verifiers.
- **A revocation authority** decides whether a group member should be removed from the group and maintains signature and key revocation lists. Each group should have at least one revocation authority.

Revocation Lists. There are two types of revocation lists:

- A key revocation list denoted by KRL lists revealed private signing keys.
- A signature revocation list denoted by SRL lists signatures created by revoked signers.

Each verifier uses one KRL and one SRL, from their chosen revocation authority. Note that key revocation provides the ability to revoke an existing signature with an updated key revocation list. However, as for any EPID scheme, signature revocation does not provide such ability because a signature can only prove that the signing key is not associated with any key in the SRL that is available during signing. This proof cannot be extended to cover any items added into the SRL later.

Algorithms/Protocols. Our EPID scheme consists of the following algorithms/protocols:

- Init(n): In the initialization algorithm, the issuer takes a security parameter n as the input, and outputs a master (group) key pair (mpk, msk). The master public key mpk is made public and the master secret key msk is stored privately by the issuer. In all other algorithms and protocols, we will assume mpk along with the security parameter n as an implicit input for all parties.
- Join(msk): the joining protocol is an interactive protocol between the issuer and a user u who wants to join the group. The issuer has a private input msk and the user does not have input. At the end of the protocol, the issuer outputs a decision: `accept` or `reject`. If `reject`, then stop. If `accept`, the user obtains its group signing key $gsk_u = (sk_u, cred_u)$ where sk_u is a secret key, and $cred_u$ is a group membership credential. sk_u is chosen and held by the user, and $cred_u$ is generated by the issuer and given to the user. Now, the user becomes a group member, who is a legitimate signer.
- Sign(gsk_u, msg, SRL): the signing algorithm allows a signer to produce an EPID signature Σ on a message $msg \in \{0,1\}^*$ using its signing key gsk_u. The signature includes proof of whether gsk_u was used to generate any signatures in the signature revocation list SRL.
- Verify(msg, Σ, KRL, SRL): the verification algorithm allows a verifier to verify whether a signature Σ is a valid signature of msg, whether the corresponding signing key has been listed on a rogue key list KRL, and whether it has been used to generate any signatures on the signature revocation list SRL.
- Revocation(KRL,SRL): The revocation algorithm allows a revocation authority to add a revealed signing key in KRL and to add a signature generated by a revoked signer in SRL.

3.2 Details of Algorithms and Protocols

Initialization Init(n): Given a security parameter n, the issuer does the following to create a group master public and secret key pair to be used for the F-SPHINCS+ signature scheme.

1. The issuer first chooses the hyper-tree node degree q and the tree height h, the values (d, k) for the underlying M-FORS scheme, a pseudorandom function prf, three hash functions $H_1 : \{0,1\}^* \rightarrow \{0,1\}^n$, $H_2 : \{0,1\}^* \rightarrow \{0,1\}^{d \cdot k}$, $H_3 : \{0,1\}^* \rightarrow \{0,1\}^{d \cdot k + (\log_2 q) \cdot h}$, and a keyed pseudorandom function $F : \{0,1\}^n \times \{0,1\}^n \rightarrow \{0,1\}^n$.
2. The issuer then runs $(sk, rpk, gp) \leftarrow$ F-SPHINCS+.keyGen(n, q, h), where (rpk, sk) is the F-SPHINCS+ public and secret key pair, and $gp = (n, q, h, d, k)$ are the hyper-tree parameters.
3. The issuer then publishes the master public key $mpk = (gp, rpk, H_1, H_2, H_3, F$, prf) and keeps the master secret key $msk = sk$ private.

4. To prove the key construction correctness, the issuer provides a Non-Interactive Zero-Knowledge Proof (NIZKP) $\pi_{\mathcal{I}}$ to demonstrate that the key pair is generated correctly, meaning that the secret and public keys are associated with each other. This NIZKP can be achieved by signing its own public key rpk using F-SPHINCS+.sign, which is similar to the issuer creating a group membership credential in the joining protocol described below.
5. In addition, the issuer initializes an empty group list GL.

Each verifier initializes two revocation lists: a key revocation list KRL and a signature revocation list SRL. All these lists are empty when initialised. Alternatively, these two revocation lists can be managed by a centralised authority and each signer and verifier can then download them for signing or verification.

Joining Protocol Join(msk, n): The joining protocol is run between a user and the issuer. Note that this protocol involves the authentication of the user by the issuer. The issuer has an authentic copy of the user's endorsement key, which is used to establish a secure and authenticated channel between the user and the issuer. Our EPID scheme does not restrict which cryptographic mechanism is used to establish this channel. In the following protocol description, it is assumed the existence of such a channel. The protocol includes the following steps:

1. A unique session ID u is assigned to the user. For simplicity, we can think of the session ID as a monotonically increasing counter, and each invocation of the joining protocol will increase it by 1. Alternatively, the value u can be computed from the user's endorsement key, which is unique to the user.
2. The user chooses a random secret key: $sk_u \xleftarrow{R} \{0,1\}^n$ as its signing key.
3. The user computes the group identifier $gid = H_1(rpk)$.
4. The user generates its entry token $et_u = F(sk_u, gid)$ together with the NIZKP $\pi_u : \mathcal{P}\{(gp, gid, et_u); (sk_u) | et_u = F(sk_u, gid)\}$.
5. The user chooses a random string $cr \xleftarrow{R} \{0,1\}^n$, computes a commitment $ct = H_1(et_u \| cr)$, then sends (u, ct) to the issuer to request joining the group.
6. Upon receiving (u, ct), the issuer checks whether an entry with the same u is in GL. If yes, the issuer rejects the user. Otherwise, if the issuer would like to accept the user, the issuer chooses a random string $gr_u \xleftarrow{R} \{0,1\}^n$ and sends it to the user, who responds by sending (et_u, cr, π_u) back. The issuer verifies $ct = H_1(et_u \| cr)$ and the NIZKP π_u. If both verifications pass, the issuer computes the group credential $(gr_u, \mathbf{S}) \leftarrow$ F-SPHINCS+.sign($et_u \| gr_u, msk, gp$) and adds $(u, et_u, gr_u, \mathbf{S})$ to GL; otherwise, the issuer rejects the user.
7. The user, if accepted by the issuer, sets its group signing key $gsk_u = (sk_u, gr_u, \mathbf{S})$. The user has now become an EPID signer for this group.

Signature Generation Sign($gsk_u, msg, $SRL): Given a message to be signed denoted by msg and a signature revocation list SRL, the user u generates an EPID signature using $gsk_u = (sk_u, gr_u, \mathbf{S})$ by performing the following steps:

1. The user gets the group public key rpk and generates a random data string $str \xleftarrow{R} \{0,1\}^n$, then computes $sid, sst, gid, et_u, mt_u, idx$ as follows:

(a) The user first computes the signature identifier $sid = H_1(msg\|str)$ and the signature signing token $sst = F(sk_u, sid)$.

(b) The user then computes the group identifier $gid = H_1(rpk)$, the group membership entry token $et_u = F(sk_u, gid)$ and $mt_u\|idx = H_3(et_u\|gr_u)$. Here $H_3(et_u\|gr_u)$ is used as F-SPHINCS+.mHash(et_u, gr_u).

2. To prove that the user has not been revoked, the user generates a random number $r \xleftarrow{R} \{0,1\}^n$, then $\forall j \in \{1, \ldots, J = |\mathsf{SRL}|\}$, the user retrieves $sid_j = H_1(msg_j\|str_j)$ and $sst_j = F(sk_j, sid_j)$ from SRL, and produces two signature proof tokens $A_j = F(F(sk_u, sid_j), r)$ and $B_j = F(sst_j, r)$. Note that if and only if $sk_u \neq sk_j$, $A_j \neq B_j$. Also note that $F(sk_u, sid_j)$ has been kept secret, so that (A_j, B_j) will not reveal any sensitive information about sk_u. As discussed in Remark 3 below, **this novel and efficient privacy-preserving inequivalence proof may have its interest.**

3. To prove the EPID credential, the user generates another random number $s \xleftarrow{R} \{0,1\}^n$ and computes $com = H_1(s\|pk_h\| \cdots \|rpk)\}$, where $pk_h, \cdots, rpk$ are the public keys for verifying the signatures in **S**, from the layer h to layer 0 (the public key at the layer 0 is rpk). The user produces an NIZKP π_E (note that recoverPK was defined in Subsect. 2.3 for M-FORS):

$$\pi_E : \mathcal{P}\{(gp,\ rpk,\ gid,\ sid,\ sst,\ com,\ r,\ \mathsf{SRL}, \forall_{j\in[1,J]}\ A_j);$$
$$(sk_u,\ et_u,\ gr_u,\ s,\ \mathbf{S} = \{\sigma_h, \cdots, \sigma_0\}) \mid sst = F(sk_u,\ sid)$$
$$\wedge \forall_{j\in[1,J]}\ A_j = F(F(sk_u,\ sid_j), r)$$
$$\wedge\ et_u = F(sk_u,\ gid)$$
$$\wedge\ mt_u\|idx = H_3(et_u\|gr_u)$$
$$\wedge\ pk_h = \mathsf{recoverPK}(\sigma_h, mt_u, (n, d, k, (h, idx)))$$
$$\wedge\ pk_{h-1} = \mathsf{recoverPK}(\sigma_{h-1}, pk_h, (n, d, k, (h-1, \lfloor\frac{idx}{q}\rfloor))) \wedge \cdots$$
$$\wedge\ rpk = \mathsf{recoverPK}(\sigma_0, pk_1, (n, d, k, (0, 0)))$$
$$\wedge\ com = H_1(s\|pk_h\| \cdots \|rpk)\}$$

4. The EPID signature is $\Sigma = (str,\ sst,\ com,\ r, \forall_{j\in[1,J]}\ A_j, \pi_E)$.

Signature Verification Verify$(msg, \Sigma, \mathsf{KRL}, \mathsf{SRL})$: Given $\Sigma = (str, sst, com, r, \forall_{j\in[1,J]}\ A_j, \pi_E)$ and msg together with two revocation lists KRL and SRL, the verifier performs the following steps to verify this signature:

1. $\forall sk_j \in \mathsf{KRL}$, the verifier computes $sst_j^* = F(sk_j, sid)$. If any $sst_j^* = sst$, rejects Σ.

2. Otherwise, $\forall j \in [1, J]$, the verifier checks if any sid_j has been used in Σ correctly. If not reject Σ. Otherwise, compute $B_j = F(sst_j, r)$ and check if any $A_j = B_j$ holds, if so reject Σ.

3. Otherwise, the verifier recomputes $sid = H_1(msg\|str)$ and $gid = H_1(rpk)$, then verifies π_E. Accept if the verification succeeds, otherwise reject.

Key and Signature Revocation Revocation(KRL,SRL): There are two cases to revoke the group membership of the user u:

1. Given sk_u, the revocation authority adds it in KRL.
2. Given a signature Σ signed by the user u together with the corresponding signed message msg, the revocation authority retrieves str and sst from Σ, computes $sid = H_1(msg\|str)$, and adds the pair (sid, sst) in SRL.

Remark 3. In the existing EPID scheme [8], an EPID signature under the signing key sk_i contains of $t = (F(sk_i, r), r)$, where r is a random value. To support signature revocation, for each revoked signature $\text{sig}_j \in$ SRL, a new EPID signature under the signing key sk_i^* includes the NIZKP for $t_{\text{sig}_j} \neq (F(sk_i^*, r_{\text{sig}_j}), r_{\text{sig}_j})$. However, the paper does not provide a concrete construction for this inequality proof in zero-knowledge. To build a practical EPID scheme from symmetric primitives, a concrete proof scheme is necessary. For the first time, we propose a non-interactive zero-knowledge inequality proof π_R:

$$\pi_R : \mathcal{P}\{(gp, \; sid, \; sst, \; r, \; \forall_{j \in [1,J]} : (sid_j, \; sst_j) \in \text{SRL}, \; A_j); (sk_u)|$$
$$sst = F(sk_u, \; sid) \wedge \forall_{j \in [1,J]} \; A_j = F(F(sk_u, \; sid_j), r)\}$$

where sk_u is the user's long-term key and r is a public nonce, which allows the verifier to compute $B_j = F(sst_j, r)$. If $A_j \neq B_j$, the verifier can be convinced that $\text{sig}_j \in$ SRL was not signed under sk_u; since otherwise it contradicts the collision-resistance of the keyed pseudorandom function F. However, if $sk_u = sk_j$, $A_j = B_j$ must hold. This proof is privacy-preserving for an unrevoked user since such proof does not reveal any sensitive information of sk_u. The proof is reasonably efficient. When SRL has J revoked signatures, it requires the NIZKP for $2J$ operations of F. In Sect. 3.5, we will discuss how to separate this revocation proof from the credential proof to optimise the performance of our EPID scheme.

3.3 The Proof π_E

The most important part in the EPID signature $\Sigma = (str, \; sst, \; com, \; r, \; \forall_{j \in [1,J]} \; A_j, \; \pi_E)$ is the proof π_E. As Σ is a signature of a message msg, the foremost thing π_E needs to prove is that the signer knows a group signing key $gsk_u = (sk_u, \; gr_u, \; \mathbf{S})$ and it was used to sign msg. Besides that, π_E also needs to prove that gsk_u is authorized by the issuer. To do that, in π_E the following is done:

1. It proves that given a nonce r, $\forall_{j \in [1,J]} \; sid_j \in$ SRL, $A_j = F(F(sk_u, sid_j), r)$ is correctly computed.
2. It proves that the same signing key sk_u used in the previous step is also used to generate two values et_u and sst, where et_u is bound with the group root public key rpk (as it is computed from $gid = H_1(rpk)$) and sst is bound with the message msg and random string str (as it is computed from $sid = H_1(msg\|str)$). sst is revealed in Σ, and et_u is hidden.
3. It proves that mt_u, which is computed from et_u, is signed under a private key in a leaf node of the hyper-tree generated by the group issuer. This is done by verifying all the signatures in $\mathbf{S}$ such that mt_u and σ_h produce the leaf public

key pk_h, which in turn with σ_{h-1} produces pk_{h-1}, and so on until reaching the root. The last public key produced is rpk which is published by the group issuer. All public keys recovered in this process match those committed in the commitment com.

Before showing the MPCitH instance of π_E, let us first introduce the notation used in such an MPCitH algorithm: $[\![x]\!]$ means that the value x is secret-shared when using an MPC algorithm, meaning that x is known by the prover but not the verifier. MPC_X means the MPC subroutine implementing the function X (e.g. MPC_F, MPC_H1, MPC_H2 and MPC_H3 implement F, H_1, H_2 and H_3). This notation will be used throughout the paper. Based on [34], in an implementation MPC_F can be used as a building block for the hash functions that we need.

Following the method of M-FORS partial verification, as shown in Subsect. 2.3, we now introduce the π_E MPC instance for the v-th block in MPCitH 1. The user uses partial signatures in the MPC. Recall that in the group signing key gsk_u, a list $\mathbf{S} = \{\sigma_h, \cdots, \sigma_0\}$ of $h+1$ signatures are stored, one for each layer in the hyper-tree of F-SPHINCS+. The signer can extract a partial signature for the v-th block from each signature, i.e. $\{\partial_{\sigma_h,v}, \cdots, \partial_{\sigma_0,v}\}$. In Line 12, an MPC subroutine MPC_partialRec that implements partialRec is used. This subroutine uses the input to compute the corresponding public key at the l-th layer in the hyper-tree (stored in $[\![M]\!]$ and also appended to $[\![COM]\!]$). After the last

---

MPCitH 1: $\pi_{E,v}$ – MPC instance for the v-th block

Public: $gp = (n,\ q,\ h,\ d,\ k)$,
$\quad rpk,\ gid,\ sid,\ sst,\ com,\ r,\ v,\ \forall_{j\in[1,J]}\ (sid_j, A_j)$
Private: $[\![sk_u]\!],\ [\![etu]\!],\ [\![gr_u]\!],\ [\![s]\!],\ [\![\partial_{\sigma_h},v]\!],\ \cdots,\ [\![\partial_{\sigma_0},v]\!]$
Output: $pk_0,\ \forall_{j\in[1,J]}\ A'_j,\ com'$
Check: $pk_0 = rpk\ \wedge\ com' = com\ \wedge\ \forall_{j\in[1,J]}\ (A'_j = A_j)$

1 **for** $j = 1;\ j \le |\mathsf{SRL}|;\ j{+}{+}$ **do**
2 $\quad$ $[\![A]\!] = \mathsf{MPC\_F}([\![sk_u]\!], sid_j)$;
3 $\quad$ $A'_j = \mathsf{MPC\_F}([\![A]\!], r)$;
4 **end**
5 $sst = \mathsf{MPC\_F}([\![sk_u]\!],\ sid)$;
6 $[\![et_u]\!] = \mathsf{MPC\_F}([\![sk_u]\!],\ gid)$;
7 $[\![mt_u]\!]\|[\![idx]\!] = \mathsf{MPC\_H3}([\![et_u]\!]\|[\![gr_u]\!])$;
8 $[\![M]\!] = [\![mt_u]\!]$;
9 $[\![COM]\!] = [\![s]\!]$;
10 **for** $l = h;\ l \ge 0;\ l{-}{-}$ **do**
11 $\quad$ parse $[\![M]\!]$ into k blocks $[\![p_0]\!], \cdots, [\![p_{k-1}]\!]$, each block is d-bits;
12 $\quad$ $[\![M]\!] = \mathsf{MPC\_partialRec}([\![\partial_{\sigma_l,v}]\!],\ [\![p_v]\!],\ [\![idx]\!],\ gp,\ l,\ v)$;
13 $\quad$ $[\![COM]\!] = \mathsf{MPC\_H1}([\![COM]\!]\|[\![M]\!])$;
14 $\quad$ $[\![idx]\!] = [\![\lfloor idx/q \rfloor]\!]$;
15 **end**
16 $com' = \mathsf{Reveal}([\![COM]\!])$;
17 $pk_0 = \mathsf{Reveal}([\![M]\!])$;

iteration, $[\![COM]\!]$ is hashed and $[\![M]\!]$ is revealed. The results will be checked by the verifier to see whether they match com and rpk. If so, the signer is likely to possess valid partial signatures along the path from the idx-th leaf node to the root node in the hyper-tree. Note that the algorithm partialRec was defined in Subsect. 2.3 for M-FORS partial proofs and the algorithm Reveal($[\![x]\!]$) is simply unmasking the value x.

3.4 Soundness Analysis of π_E

In π_E, k instances of MPC are run. In the ith instance, the partial verification procedure is used to verify every M-FORS signature in $\mathbf{S}$, but only the i-th block of the hash value being signed. Out of the k blocks, the adversary may have learned the secret strings correspond to λ_1 blocks through queries and has to cheat in all the remaining $k - \lambda_1$ blocks. For each MPC instance, the verifier opens the views of a subset of the MPC parties and a cheat prover can be detected with a probability $1 - \epsilon$. Therefore, if using an MPC protocol without pre-processing, then the soundness error is;

$$\sum_{i=0}^{k} \Pr[\lambda_1 = i] \cdot \epsilon^{k-i}$$

If using an MPC protocol with pre-processing, then the adversary can also cheat in the pre-processing phase. If the adversary cheats in λ_2 (out of M) copies of pre-processing data, and not being detected when checking the pre-processing data (the probability is denoted as $\mathrm{Succ}^{pre}(\lambda_2, k, M)$), then it needs to cheat in $k - \lambda_1 - \lambda_2$ MPC instances. The soundness error is:

$$\sum_{i=0}^{k} \Pr[\lambda_1 = i] \left(\sum_{\lambda_2=0}^{k-\lambda_1} \mathrm{Succ}^{pre}(\lambda_2, k, M) \cdot \epsilon^{k-\lambda_1-\lambda_2} \right)$$

As a concrete example, let us consider a case in which we implement π_E using KKW [37]. Then we have:

$$\Pr[\lambda_1 = i] = \binom{k}{i}(1 - (1 - 2^{-d})^q)^i ((1 - 2^{-d})^q)^{k-i},$$

$$\mathrm{Succ}^{pre}(\lambda_2, k, M) = \frac{\binom{M-\lambda_2}{M-k}}{\binom{M}{M-k}}, \quad \epsilon = \frac{1}{N}$$

In the above, d, k, q are the parameters for the M-FORS signature, M is the number of pre-processing data generated, and N is the number of MPC parties. When $d = 16, k = 70, q = 1024, M = 1120$, and $N = 16$, then the soundness error is $2^{-257.769}$; when $d = 16, k = 35, q = 1024, M = 560$, and $N = 16$, then the soundness error is $2^{-128.987}$.

3.5 Splitting Revocation and Credential Proofs

The cost of proving or verifying that a signer is not revoked based on a given SRL is dependent on the size of SRL, while the cost of proving or verifying that a signer holds a valid group credential is related to the group size. The previous specification of π_E in Subsect. 3.3 includes these two proofs in a single NIZKP. This may not be the best choice if the costs of these two proofs are not balanced, so optionally we split the proof π_E into two separate NIZKPs, one for revocation denoted by π_R and another for the credential denoted by π_C, i.e., $\pi_E = (\pi_R, \pi_C)$. We specify them in MPCitH 2 and MPCitH 3 respectively. Note that π_R does not use a partial proof but π_C does. The connection between these two NIZKPs is that they share the same sid and sst values, which indicates that these two NIZKPs are created by the same sk_u.

MPCitH 2: π_R – MPC Instance for Revocation

Public: $gp = (n,\ q,\ h,\ d,\ k)$, sid, sst, r, $\forall_{j \in [1,J]}\ (sid_j, A_j)$
Private: $[\![sk_u]\!]$
Output: sst', $\forall_{j \in [1,J]}\ A'_j$
Check: $sst = sst'\ \wedge\ \forall_{j \in [1,J]}\ A'_j = A_j$
1 $sst' = \mathsf{MPC\_F}([\![sk_u]\!],\ sid)$;
2 **for** $j = 1;\ j \leq |\mathsf{SRL}|;\ j{+}{+}$ **do**
3 $\quad$ $[\![A]\!] = \mathsf{MPC\_F}([\![sk_u]\!], sid_j)$;
4 $\quad$ $A'_j = \mathsf{MPC\_F}([\![A]\!], r)$;
5 **end**

---

4   UC-Based EPID Security Model

In this section, we recall the definition of the EPID UC model from [28], which is a modification of the DAA UC model given by Camenisch et al. in [17]. The changes include replacing linkability with a revocation interface and adding the signature revocation check from [16]. The model covers the following security properties:

Correctness: If a group member has completed the Join procedure and neither its key nor any of its signatures have been revoked, that group member's signatures should successfully verify.

Anonymity: Given two signatures, no adversary can distinguish whether they were created by one honest signer or two different honest signers.

Unforgeability: When the issuer is honest, no adversary can create a signature on behalf of an honest signer.

Non-frameability: Regardless of whether the issuer is honest or not, no adversary can create a signature that, if put in SRL, can revoke any honest signers' signatures.

MPCitH 3: $\pi_{C,v}$ – MPC instance for the v-th block

Public: $gp = (n, q, h, d, k)$, rpk, gid, sid, sst, com, v
Private: $[\![sk_u]\!]$, $[\![etu]\!]$, $[\![gr_u]\!]$, $[\![s]\!]$, $[\![\partial_{\sigma_h}, v]\!]$, $\cdots$, $[\![\partial_{\sigma_0}, v]\!]$
Output: pk_0, com', sst'
Check: $pk_0 = rpk \ \wedge \ com' = com \ \wedge \ sst' = sst$

1 $sst' = \mathsf{MPC\_F}([\![sk_u]\!], sid)$;
2 $[\![etu]\!] = \mathsf{MPC\_F}([\![sk_u]\!], gid)$;
3 $[\![mt_u]\!]\|[\![idx]\!] = \mathsf{MPC\_H3}([\![etu]\!]\|[\![gr_u]\!])$;
4 $[\![M]\!] = [\![mt_u]\!]$;
5 $[\![COM]\!] = [\![s]\!]$;
6 **for** $l = h;\ l \geq 0;\ l--$ **do**
7 $\quad$ parse $[\![M]\!]$ into k blocks $[\![p_0]\!], \cdots, [\![p_{k-1}]\!]$, each block is d-bit;
8 $\quad$ $[\![M]\!] = \mathsf{MPC\_partialRec}([\![\partial_{\sigma_i,v}]\!], [\![p_v]\!], [\![idx]\!], gp, l, v)$;
9 $\quad$ $[\![COM]\!] = \mathsf{MPC\_H1}([\![COM]\!]\|[\![M]\!])$;
10 $\quad$ $[\![idx]\!] = [\![\lfloor idx/q \rfloor]\!]$;
11 **end**
12 $com' = \mathsf{Reveal}([\![COM]\!])$;
13 $pk_0 = \mathsf{Reveal}([\![M]\!])$;

Generally speaking, security in the UC framework follows the simulation-based paradigm, where a protocol is secure when it is as secure as an ideal functionality that performs the desired tasks in a way that is secure by design. In a UC model, an environment $\mathcal{E}$ passes inputs and outputs to the protocol parties. The network is controlled by an adversary $\mathcal{A}$ that may communicate freely with $\mathcal{E}$. In the ideal world, the parties forward their inputs to the ideal functionality $\mathcal{F}$, which then (internally) performs the defined task and creates outputs that the parties forward to $\mathcal{E}$. A real-world protocol Π is said to securely realize a functionality $\mathcal{F}$, if the real world is indistinguishable from the ideal world, meaning for every adversary performing an attack in the real world, there is an ideal world adversary (often called simulator) $\mathcal{S}$ that performs the same attack in the ideal world. More precisely, a protocol Π is secure if for every adversary $\mathcal{A}$, there exists a simulator $\mathcal{S}$ such that no environment $\mathcal{E}$ can distinguish executing the real world with Π and $\mathcal{A}$, and executing the ideal world with $\mathcal{F}$ and $\mathcal{S}$.

The ideal functionality $\mathcal{F}_{\mathsf{EPID}}$ is formally defined under the assumption of static corruption, i.e., the adversary decides beforehand which parties are corrupt and informs $\mathcal{F}_{\mathsf{EPID}}$ about them. $\mathcal{F}_{\mathsf{EPID}}$ has five interfaces (SETUP, JOIN, SIGN, VERIFY, REVOKE) described below. Several sessions of the protocol are allowed to run at the same time and each session will be given a global identifier SID that consists of an issuer $\mathcal{I}$ and a unique string SID', i.e. SID $= (\mathcal{I}, \text{SID}')$. We also define the JOIN and SIGN sub-sessions by JSID and SSID. We also define the algorithms that will be used inside the functionality as follows:

- Kgen(1^λ): A probabilistic algorithm that takes a security parameter λ and generates keys tsk for honest signers.

- sig(tsk, msg): A probabilistic algorithm used for honest signers. On input of a key tsk, it calculates the signature identifier $sid = H_1(msg, str)$ for a random $str \leftarrow \{0,1\}^n$ and outputs a signature Σ.
- ver(Σ, msg, KRL, SRL): A deterministic algorithm that is used in the VERIFY interface. On input of a signature Σ, it outputs $f = 1$ if the signature is valid, $f = 0$ otherwise.
- Identify(tsk, Σ, msg): A deterministic algorithm that will be used to ensure consistency with the ideal functionality $\mathcal{F}_{\mathsf{EPID}}$'s internal records. It outputs 1 if a key tsk was used to produce a signature Σ on sid, 0 otherwise.
- Revoke(tsk^*, Σ^*, KRL, SRL): A deterministic algorithm that takes input tsk^* or Σ^*, it adds tsk^* to KRL or Σ^* to SRL respectively.

The UC framework allows us to focus on the analysis of a single protocol instance with a globally unique session identifier SID. $\mathcal{F}_{\mathsf{EPID}}$ uses session identifiers of the form SID $= (\mathcal{I}, \text{SID}')$ for some issuer $\mathcal{I}$ and a unique string SID$'$. In the procedures, functions CheckTtdHonest and CheckTtdCorrupt are used that return '1' when a key belongs to a honest signer that has produced no signature, and when a key belongs to a corrupt user such that there is no signature simultaneously linking back to the inputted key and another one, respectively; and return '0' otherwise. We label the checks that are done by the ideal functionality in roman numerals.

$\mathcal{F}_{\mathsf{EPID}}$ SETUP: On input (SETUP, SID) from the issuer $\mathcal{I}$, $\mathcal{F}_{\mathsf{EPID}}$ verifies that $(\mathcal{I}, \text{SID}') = \text{SID}$ and outputs (SETUP, SID) to $\mathcal{S}$. $\mathcal{F}_{\mathsf{EPID}}$ receives from the simulator $\mathcal{S}$ the algorithms Kgen, sig, ver, Identifyand revoke. These algorithms are responsible for generating keys for honest signers, creating signatures for honest signers, verifying the validity of signatures, checking whether a signature was generated by a given key, and updating the revocation lists respectively. $\mathcal{F}_{\mathsf{EPID}}$ stores the algorithms, checks that the algorithms ver, Identify and Revoke are deterministic [Check I], and outputs (SETUPDONE, SID) to $\mathcal{I}$.

$\mathcal{F}_{\mathsf{EPID}}$ JOIN:

1. JOIN REQUEST: On input (JOIN, SID, JSID) from a signer Signer, create a join session $\langle$JSID, Signer, request$\rangle$. Output (JOINSTART, SID, JSID, Signer) to $\mathcal{S}$.
2. JOIN REQUEST DELIVERY: Proceed upon receiving delivery notification from $\mathcal{S}$ by updating the session record to $\langle$JSID, Signer, delivery$\rangle$.
   - If $\mathcal{I}$ or Signer is honest and $\langle$Signer, $\star, \star\rangle$ is already in Member List ML, output $\bot$ [Check II].
   - Output (JOINPROCEED, SID, JSID, Signer) to $\mathcal{I}$.
3. JOIN PROCEED: Upon receiving an approval from $\mathcal{I}$, $\mathcal{F}_{\mathsf{EPID}}$ updates the session record to $\langle$JSID, SID, Signer, complete$\rangle$. Then it outputs (JOINCOMPLETE, SID, JSID) to $\mathcal{S}$.
4. KEY GENERATION: On input (JOINCOMPLETE, SID, JSID, tsk) from $\mathcal{S}$.
   - If the signer is honest, set $tsk = \bot$, else verify that the provided tsk is eligible by performing the following two checks that are described above:

- CheckTtdHonest(tsk)=1 [Check III].
- CheckTtdCorrupt(tsk)=1 [Check IV].
- Insert ⟨Signer, tsk⟩ into Member List ML, and output JOINED.

$\mathcal{F}_{\mathsf{EPID}}$ SIGN:

1. SIGN REQUEST: On input a request (SIGN, SID, SSID, Signer, msg) from the signer, the ideal functionality calculates the signature identifier sid and aborts if $\mathcal{I}$ is honest and no entry ⟨Signer, ⋆⟩ exists in ML [Check V], else creates a sign session ⟨SSID, Signer, msg, request⟩ and outputs (SIGNSTART, SID, SSID, Signer, msg)) to $\mathcal{S}$.
2. SIGN PROCEED: On input (SIGNPROCEED, SID, SSID, msg) from Signer, $\mathcal{F}_{\mathsf{EPID}}$ outputs (SIGNCOMPLETE, SID, SSID, KRL, SRL, msg) to $\mathcal{S}$, where KRL and SRL represent the key and the signature revocation lists respectively.
3. SIGNATURE GENERATION: On input (SIGNCOMPLETE, SID, SSID, Σ, KRL, SRL) from $\mathcal{S}$, if Signer is honest then $\mathcal{F}_{\mathsf{EPID}}$ will:
   - Ignore an adversary's signature Σ, and generate the signature for a fresh or established tsk.
   - Check CheckTtdHonest(tsk)=1 [Check VI], and store ⟨Signer, tsk⟩ in DomainKeys.
   - Generate the signature $\Sigma \leftarrow \mathrm{sig}(tsk, msg)$.
   - Check ver(Σ, msg, KRL, SRL)=1 [Check VII], and check Identify(Σ, msg, tsk) = 1 [Check VIII].
   - Check that there is no signer other than Signer with key tsk' registered in ML or DomainKeys such that Identify(Σ, msg, tsk')=1 [Check IX].
   - For all $(\Sigma^*, msg^*) \in$ SRL, find all $(tsk^*, \mathsf{Signer}^*)$ from ML and DomainKeys such that Identify(Σ^*, msg^*, tsk^*) = 1
     - Check that no two distinct keys tsk^* trace back to Σ^* [Check X].
     - Check that no pair (tsk^*, Signer) was found [Check IX].
   - If Signer is honest, then store ⟨Σ, Signer, sid⟩ in Signed and output (SIGNATURE, SID, SSID, Σ, msg, KRL, SRL).

$\mathcal{F}_{\mathsf{EPID}}$ VERIFY: On input (VERIFY, SID, msg, Σ, KRL, SRL), from a party $\mathcal{V}$ to check whether Σ is a valid signature on sid, KRL and SRL, the ideal functionality does the following:

- Extract all pairs (tsk', Signer') from the DomainKeys and ML, for which Identify(tsk', Σ, msg)=1. Set $b = 0$ if any of the following holds:
  - More than one key tsk_i was found [Check XII].
  - $\mathcal{I}$ is honest and no pair (tsk, Signer) was found [Check XIII].
  - An honest Signer was found, but no entry ⟨⋆, Signer, msg, str⟩ was found in Signed [Check XIV].
  - There is a key $tsk^* \in$ KRL, such that Identify(Σ, msg, tsk^*)=1 and no pair (tsk, Signer) for an honest Signer was found [Check XV].
  - For some matching tsk and $(\Sigma^*, msg^*) \in$ SRL, Identify(tsk, Σ^*, msg^*) = 1 [Check XVI]

- If $b \neq 0$, set $b \leftarrow \mathrm{ver}(\varSigma, msg, \mathrm{SRL}, \mathrm{KRL})$.
- Add $\langle \varSigma, msg, \mathrm{KRL}, \mathrm{SRL}, b \rangle$ to VerResults, and output (VERIFIED, SID, b) to $\mathcal{V}$.

$\mathcal{F}_{\mathsf{EPID}}$ REVOKE: On input (tsk^*, KRL), the ideal functionality replaces KRL with KRL $\cup$ tsk^*. On input $(\varSigma^*, msg^*, \mathrm{SRL})$, the ideal functionality replaces SRL with SRL $\cup$ $\varSigma^*$ after verifying $\varSigma^*$.

We emphasize that our model catches all the required EPID security properties. The *Correctness* property is achieved since honestly generated signatures always pass through verification check via the algorithm $\mathrm{ver}(\varSigma, msg, \mathrm{KRL}, \mathrm{SRL})$ [Check VIII]. This, in the real world, means that honestly generated signatures are always accepted by the verifier and not being revoked. The *Anonymity* property is guaranteed due to the random choice of the key tsk if the key belongs to an honest signer. In the case of a corrupt signer, the simulator is allowed to provide a signature that may reveal the signer's identity, as the signing key can be extracted from the respective signer key pair. This reflects that the anonymity of an EPID signer is guaranteed only when the signer is honest. The *Unforgeability* property is due to [Check XIII] and [Check XV] and the *Non-frameability* property is due to the [Check IX]. Furthermore, CheckTtdHonest prevents registering an honest tsk in the Join interface that matches an existing signature so that conflicts can be avoided and signatures can always be traced back to the original signer [Check III]. This ensures that honestly generated signatures are not revoked due to the identified algorithm being deterministic in our model. CheckTtdCorrupt [Check IV] is done when storing a new tsk that belongs to a corrupt Signer, it checks that the new tsk does not break the identifiability of signatures, i.e., it checks that there is no other known Signer key tsk', unequal to tsk, such that both keys are identified as the owner of a signature.

5 UC Security Proof of the EPID Scheme

In this section, we provide a high-level description of the UC-based security proof of our hash-based EPID scheme, which was described in Sect. 3. We present a sequence of games to show that there exists no environment $\mathcal{E}$ that can distinguish the real-world protocol denoted by $\varPi$ with an adversary $\mathcal{A}$, from the ideal world $\mathcal{F}$ with a simulator $\mathcal{S}$. Each of these games contains further checks that guarantee a desired security requirement while proving game-to-game indistinguishability. At the end of the proof, we showcase that our real protocol guarantees the desired security requirements that the ideal world provides.

We start with the real-world protocol execution in Game 1. In the next game, we construct one entity C that runs the real-world protocol for all honest parties. Then we split C into two pieces, an ideal functionality $\mathcal{F}$ and a simulator $\mathcal{S}$ that simulates the real-world parties. Initially, we start with an "empty" functionality $\mathcal{F}$. With each game, we gradually change $\mathcal{F}$ and update $\mathcal{S}$ accordingly, moving from the real world to the ideal world, and culminating to the full $\mathcal{F}_{\mathsf{EPID}}$ being realized as part of the ideal world, thus, proving our proposed security model presented in Sect. 4. The endmost goal of our proof is to prove the indistinguishability between Game 1 and Game 14, i.e., between the complete real world and the fully functional ideal world. This is done by proving that each game is indistinguishable from the previous one starting from Game 1 to reach Game 14. As aforementioned, our proof starts with setting up the real-world games (Game 1 and Game 2), followed by introducing the ideal functionality in Game 3. At this stage, the ideal functionality $\mathcal{F}$ only forwards its inputs to the simulator which simulates the real world. From Game 4 onward, $\mathcal{F}$ starts executing the setup interface on behalf of the Issuer. Moving on to Game 5, $\mathcal{F}$ handles simple verification and consistency checks without performing any detailed checks at this stage; i.e., it only checks if the signer belongs to a revocation list. In Games 6-7, $\mathcal{F}$ executes the join interface while performing checks to maintain the registered keys' consistency. It also adds checks that allow only the devices that have successfully been enrolled to create signatures. Game 8 proves the anonymity of EPID by letting $\mathcal{F}$ handle the sign queries on behalf of an honest Signer using freshly generated random key instead of running the sign algorithm using the signer's signing key. At the end of this game, we prove that an external environment will notice no change from previous games where the real-world sign algorithm was executed. Now moving to Games 9–14, we let $\mathcal{F}$ perform all other checks that are explained in our UC model that ends with the ideal functionality $\mathcal{F}_{\mathsf{EPID}}$ defined in Sect. 4.

Proof. **Game 1 (Real Word)**: This is the real world protocol.

Game 2 (Transition to the Ideal World): An entity C is introduced. C receives all inputs from the honest parties and simulates the real-world protocol for them. This is equivalent to Game 1, as this change is invisible to $\mathcal{E}$.

Game 3 (Transition to the Ideal World with Different Structure): We now split C into two parts, $\mathcal{F}$ and $\mathcal{S}$, where $\mathcal{F}$ behaves as an ideal functionality. It receives all the inputs and forwards them to $\mathcal{S}$, which simulates the real-world protocol for honest parties and sends the outputs to $\mathcal{F}$. $\mathcal{F}$ then forwards these outputs to $\mathcal{E}$. This game is essentially equivalent to Game 2 with a different structure which is invisible to $\mathcal{E}$.

Game 4 ($\mathcal{F}$ Handles the Setup): $\mathcal{F}$ now behaves differently in the setup interface, as it stores the algorithms defined in Sect. 4 that are provided by $\mathcal{S}$ from real-world protocol. $\mathcal{F}$ stores the algorithms, and checks that the algorithms ver, Identify and Revoke are deterministic [Check I], such check is indistinguishable from the real world since the algorithms are adopted from the real-world protocol. $\mathcal{F}$ also performs checks and ensures that the structure of SID, which represents the issuer's unique session identifier defined in Sect. 4, is correct for an honest $\mathcal{I}$, and aborts if not. When $\mathcal{I}$ is honest, $\mathcal{S}$ will start simulating it. Since $\mathcal{S}$ is now running the Issuer, it knows its secret key. In case $\mathcal{I}$ is corrupt, $\mathcal{S}$ extracts $\mathcal{I}$'s secret key from $\pi_{\mathcal{I}}$ when the issuer registers his key with $\mathcal{F}_{ca}$, a common certificate authority functionality that is available to all parties and controlled by the simulator, then proceeds to the setup interface on behalf of $\mathcal{I}$. By the simulation soundness of $\pi_{\mathcal{I}}$, this game transition is indistinguishable from the previous game (Game 4 $\approx$ Game 3).

Game 5 ($\mathcal{F}$ handles the verification and the revocation checks): $\mathcal{F}$ now performs the verification and the revocation checks instead of forwarding them to $\mathcal{S}$. There are no protocol messages and the outputs are exactly as in the real-world protocol. Knowing the lists KRL and SRL for corrupt signers, $\mathcal{F}$ can perform the revocation checks, and the outcomes of these checks are equal to the real-world protocol (Game 5 ≈ Game 4).

Game 6: ($\mathcal{F}$ handles the join queries): $\mathcal{F}$ stores in its records the members that have joined. If $\mathcal{I}$ is honest, $\mathcal{F}$ stores the secret key tsk, extracted from $\mathcal{S}$, for a corrupt signer. $\mathcal{S}$ always has enough information to simulate the real-world protocol except when the issuer is the only honest party. In this case, $\mathcal{S}$ does not know who initiated the join, and so cannot make a join query with $\mathcal{F}$ on the signer's behalf. Thus, to deal with this case, $\mathcal{F}$ can safely choose any corrupt signer and put it into ML. The identities of signers are only used for creating signatures for honest signers, so corrupted signers do not matter. In the case that the signer is already registered in ML, $\mathcal{F}$ would abort the protocol [Check II], but $\mathcal{I}$ will have already tested this case before continuing with the proceeding with the join query. Hence $\mathcal{F}$ will not abort. Thus in all cases, $\mathcal{F}$ and $\mathcal{S}$ can interact to simulate the real-world protocol, so Game 6 ≈ Game 5.

Game 7: ($\mathcal{F}$ performs pre-sign checks): If $\mathcal{I}$ is honest, then $\mathcal{F}$ now only allows members that joined to sign [Check V]. An honest signer will always check whether it has successfully joined (i.e., has been issued a valid credential) before signing in the real-world protocol, so there is no difference for honest signers. Therefore Game 7 ≈ Game 6.

Game 8: ($\mathcal{F}$ handles the sign queries by simulating the Signer without knowing the secret): We now transform $\mathcal{F}$ such that it internally handles the signing queries of honest signers instead of merely forwarding them to $\mathcal{S}$ that simulates the Signer and creates a signature using the Signer's key $tsk = sk_u$ as in the games before. When the Signer is honest, $\mathcal{F}$ creates the signatures internally as follows: It chooses a new key $key \leftarrow \{0,1\}^n$ per signature and then runs the sign algorithm $\text{sig}(key, msg)$ defined in Sect. 4 for that fresh key. To prove the anonymity of our EPID scheme, we show that if there exists an environment that can distinguish a signature of an honest party using $tsk = sk_u$ from a signature using a random key $key \leftarrow \{0,1\}^n$, then the environment can break the pseudorandom property of the function F.

Suppose that $\mathcal{E}$ is given tuples $\Sigma = (str, sst, com, r, \forall_{j \in [1,J]} A_j, \pi_E)$, where J denote the total number of the revoked signatures. In the reduction, we have to be able to simulate the Signer u without knowing the secret sk_u. Let key be a randomly sampled key from $\{0,1\}^n$ that will be used to generate signatures on behalf of the honest Signer rather than using the real Signer secret key sk_u. Since the issuer's secret key msk can be extracted from the issuer's zero-knowledge proof $\pi_{\mathcal{I}}$ for the correctness of the master secret and public key pair due to the soundness of the proof $\pi_{\mathcal{I}}$ and getting access to $\mathcal{F}_{crs}$, a common reference string functionality that provides participants with all system parameters. Then a credential can be created on $et'_u = F(key, gid)$ by running the signing algorithm of F-SPHINCS+ with the input (et'_u, msk, gp). After getting a credential on et'_u, sst will be calculated as functions of key such that $sst = F(key, sid)$ where $sid = H(msg, str)$. All other parts of the signature follow the same real-world protocol (i.e. when using the Signer's sk_u). The commitment com is calculated as our defined sign algorithm and the proof π_E can then be perfectly simulated using the random secret key. Due to the zero-knowledge property of the proof π_E and the pseudorandom outputs of the function F, we argue that an external environment cannot distinguish between 1) a signature generated using the Signer's (sk_u, et_u) and 2) a signature generated by a random (key, et'_u). The signature will not match one of the revoked signatures $\Sigma_j \in$ SRL with an overwhelming probability, because the probability that Σ matches one of the revoked signatures is that key matches one of the keys that were used to generate Σ_j which is $J/2^n$. For large n, this becomes negligible. With a high probability the signature that is generated from a random key r will not be revoked, so Game 8 $\approx$ Game 7.

Game 9: ($\mathcal{F}$ performs pre-signing checks): When storing a new $tsk = sk_u$, $\mathcal{F}$ checks CheckTtdCorrupt(tsk)=1 [Check IV] or CheckTtdHonest(tsk)=1 [Check III] . We want to show that these checks will always pass. A valid signatures always satisfy $et_u = F(sk_u, gid)$, $sst = F(sk_u, sid)$ and $(gr_u, \mathbf{S}) \leftarrow$ F-SPHINCS+.sign(et_u, msk, gp) where et_u corresponds to a signing key sk_u. In the real-world protocol, we have $tsk = sk_u$. By the soundness property of π_E that is proved in Sect. 3.4, there exists one sst that matches this signature. Thus, CheckTtdCorrupt(tsk) = 1 will always give the correct output. Also, due to the large min-entropy of the uniform distribution the probability that sampling a selected sk_u is negligible for large n with probability equal to $1/2^n$, with overwhelming probability, there doesn't exist a signature already using the same sk_u, which implies that CheckTtdHonest(tsk) = 1 will give the correct output with overwhelming probability. Hence, Game 9 $\approx$ Game 8.

Game 10: ($\mathcal{F}$ checks the correctness of the protocol): In this game $\mathcal{F}$ checks that any honestly generated signature $\Sigma = (str, sst, com, \pi_E)$ is always valid due to the completeness property of π_E and the correctness of the F-SPHINCS+ signature. A valid proof π_E on the credential ensures that the credential has the correct structure and always leads to the correct extraction of the issuer public key rpk due to the soundness of π_E and the correctness of the F-SPHINCS+ signature. Second, $\mathcal{F}$ makes sure identify(tsk, Σ, msg) = 1, which is also achieved in the real-world protocol due to the soundness of π_E. $\mathcal{F}$ checks, using its internal records ML and DomainKeys that honest users are not sharing the same secret key tsk. The soundness of π_E also ensures that the honestly generated signatures will not match any revoked signature, this is checked by $\mathcal{F}$ [Check XV] and [Check XVI] in the ideal world. This due to the calculations of $A_j = F(F(sk_u, sid_j), r)$ and $B_j = F(sst_j, r)$ for $\forall \Sigma_j \in$ SRL, where $sst_j = F(sk_j, sid_j)$ and $r \xleftarrow{R} \{0, 1\}^n$, if $A_j \neq B_j$ then $F(sk_j, sid_j) \neq F(sk_u, sid_j)$ and hence $sk_j \neq sk_u$ due to the collision resistance property of the function F. Therefore Game 10 $\approx$ Game 9.

Game 11 ($\mathcal{F}$ checks that valid signatures are deterministic): Add [Check IX] to ensure that there are no multiple sk_u values matching to one signature. However, since there exists only one sk_u such that $sst = F(sk_u, sid) \wedge$ $et_u = F(sk_u, gid) \wedge com = H_1(s||pk_h||\cdots||rpk)$ due to collision resistance of the function F and the binding property of the commitment com, thus two different signatures cannot share the same sk_u. In general, if there exist two signatures sharing the same sk_u then this breaks the soundness of π_E, thus any valid signature should be identified to one sk_u. Thus Game 11 $\approx$ Game 10.

Game 12 ($\mathcal{F}$ checks the unforgeability of a credential): To prevent accepting signatures whose corresponding credentials are not issued by the honest issuer, $\mathcal{F}$ adds a further check [Check XIII]. This follows the unforgeability property of the F-SPHINCS+ scheme as analysed in Appendix A. In our EPID scheme, a membership credential is the issuer's F-SPHINCS+ signature on the Signer's public key, so we get Game 12 $\approx$ Game 11.

Game 13 ($\mathcal{F}$ checks the unforgeability of EPID signatures): [Check XIV] is added to $\mathcal{F}$ to prevent anyone forging a signature, which should be signed under honest signer's group signing key $gsk_u = (sk_u, gr_u, \mathbf{S})$. If such a signature is verified then due to the binding property of the commitment scheme used to generate $com = H_1(s||pk_h||\cdots||rpk)$, where s is a nonce and $pk_h, \cdots, rpk$ are the root values of a chained M-FORS trees. These keys are used to verify the F-SPHINCS+ signature $\mathbf{S}$. The signature should correctly verify on an entry token $(et_u||gr_u)$ under the first committed verification key pk_h, where $et_u = F(sk_u, gid)$ for some honest signer's signing key sk_u. We argue that any modification in the committed verification keys would end with a failed verification of the signature $\mathbf{S}$ on the user entry token $(et_u||gr_u)$ due to the correctness of F-SPHINCS+. Now suppose that an adversary knows the credential $(gr_u, \mathbf{S})$ but not sk_u. The adversary chooses a random sk'_u and proceeds with the MPCitH NIZKPs for the construction of $et'_u = F(sk'_u, gid)$. Due to the soundness of π_E, the proof cannot be simulated unless $(et'_u||gr_u)$ verifies to be correctly signed under $pk_h, \cdots, rpk$ used in com. This would only happen if $et'_u = et_u$ due to F-SPHINCS+ being a q-EU-CMA secure signature (see Appendix A for a proof). Therefore sk'_u should match sk_u. The probability of this to happen is $1/2^n$, then the advantage of the adversary is negligible for large n. Therefore, Game 13 $\approx$ Game 12 with overwhelming probability.

Game 14 ($\mathcal{F}$ checks the correct revocation): [Check XV] and [Check XVI] are added to $\mathcal{F}$ to ensure that honestly generated signatures are not being revoked. If there exists a matching revoked key $sk_u^* \in$ KRL which belongs to an honest signer and is not revoked, then this breaks the collision resistance property of F. Suppose that there exists a $\Sigma_j \in$ SRL, such that Identify$(sk_u^*, \Sigma_j, msg_j) = 1$, i.e., the equation $A_j = B_j$ holds. This means $F(F(sk_u^*, sid_j), r) = F(sst_j, r)$, where $sst_j = F(sk_j, sid_j) \in \Sigma_j$. Due to the soundness of the MPCitH proof of F, sk_u^* will match to sk_j which was used to generate $\Sigma_j \in$ SRL. However, as we assumed that sk_u^* is not revoked, so $A_j \neq B_j$ will hold for all $\Sigma_j \in$ SRL. Therefore, Game 14 $\approx$ Game 13. $\qquad\square$

6 Implementation and Comparison

We implemented the signature revocation algorithm to show its feasibility and assess its performance[1]. The implementation was in C++ and used much of the code provided by Chen et al. [22] in support of their paper on hash-based group signatures. This code was itself based on the Picnic KKW scheme (namely picnic3) and used some subroutines from the Picnic implementation [48] submitted to the NIST Post-Quantum Cryptography Standardization project [42]. In their implementation, Chen et al. used two different security parameters, i.e. $n = 129$ and $n = 255$ and we use these same values for our tests. For the MPC-in-the-Head parameters, we use those from the Picnic implementations. Namely for $n = 129$, $NR = 250$ and $NO = 36$, while for $n = 255$, $NR = 601$ and $NO = 68$. NR and NO are the total number of MPC instances and the number of opened MPC instances respectively.

We measure the performance of our EPID revocation scheme based on our C++ implementation. The programs were compiled using the GNU GCC compiler [30] version 12.3.0 and executed on a laptop (Intel i7-8850H CPU @2.6 GHz: 32 Gb RAM) with the Ubuntu operating system. Although the CPU has multiple cores, the timings were obtained using a single core. The performance figures are given in Table 1 and are the averages for 10 runs. The timings were obtained using the C++ timing routines. It should be noted that, unlike the credential signing times these times are independent of the group size. They are, as to be expected, approximately linear in the revocation list size.

Table 1. Revocation test results for different signature revocation list sizes.

n	SRL size	sign	verify	π_R size
129	10	0.7	0.3	0.12
	100	6.7	3.2	1.0
	500	34.3	16.3	5.2
	1000	67.5	32.5	10.4
255	10	3.4	1.6	0.43
	100	33.1	15.7	3.9
	500	164.2	78.0	19.2
	1000	328.0	155.8	38.2

Table 2. Test results from Chen et al. [22] for various group sizes.

n	group size	sign	verify	sig. size
129	2^{10}	8.7	4.4	0.56
	2^{20}	12.9	6.3	0.83
	2^{40}	21.4	10.2	1.39
	2^{60}	29.4	13.9	1.95
255	2^{10}	36.4	17.3	2.28
	2^{20}	53.0	25.6	3.40
	2^{40}	89.4	43.0	5.65
	2^{60}	125.1	60.0	7.91

In this table times are given in seconds and sizes in MB.

The timings are consistent with those obtained by Chen et al. but are very slow when compared against the results reported for the reference Picnic implementation. We are currently investigating this discrepancy. As, to support confidentiality, the code allows the inputs and outputs to the LowMC function to be masked this introduces extra overheads when calculating each single LowMC function and this may partially explain the discrepancy. This idea is supported

---

[1] The revocation code is available at: https://github.com/UoS-SCCS/HB_EPID_Revocation.

by the results of profiling the code when approximately 60% of the time is reportedly spent in the (Picnic) tape generation and bit manipulation routines.

To enable comparison with other post-quantum EPID schemes we combine the measurements from Chen *et al.* [22] (reproduced in Table 2) with those that we obtained for π_R to give us an estimate of the signing times and signature sizes for our EPID scheme. In Table 3 we show a comparison with several lattice-based EPID implementations for which data is available. For these implementations figures were given for a signature revocation list containing 1000 items and to make the comparison we use our figures for 1000 items and group sizes of 2^{40} and 2^{60}. While our scheme is clearly better when considering the user private key and signature sizes, the situation is less clear for the timings; We are certainly on a par with the lattice-based schemes for $n = 129$, but lose out when the security parameter is increased to $n = 255$. However, it should be noted that this is a reference implementation in C++ with no attempt at optimisation or adaptation to use more efficient, but processor specific, processor instructions. There is much scope for improving these timings.

Table 3. Comparison with lattice-based EPID schemes (signature sizes in MB and times in seconds).

scheme	private-key	signing	verification	sig. size
LEPID [20]	58 KB	200	80	9[†]
LEPID [28]	100 KB	374	121	854
$n = 129, GS = 2^{40}$	17 bytes	89	43	11.8
$n = 129, GS = 2^{60}$	17 bytes	97	46	12.4
$n = 255, GS = 2^{40}$	32 bytes	417	199	43.9
$n = 255, GS = 2^{60}$	32 bytes	453	216	46.1

† This figure is estimated from the signature revocation size in [28] and the signature size in [23].

7   Conclusions

This paper proposes a new EPID scheme from symmetric primitives. Following recent research on group signatures and direct anonymous attestation, we make use of a modified SPHINCS+ signature as a group membership credential and use an MPCitH-based signature to prove the possession of that credential. This choice allows our EPID scheme to handle a large group size (up to 2^{60}), which is suitable for rapidly increasing cyber security and trusted computing applications. Our EPID scheme has an efficient signature-based revocation method. The security of the EPID scheme is proved under the UC framework. We present several optimizations to improve performance and provide a prototype implementation. For future work, we will investigate ways of improving performance and obtaining more practical benchmarks.

Acknowledgments. We thank the European Union's Horizon research and innovation program for support under grant agreement numbers: 779391 (FutureTPM), 952697 (ASSURED), 101019645 (SECANT), 101069688 (CONNECT), 101070627 (REWIRE) and 101095634 (ENTRUST). These projects are funded by the UK government's Horizon Europe guarantee and administered by UKRI. We also thank the National Natural Science Foundation of China for support under grant agreement numbers: 62072132 and 62261160651. Finally, we appreciate the valuable comments from the anonymous reviewers; particularly, the suggestion that removing B_j values from a signature would improve the performance of our scheme.

Appendix

A Security Analysis: F-SPHINCS+

The standard security definition for digital signature schemes is existential unforgeability under adaptive chosen-message attacks (EU-CMA). It can be extended to a few-time signature by limiting the adversary's call to the sign oracle to q times where q is the maximum number of signatures that the few-time signature scheme is allowed to generate for each signing key. Let $SIG = (kg, sign, vf)$ be a q-time signature scheme, Fig. 4 shows the q-EU-CMA game.

Experiment $\text{Exp}_{SIG,A}^{q\text{-EU-CMA}}(n)$

- $(sk, pk) \leftarrow kg$
- $(M^*, \sigma^*) \leftarrow A^{sign(sk,\cdot)}(pk)$, and A can query the *sign* Oracle at most q times.
- Return 1 iff $vf(pk, M^*, \sigma^*) = 1 \wedge M^* \notin \{M_i\}_{i=1}^q$

Fig. 4. q-EU-CMA game.

Definition 1 (q-EU-CMA). *Let SIG be a digital signature scheme. It is said to be q-EU-CMA secure, if for any adversary A, the following holds:*

$$Succ_{SIG}^{q\text{-EU-CMA}}(A(n)) = Pr\left[\text{Exp}_{SIG,A}^{q\text{-EU-CMA}}(n) = 1\right] \leq negl(n)$$

Theorem 1. *For suitable parameters, n, d, k, h, q, the F-SPHINCS+ signature is q^h-EU-CMA secure if:*

- *H_1 is SM-TCR and SM-DSPR secure;*
- *H_2 is TSR secure with at most q queries;*
- *H_3 is ITSR secure with at most q^h queries;*
- *prf is a secure pseudorandom function.*

Proof. To successfully forge a group issuer's signature on a message M chosen by the adversary, there are the following mutually exclusive cases:

1 Let $MD||idx = H_3(M||gr)$ for some gr. In the forged signature, All secret strings corresponding to $MD = p_0||\cdots||p_{k-1}$, i.e. $\{\mathbf{x}_{p_i}^{(i)}\}_{i=0}^{k-1}$, are the same as generated from leaf_{idx}'s secret key. This case consists of the following sub-cases:

  1.1 The adversary learns all secret strings from signatures obtained in the query phase.

  1.2 Some secret strings are not leaked from previous signatures, and for each of them, the adversary either:

    1.2.1 learns it by breaking the pseudorandom function that is used to expand the secret key into $\mathbf{x}_i$;

    1.2.2 or learns it by looking at their H_1 hash values and find the pre-images.

2 Let $MD||idx = H_3(M||gr)$ for some gr. In the forged signature, some secret strings corresponding to $MD = p_0||\cdots||p_{k-1}$, i.e. $\{\mathbf{x}_{p_i}^{(i)}\}_{i=0}^{k-1}$, are NOT the same as generated from leaf_{idx}'s secret key. Then let $\mathbf{S}$ be the list of $h+1$ M-FORS signatures in the forged signature, we can find i such that when verifying the i-th signature ($0 \leq i \leq h$), we obtain the same public key as would be generated by the signer, but for all $0 \leq j < i$, we obtain a different public key as would be generated by the signer. This means:

  2.1 The adversary has found at least one second-preimages of H_1 so that some Merkle trees in the ith signature are computed with the second-preimages. They end up having the same roots as the trees computed by the group issuer.

  2.2 The adversary knows all secret strings corresponding to the public key produced from verifying the $(i-1)$th signature. This public key is different from the public key at the same location generated by the group issuer. This can be done by either:

    2.2.1 learning all from previous signature queries;

    2.2.2 or breaking the pseudorandom function;

    2.2.3 or finding some pre-images of H_1.

Given the above, we analyze the F-SPHINCS+ signature scheme through a series of games:

Game 0: The original EU-CMA game in which the adversary needs to forge a valid group issuer's signature after q_s queries.

Game 1: Exactly as Game 0 except all output of prf are replaced by truly random n-bit strings. We eliminate from the above list Case 1.2.1 and 2.2.2 by this modification. Since each call to prf uses a secret key and a distinct value as input, assuming prf is a pseudorandom function, we have:

$$|\text{Succ}^{Game0}(A(n)) - \text{Succ}^{Game1}(A(n))| \leq negl(n)$$

Game 2: Game 2 differs from Game 1 in that we consider the adversary lost if the adversary outputs a forgery by breaking the ITSR security of H_3. This modification eliminates from the above list Case 1.1. The winning condition in Fig. 4 is changed to:

- Return 1 iff $ITSR(H_3, M^*) = 0 \land vf(pk, M^*, \sigma^*) = 1 \land M^* \notin \{M_i\}_{i=1}^{q^h}$.

The predicate $ITSR$ is defined as the following:

- Let M^* be the message that the adversary chooses to generate the forgery on, and gr^* the random string used by the adversary to compute $MD^*||idx^* = H_3(M^*||gr^*)$.
- Parse $MD^* = p_0^*||\cdots||p_{k-1}^*$ where each $p_j^* \in [0, 2^d - 1]$. From the above we obtain a set $C^* = ((idx^*, 0, p_0^*), \cdots, (idx^*, k-1, p_{k-1}^*))$.
- For each message queried in the query phase M_i $(1 \leq i \leq q^h)$, and gr_i the random string, compute $MD_i||idx_i = H_3(M_i||gr_i)$ and obtain $C_i = ((idx_i, 0, p_{i,0}), \cdots, (idx_i, k-1, p_{i,k-1}))$.
- Return 1 iff $C^* \subseteq \bigcup_{i=1}^{q^h} C_i$.

We can see that $ITSR(H_3, M^*) = 0$ iff the adversary can break the ITSR security of H_3. Hence, we have:

$$|\text{Succ}^{Game1}(A(n)) - \text{Succ}^{Game2}(A(n))| \leq \text{Succ}_{H_3, q^h}^{ITSR}(A) \leq negl(n)$$

Game 3: Game 3 differs from Game 2 in that we consider the adversary lost if the forgery contains a second preimage for an input to H_1 that was part of a signature returned as a signing-query response. Here the second preimage can be included explicitly in the signature, or implicitly observed when verifying the signature. This eliminates from the above list Case 2.1. Then we have:

$$|\text{Succ}^{Game2}(A(n)) - \text{Succ}^{Game3}(A(n))| \leq \text{Succ}_{H_1, q}^{SM-TCR}(A) \leq negl(n)$$

Game 4: Game 4 differs from Game 3 in that we consider the adversary lost if the adversary outputs a forgery by breaking the TSR security of H_2, which allows the adversary to forge an intermediate signature in **S**, and then any signature earlier in the chain. This eliminates from the above list Case 2.2.1. The winning condition in Fig. 4 is changed to:

- Return 1 iff $TSR(H_2, M^*) = 0 \land ITSR(H_3, M^*) = 0 \land vf(pk, M^*, \sigma^*) = 1 \land M^* \notin \{M_i\}_{i=1}^{q^h}$.

The predicate TSR is defined as the following:

- The adversary chooses an intermediate node in the hyper-tree at address (a, b), and two n-bit string L^*, R^*.
- For each signature obtained in the query phase, if $\mathbf{S}_i$ includes a signature generated using the secret key in node (a, b) over the public key in one of its child node, parse this public key into k blocks, each of d-bit $pk_i = p_{i,0}||\cdots||p_{i,k-1}$, and generate a set $C_i = \{(j, p_{i,j})\}_{j=0}^{k-1}$.
- Compute $pk^* = H_2(\text{aux}||k||0||0||L^*||R^*)$, parse pk^* into $p_0^*||\cdots||p_{k-1}^*$, and generate a set $C^* = \{(j, p_j^*)\}_{j=0}^{k-1}$.
- Return 1 iff $C^* \subseteq \bigcup_{i=1}^{q} C_i$.

Note that each M-FORS public key is the root of a Merkle tree generated from pseudorandom strings. Also for each intermediate node in a hyper-tree, it has at most q children, hence no more than q signatures signed by the secret key in this intermediate node can be obtained by the adversary. So $TSR(H_2, M^*) = 0$ iff the adversary can break the TSR security of H_2. Hence, we have:

$$|\mathrm{Succ}^{Game3}(A(n)) - \mathrm{Succ}^{Game4}(A(n))| \le \mathrm{Succ}^{TSR}_{H_2,q}(A) \le negl(n)$$

Now the cases in which the adversary can forge a signature are all eliminated except Case 1.2.2 and 2.2.3, which requires the adversary to find a pre-image of at least one hash values produced by H_1. The success probability of finding a pre-image is as analyzed in [4]:

$$\mathrm{Succ}^{Game4}(A) \le 3 \cdot \mathrm{Succ}^{SM-TCR}_{H_1,p}(A) + \mathrm{Adv}^{SM-DSPR}_{H_1,p}(A)$$
$$\le negl(n)$$

So overall, the advantage of the adversary is negligible. $\qquad\square$

TSR security of H_2. In any case, q signatures can be generated under the secret key of a non-leaf node in the hyper-tree. Assuming the adversary knows all of them, then for each block of the chosen pk^*, the probability of the secret string has been leaked is $1 - (1 - \frac{1}{2^d})^q$, so all secret string have been leaked is $(1 - (1 - \frac{1}{2^d})^q)^k$. For $d = 16, q = 1024, k = 68$, this probability is $2^{-468.87}$, if $k = 35$, this probability is $2^{-210.39}$.

ITSR security of H_3. For a leaf node of the hyper-tree, it may have been used to sign γ signatures out of the total q_s signature queries. So the probability that all secret string of a chosen message M being leaked through query is:

$$\sum_{\gamma}(1 - (1 - \frac{1}{2^d})^{\gamma})^k \binom{q_s}{\gamma}(1 - \frac{1}{q^h})^{q_s - \gamma}\frac{1}{q^{h\gamma}}$$

For $d = 16, q = 1024, k = 68, h = 6, q_s = 2^{60}$, this probability is $2^{-407.32}$, if $k = 35$, this probability is $2^{-208.95}$.

References

1. Baum, C., et al.: Publicly verifiable zero-knowledge and post-quantum signatures from VOLE-in-the-Head. In: Handschuh, H., Lysyanskaya, A. (eds.) CRYPTO. LNCS, vol. 14085, pp. 581–615. Springer, Heidelberg (2023). https://doi.org/10.1007/978-3-031-38554-4_19
2. Baum, C., de Saint Guilhem, C.D., Kales, D., Orsini, E., Scholl, P., Zaverucha, G.: Banquet: short and fast signatures from AES. In: Garay, J.A. (ed.) PKC 2021. LNCS, vol. 12710, pp. 266–297. Springer, Cham (2021). https://doi.org/10.1007/978-3-030-75245-3_11

3. Ben-Sasson, E., Chiesa, A., Riabzev, M., Spooner, N., Virza, M., Ward, N.P.: Aurora: transparent succinct arguments for R1CS. In: Ishai, Y., Rijmen, V. (eds.) EUROCRYPT 2019. LNCS, vol. 11476, pp. 103–128. Springer, Cham (2019). https://doi.org/10.1007/978-3-030-17653-2_4

4. Bernstein, D.J., Hülsing, A., Kölbl, S., Niederhagen, R., Rijneveld, J., Schwabe, P.: The SPHINCS$^+$ signature framework. In: ACM CCS, pp. 2129–2146 (2019)

5. Bhadauria, R., Fang, Z., Hazay, C., Venkitasubramaniam, M., Xie, T., Zhang, Y.: Ligero++: a new optimized sublinear IOP. In: ACM CCS, pp. 2025–2038 (2020)

6. Biswas, C., Dutta, R., Sarkar, S.: An efficient post-quantum secure dynamic EPID signature scheme using lattices. Multimedia Tools Appl. **85**, 13791–13820 (2023)

7. Blanchet, B., et al.: Modeling and verifying security protocols with the applied Pi calculus and ProVerif. Found. Trends® Priv. Secur. **1**(1-2), 1–135 (2016)

8. Boneh, D., Eskandarian, S., Fisch, B.: Post-quantum EPID signatures from symmetric primitives. In: CT-RSA, pp. 251–271 (2019)

9. Boneh, D., Shacham, H.: Group signatures with verifier-local revocation. In: ACM CCS, pp. 168–177 (2004)

10. Bootle, J., Lyubashevsky, V., Nguyen, N.K., Sorniotti, A.: A framework for practical anonymous credentials from lattices. Cryptology ePrint Archive, Paper 2023/560 (2023). https://eprint.iacr.org/2023/560

11. Brickell, E.F., Camenisch, J., Chen, L.: Direct anonymous attestation. In: ACM CCS, pp. 132–145 (2004)

12. Brickell, E., Li, J.: Enhanced privacy ID: a direct anonymous attestation scheme with enhanced revocation capabilities. In: Proceedings of the 2007 ACM Workshop on Privacy in Electronic Society, pp. 21–30 (2007)

13. Brickell, E., Li, J.: Enhanced Privacy ID from bilinear pairing. Cryptology ePrint Archive, Paper 2009/095 (2009). https://eprint.iacr.org/2009/095

14. Brickell, E., Li, J.: Enhanced privacy ID from bilinear pairing for hardware authentication and attestation. Int. J. Inf. Priv. Secur. Integr. 2 **1**(1), 3–33 (2011)

15. Brickell, E., Li, J.: Enhanced privacy ID: a direct anonymous attestation scheme with enhanced revocation capabilities. IEEE Trans. Depend. Secur. Comput. **9**(3), 345–360 (2012)

16. Camenisch, J., Chen, L., Drijvers, M., Lehmann, A., Novick, D., Urian, R.: One TPM to bind them all: fixing TPM 2.0 for provably secure anonymous attestation. In: IEEE Symposium on Security and Privacy, pp. 901–920. IEEE (2017)

17. Camenisch, J., Drijvers, M., Lehmann, A.: Universally composable direct anonymous attestation. In: Cheng, C.-M., Chung, K.-M., Persiano, G., Yang, B.-Y. (eds.) PKC 2016. LNCS, vol. 9615, pp. 234–264. Springer, Heidelberg (2016). https://doi.org/10.1007/978-3-662-49387-8_10

18. Chase, M., et al.: Post-quantum zero-knowledge and signatures from symmetric-key primitives. In: ACM CCS, pp. 1825–1842 (2017)

19. Chaum, D., van Heyst, E.: Group signatures. In: Davies, D.W. (ed.) EUROCRYPT 1991. LNCS, vol. 547, pp. 257–265. Springer, Heidelberg (1991). https://doi.org/10.1007/3-540-46416-6_22

20. Chen, L., Xu, Z., Tu, T., Wang, Z.: Lattice-based privacy enhanced identity protocol for SDO services. In: International Conference on Signal and Image Processing (ICSIP), pp. 609–613 (2023)

21. Chen, L., Dong, C., El Kassem, N., Newton, C.J., Wang, Y.: Hash-based direct anonymous attestation. In: Johansson, T., Smith-Tone, D. (eds.) PQCrypto. LNCS, vol. 14154, pp. 565–600. Springer, Heidelberg (2023). https://doi.org/10.1007/978-3-031-40003-2_21

22. Chen, L., Dong, C., Newton, C.J., Wang, Y.: Sphinx-in-the-head: group signatures from symmetric primitives. ACM Trans. Priv. Secur. **27**, 1–35 (2023)

23. Chen, L., El Kassem, N., Lehmann, A., Lyubashevsky, V.: A framework for efficient lattice-based DAA. In: Proceedings of the 1st ACM Workshop on Workshop on Cyber-Security Arms Race, pp. 23–34 (2019)

24. Chen, M.S., et al: Preon: zk-SNARK based signature scheme. NIST PQ Signatures submissions (2023). https://csrc.nist.gov/csrc/media/Projects/pqc-dig-sig/documents/round-1/spec-files/Preon-spec-web.pdf

25. Dall, F., et al.: Cachequote: efficiently recovering long-term secrets of SGX EPID via cache attacks. ICAR Trans. Cryptogr. Hardw. Embed. Syst. 171–191 (2018)

26. Dobraunig, C., Kales, D., Rechberger, C., Schofnegger, M., Zaverucha, G.: Shorter signatures based on tailor-made minimalist symmetric-key crypto. In: ACM CCS, pp. 843–857 (2022)

27. El Kassem, N.: Lattice-based direct anonymous attestation. Ph.D. thesis, University of Surrey (2020)

28. EL Kassem, N., Fiolhais, L., Martins, P., Chen, L., Sousa, L.: A lattice-based enhanced privacy ID. In: Laurent, M., Giannetsos, T. (eds.) WISTP 2019. LNCS, vol. 12024, pp. 15–31. Springer, Cham (2020). https://doi.org/10.1007/978-3-030-41702-4_2

29. Faonio, A., Fiore, D., Nizzardo, L., Soriente, C.: Subversion-resilient enhanced privacy ID. In: Galbraith, S.D. (ed.) CT-RSA 2022. LNCS, vol. 13161, pp. 562–588. Springer, Cham (2022). https://doi.org/10.1007/978-3-030-95312-6_23

30. Free Software Foundation, Inc.: GCC, the GNU Compiler Collection (2022). https://ggcc.gnu.org

31. Fu, S., Gang, G.: Polaris: transparent succinct zero-knowledge arguments for R1CS with efficient verifier. In: Proceedings on Privacy Enhancing Technologies, pp. 544–564 (2022)

32. Giacomelli, I., Madsen, J., Orlandi, C.: Zkboo: faster zero-knowledge for boolean circuits. In: USENIX Security, pp. 1069–1083 (2016)

33. Ishai, Y., Kushilevitz, E., Ostrovsky, R., Sahai, A.: Zero-knowledge from secure multiparty computation. In: STOC, pp. 21–30 (2007)

34. ISO/IEC 10118-2:2010: Information technology - Security techniques - Hash-functions - Part 2: Hash-functions using an n-bit block cipher. Standard, International Organization for Standardization, Geneva, CH (2010). https://www.iso.org/standard/44737.html

35. ISO/IEC 20008-2:2013: Information technology - Security techniques - Anonymous digital signatures - Part 2: Mechanisms using a group public key. Standard, International Organization for Standardization, Geneva, CH (2013). https://www.iso.org/standard/56916.html

36. Kales, D., Zaverucha, G.: Efficient lifting for shorter zero-knowledge proofs and post-quantum signatures. Cryptology ePrint Archive, Paper 2022/588 (2022). https://eprint.iacr.org/2022/588

37. Katz, J., Kolesnikov, V., Wang, X.: Improved non-interactive zero knowledge with applications to post-quantum signatures. In: ACM CCS, pp. 525–537 (2018)

38. Kim, S., et al.: AIM: symmetric primitive for shorter signatures with stronger security. In: ACM CCS, pp. 401–415 (2023)

39. Lamport, L.: Constructing digital signatures from a one-way function. SRI International Computer Science Laboratory, Technical Report (1979)

40. Lyubashevsky, V., Nguyen, N.K., Plançon, M.: Lattice-based zero-knowledge proofs and applications: shorter, simpler, and more general. In: Dodis, Y., Shrimp-

ton, T. (eds.) CRYPTO. LNCS, vol. 13508, pp. 71–101. Springer, Heidelberg (2022). https://doi.org/10.1007/978-3-031-15979-4_3

41. Merkle, R.C.: A certified digital signature. In: Brassard, G. (ed.) CRYPTO 1989. LNCS, vol. 435, pp. 218–238. Springer, New York (1990). https://doi.org/10.1007/0-387-34805-0_21

42. NIST: Post-quantum cryptography standardization (2017–2022). https://csrc.nist.gov/projects/post-quantum-cryptography/post-quantum-cryptography-standardization

43. NIST: Nist announces first four quantum-resistant cryptographic algorithms (2022). https://nist.gov/news-events/news/2022/07/nist-announces-first-four-quantum-resistant-cryptographic-algorithms

44. de Saint Guilhem, C.D., De Meyer, L., Orsini, E., Smart, N.P.: BBQ: using AES in picnic signatures. In: Paterson, K.G., Stebila, D. (eds.) SAC 2019. LNCS, vol. 11959, pp. 669–692. Springer, Cham (2020). https://doi.org/10.1007/978-3-030-38471-5_27

45. de Saint Guilhem, C.D., Orsini, E., Tanguy, T.: Limbo: efficient zero-knowledge MPCitH-based arguments. In: ACM CCS, pp. 3022–3036 (2021)

46. Sardar, M.U., Fetzer, C., et al.: Towards formalization of enhanced privacy ID (EPID)-based remote attestation in Intel SGX. In: Euromicro Conference on Digital System Design (DSD), pp. 604–607 (2020)

47. TCG: TPM 2.0 library specification. https://trustedcomputinggroup.org/resource/tpm-library-specification/

48. Zaverucha, R., Kales, G.: Reference implementation of the Picnic post-quantum signature scheme (2020). https://github.com/Microsoft/Picnic

49. Zaverucha, G.: The Picnic signature algorithm specification (2020). Supporting Documentation in https://github.com/Microsoft/Picnic

Code-Based Cryptography

The Blockwise Rank Syndrome Learning Problem and Its Applications to Cryptography

Nicolas Aragon[1], Pierre Briaud[2,3], Victor Dyseryn[1], Philippe Gaborit[1], and Adrien Vinçotte[1(✉)]

[1] XLIM, Université de Limoges, Limoges, France
adrien.vincotte@unilim.fr
[2] Inria Paris, Paris, France
[3] Sorbonne Université, Paris, France

Abstract. A notion of blockwise errors in the context of rank-based cryptography has recently been introduced in [28]. It allowed to choose more interesting parameters for the original LRPC and RQC schemes, which contributed to greatly improve their performances. Prior to that, it had been proposed in [3,16] to consider several decoding instances which are correlated (this is called the multi-syndromes approach). The goal was similar and these works also lead to new schemes with very competitive public key and ciphertext sizes.

In this paper, we show that these two approaches can be combined to construct even more efficient generalized RQC and LRPC schemes. We introduce the ℓ-RSL problem, which is a version of the Rank Support Learning problem relevant to the multi-syndrome approach but where the errors have a blockwise structure. Our generalizations rely on its difficulty. Concretely, we can obtain very interesting sizes. For 128-bit security, we propose parameters for which the sum of the public key and the ciphertext is only 1.4 kB for our generalized RQC and 1.7 kB for our generalized LRPC scheme. This is a 40% gain compared to [16,28], our RQC doing even better than KYBER which features 1.5 kB.

Besides these new schemes, we provide new attacks on the ℓ-RD problem introduced in [28]. In particular, they allow us to cryptanalyze all blockwise LRPC parameters proposed in [28] (with an improvement of more than 40 bits for structural attacks). We also describe combinatorial and algebraic attacks for the ℓ-RSL problem we introduce.

Keywords: rank metric · LRPC codes · Gabidulin codes · multiple syndromes · blockwise errors

1 Introduction

Background on Rank Metric Code-Based Cryptography. Classical code-based cryptography relies on the Hamming distance but it is also possible to use another metric: the rank metric. This metric, introduced in 1985 by Gabidulin [17], is very different from the Hamming distance. In recent years, the rank metric has received very strong attention from the coding community because of its

© The Author(s), under exclusive license to Springer Nature Switzerland AG 2024
M.-J. Saarinen and D. Smith-Tone (Eds.): PQCrypto 2024, LNCS 14771, pp. 75–106, 2024.
https://doi.org/10.1007/978-3-031-62743-9_3

relevance to network coding. Moreover, this metric can also be used for cryptography. Indeed, it is possible to construct rank-analogues of Reed-Solomon codes: the Gabidulin codes. These codes are used in early cryptosystems, like the GPT cryptosystem [18] which consists of an instanciation of the McEliece cryptosystem with Gabidulin codes, but they were found to be inherently vulnerable due to the very strong structure of the underlying codes. More recently, considering an approach similar to NTRU [22] (and also MDPC codes [24]), it was possible to construct a very efficient cryptosystem based on weakly structured rank codes: the LRPC cryptosystem [20]. Overall, the main interest of rank-metric based cryptography is that the complexity of the best known attack grows very quickly with the size of the parameters, it means than in practice it is possible to obtain cryptosystems with a size (public key + ciphertext) of only a few thousand bytes without adding any cyclic or ideal structure, while such parameter sizes can only be obtained with an additional structure (quasi-cyclic for example) for Hamming code-based cryptography. At the 2017 NIST standardization process, several schemes based on rank metric were proposed: LAKE, LOCKER, OUROBOROS-R and RQC. The three schemes LAKE, LOCKER and OUROBOROS-R were merged in the ROLLO 2nd round submission and the RQC submission remained as an independent submission. Eventually, due to incertitudes brought by algebraic attacks [12,14] which attacked NIST proposed parameters for rank metric, the schemes did not reach the 3rd round of the NIST standardization. However, the overall process permitted to reach a new audience for the potentiality of rank-based cryptosystems. The Loidreau cryptosystem [23] and its recent improvement [7] are another example of rank-based cryptosystem. In this paper we focus on the LRPC (also called ILRPC after considering ideal codes rather than quasi-cyclic codes) and RQC cryptosystems.

Background on LRPC and RQC Cryptosystems. The original LRPC cryptosystem was introduced in 2014 [20], although the system leads to very small parameters its main drawback relies in its Decoding Failure Rate (DFR) which is related to the block size n of the code. In practice finding very good parameters for 2^{-30} is easy but decreasing the DFR to IND-CCA2 compliant values like 2^{-128} implies a strong increase of parameters. The RQC cryptosystem is an equivalent in rank metric of the HQC scheme submitted to the NIST standardization process. One of the strong feature of the scheme is that because of the use of Gabidulin codes the DFR of the scheme is zero, but it comes at a cost of having parameters bigger than for LRPC. The scheme also reduces to general ideal instances of rank based problems. Taking account of algebraic attacks of [12] had obliged to increase parameters of both systems so that eventually for a DFR of 2^{-128} parameters were more than 4 kBytes. There was not any major breakthrough for LRPC until the introduction in 2022 [3] of the multiple syndromes approach: this approach, based on the Rank Support Learning problem, permits to consider several syndromes and hence to decrease more easily the DFR of the system, in practice it permitted to obtain 2.4 kBytes parameters (pk+ct). The same approach of multiple syndromes (together with the introduction of Augmented Gabidulin codes) was also proposed for RQC [16], which gave also small parameters down to 2.7 kB (pk+ct).

Recent Results and Introduction of Blockwise Rank Errors for Rank Codes for LRPC and RQC Schemes. Very recently in [28], the authors introduced the notion of rank blockwise errors, which permits to decrease the weight of decoded errors for the LRPC and RQC schemes. The main idea of this approach is to consider words formed of blocks of respective length $n_1, ..., n_\ell$ with each block being associated to a given error e_i of rank r_i with support E_i, such that the supports E_i intersect only in 0. The case of $\ell = 2$ permits to get an error to decode for LRPC of smaller weight $r_1.d_1 + r_2.d_2$ rather than $r.d$ in the case of classical LRPC. In fact, to give a general idea one exchanges the complexity of searching for an error of weight $2r$ and length $2n$ by the complexity of searching for a blockwise error of weight (r, r) associated to two blocks of length n. If one considers $r = d$ and $r_1 = r_2 = d_1 = d_2 = \frac{r}{2}$, the classical LRPC approach with homogeneous errors gives a syndrome of weight $r.d = r^2$, whereas in the case of blockwise error the syndrome would have weight $r_1.d_1 + r_2.d_2 = \frac{r^2}{2}$. Having to decode errors of smaller weight can have a strong impact for decoding. In their paper [28], the authors then generalize previously known attacks in their blockwise rank error case (both for combinatorial and algebraic attacks) following recent results on non-homogeneous errors. They show that considering the blockwise approach rather than the classical homogeneous approach may be advantageous in some cases. The approach is especially interesting for the RQC scheme, for which they propose parameters with size 2.5 kB (public key + ciphertext), and a little less for the ILRPC case: with high DFR 2^{-30}, their parameters are 15% smaller than ROLLO-I (ex-LAKE, even if we will later explain that their proposed parameters can be broken). Overall, the approach they propose is very interesting and completely develop the potential of rank metric.

Blockwise Rank Errors: Why this New Error Structure is Completely Suited for Rank Metric Based Cryptography. As a well known notion, the rank metric benefits from strange properties. Indeed, suppose one wants to solve the RSD problem: $H.e^t = s$ (for e a codeword of $\mathbb{F}_{q^m}^n$ of weight r and H a random $(n-k) \times n$ matrix). In practice, the complexity of best attacks becomes linear whenever n becomes large enough. This property is directly related to the notion of support of the error: when the error length increases, the support of the error does not change. This peculiar property leads to the fact that it is easily possible to construct simple codes which can decode up to the rank Gilbert-Varshamov bound [19]. Notice that this type of feature is not present for Hamming or Euclidean distance. This property also explains why a straight-forward adaptation of the Learning Parity with Noise (LPN) or Learning With Errors (LWE) problem does not work for rank metric: it is possible to polynomially solve the system after a quadratic number of given syndromes. A way to obtain an equivalent approach for LPN or LWE in rank metric is proposed in [15]: rather than adding errors with always the same support, one adds fixed

length block errors with different error supports. This Learning with Rank Errors
(LRE) approach permits to get an equivalent notion to LPN and LWE. The previous LRE approach is very close to the approach proposed in [28] and is also
closely related to the sum-rank approach. The non homogeneous approach of [13]
can also be seen as a particular case of blockwise rank errors. In practice, the
rank blockwise error approach permits to efficiently counter the attack in which,
for a given m, one dramatically increases the length n of the code. The best
combinatorial attacks have a complexity with roughly an exponent in krm/n,
the blockwise structured error support counters the m/n effect, so that the best
attacks essentially remains in kr for the exponent. This type of structured error
is especially resistant for $[\ell n, n]$ codes with blocks of size n and $m = n$. This type
of parameters is very well suited for ideal LRPC and RQC schemes, for which
the main attacks correspond precisely to this case.

Contributions. We combine in this paper the two previous approaches: multiple syndromes (together with Augmented Gabidulin codes) and blockwise errors
for LRPC and RQC schemes. This new combined approach is especially efficient
for the RQC scheme for which it permits to obtain parameters of size 1.4 kB
(public key + ciphertext) for 128 bit security, since the blockwise approach counters the $[3n, n]$ security reduction. However the approach in the case of LRPC
codes combined with the xMS approach of [3] also remains interesting with a 1.7
kB size. These results are really a big step compared to previous results with a
40% decrease in terms of parameters size, giving parameters even smaller than
KYBER (1.5 kB). It is the first time that one gets so small parameters in rank
metric (and codes in general), along with very small DFR.

Besides these main results the contributions are the following:

- We define a new problem: the Blockwise Rank Syndrome Learning problem
  which permits to design new generalized LRPC and RQC schemes using multiple syndromes and blockwise rank error approaches. We generalize the xMS
  approach of [3] for the case of rank block errors.
- We give new attacks for the ℓ-RD blockwise error problem, in particular we
  break all parameters of [28] for their LRPC variations. Notice that it does
  not alter the confidence we can have in the scheme, since parameters can be
  increased to thwart this attack.
- We give generalized combinatorial and algebraic attacks for the new Blockwise
  Rank Syndrome Learning problem.
- We revisit some combinatorial and algebraic attacks described in [28].

Organisation of the Paper. Section 1 gives a general overview of the situation for LRPC and RQC schemes and also gives a perspective on the blockwise rank error approach. Section 2 gives the general background on rank metric
and cryptographic schemes. Section 3 describes the new blockwise RSL problem
together with the generalization of the xMS approach in the case of blockwise
rank errors. Section 4 gives a description of our new generalized RQC and LRPC
schemes. Sections 5 and 6 gives details for combinatorial and algebraic attacks

for the problem we consider, but also revisit some complexities of [28]. Section 7 describes the cryptanalyze of LRPC parameters of [28]. Section 8 describes new parameters with our new approach and compares to other schemes.

2   Preliminaries

2.1   Background on the Rank Metric

Definition 1 (Rank metric over $\mathbb{F}_{q^m}^n$). *For a vector $\boldsymbol{x} = (x_1, \ldots, x_n) \in \mathbb{F}_{q^m}^n$, we define the support $\mathsf{Supp}(\boldsymbol{x}) \stackrel{def}{=} \langle x_1, \ldots, x_n \rangle_{\mathbb{F}_q}$. The rank weight of $\boldsymbol{x}$ is equal to $\|\boldsymbol{x}\| \stackrel{def}{=} \dim(\mathsf{Supp}(\boldsymbol{x}))$.*

In the following, the set of vectors in $\mathbb{F}_{q^m}^n$ of rank weight r will be denoted by:

$$S_r^n(\mathbb{F}_{q^m}) \stackrel{def}{=} \left\{ \mathbf{x} \in \mathbb{F}_{q^m}^n \mid \|\mathbf{x}\| = r \right\}.$$

We will also use

$$S_{r,1}^n(\mathbb{F}_{q^m}) \stackrel{def}{=} \{ \mathbf{x} \in \mathbb{F}_{q^m}^n \mid \|x\| = r, 1 \in \mathsf{Supp}(\mathbf{x}) \}.$$

Definition 2 ($\mathbb{F}_{q^m}$-linear code). *An $\mathbb{F}_{q^m}$-linear code of parameters $[n, k]_{q^m}$ is an $\mathbb{F}_{q^m}$-subspace of $\mathbb{F}_{q^m}^n$ of dimension k.*

Such a code $\mathcal{C}$ can be represented by a full-rank generator matrix $\mathbf{G} \in \mathbb{F}_{q^m}^{k \times n}$ or by a full-rank parity-check matrix $\mathbf{H} \in \mathbb{F}_{q^m}^{(n-k) \times n}$.

2.2   Rank Decoding and Rank Support Learning Problems

The decoding problem relevant for all rank-based constructions is:

Definition 3 (RD Problem). *Given $(\boldsymbol{G}, \boldsymbol{y}) \in \mathbb{F}_{q^m}^{k \times n} \times \mathbb{F}_{q^m}^n$, the Rank Decoding problem $\mathsf{RD}(n, k, r)$ asks to compute $\boldsymbol{e} \in \mathbb{F}_{q^m}^n$ such that $\boldsymbol{y} = \boldsymbol{xG} + \boldsymbol{e}$ and $\|\boldsymbol{e}\| \leq r$. We will write RSD for the equivalent version written with a parity-check matrix.*

Even if RD is not known to be NP-complete, [26] gives a randomized reduction to the decoding problem in the Hamming metric, this time NP-complete. The Rank Support Learning problem [19] is a generalization of RD where we are given N instances with the same generator matrix (or the same parity-check matrix for RSD) and where the errors have the same support.

Definition 4 (RSL Problem). *Given $(\boldsymbol{H}, \boldsymbol{S}) \in \mathbb{F}_{q^m}^{(n-k) \times n} \times \mathbb{F}_{q^m}^{N \times (n-k)}$, the Rank Support Learning Problem $\mathsf{RSL}(n, k, r, N)$ asks to compute a subspace $E \subset \mathbb{F}_{q^m}$ of dimension r for which there exists a matrix $\boldsymbol{V} \in E^{\ell \times n}$ such that $\boldsymbol{HV}^{\mathsf{T}} = \boldsymbol{S}^{\mathsf{T}}$.*

2.3   Ideal Codes

Let $P \in \mathbb{F}_q[X]$ be an irreducible polynomial of degree n. We define the internal product of two vectors $\mathbf{x}$, $\mathbf{y}$ in $\mathbb{F}_{q^m}^n$ as $\mathbf{x} \cdot \mathbf{y} \overset{\text{def}}{=} \mathbf{X}(X)\mathbf{Y}(X) \bmod P$, where $\mathbf{X}(X) = \sum_{i=0}^{k-1} x_i X^i$ and $\mathbf{Y}(X) = \sum_{i=0}^{k-1} y_i X^i$.

Definition 5 (Ideal matrix). *Let $P \in \mathbb{F}_q[X]$ be a polynomial of degree n and let $\mathbf{v} \in \mathbb{F}_{q^m}^n$. The ideal matrix generated by $\mathbf{v}$ and P, denoted by $\mathcal{IM}_P(\mathbf{v})$ (or $\mathcal{IM}(\mathbf{v})$ if there is no ambiguity on P), is the element of $\mathbb{F}_{q^m}^{n \times n}$ defined by*

$$\mathcal{IM}_P(\mathbf{v}) \overset{\text{def}}{=} \begin{pmatrix} \mathbf{v}(X) \quad \bmod P \\ X\mathbf{v}(X) \quad \bmod P \\ \vdots \\ X^{k-1}\mathbf{v}(X) \quad \bmod P \end{pmatrix}.$$

One can see that $\mathbf{u} \cdot \mathbf{v} = \mathbf{u}\mathcal{IM}(\mathbf{v}) = \mathbf{v}\mathcal{IM}(\mathbf{u}) = \mathbf{v} \cdot \mathbf{u}$, so that the internal product is a matrix-vector product by the ideal matrix. An ideal code of parameters $[sn, tn]_{q^m}$ is an $\mathbb{F}_{q^m}$-linear code which admits a generator matrix made of $s \times t$ ideal matrix blocks. A crucial point is that if $P \in \mathbb{F}_q[X]$ is irreducible and if n and m are prime, then this code admits a systematic generator matrix made of ideal blocks [1]. In the following, we will restrict ourselves to $t = 1$.

Definition 6 (Ideal codes). *Let $P(X) \in \mathbb{F}_q[X]$ be a polynomial of degree n and let $\mathbf{g}_i \in \mathbb{F}_{q^m}^n$ for $i \in \{1, ..., s-1\}$. We call the $[sn, n]_{q^m}$ ideal code $\mathcal{C}$ of generators $(\mathbf{g}_1, ..., \mathbf{g}_{s-1})$ the code with generator matrix $\mathbf{G} = (I_n \; \mathcal{IM}(\mathbf{g}_1) \; ... \; \mathcal{IM}(\mathbf{g}_{s-1})) \in \mathbb{F}_{q^m}^{n \times sn}$. Equivalently, the code $\mathcal{C}$ admits a parity-check matrix of the form*

$$\mathbf{H} = \begin{pmatrix} & \mathcal{IM}(\mathbf{h}_1) \\ I_{n(s-1)} & \vdots \\ & \mathcal{IM}(\mathbf{h}_{s-1}) \end{pmatrix}.$$

Definition 7 (IRSD Problem). *Given $\mathbf{H} \in \mathbb{F}_{q^m}^{(s-1)n \times sn}$ a parity-check matrix of an $[sn, n]_{q^m}$-ideal code and $\mathbf{s} \in \times \mathbb{F}_{q^m}^{(s-1)n}$, the Ideal Rank Support Decoding Problem $\mathsf{IRSD}(n, s, r)$ asks to compute $\mathbf{e} \in \mathbb{F}_{q^m}^{ns}$ such that $\|\mathbf{e}\| \leq r$ and $\mathbf{H}\mathbf{e}^\mathsf{T} = \mathbf{s}^\mathsf{T}$.*

Definition 8 (IRSL Problem). *Given $\mathbf{H} \in \mathbb{F}_{q^m}^{(s-1)n \times sn}$ a parity-check matrix of an $[sn, n]_{q^m}$-ideal code and $\mathbf{S} \in \times \mathbb{F}_{q^m}^{N \times (s-1)n}$, the Ideal Rank Support Learning Problem $\mathsf{IRSL}(n, s, r, N)$ asks to compute a subspace E of $\mathbb{F}_{q^m}$ of dimension r for which there exists a matrix $\mathbf{V} \in E^{N \times n}$ such that $\mathbf{H}\mathbf{V}^\mathsf{T} = \mathbf{S}^\mathsf{T}$.*

2.4   LRPC Codes and Early LRPC-Based Schemes

LRPC codes were introduced in [20] as the rank metric analogue of LDPC codes.

Definition 9 (LRPC code). *An $[n, k]_{q^m}$-linear code $\mathcal{C}$ is said to be LRPC of dual weight d if it admits a parity-check matrix $\boldsymbol{H} \in \mathbb{F}_{q^m}^{(n-k) \times n}$ whose coefficients span an $\mathbb{F}_q$-vector space F of dimension d. Such a matrix $\boldsymbol{H}$ will be called a homogeneous matrix of weight d and support F.*

Introduced in [20], the Rank Support Recovery (RSR) algorithm allows to decode efficiently if the support F of an homogeneous parity-check matrix is known. The following definition combines Definition 6 and Definition 9, as we can clearly construct codes which admit the two properties:

Definition 10 (Ideal-LRPC code). *An Ideal-LRPC code is both an Ideal code and an LRPC code.*

Presented in Fig. 1, the LOCKER Public Key Encryption scheme [6] uses such an Ideal-LRPC code. Its security relies on the difficulty of the IRSD problem.

KeyGen(1^λ):

  - Sample uniformly at random $\mathbf{x}, \mathbf{y} \xleftarrow{\$} S_d^n(\mathbb{F}_{q^m})$
  - Compute $\mathbf{h} = \mathbf{x}^{-1} \cdot \mathbf{y} \mod P$, where $P \in \mathbb{F}_q[X]$ is irreducible of degree n
  - Output pk = $\mathbf{h}$ and sk = $(\mathbf{x}, \mathbf{y})$

Encrypt(pk, $\mathbf{m}$):

  - Sample uniformly at random $\mathbf{e}_1, \mathbf{e}_2 \xleftarrow{\$} S_r^{2n}(\mathbb{F}_{q^m})$
  - Compute $E = \mathsf{Supp}(\mathbf{e}_1, \mathbf{e}_2)$ and $cipher = \mathbf{m} \oplus \mathsf{H}(E)$, where $\oplus$ is the bitwise XOR
  - Compute $\mathbf{c} = \mathbf{e}_1 + \mathbf{e}_2 \cdot \mathbf{h}$ and output ct = $(cipher, \mathbf{c})$

Decrypt(sk, ct):

  - Compute $\mathbf{s} = \mathbf{x}\mathbf{c}$, set $F = \mathsf{Supp}(\mathbf{x}, \mathbf{y})$ and retrieve $E = \mathsf{RSR}(F, \mathbf{s}, r)$
  - Output $\mathbf{m} = cipher \oplus \mathsf{H}(E)$

Fig. 1. Description of the LOCKER scheme

The following Key Encapsulation Mechanism (KEM) given in Fig. 2 is due to [3]. It exploits several syndromes whose errors have the same support in order to improve the initial LRPC decoder. Its security relies on the IRSL problem.

2.5 Augmented Gabidulin Codes and the RQC-MS-AG Scheme

Augmented Gabidulin codes were introduced in [16]. The idea is to add a sequence of zeros at the end of a Gabidulin code.

Definition 11 (Augmented Gabidulin codes). *Let $(k, n, n', m) \in \mathbb{N}^4$ such that $k \leq n' < m < n$. Let $\boldsymbol{g} = (g_1, \ldots, g_{n'}) \in \mathbb{F}_{q^m}^{n'}$ such that $\|\boldsymbol{g}\| = n'$ and let*

KeyGen(1^λ):

  - Sample uniformly at random a subspace F of $\mathbb{F}_{q^m}$ of dimension d.

  - Sample uniformly at random $\mathbf{U} = (\mathbf{A}|\mathbf{B}) \xleftarrow{\$} F^{(n-k)\times n}$.

  - Output $\mathbf{H} = (\mathbf{I}_{n-k}|\mathbf{A}^{-1}\mathbf{B})$ the systematic form of $\mathbf{U}$.

Encap($\mathbf{H}$):

  - Sample uniformly at random E of dimension r.

  - Sample uniformly at random $\mathbf{V} \xleftarrow{\$} E^{n\times N}$

  - Output $\mathbf{C} = \mathbf{HV}$

  - Define $K = \mathsf{H}(E)$

Decap($\mathbf{C}, \mathbf{U}$):

  - Compute $\mathbf{S} = \mathbf{AC}$

  - Recover $E \leftarrow \mathsf{RSR}(F, \mathbf{S}, r)$

  - Return $K = \mathsf{H}(E)$ or $\perp$ if RSR failed.

Fig. 2. Algorithms of the Key Encapsulation Mechanism ILRPC-MS

$\overline{g} \stackrel{def}{=} (g \,|\, \mathbf{0}_{n-n'}) \in \mathbb{F}_{q^m}^n$. *The* Augmented Gabidulin code $\mathcal{G}_{\overline{g}}^+(n, n', k, m)$ *is the code of parameters* $[n, k]_{q^m}$ *defined by:*

$$\mathcal{G}_{\overline{g}}^+(n, n', k, m) \stackrel{def}{=} \left\{ P(\overline{g}), \ \deg_q(P) < k \right\},$$

where $P(\overline{g}) \stackrel{def}{=} (P(g_1), \dots, P(g_{n'}), \mathbf{0}_{n-n'})$ *and P is a q-polynomial.*

The idea is to benefit from elements of the support of the error in the last positions when we decode. They correspond to *support erasures* in a rank metric context. More precisely, *support erasures* are defined as a subspace of the vector space spanned by the error coordinates, i.e., the support of the error. Overall, these codes allow to improve the decoding capacity $\left\lfloor \frac{n'-k}{2} \right\rfloor$ of the original Gabidulin code but this comes at the price of a non-zero decryption failure rate.

Proposition 1 (Decoding Algorithm for Augmented Gabidulin codes).
Let $\mathcal{G}_{\overline{g}}^+(n, n', k, m)$ be an augmented Gabidulin code and let $\varepsilon \in \{1, 2, \dots, \min(n - n', n'-k)\}$ be the dimension of the vector space generated by the support erasures. There exists an efficient decoding algorithm correcting errors of rank weight up to $\delta \stackrel{def}{=} \left\lfloor \frac{n'-k+\varepsilon}{2} \right\rfloor$ with a decryption failure rate (DFR) of:

$$DFR(n, n', \delta, \varepsilon) = q^{\delta(n'-n)} \sum_{i=1}^{\varepsilon} \prod_{j=0}^{i-1} \frac{(q^\delta - q^j)(q^{n-n'} - q^j)}{q^i - q^j}.$$

Using such codes together with the multi syndrome approach of [3] allowed to devise an improvement of RQC called RQC-MS-AG [16]. This scheme is declined in two versions. What is important for our purposes is that one uses *non-homogeneous* errors. A non-homogeneous vector of weight (ω_1, ω_2) in $\mathbb{F}_{q^m}^{3n}$ is an element of

$$\mathcal{S}_{(\omega_1,\omega_2)}^{3n}(\mathbb{F}_{q^m}) \stackrel{\text{def}}{=} \{\mathbf{x} = (\mathbf{x}_1, \mathbf{x}_2, \mathbf{x}_3) \in \mathbb{F}_{q^m}^{3n} \mid \|(\mathbf{x}_1, \mathbf{x}_3)\| = \omega_1,$$
$$\|\mathbf{x}_2\| = \omega_1 + \omega_2, \mathsf{Supp}(\mathbf{x}_1, \mathbf{x}_3) \subset \mathsf{Supp}(\mathbf{x}_2)\}.$$

The use of several syndromes requires to extend this notion to matrices (the support still corresponding to the vector space spanned by its coefficients):

$$\mathcal{S}_{(\omega_1,\omega_2)}^{N\times 3n}(\mathbb{F}_{q^m}) \stackrel{\text{def}}{=} \{\mathbf{M} = (\mathbf{M}_1 \mid \mathbf{M}_2 \mid \mathbf{M}_3) \in \mathbb{F}_{q^m}^{N\times 3n}, \ \dim(\mathsf{Supp}(\mathbf{M}_1 \mid \mathbf{M}_3)) = \omega_1,$$
$$\dim(\mathsf{Supp}(\mathbf{M}_2)) = \omega_1 + \omega_2, \ \mathsf{Supp}(\mathbf{M}_1 \mid \mathbf{M}_3) \subset \mathsf{Supp}(\mathbf{M}_2)\}.$$

Fig. 3 presents the RQC-MS-AG scheme using non-homogeneous errors. As it also uses ideal codes, we consider n_1 and n_2 two integers and $P \in \mathbb{F}_q[X]$ an irreducible polynomial of degree n_2. For a vector $\mathbf{v} \in \mathbb{F}_{q^m}^{n_2}$ and a matrix $\mathbf{M} \in \mathbb{F}_{q^m}^{n_2 \times n_1}$, we generalize the internal product between vectors by

$$\mathbf{v} \cdot \mathbf{M} \stackrel{\text{def}}{=} ((\mathbf{v} \cdot \mathbf{m}_1)^{\mathsf{T}}, \ldots, (\mathbf{v} \cdot \mathbf{m}_{n_1})^{\mathsf{T}}),$$

where $\mathbf{m}_i$ is the i-th column of $\mathbf{M}$ for $i \in \{1, ..., n_1\}$ and where the products at the right hand side are standard internal products. The procedure Fold turns the vector $\mathbf{v} = (\mathbf{v}_1, \ldots, \mathbf{v}_{n_1}) \in (\mathbb{F}_{q^m}^{n_2})^{n_1}$ into $\mathsf{Fold}(\mathbf{v}) \stackrel{\text{def}}{=} (\mathbf{v}_1^{\mathsf{T}}, \ldots, \mathbf{v}_{n_1}^{\mathsf{T}}) \in \mathbb{F}_{q^m}^{n_2 \times n_1}$. The inverse map is denoted by Unfold.

KeyGen(1^λ):

- Sample uniformly at random $\mathbf{h} \xleftarrow{\$} \mathbb{F}_{q^m}^{n_2}$, $\mathbf{g} \xleftarrow{\$} \mathcal{S}_{n'}^{n'}(\mathbb{F}_{q^m})$ and $(\mathbf{x}, \mathbf{y}) \xleftarrow{\$} \mathcal{S}_{\omega,1}^{2n_2}(\mathbb{F}_{q^m})$.

- Compute $\mathbf{s} = \mathbf{x} + \mathbf{h} \cdot \mathbf{y} \mod P$

- Output $\mathsf{pk} = (\mathbf{g}, \mathbf{h}, \mathbf{s})$ and $\mathsf{sk} = (\mathbf{x}, \mathbf{y})$

Encrypt($\mathsf{pk}, \mathbf{m}$):

- Compute a generator matrix $\mathbf{G} \in \mathbb{F}_{q^m}^{k \times n_1 n_2}$ for $\mathcal{G}_{\overline{\mathbf{g}}}^+(n_1 n_2, n', k, m)$, $\overline{\mathbf{g}} \stackrel{\text{def}}{=} (\mathbf{g} \mid \mathbf{0}_{n_1 n_2 - n'})$

- Sample uniformly at random $(\mathbf{R}_1, \mathbf{E}, \mathbf{R}_2) \xleftarrow{\$} \mathcal{S}_{(\omega_1,\omega_2)}^{n_2 \times 3n_1}(\mathbb{F}_{q^m})$

- Compute $\mathbf{U} = \mathbf{R}_1 + \mathbf{h} \cdot \mathbf{R}_2$ and $\mathbf{V} = \mathsf{Fold}(\mathbf{mG}) + \mathbf{s} \cdot \mathbf{R}_2 + \mathbf{E}$

- Output $\mathbf{C} = (\mathbf{U}, \mathbf{V})$

Decrypt($\mathsf{sk}, \mathbf{C}$):

- Output $\mathcal{G}_{\overline{\mathbf{g}}}^+.\mathsf{Decode}(\mathsf{Unfold}(\mathbf{V} - \mathbf{y} \cdot \mathbf{U}))$

Fig. 3. Description of the RQC-MS-AG scheme

2.6 Blockwise Errors and Related Problems

Blockwise errors have been recently introduced in [28]. Their particular structure was used to increase the capacity of LRPC decoding.

Definition 12 (Blockwise ℓ-error). *Let* $\boldsymbol{n} = (n_1, ..., n_\ell) \in \mathbb{N}^\ell$, $\boldsymbol{r} = (r_1, ..., r_\ell) \in \mathbb{N}^\ell$ *and* $n \stackrel{def}{=} \sum_{i=1}^\ell n_i$. *An error* $\boldsymbol{e} \in \mathbb{F}_{q^m}^n$ *is said to be an ℓ-error with parameters* $\boldsymbol{n}$ *and* $\boldsymbol{r}$ *if it is the concatenation of ℓ errors* $\boldsymbol{e}_i \in \mathbb{F}_{q^m}^{n_i}$ *such that*

- *for all* $i \in \{1, ..., \ell\}$, $\|\boldsymbol{e}_i\| = r_i$,
- *for all* $i \neq j$, $\mathsf{Supp}(\boldsymbol{e}_i) \cap \mathsf{Supp}(\boldsymbol{e}_j) = \{0\}$.

We denote $\mathcal{S}_{\mathbf{r}}^{\mathbf{n}}(\mathbb{F}_{q^m})$ as the set of blockwise errors with parameters $\mathbf{n}$ and $\mathbf{r}$. For an integer N and vectors $\mathbf{n}$ and $\mathbf{r}$, we can similarly define $\mathcal{S}_{\mathbf{r}}^{N \times \mathbf{n}}(\mathbb{F}_{q^m})$ the set of matrices of size $N \times n_i$ whose elements are block matrices $\mathbf{M} = (\mathbf{M}_1 \mid \cdots \mid \mathbf{M}_\ell)$ such that $\dim(\mathsf{Supp}(\mathbf{M}_i)) = r_i$. We can naturally define restrictions of the RD and IRSD problems to blockwise errors.

Definition 13 (ℓ-RD problem). *Let* $\boldsymbol{n} = (n_1, ..., n_\ell) \in \mathbb{N}^\ell$, $\boldsymbol{r} = (r_1, ..., r_\ell) \in \mathbb{N}^\ell$ *and* $n \stackrel{def}{=} \sum_{i=1}^\ell n_i$. *Given a full-rank matrix* $\boldsymbol{G} \in \mathbb{F}_{q^m}^{k \times n}$ *and* $\boldsymbol{y} \stackrel{def}{=} \boldsymbol{x}\boldsymbol{G} + \boldsymbol{e}$ *such that* $\boldsymbol{x} \in \mathbb{F}_{q^m}^k$ *is uniformly sampled and* $\boldsymbol{e} \in \mathcal{S}_{\boldsymbol{r}}^{\boldsymbol{n}}$, *the Blockwise Rank Decoding problem* $\mathsf{RD}(\boldsymbol{n}, k, \boldsymbol{r}, m)$ *asks to find* $\boldsymbol{x}$ *and* $\boldsymbol{e}$.

Definition 14 (ℓ-IRSD problem). *Let* $\boldsymbol{n} = (n_1, ..., n_\ell) \in \mathbb{N}^\ell$, $\boldsymbol{r} = (r_1, ..., r_\ell) \in \mathbb{N}^\ell$ *and* $n \stackrel{def}{=} \sum_{i=1}^\ell n_i$. *Let* $\boldsymbol{H} \in \mathbb{F}_{q^m}^{(n-1)s \times ns}$ *be a parity-check matrix of an* $[sn, n]$ *ideal code. On input* $(\boldsymbol{H}, \boldsymbol{s})$ *where* $\boldsymbol{s}^\mathsf{T} = \boldsymbol{H}\boldsymbol{e}^\mathsf{T}$ *and* $\boldsymbol{e} \in \mathcal{S}_{\boldsymbol{r}}^{\boldsymbol{n}}$, *the Blockwise Ideal Rank Syndrome Decoding problem* $\mathsf{IRSD}(\boldsymbol{n}, k, \boldsymbol{r}, m)$ *asks to find* $\boldsymbol{e}$.

An improved version of LOCKER based on 2-IRSD was given in [28].

3 ℓ-LRPC Codes and Decoding with Several Syndromes

In this paper, we combine the multi syndrome approach of [3] together with the blockwise structure of [28]. Thus, Sect. 3.1 starts by describing new restrictions of RSL to this error structure.

3.1 New Problems Related to Blockwise Errors

Definition 15 (ℓ-RSL problem). *Given* $(\boldsymbol{H}, \boldsymbol{H}\boldsymbol{E}^\mathsf{T})$, *where* $\boldsymbol{H} \in \mathbb{F}_{q^m}^{(n-k) \times n}$ *is full-rank and where* $\boldsymbol{E} = (\boldsymbol{E}_1 \mid \cdots \mid \boldsymbol{E}_\ell) \in \mathbb{F}_{q^m}^{N \times n}$ *is such that for* $i \in \{1, ..., \ell\}$, *the matrix* $\boldsymbol{E}_i \in \mathbb{F}_{q^m}^{N \times n_i}$ *is homogeneous of support* $\mathcal{V}_i$, $\dim \mathcal{V}_i = r_i$, $\mathcal{V}_i \cap \mathcal{V}_j = \{0\}$ *for* $i \neq j$, *the Blockwise Rank Support Learning problem* ℓ-$\mathsf{RSL}(m, \boldsymbol{n}, \boldsymbol{r}, k, N)$ *asks to find the set of subspaces* $(\mathcal{V}_i)_{i \in \{1, ..., \ell\}}$.

We can also define a variant of this problem for an ideal code of parameters $[sn, n]_{q^m}$ and where the s-errors have blocks of the same length n.

Definition 16 (*s*-IRSL **problem**). *Let* $\boldsymbol{H}$ *be a parity check matrix of an* $[sn, n]_{q^m}$ *ideal code and let* $\boldsymbol{r} = (r_1, ..., r_s) \in \mathbb{N}^s$. *Given* $(\boldsymbol{H}, \boldsymbol{S}) \in \mathbb{F}_{q^m}^{(s-1)n \times sn} \times \mathbb{F}_{q^m}^{N \times (s-1)n}$, *the Blockwise Ideal Rank Support Learning problem* IRSL$(s, n, \boldsymbol{r}, N)$ *asks to compute a set of* s *subspaces* $\mathcal{V} = (\mathcal{V}_1, \ldots, \mathcal{V}_s)$ *such that* $\dim \mathcal{V}_i = r_i$, $\mathcal{V}_i \cap \mathcal{V}_j = \{0\}$ *for* $i \neq j$ *and such that there exists a matrix* $\boldsymbol{V} = (\boldsymbol{V}_1 \mid \cdots \mid \boldsymbol{V}_s) \in \mathbb{F}_{q^m}^{N \times sn}$ *such that* $\boldsymbol{HV}^{\mathsf{T}} = \boldsymbol{S}^{\mathsf{T}}$ *and whose* i-*th block is homogeneous of support* $\mathcal{V}_i$ *for all* $i \in \{1..s\}$.

In the rest of the section, we study decoding algorithms for ℓ-LRPC codes, introduced in [28]. Their definition is recalled below.

Definition 17. *Let* $\boldsymbol{H} = (\boldsymbol{H}_1 \mid \cdots \mid \boldsymbol{H}_\ell) \in \mathbb{F}_{q^m}^{(n-k) \times n}$ *full-rank such that* $\boldsymbol{H}_i \in \mathbb{F}_{q^m}^{(n-k) \times n_i}$ *is homogeneous of weight* d_i *and support* F_i *for* $i \in \{1..\ell\}$ *and such that for all* $i \neq j$, $F_i \cap F_j = \{0\}$. *The code* $\mathcal{C}$ *with parity-check matrix* $\boldsymbol{H}$ *is said to be an* ℓ-*LRPC code (with dual weight* $(d_1, \ldots, d_\ell)$).

In Sect. 3.2, we extend the decoding algorithm of [28] to multiple syndromes. In Sect. 3.3, we propose a way to improve its DFR by using a trick from [3].

3.2 Decoding Algorithm with Multiple Syndromes

Our new algorithm is described in Algorithm 1. Its correctness easily follows from the one of the algorithms of [8,28].

Algorithm 1. Decoding algorithm of ℓ-LRPC codes for ℓ-errors

Input: A collection of N syndromes $(\mathbf{s}_1, \ldots, \mathbf{s}_N) \in \mathbb{F}_{q^m}^{(n-k) \times N}$ and the parity-check matrix $\mathbf{H} \in \mathbb{F}_{q^m}^{(n-k) \times k}$

Output: The ℓ-error $\mathbf{e}$, or **error**

    Compute the syndrome space $S = \langle s_{1,1}, \ldots s_{N,n-k} \rangle$

    Let $\{F_{i1}, \ldots F_{id_i}\}$ be a basis of F_i for all i

    Compute $S_{ij} = F_{ij}^{-1} S$ for all $i \in \{1, \ldots, \ell\}$ and $j \in \{1, \ldots, d_i\}$

    Compute $E_i = \bigcap_{j=1}^{d_i} S_{ij}$

    if $\dim(E_i) \neq r_i$ for any i **then**

        return error

    else

        Recover $E = \sum_{i=1}^{\ell} E_i$

        Solve the linear system $\mathbf{He}^{\mathsf{T}} = \mathbf{s}^{\mathsf{T}}$ with $\mathbf{e} \in E^n$ as unknown

        return e

This algorithm has a non-zero DFR. There are two cases that can make it fail:

1. the dimension of the syndrome space S is lower than the dimension of the whole product space $\sum_{i=1}^{\ell} E_i F_i$;

2. there exists $i \in \{1..\ell\}$ such that $E_i \supsetneq \bigcap_{j=1}^{d_i} S_{ij}$.

An upper bound of this DFR is given in Theorem 1.

Theorem 1. *Let $\mu = \sum_{i=1}^{\ell} r_i d_i$ and let N be the number of syndromes. Under the assumption that each element of the syndrome space as a random element of $P \overset{def}{=} \sum_{i=1}^{\ell} E_i F_i$, the decoding failure probability of Algorithm 1 is bounded by:*

$$q^{-(N(n-k)-\mu)} + \sum_{i=1}^{\ell} q^{-(d_i-1)(m-\mu)+\mu-r_i}. \tag{1}$$

To prove it, we need the following result from [6]:

Proposition 2. *Let r, d and μ be three integers. Let E be a fixed subspace of dimension r and let $R_i, 1 \leqslant i \leqslant d$, be d independently chosen random subspaces of dimension μ containing the subspace E. The probability that $\dim \bigcap_{i=0}^{d} R_i > r$ is bounded from above by:*

$$q^{\mu-r} \left(\frac{q^\mu - q^r}{q^m} \right)^{d-1} \approx q^{-(d-1)(m-\mu)+\mu-r}$$

Proof (of Theorem 1). First, we study the probability that $\dim(S) < \dim(\sum E_i F_i)$. Each s_{ij} is an element of the product space $P = \sum E_i F_i$. Thus, we can write the set of coefficients of all syndromes as an element in $\mathbb{F}_q^{N(n-k) \times \mu}$ whose rows are obtained by unfolding the s_{ij}'s in a fixed basis of P. By assumption, this matrix behaves as a random matrix. Under this assumption, the probability that $\dim(S) < \dim(P)$ is thus equal to the probability that a random $N(n-k) \times \mu$ matrix is not full-rank. This probability can be upper-bounded by $q^{-(N(n-k)-\mu)}$ and this gives the first term in Eq. (1). The second case which leads to a decoding failure is when there is $i \in \{1..\ell\}$ such that $E_i \supsetneq \bigcap S_{ij}$. By Proposition 2, the probability that $E_i \supsetneq \bigcap S_{ij}$ can be upper bounded by $q^{-(d_i-1)(m-\mu)+\mu-r}$ for $i \in \{1..\ell\}$. We need to recover E_i for all $1 \leqslant i \leqslant \ell$, hence the result. $\square$

3.3   Improving its DFR

By using a technique introduced in the xMS protocol [3], we extend Algorithm 1 to reduce its DFR. The resulting algorithm corresponds to Algorithm 2.

Algorithm 2. Decoding algorithm of ℓ-LRPC codes for ℓ-errors

Input: A collection of N syndromes $(\mathbf{s}_1, \ldots, \mathbf{s}_N) \in \mathbb{F}_{q^m}^{(n-k) \times N}$, the parity-check matrix
$\mathbf{H} \in \mathbb{F}_{q^m}^{(n-k) \times k}$ and an algorithm parameter c
Output: The ℓ-error $\mathbf{e}$, or **error**
  Compute the syndrome space $S = \langle s_{1,1}, \ldots s_{N,n-k} \rangle$
  Let $\{F_{i1}, \ldots F_{id_i}\}$ be a basis of F_i for all i
  Compute $S_{ij} = F_{ij}^{-1} S$ for all $i \in \{1, \ldots, \ell\}$ and $j \in \{1, \ldots, d_i\}$
  Compute $E_i = \bigcap_{j=1}^{d_i} S_{ij}$
  if $\dim(E_i) > r_i + c$ for any i **then**
    return error
  else
    $E' = \sum_{i=1}^{\ell} E_i$
    Solve the linear system $\mathbf{He}^\mathsf{T} = \mathbf{s}^\mathsf{T}$ with $\mathbf{e} \in E'^n$ as unknown
    return e

Correctness. The parameter c must be chosen so that the linear system over $\mathbb{F}_q$ derived from $\mathbf{He}^\mathsf{T} = \mathbf{s}^\mathsf{T}$ with the knowledge of E' has more linearly independent equations than the number of unknowns. If these equations are linearly independent, this condition is met when $(n-k)m \geq \sum n_i \dim(E_i)$, hence a fortiori when $(n-k)m \geq \sum n_i(r_i + c)$. When the system has a unique solution, the rest of the algorithm works in the same way as in Algorithm 1.

Theorem 2. *Let* $\mu = \sum r_i d_i$ *and let* N *be the number of given syndromes. Under the same assumption as in Theorem 1, the decoding failure probability (DFR) of the extended decoding algorithm for ℓ-LRPC codes is bounded by:*

$$q^{-(N(n-k)-\mu)} + \frac{1}{\phi(q^{-1})} \sum_{i=1}^{\ell} q^{(c+1)(\mu - r_i - (c+1) + (d_i-1)(\mu-m))},$$

where ϕ is the Euler function $\phi(x) \stackrel{\text{def}}{=} \prod_{k=1}^{+\infty} (1 - x^k)$, $|x| < 1$.

Proof. The improvement is in the second term, the first term $q^{-(N(n-k)-\mu)}$ being similar to the one of Theorem 1. Another possibility for Algorithm 2 to fail is if $\dim(E_i) > r_i + c$ for at least one $i \in \{1..\ell\}$. By [3, Proposition 3], we have

$$P\left(\dim\left(\bigcap_{j=1}^{d_i} S_{ij}\right) > r_i + c\right) \leq \frac{1}{\phi(q^{-1})} q^{(c+1)(\mu - r_i - (c+1) + (d_i-1)(\mu-m))}.$$

As in the proof of Theorem 1, the second term follows by summing the upper bounds for $i \in \{1..\ell\}$. $\qquad\square$

4 New Cryptographic Schemes Based on ℓ-RSL and ℓ-IRSL

4.1 RQC-MS-AG Scheme with Blockwise Errors

We propose an improvement of the RQC-MS-AG by using 2-errors and 3-errors. A description of the resulting scheme can be found in Fig. 4.

Comments. The Augmented Gabidulin code has parameters $(n_1 n_2, m, k, m)$ and Decode is an efficient decoding algorithm that can correct up to $\delta = \lfloor \frac{m-k+\varepsilon}{2} \rfloor$ errors, where $\varepsilon \leq \min(m-k, n_1 n_2 - m)$ is fixed as a parameter (in this case, the DFR is estimated by Proposition 1). The main difference with the former RQC-MS-AG scheme is that $(\mathbf{x}, \mathbf{y})$ is a 2-blockwise error rather than a random error of length $2n_2$ whose support contains 1 and that the triple $(\mathbf{R}_1, \mathbf{E}, \mathbf{R}_2)$ sampled at the encryption is a set of 3-blockwise errors instead of being a set of non-homogeneous errors with the same support. The rest of the scheme is rather similar and we keep the same notation as in Fig. 3.

KeyGen(1^λ):

- Sample uniformly at random: $\mathbf{g} \xleftarrow{\$} \mathcal{S}_m^m(\mathbb{F}_{q^m})$, $\mathbf{h} \xleftarrow{\$} \mathbb{F}_{q^m}^{n_2}$ and $(\mathbf{x}, \mathbf{y}) \xleftarrow{\$} \mathcal{S}_{(r_\mathbf{x}, r_\mathbf{y})}^{(n_2, n_2)}(\mathbb{F}_{q^m})$

- Compute $\mathbf{s} = \mathbf{x} + \mathbf{h} \cdot \mathbf{y} \mod P$

- Output $\mathsf{pk} = (\mathbf{g}, \mathbf{h}, \mathbf{s})$ and $\mathsf{sk} = (\mathbf{x}, \mathbf{y})$

Encrypt($\mathsf{pk}, \mathbf{m}$):

- Compute a generator matrix $\mathbf{G} \in \mathbb{F}_{q^m}^{k \times n_1 n_2}$ for $\mathcal{G}_{\overline{\mathbf{g}}}^+(n_1 n_2, m, k, m)$, $\overline{\mathbf{g}} \overset{\text{def}}{=} (\mathbf{g} \mid 0_{n_1 n_2 - m})$

- Sample $(\mathbf{R}_1, \mathbf{R}_2, \mathbf{E}) \xleftarrow{\$} \mathcal{S}_{(r_1, r_2, r_e)}^{n_2 \times (n_1, n_1, n_1)}(\mathbb{F}_{q^m})$

- Compute $\mathbf{U} = \mathbf{R}_1 + \mathbf{h} \cdot \mathbf{R}_2$ and $\mathbf{V} = \mathsf{Fold}(\mathbf{mG}) + \mathbf{s} \cdot \mathbf{R}_2 + \mathbf{E}$

- Output $\mathbf{C} = (\mathbf{U}, \mathbf{V})$

Decrypt($\mathsf{sk}, \mathbf{C}$):

- Output $\mathsf{Decode}(\mathsf{Unfold}(\mathbf{V} - \mathbf{y} \cdot \mathbf{U}))$

Fig. 4. Description of the RQC-MS-AG scheme with blockwise errors

The parameters need to be chosen according to the following proposition.

Proposition 3. *Decryption is correct as long as*

$$\|\mathsf{Unfold}(\boldsymbol{x} \cdot \boldsymbol{R}_2 - \boldsymbol{y} \cdot \boldsymbol{R}_1 + \boldsymbol{E})\| \leq \delta.$$

Proof. We have $\mathbf{U} = \mathbf{R}_1 + \mathbf{h} \cdot \mathbf{R}_2$ and $\mathbf{V} = \mathsf{Fold}(\mathbf{mG}) + \mathbf{s} \cdot \mathbf{R}_2 + \mathbf{E}$, so that

$$\mathbf{V} - \mathbf{y} \cdot \mathbf{U} = \mathsf{Fold}(\mathbf{mG}) + (\mathbf{x} + \mathbf{hy}) \cdot \mathbf{R}_2 + \mathbf{E} - \mathbf{y} \cdot (\mathbf{R}_1 + \mathbf{hR}_2)$$
$$= \mathsf{Fold}(\mathbf{mG}) + \mathbf{x} \cdot \mathbf{R}_2 - \mathbf{y} \cdot \mathbf{R}_1 + \mathbf{E}.$$

This implies $\mathsf{Unfold}(\mathbf{V} - \mathbf{y} \cdot \mathbf{U}) = \mathbf{mG} + \mathsf{Unfold}(\mathbf{x} \cdot \mathbf{R}_2 - \mathbf{y} \cdot \mathbf{R}_1 + \mathbf{E})$. Therefore, the algorithm Decode will output $\mathbf{m}$ (there is still a DFR) as long as $\|\mathsf{Unfold}(\mathbf{x} \cdot \mathbf{R}_2 - \mathbf{y} \cdot \mathbf{R}_1 + \mathbf{E})\| \leq \delta$. □

4.2 ILRPC-MS with Blockwise Errors

We also improve the ILRPC-MS scheme of [3] described in Fig. 2 by using 2-errors. Our new scheme is presented in Fig. 5.

Let $\mathcal{V} = (\mathcal{V}_i)_{i \in \{1,...,\ell\}}$ a finite sequence of subspaces of $\mathbb{F}_{q^m}$ such that $\dim \mathcal{V}_i = r_i$ and for all $i \neq j$: $\mathcal{V}_i \cap \mathcal{V}_j = \{0\}$. We denote $\mathcal{S}_{\mathbf{r}}^{\mathbf{n}}(\mathcal{V})$ the set of vectors of the form $\mathbf{x} = (\mathbf{x}_1, ..., \mathbf{x}_\ell)$, such that for all $i \in \{1, ..., \ell\}$, the coefficients of each vector $\mathbf{x}_i \in \mathbb{F}_{q^m}^{n_i}$ belongs to $\mathcal{V}_i$.

KeyGen(1^λ):
- Choose uniformly at random two subspaces F_1 and F_2 in $\mathbb{F}_{q^m}$ of respective dimensions d_1 and d_2.
- Sample a couple of polynomials whose coefficients belong to F: $(\mathbf{x}, \mathbf{y}) \xleftarrow{\$} F_1^{n_2} \times F_2^{n_2}$.
- Compute $\mathbf{h} = \mathbf{x}^{-1}\mathbf{y} \mod P$
- Output $\mathsf{pk} = \mathbf{h}$ and $\mathsf{sk} = (\mathbf{x}, \mathbf{y})$

Encap(pk):
- Choose uniformly at random $\mathcal{V} = (\mathcal{V}_1, \mathcal{V}_2)$ such that $\dim \mathcal{V}_i = r_i$ and $\mathcal{V}_1 \cap \mathcal{V}_2 = \{0\}$.
- Sample uniformly n_1 polynomials whose coefficients belong to $\mathcal{S}_{\mathbf{r}}^{(n_2,n_2)}(\mathcal{V})$:

$(\mathbf{e}_1, ..., \mathbf{e}_{n_1}) \xleftarrow{\$} (\mathcal{S}_{\mathbf{r}}^{(n_2,n_2)}(\mathcal{V}))^{n_1}$
- Write each vector $\mathbf{e}_i$ as concatenation of $\mathbf{e}_{i,1}$ and $\mathbf{e}_{i,2}$, i.e. $\mathbf{e}_i = (\mathbf{e}_{i,1}|\mathbf{e}_{i,2})$
- Compute $\mathbf{c}_i = \mathbf{e}_{i,1} + \mathbf{e}_{i,2}\mathbf{h}$ for all integer i from 1 to n_1.
- Define $K = \mathsf{H}(\mathcal{V})$ and output $\mathbf{c} = (\mathbf{c}_1, ..., \mathbf{c}_{n_1})$

Decap(sk, c):
- Compute $\mathbf{S} = (\mathbf{xc}_1, ..., \mathbf{xc}_{n_1})$
- Recover $\mathcal{V} \leftarrow \mathsf{Decode}(F, \mathbf{S}, \mathbf{r})$
- Return $K = \mathsf{H}(\mathcal{V})$ or $\perp$ if the Decode algorithm failed.

Fig. 5. Algorithms KeyGen, Encap and Decap of the Key Encapsulation Mechanism ILRPC-Block-MS

Comments. As ideal codes are used, we recall that the vectors $\mathbf{x}$, $\mathbf{y}$ in this figure must be seen as elements in $\mathbb{F}_{q^m}[X]$ taken modulo an irreducible polynomial $P \in \mathbb{F}_q[X]$ of degree n. The Decode algorithm is a decoding algorithm for LRPC codes in the case of blockwise errors. It can be either Algorithm 1 or Algorithm 2. More precisely, we call our scheme ILRPC-Block-MS when Algorithm 1 is used and ILRPC-Block-XMS($r + c$) otherwise, where c is the extra parameter in Algorithm 2. These two algorithms output the error vector rather than its support but they are somehow equivalent to RSR because it is straightforward to recover the full error vector once its support is known.

5 Combinatorial Attacks

In this section, we present combinatorial attacks against three difficult problems adapted to blockwise errors:

1. For the $\ell - $ RD problem, we present an adaptation of the AGHT attack, different from [28], as well as a new attack called *Shortening and Truncating*. We compare these attacks on a specific parameter case;
2. For the $\ell - $ RSL problem
3. A structural attack against ℓ-LRPC codes.

5.1 Combinatorial Attacks Against ℓ-RD

To study the complexity of solving the ℓ-RD problem with combinatorial attacks, we will adapt and derive the new complexity of the attacks from [9,21,25] to the case of ℓ-errors. in this section, we present results in a simplified situation where $n_1 = \cdots = n_\ell = n$, $k = n$ and $r_1 \leq r_2 \leq \cdots \leq r_\ell$.

These attacks are similar to what was presented in [27], although it does not require the support to be disjoint. Another difference is that we take advantage of simplified situations as explained in the previous paragraph.

5.1.1 The Ourivski-Johansonn Attack

As presented in [28], the complexity of the OJ attack is

$$\mathcal{O}((m(r - 1) + (n - r_1))^\omega q^{(r_1-1)(n-r_1)+r_\ell}).$$

5.1.2 The AGHT Attack

In order to adapt the algorithm from [9] to the case of ℓ-errors, we will sample ℓ different vector spaces F_i of dimension t_i, and the algorithm will succeed if $\exists \alpha$ such that $\forall i, \alpha E_i \subset F_i$. Using the same techniques as in [9] this probability can be approximated by:

$$\frac{q^m - 1}{q - 1} \prod_{i=1}^{\ell} q^{-r_i(m-t_i)}$$

Which gives a total complexity of:

$$\mathcal{O}((n - k)^3 \, m^3 q^{-m+\sum\limits_{i=1}^{\ell} r_i(m-t_i)}) \tag{2}$$

Recall that we restrict ourselves to the case where $\forall i, n_i = \frac{n}{\ell}$.

The total complexity depends on the choice of t_is. First we must choose these values such that $\sum\limits_{i=1}^{\ell} t_i n_i \leqslant m - \lceil \frac{m(k+1)}{n} \rceil$ for the system to have more equations than unknowns, and $t_i > r_i$ for having a non-zero probability that $E_i \subset F_i$. Then there are two cases:

1. All of the r_is are equal. In this case the choice of the t_is does not change the complexity, and the complexity is the same for ℓ-errors and an error of weight r.
2. The r_is are not equal. In this case the optimal strategy is to try to make perfect guesses for the smaller r_is (i.e. choosing $t_i = r_i$) in order to have the highest possible value for the t_i corresponding to the highest r_i.

The more the r_is are different, the bigger the advantage of specifically targeting ℓ-errors instead of errors of weight r Fig. 6.

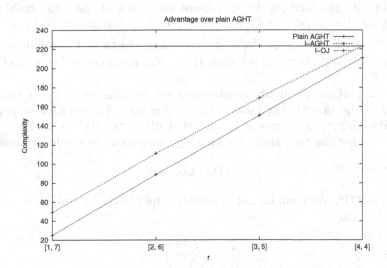

Fig. 6. Complexities of the AGHT algorithm targeting an error of rank r (plain) and adapted to ℓ-errors for parameters $m = 61, n = 134, k = 67$ and different values of **r**.

Comparison with [28]

In [28, Sect. 3.3], the authors propose an adaptation of the AGHT attack to the case of ℓ-errors. We claim their adaptation misestimates the complexity of ℓ-AGHT attack. We give below two arguments to support our assertion.

First, in the demonstration of their Lemma 3.5 (cf. [28, Appendix C.1]), they seem to imply that the number of subspaces of $\mathbb{F}_{q^m}$ of dimension t_2 disjoint from a fixed E_1 is exactly equal to the number of subspaces of $\mathbb{F}_{q^m}/E_1$ of dimension t_1, which is not the case. In particular, in their $\ell = 2$ example, they guess a subspace F_2 in $\mathbb{F}_{q^m}/E_1$, but in order to perform the rest of the attack, this F_2 needs to be lifted in $\mathbb{F}_{q^m}$ into a $\widehat{F}_2$. Even though F_2 contains E_2/E_1, it is not guaranteed that $\widehat{F}_2$ will contain E_2, as it depends on the choice of the representatives for the lifting.

Second, as we understood their attack, sampling F_ℓ requires a correct guess for each $E_1, \ldots, E_{\ell-1}$. Therefore $F_1, \ldots, F_{\ell-1}$ play no role in the attack, which sounds somewhat strange.

5.1.3   Hybrid Shortening and Truncating Attack

This new attack is an hybrid between Ourivski-Johansonn and other attacks against the plain RD problem. The attack consists of reducing the problem to solving the same problem in a code with smaller dimension (shortening), and then considering only the part of the code associated to error coordinates belonging to vectorial space of dimension r_1 (truncating). Then, we obtain a Rank Decoding problem instance with a homogeneous error of smaller dimension. It is related to the hybrid attack presented in [13, Sect. 5.5], with the difference that the truncating part was previously unpublished.

To simplify the analysis, let us present an attack of the 2-RD problem in a code $\mathcal{C}$ of size $[2n, n]$: let $\mathbf{G} \in \mathbb{F}_{q^m}^{n \times 2n}$ the generator matrix of $\mathcal{C}$, an error $\mathbf{e} \in S_{(r_1, r_2)}^{(n,n)}$ with $(r_1, r_2) \in \mathbb{N}^2$. We reduce the problem to the resolution of a homogeneous RD problem, in a code with smaller parameters. Let $\mathbf{y} = \mathbf{x}\mathbf{G} + \mathbf{e}$ with $\mathbf{x} \in \mathbb{F}_{q^m}^n$.

We can perform $\mathbb{F}_q$-linear combinations on coordinates of $\mathbf{e}_1$, in order to obtain 0 in the first t_1 coordinates. In other words, it is possible to apply a matrix $\mathbf{P}$ with $r_1 t_1$ unknowns in $\mathbb{F}_q$ such that $\mathbf{e}\mathbf{P}$ is $(0...0 \,|\, \mathbf{e}_1' \,|\, \mathbf{e}_2)$.

The attacker can then apply the same operations on the syndrome, and gets

$$\mathbf{y}' = \mathbf{y}\mathbf{P} = \mathbf{x}\mathbf{G}' + \mathbf{e}'$$

with $\mathbf{G}' = \mathbf{G}\mathbf{P}$. Without loss of generality, the matrix $\mathbf{G}$ can be in a semi-systematic form

$$\mathbf{G}' = \left(\begin{array}{c|c} I_t & * \\ \hline 0 & * \end{array} \right)$$

Operations on the columns can then be performed to cancel to top-right block of $\mathbf{G}'$, i.e. there exists an invertible matrix $\mathbf{Q}$ such that

$$\mathbf{G}'\mathbf{Q} = \left(\begin{array}{c|c} I_t & 0 \\ \hline 0 & \mathbf{A} \end{array} \right)$$

Because the error $\mathbf{e}'$ has its first t coordinates set to 0, $\mathbf{e}'\mathbf{Q} = \mathbf{e}'$ hence by writing:

$$\mathbf{y}'', \text{ the } n \text{ rightmost coordinates of } \mathbf{y}'\mathbf{Q}$$
$$\mathbf{x}'', \text{ the } n - t \text{ rightmost coordinates of } \mathbf{x}$$
$$\mathbf{G}'', \text{ the } n \text{ rightmost columns of } \mathbf{A}$$

we get

$$\mathbf{y}'' = \mathbf{x}''\mathbf{G}'' + \mathbf{e}_2$$

which is an instance of the RD problem in a code of parameters $[n, n - t_1, r_2]$. The cost of transforming the initial instance in this reduced instance is $q^{r_1 t_1}$ (for finding the correct matrix $\mathbf{P}$) times n^2 (for calculating the matrix $\mathbf{Q}$).

By symmetry, another variant of the attack consists in canceling t_2 coordinates in the rightmost part of the error of weight r_2, and then solving an RD instance in a code with parameters $[n, n - t_2, r_1]$.

In the above explanation, the attacker *truncates* until obtaining a plain RD instance. Another possibility is to truncate only $t_1 \leq u_1 < n$ columns of $\mathbf{G}''$, yielding a 2-RD instance $(n - u_1, n)$ with weights (r_1, r_2).

We can then deduce the following proposition:

Proposition 4. *The complexity of solving the 2-RD problem in a code of size (n, n) by the Shortening and Truncating attack is estimated as:*

$$n^2 \cdot \min_{\substack{1 \leq t_1 \leq n \\ 1 \leq t_2 \leq n \\ t_1 \leq u_1 \leq n \\ t_2 \leq u_2 \leq n}} \left(q^{r_1 t_1} \times \mathcal{T}_{2-\text{RD}}\left((n - u_1, n), n - t_1, (r_1, r_2), m\right), q^{r_2 t_2} \times \mathcal{T}_{2-\text{RD}}\left((n, n - u_2), n - t_2, (r_1, r_2), m\right) \right)$$

$$(3)$$

where $\mathcal{T}_{2-\text{RD}}(n, k, r, m)$ is the complexity of the best algorithm for solving an instance of $2 - \text{RD}(n, k, r, m)$ problem.

5.2   Combinatorial Attacks on ℓ-RSL

The first combinatorial attack on plain RSL was given in [19] when this problem was introduced. A more efficient attack was proposed in [16]. In particular, it showed that RSL can be solved in polynomial time for a number N of syndromes which is in general much smaller than the former bound $N \geq nr$ from [19].

Complexity of the [16] attack on plain RSL, where $a = \lfloor \frac{N}{r} \rfloor$

$$\begin{cases} \text{polynomial when } a - N/m \geq k, \text{ hence a fortiori when } N \geq (k+1)\frac{m}{m-r} \\ \mathcal{O}\left(q^{r\left(m - \lfloor \frac{m(n-k)-N}{n-a} \rfloor\right)}\right) \text{ otherwise.} \end{cases}$$

This attack exploits the fact that there exists an $\mathbb{F}_q$-linear combination of the errors $\mathbf{e}_i$, $i \in \{1..N\}$ with $a = \lfloor \frac{N}{r} \rfloor$ zeroes in the leftmost positions. For instance, the goal is to find scalars $(\lambda_1, \ldots, \lambda_\ell) \in \mathbb{F}_q^\ell$ and $\widetilde{\mathbf{e}} \in E^{n-a}$ such that

$$(\mathbf{0} \,|\, \widetilde{\mathbf{e}}) = \sum_{i=1}^{\ell} \lambda_i \mathbf{e}_i.$$

Then, the linear equation

$$(\mathbf{0} \,|\, \widetilde{\mathbf{e}}) \mathbf{H}^\mathsf{T} = \sum_{i=1}^{\ell} \lambda_i \mathbf{s}_i$$

is rewritten as a linear system over $\mathbb{F}_q$ in $m(n-k)$ equations and $(n-a)m+N$ unknowns. When it is overdefined, solving this system takes polynomial time. Otherwise, [16] applies the same techniques as in combinatorial attacks on RD by sampling a random subspace F of dimension t. However, contrary to AGHT, the guess is successful when $E \subset F$ but not when $\alpha E \subset F$ for an arbitrary $\alpha \in \mathbb{F}_{q^m}^*$ (as we only consider $\mathbb{F}_q$-linear combinations of the $\mathbf{e}_i$'s).

Adaptation to ℓ-RSL. We modify this algorithm in the same way as what we did for ℓ-RD. In the following, we restrict ourselves to the case when $n_1 = \cdots = n_\ell = n$, $k = n$, $r = r_1 = \cdots = r_\ell$ and $N \le nr_1$. The condition on N implies that we cannot hope to "kill" completely one of the ℓ blocks of the error by putting zeroes. The complexity of this adaption is given below.

> **Complexity of our adapation on ℓ-RSL, where $a = \left\lfloor \frac{N}{r_1} \right\rfloor$**
> (when $n_1 = \cdots = n_\ell = n$, $k = n$, $r = r_1 = \cdots = r_\ell$ and $N \le nr_1$)
>
> $$\mathcal{O}\left(q^{r\left(m-\left\lfloor \frac{m(n\ell-\ell)-N-(\ell-1)nr}{n-a} \right\rfloor\right)+(\ell-1)r(m-r)}\right).$$

Proof. The condition on N makes that we cannot attack a support which is smaller than the common support E. Thus, we only care about fixing the maximum number of zeroes. Without loss of generality, we fix $a = \left\lfloor \frac{N}{r_1} \right\rfloor$ zeroes all in the first block. By doing so, the error $(\mathbf{0} \mid \widetilde{\mathbf{e}})$ we end up with is still blockwise and of the same support. We use the blockwise structure as in the AGHT adaptation. The probability of a correct guess $E_i \subset F_i$ for $i \in \{1..\ell\}$ is now

$$\prod_{i=1}^{\ell} q^{-r_i(m-t_i)},$$

and we want

$$(n-a)t_1 + \sum_{i=2}^{\ell} nt_i \le m(n\ell - \ell) - N. \tag{4}$$

As the goal is to maximize the sum $\sum_{i=1}^{\ell} r_i t_i$ to maximize the probability that $E_i \subset F_i$ for $i \in \{1..\ell\}$, we take $t_i = r$ for $i > 1$, and thus $t_1 = \left\lfloor \frac{m(n\ell-\ell)-N-(\ell-1)nr}{n-a} \right\rfloor$, the highest value satisfying Eq. 4. □

5.3 A Structural Attack Against 2-LRPC Codes

It is also possible to consider structural attacks, by exploiting a possible particular structure of the code to recover the secret key $\mathbf{H}$. For example: in the case of an 2-LRPC code.

Proposition 5. *The complexity of recovering the structure of a 2-LRPC code* $\mathcal{C}$ *of size* (n, n) *by the Shortening and Truncating attack is estimated as:*

$$n^2 \cdot \min_{\substack{1 \leq t_1 \leq n \\ 1 \leq t_2 \leq n \\ t_1 + \lfloor n/d_1 \rfloor \leq u_1 \leq n \\ t_2 + \lfloor n/d_2 \rfloor \leq u_2 \leq n}} \left(\begin{array}{l} q^{r_1 t_1} \times \mathcal{T}_{2-\mathsf{RD}}((n - u_1, n), n - t_1 - \lfloor \frac{n}{d_1} \rfloor, (r_1, r_2), m), \\[2mm] q^{r_2 t_2} \times \mathcal{T}_{2-\mathsf{RD}}((n, n - u_2), n - t_2 - \lfloor \frac{n}{d_2} \rfloor, (r_1, r_2), m) \end{array} \right)$$

(5)

Proof. We explain using the attack described in [21] why we can reduce it to a subcode of $\mathcal{C}$ with smaller parameters.

Let $\mathbf{H} \in \mathbb{F}_{q^m}^{n \times 2n}$ the parity check matrix of $\mathcal{C}$. We can define the matrix as $\mathbf{H} = (\mathbf{H}_1 \mathbf{H}_2)$, where $\mathbf{H}_1, \mathbf{H}_2 \in \mathbb{F}_{q^m}^{n \times n}$ and $\mathbf{H}_1$ (resp. $\mathbf{H}_2$) has its coefficients belong to the same subspace F_1 (resp. F_2, disjoint to F_1) of dimension d_1 (resp. d_2).

Let $\mathcal{D}$ the dual code of $\mathcal{C}$, whose $\mathbf{H} = (\mathbf{H}_1 \mathbf{H}_2)$ is a generator matrix. We denote by $(H_i)_{i \in \{1, \ldots, n\}}$ the rows of $\mathbf{H}$, and we consider a word $\mathbf{x} \in \mathcal{D}$ obtained from linear combination in $\mathbb{F}_q$: $\mathbf{x} = \sum_{i=1}^{n} a_i H_i$, with $a_i \in \mathbb{F}_q$. Consider the block $\mathbf{H}_2$, whose coefficients belong to F_2. Since F_2 has dimension d_2, choose d_2 variables a_i correctly allows to put to 0 a coordinate of $\mathbf{x}$. Since there are n variables a_i, one can put to 0 with a good probability $\lfloor n/d_2 \rfloor$ coefficients of $\mathbf{x}$. Therefore, the dual code $\mathcal{C}^\perp$ contains with a good probability a word $\mathbf{x} = (\mathbf{x}_1 \mathbf{x}_2)$, whose the coefficients of $\mathbf{x}_1$ belongs to F_1 and the $\lfloor n/d_2 \rfloor$ first coordinates of $\mathbf{x}_2$ are equal to zero (without loss of generality). Then, the attacker can perform the Shortening and Truncating attack on $\mathcal{D}$, knowing that the dimension of the code has already been reduced.   □

6 Algebraic Attacks

The algebraic attacks of [28] on ℓ-RD are an adaptation of the known techniques for RD [12–14] by taking advantage of the block structure. They do not exploit the fact that the supports are pairwise disjoint. Since we introduce the ℓ-RSL problem, we also adapt the algebraic attack of [11] in a similar way. In this section, we will heavily rely on the fact that for a vector $\mathbf{x} \in \mathbb{F}_{q^m}^n$ and a basis $\beta \in \mathbb{F}_{q^m}$ for the extension field, there exists a unique matrix $\mathbf{M}(\mathbf{x}) \in \mathbb{F}_q^{m \times n}$ such that $\mathbf{x} = \beta \mathbf{M}(\mathbf{x})$.

6.1 MaxMinors Attack

As in the most recent combinatorial attacks, RD is reduced to the problem of finding a weight r codeword in the code $\mathcal{C}_{\mathbf{y}} \stackrel{def}{=} \mathcal{C} \oplus \langle \mathbf{y} \rangle_{\mathbb{F}_{q^m}}$. The error vector satisfies the equation

$$\mathbf{e} \mathbf{H}_{\mathbf{y}}^{\mathsf{T}} = \mathbf{0},$$

where $\mathbf{H_y} \in \mathbb{F}_{q^m}^{(n-k-1) \times n}$ is a systematic parity-check matrix for $\mathcal{C}_y$. We then express $\mathbf{M(e)} \in \mathbb{F}_q^{m \times n}$ as a product $\mathbf{SC}$, where $\mathbf{S} \in \mathbb{F}_q^{m \times r}$ and $\mathbf{C} \in \mathbb{F}_q^{r \times n}$ are the support and coefficient matrices respectively. Finally, the matrix $\mathbf{SCH}_y^\mathsf{T} \in \mathbb{F}_{q^m}^{r \times (n-k-1)}$ is not full-rank because $\beta \mathbf{SCH}_y^\mathsf{T} = \mathbf{0}$.

Modeling 1 (MaxMinors). *Let $\boldsymbol{H_y} \in \mathbb{F}_{q^m}^{(n-k-1) \times n}$ be a systematic parity-check matrix for $\mathcal{C}_y = \mathcal{C} \oplus \langle \boldsymbol{y} \rangle_{\mathbb{F}_{q^m}}$ and let $\boldsymbol{C} \in \mathbb{F}_q^{r \times n}$ be the secret coefficient matrix associated to $e \in \mathbb{F}_{q^m}^n$. The MaxMinors modeling is the system defined by $\{P_J\}_{J \subset \{1..n-k-1\}, \, \#J=r}$, where*

$$P_J \overset{def}{=} \left| C(H_y^\mathsf{T})_{*,J} \right|.$$

By using the Cauchy-Binet formula, this system is known to be linear (over $\mathbb{F}_{q^m}$) in the maximal minors $c_T \overset{def}{=} |\mathbf{C}|_{*,T}$ of $\mathbf{C}$ for $T \subset \{1..n\}$, $\#T = r$. As these minors are over $\mathbb{F}_q$, the attack proceeds by solving a system projected over $\mathbb{F}_q$ containing $m\binom{n-k-1}{r}$ equations.

In order to solve ℓ-RD, [28] propose to fix certain variables in the MaxMinors system. A previous attempt of the same type can be found in the RQC submission on non-homogeneous errors [1]. To attack an ℓ-RD instance of block size $n \overset{def}{=} \sum_{i=1}^\ell n_i$ and dimension k with $r \overset{def}{=} \sum_{i=1}^\ell r_i$, the idea is to write the coefficient matrix as

$$\mathbf{C} = \begin{pmatrix} \mathbf{C}_1 & & & \\ & \mathbf{C}_2 & & \\ & & \ddots & \\ & & & \mathbf{C}_\ell \end{pmatrix} \in \mathbb{F}_q^{r \times n}, \quad \mathbf{C}_i \in \mathbb{F}_q^{r_i \times n_i}. \tag{6}$$

If we set $n_{\leq j} \overset{def}{=} \sum_{i=1}^j n_i$, we notice that the minor variables that are possibly non-zero are such that $T_j \overset{def}{=} (T - n_{\leq j-1}) \cap \{1..n_j\}$ is of size r_j for $j \in \{1..\ell\}$. This allows to consider $\prod_{i=1}^\ell \binom{n_i}{r_i}$ unknowns instead of $\binom{n}{r}$. Moreover, such minors can be seen as product of smaller ones, i.e. ,

$$c_T = \prod_{i=1}^\ell c_{i,T_i}, \quad c_{i,T_i} \overset{def}{=} |\mathbf{C}_i|_{*,T_i}. \tag{7}$$

The question left open in [28] is the study of linear dependencies between the MaxMinor equations by zeroing the rest of the variables.

We attempted to study such relations in the system over $\mathbb{F}_{q^m}$, mainly for blocks of the same size. In turns out that there always exist some when $\ell \geq 3$. In that respect, the situation is comparable to that of [16]. When $\ell = 2$, there is a collision between leading terms which does not occur in the random case but we observed in our tests that the equations remained linearly independent.

Message Attack. We restrict ourselves to blocks of the same size, for $\ell = 2$ and $\ell = 3$. Estimate 1 is based upon the assumption that the equations remain linearly independent when $\ell = 2$. We set $N_2(n, r_1, r_2) \overset{def}{=} \binom{n-1}{r_1+r_2}$.

Estimate 1 (2 blocks). *We expect to solve a 2-RD instance of parameters* $(m, n_1 = n, n_2 = n, k = n, (r_1, r_2))$ *by Gaussian elimination on the MaxMinors system whenever*

$$mN_2(n, r_1, r_2) \geq \binom{n}{r_1}\binom{n}{r_2} - 1, \tag{8}$$

with cost $\mathcal{O}\left(mN_2(n, r_1, r_2)\binom{n}{r_1}^{\omega-1}\binom{n}{r_2}^{\omega-1}\right)$, $2 \leq \omega \leq 3$. *When Eq.* (8) *does not hold, we estimate the cost of the hybrid approach of by*

$$\mathcal{O}\left(\min_{\substack{(a_1, a_2) \\ mN_2(n,r_1,r_2) \geq \binom{n-a_1}{r_1}\binom{n-a_2}{r_2}-1}} \left(q^{a_1 r_1 + a_2 r_2} mN_2(n, r_1, r_2)\binom{n-a_1}{r_1}^{\omega-1}\binom{n-a_2}{r_2}^{\omega-1}\right)\right).$$

When $\ell = 3$, we replace the total number of equations $m\binom{2n-1}{r_1+r_2+r_3}$ by the following sharper bound on the number of linearly independent equations (obtained from preliminary analysis):

$$mN_3(n, r_1, r_2, r_3) \overset{def}{=} m\sum_{j=r_2-1}^{r_1+r_2} \binom{n-1}{j}\binom{n-1}{r_1+r_2+r_3-j}.$$

On our parameters, this value is still quite close to the maximum number of equations.

Estimate 2 (3 blocks). *We expect to solve a 3-RD instance of parameters* $(m, n_1 = n, n_2 = n, n_3 = n, k = n, (r_1, r_2, r_3))$ *by Gaussian elimination on the MaxMinors system whenever*

$$mN_3(n, r_1, r_2, r_3) \geq \binom{n}{r_1}\binom{n}{r_2}\binom{n}{r_3} - 1, \tag{9}$$

with cost $\mathcal{O}\left(mN_3(n, r_1, r_2, r_3)\binom{n}{r_1}^{\omega-1}\binom{n}{r_2}^{\omega-1}\binom{n}{r_3}^{\omega-1}\right)$, $2 \leq \omega \leq 3$. *When Eq.* (9) *does not hold, we estimate the cost of the hybrid approach of by*

$$\mathcal{O}\left(\min_{\substack{(a_1, a_2, a_3) \\ mN_3(n,r_1,r_2,r_3) \geq \binom{n-a_1}{r_1}\binom{n-a_2}{r_2}\binom{n-a_3}{r_3}-1}} \left(q^{a_1 r_1 + a_2 r_2 + a_3 r_3} mN_3(n, r_1, r_2, r_3)\binom{n-a_1}{r_1}^{\omega-1}\binom{n-a_2}{r_2}^{\omega-1}\binom{n-a_3}{r_3}^{\omega-1}\right)\right).$$

Structural Attack. In this case, we have more freedom to fix coordinates to zero in the error vector. We reduce to a problem with a unique solution with probability 1 and we then proceed as before. On an instance with parameters $(m, n_1 = n, n_2 = n, k = n, (d_1, d_2))$, we can freely

- fix b_1 on the left and then the rest $b_2 = \left\lfloor \frac{n_1 + n_2 - k - r_1 b_1}{r_2} \right\rfloor$ on the right;
- fix b_2 zeroes on the right first and then $b_1 = \left\lfloor \frac{n_1 + n_2 - k - r_2 b_2}{r_1} \right\rfloor$ on the left.

By doing so, we expect to attack a new instance with block size $n_1 = n - b_1$, $n_2 = n - b_2$ and with dimension $n - b_1 - b_2$. The codimension remains $(2n - b_1 - b_2) - (n - b_1 - b_2) = n$.

Estimate 3. *The complexity of this attack is* $\mathcal{O}(m \times \min(A, B))$, *where*

$$A = \min_{\substack{0 \le b_1 \le \lfloor n/d_1 \rfloor \\ b_2 = \left\lfloor \frac{n - r_1 b_1}{d_2} \right\rfloor}} \left(\min_{\substack{(a_1, a_2) \\ m N_2(n, d_1, d_2) \ge \binom{n - b_1 - a_1}{d_1} \binom{n - b_2 - a_2}{d_2} - 1}} q^{a_1 d_1 + a_2 d_2} N_2(n, d_1, d_2) \binom{n - b_1 - a_1}{d_1}^{\omega - 1} \binom{n - b_2 - a_2}{d_2}^{\omega - 1} \right),$$

$$B = \min_{\substack{0 \le b_2 \le \lfloor n/d_2 \rfloor \\ b_1 = \left\lfloor \frac{n - d_2 b_2}{d_1} \right\rfloor}} \left(\min_{\substack{(a_1, a_2) \\ m N_2(n, d_1, d_2) \ge \binom{n - b_1 - a_1}{d_1} \binom{n - b_2 - a_2}{d_2} - 1}} q^{a_1 d_1 + a_2 d_2} N_2(n, d_1, d_2) \binom{n - b_1 - a_1}{d_1}^{\omega - 1} \binom{n - b_2 - a_2}{d_2}^{\omega - 1} \right).$$

6.2   Attack Based on Support-Minors

The Support-Minors system was introduced in [14] as a new modeling for the MinRank problem but its analysis in the context of RD was inaccurate. This was corrected in [13] where they propose the SM-$\mathbb{F}_{q^m}^{+}$ attack. When MaxMinors projected over $\mathbb{F}_q$ cannot be solved by direct linearization, it consists in adding the following equations:

Modeling 2 (Support-Minors for RD). *Let* $\boldsymbol{G} \in \mathbb{F}_{q^m}^{k \times n}$ *be a systematic generator matrix of* $\mathcal{C}$ *and let* $\boldsymbol{C} \in \mathbb{F}_q^{r \times n}$ *be the secret coefficient matrix associated to* $\boldsymbol{e} \in \mathbb{F}_{q^m}^n$. *The Support-Minors modeling is the system defined by* $\{Q_I\}_{I \subset \{1..n\}, \ \#I = r+1}$, *where*

$$Q_I \overset{def}{=} \left| \begin{pmatrix} \boldsymbol{x}\boldsymbol{G} + \boldsymbol{y} \\ \boldsymbol{C} \end{pmatrix}_{*, I} \right|.$$

This is a bilinear system in $c_T \in \mathbb{F}_q$ *and* $x_j \in \mathbb{F}_{q^m}$ *for* $j \in \{1..k\}$.

On some RD instances, it can lead to better complexities than the hybrid MaxMinors attack.

However, we observe that Support-Minors is much sparser than MaxMinors. In particular, a lot more relations are to be expected when we apply it to ℓ-RD. By Laplace expansion along the first row, the c_T variables present in Q_I are included in the set $\{c_{I \setminus \{i\}}, \ i \in I\}$. Now, a $c_{I \setminus \{i\}}$ that remains after specialization is necessarily as in Eq. (7). In other words, this means that $(I \setminus \{i\} - n_{\le j-1}) \cap \{1..n_j\}$ is of size r_j for all j. It imposes that $(I - n_{\le j-1}) \cap \{1..n_j\}$ is of size r_j except for one j where it is of size $r_j + 1$. Conversely, for such an I and j_0 for which $(I - n_{\le j_0-1}) \cap \{1..n_{j_0}\}$ is of size $r_{j_0} + 1$ and the rest of the intersections are of size r_j, the c_T present are of the form $c_{I \setminus \{i\}}, \ i \in I \cap \{n_{\le j_0-1} + 1..n_{\le j_0}\}$.

We have not studied the full SM-$\mathbb{F}_{q^m}^{+}$ modeling. For this reason and as the progress over MaxMinors in the random case was often only by a few bits, we adopt Estimate 4:

Estimate 4. *We do not take into account SM-$\mathbb{F}_{q^m}^{+}$ to derive our parameters.*

6.3   Algebraic Attack on ℓ-RSL

We start by describing the approach of [11] on a plain RSL instance. As in the above combinatorial attack, it targets a specific vector $\mathbf{e} \in \mathbb{F}_{q^m}^n$ which is a linear combination over $\mathbb{F}_q$ between the N errors $\mathbf{e}^{(i)}$, $i \in \{1..N\}$. By keeping the same notation as in the RD case, we may write

$$\mathbf{e}\mathbf{H}^{\mathsf{T}} = \left(\sum_{i=1}^N \lambda_i \mathbf{e}^{(i)}\right) \mathbf{H}^{\mathsf{T}} = \left(\sum_{i=1}^N \lambda_i \beta \mathbf{S}\mathbf{C}^{(i)}\right) \mathbf{H}^{\mathsf{T}} = \beta\mathbf{S}\mathbf{C}\mathbf{H}^{\mathsf{T}}, \qquad (10)$$

where $\mathbf{S} \in \mathbb{F}_q^{m \times r}$ is the support matrix common to all the errors, where $\mathbf{C}^{(i)} \in \mathbb{F}_q^{r \times n}$ is the coefficient matrix of $\mathbf{e}_i$ and where $\mathbf{C} \stackrel{def}{=} \sum_{i=1}^N \lambda_i \mathbf{C}^{(i)}$. In order to solve a problem with a unique solution, [11] targets a vector $\mathbf{e}$ such that the matrix $\mathbf{C}$ is of rank $< r$ and/or contains zero columns (corresponding to zeroes in $\mathbf{e}$). To be consistent with what was presented in the combinatorial attack, we will restrict ourselves to looking for a full-rank matrix $\mathbf{C}$ which contains as many zero columns as possible to belong to the space generated by the $\mathbf{C}_i$'s, i.e., $a = \lfloor \frac{N}{r} \rfloor$. In other words, we will consider $\mathbf{C} \stackrel{def}{=} \left(\mathbf{0}_{a \times r} \ \widetilde{\mathbf{C}}\right)$, where $\widetilde{\mathbf{C}}\mathbb{F}_q^{r \times (n-a)}$ is of full-rank. Note that $\mathbf{C}\mathbf{H}^{\mathsf{T}} = \widetilde{\mathbf{C}}\widetilde{\mathbf{H}}^{\mathsf{T}}$, where $\widetilde{\mathbf{H}} \stackrel{def}{=} \mathbf{H}_{*,[a+1,n]}$. For $i \in \{1..N\}$, let $\mathbf{s}^{(i)} \in \mathbb{F}_{q^m}^{n-k}$ be the syndrome associated to $\mathbf{e}^{(i)}$. By Equation (10), the syndrome $\mathbf{e}\mathbf{H}^{\mathsf{T}} = \sum_{i=1}^N \lambda_i \mathbf{s}^{(i)}$ is a linear combination over $\mathbb{F}_{q^m}$ between the rows of $\mathbf{C}\mathbf{H}^{\mathsf{T}}$. Thus, the matrix

$$\boldsymbol{\Delta} \stackrel{def}{=} \begin{pmatrix} \sum_{i=1}^N \lambda_i \mathbf{s}^{(i)} \\ \widetilde{\mathbf{C}}\widetilde{\mathbf{H}}^{\mathsf{T}} \end{pmatrix} \in \mathbb{F}_{q^m}^{(r+1) \times (n-k)}$$

is of rank at most r.

Modeling 3 (RSL-Minors). *Let $a = \lfloor \frac{N}{r} \rfloor$, let $\widetilde{C} \in \mathbb{F}_q^{r \times (n-a)}$ be the coefficient matrix associated to the secret $\widetilde{e}$ in the target vector $e = (0 \mid \widetilde{e})$ and let $\widetilde{H} \stackrel{def}{=} H_{*,[a+1,n]}$. The RSL-Minors modeling is the defined by $\{\boldsymbol{\Delta}_J\}_{J \subset \{1..n-k\}, \#J=r+1}$, where*

$$\boldsymbol{\Delta}_J \stackrel{def}{=} |\boldsymbol{\Delta}_{*,J}| = \left| \begin{pmatrix} \sum_{i=1}^N \lambda_i s^{(i)} \\ \widetilde{C}\widetilde{H}^{\mathsf{T}} \end{pmatrix}_{*,J} \right|.$$

Using the Cauchy-Binet formula, this system can be seen as bilinear in the λ_i variables and the maximal minors of $\widetilde{C}$ (that we still denote by c_T).

Once again, as the equations have coefficients in $\mathbb{F}_{q^m}$ and as the variables are searched in $\mathbb{F}_q$, [11] solves a system projected over $\mathbb{F}_q$ containing $m\binom{n-k}{r+1}$ equations.

In the ℓ-RSL case, all the coefficient matrices $\mathbf{C}^{(i)}$ are block diagonal as in Eq. (6). This property is preserved by linear combination, which means that we can use the same specialization as in the ℓ-RD case. The adaptation of the above would then be to target a matrix $\mathbf{C}$ such that the j-th diagonal block $\mathbf{C}_j$ contains a_j zero columns, for $j \in \{1..\ell\}$, under the constraint $\sum_{j=1}^\ell a_j r_j \leq N$. Assuming that the number of linearly independent equations remains the same in all cases, we would like to minimize the number of non-zero c_T variables $\prod_{i=1}^\ell \binom{n_i - a_i}{r_i}$.

Note that there is no formula for this minimum in the general case and that some particular ways of fixing zero columns might create algebraic relations.

For the parameter we consider (see the Sect. 8), the number of given syndromes is very low, and far from being big enough, so that the attacks based on the ℓ-RSL problem impacts the security. In practice, for the parameters we consider, the best attacks are the attacks against ℓ-RSD problem.

7   Application to Cryptanalysis

In this section, we apply the above attacks on the parameters given by [28] for their improvement of Lake (ROLLO-I), based on 2-LRPC codes. There are two types of attacks to consider for the security of their parameters, the structural attacks targeting weights (d_1, d_2) and the message attacks targeting weights (r_1, r_2). In our case we propose two new structural attacks to recover the secret key of the system.

A first attack (attack1) corresponds to the attack against 2-LRPC codes explained in Sect. 5.3. The idea of the attack is to shorten as much as possible the block corresponding to the higher d_i, then shorten on these $\frac{n}{d_i}$ positions and then truncate the block corresponding to d_i, then one gets an homogeneous error that we can attack with algebraic attacks for homogeneous errors. It is also possible to increase the number of terms shortened by guessing zero positions on the d_i part at a cost of 2^{d_i} per new zero coordinate. In practice the best results are obtained when guessing sufficiently many more zeros coordinates the part corresponding to the case where the MaxMinor attack is the most efficient, in that case we estimated the polynomial part at the cost of n^2 as it is usually the case for attacks and parameters and also we consider $w = 2.8$ the Strassen exponent.

A second attack consists in having the same Shortening and Truncating approach but rather than truncating, we just attack directly the code with algebraic attacks for blockwise errors described in [28], notice that at the difference of Attack1, it is more efficient to shorten on the smallest r_i, which permits to better decrease the dimension of the code.

The table in Fig. 7 gathers the complexities of our cryptanalyzes of parameters on Lake, given by [28], and their claimed security.

n	m	(d_1, d_2)	(r_1, r_2)	Security	Claimed M.A.S.	Claimed S.A.S.	Attack 1	Attack 2
67	61	(5,4)	(4,4)	128	145	160	132	116
79	71	(5,5)	(5,5)	192	225	255	181	166
89	79	(6,5)	(5,5)	256	281	266	246	224

Fig. 7. Security of parameters on Lake given by [28]. We refers as M.A.S. (resp. S.A.S.) for Message (resp. Structural) Attack Security.

Our new attack is very efficient against LAKE parameters given in [28], outperforming by 44 bits the security for structural attacks for the 128 bits NIST type parameters.

8 Parameters

We discuss here on the security and parameters of our two new schemes. For all our protocols, both 128 and 192 bits security level are considered. Parameters proposed are compliant with NIST security levels 1 and 3 of 143 and 207 classical bit security. Two sets of parameters are proposed for each of the schemes: the first designed to resist attacks with $\omega = 2.8$ as the Strassen constant (value with which common attacks are considered), the second (still compliant with the NIST security definition of Level 1 and Level 3) corresponds to a higher security constraint with $\omega = 2$, for which no practical attack is known for the moment.

To have available both several syndromes and blockwise errors allows to achieve excellent sizes: the first idea allows to obtain more coordinates to guess the support error, and the second gives syndromes relying to smaller spaces, which makes decoding easier.

8.1 Parameters of ILRPC-Block-MS

The security of the scheme relies on the hardness to solve the instance of a 2-IRSL problem on a code $[2n_2, n_2]_{q^m}$ with parity check matrix: $(\mathbf{1} \ \mathbf{h})$, where n_1 syndromes with the same block support of size (n_2, n_2) and dimension (r_1, r_2) are given in input. However, the attacks against 2-IRSL are not the best because the number of syndromes given is too small within the parameters we propose. One refers to this attack as Attack 1. One must also consider the structural attack against LRPC (Attack 2).

Parameters and resulting sizes are presented in Fig. 8 for $\omega = 2.8$, and in Fig. 9 for $\omega = 2$. Since the ideal parity check matrix is completely determined by the polynomial $\mathbf{h}$, its size is reduced to $\lfloor \frac{n_2 m}{8} \rfloor$ bytes. The $\mathbf{c}$ is made of n_1 polynomials of degree n_2 whose coefficients belong to $\mathbb{F}_{q^m}$, so its size is $\lfloor \frac{n_1 n_2 m}{8} \rfloor$ bytes. The parameters we obtain compare very well with previous results: 3.8 kB for 128 bits security in [28] and 2.4 kB for the multiple syndromes approach [3]. Indeed as explained in the introductory section, the blockwise approach is essentially interesting for RQC and less for LRPC, since blockwise small weight

Scheme	n_2	m	(d_1, d_2)	(r_1, r_2)	n_1	DFR	Att. 1	Att. 2	pk + ct (kB)
ILRPC-Block-xMS-128 $(r+3)$	84	59	(5,5)	(4,4)	2	-128	154	176	1.8
ILRPC-Block-xMS-128 $(r+5)$	84	53	(5,5)	(4,4)	2	-128	162	185	1.7
ILRPC-Block-xMS-192 $(r+2)$	83	83	(6,5)	(5,5)	3	-192	242	204	3.4
ILRPC-Block-xMS-192 $(r+3)$	79	83	(6,5)	(5,5)	3	-194	235	202	3.3

Fig. 8. Comparaison of parameters of ILRPC schemes, security for $\omega = 2.8$

errors are more vulnerable to the Shortening and Truncating approach of Sect. 5, indeed the smallest the d_i the greater the zeros set for shortening. Overall the approach becomes more interesting when one considers the XMS approach (originally described in [3]) that uses an extended decoding algorithm for LRPC, decoding algorithm that we generalize in Sect. 3 to the case of blockwise rank errors.

8.2   Parameters of RQC-Block-MS-AG Scheme

The attacks 1 and 2 relies on the algebraic attack which consists on solving the 2-IRSD (on the $[2n_2, n_2]_{q^m}$ ideal code with parity check matrix $(1\ h)$) and 3-IRSL problem (on the $[3n_2, n_2]_{q^m}$ ideal code whose $\begin{pmatrix} 1 & 0 & h \\ 0 & 1 & s \end{pmatrix}$ is a parity check matrix). The attack 3 is the Shortening and Truncating attack on the 2-IRSD instance. Note that there is currently no attack that takes advantage of the ideal structure of the parity check matrix, this is why these instances are considered as difficult to solve as 2-RSD and 3-RSL instances.

Scheme	m	n_2	(d_1, d_2)	(r_1, r_2)	n_1	DFR	Att. 1	Att. 2	pk + ct (kB)
ILRPC-Block-xMS-128 $(r+4)$	61	95	(5,5)	(5,4)	2	-145	179	147	2.2
ILRPC-Block-xMS-128 $(r+6)$	59	89	(5,5)	(5,4)	2	-133	177	145	2.0
ILRPC-Block-xMS-192 $(r+2)$	89	84	(6,6)	(5,5)	3	-192	204	213	3.7
ILRPC-Block-xMS-192 $(r+3)$	83	85	(6,6)	(5,5)	3	-195	209	213	3.5

Fig. 9. Parameters for ILRPC schemes with $\omega = 2$

The decoding algorithm takes as input n_2 vectors having the same errors support, that is to say it has $n_1 n_2$ available coordinates to compute the support. We use a public Augmented Gabidulin code of length $n_1 n_2$ and dimension k, constructed from a vector $\mathbf{g}$ of size m. Let ε the number of erasure coordinates one uses to recover the support error. The values above must be chosen such that the decoding capacity of the code thus obtained: $\delta = \lfloor \frac{m-k+\varepsilon}{2} \rfloor$, must be greater than or equal to the weight of the error which is $r_{\mathbf{x}} r_1 + r_{\mathbf{y}} r_2 + r_{\mathbf{e}}$. On the other hand, the resulting decryption failure rate (see Proposition 1) must be remain low.

The resulting parameters for 128 and 192 bits of security are presented in Fig. 10. The sizes are computing according to the following formulas: $|\mathsf{pk}| = \lceil \frac{n_2 m}{8} \rceil + \frac{2\lambda}{8}$ and $|\mathsf{ct}| = \lceil \frac{2n_1 n_2 m}{8} \rceil$. Since $\mathbf{g}$ and $\mathbf{h}$ are uniformly sampled from their respective spaces, they can be represented as seeds of size λ bits. The ciphertext ct contains two matrices lying in $\mathbb{F}_{q^m}^{n_2 \times n_1}$. The decrease in size of public key and ciphertext over time is a direct consequence of the decrease in the size of the parameters.

For comparison, we also present the parameters of previous versions of RQC. We observe that the different developments have made it possible to consider

Scheme	m	n_2	q	k	ε	r_x	r_y	r_1	r_2	r_e	n_1	Att. 1	Att. 2	Att. 3	DFR	pk + ct (kB)
RQC-Block-MS-AG-128	43	52	2	3	32	4	4	4	4	4	2	145	153	154	-145	1.4
RQC-Block-MS-AG-192	67	68	2	3	45	5	5	5	5	6	2	228	206	231	-206	2.8
RQC-Block-MS-AG-256	83	83	2	3	58	6	5	5	6	9	2	289	299	304	-262	4.3

Fig. 10. Parameters for RQC-Block-MS-AG and resistance to attacks, $\omega = 2.8$

Scheme		m	n_2	q	k	ε	r_x	r_y	r_1	r_2	r_e	n_1	DFR	pk + ct (kB)
RQC-Block-MS-AG-128	(this paper)	43	52	2	3	32	4	4	4	4	4	2	-145	1.4
RQC-Block-128 [28]		83	79	2	7	-	4	4	4	4	4	1	-	2.5
RQC-NH-MS-AG-128 [16]		61	50	2	3	51	7	7	7	5	12	3	-158	2.7
RQC-128 [1]		127	113	2	3	-	7	7	7	7	13	1	-	5.3
RQC-Block-MS-AG-192	(this paper)	67	68	2	3	45	5	5	5	5	6	2	-206	2.8
RQC-Block-192		127	113	2	3	-	5	5	5	5	5	1	-	5.3
RQC-NH-MS-AG-192		79	95	2	5	65	8	8	8	5	13	2	-238	4.7
RQC-192		151	149	2	5	-	8	8	8	8	16	1	-	8.3

Fig. 11. Comparaison of parameters of different RQC schemes, $\omega = 2.8$

increasingly smaller parameters, particularly due to the weight of the error in the message to decode which decreases for the same security (Fig. 11).

Likewise for the ILRPC scheme, one also proposes parameters which achieve 128 and 192 bits of security against attacks with $\omega = 2$. The new resulting parameters can be found in Fig. 12.

Scheme	m	n_2	q	k	ε	r_x	r_y	r_1	r_2	r_e	n_1	Att. 1	Att. 2	Att. 3	DFR	pk + ct (kB)
RQC-Block-MS-AG-128	59	61	2	3	42	5	4	5	4	9	2	147	151	170	-138	2.3
RQC-Block-MS-AG-192	67	81	2	3	56	5	5	5	5	10	2	213	208	250	-195	3.4
RQC-Block-MS-AG-256	97	92	2	3	68	6	6	6	6	9	2	313	275	347	-278	5.6

Fig. 12. Parameters for RQC-Block-MS-AG schemes, $\omega = 2$

8.3 Comparison with Other Schemes

For comparison, we compare our sizes with those of other encryption schemes, see Fig. 13. We can see that our scheme has very competitive performances for

Scheme		128 bits	192 bits
RQC-Block-MS-AG	(this paper, Figure 11)	1.4	2.8
ILRPC-Block-MS	(this paper, Figure 8)	1.7	3.3
KYBER [10]		1.5	2.2
BIKE [5]		3.1	6.2
HQC [2]		6.7	13.5
Classic McEliece [4]		261.2	624.3

Fig. 13. Comparison of different schemes, the sizes represent the sum of the key and the ciphertext, expressed in kB

128 bits of security, by getting slightly smaller sizes than the lattice-based scheme KYBER.

9   Further Work

We showed in this paper that combine the blockwise errors and multiple syndromes approach allowed to reach small parameters than the previous versions of the RQC and LRPC schemes. However, it is possible to decrease the decoding failure rate of the Augmented Gabidulin code $\mathcal{G}$ that we use in our RQC-Block-MS-AG scheme (see Fig. 4). We recall that the error to decode is $\mathbf{x} \cdot \mathbf{R}_2 - \mathbf{y} \cdot \mathbf{R}_1 + \mathbf{E}$. One can impose 1 to be in the support of $\mathbf{R}_2$. By doing this, we would make sure that the support of $\mathbf{x}$ is included in the support of the error to decode. Consequently, we could deduce a subspace of the support of the error of dimension r_x, allowing to further reduce the parameters for the same security.

References

1. Melchor, C.A., et al.: Rank quasi cyclic (RQC). Second Round submission to NIST Post-Quantum Cryptography call, April 2020
2. Melchor, C.A., et al.: HQC. Round 3 Submission to the NIST Post-Quantum Cryptography Call, June 2021. https://pqc-hqc.org/
3. Aguilar-Melchor, C., Aragon, N., Dyseryn, V., Gaborit, P., Zémor, G.: LRPC codes with multiple syndromes: near ideal-size KEMs without ideals. In: Cheon, J.H., Johansson, T. (eds.) International Conference on Post-Quantum Cryptography, vol. 13512, pp. 45–68. Springer, Cham (2022). https://doi.org/10.1007/978-3-031-17234-2_3
4. Albrecht, M.R., et al.: Classic McEliece: conservative code-based cryptography. Third round submission to the NIST post-quantum cryptography call, October 2020
5. Aragon, N., et al.: BIKE. NIST Round 1 submission for Post-Quantum Cryptography, November 2017
6. Aragon, N., et al.: ROLLO (merger of Rank-Ouroboros, LAKE and LOCKER). Second round submission to the NIST post-quantum cryptography call, March 2019
7. Aragon, N., Dyseryn, V., Gaborit, P., Loidreau, P., Renner, J., Wachter-Zeh, A.: LowMS: a new rank metric code-based KEM without ideal structure. Cryptology ePrint Archive (2022)
8. Aragon, N., Gaborit, P., Hauteville, A., Ruatta, O., Zémor, G.: Low rank parity check codes: new decoding algorithms and applications to cryptography. IEEE Trans. Inf. Theory **65**(12), 7697–7717 (2019)
9. Aragon, N., Gaborit, P., Hauteville, A., Tillich, J.-P.: A new algorithm for solving the rank syndrome decoding problem. In: 2018 IEEE International Symposium on Information Theory (ISIT), pp. 2421–2425. IEEE (2018)
10. Avanzi, R., et al.: Crystals-Kyber. Third round submission to the NIST post-quantum cryptography call, August 2021
11. Bardet, M., Briaud, P.: An algebraic approach to the rank support learning problem. In: Cheon, J.H., Tillich, J.-P. (eds.) PQCrypto 2021 2021. LNCS, vol. 12841, pp. 442–462. Springer, Cham (2021). https://doi.org/10.1007/978-3-030-81293-5_23

12. Bardet, M., et al.: An algebraic attack on rank metric code-based cryptosystems. In: Canteaut, A., Ishai, Y. (eds.) EUROCRYPT 2020. LNCS, vol. 12107, pp. 64–93. Springer, Cham (2020). https://doi.org/10.1007/978-3-030-45727-3_3

13. Bardet, M., Briaud, P., Bros, M., Gaborit, P., Tillich, J.-P.: Revisiting algebraic attacks on MinRank and on the rank decoding problem. Des. Codes Cryptogr. **91**, 3671–3707 (2023)

14. Bardet, M., et al.: Improvements of algebraic attacks for solving the rank decoding and MinRank problems. In: Moriai, S., Wang, H. (eds.) ASIACRYPT 2020. LNCS, vol. 12491, pp. 507–536. Springer, Cham (2020). https://doi.org/10.1007/978-3-030-64837-4_17

15. Bettaieb, S., Bidoux, L., Connan, Y., Gaborit, P., Hauteville, A.: The learning with rank errors problem and an application to symmetric authentication. In: 2018 IEEE International Symposium on Information Theory (ISIT), pp. 2629–2633. IEEE (2018)

16. Bidoux, L., Briaud, P., Bros, M., Gaborit, P.: RQC revisited and more cryptanalysis for rank-based cryptography. arXiv preprint arXiv:2207.01410 (2022)

17. Gabidulin, E.M.: Theory of codes with maximum rank distance. Problemy peredachi informatsii **21**(1), 3–16 (1985)

18. Gabidulin, E.M., Paramonov, A.V., Tretjakov, O.V.: Ideals over a non-commutative ring and their application in cryptology. In: Davies, D.W. (eds.) Advances in Cryptology-EUROCRYPT 1991: Workshop on the Theory and Application of Cryptographic Techniques Brighton, UK, 8–11 April 1991 Proceedings 10, pp. 482–489. Springer, Cham (1991). https://doi.org/10.1007/3-540-46416-6_41

19. Gaborit, P., Hauteville, A., Phan, D.H., Tillich, J.-P.: Identity-based encryption from codes with rank metric. In: Katz, J., Shacham, H. (eds.) CRYPTO 2017. LNCS, vol. 10403, pp. 194–224. Springer, Cham (2017). https://doi.org/10.1007/978-3-319-63697-9_7

20. Gaborit, P., Murat, G., Ruatta, O., Zémor, G.: Low rank parity check codes and their application to cryptography. In: Proceedings of the Workshop on Coding and Cryptography WCC, vol. 2013 (2013)

21. Gaborit, P., Ruatta, O., Schrek, J., Zémor, G.: New results for rank-based cryptography. In: Pointcheval, D., Vergnaud, D. (eds.) Progress in Cryptology–AFRICACRYPT 2014: 7th International Conference on Cryptology in Africa, Marrakesh, Morocco, 28–30 May 2014, Proceedings 7, pp. 1–12. Springer, Cham (2014). https://doi.org/10.1007/978-3-319-06734-6_1

22. Hoffstein, J., Pipher, J., Silverman, J.H.: NTRU: a ring-based public key cryptosystem. In: Buhler, J.P. (ed.) ANTS 1998. LNCS, vol. 1423, pp. 267–288. Springer, Heidelberg (1998). https://doi.org/10.1007/BFb0054868

23. Loidreau, P.: A new rank metric codes based encryption scheme. In: Lange, T., Takagi, T. (eds.) Post-Quantum Cryptography: 8th International Workshop, PQCrypto 2017, Utrecht, The Netherlands, 26–28 June 2017, Proceedings 8, pp. 3–17. Springer, Cham (2017). https://doi.org/10.1007/978-3-319-59879-6_1

24. Misoczki, R., Tillich, J.-P., Sendrier, N., Barreto, P.S.L.M.: MDPC-McEliece: new McEliece variants from moderate density parity-check codes. In: 2013 IEEE International Symposium on Information Theory, pp. 2069–2073. IEEE (2013)

25. Ourivski, A.V., Johansson, T.: New technique for decoding codes in the rank metric and its cryptography applications. Probl. Inf. Transm. **38**, 237–246 (2002)

26. Philippe, G., Gilles, Z.: On the hardness of the decoding and the minimum distance problems for rank codes (2014)

27. Puchinger, S., Renner, J., Rosenkilde, J.: Generic decoding in the sum-rank metric. IEEE Trans. Inf. Theory **68**(8), 5075–5097 (2022)
28. Song, Y., Zhang, J., Huang, X., Wu, W.: Blockwise rank decoding problem and LRPC codes: cryptosystems with smaller sizes. Cryptology ePrint Archive (2023)

Reducing Signature Size
of Matrix-Code-Based Signature Schemes

Tung Chou[1(✉)], Ruben Niederhagen[1,2(✉)], Lars Ran[3(✉)],
and Simona Samardjiska[3(✉)]

[1] Academia Sinica, Taipei, Taiwan
blueprint@crypto.tw
[2] University of Southern Denmark, Odense, Denmark
ruben@polycephaly.org
[3] Radboud University, Nijmegen, Netherlands
{lran,simonas}@cs.ru.nl

Abstract. This paper shows novel techniques to reduce the signature size of the code-based signature schemes MEDS and ALTEQ, by a large factor. For both schemes, the signature size is dominated by the responses for rounds with nonzero challenges, and we reduce the signature size by reducing the size of these responses. For MEDS, each of the responses consists of m^2+n^2 field elements, while in our new protocol each response consists of only $2k$ (k is usually chosen to be close to m and n) field elements. For ALTEQ, each of the responses consists of n^2 field elements, while in our new protocol each response consists of about $\sqrt{2}n^{3/2}$ field elements. In both underlying Σ-protocols of the schemes, the prover generates a random isometry and sends the corresponding isometry to the verifier as the response. Instead of doing this, in our new protocols, the prover derives an isometry from some random code words and their presumed (full or partial) images. The prover sends the corresponding code words and images to the verifier as the response, so that the verifier can derive an isometry in the same way. Interestingly, it turns out that each response takes much fewer field elements to represent in this way.

Keywords: Code-based cryptography · Digital signature schemes · Post-quantum cryptography

1 Introduction

In recent years, post-quantum cryptography has come into the spotlight of the cryptographic community as a result of several standardization efforts including that of the National Institute of Standards and Technology of the USA (NIST) [20]. With the goal of standardizing post-quantum key encapsulation mechanisms and digital signatures, NIST standardization process has spurred

This research has been partially supported by the Dutch government through the NWO grant OCNW.M.21.193 (ALPaQCa) and by the Taiwanese government through the NSTC grants 112-2634-F-001-001-MBK and 112-2222-E-0001-003.

M.-J. Saarinen and D. Smith-Tone (Eds.): PQCrypto 2024, LNCS 14771, pp. 107–134, 2024.
https://doi.org/10.1007/978-3-031-62743-9_4

an enormous amount of new design and cryptanalytic ideas. We now evidently have achieved great progress in understanding the security of new, but also relatively old proposals. In fact, some breakthrough cryptanalytic results against candidates [4,23] in the final round for standardization urged NIST to open an additional round for digital signatures [1] expecting to achieve more diversity in underlying hard problems and ratio between signature and key sizes. In this additional round, NIST indicated that they would like to select schemes with small signatures and fast verification that are not based on structured lattices. Immediate candidates that fit the description are multivariate signatures based on UOV [19], which inherently have very small signatures. The downside of these is that they typically have huge public keys and no guarantees about the security of the construction.

On the other end of the spectrum, lie the heavy but provably secure Fiat-Shamir signatures. In a course of a few years, thanks to generic huge improvements in signature size, they moved from extremely inefficient to reasonable candidates for standardization. There are now more than 12 candidates in the additional round based on the Fiat-Shamir paradigm. Three of these, MEDS [11], ALTEQ [22] and LESS [3] use the GMW Σ-protocol [17] by Goldreich, Micali and Wigderson, that was originally presented over the graph-isomorphism problem, but can be constructed from any hard equivalence problem. For example, MEDS uses the matrix code equivalence problem, in which the objects are matrix codes and the equivalences are two-sided bijective linear transformations. ALTEQ uses alternating trilinear form equivalence with equivalences again from the general linear group, but now acting on three "sides". Finally, LESS uses linear code equivalence where the objects are Hamming codes and the equivalences scaled permutations.

In all of these schemes the isometries are encoded in the signature and actually constitute most of it. Finding a compact representation of isometries thus directly influences the size of the signature. In this paper, our aim to encode isometries more efficiently while keeping the impact on the other performance metrics (public key size and computational performance) moderate.

1.1   Our Contribution

This paper shows novel techniques to reduce the signature size of the code-based signature schemes MEDS and ALTEQ, by a large factor. For both schemes, the signature size is dominated by the responses for rounds with nonzero challenges, and we reduce the signature size by reducing the size of these responses. For MEDS, each of these responses consists of $m^2 + n^2$ field elements, while in our new protocol each consists of only $2k$ (k is usually chosen to be close to m and n) field elements. For ALTEQ, each of these responses consists of n^2 field elements, while in our new protocol each consists of about $\sqrt{2}n^{3/2}$ field elements. Furthermore, using a similar technique, we can reduce the public key size by roughly $n(n - \sqrt{2n})$ field elements.

Concrete signature sizes can be found in Table 1 and Table 3. For NIST security level I, the smallest signature size in the MEDS submission is 9896 bytes, while Table 1 shows a parameter set with 2886-byte signatures when our new protocol is used. Also for NIST security level I, the smallest signature size of the ALTEQ submission is 9528 bytes, while Table 3 shows a parameter set with 3752-byte signatures when our new protocol is used. These smaller signature sizes are obtained without increasing the public key sizes.

1.2 Techniques

In the underlying Σ-protocols of both schemes, the prover generates a random isometry and sends the isometry, corresponding to the challenge, to the verifier as the response. Instead of doing this, in our new protocols, the prover derives an isometry from some random codewords and their presumed (full or partial) images. The prover sends the corresponding codewords and images to the verifier as the response, so that the verifier can derive the corresponding isometry in the same way. Each response takes much fewer field elements to represent in this way, as the codewords can be represented as their coordinates with respect to a basis of the code, and as the images do not even have to be sent, but can be simply considered as public data.

We take inspiration from the public key reduction technique introduced for MEDS in [11]. There, the fact that an isometry can be efficiently derived from a small number of matching codewords in the two codes is used in the key-generation process. Using it, it becomes possible to generate part of the public key from a public seed, and thus to reduce the overall size of the public key.

Although in this paper we only show new protocols for matrix-code-based signature schemes, our technique is a general approach for representation of isometries, and thus it might be efficiently applicable to other schemes as well. We leave this as future work.

1.3 Related Work: CF-LESS

Since LESS is constructed in a way similar to MEDS and ALTEQ, it seems reasonable to mention the recent paper [12], which is about reducing signature size of LESS. The technique of [12] looks quite different from ours. Roughly speaking, the main idea of [12] is to define an equivalence relation for the set of all possible codes and to set the commitment to be the canonical element in an equivalence class. In this way, each response does not need to contain the information for indicating which code in the equivalence class is the actual target, so the response size can be saved. In the Σ-protocol for the LESS submission [2], each response takes $k \cdot (\lceil \log_2 n \rceil + \lceil \log_2(q - 1) \rceil)$ bits (where k is the code dimension, n is the code length, and q is the field size), while in the best Σ-protocol of [12], each response takes only n bits.

1.4 Structure of This Paper

Section 2 specifies notations that are useful for the remaining sections. Section 3 reviews how MEDS was designed. Section 4 presents our new Σ-protocols for

MEDS. Section 5 reviews how ALTEQ was designed and presents our new Σ-protocols for ALTEQ.

2   Notations

We denote by $\mathsf{RS}(\mathbf{G})$ the row space of a matrix $\mathbf{G}$. We denote by $\mathsf{RREF}(\mathbf{G})$ reduced row echelon form of a matrix $\mathbf{G}$. $\mathsf{SF}(\mathbf{G})$ is defined to be $\mathsf{RREF}(\mathbf{G})$, if that happens to be of the form $(\mathbf{I} \mid \mathbf{H})$ (i.e., systematic form), or $\perp$ otherwise. We define $\mathsf{SF}^*(\mathbf{G})$ as follows.

$$\mathsf{SF}^*(\mathbf{G}) = \begin{cases} (\perp, \perp), & \text{if } \mathsf{SF}(\mathbf{G}) = \perp. \\ (\mathsf{SF}(\mathbf{G}), \mathbf{T}), \text{ such that } \mathsf{SF}(\mathbf{G}) = \mathbf{T} \cdot \mathbf{G}, & \text{otherwise.} \end{cases}$$

For any $\mathbf{v} \in \mathbb{F}_q^{mn}$, $\mathsf{matrix}(\mathbf{v})$ is defined as

$$\begin{bmatrix} \mathbf{v}_0 & \cdots & \mathbf{v}_{n-1} \\ \mathbf{v}_n & \cdots & \mathbf{v}_{2n-1} \\ \vdots & & \vdots \\ \mathbf{v}_{(m-1)n} & \cdots & \mathbf{v}_{mn-1} \end{bmatrix} \in \mathbb{F}_q^{m \times n}.$$

vector performs the inverse operation of matrix. Given $\mathbf{A}, \mathbf{B} \in \mathrm{GL}_m(q) \times \mathrm{GL}_n(q)$, $\pi_{\mathbf{A},\mathbf{B}}(\mathbf{v})$ is defined as $\mathsf{vector}(\mathbf{A} \cdot \mathsf{matrix}(\mathbf{v}) \cdot \mathbf{B})$. Similarly, $\pi_{\mathbf{A},\mathbf{B}}$ can take a matrix of mn columns as input and outputs the result of applying the operation to each row. Here are some obvious but useful properties of the operator[1] π:

- $\mathbf{G}' = \pi_{\mathbf{A},\mathbf{B}}(\mathbf{G}) \iff \mathbf{G} = \pi_{\mathbf{A}^{-1},\mathbf{B}^{-1}}(\mathbf{G}')$.
- $\pi_{\mathbf{A}' \cdot \mathbf{A},\mathbf{B} \cdot \mathbf{B}'}(\mathbf{G}) = \pi_{\mathbf{A}',\mathbf{B}'}(\pi_{\mathbf{A},\mathbf{B}}(\mathbf{G}))$.
- $\mathbf{T} \cdot \pi_{\mathbf{A},\mathbf{B}}(\mathbf{G}) = \pi_{\mathbf{A},\mathbf{B}}(\mathbf{T} \cdot \mathbf{G})$.

3   The MEDS Signature Scheme

This section briefly reviews how the MEDS signature scheme [10] was designed. In particular, we explain the underlying hard problem, the underlying Σ-protocol, and how the signature scheme is constructed by applying the Fiat-Shamir transform and various optimizations to the basic Σ-protocol.

3.1   The Matrix Code Equivalence Problem

Definition 1. *Let $\mathcal{C}$ and $\mathcal{D}$ be two $[m \times n, k]$ matrix codes over $\mathbb{F}_q$. We say that $\mathcal{C}$ and $\mathcal{D}$ are equivalent if there exist two matrices $\mathbf{A} \in \mathrm{GL}_m(q)$ and $\mathbf{B} \in \mathrm{GL}_n(q)$ such that $\mathcal{D} = \mathbf{A} \cdot \mathcal{C} \cdot \mathbf{B}$, i.e. for all $\mathbf{C} \in \mathcal{C}$, $\mathbf{A} \cdot \mathbf{C} \cdot \mathbf{B} \in \mathcal{D}$.*

---

[1] The operator $\pi_{\mathbf{A},\mathbf{B}}$ can also be represented as the matrix $\mathbf{B}^\top \otimes \mathbf{A}$ where $-\otimes-$ is the Kronecker product.

Public Data

$q, m, n, k \in \mathbb{N}$.
$\mathbf{A}_0 = \mathbf{I}_m \in \mathrm{GL}_m(q)$,
$\mathbf{B}_0 = \mathbf{I}_n \in \mathrm{GL}_n(q)$.

I. Keygen()

1. $\mathbf{G}_0 \xleftarrow{\$} \mathbb{F}_q^{k \times mn}$.
2. $\mathbf{A}_1, \mathbf{B}_1 \xleftarrow{\$} \mathrm{GL}_m(q) \times \mathrm{GL}_n(q)$.
3. $\mathbf{G}_1, \mathbf{T}_1 \leftarrow \mathsf{SF}^*(\pi_{\mathbf{A}_1, \mathbf{B}_1}(\mathbf{G}_0))$.
   If $\mathbf{G}_1 = \perp$, go to the 2nd step.
4. $\mathsf{sk} \leftarrow (\mathbf{A}_1, \mathbf{B}_1, \mathbf{T}_1)$ and $\mathsf{pk} \leftarrow (\mathbf{G}_0, \mathbf{G}_1)$.
   Return $(\mathsf{sk}, \mathsf{pk})$.

II. Commit(pk)

1. Set $\tilde{\mathbf{A}}, \tilde{\mathbf{B}} \xleftarrow{\$} \mathrm{GL}_m(q) \times \mathrm{GL}_n(q)$.
2. $\tilde{\mathbf{G}} \leftarrow \mathsf{SF}(\pi_{\tilde{\mathbf{A}}, \tilde{\mathbf{B}}}(\mathbf{G}_0))$.
   If $\tilde{\mathbf{G}} = \perp$, go to the 1st step.
3. $\mathsf{cmt} \leftarrow \tilde{\mathbf{G}}$. Return cmt.

III. Challenge()

1. $\mathsf{ch} \xleftarrow{\$} \{0, 1\}$. Return ch.

V. Verify(pk, cmt, ch, rsp)

1. Parse rsp into $(\mathbf{A}', \mathbf{B}')$. If $\mathbf{A}' \notin \mathrm{GL}_m(q)$
   or $\mathbf{B}' \notin \mathrm{GL}_n(q)$, return "reject".
2. $\mathsf{cmt}' \leftarrow \mathsf{SF}(\pi_{\mathbf{A}', \mathbf{B}'}(\mathbf{G}_{\mathsf{ch}}))$.
   If $\mathsf{cmt}' = \perp$, return "reject".
3. If $\mathsf{cmt}' = \mathsf{cmt}$, return "accept". Otherwise, return "reject".

IV. Response(sk, pk, cmt, ch)

1. $\mathsf{rsp} \leftarrow (\tilde{\mathbf{A}} \cdot \mathbf{A}_{\mathsf{ch}}^{-1}, \mathbf{B}_{\mathsf{ch}}^{-1} \cdot \tilde{\mathbf{B}})$.
   Return rsp.

Fig. 1. MEDS Σ-protocol. Note that $\mathbf{T}_1$ is not used in this protocol actually, but it will be used for the protocols in Fig. 2 and Fig. 4.

The underlying hard problem in MEDS is the Matrix Code Equivalence (MCE) Problem. The problem is known to be at least as difficult as the Linear Code Equivalence problem (LCE) and as difficult as the Isomorphism of polynomials (IP) problem [7] and the Alternating Trilinear Form Equivalence (ATFE) problem [18, 22]. The computational version of it, which is relevant for the MEDS signature construction as well as our optimization is defined as follows.

Problem 1 (Matrix Code Equivalence). $\mathsf{MCE}(k, n, m, \mathcal{C}, \mathcal{D})$:
Given: Two k-dimensional matrix codes $\mathcal{C}, \mathcal{D} \subset \mathbb{F}_q^{m \times n}$.
Goal: Find - if any - $\mathbf{A} \in \mathrm{GL}_m(q), \mathbf{B} \in \mathrm{GL}_n(q)$ such that $\mathcal{D} = \mathbf{A} \cdot \mathcal{C} \cdot \mathbf{B}$.

The map $(\mathbf{A}, \mathbf{B}) : \mathbf{C} \mapsto \mathbf{A} \cdot \mathbf{C} \cdot \mathbf{B}$ is called an *isometry* between $\mathcal{C}$ and $\mathcal{D}$, in the sense that it preserves the rank i.e. $\mathrm{Rank}(\mathbf{C}) = \mathrm{Rank}(\mathbf{A} \cdot \mathbf{C} \cdot \mathbf{B})$.

3.2 The MEDS Σ-Protocol

The MEDS scheme is based on a three-pass Σ-protocol, of which the security is based on MCE. In matrix notation, the main structure of the protocol is given in Fig. 1. The key generation algorithm generates two codes by generating the corresponding generator matrices $\mathbf{G}_0, \mathbf{G}_1$ such that $\mathbf{G}_1 = \mathbf{T}_1 \cdot \pi_{\tilde{\mathbf{A}}_1, \tilde{\mathbf{B}}_1}(\mathbf{G}_0)$. In the commitment algorithm, the prover generates a random isometry $(\tilde{\mathbf{A}}, \tilde{\mathbf{B}})$, applies the isometry to the code generated by $\mathbf{G}_0$, and sets the commitment cmt to (systematic form of a generator matrix of) the resulting code. The prover sets the response rsp to $(\tilde{\mathbf{A}}, \tilde{\mathbf{B}})$ if the challenge ch is equal to 0, or $(\tilde{\mathbf{A}} \cdot \mathbf{A}_1^{-1}, \mathbf{B}_1^{-1} \cdot \tilde{\mathbf{B}})$

if the challenge ch is equal to 1. The verifier parses the response as an isometry $(\mathbf{A}', \mathbf{B}')$, applies the isometry to the code generated by $\mathbf{G}_{ch} \in \{\mathbf{G}_0, \mathbf{G}_1\}$, and returns "accept" or "reject" depending on whether the resulting code is equal to the code represented by cmt.

3.3   Fiat-Shamir and Common Tricks to Reduce Signature Size

MEDS, as many other signature schemes, is constructed by applying the Fiat-Shamir transform [14] to the underlying Σ-protocol. The signature scheme consists of t rounds of the Σ-protocol. The challenges $ch^{(0)}, \ldots, ch^{(t-1)}$ for all rounds are derived from a hash value of the commitments and the message. MEDS makes use of some common techniques to reduce signature size:

1. **Using more than two matrix codes in the public key.** Instead of the matrix code equivalence problem, it is possible to use the **multiple matrix code equivalence problem**, where the attacker is asked to find the isometry between any 2 of s matrix codes. This problem is polynomial-time-equivalent to the MCE problem, therefore there is no need to use it in MEDS in addition to the MCE problem. When applying this optimization, the public key becomes s generator matrices $\mathbf{G}_0, \ldots, \mathbf{G}_{s-1}$, and $(ch^{(0)}, \ldots, ch^{(t-1)})$ becomes a random element in $\{0, \ldots, s-1\}^t$ (instead of $\{0,1\}^t$) [13]. This has the benefit of reducing the soundness error to $1/s < 1/2$, and thus it reduces the number of rounds t required in the resulting signature scheme. For simplicity, Fig. 1 and all other Σ-protocols in this paper are presented under the assumption $s = 2$. Note that this trick reduces the signature size, at the cost of much larger public keys.
2. **Seeding responses when $ch^{(i)} = 0$.** The idea is to generate the isometry in the commitment algorithm by expanding a short seed [5]. In this way, signature size can be saved by sending the seed as the response whenever the challenge is 0. Each response still consists of a random isometry when the challenge is nonzero.
3. **Using fixed-weight challenges.** Instead of making $(ch^{(0)}, \ldots, ch^{(t-1)})$ a random element in $\{0, \ldots, s-1\}^t$, the idea is to make it a vector of Hamming weight w [5]. w is often chosen to be small compared to t. In this way, the main components of each signature become $t - w$ seeds and w isometries. This helps to reduce the signature size, as an isometry typically takes much more bits to represent than a seed.
4. **Generating seeds from a seed tree.** The previous trick can be refined to obtain even smaller signatures. The idea is to build a binary tree of seeds [5], such that the children of each node can be obtained by hashing the node, together with a salt for the tree to mitigate collision attacks. In this way, the $t - w$ seeds can be compressed into a smaller number of seeds (using a *puncturable* PRF [16]). The number of required seeds depends on the actual challenges. [8] shows that the number of required seeds is upper bounded by $\mathcal{N}(t, w) := 2^{\lceil \log_2 w \rceil} + w \cdot (\lceil \log_2 t \rceil - \lceil \log_2 w \rceil - 1)$.

Overall, with the tricks above, the signature size in bytes can be calculated as

$$w \cdot \lceil \mathsf{isobits}/8 \rceil + \mathcal{N}(t, w) \cdot \ell_{\text{tree\_seed}} + \ell_{\text{salt}} + \ell_{\text{digest}}. \tag{1}$$

Here, isobits is the number of bits each response takes when $\mathsf{ch}^{(i)} \neq 0$, which is same as the number of bits every response takes before applying the tricks. Since in Fig. 1 each response consists of a matrix in $\mathbb{F}_q^{m \times m}$ and a matrix in $\mathbb{F}_q^{n \times n}$, isobits is set to be $(m^2 + n^2) \cdot \lceil \log_2(q) \rceil$. $\ell_{\text{tree\_seed}}$ is the byte-length of each node in the seed tree. ℓ_{salt} is the byte-length of the salt. ℓ_{digest} is the byte-length of the hash value of the commitments and the message. The values of $\ell_{\text{tree\_seed}}$, ℓ_{salt}, and ℓ_{digest} for the MEDS submission are specified in [10, Table 2].

3.4 Reducing Public-Key Size

The multiple public keys optimization discussed in the previous section can reduce the signature size quite substantially, but there is a prize to pay - the public key increases. In order to reduce the impact on the public key of this nice optimization (and to allow for even shorter signatures by reparametrization) a technique for public key compression was introduced in [11]. It basically trades public key size for efficiency, and allows part of the public key to be generated from a public seed, and then be used together with (part of) the secret key to derive the whole secret isometry and the rest of the public key. Typically, the whole isometry can be derived from two seeded codewords in the public key, resulting in reduction of the public key size by $2s(mn - k)$.

4 Optimizing the MEDS Σ-Protocol

This section presents our new Σ-protocols for MEDS. Each response in the new Σ-protocols is represented with fewer field elements than those in the original MEDS Σ-protocol (Fig. 1) when k is not too large compared to m and n. The new protocols are inspired by the public key compression trick (see Sect. 3.4).

Before explaining the new protocols, let us introduce some notation and terms from the original MEDS Σ-protocol. We define $\mathcal{C}_i = \{\mathsf{matrix}(\mathbf{v}) \mid \mathbf{v} \in \mathsf{RS}(\mathbf{G}_i)\}$. The code $\mathcal{C}_0$ is considered as the "domain code" for the prover, while $\mathcal{C}_{\mathsf{ch}}$ is considered as the "domain code" for the verifier. In the commitment algorithm, with $(\tilde{\mathbf{A}}, \tilde{\mathbf{B}})$ and $\mathcal{C}_0$, the prover derives its "image code"

$$\tilde{\mathbf{A}} \cdot \mathcal{C}_0 \cdot \tilde{\mathbf{B}} = \{\mathsf{matrix}(\mathbf{v}) \mid \mathbf{v} \in \mathsf{RS}(\pi_{\tilde{\mathbf{A}}, \tilde{\mathbf{B}}}(\mathbf{G}_0))\}$$

and represent it as $\mathsf{cmt} = \mathsf{SF}(\pi_{\tilde{\mathbf{A}}, \tilde{\mathbf{B}}}(\mathbf{G}_0))$. Similarly, in the verification algorithm, with $(\mathbf{A}', \mathbf{B}')$ and $\mathcal{C}_{\mathsf{ch}}$, the verifier derives its "image code"

$$\mathbf{A}' \cdot \mathcal{C}_{\mathsf{ch}} \cdot \mathbf{B}' = \{\mathsf{matrix}(\mathbf{v}) \mid \mathbf{v} \in \mathsf{RS}(\pi_{\mathbf{A}', \mathbf{B}'}(\mathbf{G}_{\mathsf{ch}}))\}$$

and represent it as $\mathsf{cmt}' = \mathsf{SF}(\pi_{\mathbf{A}', \mathbf{B}'}(\mathbf{G}_{\mathsf{ch}}))$. In our new Σ-protocols, each of the prover and verifier still needs to derive the image code from the domain code and an isometry, but the isometry is obtained in a different way.

In our new protocols, codewords in domain codes are represented as their **coordinate vectors**: the coordinate vector of $\mathbf{C} \in \mathcal{C}_i$ (with respect to $\mathbf{G}_i$) is defined as the vector $\mathbf{c} \in \mathbb{F}_q^k$ such that $\mathbf{C} = \mathsf{matrix}(\mathbf{c} \cdot \mathbf{G}_i)$. Such a representation is crucial for reducing the number for field elements each response takes.

For ease of understanding, the reader can simply assume that $k \in \{m, n\}$ in this section, which holds for all parameter sets shown in Sect. 4.4, and we have $m = n = k$ for all the parameter sets proposed in the MEDS submission [10].

4.1   New Σ-Protocol for MEDS with $m = n$

Our first new protocol for MEDS requires that $m = n$. Instead of generating an isometry directly and using it to derive the image code, the prover derives an isometry $(\tilde{\mathbf{A}}, \tilde{\mathbf{B}})$ from a codeword $\tilde{\mathbf{C}} \in \mathrm{GL}_n(q)$ in the domain code and a presumed codeword $\mathbf{D} \in \mathrm{GL}_n(q)$ in the image code such that $\mathbf{D} = \tilde{\mathbf{A}} \cdot \tilde{\mathbf{C}} \cdot \tilde{\mathbf{B}}$. Instead of receiving an isometry directly and using it to derive the image code, the verifier derives an isometry $(\mathbf{A}', \mathbf{B}')$ from a codeword $\mathbf{C}' \in \mathrm{GL}_n(q)$ in the domain code and the same presumed codeword $\mathbf{D} \in \mathrm{GL}_n(q)$ in the image code, such that $\mathbf{D} = \mathbf{A}' \cdot \mathbf{C}' \cdot \mathbf{B}'$. To make sure that there is only 1 possibility for isometry $(\tilde{\mathbf{A}}, \tilde{\mathbf{B}})$ or $(\mathbf{A}', \mathbf{B}')$, $\tilde{\mathbf{A}}$ is generated in the commitment algorithm, and $\mathbf{A}'$ is included in the response, as in Fig. 1. Each response then takes only $n^2 + k$ (instead of $2n^2$) field elements: n^2 for $\mathbf{A}'$, and k for the coordinate vector of the codeword $\mathbf{C}'$ in the domain code for the verifier. The codeword $\mathbf{D}$ is considered as public data, so it is not included in rsp.

The new protocol is presented in Fig. 2. The public data and the key generation algorithm are mostly same as in Fig. 1, except for the public matrices $\mathbf{D} \in \mathrm{GL}_n(q)$ and $\mathbf{T}_0 = \mathbf{I}_k$. In the commitment algorithm, the prover selects a random codeword $\tilde{\mathbf{C}} \in \mathrm{GL}_n(q) \cap \mathcal{C}_0$, generates a random matrix $\tilde{\mathbf{A}} \in \mathrm{GL}_n(q)$, and derives $\tilde{\mathbf{B}}$ as $(\tilde{\mathbf{A}}\tilde{\mathbf{C}})^{-1}\mathbf{D}$. The prover includes $\mathbf{A}' = \tilde{\mathbf{A}} \cdot \mathbf{A}_{\mathsf{ch}}^{-1}$ and the coordinate vector $\tilde{\mathbf{c}} \cdot \mathbf{T}_{\mathsf{ch}}^{-1}$ of $\mathbf{C}' = \mathbf{A}_{\mathsf{ch}} \cdot \tilde{\mathbf{C}} \cdot \mathbf{B}_{\mathsf{ch}} \in \mathrm{GL}_n(q) \cap \mathcal{C}_{\mathsf{ch}}$ in the response. Note that $\mathbf{C}'$ can be viewed as the codeword in $\mathcal{C}_{\mathsf{ch}}$ corresponding to $\tilde{\mathbf{C}}$. In the verification algorithm, the verifier derives $\mathbf{B}'$ as $(\mathbf{A}'\mathbf{C}')^{-1}\mathbf{D}$.

Theorem 1. *The protocol in Fig. 2 is a Σ-protocol for the MCE relation.*

Proof. In order to show that the protocol is a Σ-protocol we need to prove the properties of completeness, special soundness and honest-verifier zero-knowledge.

Completeness: Given an honestly generated commitment-response pair (cmt_0, rsp_0) for $\mathsf{ch} = 0^2$, it is easy to see that $\mathbf{Verify}(\mathsf{pk}, \mathsf{cmt}_0, 0, \mathsf{rsp}_0) = $ "accept" as $\mathbf{C}' = \tilde{\mathbf{C}}$ and $\mathbf{A}' = \tilde{\mathbf{A}}$.

Given an honestly generated commitment-response pair ($\mathsf{cmt}_1, \mathsf{rsp}_1 = (\mathbf{A}', \mathbf{c}')$) for $\mathsf{ch} = 1$, we have

$$\mathbf{C}' = \mathsf{matrix}(\mathbf{c}' \cdot \mathbf{G}_1) = \mathsf{matrix}(\tilde{\mathbf{c}} \cdot \mathbf{T}_1^{-1} \cdot \mathbf{G}_1) = \mathbf{A}_1 \cdot \tilde{\mathbf{C}} \cdot \mathbf{B}_1, \tag{2}$$

---

[2] "Honestly generated" means that the pair is obtained by running $\mathsf{cmt}_0 \leftarrow$ **Commit**(pk) and then $\mathsf{rsp}_0 \leftarrow$ **Response**(sk, pk, cmt_0, ch).

Public Data

$q, m, n, k \in \mathbb{N}$, such that $m = n$.

$\mathbf{A}_0 = \mathbf{B}_0 = \mathbf{I}_n \in \mathrm{GL}_n(q)$. $\mathbf{T}_0 = \mathbf{I}_k \in \mathrm{GL}_k(q)$.

$\mathbf{D} \in \mathrm{GL}_n(q)$.

II. Commit(pk)

1. Set $\tilde{\mathbf{c}} \xleftarrow{\$} \mathbb{F}_q^k$. $\tilde{\mathbf{C}} \leftarrow \mathrm{matrix}(\tilde{\mathbf{c}} \cdot \mathbf{G}_0)$.
   If $\tilde{\mathbf{C}} \notin \mathrm{GL}_n(q)$, repeat this step.
2. Set $\tilde{\mathbf{A}} \xleftarrow{\$} \mathrm{GL}_n(q)$. $\tilde{\mathbf{B}} \leftarrow (\tilde{\mathbf{A}}\tilde{\mathbf{C}})^{-1}\mathbf{D}$.
3. $\tilde{\mathbf{G}} \leftarrow \mathsf{SF}(\pi_{\tilde{\mathbf{A}},\tilde{\mathbf{B}}}(\mathbf{G}_0))$.
   If $\tilde{\mathbf{G}} = \perp$, go to the 1st step.
4. $\mathsf{cmt} \leftarrow \tilde{\mathbf{G}}$. Return cmt.

IV. Response(sk, pk, cmt, ch)

1. $\mathsf{rsp} \leftarrow (\tilde{\mathbf{A}} \cdot \mathbf{A}_{\mathsf{ch}}^{-1}, \tilde{\mathbf{c}} \cdot \mathbf{T}_{\mathsf{ch}}^{-1})$.
   Return rsp.

III. Challenge()

1. $\mathsf{ch} \xleftarrow{\$} \{0,1\}$. Return ch.

V. Verify(pk, cmt, ch, rsp)

1. Parse rsp into $(\mathbf{A}', \mathbf{c}')$.
   If $\mathbf{A}' \notin \mathrm{GL}_n(q)$, return "reject".
2. $\mathbf{C}' \leftarrow \mathrm{matrix}(\mathbf{c}' \cdot \mathbf{G}_{\mathsf{ch}})$.
   If $\mathbf{C}' \notin \mathrm{GL}_n(q)$, return "reject".
3. $\mathbf{B}' \leftarrow (\mathbf{A}'\mathbf{C}')^{-1}\mathbf{D}$.
4. $\mathsf{cmt}' \leftarrow \mathsf{SF}(\pi_{\mathbf{A}',\mathbf{B}'}(\mathbf{G}_{\mathsf{ch}}))$.
   If $\mathsf{cmt}' = \perp$, return "reject".
5. If $\mathsf{cmt} = \mathsf{cmt}'$, return "accept".
   Otherwise, return "reject".

Fig. 2. New MEDS Sigma Protocol for $m = n$. Keygen as in Fig. 1.

and thus $\mathbf{B}' = (\mathbf{A}'\mathbf{C}')^{-1}\mathbf{D} = (\tilde{\mathbf{A}} \cdot \tilde{\mathbf{C}} \cdot \mathbf{B}_1)^{-1}\mathbf{D} = \mathbf{B}_1^{-1} \cdot \tilde{\mathbf{B}}$. Therefore,

$$\mathsf{RS}(\pi_{\mathbf{A}',\mathbf{B}'}(\mathbf{G}_1)) = \mathsf{RS}(\pi_{\tilde{\mathbf{A}} \cdot \mathbf{A}_1^{-1}, \mathbf{B}_1^{-1} \cdot \tilde{\mathbf{B}}}(\mathbf{G}_1)) = \mathsf{RS}(\pi_{\tilde{\mathbf{A}},\tilde{\mathbf{B}}}(\mathbf{G}_0)), \qquad (3)$$

which implies that $\mathsf{SF}(\pi_{\mathbf{A}',\mathbf{B}'}(\mathbf{G}_1)) = \mathsf{SF}(\pi_{\tilde{\mathbf{A}},\tilde{\mathbf{B}}}(\mathbf{G}_0)) = \mathsf{cmt}_1$.

Zero-Knowledge: To simulate a commitment-response pair for $\mathsf{ch} = 0$, apparently the simulator can simply run $\hat{\mathsf{cmt}}_0 \leftarrow$ **Commit**(pk) and also provide $\hat{\mathsf{rsp}}_0 \leftarrow$ **Response**(sk^*, pk, $\hat{\mathsf{cmt}}_0$, 0), where sk^* is a dummy argument that is not actually used.

Let **Commit**$^{(\mathbf{G}_1)}$ be the modified version of **Commit** where $\mathbf{G}_0$ is replaced by $\mathbf{G}_1$. We claim that for $\mathsf{ch} = 1$, the simulator can simulate a commitment-response pair by running $\hat{\mathsf{cmt}}_1 \leftarrow$ **Commit**$^{(\mathbf{G}_1)}$(pk) and correspondingly $\hat{\mathsf{rsp}}_1 = (\hat{\mathbf{A}}, \hat{\mathbf{c}}) \leftarrow$ **Response**(sk*, pk, $\hat{\mathsf{cmt}}_1$, 0). In other words, we claim that an honestly generated pair $(\mathsf{cmt}_1, \mathsf{rsp}_1 = (\tilde{\mathbf{A}} \cdot \mathbf{A}_1^{-1}, \tilde{\mathbf{c}} \cdot \mathbf{T}_1^{-1}))$ for $\mathsf{ch} = 1$ has exactly the same distribution as $(\hat{\mathsf{cmt}}_1, \hat{\mathsf{rsp}}_1)$.

To see that the claim is true, first consider a modified version of the protocol, where each SF is replaced by RREF (replacement also happens in **Commit**$^{(\mathbf{G}_1)}$). With procedures in this modified protocol, $\hat{\mathbf{A}}$ will be a uniform random element in $\mathrm{GL}_n(q)$, and $\hat{\mathbf{c}}$ will be the coordinate vector of a uniform random element in $\mathcal{C}_1 \cap \mathrm{GL}_n(q)$. $(\tilde{\mathbf{A}} \cdot \mathbf{A}_1^{-1}, \tilde{\mathbf{c}} \cdot \mathbf{T}_1^{-1})$ has the same distribution as $(\hat{\mathbf{A}}, \hat{\mathbf{c}})$: $\tilde{\mathbf{A}}$ is uniform random in $\mathrm{GL}_n(q)$, and $Eq.\,(2)$ shows that $\tilde{\mathbf{c}} \cdot \mathbf{T}_1^{-1}$ has the same distribution as $\hat{\mathbf{c}}$.

Then, the proof of completeness shows that there is a deterministic procedure that can be used to derive cmt_1 from $(\mathsf{rsp}_1, \mathbf{G}_1, \mathbf{D})$ and to derive $\hat{\mathsf{cmt}}_1$ from

---

Input: $C_0, C_1, D_0, D_1 \in \mathbb{F}_q^{m \times n}$.
Output: $(A, B) \in \mathrm{GL}_m(q) \times \mathrm{GL}_n(q)$ such that $AC_0B = D_0$ and $AC_1B = D_1$, or $\bot$.

1. Build a linear system of $2nm$ equations and $m^2 + n^2$ variables by considering

$$AC_0 = D_0 B^{-1}, AC_1 = D_1 B^{-1},$$

   where entries in A and B^{-1} are considered as variables.
2. If the solution space of the linear system does not have dimension 1, return $\bot$.
3. Pick any nontrivial solution in the solution space to obtain $(A, B^{-1}) \in \mathbb{F}_q^{m \times m} \times \mathbb{F}_q^{n \times n}$. If $A \notin \mathrm{GL}_m(\mathbb{F}_q)$ or $B^{-1} \notin \mathrm{GL}_n(\mathbb{F}_q)$, return $\bot$. Otherwise, return (A, B).

Fig. 3. The function **Solve**.

$(r\hat{s}p_1, G_1, D)$, so (rsp_1, cmt_1) has the same distribution as $(r\hat{s}p_1, c\hat{m}t_1)$. Finally, changing RREF back to SF simply means adding the same constraint to cmt_1 and $c\hat{m}t_1$, so (rsp_1, cmt_1) still has the same distribution as $(r\hat{s}p_1, c\hat{m}t_1)$ when the original protocol is considered.

Special Soundness: Given cmt, rsp_0, rsp_1 such that $\textbf{Verify}(pk, cmt, 0, rsp_0) =$ "accept" $= \textbf{Verify}(pk, cmt, 1, rsp_1)$, there exists an efficient algorithm that outputs $\tilde{A}, \tilde{B}, A', B'$, such that

$$SF(\pi_{\tilde{A}, \tilde{B}}(G_0)) = cmt = SF(\pi_{A', B'}(G_1)).$$

Then, $((A')^{-1} \cdot \tilde{A}, \tilde{B} \cdot (B')^{-1})$ yields a solution to the MCE instance (G_0, G_1). □

One might expect that the protocol still works:

– if the prover simply picks an arbitrary $(\tilde{A}, \tilde{B})$ such that $\tilde{A} \cdot \tilde{C} \cdot \tilde{B} = D$, and
– if the verifier simply picks an arbitrary (A', B') such that $A' \cdot C' \cdot B' = D$.

In this way, rsp does not need to include A'. However, now it is no longer guaranteed that $(A', B') = (\tilde{A} \cdot A_{ch}^{-1}, B_{ch}^{-1} \cdot \tilde{B})$. Consequently, it is very likely that $SF(\pi_{\tilde{A}, \tilde{B}}(G_0)) \neq SF(\pi_{A', B'}(G_{ch}))$, which means completeness is broken.

Variants of the Protocol. There are some natural variants of the protocol. For example, instead of having D as public data, D can be considered as a part of the public key. As another example, D can be chosen as a random invertible matrix and included in the response. The proof for Theorem 1 also applies to these variants. We note that in the second variant, to save signature size, the signer can send a short seed from which D's for all rounds can be derived in a pseudo-random fashion.

Public Data

$q, m, n, k \in \mathbb{N}$, such that $|m - n| \le 1$.

$\mathbf{A}_0 = \mathbf{I}_m \in \mathrm{GL}_m(q)$.

$\mathbf{B}_0 = \mathbf{I}_n \in \mathrm{GL}_n(q)$.

$\mathbf{T}_0 = \mathbf{I}_k \in \mathrm{GL}_k(q)$.

Full-rank, linearly independent $\mathbf{D}_0, \mathbf{D}_1 \in \mathbb{F}_q^{m \times n}$.

II. Commit(pk)

1. Set $(\tilde{\mathbf{c}}_0, \tilde{\mathbf{c}}_1) \xleftarrow{\$} \mathbb{F}_q^k \times \mathbb{F}_q^k$. If $\tilde{\mathbf{c}}_0$ and $\tilde{\mathbf{c}}_1$ are linearly dependent, repeat this step.

2. For $i \in \{0, 1\}$, $\tilde{\mathbf{C}}_i \leftarrow \mathrm{matrix}(\tilde{\mathbf{c}}_i \cdot \mathbf{G}_0)$. If $\tilde{\mathbf{C}}_0$ or $\tilde{\mathbf{C}}_1$ is not full rank, go to the 1st step.

3. $(\tilde{\mathbf{A}}, \tilde{\mathbf{B}}) \leftarrow \mathrm{Solve}(\tilde{\mathbf{C}}_0, \tilde{\mathbf{C}}_1, \mathbf{D}_0, \mathbf{D}_1)$. If $(\tilde{\mathbf{A}}, \tilde{\mathbf{B}}) = \perp$, go to the 1st step.

4. $\tilde{\mathbf{G}} \leftarrow \mathrm{SF}(\pi_{\tilde{\mathbf{A}}, \tilde{\mathbf{B}}}(\mathbf{G}_0))$. If $\tilde{\mathbf{G}} = \perp$, go to the 1st step.

5. $\mathrm{cmt} \leftarrow \tilde{\mathbf{G}}$. Return cmt.

IV. Response(sk, pk, cmt, ch)

1. $\mathrm{rsp} \leftarrow (\tilde{\mathbf{c}}_0 \cdot \mathbf{T}_{\mathrm{ch}}^{-1}, \tilde{\mathbf{c}}_1 \cdot \mathbf{T}_{\mathrm{ch}}^{-1})$. Return rsp.

III. Challenge()

1. $\mathrm{ch} \xleftarrow{\$} \{0, 1\}$. Return ch.

V. Verify(pk, cmt, ch, rsp)

1. Parse rsp into $(\mathbf{c}_0', \mathbf{c}_1')$. If $\mathbf{c}_0'$ and $\mathbf{c}_1'$ are linearly dependent, return "reject".

2. For $i \in \{0, 1\}$, $\mathbf{C}_i' \leftarrow \mathrm{matrix}(\mathbf{c}_i' \cdot \mathbf{G}_{\mathrm{ch}})$. If $\mathbf{C}_0'$ or $\mathbf{C}_1'$ is not full rank, return "reject".

3. $(\mathbf{A}', \mathbf{B}') \leftarrow \mathrm{Solve}(\mathbf{C}_0', \mathbf{C}_1', \mathbf{D}_0, \mathbf{D}_1)$. If $(\mathbf{A}', \mathbf{B}') = \perp$, return "reject".

4. $\mathrm{cmt}' \leftarrow \mathrm{SF}(\pi_{\mathbf{A}', \mathbf{B}'}(\mathbf{G}_{\mathrm{ch}}))$. If $\mathrm{cmt}' = \perp$, return "reject".

5. If $\mathrm{cmt} = \mathrm{cmt}'$, return "accept". Otherwise, return "reject".

Fig. 4. New MEDS Sigma Protocol for $|m - n| \le 1$. Keygen as in Fig. 1.

4.2 New Σ-Protocol for MEDS with $|m - n| \le 1$

The second new Σ-protocol for MEDS requires that $|m - n| \le 1$. The main idea of the new protocol is that each of the prover and verifier derives an isometry that maps a pair of codewords in the domain code to a pair of presumed codewords in the image code. The prover generated the codewords in the domain code. For the verifier, the codewords in the domain code are included in the response. Since the codewords in the response are represented as coordinate vectors, the response takes only $2k$ field elements to represent. As in the protocol shown in the previous subsection, the presumed codewords are considered as public data, so they are not included in the response.

The prover and verifier make use of the procedure **Solve** (c.f. Fig. 3) to derive an isometry mapping $\mathbf{C}_0, \mathbf{C}_1 \in \mathbb{F}_q^{m \times n}$ in the domain code to $\mathbf{D}_0, \mathbf{D}_1 \in \mathbb{F}_q^{m \times n}$ in the image code. The procedure computes an isometry by solving the linear system of $2mn$ equations and $m^2 + n^2$ equations formed by

$$\mathbf{A}\mathbf{C}_0 = \mathbf{D}_0\mathbf{B}^{-1}, \mathbf{A}\mathbf{C}_1 = \mathbf{D}_1\mathbf{B}^{-1},$$

where entries in $\mathbf{A}$ and $\mathbf{B}^{-1}$ are considered as variables. Note that **Solve** is allowed to return any $(\mathbf{A}, \mathbf{B})$ as long as $(\mathbf{A}, \mathbf{B}^{-1}) \in \mathrm{GL}_m(q) \times \mathrm{GL}_n(q)$ is in the solution space, under the condition that the solution space has dimension exactly 1. This makes sense: Under the condition, the set of all valid solutions must be of the form $\{(\alpha\mathbf{A}, \alpha\mathbf{B}^{-1}) \mid \alpha \in \mathbb{F}_q^*\}$, and $\pi_{\alpha\mathbf{A},\alpha^{-1}\mathbf{B}}(\mathbf{G})$ is independent of the choice of α.

In the new protocol shown in Fig. 4, the public data and the key generation algorithm is mostly same as in Fig. 1, except for the public matrices $\mathbf{T}_0 = \mathbf{I}_k$ and $\mathbf{D}_0, \mathbf{D}_1 \in \mathbb{F}_q^{m \times n}$. In the commitment algorithm, the prover generates two full-rank, linearly independent codewords $\tilde{\mathbf{C}}_0, \tilde{\mathbf{C}}_1 \in \mathcal{C}_0$ and uses **Solve** to find an isometry $(\tilde{\mathbf{A}}, \tilde{\mathbf{B}})$ that maps $\tilde{\mathbf{C}}_0, \tilde{\mathbf{C}}_1$ to $\mathbf{D}_0, \mathbf{D}_1$. The response $(\tilde{\mathbf{c}}_0 \cdot \mathbf{T}_{\mathsf{ch}}^{-1}, \tilde{\mathbf{c}}_1 \cdot \mathbf{T}_{\mathsf{ch}}^{-1})$ is essentially the coordinate vectors (w.r.t. $\mathbf{G}_{\mathsf{ch}}$) of the two codewords in $\mathcal{C}_{\mathsf{ch}}$ corresponding to $\tilde{\mathbf{C}}_0$ and $\tilde{\mathbf{C}}_1$. In the verification algorithm, the verifier derives two codewords $\mathbf{C}_0', \mathbf{C}_1' \in \mathcal{C}_{\mathsf{ch}}$ from the coordinate vectors in the response, and uses **Solve** to find an isometry $(\mathbf{A}', \mathbf{B}')$ that maps $\mathbf{C}_0', \mathbf{C}_1'$ to $\mathbf{D}_0, \mathbf{D}_1$.

As in the previous section, $\mathbf{D}_i$'s can also be considered as a part of the public key or chosen as random matrices. The proof for the following theorem also applies to these variants.

Theorem 2. *The protocol in Fig. 4 is a Σ-protocol for the* MCE *relation.*

Proof. We show completeness, zero knowledge, and special soundness:

Completeness. Given an honestly generated commitment-response pair $(\mathsf{cmt}_0, \mathsf{rsp}_0)$ for $\mathsf{ch} = 0$, it is easy to see that **Verify**$(\mathsf{pk}, \mathsf{cmt}_0, 0, \mathsf{rsp}_0) = $ "accept" as $(\mathbf{A}', \mathbf{B}') = (\alpha\tilde{\mathbf{A}}, \alpha^{-1}\tilde{\mathbf{B}})$ for some $\alpha \in \mathbb{F}_q^*$.

Given an honestly generated commitment-response pair $(\mathsf{cmt}_1, \mathsf{rsp}_1 = (\mathbf{c}_0', \mathbf{c}_1'))$ for $\mathsf{ch} = 1$, we have $\mathbf{C}_i' = \mathbf{A}_1 \cdot \tilde{\mathbf{C}}_i \cdot \mathbf{B}_1$ for $i \in \{0,1\}$ according to the completeness proof of Theorem 1. This implies that

$$\mathbf{A} \cdot \mathbf{C}_i' \cdot \mathbf{B} = \mathbf{D}_i, \text{ for } i \in \{0,1\} \implies \mathbf{A}\mathbf{A}_1 \cdot \tilde{\mathbf{C}}_i \cdot \mathbf{B}_1\mathbf{B} = \mathbf{D}_i, \text{ for } i \in \{0,1\}$$

and

$$\mathbf{A} \cdot \tilde{\mathbf{C}}_i \cdot \mathbf{B} = \mathbf{D}_i, \text{ for } i \in \{0,1\} \implies \mathbf{A}\mathbf{A}_1^{-1} \cdot \mathbf{C}_i' \cdot \mathbf{B}_1^{-1}\mathbf{B} = \mathbf{D}_i, \text{ for } i \in \{0,1\}.$$

In other words, there is a bijective map between the set of $(\mathbf{A}, \mathbf{B})$'s mapping $\tilde{\mathbf{C}}_i$'s to $\mathbf{D}_i$'s and the set of $(\mathbf{A}, \mathbf{B})$'s mapping $\mathbf{C}_i'$'s to $\mathbf{D}_i$'s, and thus the two sets have the same cardinality. Therefore, the solution space for $\mathbf{A}', (\mathbf{B}')^{-1}$ (in the verification algorithm) must be of dimension 1, and $(\mathbf{A}', \mathbf{B}') = (\alpha\tilde{\mathbf{A}}\mathbf{A}_1^{-1}, \alpha^{-1}\mathbf{B}_1^{-1}\tilde{\mathbf{B}})$ for some $\alpha \in \mathbb{F}_q^*$. We conclude that Eq. (3) holds and thus $\mathsf{SF}(\pi_{\mathbf{A}',\mathbf{B}'}(\mathbf{G}_1)) = \mathsf{SF}(\pi_{\tilde{\mathbf{A}},\tilde{\mathbf{B}}}(\mathbf{G}_0)) = \mathsf{cmt}_1$.

Zero Knowledge. The $\mathsf{ch} = 0$ case is trivial as in the proof for zero knowledge for Theorem 1. We claim that for $\mathsf{ch} = 1$, the simulator can simulate a commitment-response pair by running $\hat{\mathsf{cmt}}_1 \leftarrow$ **Commit**$^{(\mathbf{G}_1)}(\mathsf{pk})$, and $\hat{\mathsf{rsp}}_1 = (\hat{\mathbf{c}}_0, \hat{\mathbf{c}}_1) \leftarrow$ **Response**$(\mathsf{sk}^*, \mathsf{pk}, \hat{\mathsf{cmt}}_1, 0)$. That is, we claim that honestly generated $(\mathsf{cmt}_1, \mathsf{rsp}_1 = (\tilde{\mathbf{c}}_0 \cdot \mathbf{T}_1^{-1}, \tilde{\mathbf{c}}_1 \cdot \mathbf{T}_1^{-1}))$ for $\mathsf{ch} = 1$ has the same distribution as $(\hat{\mathsf{cmt}}_1, \hat{\mathsf{rsp}}_1)$.

We follow the proof for zero knowledge for Theorem 1 to first consider the modified protocol where SF is replaced by RREF. With the modified procedures, $(\hat{\mathbf{c}}_0, \hat{\mathbf{c}}_1)$ is going to be coordinate vectors (w.r.t. $\mathbf{G}_1$) of 2 uniform random codewords $\hat{\mathbf{C}}_0, \hat{\mathbf{C}}_1 \in \mathcal{C}_1$ such that

- $\hat{\mathbf{C}}_0, \hat{\mathbf{C}}_1$ are linearly independent and full-rank and
- $\mathbf{Solve}(\hat{\mathbf{C}}_0, \hat{\mathbf{C}}_1, \mathbf{D}_0, \mathbf{D}_1) \neq \perp$.

The proof for completeness shows that $(\tilde{\mathbf{c}}_0 \cdot \mathbf{T}_1^{-1}, \tilde{\mathbf{c}}_1 \cdot \mathbf{T}_1^{-1})$ has the same distribution as $(\hat{\mathbf{c}}_0, \hat{\mathbf{c}}_1)$. The remainder of the proof is similar to the proof for zero knowledge for Theorem 1.

Special Soundness. The proof is essentially the same as the one for Theorem 1, so we do not repeat it here.   □

Why is the Dimension of the Solution Space Restricted to 1 in **Solve***?* When the dimension is 0, the only solution of the linear system will lead to $(\mathbf{A}, \mathbf{B}^{-1}) = (0,0)$, which is not desired. When the dimension is larger than 1, it is no longer guaranteed that $(\mathbf{A}', \mathbf{B}') = (\alpha \tilde{\mathbf{A}} \mathbf{A}_1^{-1}, \alpha^{-1} \mathbf{B}_1^{-1} \tilde{\mathbf{B}})$, so completeness is broken. This also explains why we require that $|m - n| \leq 1$: When $|m - n| > 1$, we have $2mn + 1 < m^2 + n^2$, so the dimension of the solution space will be larger than 1.

Success Probability of **Solve***.* The linear systems in **Solve** are highly structured and should not be considered as random linear systems. Nevertheless, for most $\mathbf{D}_i$'s, experiment results show that the probability **Solve** returns an isometry is close to the probability that a random matrix in $\mathbb{F}_q^{2mn \times (m^2 + n^2)}$ has a kernel space of dimension 1. This means that when $m = n$, **Solve** returns $\perp$ with a high probability, so the signing algorithm is expected to be inefficient. In the next subsection, we give some arguments regarding the success probability (and complexity) of **Solve** for a specific choice of $\mathbf{D}_0, \mathbf{D}_1 \in \mathbb{F}_q^{m \times n}$ with $n = m + 1$.

4.3 A Specific Choice for $\mathbf{D}_0, \mathbf{D}_1$

For the $|m - n| \leq 1$ protocol (c.f. Fig. 4) introduced in the previous subsection, the linear systems in **Solve** are of the form $\mathbf{Lx} = 0$, where $\mathbf{L} \in \mathbb{F}_q^{2mn \times (m^2 + n^2)}$. In general, one would expect that it takes $O(n^6)$ field operations to solve such a linear system. However, we found that, due to setting $n = m + 1$ and by using $\mathbf{D}_0 = (\mathbf{I}_m \mid 0) \in \mathbb{F}_q^{m \times n}$, $\mathbf{D}_1 = (0 \mid \mathbf{I}_m) \in \mathbb{F}_q^{m \times n}$, we can obtain a much more sparse and structured linear system such that the cost can be reduced to only $O(n^3)$ field operations.

With such a choice for $\mathbf{D}_i$'s, the matrix $\mathbf{L}$ is going to be in the shape illustrated in Fig. 5a. After various row operations are applied, the matrix is transformed into the form illustrated by Fig. 5f, which is almost in row echelon form. Then, computing reduced row echelon form of $\mathbf{L}$ boils down to computing reduced row echelon form of $\mathbf{M} \in \mathbb{F}_q^{(m-1) \times m}$ plus backward substitutions. Note that checking whether $\mathbf{L}$ has a dimension-1 kernel space also boils down to checking whether $\mathbf{M}$ has a dimension-1 kernel space. Below we explain why $\mathbf{L}$ is of the shape of Fig. 5a and how the matrix in Fig. 5f is obtained by applying a sequence of row operations.

Let $a_{i,j}$ be the variable for $\mathbf{A}_{i,j}$, and let $b_{i,j}$ be the variable for $(\mathbf{B}^{-1})_{i,j}$. Consider $\mathbf{D}_0 \mathbf{B}^{-1} - \mathbf{A} \mathbf{C}_0 = 0$. We have $(\mathbf{AC}_0)_{i,j} = \sum_k \mathbf{A}_{i,k} (\mathbf{C}_0)_{k,j}$, and $\mathbf{D}_0 \mathbf{B}^{-1}$

is simply the first m rows of $\mathbf{B}^{-1}$. This leads to equations $b_{i,j} - \sum_{k=0}^{m-1} (\mathbf{C}_0)_{k,j} a_{i,k}$, for $i = 0, \ldots, n-2$ and $j = 0, \ldots, n-1$. This explains the first mn rows of Fig. 5a: for any (i,j), the equation is represented in row $in + j$ of $\mathbf{L}$, while the first n^2 columns of $\mathbf{L}$ correspond to

$$b_{0,0}, \ldots, b_{0,n-1}, b_{1,0}, \ldots, b_{1,n-1}, \ldots, b_{n-1,0}, \ldots, b_{n-1,n-1},$$

and the last m^2 columns of $\mathbf{L}$ correspond to

$$a_{0,0}, \ldots, a_{0,m-1}, a_{1,0}, \ldots, a_{1,m-1}, \ldots, a_{m-1,0}, \ldots, a_{m-1,m-1},$$

Following the discussion above, it is easy to see that the last mn rows of Fig. 5a are for $\mathbf{D}_1 \mathbf{B}^{-1} - \mathbf{A}\mathbf{C}_1 = 0$.

Figure 5f is derived from Fig. 5a by carrying out the steps below.

- Figure 5b is obtained by rearranging rows in Fig. 5a. This step takes 0 field operations.
- Figure 5c is obtained by eliminating the $\mathbf{I}_n$'s in the last $(m-1)n$ rows of Fig. 5b. This step takes 0 field operations as we only need to replace the $\mathbf{I}_n$'s by 0 and replace some zero submatrices by $\mathbf{C}_0^{\mathsf{T}}$.
- Figure 5d is obtained by applying Gaussian eliminations to the $(-\mathbf{C}_1^{\mathsf{T}} \mid \mathbf{C}_0^{\mathsf{T}})$ blocks in Fig. 5c. Note that we can always reduce $(-\mathbf{C}_1^{\mathsf{T}} \mid \mathbf{C}_0^{\mathsf{T}})$ to the form

$$\begin{bmatrix} \mathbf{I}_m & \mathbf{N} \\ 0 & \mathbf{v} \end{bmatrix}$$

where $\mathbf{v} \in \mathbb{F}_q^m$, as $\mathbf{C}_1$ is full rank. This step takes $O(n^2 m) = O(n^3)$ field operations.
- Figure 5e is obtained by rearranging rows in Fig. 5d. This step takes 0 field operations.
- Figure 5f is obtained by eliminating elements in the last $m-1$ rows in Fig. 5e. It turns out that the rows of $\mathbf{M}$ are determined by $\mathbf{v}$ and $\mathbf{N}$ as we have:

$$\mathbf{M} = \begin{bmatrix} \mathbf{v} \cdot (-\mathbf{N})^0 \\ \mathbf{v} \cdot (-\mathbf{N})^1 \\ \mathbf{v} \cdot (-\mathbf{N})^2 \\ \vdots \\ \mathbf{v} \cdot (-\mathbf{N})^{m-2} \end{bmatrix} \in \mathbb{F}_q^{(m-1)\times m}.$$

Therefore, this step takes $O(n^3)$ field operations, if each row is computed as the product of the previous row and $-\mathbf{N}$.

Computing reduced row echelon form of $\mathbf{M}$ takes $O(n^3)$ field operations. Backward substitutions also take $O(n^3)$ field operations. Checking whether $\mathbf{A}$ and $\mathbf{B}^{-1}$ are invertible again takes $O(n^3)$ field operations. Therefore, we conclude that **Solve** takes $O(n^3)$ field operations in total. For comparison, each of the $\pi_{\tilde{\mathbf{A}},\tilde{\mathbf{B}}}$, $\pi_{\mathbf{A}',\mathbf{B}'}$, and SF operations in the commitment and verification algorithms takes $O(n^4)$ field operations, under the assumption that $k = O(n)$.

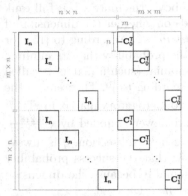

(a) Initial sparse system matrix.

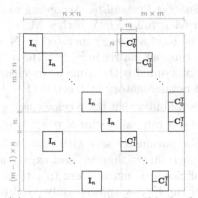

(b) After moving the last block of m rows upwards.

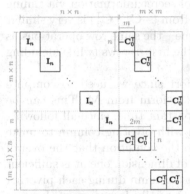

(c) After eliminating the left bottom quadrant.

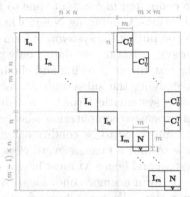

(d) After Gaussian elimination of the subsystem $(-\mathbf{C}_1^{\mathsf{T}}|\mathbf{C}_0^{\mathsf{T}})$.

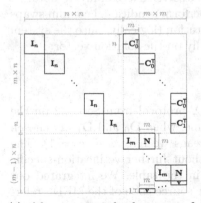

(e) After moving the last row of each row block downwards.

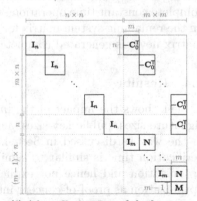

(f) After elimination of the last $m-1$ rows, which gives subsystem M.

Fig. 5. Process of solving the block diagonal system.

Success Probability. According to the discussion above, the matrix $\mathbf{L}$ is full rank if $\mathbf{M}$ is full rank. Whether $\mathbf{M}$ is full rank depends on whether the dimension of the Krylov space generated by $\mathbf{N}$ and $\mathbf{v}$ is at least $m - 1$. According to [15], for a random matrix in $\mathbb{F}_q^{m \times m}$, the $m \to \infty$ limit of the probability that its minimal polynomial is the same as its characteristic polynomial (such a matrix is called a nonderogatory matrix), is $(1 - \frac{1}{q^5})/(1 + \frac{1}{q^3})$. According to [9, Theorem 9], the probability that the Krylov space generated by a nonderogatory matrix in $\mathbb{F}_q^{m \times m}$ and a random vector $\mathbf{v} \in \mathbb{F}_q^m$ is of dimension m, is lower bounded by $\frac{0.218}{1 + \log_q m}$. For parameter sets with $n = m + 1$ shown in the next subsection, q is always much larger than m, and experiment results show that the success probability of **Solve** is much closer to 1 than to 0.218, presumably because the dimension of the Krylov space is only required to be at least $m - 1$.

Constant Time Implementation. For the signing operation, system solving must be computed in constant time to avoid leakage of secret information via timing variations. Computing $\mathbf{N}$ and v in constant time from $(-\mathbf{C}_1^{\mathsf{T}} \mid \mathbf{C}_0^{\mathsf{T}})$ is very similar to computing the systematic form in constant time—the same row operations as for systemization are simply only performed for the first m rows (while including the last row in pivoting and elimination).

Solving the subsystem $\mathbf{M}$ requires more effort since we need to compute not a systematic form but a reduced row echelon form from $\mathbf{M}$. This can be an expensive computation when performed in constant time, since all following columns need to be conditionally swapped with with pivoting column to make sure to find a pivot. Nevertheless, since we have the condition that the overall system and hence $\mathbf{M}$ must have a solution space of dimension one, it is sufficient to perform a single conditional swap with the last column during each pivoting operation. We count how often a column swap actually is necessary: If more than one swap needs to be performed, $\mathbf{M}$ has more than one solution and system solving is aborted with an error code. If $\mathbf{M}$ can be solved successfully, to obtain a complete constant time operation, we need to perform conditional column swaps on the remaining system matrix for back-substitution (logically, since the system matrix never is generated completely) and finally on the solution vector.

4.4   Results

Table 1 shows the impact of the $|m - n| \leq 1$ Σ-protocol from Sect. 4.2 on the signature sizes, public key sizes, and signing time, when $\mathbf{D}_0$ and $\mathbf{D}_1$ are chosen in the way as discussed in Sect. 4.3 (which means we have $n - m = 1$). The verification time is similar to signing time without further verification-specific optimization and hence not explicitly shown in the table. We integrated our optimization as proof-of-concept into the public source code of the MEDS reference implementation[3]. For a fair comparison, as the reference implementation, our modifications are constant time. The cycle counts were obtained on a AMD Ryzen 7 PRO 5850U.

---

[3] https://github.com/MEDSpqc/meds.

For each parameter set, the first row ("spec [10]") shows the performance of the original MEDS reference implementation without our optimization. Also the second row ("spec n++") is without our optimization, but n is changed to $m+1$ (i.e., incremented by one) to identify what impact on performance is due to the parameter change and what impact is due to the additional computation for the signature size optimization. The third row ("sig opt") shows the performance including our $|m - n| \leq 1$ signature size optimization from Sect. 4.2. The signature size for the "sig opt" cases can be computed using Eq. (1) and by setting isobits to $2k\lceil\log_2(q)\rceil$.

In all six parameter set cases, the increase in computing time for signing when using the signature optimization compared to the original parameter set is less than 50% and when focusing just on the change for $n = m + 1$ the increase is less than 30%. The impact is more moderate for higher parameter sets due to other dominating computations that are the same with and without the optimization. For the Level I parameter set, our optimization reduces the signature size to under one quarter. Since the size of w non-seeded responses drops from quadratic to linear in the security parameters ($m^2 + n^2$ to $2k$), we obtain a particularly strong up to over $20\times$ improvement in signature size for the larger parameter sets.

However, for Level I and III, the attack cost actually is reduced when incrementing n by one, based on the attacks described in the MEDS specification [10]. Hence, to maintain the security level, we need to increase m, n, and k by one, which increases all public key size, signature size, and signing time, as shown in the fourth row of the Level I and III parameter sets. Nevertheless, due to the significant reduction of the signature size compared to the original "spec [10]" case, we can compensate for these performance penalties by modifying the performance parameters, i.e., by reducing s (to reduce the public key size), by reducing t (to reduce signing time), and by increasing w correspondingly (which increases the signature size). The result of this is shown in the fifth row for the Level I and III parameter sets and in the fourth row for the Level V parameters.

Overall, our signature optimization allows us to reduce the signature size significantly to about 30% at Level I, to about 12% at Level III, and to about 6% on Level V at little to no negative impact on public key size and signing time (which for smaller parameter sets even can be improved as well depending on what trade-offs are chosen for the performance parameters s, t, and w).

5   Extending Our Technique to ALTEQ

Our technique is designed to apply to group-action Fiat-Shamir signatures using matrix codes. It is however not immediately clear whether it is still a valid approach under specific constraints. In this section we answer positively this question for the case of matrix codes arising from alternating trilinear forms used by ALTEQ [6,22]. In this case the isometries can be represented by a single matrix, and the matrix codes show a specific symmetry, coming from the alternating-ness, not present in random matrix codes.

Table 1. Comparison of the $|m - n| \leq 1$ signature size optimization from Sect. 4.2 ("sig opt") in several variants with the original parameter sets ("spec [10]") and the original parameter sets using $n = m + 1$ ("spec n++").

		q	n	m	k	bit sec.	s	t	w	pk (byte)	sig (byte)	sign (mcyc)
NIST Security Level I												
Ia 1	spec [10]	4093	14	14	14	146.52	4	1152	14	9 923	9 896	486.89
Ia 2	spec n++		15			130.05†				10 685	10 512	551.40
Ia 3	sig opt		15			130.05†				10 616	2 252	708.81
Ia 4	sig opt		16	15	15	148.61				13 196	2 294	896.85
Ia 5	sig opt		16			148.61	2	256	30	4 420	2 886	199.24
Ib 1	spec [10]	4093	14	14	14	146.52	5	192	20	13 220	12 976	82.34
Ib 2	spec n++		15			130.05†				14 236	13 856	88.38
Ib 3	sig opt		15			130.05†				14 144	2 056	120.43
Ib 4	sig opt		16	15	15	148.61				17 584	2 116	147.61
Ib 5	sig opt		16			148.61	2	144	48	4 420	4 016	112.22
NIST Security Level III												
IIIa 1	spec [10]	4093	22	22	22	216.83	4	608	26	41 711	41 080	1 244.56
IIIa 2	spec n++		23			195.38†				43 697	42 848	1 325.20
IIIa 3	sig opt		23			195.38†				43 592	5 044	1 730.32
IIIa 4	sig opt		24	23	23	213.64				50 024	5 122	2 027.83
IIIa 5	sig opt		24			213.64	3	480	31	33 360	5 203	1 572.73
IIIb 1	spec [10]	4093	22	22	22	216.83	5	160	36	55 604	54 736	332.91
IIIb 2	spec n++		23			195.38†				58 252	57 184	361.72
IIIb 3	sig opt		23			195.38†				58 112	4 840	450.68
IIIb 4	sig opt		24	23	23	213.64				66 688	4 948	524.62
IIIb 5	sig opt		24			213.64	3	128	69	33 360	6 241	425.93
NIST Security Level V												
Va 1	spec [10]	2039	30	30	30	291.31	5	192	52	134 180	132 528	1 229.89
Va 2	spec n++		31			298.24				138 804	136 896	1 285.49
Va 3	sig opt		31			298.24				138 632	8 092	1 623.09
Va 4	sig opt		31			298.24	4	144	74	103 982	10 302	1 257.84
Vb 1	spec [10]	2039	30	30	30	291.31	6	112	66	167 717	165 464	726.48
Vb 2	spec n++		31			298.24				173 497	171 008	750.95
Vb 3	sig opt		31			298.24				173 282	7 526	955.19
Vb 4	sig opt		31			298.24	5	112	86	138 632	8 546	955.76

†For these cases, incesing n to $m + 1$ reduces the security under the desired level. To compensate for this, the security paramters need to be increased.

Alternating Trilinear Forms. An alternating trilinear form (ATF) on $\mathbb{F}_q^n$ is a function

$$\phi : \mathbb{F}_q^n \times \mathbb{F}_q^n \times \mathbb{F}_q^n \to \mathbb{F}_q$$

such that it is:

- *Trilinear:* It is linear in each of its three arguments.
- *Alternating:* Whenever $\mathbf{x}_i = \mathbf{x}_j$, for some $i \neq j$, then $\phi(\mathbf{x}_1, \mathbf{x}_2, \mathbf{x}_3) = 0$.

The vector space of alternating trilinear forms on $\mathbb{F}_q^n$ is denoted by $\bigwedge^3 \mathbb{F}_q^n$. When q is odd, every alternating form is also skew-symmetric, i.e. $\phi(\mathbf{x}_1, \mathbf{x}_2, \mathbf{x}_3) = -\phi(\mathbf{x}_{\tau(1)}, \mathbf{x}_{\tau(2)}, \mathbf{x}_{\tau(3)})$ for any transposition $\tau \in \mathcal{S}_3$.

A trilinear form is, by trilinearity, completely determined by its value on all triples of basis vectors $c_{ijk} = \phi(\mathbf{e}_i, \mathbf{e}_j, \mathbf{e}_k)$ for $1 \leq i, j, k \leq n$. If in addition the form is alternating, there is redundancy in these values, since $c_{ijk} = -c_{ikj} = c_{kij} = -c_{jik} = c_{jki} = -c_{kji}$ Therefore, an ATF is completely determined by $c_{ijk} = \phi(\mathbf{e}_i, \mathbf{e}_j, \mathbf{e}_k)$ for $1 \leq i < j < k \leq n$ and can be represented by $\binom{n}{3}$ field elements.

For a given $\mathbf{v} \in \mathbb{F}_q^n$, we will use the notation $\phi_{\mathbf{v}} = \phi(-, -, \mathbf{v})$ to denote a partially fixed trilinear form. Similarly, we will write $\phi_i = \phi_{\mathbf{e}_i} = \phi(-, -, \mathbf{e}_i)$ in the case of basis vectors. By abuse of notation we will sometimes write $\phi_{\mathbf{v}}$ for the skew-symmetric matrix $(\phi_{\mathbf{v}})_{jk} = \phi_{\mathbf{v}}(\mathbf{e}_j, \mathbf{e}_k)$. In our optimization we will make use of the following observation:

$$\phi(\mathbf{u}, \mathbf{v}, \mathbf{w}) = [\phi_1(\mathbf{u}, \mathbf{v}), \ldots, \phi_n(\mathbf{u}, \mathbf{v})] \cdot \mathbf{w}, \quad \forall\, \mathbf{u}, \mathbf{v}, \mathbf{w} \in \mathbb{F}_q^n$$

Here · represents the standard inner product. For simplicity we will denote

$$\phi_{\mathbf{u}, \mathbf{v}} = [\phi_1(\mathbf{u}, \mathbf{v}), \ldots, \phi_n(\mathbf{u}, \mathbf{v})] \in \mathbb{F}_q^n.$$

Note that alternating-ness implies that $\phi_{\mathbf{u}, \mathbf{v}} = \phi_{\mathbf{v}, \mathbf{u}}$.

A Cryptographic Group Action. The Alternating Trilinear Form Equivalence problem can be seen as the vectorization problem of a group action of $\mathrm{GL}_n(q)$ on $\bigwedge^3 \mathbb{F}_q^n$. This group action can be constructed as follows, given a linear transformation $\mathbf{A} \in \mathrm{GL}_n(q)$ we can naturally lift this to $\bigwedge^3 \mathbb{F}_q^n$ via

$$\phi \cdot \mathbf{A} = \phi \circ \mathbf{A} = \phi(\mathbf{A}(-), \mathbf{A}(-), \mathbf{A}(-)).$$

In this way we get a right group action of $\mathrm{GL}_n(q)$ on $\bigwedge^3 \mathbb{F}_q^n$. Now, given the group action, we define the Alternating Trilinear Form Equivalence (ATFE) problem:

Problem 2 (Alternating Trilinear Form Equivalence). ATFE(n, ϕ, ψ):
Input: Two alternating trilinear forms ϕ, ψ.
Question: Find – if any – $\mathbf{A} \in \mathrm{GL}_n(q)$ such that $\phi \cdot \mathbf{A} = \psi$ i.e.:

$$\phi(\mathbf{Ax}, \mathbf{Ay}, \mathbf{Az}) = \psi(\mathbf{x}, \mathbf{y}, \mathbf{z}) \quad \forall \mathbf{x}, \mathbf{y}, \mathbf{z} \in \mathbb{F}_q^n.$$

Since ATFE is a hard problem, we obtain a cryptographic group action.

The ATFE problem can be restated in terms of matrix codes. Given an alternating trilinear form ϕ, we denote by $\langle\phi_1,\ldots,\phi_n\rangle$ the code generated by the matrices $\phi_1,\ldots,\phi_n$. We will say that this code is the matrix code representation of ϕ. We now have the following formulation:

Problem 3 (Alternating Trilinear Form Equivalence (Matrix Code formulation)). ATFE(n,ϕ,ψ):
Input: Two alternating trilinear forms in matrix code representation $\langle\phi_1,\ldots,\phi_n\rangle$, $\langle\psi_1,\ldots,\psi_n\rangle$.
Question: Find – if any – $\mathbf{A}\in\mathrm{GL}_n(q)$ such that $\mathbf{A}^\top\phi_i\mathbf{A}\in\langle\psi_1,\ldots,\psi_n\rangle\subset\mathbb{F}_q^{n\times n}$ for all $1\leq i\leq n$.

This restatements shows that ATFE can be considered as a matrix code equivalence problem with restriction on the type of isometry and the structure of the codes. Note that both MCE and ATFE are TI-complete as shown in [21] and [18].

5.1   The Basic ALTEQ Protocol

The basic ALTEQ protocol is a straightforward application of Fiat-Shamir to an equivalence problem. It is similar to the basic MEDS protocol except that the ATF is represented using its compact representation that requires only $\binom{n}{3}$ entries (as opposed to a matrix code representation that requires n^3 entries). It is given in Fig. 6. Note that the basic ALTEQ protocol can be optimized similarly to other group-action Fiat-Shamir signatures using standard techniques such as multiple public keys, fixed-weight challenges and seed-trees (see Sect. 3). The authors in [6] consider as part of their submission only the first two. They provide an implementation of seed-trees as well, but leave as open their usage for optimization of the signature size.

Remark 1. The ALTEQ specifications [6] considers a left group action instead of a right group action. These two can be easily translated to each other since acting on the right with $\mathbf{A}$ is equivalent to acting on the left with $\mathbf{A}^\top$ and vice-versa. It is clear that choosing either has no impact on the validity or security of the protocol. For the sake of this exposition and for reducing the amount of transpose symbols, we will use the right group action throughout. Therefore we also state the basic ALTEQ protocol with a right group action in Fig. 6.

5.2   The Solve Procedure for ALTEQ

The main idea of our technique introduced in the previous sections is to recover the full isometry from a small given part of the isometry itself and matching pairs of codewords from the two isometric codes that the isometry maps one to another. In MEDS, the isometry is the most general one, so it is rather easy to find $\tilde{\mathbf{A}}$ and $\tilde{\mathbf{B}}$ from part of $\tilde{\mathbf{T}}$ and two pairs of matching codewords.

Public Data

$q, n, \lambda \in \mathbb{N}$.

$\mathbf{A}_0 = \mathbf{I}_n \in \mathrm{GL}_n(q)$.

I. Keygen()

1. $\phi_0 \xleftarrow{\$} \bigwedge^3 \mathbb{F}_q^n$.
2. $\mathbf{A}_1 \xleftarrow{\$} \mathrm{GL}_n(q)$.
3. $\phi_1 \leftarrow \phi_0 \cdot \mathbf{A}_1$.
4. $\mathsf{sk} \leftarrow \mathbf{A}_1$ and $\mathsf{pk} \leftarrow (\phi_0, \phi_1)$.
5. Return $(\mathsf{sk}, \mathsf{pk})$.

II. Commit(pk)

1. $\tilde{\mathbf{A}} \xleftarrow{\$} \mathrm{GL}_n(q)$.
2. $\psi \leftarrow \phi_0 \cdot \tilde{\mathbf{A}}$.
3. $\mathsf{cmt} \leftarrow \psi$.
4. Return cmt.

III. Challenge()

1. $\mathsf{ch} \xleftarrow{\$} \{0,1\}$. Return ch.

V. Verify(pk, cmt, ch, rsp)

1. Parse rsp into $\mathbf{A}'$.
2. If $\mathbf{A}' \notin \mathrm{GL}_n(q)$, return "reject".
3. $\mathsf{cmt}' \leftarrow \phi_{\mathsf{ch}} \cdot \mathbf{A}'$.
4. If $\mathsf{cmt}' = \mathsf{cmt}$, return "accept". Otherwise, return "reject".

IV. Response(sk, pk, cmt, ch)

1. $\mathsf{rsp} \leftarrow \mathbf{A}_{\mathsf{ch}}^{-1} \cdot \tilde{\mathbf{A}}$.
2. Return rsp.

Fig. 6. ALTEQ Sigma Protocol.

In ALTEQ, if we view it in matrix code representation, we have $\tilde{\mathbf{A}} = \tilde{\mathbf{B}} = \tilde{\mathbf{T}}$. Trying to find algebraically the coefficients of $\tilde{\mathbf{A}}$ and $\tilde{\mathbf{A}}^{-1}$ as in MEDS, might not be the best strategy. The matrices being the same seems to cause a problem and next, we see why. Nevertheless, we show how we can actually make use of it to achieve a similar effect as in MEDS.

Let us fix the first α columns of $\tilde{\mathbf{A}}$. Denote by A_i the ith column of $\tilde{\mathbf{A}}$. Now, since for $i \leq \alpha$, we know that $\tilde{\mathbf{A}}e_i = A_i$, we can compute the matrices:

$$\phi(\tilde{\mathbf{A}}e_i, \tilde{\mathbf{A}}(-), \tilde{\mathbf{A}}(-)) = \phi_{A_i}(\tilde{\mathbf{A}}(-), \tilde{\mathbf{A}}(-)), \quad \forall i \leq \alpha.$$

Now, just as in MEDS we can consider these to be codewords, fix matching target codewords in the ephemeral ATF , and build a system of equations to find the rest of the isometry. For example, we can fix a skew-symmetric matrix ψ_i and create a system using the following equality:

$$\phi_{A_i}(\tilde{\mathbf{A}}(-), \tilde{\mathbf{A}}(-)) = \psi_i(-, -).$$

However, as we can see, this expression is quadratic in the $\tilde{\mathbf{A}}$ variables, which would be too inefficient to solve during signing. We could try to take one $\tilde{\mathbf{A}}$ to the other side:

$$\phi_{A_i}(\tilde{\mathbf{A}}(-), -) = \psi_i(-, \tilde{\mathbf{A}}^{-1}(-)).$$

However, to make sure that $\tilde{\mathbf{A}}$ and $\tilde{\mathbf{A}}^{-1}$ are in fact each others inverses, we again need quadratic equations, which is a problem since the final system will likely be inefficient to solve.

What we can do to avoid quadratic equations, is fix one more argument in ϕ. Now we calculate, for $i \neq j$ and $i \leq \alpha$

$$\phi(\tilde{\mathbf{A}}e_i, \tilde{\mathbf{A}}e_j, \tilde{\mathbf{A}}(-)) = \phi(A_i, A_j, \tilde{\mathbf{A}}(-)) = \phi_{A_i, A_j} \cdot \tilde{\mathbf{A}}.$$

Now, this is promising, as $\phi_{A_i,A_j} \cdot \tilde{\mathbf{A}}$ is just a linear expression. If we fix a target vector $\bar{\Psi}_{i,j} \in \mathbb{F}_q^n$ to match it with, we should get n equations in the $\tilde{\mathbf{A}}$ variables. Or at least, so it seems: We do have to be careful here, because for $k \leq \alpha$,

$$(\bar{\Psi}_{i,j})_k = (\phi_{A_i,A_j} \cdot \tilde{\mathbf{A}})_k = \phi_{A_i,A_j} \cdot \tilde{\mathbf{A}} \cdot \mathbf{e}_k = \phi_{A_i,A_j} \cdot A_k.$$

But this equation does not contain any $\tilde{\mathbf{A}}$ variables! So it will almost surely be an inconsistent equation. To avoid this from happening, we fix the last $n - \alpha$ positions of the vector $\bar{\Psi}_{i,j}$ as $\Psi_{i,j} \in \mathbb{F}_q^{n-\alpha}$ and consider only the last $n - \alpha$ columns of $\tilde{\mathbf{A}}$, which we denote by $\tilde{\mathbf{A}}_x$, resulting in:

$$\Psi_{i,j} = \phi_{A_i,A_j} \cdot \tilde{\mathbf{A}}_x$$

Now since we fixed αn entries of our isometry, and for every pair $i, j \leq \alpha$ we get $n - \alpha$ equations, we need to choose target vectors for n pairs $i, j \leq \alpha$. Furthermore, by symmetry, $\phi_{A_i,A_j} = \phi_{A_j,A_i}$, so $\Psi_{i,j} = \Psi_{j,i}$. In other words, we need n pairs with $i \leq j \leq \alpha$. This gives the condition $\binom{\alpha}{2} \geq n$ which determines how big must α be.

Let $(i_1, j_1), \ldots, (i_n, j_n)$ be such a list of n distinct pairs with $i_k \leq j_k \leq \alpha$. Then let us construct the following matrices:

$$\Phi_{\tilde{\mathbf{A}}} = \begin{bmatrix} \phi_{A_{i_1}, A_{j_1}} \\ \vdots \\ \phi_{A_{i_n}, A_{j_n}} \end{bmatrix} \in \mathbb{F}_q^{n \times n} \quad \text{and} \quad \Psi = \begin{bmatrix} \Psi_{i_1, j_1} \\ \vdots \\ \Psi_{i_n, j_n} \end{bmatrix} \in \mathbb{F}_q^{n \times (n-\alpha)}.$$

We can now write our equations as:

$$\Phi_{\tilde{\mathbf{A}}} \cdot \tilde{\mathbf{A}}_x = \Psi.$$

When $\Phi_{\tilde{\mathbf{A}}}$ is invertible, which happens with probability $1/q$, we can compute the remaining values of $\tilde{\mathbf{A}}$ as $\tilde{\mathbf{A}}_x = \Phi_{\tilde{\mathbf{A}}}^{-1} \cdot \Psi$. Since we want an isometry, we only have to check that the entire $\tilde{\mathbf{A}}$ is full rank, which happens with chance $1/q$.

Thus to conclude, if we fix α columns of our isometry and a random matrix $\Psi \in \mathbb{F}_q^{n \times (n-\alpha)}$, then we can create a system in the remaining entries of $\tilde{\mathbf{A}}$ that has at most one solution with chance roughly $2/q$. We summarize the above discussion in the procedure $\mathbf{Solve}_\Psi$ given in Fig. 7. In the description, we use an injective function $\mathfrak{I} = (\mathfrak{I}_1, \mathfrak{I}_2) : \{1, \ldots, n\} \to \{(i,j) \mid 1 \leq i < j \leq \alpha\}$ whose purpose is to ease the notation by providing an ordering on the two-dimensional indices relevant in the construction.

5.3 The Optimized Protocol

The above method, following the same reasoning as for MEDS in the previous sections, suggests to execute the protocol using a specific, fixed choice of Ψ for all alternating forms we use. Denote the set of all alternating forms $\phi \in \bigwedge^3 \mathbb{F}_q^n$ with this fixed Ψ by $\mathcal{A}_\Psi$.

Constants: $\Psi \in \mathbb{F}_q^{n \times (n-\alpha)}$, and an injective function $\mathfrak{I} : \{1, \ldots, n\} \to \{(i,j) \mid 1 \leq i < j \leq \alpha\}$.
Input: $\phi_0 \in \bigwedge^3 \mathbb{F}_q^n$, $A_i \in \mathbb{F}_q^n$ for $i \leq \alpha$.
Output: $\tilde{A} \in \mathrm{GL}_n(q)$ such that
$\tilde{A}_i = A_i$ for $i \leq \alpha$ and $(\phi_0 \cdot \tilde{A})(e_{\mathfrak{I}_1(i)}, e_{\mathfrak{I}_2(i)}, e_{j+\alpha}) = \Psi_{i,j}$, or $\perp$.

1. Construct $\Phi_{\tilde{A}} = \{\phi_0 \left(A_{\mathfrak{I}_1(i)}, A_{\mathfrak{I}_2(i)}, e_j\right)\}_{i,j}$
2. If $\Phi_{\tilde{A}} \notin \mathrm{GL}_n(q)$, return $\perp$.
3. $\tilde{A} = (A_1 \cdots A_\alpha \mid \Phi_{\tilde{A}}^{-1}\Psi)$.
4. If $\tilde{A} \notin \mathrm{GL}_n(q)$, return $\perp$. Otherwise return $\tilde{A}$.

Fig. 7. The function Solve_Ψ.

To see that restricting the protocol to $\mathcal{A}_\Psi$ does not impact the security we make the following argument.

Let us assume that ATFE restricted to $\mathcal{A}_\Psi$ is an easy problem, i.e. given $\tilde{\phi}, \tilde{\psi} \in \mathcal{A}_\Psi$, we can find an isometry $\tilde{\phi} \xrightarrow{\mathbf{A}} \tilde{\psi}$ efficiently. Now we want to show that with assumption, ATFE is easy as well to obtain a contradiction.

Let $\phi, \psi \in \bigwedge^3 \mathbb{F}_q^n$, then we can, using **Solve**, efficiently find $\tilde{\phi}, \tilde{\psi} \in \mathcal{A}_\Psi$ and $\tilde{\mathbf{A}}, \tilde{\mathbf{B}} \in \mathrm{GL}_n(q)$ with $\phi \xrightarrow{\tilde{\mathbf{A}}} \tilde{\phi}$ and $\psi \xrightarrow{\tilde{\mathbf{B}}} \tilde{\psi}$. But now, using our assumption, we can efficiently find an isometry $\tilde{\phi} \xrightarrow{\mathbf{A}} \tilde{\psi}$. Using this we can construct the isometry $\tilde{\mathbf{B}}^{-1} \circ \mathbf{A} \circ \tilde{\mathbf{A}} : \phi \to \psi$. Hence we could solve ATFE efficiently, which is a contradiction.

To summarize the discussion, we present our optimized protocol in Fig. 8. We formally show its security with the following theorem.

Theorem 3. *The protocol in Fig. 8 is a Σ-protocol for the* ATFE *relation.*

Proof. We prove as usual the properties of completeness, special soundness and honest-verifier zero-knowledgeness.

Completeness: For $(\mathsf{cmt}_0, \mathsf{rsp}_0)$ being an honestly generated commitment-response pair for $\mathsf{ch} = 0$, rsp_0 consists of the first α columns, $A_1, \ldots, A_\alpha$, of $\tilde{A}$. This means that $\mathbf{A}'$ is parsed into exactly these columns which results in $\tilde{A}' = \tilde{A}$ and $\mathrm{Verify}(\mathsf{pk}, \mathsf{cmt}_0, 0, \mathsf{rsp}_0) = $ "accept".

For ch_1, the response rsp_1 consists of the columns $A_i' = \mathbf{A}_1^{-1}A_i$ for $1 \leq i \leq \alpha$. Now for $i \leq j \leq \alpha$ we have the following equality:

$$\psi_{A_i', A_j'} = \psi(\mathbf{A}_1^{-1}A_i, \mathbf{A}_1^{-1}A_j, \mathbf{A}_1^{-1}\mathbf{A}_1-)$$
$$= \phi(A_i, A_j, \mathbf{A}_1-)$$
$$= \phi_{A_i, A_j} \cdot \mathbf{A}_1.$$

Public Data

$q, n, \lambda \in \mathbb{N}$.

$\mathbf{A}_0 = \mathbf{I}_n \in \mathrm{GL}_n(q)$.

$\alpha = \min\{m \mid m \in \mathbb{N}, \binom{m}{2} \geq n\}$.

An injective function

$\mathfrak{I} : \{1, \ldots, n\} \to \{(i,j) | 1 \leq i < j \leq \alpha\}$.

$\Psi \in \mathbb{F}_q^{n \times (n-\alpha)}$.

I. Keygen()

1. $\phi_0 \xleftarrow{\$} \mathcal{A}_\Psi$.
2. $A_i \xleftarrow{\$} \mathbb{F}_q^n$ for $1 \leq i \leq \alpha$.
3. $\mathbf{A}_1 \leftarrow \mathbf{Solve}_\Psi(\phi_0, \{A_i\})$
4. $\phi_1 \leftarrow \phi_0 \cdot \mathbf{A}_1$.
5. $\mathsf{sk} \leftarrow \mathbf{A}_1$ and $\mathsf{pk} \leftarrow (\phi_0, \phi_1)$.
6. Return $(\mathsf{sk}, \mathsf{pk})$.

II. Commit(pk)

1. $A_i \xleftarrow{\$} \mathbb{F}_q^n$ for $1 \leq i \leq \alpha$.
2. $\tilde{\mathbf{A}} \leftarrow \mathbf{Solve}_\Psi(\phi_0, \{A_i\})$
3. If $\tilde{\mathbf{A}} = \bot$, restart at 1.
4. $\psi \leftarrow \phi_0 \cdot \tilde{\mathbf{A}}$.
5. $\mathsf{cmt} \leftarrow \psi$.
6. Return cmt.

III. Challenge()

1. $\mathsf{ch} \xleftarrow{\$} \{0, 1\}$. Return ch.

V. Verify(pk, cmt, ch, rsp)

1. Parse rsp into $\mathbf{A}' \in \mathbb{F}_q^{n \times \alpha}$.
2. $A_i' \leftarrow \mathbf{A}' \mathbf{e}_i$, for $1 \leq i \leq \alpha$.
3. $\tilde{\mathbf{A}}' \leftarrow \mathbf{Solve}_\Psi(\phi_{\mathsf{ch}}, \{A_i'\})$
4. If $\tilde{\mathbf{A}}' = \bot$, return "reject".
5. $\psi \leftarrow \phi_{\mathsf{ch}} \cdot \tilde{\mathbf{A}}'$.
6. $\mathsf{cmt}' \leftarrow \psi$.
7. If $\mathsf{cmt}' = \mathsf{cmt}$, return "accept". Otherwise, return "reject".

IV. Response(sk, pk, cmt, ch)

1. $\mathsf{rsp} \leftarrow \mathbf{A}_{\mathsf{ch}}^{-1} \cdot (A_1 \cdots A_\alpha) \in \mathbb{F}_q^{n \times \alpha}$.
2. Return rsp.

Fig. 8. Optimized Σ-protocol for ALTEQ.

Thus, in our **Solve** procedure the matrix $\Phi_{\tilde{\mathbf{A}}'}$ that we build from ψ and A_i's is equal to:

$$\Phi_{\tilde{\mathbf{A}}'} = \begin{bmatrix} \psi_{A_{i_1}', A_{j_1}'} \\ \vdots \\ \psi_{A_{i_n}', A_{j_n}'} \end{bmatrix} = \begin{bmatrix} \phi_{A_{i_1}, A_{j_1}} \cdot \mathbf{A}_1 \\ \vdots \\ \phi_{A_{i_n}, A_{j_n}} \cdot \mathbf{A}_1 \end{bmatrix} = \Phi_{\tilde{\mathbf{A}}} \cdot \mathbf{A}_1$$

A first conclusion is that invertibility of $\Phi_{\tilde{\mathbf{A}}}$ is equivalent to invertibility of $\Phi_{\tilde{\mathbf{A}}'}$. Then, when we solve $\Phi_{\tilde{\mathbf{A}}'} \mathbf{A}' = \Psi$, we obtain

$$\mathbf{A}' = \Phi_{\tilde{\mathbf{A}}'}^{-1} \Psi = \mathbf{A}_1^{-1} \Phi_{\tilde{\mathbf{A}}}^{-1} \Psi = \mathbf{A}_1^{-1} \tilde{\mathbf{A}}.$$

In other words $\mathbf{A}' = \mathbf{A}_1^{-1} \tilde{\mathbf{A}}$ proving completeness.

Zero-Knowledge: The proof for Zero-knowledge again follows a similar structure as the ones for the optimized MEDS protocols. The case of ch_0 is straightforward to simulate since the honest procedure for obtaining the pair $(\mathsf{cmt}_0, \mathsf{rsp}_0)$ does not involve the secret key. Because of completeness, we can immediately conclude that running the honest commit procedure without the secret key but instead of ϕ, using ψ produces a valid transcript $(\mathsf{cmt}_1, \mathsf{ch}_1, \mathsf{rsp}_1)$. Now since we can sample from $\{\tilde{\mathbf{A}} \in \mathrm{GL}_n(q) \mid \psi \cdot \tilde{\mathbf{A}} \in \mathcal{A}_\Psi\}$ uniformly random and the ephemeral isometry is sampled uniformly random from $\{\tilde{\mathbf{A}} \in \mathrm{GL}_n(q) \mid \phi \cdot \tilde{\mathbf{A}} \in \mathcal{A}_\Psi\}$, it follows that distribution of the transcripts of the honest and simulated protocol are the same, so we have zero-knowledge.

Special-Soundness: The premise of the optimization of the protocol is to send isometries with less information. Since one can construct the respective isometry from each response, special soundness is evident.

5.4   New Sizes

For the comparison of the new sizes to the original protocol we take the same conventions. We denote by C the amount of public keys (excluding ϕ_0), by r the number of rounds in the Fiat-Shamir construction, and by K the amount of rounds with non-zero challenge. Furthermore we denote by λ the security parameter and the size of our seeds. Now the security of the Fiat-Shamir construction can still be calculated as:

$$\binom{r}{K} \cdot C^K$$

The new public key-size and signature size can be computed as:

$$\text{PubKeySize} = C\left(\binom{n}{3} - n(n-\alpha)\right) \cdot \lceil \log_2 q \rceil + \lambda$$

$$\text{SigSize} = (r - K + 2) \cdot \lambda + K \cdot \alpha \cdot n \cdot \lceil \log_2 q \rceil$$

For NIST Security Level I, III, and V we take λ to be 128, 192 and 256 respectively, in line with the original ALTEQ specification.

Since the sizes of the public keys and isometries have changed, it can be worthwhile to re-optimize the Fiat-Shamir parameters. For the balanced parameters we optimized on pk + sig. For the ShortSig parameter sets we limited the public key to be of size 512 KB, 1 MB, and 2 MB respectively, in line with the original specs. These re-optimizations of the Fiat-Shamir parameters are indicated by a "+"-sign. In the re-optimizations we did not take computational speed into account. One could always limit the number of rounds and re-optimize.

These size reductions come at a small computational cost. We call C_{iso} the cost of a group action computation, C_{multi} the cost of a matrix multiplication and C_{inverse} the cost of matrix inversion then we can state the costs of the original protocol as follows:

$$C_{\text{Keygen}} = C \cdot C_{\text{iso}}$$
$$C_{\text{Commit}} = r \cdot C_{\text{iso}} + K \cdot C_{\text{multi}}$$
$$C_{\text{Verify}} = r \cdot C_{\text{iso}}$$

In the optimized protocol we have the added computational cost of **Solve**. If we assume that computing $\Phi_{\tilde{A}}$ in **Solve** is as costly as C_{iso} then we can state its computational costs as follows:

$$C'_{\text{Keygen}} = C \cdot (2 \cdot C_{\text{iso}} + C_{\text{multi}} + C_{\text{inverse}})$$
$$C'_{\text{Commit}} = r \cdot (2 \cdot C_{\text{iso}} + C_{\text{multi}} + C_{\text{inverse}}) + K \cdot C_{\text{multi}}$$
$$C'_{\text{Verify}} = r \cdot (2 \cdot C_{\text{iso}} + C_{\text{multi}} + C_{\text{inverse}})$$

This is a small price for the reduction in signature size (Table 2).

Table 2. Comparison of the public key and signature sizes after optimization using the "Balanced" parameter sets from ("spec [6]").

		n	α	C	r	K	pk (byte)	sig (byte)	pk + sig (byte)
				NIST Security Level I					
Balanced	spec [6]	13	–	7	84	22	8 024	15 896	23 920
Balanced	optimized	13	6	7	84	22	5 476	7 888	13 364
Balanced+	optimized	13	6	3	160	23	2 356	9 400	11 756
				NIST Security Level III					
Balanced	spec [6]	20	–	7	201	28	31 944	49 000	80 944
Balanced	optimized	20	7	7	201	28	24 664	19 880	44 544
Balanced+	optimized	20	7	2	306	36	7 064	26 688	33 752
				NIST Security Level V					
Balanced	spec [6]	25	–	8	119	48	73 632	122 336	195 968
Balanced	optimized	25	8	8	119	48	60 032	40 736	100 768
Balanced+	optimized	25	8	2	424	47	15 032	49 728	64 760

Table 3. Comparison of the public key and signature sizes after optimization using the "ShortSig" parameter sets from ("spec [6]").

		n	α	C	r	K	pk (byte)	sig (byte)
				NIST Security Level I				
ShortSig	spec [6]	13	–	458	16	14	523 968	9 528
ShortSig	optimized	13	6	458	16	14	357 256	4 432
ShortSig+	optimized	13	6	657	29	11	512 476	3 752
				NIST Security Level III				
ShortSig	spec [6]	20	–	229	39	20	1 044 264	32 504
ShortSig	optimized	20	7	229	39	20	806 104	11 704
ShortSig+	optimized	20	7	297	69	17	1 045 464	10 816
				NIST Security Level V				
ShortSig	spec [6]	25	–	227	67	25	2 088 432	63 908
ShortSig	optimized	25	8	227	67	25	1 702 532	21 408
ShortSig+	optimized	25	8	276	88	23	2 070 032	20 544

References

1. NIST additioal signature round announcement. NIST Official Website (2021). https://csrc.nist.gov/projects/pqc-dig-sig
2. Baldi, M., et al.: LESS: linear equivalence signature scheme (2023). https://www.less-project.com/LESS-2023-08-18.pdf

3. Barenghi, A., Biasse, J.-F., Persichetti, E., Santini, P.: LESS-FM: fine-tuning signatures from the code equivalence problem. In: Cheon, J.H., Tillich, J.-P. (eds.) PQCrypto 2021 2021. LNCS, vol. 12841, pp. 23–43. Springer, Cham (2021). https://doi.org/10.1007/978-3-030-81293-5_2

4. Beullens, W.: Breaking rainbow takes a weekend on a laptop. In: Dodis, Y., Shrimpton, T. (eds.) CRYPTO 2022. LNCS, vol. 13508, pp. 464–479. Springer, Cham (2022). https://doi.org/10.1007/978-3-031-15979-4_16

5. Beullens, W., Katsumata, S., Pintore, F.: Calamari and falafl: logarithmic (linkable) ring signatures from isogenies and lattices. In: Moriai, S., Wang, H. (eds.) ASIACRYPT 2020. LNCS, vol. 12492, pp. 464–492. Springer, Cham (2020). https://doi.org/10.1007/978-3-030-64834-3_16

6. Bläser, M., et al.: The alteq signature scheme: algorithm specifications and supporting documentation (2023). https://pqcalteq.github.io/ALTEQ_spec_2023.09.18.pdf

7. Bouillaguet, C., Fouque, P.-A., Véber, A.: Graph-theoretic algorithms for the "isomorphism of polynomials" problem. In: Johansson, T., Nguyen, P.Q. (eds.) EUROCRYPT 2013. LNCS, vol. 7881, pp. 211–227. Springer, Heidelberg (2013). https://doi.org/10.1007/978-3-642-38348-9_13

8. Boyar, J., Erfurth, S., Larsen, K.S., Niederhagen, R.: Quotable signatures for authenticating shared quotes. In: Aly, A., Tibouchi, M. (eds.) Progress in Cryptology – LATINCRYPT 2023. LNCS, vol. 14168, pp. 273–292. Springer, Cham (2023). https://doi.org/10.1007/978-3-031-44469-2_14

9. Brent, R.P., Gao, S., Lauder, A.G.: Random krylov spaces over finite fields. SIAM J. Discret. Math. 16(2), 276–287 (2003)

10. Chou, T., et al.: MEDS – matrix equivalence digital signature (2023). https://meds-pqc.org/spec/MEDS-2023-05-31.pdf, submission to the NIST Digital Signature Scheme standardization process

11. Chou, T., et al.: Take your MEDS: digital signatures from matrix code equivalence. In: Mrabet, N.E., Feo, L.D., Duquesne, S. (eds.) Progress in Cryptology — AFRICACRYPT 2023. LNCS, vol. 14064, pp. 28–52. Springer, Cham (2023). https://doi.org/10.1007/978-3-031-37679-5_2

12. Chou, T., Persichetti, E., Santini, P.: On linear equivalence, canonical forms, and digital signatures (2023). https://eprint.iacr.org/2023/1533.pdf

13. De Feo, L., Galbraith, S.D.: SeaSign: compact isogeny signatures from class group actions. In: Ishai, Y., Rijmen, V. (eds.) EUROCRYPT 2019. LNCS, vol. 11478, pp. 759–789. Springer, Cham (2019). https://doi.org/10.1007/978-3-030-17659-4_26

14. Fiat, A., Shamir, A.: How To Prove Yourself: Practical Solutions to Identification and Signature Problems. In: Odlyzko, A.M. (ed.) CRYPTO 1986. LNCS, vol. 263, pp. 186–194. Springer, Heidelberg (1987). https://doi.org/10.1007/3-540-47721-7_12

15. Fulman, J.: Random matrix theory over finite fields. Bull. Am. Math. Soc. 39(1), 51–85 (2002)

16. Goldreich, O., Goldwasser, S., Micali, S.: How to construct random functions. J. ACM 33(4), 792–807 (1986)

17. Goldreich, O., Micali, S., Wigderson, A.: Proofs that yield nothing but their validity or all languages in np have zero-knowledge proof systems. J. ACM 38(3), 690-728 (1991). https://doi.org/10.1145/116825.116852

18. Grochow, J.A., Qiao, Y., Tang, G.: Average-case algorithms for testing isomorphism of polynomials, algebras, and multilinear forms. J. Groups, Complexity, Cryptology 14(1) (2022).https://doi.org/10.46298/jgcc.2022.14.1.9431, https://

gcc.episciences.org/9836, preliminary version appeared in STACS '21, https://doi.org/10.4230/LIPIcs.STACS.2021.38. Preprint available at arXiv:2012.01085

19. Kipnis, A., Patarin, J., Goubin, L.: Unbalanced oil and vinegar signature schemes. In: Stern, J. (ed.) EUROCRYPT 1999. LNCS, vol. 1592, pp. 206–222. Springer, Heidelberg (1999). https://doi.org/10.1007/3-540-48910-X_15

20. National Institute for Standards and Technology: Post-Quantum Cryptography Standardization (2017). https://csrc.nist.gov/Projects/Post-Quantum-Cryptography

21. Reijnders, K., Samardjiska, S., Trimoska, M.: Hardness estimates of the code equivalence problem in the rank metric. Des. Codes Cryptogr. (2024). https://doi.org/10.1007/s10623-023-01338-x

22. Tang, G., Duong, D.H., Joux, A., Plantard, T., Qiao, Y., Susilo, W.: Practical post-quantum signature schemes from isomorphism problems of trilinear forms. In: EUROCRYPT 2022. Lecture Notes in Computer Science, vol. 13277, pp. 582–612. Springer (2022). https://doi.org/10.1007/978-3-031-07082-2_21

23. Tao, C., Petzoldt, A., Ding, J.: efficient key recovery for all HFE signature variants. In: Malkin, T., Peikert, C. (eds.) CRYPTO 2021. LNCS, vol. 12825, pp. 70–93. Springer, Cham (2021). https://doi.org/10.1007/978-3-030-84242-0_4

Group-Action-Based Cryptography

CCA Secure Updatable Encryption from Non-mappable Group Actions

Jonas Meers[1]([✉])[iD] and Doreen Riepel[2]([✉])[iD]

[1] Ruhr University Bochum, Bochum, Germany
jonas.meers@rub.de
[2] University of California San Diego, La Jolla, USA
driepel@ucsd.edu

Abstract. Ciphertext-independent updatable encryption (UE) allows
to rotate encryption keys and update ciphertexts via a token without the need to first download the ciphertexts. Although, syntactically,
UE is a symmetric-key primitive, ciphertext-independent UE with forward secrecy and post-compromise security is known to imply public-key
encryption (Alamati, Montgomery and Patranabis, CRYPTO 2019).

Constructing post-quantum secure UE turns out to be a difficult task.
While lattices offer the necessary homomorphic properties, the introduced noise allows only a bounded number of updates. Group actions
have become an important alternative, however, their structure is limited. The only known UE scheme by Leroux and Roméas (IACR ePrint
2022/739) uses effective triple orbital group actions which uses additional algebraic structure of CSIDH. Using an ideal cipher, similar to
the group-based scheme SHINE (Boyd et al., CRYPTO 2020), requires
the group action to be mappable, a property that natural isogeny-based
group actions do not satisfy. At the same time, other candidates based
on non-commutative group actions suffer from linearity attacks.

For these reasons, we explicitly ask how to construct UE from group
actions that are not mappable. As a warm-up, we present BIN-UE which
uses a bit-wise approach and is CPA secure based on the well-established
assumption of weak pseudorandomness and in the standard model. We
then construct the first actively secure UE scheme from post-quantum
assumptions. Our scheme COM-UE extends BIN-UE via the Tag-then-
Encrypt paradigm. We prove CCA security in the random oracle model
based on a stronger computational assumption. We justify the hardness
of our new assumption in the algebraic group action model.

Keywords: Updatable encryption · group actions · isogenies ·
algebraic group action model

1 Introduction

Updatable encryption (UE) allows to update a ciphertext to a new key without first decrypting the ciphertext and then re-encrypting it with the new key.
Instead, the owner of the encryption key computes an update *token* which can

M.-J. Saarinen and D. Smith-Tone (Eds.): PQCrypto 2024, LNCS 14771, pp. 137–169, 2024.
https://doi.org/10.1007/978-3-031-62743-9_5

then be used by a different party to update the ciphertext on behalf of the owner. This is especially useful in the context of cloud storage where a user might want to update the encryption key of some large encrypted file without the need to first download the file and re-encrypt it locally. This and other real-world applications have contributed to the fact that UE is a very active field of research [11,29,30,32,33,37,42]. All these works are concerned with the most general setting, where tokens can be created independently (i. e., they only depend on the old and new key) and allow to update all ciphertexts encrypted under the old key. This will also be our focus.

SECURITY OF UE. Since the introduction of UE by Boneh, Lewi, Montgomery and Raghunathan [9], security definitions have evolved. Definitions for standard symmetric encryption (SE) have been adapted to the setting of UE, capturing confidentiality and integrity of messages. In contrast to the standard SE setting, however, updating keys aims to provide stronger security, namely, forward secrecy and post-compromise security. This is captured in security definitions based on *epochs*, where some encryption keys and tokens may be revealed. Even in the presence of adaptive corruptions, we ask for indistinguishability under chosen message attacks and unlinkability of ciphertexts across updates, both of which are captured in the IND-UE-CPA definition of [11]. However, defining trivial attacks has turned out to be a complex and subtle task; various properties of UE schemes, which affect the "inferred" knowledge after a corruption, have been identified and result in slight adaptations [28,42]. For sake of clarity, we will not elaborate further at this point and explain the necessary details in the main body of the paper. In this work, we also aim for stronger security for UE capturing chosen ciphertext attacks (IND-UE-CCA), where the adversary is given additional access to a decryption oracle.

CONSTRUCTIONS OF UE. In order for a scheme to allow for rotating keys and updates, proposed schemes make use of public-key primitives with homomorphic properties. Indeed, Alamati, Montgomery and Patranabis [3] show that any ciphertext-independent UE scheme that is forward and post-compromise secure implies public-key encryption. We provide an overview of existing constructions in Table 1. There exist various constructions that rely on (elliptic-curve) groups, e. g., RISE [32], SHINE [11] and the DDH-based instantiation of the Encrypt-and-MAC (E&M) construction in [30]. While one might hope that these schemes can be easily transferred to the group action setting, current candidates for group actions do not allow for this. We will elaborate more on these constructions in Sect. 1.1.

The emergence of quantum computers poses an undeniable threat to all UE constructions based on prime-order groups. Therefore, the interest in post-quantum secure constructions for UE has grown in recent years. One promising approach constructs UE based on lattices [28,29,42]. The security of these schemes relies on the Learning with Error (LWE) assumption and updates are computed using the homomorphic properties of the underlying lattice. More specifically, the UE constructions rely on a key homomorphic PKE. When using a key and message homomorphic PKE, an even stronger security notion that captures uni-directional updates can be achieved, albeit at the price of cipher-

Table 1. Overview of existing ciphertext-independent UE constructions and our new constructions BIN-UE and COM-UE. For each scheme, we note whether updates are performed using randomness (rand) or deterministically (det). Most schemes are analyzed using the IND-UE security definition from [11], while others use the weaker IND-ENC and IND-UPD definitions [32]. For a formal comparison of these definitions, we refer the reader to [11]. The definition of RCCA security [30] has been established for constructions with randomized updates.

	Scheme	Security (IND)	Assumption	Model
Groups	RISE [32]	(rand, UE, CPA)	DDH	Standard
	E&M [30]	(det, ENC/UPD, CCA)	DDH	ROM
	SHINE0 [11]	(det, UE, CCA)	DDH	Ideal Cipher
Pairings	NYUAE [30]	(rand, ENC/UPD, RCCA)	SXDH	Standard
	SS23 [49]	(rand, UE, CPA)$^+$	SXDH	Standard
Lattices	Jia20 [29]	(rand, UE, CPA)	LWE	Standard
	Nis22 [42]	(rand, UE, CPA)	LWE	Standard
	GP23 [28]	(rand, UE, CPA)	LWE	Standard
Group Actions	GAINE0* [33]	(det, UE, CCA)	Wk-PR	Ideal Cipher
	TOGA-UE [33]	(det, UE, CPA)	P-CSSDDH	Standard
	BIN-UE (Sec. 3)	(det, UE, CPA)	Wk-PR	Standard
	COM-UE (Sec. 4)	(det, UE, CCA)	DLAI	ROM + AGAM

*no secure instantiation known
$^+$satisfies a stronger definition with expiry

texts and keys growing with the number of epochs. For more details, we refer to Sect. 1.3. The main drawback of these schemes, however, is the fact that encryption noise increases with each update, resulting in a finite number of updates that the schemes support. Furthermore, these schemes are currently not IND-UE-CCA secure.

1.1   The Difficulty of Constructing UE from Group Actions

Cryptographic group actions offer a post-quantum secure alternative to prime-order groups and are therefore another natural candidate for constructing post-quantum secure UE. Let $(\mathcal{G}, \cdot)$ be a group and $\mathcal{X}$ some set. A group action $\star : \mathcal{G} \times \mathcal{X} \to \mathcal{X}$ defines a map which is compatible with the group operation, i.e., $e \star x = x$ and $(g \cdot h) \star x = g \star (h \star x)$ for all $x \in \mathcal{X}$, $g, h \in \mathcal{G}$, where $e \in \mathcal{G}$ is the neutral element. Note in particular, that we do not assume any structure on $\mathcal{X}$ which will be one limiting factor in constructing efficient UE schemes. One popular instantiation of a cryptographic group action is CSIDH [15] which is based on isogenies between supersingular elliptic curves. Besides close variants like CSURF [12] and SCALLOP [22], CSIDH is the only known commutative group action that is believed to offer post-quantum security.

USING ELGAMAL ENCRYPTION. The group-based UE scheme RISE [32] uses the homomorphic properties of the ElGamal encryption scheme. Recall that the message in (standard) ElGamal encryption is represented by a group element which is then multiplied with the public key raised to an ephemeral secret. Due to the limited structure of group actions, however, we cannot adapt this approach. For PKE, this issue can be resolved by applying a hash function first and then encrypt the message. For UE, this will destroy all the properties required for updatability. An alternative approach is that of SiGamal [38], which we will further discuss below.

USING IDEAL CIPHERS. We now turn to SHINE which is the group-based UE scheme from [11]. SHINE makes use of an ideal permutation to map the message (and a nonce) to a group element. Encryption is then simply exponentiation using the secret key. IND-UE-CPA security assumes DDH and the proof is carried out in the ideal cipher model which dates back to Shannon [48]. The advantage is that only exponentiation is used, thus, there is a straightforward generalization to the group action setting. The resulting scheme GAINE has been proposed by Leroux and Roméas [33] and they prove IND-UE-CPA security in the ideal cipher model, assuming weak pseudorandomness (Wk-PR) of the group action. The scheme can further be made IND-UE-CCA secure by adding a zero-padding to the message (and nonce), resulting in schemes SHINE0 and GAINE0. However, the way the ideal cipher is used adds an additional requirement, namely, the group action must be *mappable*. In short, a mappable group action comes equipped with an efficiently computable bijection $\pi : \{0,1\}^N \to \mathcal{X}$ which allows mapping a message to a set element and vice versa. It turns out that for many popular group actions like CSIDH, it is notoriously hard to define such a mapping [10,39]. At the same time, there is currently no other (non-commutative) group action that is both mappable and satisfies Wk-PR. In fact, it was recently shown that many non-commutative group actions are susceptible to linearity attacks, making them unsuitable for UE [20]. This leaves us with no secure candidate instantiation for GAINE.

TRIPLE ORBITAL GROUP ACTIONS. For the reasons identified above, the authors in [33] define a new algebraic abstraction called *Triple Orbital Group Action* (TOGA). It combines a mappable group action and a weakly pseudorandom group action into a single structure. The resulting scheme, TOGA-UE, can then be instantiated with isogenies based on ideas developed for the SiGamal encryption scheme [38]. While TOGA-UE seems like a promising approach to avoid the ideal cipher model in the first place, its security relies on the weak-pseudorandomness of the *whole* TOGA. More precisely, for the instantiation given in [33] based on CSIDH this results in an assumption close to the P-CSSDDH assumption first defined in [38, Definition 10]. Unfortunately, P-CSSDDH does not reduce to the standard Wk-PR of CSIDH since in P-CSSDDH additional torsion point information is revealed. Although the revealed information is not sufficient to apply the SIDH attacks [13,35,47], it makes the hardness of P-CSSDDH less well understood. Further, apart from CSIDH and its variations there is currently no other (post-quantum secure) instantiation of TOGA as its definition is rather dedicated to SiGamal. Lastly, the authors point out that their construction is malleable; thus, IND-UE-CCA security of TOGA-UE or an adaptation of it seems currently out of reach.

CCA SECURITY VIA ENCRYPT-AND-MAC. As of now, we do not have any post-quantum secure UE scheme that achieves IND-UE-CCA security. Klooß, Lehmann and Rupp [30] give a DDH-based UE scheme based on the Encrypt-and-MAC (E&M) paradigm. Their scheme combines the above-mentioned ElGamal encryption scheme with an updatable PRF based on the construction by Naor, Pinkas and Reingold [41]. Ignoring for now that we cannot use the same ElGamal approach as elaborated above, we want to point out that the updatable PRF requires hashing into the group (i.e., for group actions this would be the set), which, although a weaker requirement than being mappable [33], is still an open question for isogeny-based group actions [10]. Given that known lattice-based construction also do not achieve IND-UE-CCA security, we do not have any actively secure UE from post-quantum assumptions.

1.2 Our Contributions

We aim to overcome these difficulties and our goal is to construct detIND-UE-CCA secure UE from any (non-commutative) group action without requiring the group action to be mappable.

Our first construction, which we call BIN-UE, maps each bit of the message to a set element in a black-box way and then encrypts each bit under a different key. More specifically, for a key $k = (k_1, \cdots, k_n) \in \mathcal{G}^n$ and a message $M = (m_1, \ldots, m_n) \in \{0,1\}^n$, the encryption algorithm computes

$$\mathsf{BIN\text{-}UE.Enc}(k, M; (x_0, x_1)) := (k_1 \star x_{m_1}, \ldots, k_n \star x_{m_n}) \,,$$

where $x_0, x_1 \in \mathcal{X}$ are random set elements used as encryption randomness. Update tokens are of the form $\Delta_i = k_i^{\mathrm{new}} \cdot (k_i^{\mathrm{old}})^{-1}$ and applied to each element of the ciphertext individually. In order to allow for correct decryption, we will have to define an order on x_0 and x_1. We will explain the technicalities in Sect. 3, where we formally introduce the scheme. Apart from being applicable to non-mappable group actions like CSIDH [15], this approach comes with several additional advantages: First, we prove IND-UE-CPA security assuming that the group action is weakly pseudorandom, which is considered a standard assumption for CSIDH. Second, our proof does not require idealized models, that is, security holds in the *standard model*. This is a direct consequence of not needing a mappable group action. A natural disadvantage of the bit-wise approach is the large key size and overall efficiency of the scheme since both grow linearly in the bit-length of the messages. In group action based cryptography, however, this is a well understood and accepted compromise [1,2,6,8,23].

We then turn to constructing a scheme that satisfies IND-UE-CCA security, which is the main contribution of this paper. Our second scheme COM-UE extends BIN-UE via the Tag-then-Encrypt paradigm, where we encrypt messages of the form $(M, T) \in \{0,1\}^{n+t}$ with BIN-UE. This means a key is now $k \in \mathcal{G}^{n+t}$. More specifically, to encrypt a message $M \in \{0,1\}^n$ with randomness r, we compute the following:

$$\mathsf{COM\text{-}UE.Enc}(k, M; r) := \mathsf{BIN\text{-}UE.Enc}(k, M \| \mathsf{H}(M, r); r) \,,$$

where hash function H is used to compute the tag. The advantage is that updatability works exactly as in BIN-UE. In Sect. 4, we further elaborate on how this approach compares to the Encrypt-*and*-MAC construction of [30] and why Tag-*then*-Encrypt seems preferable here. While the composition is not secure in general [5], we prove that COM-UE is IND-UE-CCA secure under a new assumption and in the random oracle model. Our assumption Multi-St-UP is a non-standard and stronger variant of weak unpredictability for group actions [2]. In order to justify its hardness, we show that in the Algebraic Group Action Model (AGAM) [24], Multi-St-UP is implied by the Discrete Logarithm Problem with Auxilary Input [4]. Lastly, COM-UE has the same set of disadvantages as BIN-UE.

To summarize, we give the first UE scheme from group actions that satisfies IND-UE-CPA security from standard assumptions. Further, we get the first UE scheme that satisfies IND-UE-CCA security from post-quantum, however non-standard, assumptions.

1.3   Further Related Work

Ciphertext-*dependent* UE, as considered in [7,9,17,18,26], generates tokens for individual ciphertexts. While, in general, this allows for more efficient constructions, it requires the owner of the data to download (a part of) the ciphertext in order to generate the update token.

The *direction of updates* plays an important role in determining the impact of key and token corruptions. While our schemes have bi-directional updates, where the old key can be derived from the new key (and token) and vice versa, recent works have studied uni- and no-directional updates [28,29,42] and their relations. While these properties are desirable in terms of security guarantees, schemes are also notoriously harder to construct. This was studied in further detail by [28] who aim at constructing UE from PKE generically. They show how to construct bi-directional UE scheme from a key homomorphic PKE scheme. Then, to construct UE with no-directional updates[1], they require PKE with key and message homomorphism. In this construction, ciphertext and key sizes grow linearly in the number of epochs. A similar construction was given in [37]. Unfortunately, it is not clear how to construct a key and message homomorphic PKE from group actions since it would require to combine set elements. Further note that the only known construction in this setting which does not have growing ciphertexts and keys relies on the strong assumption of indistinguishability obfuscation [42].

A *constructive* and *composable* view on UE was taken in [27,34], respectively. Further, Slamanig and Striecks [49] study a stronger security definition with more *fine-grained forward secrecy* via expiry epochs.

Updatable MACs [19] are a useful tool to ensure ciphertext integrity in UE. Unfortunately, known group-based constructions require hashing into the group

---

[1] No-directional and backward-leak uni-directional updates are shown to be equivalent [28]. They provide strictly stronger security than bi-directional updates which have been shown to be equivalent to forward-leak unidirectional updates [29].

and thus, do not directly transfer to the group action setting. Extending UE with signed ciphertext was recently considered in [46].

Proxy re-encryption is a public-key primitive which enables to re-encrypt a ciphertext, encrypted to one party's public key, such that it can be decrypted by another party's secret key. Constructions and security models have been considered in [16,21,31,37,44,45] and also compared to the UE setting [21,31].

Updatable *public-key* encryption has been constructed from isogenies [25], however, the goal here is to update public and secret keys asynchronously (and not to update ciphertexts) to achieve forward secrecy in messaging applications.

2   Preliminaries

NOTATION. We denote by $\prec_{\mathsf{lex}}$ the lexicographical order. For integers m, n where $m < n$, $[m, n]$ denotes the set $\{m, m + 1, ..., n\}$. For $m = 1$, we simply write $[n]$. For a set S, $s \xleftarrow{\$} S$ denotes that s is sampled uniformly and independently at random from S. $y \leftarrow \mathcal{A}(x_1, x_2, ...)$ denotes that on input $x_1, x_2, ...$ the probabilistic algorithm $\mathcal{A}$ returns y. $\mathcal{A}^O$ denotes that algorithm $\mathcal{A}$ has access to oracle O. An adversary is a probabilistic algorithm. We will use game-based security notions, where $\Pr[G(\mathcal{A}) \Rightarrow 1]$ denotes the probability that the final output of game G running adversary $\mathcal{A}$ is 1. The notation $[\![X]\!]$ denotes a boolean test which returns 1 if the statement X is true and 0 otherwise.

2.1   Group Actions

We recall the definition of (restricted) effective group actions from [2], which provides an abstract framework to build cryptographic primitives relying on isogeny-based assumptions such as CSIDH.

Definition 1 (Group Action). *Let $(\mathcal{G}, \cdot)$ be a group with identity element $e \in \mathcal{G}$, and $\mathcal{X}$ a set. A map*

$$\star : \mathcal{G} \times \mathcal{X} \to \mathcal{X}$$

is a group action if it satisfies the following properties:

1. *Identity: $e \star x = x$ for all $x \in \mathcal{X}$.*
2. *Compatibility: $(g \cdot h) \star x = g \star (h \star x)$ for all $g, h \in \mathcal{G}$ and $x \in \mathcal{X}$.*

Remark 1. Throughout this paper, we assume the group action to be commutative and regular. The latter means that for any $x, y \in \mathcal{X}$ there exists precisely one $g \in \mathcal{G}$ satisfying $y = g \star x$.

Definition 2 (Effective Group Action). *Let $(\mathcal{G}, \mathcal{X}, \star)$ be a group action satisfying the following properties:*

1. *$\mathcal{G}$ is finite and there exist efficient (PPT) algorithms for membership testing, equality testing, (random) sampling, group operation and inversion.*
2. *The set $\mathcal{X}$ is finite and there exist efficient algorithms for membership testing and to compute a unique representation.*

Games $G_{\mathsf{EGA}}^{\mathsf{Wk\text{-}PR}\text{-}b}(\mathcal{A})$	Oracle SAMPLE
00 $g \xleftarrow{\$} \mathcal{G}$	03 $x, y \xleftarrow{\$} \mathcal{X}$
01 $b' \leftarrow \mathcal{A}^{\mathrm{SAMPLE}}$	04 if $b = 0$: return (x, y)
02 return b'	05 if $b = 1$: return $(x, g \star x)$

Fig. 1. Games $G_{\mathsf{EGA}}^{\mathsf{Wk\text{-}PR}\text{-}b}$, where $b \in \{0, 1\}$, capturing weak pseudorandomness of EGA.

3. *There exists a distinguished element $\tilde{x} \in \mathcal{X}$ with known representation.*
4. *There exists an efficient algorithm to evaluate the group action, i.e. to compute $g \star x$ given g and x.*

Then we call $\tilde{x} \in \mathcal{X}$ the origin and $(\mathcal{G}, \mathcal{X}, \star, \tilde{x})$ an effective group action (EGA).

Remark 2 (Mappable EGA). Recalling the definition of [33], a mappable effective group action comes with a bijection $\pi : \{0, 1\}^N \to \mathcal{X}$ such that $N = \log|\mathcal{X}|$. Since it is unclear whether such a mapping exists for isogeny-based group actions [10,39], we explicitly avoid making this assumption.

We will use the definition of weak pseudorandomness [2] which can be viewed as a multi-instance decisional Diffie-Hellman assumption for group actions.

Definition 3 (Weak Pseudorandomness). *Let* EGA $= (\mathcal{G}, \mathcal{X}, \star, \tilde{x})$ *be an effective group action. Consider the games $G_{\mathsf{EGA}}^{\mathsf{Wk\text{-}PR}\text{-}0}$ and $G_{\mathsf{EGA}}^{\mathsf{Wk\text{-}PR}\text{-}1}$ for an adversary $\mathcal{A}$ as defined in Fig. 1. We define the advantage of $\mathcal{A}$ in distinguishing the two games as*

$$\mathsf{Adv}_{\mathsf{EGA}}^{\mathsf{Wk\text{-}PR}}(\mathcal{A}) := |\Pr[G_{\mathsf{EGA}}^{\mathsf{Wk\text{-}PR}\text{-}1}(\mathcal{A}) \Rightarrow 1] - \Pr[G_{\mathsf{EGA}}^{\mathsf{Wk\text{-}PR}\text{-}0}(\mathcal{A}) \Rightarrow 1]|.$$

2.2 Updatable Encryption

We recall the definition of an updatable encryption scheme and security definitions from [11].

SYNTAX. An updatable encryption scheme UE for message space **M**, key space **K** and ciphertext space **C** consists of the following algorithms:

- KeyGen $\to k$: The key generation algorithm outputs a key $k \in \mathbf{K}$.
- Enc$(k, M) \to C$: On input a key $k \in \mathbf{K}$ and a message $M \in \mathbf{M}$, the encryption algorithm computes a ciphertext C.
- Dec$(k, C) \to \{M, \bot\}$: On input a key $k \in \mathbf{K}$ and a ciphertext $C \in \mathbf{C}$, the decryption algorithm outputs a message M or a special symbol $\bot$ indicating failure.
- TokenGen$(k, k') \to \Delta$: On input two keys $k, k' \in \mathbf{K}$, the token generation algorithm outputs an update token Δ.
- Upd$(\Delta, C) \to C'$: On input a token Δ and a ciphertext $C \in \mathbf{C}$, the update algorithm computes an updated ciphertext C'.

If a scheme is defined relative to some public parameters, we assume that they are implicit input to all algorithms. In this work, we only consider schemes where Dec, TokenGen and Upd are deterministic algorithms, which we will indicate accordingly when assigning outputs. Furthermore, we will sometimes make the encryption randomness and randomness space explicit and denote them with r and $\mathbf{R}$, respectively.

The execution of the scheme can be described by epochs. Each key and ciphertext belong to one epoch $e \in \mathbb{N}$ which we write as $k^{(e)}$ and $C^{(e)}$, respectively. A token $\Delta^{(e+1)}$ allows to update a ciphertext from epoch e to the next epoch $e+1$. For correctness, we ask that an updated ciphertext still decrypts correctly under the respective key. This is captured in the following definition.

Definition 4 (Correctness of UE). *Let* UE *be an updatable encryption scheme and $n_e \in \mathbb{N}$. We say that* UE *is perfectly correct if for any $M \in \mathbf{M}$, for $e \in [n_e - 1]$, it holds that*

$$\Pr[\mathsf{Dec}(k^{(n_e)}, C^{(n_e)}) = M] = 1 \,,$$

where

- $k^{(e)}, \dots, k^{(n_e)} \leftarrow \mathsf{KeyGen}$,
- $C^{(e)} \leftarrow \mathsf{Enc}(k^{(e)}, M)$, *and*
- $\Delta^{(i+1)} := \mathsf{TokenGen}(k^{(i)}, k^{(i+1)})$, $C^{(i+1)} := \mathsf{Upd}(\Delta^{(i+1)}, C^{(i)})$ *for $i \in [e, n_e - 1]$.*

We will use the security definitions for UE schemes with deterministic and bi-directional updates from [11]. Below, we describe and define three different games, capturing detIND-UE-CPA, detIND-UE-CCA and INT-CTXT security, respectively.

CONFIDENTIALITY. In the game $G_{\mathsf{UE}}^{\mathsf{detIND\text{-}UE\text{-}CPA\text{-}}b}$ (cf. Fig. 2), which is parameterized by $b \in \{0, 1\}$, the adversary $\mathcal{A}$ has access to a (non-challenge) encryption oracle ENC, a challenge oracle CHALL, an oracle NEXT to proceed to the next epoch, an update oracle UPD, an update oracle for challenges UPD$\tilde{C}$ and corruption oracles CORRKEY and CORRTOKEN to reveal keys and tokens, respectively.

At the beginning of the game, an initial key $k^{(0)}$ is drawn. The game then initializes variables: an epoch counter e, an encryption counter c, a challenge flag chall and empty sets $(\mathcal{L}, \tilde{\mathcal{L}}, \mathcal{C}, \mathcal{K}, \mathcal{T})$, where

- Set $\mathcal{L}$ stores non-challenge ciphertexts produced by ENC or UPD. It records tuples of the form (c, C, e). Oracle UPD only updates ciphertexts in $\mathcal{L}$.
- Set $\tilde{\mathcal{L}}$ stores the challenge ciphertext and updated versions of it. The first entry will always be the challenge ciphertext $\tilde{C}$ together with the epoch $\tilde{e}$. Any call to NEXT automatically updates the challenge ciphertext into the new epoch, which $\mathcal{A}$ can fetch via UPD$\tilde{C}$.
- Set $\mathcal{C}$ stores all epochs in which $\mathcal{A}$ learned an updated version of the challenge ciphertext.
- Set $\mathcal{K}$ stores all epochs in which $\mathcal{A}$ corrupted the secret key.
- Set $\mathcal{T}$ stores epochs in which $\mathcal{A}$ corrupted the update token.

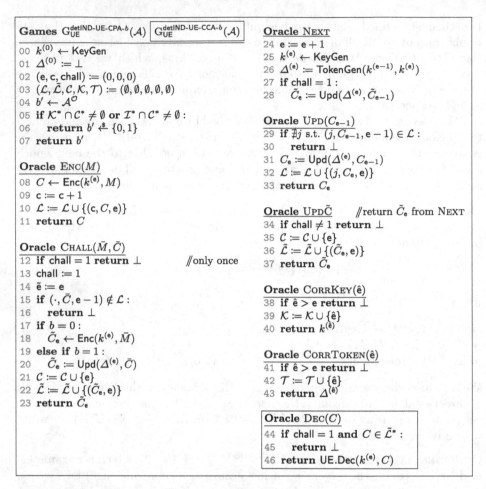

Fig. 2. Games $G_{UE}^{detIND-UE-CPA-b}$ (without code in boxes) and $G_{UE}^{detIND-UE-CCA-b}$ (including code in boxes), where $b \in \{0,1\}$ and adversary $\mathcal{A}$ has access to oracles $\mathcal{O} := \{ENC, CHALL, NEXT, UPD, UPD\tilde{C}, CORRKEY, CORRTOKEN\}$. In $G_{UE}^{detIND-UE-CCA-b}$, $\mathcal{A}$ additionally has access to oracle DEC. The definition of sets $\mathcal{K}^*, \mathcal{C}^*, \mathcal{I}^*$ and $\tilde{\mathcal{L}}^*$ to prevent trivial wins is given in the textual description.

The challenge oracle CHALL takes as input a message $\bar{M}$ and a ciphertext $\bar{C}$ such that the ciphertext was the output of a query to ENC from the previous epoch. Then, depending on the bit b, the game either computes a fresh encryption of $\bar{M}$ or an update of ciphertext $\bar{C}$. As shown in [11], this captures indistinguishability of ciphertexts as well as unlinkability of updates at the same time. All oracles can be queried adaptively and multiple times, except the challenge oracle which may only be queried once.

At some point, $\mathcal{A}$ stops and outputs a bit b'. The game checks whether $\mathcal{A}$ could have trivially learned the bit based on its queries and the inferred knowledge. In order to perform the check, the following sets need to be computed:

- Set $\mathcal{K}^*$ contains all epochs for which the adversary corrupted the key or learned the key via a token. Here, it is important to note that we look at bi-directional updates, meaning the knowledge of a key $k^{(e)}$ and tokens $\Delta^{(e)}, \Delta^{(e+1)}$ allows to compute both $k^{(e-1)}, k^{(e+1)}$. More formally, the set $\mathcal{K}^*$ is defined as $\mathcal{K}^* := \{e \in [0, n] \mid \mathsf{CorrK}(e) = \mathbf{true}\}$, where

$$\mathsf{CorrK}(e) = \mathbf{true} \iff (e \in \mathcal{K}) \vee (\mathsf{CorrK}(e-1) \wedge e \in \mathcal{T})$$
$$\vee (\mathsf{CorrK}(e+1) \wedge e+1 \in \mathcal{T}).$$

- Set $\mathcal{T}^*$ contains all epochs for which the adversary corrupted the token or learned the token via a key. For this note that bi-directional updates allow to compute a token $\Delta^{(e)}$ from keys $k^{(e-1)}$ and $k^{(e)}$, where we additionally consider keys contained in $\mathcal{K}^*$. More formally, we define the set of tokens as $\mathcal{T}^* := \{e \in [0, n] \mid (e \in \mathcal{T}) \vee (e \in \mathcal{K}^* \wedge e-1 \in \mathcal{K}^*)\}$.
- Set $\mathcal{C}^*$ contains the challenge epoch as well as all epochs for which the adversary knows updated versions of the challenge ciphertext. Since we consider deterministic updates, the knowledge of a ciphertext $\tilde{C}_e$ along with tokens $\Delta^{(e)}, \Delta^{(e+1)}$ allows to compute both corresponding ciphertexts $\tilde{C}_{e-1}$ and $\tilde{C}_{e+1}$. More formally, $\mathcal{C}^* := \{e \in [0, n] \mid \mathsf{ChallEq}(e) = \mathbf{true}\}$, where

$$\mathsf{ChallEq}(e) = \mathbf{true} \iff (e \in \mathcal{C}) \vee (\mathsf{ChallEq}(e-1) \wedge e \in \mathcal{T}^*)$$
$$\vee (\mathsf{ChallEq}(e+1) \wedge e+1 \in \mathcal{T}^*).$$

Let c be the counter value for the ciphertext used in the challenge and was previously output by ENC. In the following, we will denote this ciphertext as the challenge-input ciphertext. We define the two following sets:

- Set $\mathcal{I}$ contains the epoch in which the challenge-input ciphertext was first created and all epochs for which the adversary learned updates of the challenge-input ciphertext via UPD. More formally, $\mathcal{I} := \{e \in [0, n] \mid (\mathsf{c}, \cdot, e) \in \mathcal{L}\}$.
- Set $\mathcal{I}^*$ contains $\mathcal{I}$ and all epochs for which the adversary has inferred knowledge about the challenge-input ciphertext via corrupted tokens (similar to $\mathcal{C}^*$). More formally, $\mathcal{I}^* := \{e \in [0, n] \mid \mathsf{ChallinputEq}(e) = \mathbf{true}\}$, where

$$\mathsf{ChallinputEq}(e) = \mathbf{true} \iff (e \in \mathcal{I}) \vee (\mathsf{ChallinputEq}(e-1) \wedge e \in \mathcal{T}^*)$$
$$\vee (\mathsf{ChallinputEq}(e+1) \wedge e+1 \in \mathcal{T}^*).$$

Finally, in order to prevent trivial attacks, the game checks whether $\mathcal{K}^* \cap \mathcal{C}^* = \emptyset$ and $\mathcal{I}^* \cap \mathcal{C}^* = \emptyset$. If both checks succeed, the game returns $\mathcal{A}$'s output b' and otherwise it returns a random bit $b' \xleftarrow{\$} \{0, 1\}$.

When considering active security in the sense of detIND-UE-CCA, the game additionally provides access to a decryption oracle DEC which allows to decrypt any ciphertext, except for the challenge ciphertext and updated versions of it. In order to detect trivial wins, we use set $\tilde{\mathcal{L}}^*$ which is updated when the challenge query is issued and when the challenge ciphertext is updated. In the full version of the paper [36] we recall the algorithm to update $\tilde{\mathcal{L}}^*$ as given in [11].

We now formally define the advantage of an adversary $\mathcal{A}$ in these games.

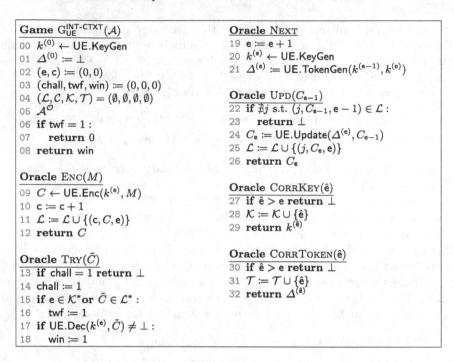

Game $G_{UE}^{INT\text{-}CTXT}(\mathcal{A})$

00 $k^{(0)} \leftarrow$ UE.KeyGen
01 $\Delta^{(0)} := \bot$
02 $(e, c) := (0, 0)$
03 $(chall, twf, win) := (0, 0, 0)$
04 $(\mathcal{L}, \mathcal{C}, \mathcal{K}, \mathcal{T}) = (\emptyset, \emptyset, \emptyset, \emptyset)$
05 $\mathcal{A}^{\mathcal{O}}$
06 **if** $twf = 1$:
07   **return** 0
08 **return** win

Oracle ENC(M)

09 $C \leftarrow$ UE.Enc$(k^{(e)}, M)$
10 $c := c + 1$
11 $\mathcal{L} := \mathcal{L} \cup \{(c, C, e)\}$
12 **return** C

Oracle TRY$(\tilde{C})$

13 **if** $chall = 1$ **return** $\bot$
14 $chall := 1$
15 **if** $e \in \mathcal{K}^*$ **or** $\tilde{C} \in \mathcal{L}^*$:
16     $twf := 1$
17 **if** UE.Dec$(k^{(e)}, \tilde{C}) \neq \bot$:
18     $win := 1$

Oracle NEXT

19 $e := e + 1$
20 $k^{(e)} \leftarrow$ UE.KeyGen
21 $\Delta^{(e)} :=$ UE.TokenGen$(k^{(e-1)}, k^{(e)})$

Oracle UPD(C_{e-1})

22 **if** $\nexists j$ s.t. $(j, C_{e-1}, e-1) \in \mathcal{L}$:
23   **return** $\bot$
24 $C_e :=$ UE.Update$(\Delta^{(e)}, C_{e-1})$
25 $\mathcal{L} := \mathcal{L} \cup \{(j, C_e, e)\}$
26 **return** C_e

Oracle CORRKEY$(\hat{e})$

27 **if** $\hat{e} > e$ **return** $\bot$
28 $\mathcal{K} := \mathcal{K} \cup \{\hat{e}\}$
29 **return** $k^{(\hat{e})}$

Oracle CORRTOKEN$(\hat{e})$

30 **if** $\hat{e} > e$ **return** $\bot$
31 $\mathcal{T} := \mathcal{T} \cup \{\hat{e}\}$
32 **return** $\Delta^{(\hat{e})}$

Fig. 3. The INT-CTXT security game for an updatable encryption scheme UE. Adversary $\mathcal{A}$ has access to oracles $\mathcal{O} = \{$ENC, NEXT, UPD, CORRKEY, CORRTOKEN, TRY$\}$.

Definition 5 (detIND-UE-CPA/CCA Security). *Let* XXX $\in \{$CPA, CCA$\}$ *and consider the games* $G_{UE}^{detIND\text{-}UE\text{-}XXX\text{-}0}$ *and* $G_{UE}^{detIND\text{-}UE\text{-}XXX\text{-}1}$ *for an updatable encryption scheme* UE *and an adversary* $\mathcal{A}$ *as defined in Fig. 2. We define the advantage of* $\mathcal{A}$ *in distinguishing the two games as*

$$\mathsf{Adv}_{UE}^{detIND\text{-}UE\text{-}XXX}(\mathcal{A}) := |\Pr[G_{UE}^{detIND\text{-}UE\text{-}XXX\text{-}1}(\mathcal{A}) \Rightarrow 1]$$
$$- \Pr[G_{UE}^{detIND\text{-}UE\text{-}XXX\text{-}0}(\mathcal{A}) \Rightarrow 1]| .$$

CIPHERTEXT INTEGRITY. In Fig. 3, we define the ciphertext integrity game. The game is similar to the confidentiality games, providing the adversary access to an encryption oracle ENC, an oracle NEXT to proceed to the next epoch, an update oracle UPD and corruption oracles CORRKEY and CORRTOKEN. We do not need a challenge oracle or challenge-update oracle. Instead, the task in this game is to produce a non-trivial ciphertext $\tilde{C}$ such that $\tilde{C}$ decrypts successfully. Here, non-trivial refers to the fact that $\tilde{C}$ must not have been an output of ENC or UPD. As in the previous game, we also need to take into account the (inferred) knowledge through key and token corruptions. This is captured in oracle TRY, where we use the sets $\mathcal{K}^*$ and $\mathcal{L}^*$. In the full version of the paper [36], we recall the algorithm how to compute $\mathcal{L}^*$, as given in [11]. Note that we only allow one query to TRY, as captured by the INT-CTXT^S notion in [11], which is equivalent to a version with multiple TRY queries. We now define INT-CTXT security as follows.

Definition 6 (INT-CTXTSecurity). *Consider the game* $G_{UE}^{INT\text{-}CTXT}$ *for an updatable encryption scheme* UE *and an adversary* $\mathcal{A}$ *as defined in Fig. 3. We define the advantage of* $\mathcal{A}$ *in winning the game as*

$$\mathsf{Adv}_{UE}^{INT\text{-}CTXT}(\mathcal{A}) := \Pr[G_{UE}^{INT\text{-}CTXT}(\mathcal{A}) \Rightarrow 1] \ .$$

Finally, we recall the statement from [11] showing that detIND-UE-CPA and INT-CTXT together imply detIND-UE-CCA.

Theorem 1 (Theorem 3 in [11]). *Let* UE *be an updatable encryption scheme. For any adversary* $\mathcal{A}$ *against the* detIND-UE-CCA *security of* UE *there exist adversaries* $\mathcal{B}, \mathcal{C}$ *against the* detIND-UE-CPA *and* INT-CTXT *security of* UE *such that*

$$\mathsf{Adv}_{UE}^{detIND\text{-}UE\text{-}CCA}(\mathcal{A}) \leq 2 \cdot \mathsf{Adv}_{UE}^{INT\text{-}CTXT}(\mathcal{B}) + \mathsf{Adv}_{UE}^{detIND\text{-}UE\text{-}CPA}(\mathcal{C}) \ ,$$

where the running times of $\mathcal{B}$ *and* $\mathcal{C}$ *are about that of* $\mathcal{A}$.

3   UE from Non-mappable Group Actions

In this section, we construct a new updatable encryption scheme called BIN-UE. Its main advantage is that BIN-UE does not require the group action to be mappable, making it possible to instantiate BIN-UE from plain CSIDH. Furthermore, its security relies on a standard assumption.

We define BIN-UE in Fig. 4. On a high level, the bits of a message are encoded into the index of two basis elements $x_0, x_1 \in \mathcal{X}$. These basis elements are chosen randomly for each encryption, which eliminates the need for either a nonce or an ideal cipher to ensure detIND-UE-CPA security. For n-bit messages, the encryption key consists of n group elements. Each bit is then encrypted individually by applying a group element to one of the basis elements.

Decryption of a message first inverts the group action and subsequently detects whether the resulting element is x_0 or x_1. Of course, without further constraints it is a priori not clear which basis element was used for the 0-bit, which is why we sort the basis elements lexicographically and use the smaller one (according to $\prec_{lex}$) for the 0-bit. To prevent decryption failures, we set the message space to be $\mathbf{M} := \{0,1\}^n \setminus \{0^n, 1^n\}$ as otherwise the messages 0^n and 1^n would be indistinguishable.

Proposition 1. *The* BIN-UE *scheme is perfectly correct.*

Proof. Let $M = (m_1, \ldots, m_n) \in \mathbf{M}$ be an arbitrary message, $k^{(0)}, k^{(1)} \leftarrow$ UE.KeyGen be two epoch keys for adjacent epochs. We show that

$$\Pr[\mathsf{UE.Dec}(k^{(1)}, C^{(1)}) = M] = 1$$

for $C^{(1)} := \mathsf{UE.Update}(\Delta^{(1)}, C^{(0)})$, $\Delta^{(1)} := \mathsf{UE.TokenGen}(k^{(0)}, k^{(1)})$ and $C^{(0)} \leftarrow \mathsf{UE.Enc}(k^{(0)}, M)$. The general case of non-adjacent epochs then follows via induction. $\square$

```
BIN-UE.KeyGen                          BIN-UE.TokenGen(k, k')
00 k := (k_1, ..., k_n) ⟸$ G^n         09 Let k = (k_1, ..., k_n) and k' = (k'_1, ..., k'_n)
01 return k                            10 return Δ := (k'_1 k_1^{-1}, ..., k'_n k_n^{-1})

BIN-UE.Update(C, Δ)                    BIN-UE.Dec(k, C)
02 Let Δ = (Δ_1, ..., Δ_n)             11 Let C = (c_1, ..., c_n) and k = (k_1, ..., k_n)
   and C = (c_1, ..., c_n)             12 for i ∈ [n] :
03 return (Δ_1 ⋆ c_1, ..., Δ_n ⋆ c_n)  13    x_i = k_i^{-1} ⋆ c_i
                                       14 if |{x_1, ..., x_n}| = 2 :
BIN-UE.Enc(k, M)                       15    Let {x̃_0, x̃_1} = {x_1, ..., x_n} and x̃_0 ≺_lex x̃_1
04 Let M = (m_1, ..., m_n)             16    for i ∈ [n] :
05 x_0, x_1 ⟸$ X     // x_0 ≺_lex x_1  17       m_i := [[x_i = x̃_1]]
06 for i ∈ [n] :                       18    return M := (m_1, ..., m_n)
07    c_i := k_i ⋆ x_{m_i}             19 return ⊥
08 return c := (c_1, ..., c_n)
```

Fig. 4. The updatable encryption scheme BIN-UE.

First, we have that

$$C^{(0)} = (C_1^{(0)}, ..., C_n^{(0)}) = (k_1^{(0)} \star x_{m_1}, ... k^{(0)} \star x_{m_n})$$

for two random set elements $x_0, x_1 \in \mathcal{X}$ with $x_0 \prec_{\text{lex}} x_1$. Essentially, we encode a bit with either the (lexicographically) larger or smaller set element. Updating the ciphertext with the token $\Delta^{(1)}$ then becomes

$$C^{(1)} = (\Delta_1^{(1)} \star C_1^{(0)}, ..., \Delta_n^{(1)} \star C_n^{(0)}) = (k_1^{(1)} \star x_{m_1}, ... k_n^{(1)} \star x_{m_n})$$

because for each entry $\Delta_i^{(1)} \cdot k_i^{(0)} = k_i^{(1)}(k_i^{(0)})^{-1} \cdot k_i^{(0)} = k_i^{(1)}$. Lastly, decrypting $C^{(1)}$ with $k^{(1)}$ yields

$$((k_1^{(1)})^{-1} \star C_1^{(1)}, ..., (k_n^{(1)})^{-1} \star C_n^{(1)}) = (x_{m_1}, ..., x_{m_n})$$

Note that since **M** does not contain the bit strings 0^n and 1^n the above tuple contains exactly two distinct set elements. We are now left with detecting at each position whether the element x_{m_i} is the (lexicographically) larger or smaller element, yielding the desired bitstring $M = (m_1, ..., m_n)$.   □

3.1   Security

In this section, we establish the security of BIN-UE. To this end, we introduce the following hardness assumption.

Definition 7 (Multi Strong Pseudorandomness (Multi-St-PR)). *Let* EGA $= (\mathcal{G}, \mathcal{X}, \star, \tilde{x})$ *and let* $n \in \mathbb{N}$. *Consider the game defined in Fig. 5. We define the advantage of an adversary $\mathcal{A}$ winning the* Multi-St-PR *game as*

$$\text{Adv}_{\text{EGA}}^{\text{Multi-St-PR}}(\mathcal{A}) := |\Pr[\text{G}_{\text{EGA}}^{\text{Multi-St-PR-1}}(\mathcal{A}) \Rightarrow 1] - \Pr[\text{G}_{\text{EGA}}^{\text{Multi-St-PR-0}}(\mathcal{A}) \Rightarrow 1]| .$$

Games $G_{\mathsf{EGA}}^{\mathsf{Multi\text{-}St\text{-}PR}\text{-}b}(\mathcal{A})$	Oracle $\mathrm{EVAL}(\beta \in \{0,1\}^n)$
00 $g_1, \ldots, g_n \xleftarrow{\$} \mathcal{G}$	03 $x_0, x_1, y_1, \ldots, y_n \xleftarrow{\$} \mathcal{X}$ $\quad$ //$x_0 \prec_{\mathsf{lex}} x_1$
01 $b' \leftarrow \mathcal{A}^{\mathrm{EVAL}}$	04 if $b = 0$:
02 return b'	05 $\quad$ return $(x_0, x_1, y_1, \ldots, y_n)$
	06 if $b = 1$:
	07 $\quad$ return $(x_0, x_1, g_1 \star x_{\beta_1}, \ldots, g_n \star x_{\beta_n})$

Fig. 5. Games $G_{\mathsf{EGA}}^{\mathsf{Multi\text{-}St\text{-}PR}\text{-}b}$ for EGA, where $b \in \{0,1\}$.

Hybrid $\mathsf{H}_i(\mathcal{A})$	Oracle $\mathrm{EVAL}(\beta)$
00 $g_1, \ldots, g_n \xleftarrow{\$} \mathcal{G}$	03 $x_0, x_1, y_1, \ldots, y_n \xleftarrow{\$} \mathcal{X}$ $\quad$ //$x_0 \prec_{\mathsf{lex}} x_1$
01 $b' \leftarrow \mathcal{A}^{\mathrm{EVAL}}$	04 return $(x_0, x_1, g_1 \star x_{\beta_1}, \ldots, g_i \star x_{\beta_i}, y_{i+1}, \ldots, y_n)$
02 return b'	

Fig. 6. The i-th hybrid.

Remark 3. The restriction that $x_0 \prec_{\mathsf{lex}} x_1$ is without loss of generality. More concretely, one could reduce the "sorted" variant of Multi-St-PR to an "unsorted" variant by just querying the unsorted EVAL oracle until the output elements are sorted (which happens with probability $1/2$). Note that an adversary can query EVAL multiple times on the same input.

Remark 4. In contrast to the definition of **M**, we do not require $\beta \neq 0^n, 1^n$ as it does not affect the reduction to the detIND-UE-CPA security of BIN-UE.

Although Multi-St-PR appears non-standard at first, we show that it reduces to the standard Wk-PR assumption.

Proposition 2 (Wk-PR $\Rightarrow$ Multi-St-PR). *Let* EGA $= (\mathcal{G}, \mathcal{X}, \star, \tilde{x})$. *For any adversary $\mathcal{A}$ against Multi-St-PR of EGA, there exists an adversary $\mathcal{B}$ against Wk-PR of EGA such that*

$$\mathsf{Adv}_{\mathsf{EGA}}^{\mathsf{Multi\text{-}St\text{-}PR}}(\mathcal{A}) \leq n \cdot \mathsf{Adv}_{\mathsf{EGA}}^{\mathsf{Wk\text{-}PR}}(\mathcal{B})$$

where n is defined as in Fig. 5 and the running time of $\mathcal{B}$ is about that of $\mathcal{A}$.

Proof. We prove the statement via a hybrid argument where in each hybrid we embed the Wk-PR challenge at one position in the Multi-St-PR tuple.

Let $\mathsf{H}_0, \ldots, \mathsf{H}_n$ be hybrids where H_i is then defined as in Fig. 6. It is clear that $\mathsf{H}_0 = G_{\mathsf{EGA}}^{\mathsf{Multi\text{-}St\text{-}PR}\text{-}0}$ and $\mathsf{H}_n = G_{\mathsf{EGA}}^{\mathsf{Multi\text{-}St\text{-}PR}\text{-}1}$. We now show that for any adversary $\mathcal{A}$ that distinguishes two adjacent hybrids there exists an adversary $\mathcal{B}$ against Wk-PR such that

$$|\Pr[\mathsf{H}_{i-1}(\mathcal{A}) \Rightarrow 1] - \Pr[\mathsf{H}_i(\mathcal{A}) \Rightarrow 1]| \leq \mathsf{Adv}_{\mathsf{EGA}}^{\mathsf{Wk\text{-}PR}}(\mathcal{B}).$$

Consider the reduction in Fig. 7. Evidently, if the oracle SAMPLE returns tuples of the form $(x, g \star x)$ for uniformly random $x \in \mathcal{X}$ and some fixed $g \in \mathcal{G}$, then $\mathcal{B}$

Adversary $\mathcal{B}^{\text{SAMPLE}}$	Oracle EVAL(β)	
00 $g_1, \ldots, g_{i-1} \xleftarrow{\$} \mathcal{G}$	03 $(x_0, y_0) \leftarrow$ SAMPLE	$/\!/ y_i = g \star x_i$ or $y_i \xleftarrow{\$} \mathcal{X}$
01 $b' \leftarrow \mathcal{A}^{\text{EVAL}}$	04 $(x_1, y_1) \leftarrow$ SAMPLE	$/\!/ $w.l.o.g. $x_0 \prec_{\text{lex}} x_1$
02 return b'	05 $y_{i+1}, \ldots, y_n \xleftarrow{\$} \mathcal{X}$	
	06 if $\beta_i = 0$:	
	07 $\tilde{y} := y_0$	
	08 else :	
	09 $\tilde{y} := y_1$	
	10 return $(x_0, x_1, g_1 \star x_{\beta_1}, \ldots, g_{i-1} \star x_{\beta_{i-1}}, \tilde{y}, y_{i+1}, \ldots, y_n)$	

Fig. 7. Adversary $\mathcal{B}$ for the proof of Proposition 2, simulating either the hybrid H_{i-1} or H_i to $\mathcal{A}$.

perfectly simulates H_i. Likewise, if SAMPLE returns tuples of the form (x, y) for uniformly random $x, y \in \mathcal{X}$, then $\mathcal{B}$ perfectly simulates H_{i-1}. Finally,

$$
\begin{aligned}
\mathsf{Adv}_{\mathsf{EGA}}^{\mathsf{Multi\text{-}St\text{-}PR}}(\mathcal{A}) &= |\Pr[\mathsf{G}^{\mathsf{Multi\text{-}St\text{-}PR\text{-}1}}(\mathcal{A}) \Rightarrow 1] - \Pr[\mathsf{G}^{\mathsf{Multi\text{-}St\text{-}PR\text{-}0}}(\mathcal{A}) \Rightarrow 1]| \\
&= |\Pr[\mathrm{H}_0(\mathcal{A}) \Rightarrow 1] - \Pr[\mathrm{H}_n(\mathcal{A}) \Rightarrow 1]| \\
&\leq \sum_{i=1}^{n} |\Pr[\mathrm{H}_{i-1}(\mathcal{A}) \Rightarrow 1] - \Pr[\mathrm{H}_i(\mathcal{A}) \Rightarrow 1]| \\
&= n \cdot \mathsf{Adv}_{\mathsf{EGA}}^{\mathsf{Wk\text{-}PR}}(\mathcal{B}) ,
\end{aligned}
$$

which concludes the proof.   □

We are now ready to establish the passive security of BIN-UE. We highlight that no ideal cipher is necessary to prove detIND-UE-CPA security of BIN-UE. Intuitively, the reason for this is that the definition of Multi-St-PR allows the adversary to supply the value β to the EVAL oracle. As we showed in the previous reduction this does not weaken the hardness of Multi-St-PR as it is essentially as hard as Wk-PR (up to a tightness loss). In the detIND-UE-CPA proof, however, this allows the reduction to directly forward messages to the EVAL oracle without needing to program an ideal cipher to ensure consistent randomness.

Theorem 2. *Let* BIN-UE *be the scheme described in Fig. 4. For any adversary* $\mathcal{A}$ *against the* detIND-UE-CPA *security of* BIN-UE*, there exists an adversary* $\mathcal{B}$ *against* Wk-PR *such that*

$$
\mathsf{Adv}_{\mathsf{BIN\text{-}UE}}^{\mathsf{detIND\text{-}UE\text{-}CPA}}(\mathcal{A}) \leq 2n(n_{\mathsf{e}} + 1)^3 \cdot \mathsf{Adv}_{\mathsf{EGA}}^{\mathsf{Wk\text{-}PR}}(\mathcal{B}) ,
$$

where n_{e} *is the number of epochs and* n *is the length of a message in bits. The running time of* $\mathcal{B}$ *is about that of* $\mathcal{A}$.

We use the same proof technique as [11,33], that is, a hybrid argument across insulated regions. Due to the strong similarities with the security proofs for GAINE and SHINE we defer the full proof to the full version of the paper [36] and provide a proof sketch below.

In each hybrid, we embed our challenge on the left boundary of the insulated region, also called the left *firewall*. Outside the insulated region, all keys and tokens are generated honestly, while inside the insulated region, tokens are simulated without knowing the corresponding keys. This allows to answer queries to both UPD and UPD$\tilde{C}$. Fresh ciphertexts are randomized using the "basis" elements x_0, x_1, eliminating the need for a nonce. Since in the Multi-St-PR game the adversary can control the bit string β, we do not need a programmable ideal cipher in order to embed messages into ciphertexts. Lastly, we note that updates are deterministic.

We give a reduction $\mathcal{B}$ which plays the Multi-St-PR game and perfectly simulates the i-th hybrid to $\mathcal{A}$ if the oracle EVAL returns "real" tuples (i.e. $b = 1$) and a random game otherwise. More specifically, the values $g_1 \star x_{\beta_1}, \ldots, g_n \star x_{\beta_n}$ returned by the EVAL oracle will be used as the ciphertext of a message $M = (\beta_1, \ldots, \beta_n)$. Therefore, we embed the elements $g_1, \ldots, g_n$ into the key of the chosen challenge epoch. Lastly, if the adversary $\mathcal{A}$ can correctly distinguish between an update and a fresh encryption, we assume that EVAL returns "real" tuples. On the other hand if the EVAL oracle returns random tuples, all encryptions and updates are truly random as well, making it impossible to distinguish an update from a fresh encryption.

3.2 Instantiation from CSIDH

CSIDH [15] is a popular cryptographic group action based on isogenies between supersingular elliptic curves over $\mathbb{F}_p$. Although CSIDH has many useful properties, it has the disadvantage of not being a *mappable* group action. Fortunately, BIN-UE does not require the group action to be mappable, which means it can be instantiated from plain CSIDH. Note that in contrast to many other (noncommutative) group actions [20], CSIDH is believed to be weakly pseudorandom, even in the post-quantum setting [14].

On the Performance of Updates. Because CSIDH is in general a *restricted* effective group action (see the full version of the paper [36]), computing an update token is very expensive. The reason is that any component $k_i^{(e)}$ of an epoch key is an element of the group $\mathcal{G}$, which is generated by the elements $(g_1, \ldots, g_\nu)$. Since the group action can only be efficiently evaluated for the elements $(g_1, \ldots, g_\nu)$ one therefore writes $k_i^{(e)}$ as a product

$$k_i^{(e)} = \prod_{j=1}^{\nu} g_j^{m_j}$$

for some exponents $m_j \in \mathbb{Z}$. For performance reasons, one further assumes that the m_j are coming from a small interval $[-\delta, \delta]$. This, however, means that a product $k_i^{(e+1)} \cdot (k_i^{(e)})^{-1}$ could result in exponents larger than $\pm\delta$. It is therefore necessary to reduce each element $k_i^{(e+1)} \cdot (k_i^{(e)})^{-1}$ modulo the so-called *lattice of relations* to get a short representation [6]. Unfortunately, a good basis for the lattice of relations is unknown in general (apart from the CSIDH-512 parameter set) and takes subexponential time to compute. Furthermore, even under the knowledge of a basis for the lattice of relation, the reduction essentially consists of a CVP instance which, depending on the quality of the lattice basis, takes subexponential time to solve asymptotically as well.

Recent developments like the SCALLOP group action [22] try to mitigate this issue, however, these alternatives are currently not practical as a single group action evaluation takes minutes to compute. Furthermore, the recently introduced group action CLAPOTIS [43] promises to be a proper EGA, however a complete description of the group action, a security analysis as well as performance results are currently not available. Lastly, we remark that the above performance issues and their possible mitigations also apply to GAINE and TOGA-UE [33].

4   An Actively Secure Variant

In this section, we introduce a generic transformation inspired by the *Tag-then-Encrypt* paradigm [40]. Although detIND-UE-CCA security of this transformation does not hold in general [5], we show that by applying the transformation to BIN-UE we get a new scheme called COM-UE that can indeed be proven detIND-UE-CCA secure in the random oracle model. The proof requires a non-standard assumption, however, we further show that in the AGAM [24] this assumption can be reduced to a variant of the group action discrete logarithm problem.

4.1   The Tag-then-Encrypt Transformation

We start by stating two important properties of an updatable encryption scheme that are needed for the transformation. To this end, let us recall the definitions of randomness-preserving and randomness-recoverable updatable encryption schemes [30].

Definition 8 (Randomness-Preserving UE). *Let* UE = (UE.KeyGen, UE.Enc, UE.Dec, UE.TokenGen, UE.Update) *be an updatable encryption scheme. Further, let* $r \in \mathbf{R}$ *be the explicit randomness of* UE.Enc, *i. e.,*

$$\mathsf{UE.Enc}(k, M) = \mathsf{UE.Enc}(k, M; r) \ .$$

The scheme is called randomness-preserving (RP) *if for all keys* $k, k' \xleftarrow{\$}$ UE.KeyGen, *tokens* $\Delta := \mathsf{UE.TokenGen}(k, k')$ *and messages* $M \in \mathbf{M}$ *we have*

$$\mathsf{UE.Update}(\Delta, \mathsf{UE.Enc}(k, M; r)) = \mathsf{UE.Enc}(k', M; r) \ .$$

Definition 9 (Randomness-Recoverable Updatable Encryption). *Let the notation be as in the previous definition. A scheme* UE *is called* randomness-recoverable (RR) *if for all keys* $k \xleftarrow{\$}$ UE.KeyGen, *messages* $M \in \mathbf{M}$ *and randomness* $r \in \mathbf{R}$:

$$\mathsf{UE.Dec}(k, \mathsf{UE.Enc}(k, M; r)) = (M, r) \ .$$

If UE fulfills both Definitions 8 and 9, then we say that UE is an RP/RR scheme or simply RP/RR for short. Evidently, BIN-UE is RP/RR with encryption randomness $r = (x_0, x_1)$.

The Transformation. Let UE = (UE.KeyGen, UE.Enc, UE.Dec, UE.TokenGen, UE.Update) be an RP/RR updatable encryption scheme with a message space that can be written as $\mathbf{M} = \mathbf{M}^+ \times \{0,1\}^t$ and randomness space $\mathbf{R}$. Further let H : $\mathbf{M}^+ \times \mathbf{R} \rightarrow \{0,1\}^t$ be a cryptographic hash function. We define a new scheme $\mathsf{UE}^+ = (\mathsf{UE.KeyGen}, \mathsf{UE}^+.\mathsf{Enc}, \mathsf{UE}^+.\mathsf{Dec}, \mathsf{UE.TokenGen}, \mathsf{UE.Update})$ that is identical to UE except for:

- The message space is $\mathbf{M}^+$.
- $\mathsf{UE}^+.\mathsf{Enc}(k, M; r)$: Compute $M' = (M \| \mathsf{H}(M, r))$ and subsequently return $C = \mathsf{UE.Enc}(k, M'; r)$.
- $\mathsf{UE}^+.\mathsf{Dec}(k, C)$: Compute $(M', r) = \mathsf{UE.Dec}(k, C)$ and parse M' as $(M \| T)$. If $T = \mathsf{H}(M, r)$ then output M, else output $\perp$.

Evidently, the transformation only applies a preprocessing on the message M and therefore does not fundamentally change the way encryption and decryption work. Thus, UE^+ inherits correctness and detIND-UE-CPA security directly from the underlying scheme UE.

Lemma 1. *The following statements hold:*

- *If UE is (perfectly) correct, then UE^+ is also (perfectly) correct.*
- *If UE is detIND-UE-CPA secure, then UE^+ is also detIND-UE-CPA secure.*

Remark 5. Making the encryption randomness implicitly accessible to the adversary via the tag does not weaken security. In fact, for any RP/RR scheme an adversary can learn the randomness of a ciphertext by issuing a key corrupt followed by a regular decryption. When transitioning to the next epoch (which might be the challenge epoch) this randomness is preserved. This is, however, not problematic as the existing security proofs for schemes like GAINE, SHINE and BIN-UE show.

4.2 A Full Description of COM-UE

By applying the transformation from Sect. 4.1 to BIN-UE we get a new scheme called COM-UE which is formally defined in Fig. 8. We let the message space be $\mathbf{M} = \{0,1\}^n \setminus \{0^n, 1^n\}$. Furthermore, we make use of a random oracle H such that H : $\{0,1\}^n \times \mathcal{X}^2 \rightarrow \{0,1\}^t$, where $t \in \mathbb{N}$ determines the length of the tag. Lastly, we set $\ell = n + t$ to be the total number of set elements in a ciphertext.

On the surface, COM-UE has some similarities with existing constructions in the literature. In particular, one could view $\mathsf{COM\text{-}UE.Enc}(k, M; r)$ as

$$\mathsf{BIN\text{-}UE.Enc}(k, M; r) \| \mathsf{BIN\text{-}UE.Enc}'(k', \mathsf{H}(M, r); r)$$

COM-UE.KeyGen	COM-UE.TokenGen(k, k')
00 $k := (k_1, \ldots, k_\ell) \xleftarrow{\$} \mathcal{G}^\ell$	10 Let $k = (k_1, \ldots, k_\ell)$ and $k' = (k'_1, \ldots, k'_\ell)$
01 return k	11 return $\Delta := (k'_1 k_1^{-1}, \ldots, k'_\ell k_\ell^{-1})$
COM-UE.Update(C, Δ)	COM-UE.Dec(k, C)
02 Let $\Delta = (\Delta_1, \ldots, \Delta_\ell)$	12 Let $C = (c_1, \ldots, c_\ell)$ and $k = (k_1, \ldots, k_\ell)$
and $C = (c_1, \ldots, c_\ell)$	13 for $i \in [\ell]$:
03 return $(\Delta_1 \star c_1, \ldots, \Delta_n \star c_\ell)$	14 $y_i := k_i^{-1} \star c_i$
	15 if $|\{y_1, \ldots, y_\ell\}| = 2$:
COM-UE.Enc(k, M)	16 Let $\{\tilde{x}_0, \tilde{x}_1\} = \{y_1, \ldots, y_\ell\}$ // $\tilde{x}_0 \prec_{\mathsf{lex}} \tilde{x}_1$
04 Let $M = (m_1, \ldots, m_n)$	17 for $i \in [\ell]$:
05 $x_0, x_1 \xleftarrow{\$} \mathcal{X}$ // $x_0 \prec_{\mathsf{lex}} x_1$	18 $m'_i := [\![y_i = \tilde{x}_1]\!]$
06 $M' := (m'_1, \ldots, m'_\ell) := (M \| \mathsf{H}(M, x_0, x_1))$	19 Parse $M' = (m'_1, \ldots, m'_\ell) = (M \| T)$
07 for $i \in [\ell]$:	20 if $T = \mathsf{H}(M, \tilde{x}_0, \tilde{x}_1)$:
08 $c_i := k_i \star x_{m'_i}$	21 return M
09 return $c := (c_1, \ldots, c_\ell)$	22 return $\perp$

Fig. 8. The scheme COM-UE. The random oracle H is defined in the main body.

for some modified BIN-UE.Enc$'$ that encrypts t bits instead of n. This resembles the Encrypt-*and*-MAC construction of [30] where a ciphertext has the form $C = (c, \tau)$ with $c = \mathsf{Enc}(k, M; r)$ and $\tau = \mathsf{PRF}(k_{\mathsf{PRF}}, (M, r))$ for some *updatable* pseudorandom function PRF.

However, on close inspection BIN-UE.Enc$(k, \mathsf{H}(M, r); r)$ cannot be viewed as an updatable PRF. First, observe that we still need to randomize the encryption, which means that the output of the supposed pseudorandom function $\widehat{\mathsf{PRF}}(k_{\mathsf{PRF}}, \cdot) = \mathsf{BIN\text{-}UE.Enc}(k_{\mathsf{PRF}}, \cdot)$ does not only depend on the key k_{PRF}, but also on some additional randomness r, which is not intended for a PRF. Second, even if we assume that we could find a consistent definition of a "randomized PRF", it seems unavoidable that $\widehat{\mathsf{PRF}}$ commits to its own randomness r, which is additionally shared with BIN-UE.Enc$(k, M; r)$. Although the latter issue can be circumvented, it still appears hard to reduce the INT-CTXT security of COM-UE exclusively to security guarantees provided by the function $\widehat{\mathsf{PRF}}$. We conclude that COM-UE cannot be viewed as a mere instantiation of the Encrypt-and-MAC construction of [30], making a dedicated security proof necessary.

4.3 Active Security of COM-UE

We now prove that in the random oracle model COM-UE is INT-CTXT secure under a new assumption that we call Multi Strong Unpredictability (Multi-St-UP). In a next step, we show that in the AGAM [24] Multi-St-UP reduces to the Discrete Logarithm Problem with Auxilary Input (DLAI). Due to Lemma 1 and Theorem 1 we get a post-quantum detIND-UE-CCA secure updatable encryption scheme from a reasonable assumption.

We begin by defining our new security assumption.

Game $G_{\mathsf{EGA}}^{\mathsf{Multi\text{-}St\text{-}UP}}(\mathcal{A})$	Oracle EVAL
00 $g_1,\ldots,g_t \xleftarrow{\$} \mathcal{G}$	06 $\beta \xleftarrow{\$} \{0,1\}^t$
01 $\gamma \xleftarrow{\$} \{0,1\}^t$	07 $x_0,x_1 \xleftarrow{\$} \mathcal{X}$ $/\!\!/ x_0 \prec_{\mathsf{lex}} x_1$
02 $(y_1,\ldots,y_t) \leftarrow \mathcal{A}^{\mathrm{EVAL},\mathrm{CHALL}}$	08 **return** $(\beta, x_0, x_1, g_1 \star x_{\beta_1}, \ldots, g_t \star x_{\beta_t})$
03 **if** $y_i = g_i \star \tilde{x}_{\gamma_i}$ **for all** $i \in [t]$:	
04 **return** 1	Oracle CHALL$(\tilde{x}_0, \tilde{x}_1)$ $/\!\!/$only one query
05 **return** 0	09 **return** γ

Fig. 9. The Multi-St-UP game for $t \in \mathbb{N}$, where we require $\tilde{x}_0 \prec_{\mathsf{lex}} \tilde{x}_1$.

Definition 10 (Multi Strong Unpredictability (Multi-St-UP)). *Let* EGA = $(\mathcal{G}, \mathcal{X}, \star, \tilde{x})$ *and* $t \in \mathbb{N}$. *Consider the game defined in Fig. 9. We define the advantage of an adversary* $\mathcal{A}$ *winning the* Multi-St-UP *game as*

$$\mathsf{Adv}_{\mathsf{EGA}}^{\mathsf{Multi\text{-}St\text{-}UP}}(\mathcal{A}) := \Pr[G_{\mathsf{EGA}}^{\mathsf{Multi\text{-}St\text{-}UP}}(\mathcal{A}) \Rightarrow 1] .$$

Intuitively, Multi-St-UP captures that for a fixed key $(g_1, \ldots, g_t)$ it should be hard to come up with a correct ciphertext for a random message γ. Of course, this is not directly applicable to COM-UE as messages are, in general, chosen by the adversary and therefore not random. However, this intuition does apply to the second part of a plaintext, which in the case of COM-UE is a hash value $\mathsf{H}(M, r)$, assuming H is a random oracle. In the ROM we can then embed the responses from the EVAL and CHALL oracles into these hash values, making the second part of the plaintext uniformly random.

Theorem 3. *Let* COM-UE *be the scheme described in Sect. 4.2. For any adversary* $\mathcal{A}$ *against the* INT-CTXT *security of* COM-UE*, there exists an adversary* $\mathcal{B}$ *against* Multi-St-UP *of* EGA *such that*

$$\mathsf{Adv}_{\mathsf{COM\text{-}UE}}^{\mathsf{INT\text{-}CTXT}}(\mathcal{A}) \leq (q + n_E)(n_e + 1) \cdot \mathsf{Adv}_{\mathsf{EGA}}^{\mathsf{Multi\text{-}St\text{-}UP}}(\mathcal{B}) + \frac{1}{2^t} + \frac{4n_E}{|\mathcal{X}|^2} ,$$

where n_e *is the number of epochs,* n_E *is the number of encryption queries and* q *is the number of queries to the random oracle. The running time of* $\mathcal{B}$ *is about that of* $\mathcal{A}$.

The following proof is based on the same idea as the INT-CTXT proof of SHINE0 [11, Theorem 5.1]. However, we improve the proof in two ways:

We first observe that the authors of [11] did not consider giving the adversary direct access to the ideal cipher[2]. Like in the random oracle model, each party should have access to the ideal cipher and therefore have the ability to query it on any input. In their proof, however, the authors implicitly assume that if the ideal cipher is defined on some input, then the output value must have been set during a call to the ENC oracle. This assumption, however, is insufficient and omits the case where an adversary queries the ideal cipher directly.

---

[2] Which plays a similar role as the random oracle in the case of COM-UE.

Secondly, our proof strategy is *tighter* than the one found in [11]. This is based on the observation that one can abort the adversary once it queried the TRY oracle. Therefore, it is only necessary to guess the left border fwl of the insulated region instead of both the left *and* right border. If the guess for fwl was correct, then the adversary calls TRY before the end of the insulated region, essentially marking the end of the region itself.

Proof. Assume that at some point, the adversary $\mathcal{A}$ submits a ciphertext $\tilde{C}$ to the TRY oracle, say in epoch e. Further, assume that no trivial win condition is triggered until that point and that $\tilde{C}$ is a well-formed BIN-UE ciphertext. Therefore, $\tilde{C}$ is a fresh ciphertext that was not produced by the game before and additionally there exists an insulated region around epoch e. Let BIN-UE.Dec$(k^{(e)}, \tilde{C}) = ((M||T), x_0, x_1) \neq \bot$ where we make explicit that BIN-UE.Dec also outputs the randomness used for the ciphertext $\tilde{C}$. In the following, we denote the random oracle by H and store queries in a list H[·], where each entry is initialized to be empty (i. e., $\bot$). We distinguish three cases:

- H$[M, x_0, x_1]$ is undefined, i. e., (M, x_0, x_1) has not been queried to the random oracle. Denote the event that the adversary wins in this case with E_0.
- H$[M, x_0, x_1]$ exists and its value was set during a direct query to H. Denote the event that the adversary wins in this case with E_1.
- H$[M, x_0, x_1]$ exists and its value was set during an encryption query. Denote the event that the adversary wins in this case with E_2.

Note that these three events are mutually exclusive. In particular, if H$[M, x_0, x_1]$ is defined then it must have been queried to oracle H before on that exact input. This can either happen via a direct query to H initiated by the adversary or via an encryption query, during which the INT-CTXT game needs to query H (cf. Figure 8 and recall that the COM-UE.Dec oracle is not present in the INT-CTXT game). We now have

$$\mathsf{Adv}_{\mathsf{COM\text{-}UE}}^{\mathsf{INT\text{-}CTXT}}(\mathcal{A}) = \Pr[\mathsf{G}_{\mathsf{COM\text{-}UE}}^{\mathsf{INT\text{-}CTXT}}(\mathcal{A}) \Rightarrow 1] \tag{1}$$

$$= \Pr[\mathsf{BIN\text{-}UE.Dec}(k^{(e)}, \tilde{C}) \neq \bot] \tag{2}$$
$$\cdot \Pr[\mathsf{G}_{\mathsf{COM\text{-}UE}}^{\mathsf{INT\text{-}CTXT}}(\mathcal{A}) \Rightarrow 1 \mid \mathsf{BIN\text{-}UE.Dec}(k^{(e)}, \tilde{C}) \neq \bot]$$
$$+ \Pr[\mathsf{BIN\text{-}UE.Dec}(k^{(e)}, \tilde{C}) = \bot]$$
$$\cdot \Pr[\mathsf{G}_{\mathsf{COM\text{-}UE}}^{\mathsf{INT\text{-}CTXT}}(\mathcal{A}) \Rightarrow 1 \mid \mathsf{BIN\text{-}UE.Dec}(k^{(e)}, \tilde{C}) = \bot]$$
$$\leq \Pr[\mathsf{G}_{\mathsf{COM\text{-}UE}}^{\mathsf{INT\text{-}CTXT}}(\mathcal{A}) \Rightarrow 1 \mid \mathsf{BIN\text{-}UE.Dec}(k^{(e)}, \tilde{C}) \neq \bot] \tag{3}$$
$$\leq \Pr[E_0] + \Pr[E_1] + \Pr[E_2] , \tag{4}$$

where in Equation (3) we used the fact that

$$\Pr[\mathsf{G}_{\mathsf{COM\text{-}UE}}^{\mathsf{INT\text{-}CTXT}}(\mathcal{A}) \Rightarrow 1 \mid \mathsf{BIN\text{-}UE.Dec}(k^{(e)}, \tilde{C}) = \bot] = 0 .$$

First, observe that $\Pr[E_0] \leq \frac{1}{2^t}$ as the reduction can simply choose a random bit string in $\{0,1\}^t$ for the value H$[M, x_0, x_1]$. The probability of this string being equal to T is exactly $\frac{1}{2^t}$, therefore $\tilde{C}$ is a well-formed COM-UE ciphertext with the same probability.

The other two probabilities follow from Lemmata 2 and 3 stated below. Collecting all the probabilities yields the statement in Theorem 3. □

Lemma 2. *Let the notation be as in Theorem 3. We then have*

$$\Pr[E_1] \leq q(n_e + 1) \cdot \mathsf{Adv}_{\mathsf{EGA}}^{\mathsf{Multi\text{-}St\text{-}UP}}(\mathcal{B}) + \frac{2n_E}{|\mathcal{X}|^2} \,,$$

where n_e is the number of epochs, n_E is the number of encryption queries and q is the number of queries to the random oracle.

Proof. Consider the reduction in Fig. 10. The main idea is to embed the group elements $(g_1, \ldots, g_t)$ of the Multi-St-UP assumption into the second half of the secret key in the challenge epoch of the INT-CTXT game. To this end, the reduction first guesses the left border fwl of the firewall around the challenge epoch, resulting in an advantage loss of $(n_e + 1)$. The reason why only the left border suffices is that we stop the adversary $\mathcal{A}$ once it queries the TRY oracle since at that point the reduction has all the necessary information to extract the solution for the Multi-St-UP assumption. To the left of the challenge epoch, the reduction simulates keys and tokens by itself, whereas inside of the firewall, the reduction simulates *partial* update tokens. Note that we do not need to simulate anything to the right of the epoch where TRY is queried. In fact, in the reduction in Fig. 10 we simulate update tokens for all epochs $e \in [\mathsf{fwl}, n_e]$ as we expect the adversary to query TRY before the end of the insulated region. If instead the adversary queries for instance the CORRKEY oracle for an epoch $\hat{e} \geq \mathsf{fwl}$ then the guess for fwl was simply wrong and the reduction aborts. Furthermore, we do not need to keep track of trivial win conditions explicitly (in particular the twf and win flags).

Of course, the reduction needs to provide consistent encryption randomness (i.e., consistent basis elements x_0, x_1) which is especially important for ciphertexts that are updated into the firewall. We get around this issue in the same way as in the proof of Theorem 2: For each encryption query to the left of the firewall, reduction $\mathcal{B}$ queries its own EVAL oracle to obtain a tuple $(\beta, x_0, x_1, y_1, \ldots, y_t)$ which it stores for later use. It then programs the random oracle such that the "tag" $T = \mathsf{H}[M, x_0, x_1]$ equals β and then encrypts $M' = (M\|T)$ with the current secret key and randomness (x_0, x_1). If $\mathsf{H}[M, x_0, x_1]$ is already set, then this programming fails and the reduction needs to abort. Note that the probability of this event is bounded by $2n_E/|\mathcal{X}|^2$ (the additional factor of 2 comes from the fact that $x_0 \prec_{\mathsf{lex}} x_1$). In the description of $\mathcal{B}$ in Fig. 10, we implicitly assume this event does not happen.

Once an update or a new encryption is requested for an epoch inside the firewall, reduction $\mathcal{B}$ uses the values $y_i = g_i \star x_{\beta_i}$ from memory to embed the elements g_i into the secret key elements $(k_{n+1}^{(\mathsf{fwl})}, \ldots, k_{n+t}^{(\mathsf{fwl})})$. Note that the first n elements of the secret key are always known to the reduction.

To embed the challenge of the Multi-St-UP game, reduction $\mathcal{B}$ guesses a query index q^* and embeds the challenge γ into the q^*-th query to the random oracle H.

Recall that for event E_1 we assume that the solution $\tilde{C}$ that $\mathcal{A}$ presents to TRY is essentially a fresh encryption of a message M since $\mathsf{H}[M, x_0, x_1]$ exists and $\mathcal{A}$ queried H on that exact input. In particular, the query $\mathsf{H}(M, x_0, x_1)$ did not occur during an ENC query. If the guess was correct and $\mathcal{A}$ successfully provided such a fresh ciphertext, then reduction $\mathcal{B}$ reverses potential (implicit) updates to the provided $\tilde{C}$, resulting in a valid ciphertext for epoch $\mathsf{e} = \mathsf{fwl}$. It is then easy to verify that the last t elements of that ciphertext are a valid solution for the Multi-St-UP assumption which completes the proof.   □

Lemma 3. *Let the notation be as in Theorem 3. We then have*

$$\Pr[E_2] \le n_E(n_{\mathsf{e}} + 1) \cdot \mathsf{Adv}_{\mathsf{EGA}}^{\mathsf{Multi\text{-}St\text{-}UP}}(\mathcal{B}) + \frac{2n_E}{|\mathcal{X}|^2} ,$$

where n_{e} is the number of epochs and n_E is the number of encryption queries.

The proof is almost identical to the proof of Lemma 2, except that now the reduction embeds the challenge during a call to ENC. We defer the full proof to the full version of the paper [36].

4.4 Hardness of Multi-St-UP

Our new assumption Multi-St-UP is non-standard, but it abstracts away all the overhead of updatable encryption and allows us to focus on a single, succinct assumption. We now show that in the AGAM introduced by [24] Multi-St-UP is essentially as hard as the Discrete Logarithm Problem with Auxiliary Input (DLAI). A more general version of DLAI was introduced in [4] and shown to be hard in the GGAM [24]. For a detailed description of the AGAM we refer the reader to the full version of the paper [36].

Definition 11 (Discrete Logarithm Problem with Auxiliary Input). *Let $\mathsf{EGA} = (\mathcal{G}, \mathcal{X}, \star, \tilde{x})$, $m \in \mathbb{N}$ be an integer and $N = ord(\mathcal{G})$ be prime. We say that an adversary $\mathcal{A}$ solves the Discrete Logarithm Problem with Auxiliary Input (DLAI) if*

$$\mathcal{A}(z_0, \dots, z_m) = h ,$$

where the z_i are given by $z_i = h^i \star \tilde{x}$ for $h \xleftarrow{\$} \mathcal{G}$.

Remark 6. The authors of [4] defined DLAI for arbitrary (composite) order groups which requires a more intricate choice of the exponents. In particular, the powers of h have to fulfill rather technical constraints related to invertibility modulo N. The results in this section can be adapted to the case of composite order groups at the expense of a much more convoluted notation. In particular, for cryptographic group actions like CSIDH one could constrain DLAI to a large prime-order subgroup of $\mathcal{G}$ as long as its group structure is known[3].

---
[3] Knowing the group structure in CSIDH is necessary for updatability already, see Sect. 3.2.

Adversary $\mathcal{B}^{\text{EVAL},\text{CHALL}}$

```
00  k^(0) ←$ BIN-UE.KeyGen
01  Δ^(0) := ⊥
02  e, c, q := 0
03  H[·] := ⊥
04  ℒ := ∅
05  fwl ←$ [0, n_e]
06  q* ←$ [1, q]
07  for j ∈ [0, fwl − 1] :
08      k^(j) ← BIN-UE.KeyGen
09      Δ^(j) := BIN-UE.TokenGen(k^(j−1), k^(j))  //†
10  for j ∈ [fwl, n_e] :
11      k_1^(j),…,k_n^(j) ←$ 𝒢^n
12  for j ∈ [fwl + 1, n_e] :
13      for ℓ ∈ [1, n] :
14          Δ_ℓ^(j) := k_ℓ^(j)/k_ℓ^(j−1)
15      for ℓ ∈ [n + 1, t] :
16          Δ_ℓ^(j) ←$ 𝒢
17  Run 𝒜^𝒪
18  return ⊥ to G_EGA^Multi-St-UP   //TRY never called
```

Oracle ENC(M)
```
19  Let M = (m_1,…,m_n)
20  c := c + 1
21  τ := (β, x_0, x_1, y_1,…,y_t) ← EVAL
22  H[M, x_0, x_1] := β
23  M' := (M||H[M, x_0, x_1])
24  if e < fwl :
25      C_j^(e) := k_j^(e) ⋆ x_{m'_j}
26  else :
27      for j ∈ [1, n] :
28          C_j^(e) := k_j^(e) ⋆ x_{m_j}
29      for j ∈ [1, t] :
30          C_{n+j}^(e) := y_j
31  C^(e) := (C_1^(e),…,C_{n+t}^(e))
32  ℒ := ℒ ∪ {(c, M', C^(e), e, τ)}
33  return C^(e)
```

Oracle NEXT
```
34  e := e + 1
```

Oracle CORRKEY(ê)
```
35  if ê > e : return ⊥
36  if ê ≥ fwl : abort       //wrong guess for fwl
37  return k^(ê)
```

Oracle TRY(C̃)
```
38  (M', x_0, x_1) := BIN-UE.Dec(k^(e), C̃)
39  Let M' = (M||T)
40  if H[M, x_0, x_1] ≠ γ : abort   //wrong guess
41  Set C^(e) = C̃
42  for ℓ ∈ [e, fwl] :       //backwards iteration
43      for j ∈ [n + 1, n + t] :
44          C_j^(ℓ−1) := (Δ_j^(ℓ))^{−1} ⋆ C_j^(ℓ)
45  return C_{n+1}^(fwl),…,C_{n+t}^(fwl) to G_EGA^Multi-St-UP
```

Oracle UPD(C^(e−1))
```
46  if ∄c : (c, M', C^(e−1), e − 1, τ) ∈ ℒ :
47      return ⊥
48  Let τ = (β, x_0, x_1, y_1,…,y_t)
49  if e < fwl :
50      Let M' = (m'_1,…,m'_{n+t})
51      C_j^(e) := k_j^(e) ⋆ x_{m'_j}
52  else :
53      Let M' = (M||T)
54      for j ∈ [1, n] :
55          C_j^(fwl) := k_j^(fwl) ⋆ x_{m_j}
56      for j ∈ [1, t] :
57          C_{n+j}^(fwl) := y_j
58      for ℓ ∈ [fwl + 1, e] :
59          C_j^(ℓ) := Δ_j^(ℓ) ⋆ C_j^(ℓ−1)
60  ℒ := ℒ ∪ {(c, M', C^(e), e, τ)}
61  return C^(e)
```

Oracle H(M, x_0, x_1)
```
62  if H[M, x_0, x_1] = ⊥ :
63      q := q + 1
64      if q = q* :
65          γ ← CHALL(x_0, x_1)
66          H[M, x_0, x_1] := γ
67      else :
68          β ←$ {0,1}^t
69          H[M, x_0, x_1] := β
70  return H[M, x_0, x_1]
```

Oracle CORRTOKEN(ê)
```
71  if ê > e : return ⊥
72  if ê = fwl : abort       //wrong guess for fwl
73  return Δ^(ê)
```

Fig. 10. The reduction $\mathcal{B}$ simulating game $G_{\text{COM-UE}}^{\text{INT-CTXT}}$ and event E_1. The set of oracles that $\mathcal{A}$ has access to is defined as $\mathcal{O} = \{\text{ENC}, \text{TRY}, \text{NEXT}, \text{UPD}, \text{CORRKEY}, \text{CORRTOKEN}, \text{H}\}$. † indicates that the computation of $\Delta^{(0)}$ is skipped.

Proposition 3 (DLAI ⇒ Multi-St-UP in the AGAM). *Let $\mathcal{A}$ be an algebraic adversary $\mathcal{A}$ against Multi-St-UP for $t \in \mathbb{N}$ such that $\mathcal{A}$ issues at most q_{EVAL} queries to oracle EVAL. Then, there exists an adversary $\mathcal{B}$ against DLAI for $m = 2q_{\text{EVAL}}(t + 1)$ such that*

$$\text{Adv}_{\text{EGA}}^{\text{Multi-St-UP}}(\mathcal{A}) \leq \frac{1}{1 - (3/4)^{t-1}} \cdot \text{Adv}_{\text{EGA}}^{\text{DLAI}}(\mathcal{B})$$

and the running time of $\mathcal{B}$ is about that of $\mathcal{A}$.

Remark 7. Recall that in COM-UE the parameter t represents the output length of the random oracle H. Therefore, the tightness loss of our reduction is close to 1 for cryptographically sized parameters.

Proof. Let q_{EVAL} be the number of queries that $\mathcal{A}$ issues to the EVAL oracle. Recall that the DLAI challenge consists of $m+1$ many set elements $(z_i)_{i \in [0,m]}$ with $z_i = h^i \star \tilde{x}$, where $m = 2q_{\text{EVAL}}(t+1)$ and t comes from the Multi-St-UP challenge. To simplify the proof and its notation, reduction $\mathcal{B}$ will not rerandomize set elements that it outputs to $\mathcal{A}$. Furthermore, we assume that adversary $\mathcal{A}$ also does not rerandomize elements it outputs. In the AGAM these simplifications are without loss of generality as we discuss in the full version of the paper [36].

Adversary $\mathcal{B}(z_0, \ldots, z_m)$

```
00  c := 0
01  γ ←$ {0,1}^t
02  y₁, ..., yₜ ← 𝒜^{EVAL,CHALL}
03  h := Extract(y₁, ..., yₜ)
04  return h
```

Oracle CHALL($\tilde{x}_0, \tilde{x}_1$) // $\tilde{x}_0 \prec_{\text{lex}} \tilde{x}_1$
```
05  return γ
```

Oracle EVAL

```
06  β ←$ {0,1}^t
07  i₀ := 1 + 2c · (t+1)
08  i₁ := 1 + (2c+1) · (t+1)
09  x₀ := z_{i₀}
10  x₁ := z_{i₁}              // w.l.o.g. x₀ ≺_lex x₁
11  c := c + 1
12  for k ∈ [t]
13     ν := k + i_{βₖ}
14     yₖ := z_ν
15  return (β, x₀, x₁, y₁, ..., yₜ)
```

Fig. 11. Adversary $\mathcal{B}$ for the proof of Proposition 3, where $m = 2q_{\text{EVAL}}(t+1)$. The Extract algorithm is described in the main body of the proof. Recall that we do not explicitly rerandomize elements as discussed in the full version of the paper [36].

Consider the reduction depicted in Fig. 11. Here, reduction $\mathcal{B}$ implicitly embeds the group elements $(h, h^2, \ldots, h^t)$ into the secret key $(g_1, \ldots, g_t)$ as follows. Assume $c = 0$, i.e. the EVAL oracle is queried for the first time. $\mathcal{B}$ first samples a random $\beta \xleftarrow{\$} \{0,1\}^t$, computes the indices $i_0 = 1$ and $i_1 = t + 2$ and subsequently defines

$$x_0 = z_1 \quad = h \star \tilde{x} \,,$$
$$x_1 = z_{t+2} = h^{t+2} \star \tilde{x} \,.$$

If the i-th bit $\beta_i = 0$, then $\mathcal{B}$ has to compute the element

$$h^i \star x_0 = h^i \star z_1 = h^i \cdot h \star \tilde{x} = z_{1+i} \,.$$

This amounts to a simple lookup of the element z_{i+1} that $\mathcal{B}$ was provided by the DLAI assumption. This method can be generalized to the case $\beta_i = 1$ and $c > 0$

Table 2. Visualization of the proof. The individual rows of the table represent different queries to the oracles. The elements h^1 through h^5 represent the secret key elements. The set elements in the main body of the table represent the elements that EVAL outputs for each query. These elements together with the basis elements are all the elements $\mathcal{A}$ receives throughout its execution. The encircled elements are those elements that $\mathcal{A}$ chooses as its base elements $\tilde{x}_0, \tilde{x}_1$. The set elements in the challenge row represent the elements $y_1, \ldots, y_t$ that $\mathcal{A}$ has to produce. The boxed elements are set elements that $\mathcal{A}$ has not yet seen and therefore their representation must contain a power of h.

Query	Bitstring	Basis	h^1	h^2	h^3	h^4	h^5
EVAL	$\beta = 10010$	$x_0 = z_1$		$\textcircled{$z_3$}$	z_4		z_6
		$x_1 = z_7$	z_8			$\textcircled{$z_{11}$}$	
EVAL	$\beta = 01110$	$x_0 = z_{13}$	z_{14}				z_{18}
		$x_1 = z_{19}$		z_{21}	z_{22}	z_{23}	
CHALL	$\gamma = 10100$	$\tilde{x}_0 = z_3$		$\boxed{z_5}$		z_7	z_8
		$\tilde{x}_1 = z_{11}$	$\boxed{z_{12}}$		z_{14}		
EVAL	$\beta = 00101$	$x_0 = z_{25}$	z_{26}	z_{27}		z_{29}	
		$x_1 = z_{31}$			z_{34}		z_{36}

(see lines 08-15 in Fig. 11). Therefore $\mathcal{B}$ successfully embeds $(h, h^2, \ldots, h^t)$ into the secret key. See also Table 2 which further illustrates this idea for $t = 5$.

Eventually, say after the c-th query, $\mathcal{A}$ calls CHALL on two basis elements $(\tilde{x}_0, \tilde{x}_1)$. Since we assume $\mathcal{A}$ to be algebraic and to not rerandomize $(\tilde{x}_0, \tilde{x}_1)$ we can write

$$\tilde{x}_0 = z_{j_0}, \quad \tilde{x}_1 = z_{j_1}, \qquad j_0, j_1 \in [0, 2c \cdot (t+1)].$$

$\mathcal{B}$ then returns a random $\gamma \xleftarrow{\$} \{0,1\}^t$ and continues simulating the EVAL oracle.

THE EXTRACT ALGORITHM. At some point $\mathcal{A}$ responds with the set elements $(y_1, \ldots, y_t)$. Since we assume $\mathcal{A}$ to be successful, we have that

$$y_i = h^i \star \tilde{x}_{\gamma_i} = \begin{cases} h^i \star z_{j_0}, & \text{if } \gamma_i = 0 \\ h^i \star z_{j_1}, & \text{if } \gamma_i = 1 \end{cases}$$

for all $i \in [1, t]$. However, since $\mathcal{A}$ is algebraic it must provide a representation (s, v) for each $y_i = h^i \star z_{j_*}$ relative to a previously received set element (which form a subset of $\{z_0, \ldots, z_m\}$). There are now two cases:

1. $\mathcal{A}$ has previously received $h^i \star z_{j_*} = z_{j_* + i}$ for each $i \in [1, t]$. In this case the representation could be trivial (up to rerandomization), i.e. $(s, v) = (1, z_{j_* + i})$.
2. $\mathcal{A}$ has not previously received $h^i \star z_{j_*}$ for at least one $i \in [1, t]$. In this case the corresponding representation (s, v) cannot be trivial. More concretely, if $v = z_\ell$ then we must have $s = h^{j_* + i - \ell} \neq 1$ (again up to rerandomization). Call this event E.

Of course, $\mathcal{B}$ can only extract h in the latter case by taking an appropriate root of s. As we will argue next, however, this case is extremely likely.

Claim. $\Pr[E] \geq 1 - \left(\frac{3}{4}\right)^{t-1}$.

We lower bound the probability by splitting it up into two disjoint events which we analyze separately:

$$\Pr[E] = \Pr[E \mid j_0, j_1 > m - t] \cdot \Pr[j_0, j_1 > m - t] + \tag{5}$$
$$\Pr[E \mid j_0 \leq m - t \vee j_1 \leq m - t] \cdot \Pr[j_0 \leq m - t \vee j_1 \leq m - t]$$
$$\geq \min \{\Pr[E \mid j_0, j_1 > m - t], \Pr[E \mid j_0 \leq m - t \vee j_1 \leq m - t]\} . \tag{6}$$

Case 1. First assume that $j_0, j_1 > m - t$. Then

$$y_t = h^t \star z_{j_b} = h^t \cdot h^{j_b} \star \tilde{x} \notin \{z_0, \ldots, z_m\} , \quad b \in \{0, 1\} ,$$

because $t + j_b > m$. In that case, the representation (s, v) for y_t is never trivial, i.e. $y_t = s \star v$ with $s = h^\kappa$ for some $\kappa > 0$ and $v = z_\ell$ for some $\ell \in [0, m]$. Therefore we have

$$\Pr[E \mid j_0, j_1 > m - t] = 1$$

and in fact Equation (6) reduces to

$$\Pr[E] \geq Pr[E \mid j_0 \leq m - t \vee j_1 \leq m - t] .$$

Case 2. Now assume that (w.l.o.g.) $j_0 \leq m - t$. If $\gamma_i = 0$ for an index $i \in [1, t]$ then by definition the adversary $\mathcal{A}$ has to produce the element z_{j_0+i} and an accompanying representation. Clearly, this representation can only be trivial if $\mathcal{A}$ has received the element z_{j_0+i} from the EVAL oracle before.

Concretely, if we let $\Delta = (\delta_1, \ldots, \delta_t) \in \{0, 1\}^t$ be defined via

$$\delta_i = \begin{cases} 1 & \text{if } z_{j_0+i} \text{ was output by EVAL} \\ 0 & \text{else} \end{cases}$$

then the previous paragraph can be rephrased as

$$\Pr[E] \geq \Pr[\exists i \in [1, t] : \delta_i = 0 \wedge \gamma_i = 0] .$$

For instance, in the running example in Table 2 we have $j_0 = 3$ and thus $\Delta = (10111)$.

Claim. δ_i is a random bit if $j_0 + i \neq 1 + k \cdot (t + 1)$ for $k \in \mathbb{N}$. In particular, the β_i and γ_i are independent.

Essentially, the claim says that δ_i is a random bit except for those i where z_{j_0+i} appeared as one of the basis elements returned by the EVAL oracle (in which case we always have $\delta_i = 1$). Note that there can be at most one such index i in the interval $[j_0 + 1, \ldots, j_0 + t]$. For all other indices we have that δ_i essentially depends on the bit string β that was chosen for the corresponding EVAL query. Since each β is uniformly random, so are the δ_i.

Concretely, for each $i \in [1, t]$ the corresponding δ_i satisfies the following equality: Assume that z_{j_0} was returned in the c-th query to EVAL, which we write explicitly as $(\beta^{(c)}, x_0^{(c)}, x_1^{(c)}, y_1^{(c)}, \ldots, y_t^{(c)})$. We then have $x_0^{(c)} = z_\mu$, $x_1^{(c)} = z_{\mu+t+1}$ and $z_{j_0} = z_{\mu+\eta}$ for some appropriate indices $\mu \le m - t$ and $0 \le \eta \le 2t + 1$. Furthermore, let $\beta^{(c+1)}$ be the bitstring returned in the subsequent EVAL query. We now have

$$
\delta_i = \begin{cases}
[\![\beta_{i+\eta}^{(c)} = 0]\!], & \text{if } i + \eta < t + 1 \\
1, & \text{if } i + \eta = t + 1 \\
[\![\beta_{i+\eta-t-1}^{(c)} = 0]\!], & \text{if } t + 1 < i + \eta < 2t + 2 \cdot \\
1 & \text{if } i + \eta = 2t + 2 \\
[\![\beta_{i+\eta-2t-3}^{(c+1)} = 0]\!], & \text{if } i + \eta > 2t + 2
\end{cases}
$$

Evidently, apart from two special cases in which $i + \eta = k \cdot (t+1)$ for some $k \in \mathbb{N}$, the δ_i only depend on the bitstrings $\beta^{(c)}, \beta^{(c+1)}$ and not on the challenge γ. In summary, we therefore have that

$$
\Pr[E] \ge 1 - \Pr[\forall i \in [1, t] : \delta_i = 1 \lor \gamma_i = 1] \ge 1 - \left(\frac{3}{4}\right)^{t-1}.
$$

Lastly, $\mathcal{B}$ can extract h from the non-trivial representation by first computing the indices j_b and ℓ. This can be done by merely comparing z_{j_b} and z_ℓ to each element z_i that $\mathcal{B}$ received from the DLAI assumption. $\mathcal{B}$ can then compute $\kappa = (j_b + t - \ell)$ and thus compute $h = s^{1/\kappa}$. $\qquad\square$

Remark 8. The assumption that $x_0 \prec_{\text{lex}} x_1$ in Fig. 11, line 13 is without loss of generality as reduction $\mathcal{B}$ can simply swap the elements x_0, x_1 if necessary. It then has to keep track of this change throughout the reduction, but this does not fundamentally change the proof. Also keep in mind that the elements x_0, x_1 are implicitly rerandomized, which means that the distribution of these elements is still correct even after a swap.

Remark 9. The proof also applies to a group action that supports *twists*. That is, a group action that comes equipped with an efficient algorithm that on input $y = g \star \tilde{x}$ computes $y^\mathsf{T} = g^{-1} \star \tilde{x}$. However, in that case the probability of the event E changes to

$$
\Pr[E] \ge 1 - \left(\frac{3}{4}\right)^{\lfloor t/2 \rfloor - 1}.
$$

This is due to the fact that, given a set element y, the adversary knows the representation of *two* set elements instead of only one (namely y and y^T). This way we can only argue for $\lfloor \frac{t}{2} \rfloor - 1$ many independent random bits δ_i, decreasing the overall probability of the event E.

Corollary 1. *Let* COM-UE *be the scheme described in Sect. 4.2. For any algebraic adversary* $\mathcal{A}$ *against the* detIND-UE-CCA *security of* COM-UE*, there exist adversaries* $\mathcal{B}, \mathcal{C}$ *against* Wk-PR *and* DLAI *in the random oracle model such that*

$$\mathsf{Adv}_{\mathsf{COM\text{-}UE}}^{\mathsf{detIND\text{-}UE\text{-}CCA}}(\mathcal{A}) \leq 2\ell(n_e+1)^3 \cdot \mathsf{Adv}_{\mathsf{EGA}}^{\mathsf{Wk\text{-}PR}}(\mathcal{B})$$
$$+ \frac{(q+n_E)(n_e+1)}{1-(3/4)^{t-1}} \cdot \mathsf{Adv}_{\mathsf{EGA}}^{\mathsf{DLAI}}(\mathcal{C}) + \frac{1}{2^t},$$

where $\ell = n+t$ *is the length of a message and tag in bits,* n_e *is the number of epochs,* n_E *is the number of encryption queries and* q *is the number of queries to the random oracle.*

Acknowledgments. We would like to thank Andre Esser, Eike Kiltz, Sabrina Kunzweiler and Edoardo Persichetti for interesting research discussions. The work of Jonas Meers and Doreen Riepel was funded by the Deutsche Forschungsgemeinschaft (DFG, German Research Foundation) under Germany's Excellence Strategy - EXC 2092 CASA - 390781972. Doreen Riepel was further supported in part by Bellare's KACST grant.

References

1. Abdalla, M., Eisenhofer, T., Kiltz, E., Kunzweiler, S., Riepel, D.: Password-authenticated key exchange from group actions. In: Dodis, Y., Shrimpton, T. (eds.) CRYPTO 2022, Part II. LNCS, vol. 13508, pp. 699–728. Springer, Heidelberg (2022). https://doi.org/10.1007/978-3-031-15979-4_24
2. Alamati, N., De Feo, L., Montgomery, H., Patranabis, S.: Cryptographic group actions and applications. In: Moriai, S., Wang, H. (eds.) ASIACRYPT 2020, Part II. LNCS, vol. 12492, pp. 411–439. Springer, Heidelberg (2020). https://doi.org/10.1007/978-3-030-64834-3_14
3. Alamati, N., Montgomery, H., Patranabis, S.: Symmetric primitives with structured secrets. In: Boldyreva, A., Micciancio, D. (eds.) CRYPTO 2019, Part I. LNCS, vol. 11692, pp. 650–679. Springer, Heidelberg (2019). https://doi.org/10.1007/978-3-030-26948-7_23
4. Baghery, K., Cozzo, D., Pedersen, R.: An isogeny-based ID protocol using structured public keys. In: Paterson, M.B. (ed.) 18th IMA International Conference on Cryptography and Coding. LNCS, vol. 13129, pp. 179–197. Springer, Heidelberg (2021). https://doi.org/10.1007/978-3-030-92641-0_9
5. Berti, F., Pereira, O., Peters, T.: Reconsidering generic composition: the tag-then-encrypt case. In: Chakraborty, D., Iwata, T. (eds.) INDOCRYPT 2018. LNCS, vol. 11356, pp. 70–90. Springer, Heidelberg (2018). https://doi.org/10.1007/978-3-030-05378-9_4
6. Beullens, W., Kleinjung, T., Vercauteren, F.: CSI-FiSh: efficient isogeny based signatures through class group computations. In: Galbraith, S.D., Moriai, S. (eds.) ASIACRYPT 2019, Part I. LNCS, vol. 11921, pp. 227–247. Springer, Heidelberg (2019). https://doi.org/10.1007/978-3-030-34578-5_9
7. Boneh, D., Eskandarian, S., Kim, S., Shih, M.: Improving speed and security in updatable encryption schemes. In: Moriai, S., Wang, H. (eds.) ASIACRYPT 2020, Part III. LNCS, vol. 12493, pp. 559–589. Springer, Heidelberg (2020). https://doi.org/10.1007/978-3-030-64840-4_19

8. Boneh, D., Guan, J., Zhandry, M.: A lower bound on the length of signatures based on group actions and generic isogenies. In: Hazay, C., Stam, M. (eds.) EURO-CRYPT 2023, Part V. LNCS, vol. 14008, pp. 507–531. Springer, Heidelberg (2023). https://doi.org/10.1007/978-3-031-30589-4_18

9. Boneh, D., Lewi, K., Montgomery, H.W., Raghunathan, A.: Key homomorphic PRFs and their applications. In: Canetti, R., Garay, J.A. (eds.) CRYPTO 2013, Part I. LNCS, vol. 8042, pp. 410–428. Springer, Heidelberg (2013). https://doi.org/10.1007/978-3-642-40041-4_23

10. Booher, J., et al.: Failing to hash into supersingular isogeny graphs. Cryptology ePrint Archive, Report 2022/518 (2022). https://eprint.iacr.org/2022/518

11. Boyd, C., Davies, G.T., Gjøsteen, K., Jiang, Y.: Fast and secure updatable encryption. In: Micciancio, D., Ristenpart, T. (eds.) CRYPTO 2020, Part I. LNCS, vol. 12170, pp. 464–493. Springer, Heidelberg (2020). https://doi.org/10.1007/978-3-030-56784-2_16

12. Castryck, W., Decru, T.: CSIDH on the surface. In: Ding, J., Tillich, J.P. (eds.) Post-Quantum Cryptography - 11th International Conference, PQCrypto 2020, pp. 111–129. Springer, Heidelberg (2020). https://doi.org/10.1007/978-3-030-44223-1_7

13. Castryck, W., Decru, T.: An efficient key recovery attack on SIDH. In: Hazay, C., Stam, M. (eds.) EUROCRYPT 2023, Part V. LNCS, vol. 14008, pp. 423–447. Springer, Heidelberg (2023). https://doi.org/10.1007/978-3-031-30589-4_15

14. Castryck, W., Houben, M., Vercauteren, F., Wesolowski, B.: On the decisional Diffie-Hellman problem for class group actions on oriented elliptic curves. Cryptology ePrint Archive, Report 2022/345 (2022). https://eprint.iacr.org/2022/345

15. Castryck, W., Lange, T., Martindale, C., Panny, L., Renes, J.: CSIDH: an efficient post-quantum commutative group action. In: Peyrin, T., Galbraith, S. (eds.) ASIACRYPT 2018, Part III. LNCS, vol. 11274, pp. 395–427. Springer, Heidelberg (2018). https://doi.org/10.1007/978-3-030-03332-3_15

16. Chandran, N., Chase, M., Liu, F.H., Nishimaki, R., Xagawa, K.: Re-encryption, functional re-encryption, and multi-hop re-encryption: a framework for achieving obfuscation-based security and instantiations from lattices. In: Krawczyk, H. (ed.) PKC 2014. LNCS, vol. 8383, pp. 95–112. Springer, Heidelberg (2014). https://doi.org/10.1007/978-3-642-54631-0_6

17. Chen, H., Galteland, Y.J., Liang, K.: CCA-1 secure updatable encryption with adaptive security. In: Guo, J., Steinfeld, R. (eds.) ASIACRYPT 2023, Part V, pp. 374–406. Springer, Singapore (2023). https://doi.org/10.1007/978-981-99-8733-7_12

18. Chen, L., Li, Y., Tang, Q.: CCA updatable encryption against malicious re-encryption attacks. In: Moriai, S., Wang, H. (eds.) ASIACRYPT 2020, Part III. LNCS, vol. 12493, pp. 590–620. Springer, Heidelberg (2020). https://doi.org/10.1007/978-3-030-64840-4_20

19. Cini, V., Ramacher, S., Slamanig, D., Striecks, C., Tairi, E.: Updatable signatures and message authentication codes. In: Garay, J. (ed.) PKC 2021, Part I. LNCS, vol. 12710, pp. 691–723. Springer, Heidelberg (2021). https://doi.org/10.1007/978-3-030-75245-3_25

20. D'Alconzo, G., Scala, A.J.D.: Representations of group actions and their applications in cryptography. Cryptology ePrint Archive, Paper 2023/1247 (2023). https://eprint.iacr.org/2023/1247

21. Davidson, A., Deo, A., Lee, E., Martin, K.: Strong post-compromise secure proxy re-encryption. In: Jang-Jaccard, J., Guo, F. (eds.) ACISP 19. LNCS, vol. 11547,

pp. 58–77. Springer, Heidelberg (2019). https://doi.org/10.1007/978-3-030-21548-4_4

22. De Feo, L., et al.: SCALLOP: scaling the CSI-FiSh. In: Boldyreva, A., Kolesnikov, V. (eds.) PKC 2023, Part I. LNCS, vol. 13940, pp. 345–375. Springer, Heidelberg (2023). https://doi.org/10.1007/978-3-031-31368-4_13

23. De Feo, L., Galbraith, S.D.: SeaSign: compact isogeny signatures from class group actions. In: Ishai, Y., Rijmen, V. (eds.) EUROCRYPT 2019, Part III. LNCS, vol. 11478, pp. 759–789. Springer, Heidelberg (2019). https://doi.org/10.1007/978-3-030-17659-4_26

24. Duman, J., Hartmann, D., Kiltz, E., Kunzweiler, S., Lehmann, J., Riepel, D.: Generic models for group actions. In: Boldyreva, A., Kolesnikov, V. (eds.) PKC 2023, Part I. LNCS, vol. 13940, pp. 406–435. Springer, Heidelberg (2023). https://doi.org/10.1007/978-3-031-31368-4_15

25. Eaton, E., Jao, D., Komlo, C., Mokrani, Y.: Towards post-quantum key-updatable public-key encryption via supersingular isogenies. In: AlTawy, R., Hülsing, A. (eds.) SAC 2021. LNCS, vol. 13203, pp. 461–482. Springer, Heidelberg (2022). https://doi.org/10.1007/978-3-030-99277-4_22

26. Everspaugh, A., Paterson, K.G., Ristenpart, T., Scott, S.: Key rotation for authenticated encryption. In: Katz, J., Shacham, H. (eds.) CRYPTO 2017, Part III. LNCS, vol. 10403, pp. 98–129. Springer, Heidelberg (2017). https://doi.org/10.1007/978-3-319-63697-9_4

27. Fabrega, A., Maurer, U., Mularczyk, M.: A fresh approach to updatable symmetric encryption. Cryptology ePrint Archive, Report 2021/559 (2021). https://eprint.iacr.org/2021/559

28. Galteland, Y.J., Pan, J.: Backward-leak uni-directional updatable encryption from (homomorphic) public key encryption. In: Boldyreva, A., Kolesnikov, V. (eds.) PKC 2023, Part II. LNCS, vol. 13941, pp. 399–428. Springer, Heidelberg (2023). https://doi.org/10.1007/978-3-031-31371-4_14

29. Jiang, Y.: The direction of updatable encryption does not matter much. In: Moriai, S., Wang, H. (eds.) ASIACRYPT 2020, Part III. LNCS, vol. 12493, pp. 529–558. Springer, Heidelberg (2020). https://doi.org/10.1007/978-3-030-64840-4_18

30. Klooß, M., Lehmann, A., Rupp, A.: (R)CCA secure updatable encryption with integrity protection. In: Ishai, Y., Rijmen, V. (eds.) EUROCRYPT 2019, Part I. LNCS, vol. 11476, pp. 68–99. Springer, Heidelberg (2019). https://doi.org/10.1007/978-3-030-17653-2_3

31. Lee, E.: Improved security notions for proxy re-encryption to enforce access control. In: Lange, T., Dunkelman, O. (eds.) LATINCRYPT 2017. LNCS, vol. 11368, pp. 66–85. Springer, Heidelberg (2019). https://doi.org/10.1007/978-3-030-25283-0_4

32. Lehmann, A., Tackmann, B.: Updatable encryption with post-compromise security. In: Nielsen, J.B., Rijmen, V. (eds.) EUROCRYPT 2018, Part III. LNCS, vol. 10822, pp. 685–716. Springer, Heidelberg (2018). https://doi.org/10.1007/978-3-319-78372-7_22

33. Leroux, A., Roméas, M.: Updatable encryption from group actions. Cryptology ePrint Archive, Report 2022/739 (2022). https://eprint.iacr.org/2022/739

34. Levy-dit-Vehel, F., Roméas, M.: A composable look at updatable encryption. Cryptology ePrint Archive, Report 2021/538 (2021). https://eprint.iacr.org/2021/538

35. Maino, L., Martindale, C., Panny, L., Pope, G., Wesolowski, B.: A direct key recovery attack on SIDH. In: Hazay, C., Stam, M. (eds.) EUROCRYPT 2023, Part V. LNCS, vol. 14008, pp. 448–471. Springer, Heidelberg (2023). https://doi.org/10.1007/978-3-031-30589-4_16

36. Meers, J., Riepel, D.: CCA secure updatable encryption from non-mappable group actions. Cryptology ePrint Archive, Paper 2024/499 (2024). https://eprint.iacr.org/2024/499

37. Miao, P., Patranabis, S., Watson, G.J.: Unidirectional updatable encryption and proxy re-encryption from DDH. In: Boldyreva, A., Kolesnikov, V. (eds.) PKC 2023, Part II. LNCS, vol. 13941, pp. 368–398. Springer, Heidelberg (2023). https://doi.org/10.1007/978-3-031-31371-4_13

38. Moriya, T., Onuki, H., Takagi, T.: SiGamal: A supersingular isogeny-based PKE and its application to a PRF. In: Moriai, S., Wang, H. (eds.) ASIACRYPT 2020, Part II. LNCS, vol. 12492, pp. 551–580. Springer, Heidelberg (2020). https://doi.org/10.1007/978-3-030-64834-3_19

39. Mula, M., Murru, N., Pintore, F.: Random sampling of supersingular elliptic curves. Cryptology ePrint Archive, Report 2022/528 (2022). https://eprint.iacr.org/2022/528

40. Namprempre, C., Rogaway, P., Shrimpton, T.: Reconsidering generic composition. In: Nguyen, P.Q., Oswald, E. (eds.) EUROCRYPT 2014. LNCS, vol. 8441, pp. 257–274. Springer, Heidelberg (2014). https://doi.org/10.1007/978-3-642-55220-5_15

41. Naor, M., Pinkas, B., Reingold, O.: Distributed pseudo-random functions and KDCs. In: Stern, J. (ed.) EUROCRYPT'99. LNCS, vol. 1592, pp. 327–346. Springer, Heidelberg (1999). https://doi.org/10.1007/3-540-48910-X_23

42. Nishimaki, R.: The direction of updatable encryption does matter. In: Hanaoka, G., Shikata, J., Watanabe, Y. (eds.) PKC 2022, Part II. LNCS, vol. 13178, pp. 194–224. Springer, Heidelberg (2022). https://doi.org/10.1007/978-3-030-97131-1_7

43. Page, A., Robert, D.: Introducing clapoti(s): Evaluating the isogeny class group action in polynomial time. Cryptology ePrint Archive, Paper 2023/1766 (2023). https://eprint.iacr.org/2023/1766

44. Phong, L.T., Wang, L., Aono, Y., Nguyen, M.H., Boyen, X.: Proxy re-encryption schemes with key privacy from LWE. Cryptology ePrint Archive, Report 2016/327 (2016). https://eprint.iacr.org/2016/327

45. Polyakov, Y., Rohloff, K., Sahu, G., Vaikuntanathan, V.: Fast proxy re-encryption for publish/subscribe systems. ACM Trans. Priv. Secur. **20**(4) (2017). https://doi.org/10.1145/3128607

46. Qian, C., Galteland, Y.J., Davies, G.T.: Extending updatable encryption: public key, tighter security and signed ciphertexts. Cryptology ePrint Archive, Paper 2023/848 (2023). https://eprint.iacr.org/2023/848

47. Robert, D.: Breaking SIDH in polynomial time. In: Hazay, C., Stam, M. (eds.) EUROCRYPT 2023, Part V. LNCS, vol. 14008, pp. 472–503. Springer, Heidelberg (2023). https://doi.org/10.1007/978-3-031-30589-4_17

48. Shannon, C.E.: Communication theory of secrecy systems. Bell Syst. Tech. J. **28**(4), 656–715 (1949)

49. Slamanig, D., Striecks, C.: Revisiting updatable encryption: controlled forward security, constructions and a puncturable perspective. In: TCC 2023 (2023)

Properties of Lattice Isomorphism as a Cryptographic Group Action

Benjamin Benčina[1]([✉]), Alessandro Budroni[2], Jesús-Javier Chi-Domínguez[2], and Mukul Kulkarni[2]

[1] Royal Holloway, University of London, London, UK
benjamin.bencina.2022@live.rhul.ac.uk
[2] Cryptography Research Center, Technology Innovation Institute, Abu Dhabi, UAE
{alessandro.budroni,jesus.dominguez,mukul.kulkarni}@tii.ae

Abstract. In recent years, the Lattice Isomorphism Problem (LIP) has served as an underlying assumption to construct quantum-resistant cryptographic primitives, e.g. the zero-knowledge proof and digital signature scheme by Ducas and van Woerden (Eurocrypt 2022), and the HAWK digital signature scheme (Asiacrypt 2022).

While prior lines of work in group action cryptography, e.g. the works of Brassard and Yung (Crypto 1990), and more recently Alamati, De Feo, Montgomery and Patranabis (Asiacrypt 2020), focused on studying the discrete logarithm problem and isogeny-based problems in the group action framework, in recent years this framing has been used for studying the cryptographic properties of computational problems based on the difficulty of determining equivalence between algebraic objects. Examples include Permutation and Linear Code Equivalence Problems used in LESS (Africacrypt 2020), and the Tensor Isomorphism Problem (TCC 2019). This study delves into the quadratic form version of LIP, examining it through the lens of group actions.

In this work we (1) give formal definitions and study the cryptographic properties of this group action (LIGA), (2) demonstrate that LIGA lacks both weak unpredictability and weak pseudorandomness, and (3) under certain assumptions, establish a theoretical trade-off between time complexity and the required number of samples for breaking weak unpredictability, for large dimensions. We also conduct experiments supporting our analysis. Additionally, we employ our findings to formulate new hard problems on quadratic forms.

Keywords: Gröbner Bases · Group Actions · Lattice-based Cryptography · Lattice Isomorphism Problem · Quadratic Forms

1 Introduction

Post-Quantum Cryptography is an active research area which aims to design public-key cryptographic primitives that can resist the threats posed by large scale quantum computers. Since most of the widely used public-key cryptographic algorithms will be affected by the attacks harnessing the computational

M.-J. Saarinen and D. Smith-Tone (Eds.): PQCrypto 2024, LNCS 14771, pp. 170–201, 2024.
https://doi.org/10.1007/978-3-031-62743-9_6

power of quantum computing, the National Institute of Standards and Technology (NIST), has already selected a few candidates for standardization [40], and more candidates are under consideration [39].

Equivalence Problems in Cryptography and Group Actions. The computational hardness of the equivalence problems for algebraic or geometric structures has emerged as an attractive underlying assumption for designing post-quantum cryptographic schemes. Informally, these are search problems which aim to find a map between two equivalent algebraic or geometric objects. Perhaps the most notable example of this approach is isogeny-based cryptography which relies on the hardness of finding isogenies between supersingular elliptic curves [1,11,19,20,23]. Cryptographic schemes have also been designed based on problems related to lattice isomorphisms [8,25], code equivalence [12], trilinear forms [44], and tensor isomorphism [32]. These have shown potential in constructing remarkable primitives, especially in the domains of proofs-of-knowledge and digital signatures [12,14,24,33]. Each of these problems is interesting in its own regard and provides different trade-offs as well as flexibility while designing cryptographic schemes, however these can also be seen as instances of a more general framework based on group actions introduced by [17] and later studied in [1,20,32]. These works show that this class of problems can be modelled as problems related to the computational hardness of inverting a group action.

Lattice Isomorphisms as a Group Action. In this work, we show how to characterize and analyze the quadratic form representation of lattice isomorphisms as a group action (LIGA). We believe that such a characterization helps in unifying the similar computational assumptions under a common framework, which can then be used to study the similarities between these hard problems.

Informally, the *Lattice Isomorphism Problem* (LIP) in its search version aims to find an isomorphism between two given isomorphic lattices. The decision version of the problem asks whether two given lattices are isomorphic or not. Lattice isomorphisms were studied and used initially in the cryptanalysis of early lattice-based schemes such as NTRU [30]. Later, Haviv and Regev studied the complexity of search-LIP [31]. More recently, two independent works by Bennett et al. [8] and by Ducas and van Woerden [25] proposed to use LIP for building cryptographic primitives. Subsequently, a digital signature scheme HAWK based on a module version of LIP has been proposed with impressive results in terms of efficiency and object sizes [24]. In [24,25] the authors focus on the quadratic form representation of the lattice isomorphism problem, which is also the focus of this paper. We find that LIGA is not a weakly unpredictable and therefore also not a weakly pseudorandom group action. These properties are stronger than one-wayness and have been studied in [1] for the isogeny-based group action. Our finding poses a significant barrier to using LIGA as a building block in the constructions of a variety of cryptographic primitives such as the Naor-Reingold-style PRF [38], along with the ones considered in [1, Sect. 4].

Shortly after the publication of the preprint version of this manuscript [18], another preprint analyzing code equivalence and other problems using a similar approach to our work was published [22].

1.1   Overview of Our Results

In this paper, we study the Lattice Isomorphism Problem (in the quadratic form setting) as defined in [25], in the framework of group actions with aim to understand its utility in building quantum-secure cryptographic primitives. Our main contributions are summarized below:

Formalizing Lattice Isomorphisms as a Group Action. In this work, we formalize LIGA as a group action and prove that it is faithful as well as transitive. We also show that LIGA is free if and only if the automorphism group of the quadratic form Q, defining the underlying equivalence class $[Q]$, is trivial.

Breaking the Weak Pseudorandomness of LIGA. We generalize the definitions of cryptographic properties of group actions presented in [1] to the setting where the underlying group and set are both infinite.[1] Assuming the conjectured hardness of LIP immediately implies that LIGA is a one-way group action. We then show that LIGA is not a weakly unpredictable (and therefore also not a weakly pseudorandom) group action, under some mild assumptions on the distribution $\mathcal{D}_{[Q]}$ used for sampling challenge instances.

Theorem 1 (Informal). *Given $O(n^2)$ instances of LIP obtained from a fixed secret isomorphism represented by $n \times n$ unimodular matrix U, it is possible to recover the secret isomorphism U in polynomial time with overwhelming probability.*

We also provide an alternate approach to recover the secret isomorphism U using Gröbner bases. At the cost of an extra multiplicative factor of $O(n^{2+(i-2)\omega})$ to the time complexity of the recovery, for a small constant $i \geq 2$ and some $\omega \in [2,3]$, one can retrieve the secret by requiring a factor of i^2 fewer samples, while assuming similar mild assumptions on the distribution $\mathcal{D}_{[Q]}$ used for sampling challenge instances.

Introducing Two New Computationally Hard Problems. We introduce two new hard problems on quadratic forms: the Transpose Quadratic Form Problem (TQFP) and the Inverse Quadratic Form Problem (IQFP). We use the aforementioned result to demonstrate the equivalence of these problems to search-LIP through dimension-preserving polynomial-time reductions, specifically for quadratic forms with a trivial automorphism group.

It is worth highlighting that such an inverse problem was previously introduced in the context of isogeny-based group actions, namely as Inv-HHS in [27]. In contrast to isogenies, we show that IQFP is as hard as LIP, while in isogenies Inv–HHS is not hard. Due to the non-linear nature of the isogeny-based group action, it appears that solving Inv–HHS does not translate to recovering the secret isogeny in polynomial time.

---

[1] This is in contrast to most of the prior works which consider group actions related to finite groups and/or sets. In [32] the authors mentioned that their definitions can be used in the setting of infinite groups and sets, specifically aiming at LIP. However, they do not present LIP in the quadratic form setting and only consider the finite groups and sets for their analysis.

Experiments. We verify our results by running experiments for lattice dimensions up to 40. Specifically, we verify that one can indeed recover the secret using estimated number of samples efficiently. We also compare the two approaches and verify that using Gröbner bases allows recovery of the secret from fewer samples. Additionally, we also conduct experiments validating the reductions from search version of LIP to the new problems introduced in this work (TQFP, and to IQFP). All these experiments are performed via a SAGEMATH [45] implementation that is available at [9].

1.2 Organization of the Paper

In Sect. 2 we give the preliminaries on lattices, group actions, and Gröbner basis computation. In Sect. 3 we formalize lattice isomorphism as a group action and provide the related results. In Sect. 4 we discuss the Gröbner basis approach along with some experimental results. In Sect. 5 we introduce two new hard problems together with their reductions from LIP. Finally, in Sect. 6 we discuss some interesting open problems.

2 Preliminaries

2.1 Notation

Let $\mathbb{N}$, $\mathbb{Z}$, $\mathbb{Q}$ and $\mathbb{R}$ denote the sets of natural, integer, rational, and real numbers, respectively. We denote vectors in boldface (e.g. v) and treat them as columns unless otherwise specified. We denote matrices by uppercase letters (e.g. M), and vectors of matrices by bold uppercase letters (e.g. $\boldsymbol{M}$). Sets are denoted with calligraphic uppercase letters (e.g. $\mathcal{S}$). For a vector $\mathbf{x}$ in $\mathbb{R}^n$, the Euclidean norm is denoted as $\|\mathbf{x}\|$.

The set of all $n \times n$ invertible matrices over $\mathbb{Z}$ is denoted by $\mathrm{GL}_n(\mathbb{Z}) := \{M \in \mathbb{Z}^{n \times n} : \det(M) = \pm 1\}$. For an invertible matrix $X \in \mathrm{GL}_n(\mathbb{Z})$, we denote the inverse of the transpose matrix X^T as $X^{-\mathsf{T}}$. Also, by I_n we denote the $n \times n$ identity matrix. For a matrix $M = [M_{i,j}] \in \mathbb{Z}^{n \times n}$, denote with $\bar{M}^{(i,j)} \in \mathbb{Z}^{(n-1) \times (n-1)}$ the minor of M with respect to $M_{i,j}$, i.e. the matrix obtained by removing the i-th row and the j-th column from M. We denote by M^* the Gram–Schmidt orthogonalization of M.

A matrix $S \in \mathbb{R}^{n \times n}$ is called *symmetric positive definite* if $S = S^\mathsf{T}$ and $\mathbf{x}^\mathsf{T} S \mathbf{x} > 0$ for all $\mathbf{x} \in \mathbb{R}^n \setminus \{\mathbf{0}\}$. The set of all $n \times n$ *symmetric positive definite* matrices over $\mathbb{R}$ is denoted by $\mathcal{S}_n^{>0}$. For $Q = [Q_{i,j}] \in \mathcal{S}_n^{>0}$ and $d := \frac{n(n+1)}{2}$, define unroll: $\mathcal{S}_n^{>0} \to \mathbb{R}^d$ as

$$\mathsf{unroll}(Q) := \begin{bmatrix} Q_{1,1} \ 2Q_{1,2} \ \dots \ 2Q_{1,n} \ Q_{2,2} \ 2Q_{2,3} \ \dots \ 2Q_{2,n} \ \dots \ Q_{n,n} \end{bmatrix}.$$

For simplicity, in the remainder of the paper, we assume both matrix multiplication and inversion take $O(n^\omega)$ integer operations for some $\omega \in [2,3]$.[2]

---

[2] The Strassen's algorithm is considered to be the best algorithm for large dimensional matrix multiplications with a running time of $O\left(n^{\log_2(7)}\right)$ operations.

Consequently, we assume that solving a linear system $Ax = B$, for some non-singular matrix $A \in \mathbb{Z}^{n \times n}$ and $B \in \mathbb{Z}^{n \times \delta}$ with $\delta \leq n$, takes time $O(n^\omega)$ since it is equivalent to computing $\mathbf{x} = A^{-1}B$.

2.2 Lattice Isomorphisms and Quadratic Forms

We refer the reader to [25] for a detailed introduction on the Lattice Isomorphism Problem. A full-rank n-dimensional lattice $\mathcal{L} = \mathcal{L}(B) := B \cdot \mathbb{Z}^n$ is generated by taking all of the possible integer combinations of the columns of a basis $B \in \mathbb{R}^{n \times n}$. Two bases B and B' generate the same lattice if and only if there exists a unimodular matrix $U \in \mathrm{GL}_n(\mathbb{Z})$ such that $B' = BU$.

Let $\mathcal{O}_n(\mathbb{F})$ be the set of all *orthonormal* matrices with entries in a field $\mathbb{F}$. Two lattices $\mathcal{L}$, $\mathcal{L}'$ are *isomorphic* if there exists an orthonormal transformation $O \in \mathcal{O}_n(\mathbb{R})$ such that $\mathcal{L}' = O \cdot \mathcal{L}$.

Definition 1 (Search Lattice Isomorphism Problem (sLIP)). *Given two isomorphic lattices $\mathcal{L}$, $\mathcal{L}' \subset \mathbb{R}^n$ find an orthonormal transformation $O \in \mathcal{O}_n(\mathbb{R})$ such that $\mathcal{L}' = O \cdot \mathcal{L}$.*

The problem in Definition 1 can be rephrased as follows. Given the bases $B, B' \in \mathbb{R}^{n \times n}$ for $\mathcal{L}$ and $\mathcal{L}'$ respectively, find $O \in \mathcal{O}_n(\mathbb{R})$ along with $U \in \mathrm{GL}_n(\mathbb{Z})$ such that $B' = OBU$. In practice, the real-valued entries of the bases and orthonormal matrices can be inconvenient to represent and result in inefficient computations. However, this can be eased by considering an equivalent problem to LIP by taking the quadratic form associated to B, i.e. the Gram matrix $Q := B^{\mathsf{T}}B$. Note that the quadratic form Q is symmetric by definition. Moreover, since B is a basis (and thus full-rank), Q is actually *symmetric positive definite*. For isomorphic lattices $\mathcal{L}, \mathcal{L}'$ with respective basis B, B', we have that $B' = OBU$ where $O \in \mathcal{O}_n(\mathbb{R})$ is orthonormal and $U \in \mathrm{GL}_n(\mathbb{Z})$ is unimodular. Then we have

$$Q' := {B'}^{\mathsf{T}}B' = U^{\mathsf{T}}B^{\mathsf{T}}O^{\mathsf{T}}OBU = U^{\mathsf{T}}B^{\mathsf{T}}BU = U^{\mathsf{T}}QU,$$

where $Q := B^{\mathsf{T}}B$ is the quadratic form of B. We call Q, Q' equivalent if such $U \in \mathrm{GL}_n(\mathbb{Z})$ exists. We also denote by $[Q]$ the equivalence class of all quadratic forms Q' equivalent to Q.

Definition 2 (sLIP$_Q$- Quadratic Form Version). *For a quadratic form $Q \in \mathcal{S}_n^{>0}$, the problem sLIP$_Q$ is, given any quadratic form $Q' \in [Q]$, to find a unimodular $U \in \mathrm{GL}_n(\mathbb{Z})$ such that $Q' = U^{\mathsf{T}}QU$.*

The squared norm of a vector $\mathbf{x}$ with respect to a quadratic form Q is defined as $\|\mathbf{x}\|_Q^2 := \mathbf{x}^{\mathsf{T}}Q\mathbf{x}$ and the inner product as $\langle \mathbf{x}, \mathbf{y} \rangle_Q := \mathbf{x}^{\mathsf{T}}Q\mathbf{y}$. The i-th minimal distance $\lambda_i(Q)$ is defined as the smallest $r > 0$ such that $\{\boldsymbol{x} \in \mathbb{Z}^n \colon \|\boldsymbol{x}\|_Q \leq r\}$ spans a space of dimension at least i. We denote by B_Q the Cholesky decomposition of Q, that is, an upper triangular matrix such that $Q = B_Q{}^{\mathsf{T}}B_Q$.

Definition 3 (Automorphisms). *Let $Q \in \mathcal{S}_n^{>0}$ be a quadratic form of dimension n. The automorphism group of Q is defined as*

$$\text{Aut}(Q) = \{V \in \text{GL}_n(\mathbb{Z}) \colon Q = V^{\mathsf{T}}QV\}.$$

We say that Q is automorphism-free if it has a trivial automorphism group $\text{Aut}(Q) = \{\pm I_n\}$.

Remark 1. Let $Q' \in [Q]$, and let $U \in \text{GL}_n(\mathbb{Z})$ be such that $Q' = U^{\mathsf{T}}QU$. Recall that for any such quadratic form Q, the group $\text{Aut}(Q)$ is always finite [42, Sect. 2.3]. The set of isomorphisms between Q and Q' can be written as $\{VU \colon V \in \text{Aut}(Q)\}$. The automorphism group of Q determines the number of isomorphisms from Q to Q' and vice versa. Therefore equivalent quadratic forms Q and Q' have the same number of automorphisms. Hence, automorphism-free quadratic forms are isomorphic only to automorphism-free quadratic forms. We provide some more details and formal justifications in Sect. 3 (Corollary 1) when we discuss orbits and stabilizers of lattice isomorphisms when viewed as a group action.

2.3 Sampling Quadratic Forms and Unimodular Matrices

Definition 4 (Discrete Gaussian Distribution w.r.t. Quadratic Forms [25, Sect. 2.3]). *For a quadratic form $Q \in \mathcal{S}_n^{>0}$, the Gaussian function on $\mathbb{R}^n$ with a parameter $s > 0$ and center $\mathbf{c}$ is defined by*

$$\forall \mathbf{x} \in \mathbb{R}^n, \ \rho_{Q,s,\mathbf{c}}(\mathbf{x}) := \exp\left(-\pi \|\mathbf{x} - \mathbf{c}\|_Q^2 / s^2\right).$$

The discrete Gaussian distribution $\mathcal{D}_{Q,s,\mathbf{c}}$ is defined as

$$\Pr_{X \sim \mathcal{D}_{Q,s,\mathbf{c}}} [X = \mathbf{x}] := \begin{cases} \frac{\rho_{Q,s,\mathbf{c}}(\mathbf{x})}{\rho_{Q,s,\mathbf{c}}(\mathbb{Z}^n)} & \text{if } \mathbf{x} \in \mathbb{Z}^n, \\ 0 & \text{otherwise} \end{cases}.$$

Brakerski et al. [16, Lemma 2.3] showed how to sample from a discrete Gaussian distribution efficiently. Ducas and van Woerden provide a polynomial time algorithm **Extract** that, taking as input a set of n linearly independent vectors Y and a quadratic form Q, returns a pair (Q', U) such that $Q' = U^{\mathsf{T}}QU$ [25, Lemma 3.1].

Definition 5 (Gaussian Form Distribution [25, Def. 3.3]). *Given a quadratic form equivalence class $[Q] \subset \mathcal{S}_n^{>0}$, the Gaussian form distribution $\mathcal{D}_s([Q])$ over $[Q]$ with a parameter $s > 0$ is defined algorithmically as follows:*

1. *Fix a representative $Q \in [Q]$.*
2. *Sample n vectors $(\mathbf{y}_1, \mathbf{y}_2, \ldots \mathbf{y}_n) := Y$ from $\mathcal{D}_{Q,s}$. Repeat until linearly independent.*
3. *$(R, U) \leftarrow \textbf{Extract}(Q, Y)$.*
4. *Return R.*

Ducas and van Woerden also provide a polynomial time algorithm to sample from $\mathcal{D}_s([Q])$ for $s \geq \max\{\lambda_n(Q), \|B_Q^*\| \cdot \sqrt{\ln(2n+4)/\pi}\}$, which returns, together with a quadratic form Q', a unimodular matrix U such that $Q' = U^\mathsf{T}QU$, and show that $Q' \leftarrow \mathcal{D}_s([Q])$ is independent from the input equivalence class representative Q [25, Lemma 3.2].

Sampling Unimodular Matrices. The algorithm **Extract** includes a method to derive a unimodular matrix from a set of independent vectors employing the Hermite Normal Form reduction that is folklore in the literature [13,36].

Algorithm 1 is a modified version of [13, Algorithm 4] for sampling unimodular matrices in polynomial time having the entries of the first $n-1$ rows uniform over the integer interval $[-T, T] \subset \mathbb{Z}$, for $T > 0$. For the context of this manuscript, it is not relevant for us whether it produces "cryptographically-strong" random unimodular matrices or not.

2.4   Cryptographic Group Actions

In this section, we present the definitions of cryptographic properties of group actions. Our definitions are inspired by those introduced in [1,20,32]. More specifically, we generalize the prior definitions to hold for infinite groups and sets, and we include the precise number of oracle calls that an adversary is allowed to make for a certain experiment, that is Definition 7 and Definition 8 give more fine-grained notions of weak unpredictability and weak pseudorandomness in comparison to their counterparts in [1, Sect. 2.1].[3]

Definition 6 (One-Way Functions). *Let P, X and Y be sets drawn from families of sets indexed by the parameter λ, and let $\mathcal{D}_P$ and $\mathcal{D}_X$ be distributions on P and X respectively. A $(\mathcal{D}_P, \mathcal{D}_X)$-OWF family is a family of efficiently computable functions $\{f_{\mathsf{pp}}(\cdot) \colon X \to Y\}_{\mathsf{pp} \in P}$ such that for all PPT adversaries $\mathcal{A}$ we have*

$$\Pr[f_{\mathsf{pp}}(\mathcal{A}(\mathsf{pp}, f_{\mathsf{pp}}(x))) = f_{\mathsf{pp}}(x)] \leq \mathsf{negl}(\lambda),$$

where $\mathsf{pp} \leftarrow \mathcal{D}_P$ and $x \leftarrow \mathcal{D}_X$.

Definition 7 (Weak Unpredictable Permutations). *Let K and X be sets drawn from families of sets indexed by the parameter λ, $\mathcal{D}_K$ and $\mathcal{D}_X$ be distributions on K and X respectively, and $t := t(\lambda) \in \mathbb{N}^+$ be a parameter. Let $F_k^\$$ be a randomized oracle that when queried samples $x \leftarrow \mathcal{D}_X$ and outputs $(x, F(k, x))$. A $(\mathcal{D}_K, \mathcal{D}_X, t)$-weak UP (wUP) is a family of efficiently computable permutations $\{F(k, \cdot) \colon X \to X\}_{k \in K}$ such that for all PPT adversaries $\mathcal{A}$ able to query $F_k^\$$ at most t times, we have*

$$\Pr[\mathcal{A}^{F_k^\$}(x^*) = F(k, x^*)] \leq \mathsf{negl}(\lambda),$$

where $k \leftarrow \mathcal{D}_K$ and $x^* \leftarrow \mathcal{D}_X$.

---

[3] This fine-grained notion of limiting the number of times the adversary calls the oracle makes our results stronger since any attacker breaking the fine-grained security property also breaks the same property in the sense of [1, Sect. 2.1] (or other prior definitions of cryptographic properties of group actions.).

Algorithm 1. Sample a unimodular matrix with all rows except the last one having entries uniformly distributed in an integer interval $[-T, T] \subset \mathbb{Z}$.

Input: A positive integer parameter $T > 0$.

Output: An $n \times n$ unimodular matrix with all rows except the last one having entries uniformly distributed in the integer interval $[-T, T] \subset \mathbb{Z}$.

1: Set a matrix $M = \{M_{i,j}\} \in \mathbb{Z}^{n \times n}$ to zero.
2: **repeat**
3:     Sample $M_{i,j} \leftarrow [-T, T]$ uniformly at random for each $i \leq n - 1$ and $j \leq n$.
4:     Use the Extended Euclidean Algorithm for computing

$$d \leftarrow \gcd\left((-1)^{n+1} \det\left(\bar{M}^{(n,1)}\right), \ldots, (-1)^{2n} \det\left(\bar{M}^{(n,n)}\right)\right),$$

along with the corresponding Bézout coefficients $M_{1,j}$'s such that

$$d = \sum_{j=1}^{n} M_{n,j} \cdot (-1)^{n+j} \det\left(\bar{M}^{(n,j)}\right) = \det(M).$$

5: **until** $d = 1$.
6: Choose the sign of $\det(M)$ as follows: sample $b \in \{0, 1\}$ uniformly at random, swap the first two rows if $b = 1$.
7: Use least-squares to find the linear combination $\sum_{j=1}^{n-1} c_j [M_{j,1} \ldots M_{j,n}]$ closest to $[M_{n,1} \ldots M_{n,n}]$, and let $\tilde{c}_i$ denote the nearest integer to c_i.
8: Update $[M_{n,1} \ldots M_{n,n}]$ as

$$[M_{n,1} \ldots M_{n,n}] - \sum_{j=1}^{n-1} \tilde{c}_j [M_{j,1} \ldots M_{j,n}].$$

9: **Return** M.

Definition 8 (Weak Pseudorandom Permutations). *Let K and X be sets drawn from families of sets indexed by the parameter λ, $\mathcal{D}_K$ and $\mathcal{D}_X$ be distributions on K and X respectively, and $t := t(\lambda) \in \mathbb{N}^+$ be a parameter. Let $\pi^\$$ be a randomized oracle that samples $x \leftarrow \mathcal{D}_X$ and outputs $(x, \pi(x))$, where π is a random permutation on X constructed adaptively by the oracle, i.e. when a new x is queried the oracle $\pi^\$$ samples $y \leftarrow \mathcal{D}_X$ until $y \neq \pi(x')$ for any previously queried $x' \in X$, and sets $\pi(x) := y$. A $(\mathcal{D}_K, \mathcal{D}_X, t)$-weak PRP (wPRP) is a family of efficiently computable permutations $\{F(k, \cdot) : X \to X\}_{k \in K}$ such that for all PPT adversaries $\mathcal{A}$ able to query the oracles $F_k^\$$ and $\pi^\$$ at most t times, we have*

$$\left| \Pr[\mathcal{A}^{F_k^\$}(1^\lambda) = 1] - \Pr[\mathcal{A}^{\pi^\$}(1^\lambda) = 1] \right| \leq \operatorname{negl}(\lambda),$$

where $k \leftarrow \mathcal{D}_K$.[4]

---

[4] As the players are PPT, we may model the "random" permutation as a random oracle that uses $\mathcal{D}_X$ to sample new images adaptively.

Definition 9 (Group Action). *A group $(G, \circ)$ is said to act on a non-empty set X if there is a map $\star \colon G \times X \to X$ that satisfies the following two properties*

1. *Identity: if e is the identity element of G, then for any $x \in X$, we have $e \star x = x$.*
2. *Compatibility: for any $g, h \in G$ and any $x \in X$, we have $(g \circ h) \star x = g \star (h \star x)$.*

We use the notation $(G, X, \star)$ to denote a group action.

If $(G, X, \star)$ is a group action, for any $g \in G$ the map $\pi_g \colon x \mapsto g \star x$ defines a permutation of X.

Definition 10 (Properties of Group Actions). *A group action $(G, X, \star)$ is said to be:*

1. ***transitive**, if for every $x_1, x_2 \in X$, there exists a group element $g \in G$ such that $x_2 = g \star x_1$ (for such a transitive group action, the set X is called a homogeneous space for G);*
2. ***faithful**, if for each group element $g \in G$, either g is the identity element or there exists a set element $x \in X$ such that $x \neq g \star x$;*
3. ***free**, if for every group element $g \in G$, g is the identity element if and only if there exists some set element $x \in X$ such that $x = g \star x$.*

Definition 11 (One-Way Group Action). *A group action $(G, X, \star)$, where G is a group and X is a set indexed by a parameter λ, is $(\mathcal{D}_G, \mathcal{D}_X)$-one-way if the family of efficiently computable functions $\{f_x \colon G \to X\}_{x \in X}$ is $(\mathcal{D}_G, \mathcal{D}_X)$-one-way, where $f_x \colon g \mapsto g \star x$, and $\mathcal{D}_G, \mathcal{D}_X$ are distributions on G, X respectively.*

Definition 12 (Weakly Unpredictable Group Action). *A group action $(G, X, \star)$ is $(\mathcal{D}_G, \mathcal{D}_X, t)$-weakly unpredictable if the family of efficiently computable permutations $\{\pi_g \colon X \to X\}_{x \in X}$ is a $(\mathcal{D}_G, \mathcal{D}_X, t)$-weak UP, where π_g is defined as $\pi_g \colon x \mapsto g \star x$ and $\mathcal{D}_X, \mathcal{D}_G$ are distributions on X, G respectively.*

Definition 13 (Weakly Pseudorandom Group Action). *A group action $(G, X, \star)$ is $(\mathcal{D}_G, \mathcal{D}_X, t)$-weakly pseudorandom if the family of efficiently computable permutations $\{\pi_g \colon X \to X\}_{x \in X}$ is a $(\mathcal{D}_G, \mathcal{D}_X, t)$-weak PRP where π_g is defined as $\pi_g \colon x \mapsto g \star x$ and $\mathcal{D}_X, \mathcal{D}_G$ are distributions on X, G respectively.*

Orbits and Stabilizers of Group Actions.

Definition 14. *Let $(G, X, \star)$ be a group action. The orbit of $x \in X$ is a subset of X defined as*

$$G \star x = \{g \star x \colon g \in G\},$$

and the stabilizer of $x \in X$ is the subgroup of G defined as

$$G_x = \{g \in G \colon g \star x = x\}.$$

Remark 2. The orbits of a group action $(G, X, \star)$ partition the set X into disjoint subsets. Moreover, the choice of the orbit representative does not matter, i.e. if $y \in G \star x$ then $G \star x = G \star y$. Note that a group action is transitive if and only if it admits a single orbit.

Remark 3. A well-known fact from group theory is that the stabilizers of set elements from the same orbit are conjugate subgroups of G, i.e. if $x_1 \in G \star x_0$ for $x_0, x_1 \in X$, then there exists $h \in G$ such that $G_{x_1} = hG_{x_0}h^{-1}$. In particular, stabilizers of elements from the same orbit have the same cardinality. Note that a group action is free if and only if all of its stabilizers are trivial. Moreover, the Orbit-Stabilizer Theorem states that for any $x \in X$ the map $f_x \colon G/G_x \to G \star x$ that maps cosets as $hG_x \mapsto h \star x$ is a bijection [35, Theorem 3.2].

2.5 Gröbner Bases and Semi-Regular Sequences

Let $\mathbb{F}$ be a field and $\mathcal{P} = \mathbb{F}[x_1, \ldots, x_n]$ a polynomial ring in n variables over $\mathbb{F}$. Let $\mathcal{M}$ be the set of monomials of $\mathcal{P}$. When $n = 1$ the natural way to order monomials is simply by comparing them by their degree. For $n > 1$, we define orderings that are admissible.

Definition 15. *A monomial order $<$ on $\mathcal{M}$ (or $\mathcal{P}$) is a well-ordering that is compatible with the product on $\mathcal{M}$, i.e. for every $u, v, w \in \mathcal{M}$ where $w \geq 1$ we have that $u < v$ implies $uw < vw$.*

We identify the set of monomials $\mathcal{M}$ with the set of their coefficients $\mathbb{Z}_{\geq 0}^n$, that is all n-tuples of non-negative integers, where $\alpha = (\alpha_1, \ldots, \alpha_n)$ is identified with the monomial $x^\alpha = x_1^{\alpha_1} \cdots x_n^{\alpha_n}$. We call α_i the degree of the monomial x at the variable x_i, and we call $|\alpha| = \sum_{i=1}^n \alpha_i$ the total degree of x. A monomial order that prioritizes ordering by total degree is called graded.

Definition 16. *The degree reverse lexicographical (DRL) order $>$ is defined by $\alpha > \beta$ if and only if $|\alpha| > |\beta|$, or $|\alpha| = |\beta|$ and the last non-zero entry of $\alpha - \beta$ is negative.*

Let $\mathcal{P}$ be equipped with the DRL monomial order. For a polynomial $f \in \mathcal{P}$, denote by $\mathrm{LM}(f)$ the leading monomial of f, that is the monomial that is the largest of all monomials of f w.r.t. the monomial order $>$. An ideal $\mathcal{I}$ of $\mathcal{P}$ is called a monomial ideal if there exists a basis for $\mathcal{I}$ consisting of monomials. By Hilbert's Basis Theorem, or more specifically Dickson's Lemma [21, Sect. 2.4, Theorem 5], such a basis can always be assumed to be finite. For a set $\mathcal{A} \subseteq \mathcal{P}$, we define $\mathrm{LM}(\mathcal{A})$ to be the set of all leading monomials of elements of $\mathcal{A}$.

Definition 17. *Let $\mathcal{I}$ be an ideal of $\mathcal{P}$. A finite subset $\mathcal{G} \subset \mathcal{I}$ is called a Gröbner basis of $\mathcal{I}$ if the set $\mathrm{LM}(\mathcal{G})$ generates the monomial ideal generated by $\mathrm{LM}(\mathcal{I})$, i.e. $\langle \mathrm{LM}(\mathcal{G}) \rangle = \langle \mathrm{LM}(\mathcal{I}) \rangle$.*

A Gröbner basis of an ideal $\mathcal{I}$ is a useful computational tool for studying the ideal $\mathcal{I}$, in particular dividing a polynomial with a Gröbner basis always gives a unique remainder, allowing one to determine membership in I. We now revise the complexity of computing Gröbner bases.

Definition 18. *A sequence of homogeneous polynomials* $(f_1, \ldots, f_m)$ *in* $\mathcal{P}$ *where* $m \leq n$ *is said to be* regular *if for all* $i = 1, \ldots, m$ *and* $g \in \mathcal{P}$ *such that* $gf_i \in \langle f_1, \ldots, f_{i-1} \rangle$ *we have that* $g \in \langle f_1, \ldots, f_{i-1} \rangle$.

Most importantly for us, a sequence $(f_1, \ldots, f_m)$ of polynomials over $\mathbb{Q}$ is regular if and only if the Hilbert series of the ideal $\mathcal{I} = \langle f_1, \ldots, f_m \rangle$ is equal to

$$S_{m,n}(z) = \frac{\prod_{i=1}^{m}(1 - z^{d_i})}{(1 - z)^n},$$

where d_i is the total degree of f_i for $i = 1, \ldots, m$. The first non-positive coefficient of the above series is called the index of regularity i_{reg} of $\mathcal{I}$. For the rest of this section, we consider polynomials over $\mathbb{Q}$.

The above construction works well for underdetermined and exactly determined systems, but we are mainly interested in the case of overdetermined polynomial systems. Note the ideals we are interested in are zero-dimensional, i.e. the set of roots of the system of equations generating the ideal is finite. The main idea is to only considered regularity up to the index of regularity [3,5,6], which is defined as follows.

Definition 19 ([6]). *Let* $\mathcal{I} = \langle f_1, \ldots, f_m \rangle$ *be an ideal of* $\mathcal{P}$. *The* index of regularity *is defined as*

$$i_{reg} = \min \left\{ d \; ; \; \dim_{\mathbb{F}}(\{f \in \mathcal{I} \; ; \; \deg(f) = d\}) = \binom{n + d - 1}{d} \right\}.$$

The above definition is equivalent to our previous one if $m \leq n$, thus subsuming it. This notion for $m > n$ will be called semi-regularity.

Definition 20 ([6, **Def.** 4]). *A sequence* $(f_1, \ldots, f_m)$ *of homogeneous polynomials in* $\mathcal{P}$ *is* semi-regular *if for all* $i = 1, \ldots, m$ *and* $g \in \mathcal{P}$ *such that* $gf_i \in \langle f_1, \ldots, f_{i-1} \rangle$ *and* $\deg(gf_i) < i_{reg}$, *we have that* $g \in \langle f_1, \ldots, f_{i-1} \rangle$.

For $m \leq n$ the definitions of regularity and semi-regularity coincide. Most importantly for us, a sequence $(f_1, \ldots, f_m)$ is semi-regular if and only if the Hilbert series of the ideal $\mathcal{I} = \langle f_1, \ldots, f_m \rangle$ is equal to $S_{m,n}(z)$ truncated after the first non-positive coefficient, whose index is precisely i_{reg}. The index of regularity bounds the complexity of Gröbner basis computation in the following way.

Lemma 1 ([6, **Prop.** 5]). *The total number of field operations in* $\mathbb{F}$ *performed by the matrix version of the* F_5 *algorithm is bounded by*

$$O\left(m i_{reg} \binom{n + i_{reg} - 1}{i_{reg}}^{\omega} \right).$$

As suggested in [6], the same complexity bound holds for non-homogeneous systems if we consider their homogeneous parts of the highest total degree [43, Thms. 1.72 and 1.73]. Moreover, we call a sequence of polynomials semi-regular if the sequence formed by their homogeneous parts of the highest total degree is semi-regular.

3   Lattice Isomorphism as a Group Action

In this section we introduce lattice isomorphism in the quadratic form setting as a group action, and provide some results related to the group action. Consider the equivalence relation $\simeq_\pm$ defined as

$$A \simeq_\pm B \iff A = \pm B,$$

and define the quotient set $\mathrm{GL}_n^\pm(\mathbb{Z}) := \mathrm{GL}_n(\mathbb{Z})/\simeq_\pm$. The elements of $\mathrm{GL}_n^\pm(\mathbb{Z})$ are equivalence classes, each containing two elements. Namely, for $A \in \mathrm{GL}_n(\mathbb{Z})$, one has a corresponding class $[A]_\pm \in \mathrm{GL}_n^\pm(\mathbb{Z})$, and $A, -A$ belong to the same class. Define the product between two classes $[A]_\pm, [B]_\pm \in \mathrm{GL}_n^\pm(\mathbb{Z})$ as

$$[A]_\pm \cdot [B]_\pm := [BA]_\pm, \tag{1}$$

where BA is the result of the matrix multiplication between two representatives B and A of the classes $[B]_\pm$ and $[A]_\pm$ respectively.

The set $\mathrm{GL}_n^\pm(\mathbb{Z})$ together with the product defined in *Equation* (1) forms a group whose identity element is $[I_n]_\pm$, the inverse of every element $[A]_\pm \in \mathrm{GL}_n^\pm(\mathbb{Z})$ is $[A^{-1}]_\pm \in \mathrm{GL}_n^\pm(\mathbb{Z})$, and with the associativity property induced by the associativity of matrix multiplication

$$([A]_\pm \cdot [B]_\pm) \cdot [C]_\pm = [BA]_\pm \cdot [C]_\pm = [CBA]_\pm = [A]_\pm \cdot [CB]_\pm = [A]_\pm \cdot ([B]_\pm \cdot [C]_\pm).$$

In what follows, we drop the notation of equivalence classes. Namely, we write $A \in \mathrm{GL}_n^\pm(\mathbb{Z})$ to indicate the class $[A]_\pm \in \mathrm{GL}_n^\pm(\mathbb{Z})$. Within the context of LIP, when we write $U^\mathsf{T} Q U$, we mean the quadratic form obtained by applying any of the two representatives of $[U]_\pm \in \mathrm{GL}_n^\pm(\mathbb{Z})$ (U and $-U$) to $Q \in \mathcal{S}_n^{>0}$. The following proposition defines lattice isomorphisms in the quadratic form representation as a group action over a non-abelian group.

Proposition 1. *Consider a quadratic form $Q \in \mathcal{S}_n^{>0}$ and let $[Q]$ be its equivalence class of isomorphic quadratic forms. Then the map*

$$\star \colon (\mathrm{GL}_n^\pm(\mathbb{Z}) \times [Q]) \to [Q], \qquad \star(V, Q_0) \mapsto V \star Q_0 := V^\mathsf{T} Q_0 V,$$

defines a group action of $\mathrm{GL}_n^\pm(\mathbb{Z})$ on $[Q]$.

Proof. Given $Q_0 \in [Q]$ and $V \in \mathrm{GL}_n(\mathbb{Z})$, then $Q_1 = V^\mathsf{T} Q_0 V$ is a quadratic form equivalent to Q_0, and therefore $Q_1 \in [Q]$. The identity element of $\mathrm{GL}_n^\pm(\mathbb{Z})$ fixes, through $\star$, any element of $[Q]$. Finally, for $U, V \in \mathrm{GL}_n^\pm(\mathbb{Z})$ we have that

$$(U \cdot V) \star Q_0 = (VU)^\mathsf{T} Q_0 VU = U^\mathsf{T}(V^\mathsf{T} Q_0 V)U = U \star (V^\mathsf{T} Q_0 V) = U \star (V \star Q_0),$$

which proves compatibility. $\qquad\qquad\qquad\qquad\qquad\qquad\qquad\qquad\qquad\qquad\quad\square$

We denote the group action based on lattice isomorphism in the quadratic form representation introduced in Proposition 1 as LIGA. Note that the map $\star$ is defined identically for any class of equivalent quadratic forms $[Q]$. Differently from most other cryptographic group actions used in the literature [1,15,33], in our case we have that both the base set and the group are infinite.[5]

We obtain the following corollary which characterizes the orbits and stabilizers of LIGA.

Corollary 1. *(a) The orbits of* LIGA *are quadratic form equivalence classes. (b) The stabilizer of a quadratic form $Q \in \mathcal{S}_n^{>0}$ w.r.t.* LIGA *is* $\mathrm{Aut}\,(Q)$.

The above corollary combined with Remark 3 implies that the automorphism groups of equivalent quadratic forms have the same size, since conjugation is a bijective map. Likewise, the above proposition combined with the Orbit-Stabilizer Theorem show that the set of isomorphisms between Q and Q' with $Q' = U^T Q U = U \star Q$ is $\{UV : V \in \mathrm{Aut}\,(Q)\}$, as this set is precisely the coset $U G_Q$ that gets mapped to Q' by f_Q in Remark 3.

We now focus on the properties of LIGA.

Proposition 2. *Let $Q \in \mathcal{S}_n^{>0}$ be the quadratic form for a basis of a lattice $\mathcal{L}$. Then the group action $(\mathrm{GL}_n^{\pm}(\mathbb{Z}), [Q], \star)$ is transitive and faithful.*

Proof. We first prove transitivity by observing that by Corollary 1, the group action $(\mathrm{GL}_n^{\pm}(\mathbb{Z}), [Q], \star)$ admits a single orbit, implying transitivity by Remark 2.

We now prove the group action is faithful by contradiction. Observe that a group action $(G, X, \star)$ is faithful if and only if for every $g \in G \setminus \{e\}$ there exists $x \in X$ such that $x \neq g \star x$, i.e. there is no group element that fixes every set element. Equivalently, the group action is faithful precisely when the subgroup $N = \bigcap_{x \in X} G_x$ of G, known as the kernel of the group action, is trivial. Since the group action $(\mathrm{GL}_n^{\pm}(\mathbb{Z}), [Q], \star)$ acts on a single orbit by Corollary 1, we have

$$N = \bigcap_{Q' \in [Q]} \mathrm{Aut}\,(Q') = \bigcap_{U \in \mathrm{GL}_n^{\pm}(\mathbb{Z})} U \,\mathrm{Aut}\,(Q)\, U^{-1},$$

where the last equality follows from the fact that if U maps Q to Q', then $\mathrm{Aut}\,(Q') = \{UVU^{-1} : V \in \mathrm{Aut}\,(Q)\} = U\,\mathrm{Aut}\,(Q)\,U^{-1}$. It follows that N is finite as a subset of $\mathrm{Aut}\,(Q)$, and normal as the intersection of the conjugacy class of $\mathrm{Aut}\,(Q)$. Notice that clearly the normal subgroup $N_{\pm} = \{\pm I_n\}$ of $\mathrm{GL}_n(\mathbb{Z})$ is also contained in N. We thus want to prove that $N/N_{\pm}$ is trivial, i.e. $N = N_{\pm}$.

Now, let us take a non-trivial $U \in N$, i.e. U fixes every element in $[Q]$, let $Q_0 \in [Q]$, and let $Q_1 = V \star Q_0 \neq Q_0$ for $V \neq \pm I_n \in \mathrm{GL}_n^{\pm}(\mathbb{Z})$. Then, $(UV) \star Q_0 = (VU) \star Q_0$ for every $Q_0 \in [Q]$, which implies $[U, V] = UVU^{-1}V^{-1} \in N$ for all $V \in \mathrm{GL}_n^{\pm}(\mathbb{Z})$. Multiplying by U^{-1} from the left yields that $VUV^{-1} \in N$ for

---

[5] Notice that LIGA, equipped with $\mathcal{D}_s([Q])$ and an efficient sampler over $\mathrm{GL}_n(\mathbb{Z})$ (Algorithm 1 or **Extract** in [25]), follows the definition of an Effective Group Action from [1], with the relaxation that the base set and group are infinite.

every $V \in \mathrm{GL}_n(\mathbb{Z})$. Therefore, the finite group N contains the entire conjugacy class of U (when viewed in $\mathrm{GL}_n(\mathbb{Z})$), which contradicts the finiteness of N.

Indeed, if the matrix U has a non-zero entry outside of the diagonal, say in the i-th row, then conjugating by V equal to the identity matrix except with $k \in \mathbb{Z}$ in the i-th entry in the first row leads to an infinite subset of the conjugacy class parametrized by $k \in \mathbb{Z}$. In the remaining case of U being a diagonal matrix with ± 1 on the diagonal and not equal to $\pm I$, we see that if U has -1 in the i-th column, then conjugating with V that has a non-trivial i-th row leads to an infinite conjugacy class.   □

The following proposition characterizes when the *free* property is satisfied.

Proposition 3. *Let $Q \in \mathcal{S}_n^{>0}$ be a quadratic form. Then, the group action $(\mathrm{GL}_n^{\pm}(\mathbb{Z}), [Q], \star)$ is free if and only if Q is automorphism-free.*

Proof. By Corollary 1, orbits are precisely equivalence classes, and because we focus on a single equivalence class $[Q]$, this implies there is a single orbit. By Remark 3, this group action is free if and only if its stabilizers are trivial, which is equivalent by Corollary 1 to the quadratic form Q (or any other orbit representative) being automorphism-free. prop

3.1   Cryptographic Properties of LIGA

We introduce in Theorem 1 a new result on the sufficient number of oracle queries to break the weak unpredictability of LIGA. More specifically, we give the necessary number of oracle calls for an adversary to invert the group action in polynomial time and space. Given the generality of the result, we do not limit it to any specific distribution on the group $\mathrm{GL}_n^{\pm}(\mathbb{Z})$ for the secret unimodular matrix. In contrast, we need the distribution on the equivalence class $[Q]$ to satisfy the following property.

Definition 21. *Let $\mathcal{D}_{[Q]}$ be a distribution over $[Q]$, for $Q \in \mathcal{S}_n^{>0}$, and let $d = \frac{n(n+1)}{2}$ and $p \geq d$ be positive integers. We say that $\mathcal{D}_{[Q]}$ induces p-linear independence if, given $Q_1, \ldots, Q_p \leftarrow \mathcal{D}_{[Q]}$, the $p \times d$ matrix $M_{\mathcal{Q}}$ whose rows are* unroll(Q_i) *(see definition in Sect. 2) is such that*

$$Pr[\mathrm{rank}(M_{\mathcal{Q}}) < d] \leq \mathsf{negl}(n).$$

For simplicity, we write that a distribution $\mathcal{D}_{[Q]}$ is p-linear when it induces p-linear independence.

The following proposition follows from Definition 21 since adding a row to a matrix does not decrease its rank.

Proposition 4. *If a distribution $\mathcal{D}_{[Q]}$ over $[Q]$ is p-linear, then it is also $(p+1)$-linear.*

Theorem 1. *Let $Q \in \mathcal{S}_n^{>0}$ and $\mathcal{D}_{\mathrm{GL}_n^{\pm}(\mathbb{Z})}$ be a distribution over $\mathrm{GL}_n^{\pm}(\mathbb{Z})$. For $d = \frac{n(n+1)}{2}$, let $\mathcal{D}_{[Q]}$ be a d-linear distribution over $[Q]$. Then the group action $(\mathrm{GL}_n^{\pm}(\mathbb{Z}), [Q], \star)$ is not a $(\mathcal{D}_{[Q]}, \mathcal{D}_{\mathrm{GL}_n^{\pm}(\mathbb{Z})}, t)$-weakly unpredictable group action for any $t \geq d$.*

Proof. We show that $(\mathrm{GL}_n^{\pm}(\mathbb{Z}), [Q], \star)$ is not a $(\mathcal{D}_{[Q]}, \mathcal{D}_{\mathrm{GL}_n^{\pm}(\mathbb{Z})}, d)$-weakly unpredictable group action by providing a polynomial-time algorithm Recover to invert the group action. Let $\mathcal{A}$ be an adversary able to make $d = \frac{n(n+1)}{2}$ queries to a randomized oracle $F_V^{\$}$ that, when queried, samples a $Q' \leftarrow \mathcal{D}_{[Q]}$ and outputs $(Q', V^{\mathsf{T}} Q' V)$. Then the adversary $\mathcal{A}$ is able to collect a list of d pairs $\mathcal{Q} := \{(Q_i, V^{\mathsf{T}} Q_i V)\}_{i=1,\ldots,d}$ such that the $d \times d$ matrix $M_{\mathcal{Q}}$ whose rows are composed by unroll(Q_i) is full-rank with overwhelming probability.

We describe first a procedure Linearize, a sub-routine of the main algorithm Recover to compute the secret unimodular V. The underlying idea takes inspiration from the work of Rasslan and Youssef [41].

Linearize. Consider one pair $(Q, Q' = V^{\mathsf{T}} Q V)$ from the set $\mathcal{Q}$. Denote with $Q_{i,j}$ (resp. $Q'_{i,j}$) the (i,j)-th entry of Q (resp. Q'). Given that Q is symmetric, we have that $Q_{i,j} = Q_{j,i}$ (resp. $Q'_{i,j} = Q'_{j,i}$). Then, we can write the equation

$$Q'_{i,j} = \sum_{k=1}^{n} \sum_{l=1}^{n} Q_{k,l} \cdot X_{(i,k),(j,l)} \tag{2}$$

where $X_{(i,k),(j,l)} = V_{i,k} \cdot V_{j,l}$ for each $i,j,k,l \in \{1,\ldots,n\}$, and $V_{i,j}$ is the (i,j)-th entry of V. Let us consider as baseline Equation (2) with $i = j$:

$$Q'_{i,i} = \sum_{k=1}^{n} \sum_{l=k+1}^{n} 2Q_{k,l} \cdot X_{(i,k),(i,l)} + \sum_{k=1}^{n} Q_{k,k} \cdot X_{(i,k),(i,k)}.$$

Writing the above equation as a d-dimensional vector-matrix multiplication, we get $Q'_{i,i} = \mathbf{Q} \cdot \mathbf{x}_i$ where

$$\mathbf{Q} = \begin{bmatrix} Q_{1,1} & 2Q_{1,2} & \cdots & 2Q_{1,n} & Q_{2,2} & 2Q_{2,3} & \cdots & 2Q_{2,n} & \cdots & Q_{n,n} \end{bmatrix}, \text{ and}$$

$$\mathbf{x}_i = \begin{bmatrix} X_{(i,1),(i,1)} & \cdots & X_{(i,1),(i,n)} & X_{(i,2),(i,2)} & \cdots & X_{(i,2),(i,n)} & \cdots & X_{(i,n),(i,n)} \end{bmatrix}^{\mathsf{T}}.$$

Denote by $\mathrm{diag}(Q') = \begin{bmatrix} Q'_{1,1} & Q'_{2,2} & \cdots & Q'_{n,n} \end{bmatrix}$ the diagonal of the matrix Q' represented as a vector. Then we have

$$\mathbf{Q} \cdot \overbrace{\begin{bmatrix} \mathbf{x}_1 & \mathbf{x}_2 & \cdots & \mathbf{x}_n \end{bmatrix}}^{d\text{-by-}n \text{ matrix}} = \mathrm{diag}(Q'). \tag{3}$$

$\downarrow$
d-dimensional vector

Recover. The procedure Linearize generates a linear system with d^2 variables and d equations. Given that we have d pairs (Q_i, Q_i') in $\mathcal{Q}$, we repeat the above technique d times to derive d^2 linearly independent equations, and proceed by finding the unique solution (up to a sign) of the associated system. We describe the algorithm to recover $\pm V$ below and refer to it as Recover:

1. For each pair (Q_i, Q_i') in $\mathcal{Q}$, apply Linearize(Q_i, Q_i') and get the following equation

$$Q_i \cdot \begin{bmatrix} x_1 & x_2 & \ldots\ldots & x_n \end{bmatrix} = \mathrm{diag}(Q_i').$$

2. Solve the linear system

$$\begin{bmatrix} Q_1 \\ \vdots \\ Q_d \end{bmatrix} \cdot \begin{bmatrix} x_1 & x_2 & \ldots\ldots & x_n \end{bmatrix} = \begin{bmatrix} \mathrm{diag}(Q_1') \\ \vdots \\ \mathrm{diag}(Q_d') \end{bmatrix} \tag{4}$$

   using Gaussian Elimination to retrieve $x_1, x_2, \ldots, x_n$.

3. Derive the entries (up to a sign) of the solution matrix U by computing first $U_{1,i} = \sqrt{x_{1,i}}$, then $U_{j,i} = \frac{x_{j,i}}{U_{1,i}}$ for $0 \leq i, j \leq n$. We have the following two scenarios:
   (a) If $U_{1,i} \neq 0$ for $i = 1, \ldots, n$ then we get (up to a sign) the i-th column V_i of V. That gives 2^n possible combinations, out of which only 2 are correct. From the perspective of the columns of V, each pair (Q, Q') in $\mathcal{Q}$ satisfies

$$V_j Q V_i = Q_{i,j}' \qquad i \leq j, \tag{5}$$

   for each $j := 1, \ldots, n$. In other words, Eq. 5 describes the inner products $\langle V_j, V_i \rangle_Q$ in the geometry given by Q.
   Thus, to get around this exponential step, we interpret them as column solution parity equations. We guess a solution for U_1, which is the first column of either V or $-V$. Then for each $i := 2, \ldots, n$, we pick the solution for U_i such that $U_i Q U_1 = Q_{1,i}'$, since the inner product given by Q is linear in both components. We thus obtain either V or $-V$, depending on our guess of the solution for U_1, after which the algorithm terminates.
   (b) If $U_{1,i} = 0$ for some $1 \leq i \leq n$, then the algorithm cannot recover the full matrix U as it would have to divide by zero. In this case, the algorithm samples a unimodular matrix R using Algorithm 1 for a parameter $T = O(n)$, and computes the set $\mathcal{Q}' := \{(Q, R^\mathsf{T} Q' R) : (Q, Q') \in \mathcal{Q}\}$, then repeats Recover with $\mathcal{Q}'$ as input. Note that $M_{\mathcal{Q}'} = M_{\mathcal{Q}}$, and so $\mathrm{rank}(M_{\mathcal{Q}'}) = d$. If the algorithm succeeds in recovering the matrix $U = VR$ (i.e., U has only non-zero entries in its first row), then it also recovers $\pm V$ as $V = UR^{-1}$, after which the algorithm terminates. Otherwise, the algorithm tries again with a different unimodular matrix R until it succeeds.

Memory and Time Complexities. Recall that $d = \frac{n(n+1)}{2}$. Step 2 from Recover requires to solve the linear system determined by Equation (4), which has a cost of $O(d^\omega) = O(n^{2\omega})$ operations. The derivation of the entries of U in Step 3 takes $O(n^2)$ integer operations. The calculations of the correct sign of the i-th column of U require $2n$ inner product calculations, which gives a total cost of $O(2n^3)$ operations. Then, the time complexity of deriving $\pm V$ becomes

$$O\left(\frac{n^\omega (n+1)^\omega}{2^\omega} + 2n^3 + n^2\right) = O(n^{2\omega})$$

operations. In terms of memory, the algorithm Recover stores one $d \times d$ matrix, two $d \times n$ matrices, and the $n \times n$ matrix U. Therefore, Recover has a memory complexity of storing

$$d^2 + 2dn + n^2 = \frac{n^2(n+1)^2}{4} + \frac{n^2(n+1)}{2} + n^2 = O(n^4)$$

matrix entries.

We are left to show that the number of tries in Step 3b in Recover is negligible and does not grow with n. Let $R_{1,1}, \ldots, R_{1,n}$ denote the entries of the first row of R which are uniformly distributed in $[-T, T] \subset \mathbb{Z}$ (because of Algorithm 1). We then have that VR has one or more zeros in its first row if and only if $(R_{1,1}, \ldots, R_{1,n})$ is a solution to the Diophantine equation

$$V_{1,j}x_1 + V_{2,j}x_2 + \cdots + V_{n,j}x_n = 0 \qquad (6)$$

for some $1 \le j \le n$. Since V is non-singular, at least one entry per row is non-zero. Without lost of generality assume $V_{n,j} \neq 0$. Then

$$x_n = -\frac{V_{1,j}}{V_{n,j}}x_1 - \frac{V_{2,j}}{V_{n,j}}x_2 - \cdots - \frac{V_{n-1,j}}{V_{n,j}}x_{n-1},$$

i.e. x_n is uniquely determined by $x_1, \ldots, x_{n-1}$, and whether or not $(x_1, \ldots, x_{n-1})$ leads to a solution or not is determined by a congruence condition modulo $V_{n,j}$. Thus, for every j there exists a rational constant $0 \le \gamma_j \le 1$ such that the number of solutions is asymptotic to $\gamma_j (2T+1)^{n-1}$. Therefore, the proportion of solutions on all the possible vectors is asymptotic to $\gamma_j/(2T+1)$. Hence, the probability that $[R_{1,1} \ldots R_{1,n}]$ is not a solution of any of Equation (6) is at least

$$\left(1 - \frac{1}{2T+1}\right)^n = \left(1 - \frac{1}{O(n)}\right)^n = \left(1 - \frac{1}{cn}\right)^n \xrightarrow{n \to \infty} e^{-1/c}$$

for some constant $c \ge 1$. □

Weak pseudorandomness of a permutation is a stronger property than weak unpredictability, therefore we obtain the following corollary.

Corollary 2. *Let* $Q \in \mathcal{S}_n^{>0}$ *and* $\mathcal{D}_{\mathrm{GL}_n^{\pm}(\mathbb{Z})}$ *be a distribution over* $\mathrm{GL}_n^{\pm}(\mathbb{Z})$. *For* $d = \frac{n(n+1)}{2}$, *let* $\mathcal{D}_{[Q]}$ *be a d-linear distribution over* $[Q]$. *Then, the group action* $(\mathrm{GL}_n^{\pm}(\mathbb{Z}), [Q], \star)$ *is not a* $(\mathcal{D}_{[Q]}, \mathcal{D}_{\mathrm{GL}_n^{\pm}(\mathbb{Z})}, t)$-*weakly pseudorandom group action, for any* $t \geq d$.

Theorem 1 and Corollary 2 also extend to the case of $\mathcal{D}_{[Q]}$ being p-linear for $p > d$, due to Proposition 4.

On d-Linear Distributions and Experimental Verification. We believe that the hypothesis on the distribution $\mathcal{D}_{[Q]}$ to be d-linear is realistic. Essentially, we require $\mathcal{D}_{[Q]}$ to output quadratic forms that are linearly independent from each other via the function unroll(). On the other hand, a distribution that outputs samples that are somewhat more likely to be linearly dependent would make them more predictable. Hence, it would likely come with serious security implications when used to build cryptographic primitives.

We were not able to prove that $\mathcal{D}_s([Q])$ (described in Definition 5, introduced and used in [25]) is d-linear theoretically. However, we experimentally observed that $\mathcal{D}_s([Q])$ behaves as a d-linear distribution. Therefore, we make the following assumption.

Assumption 1. *For a quadratic form* $Q \in \mathcal{S}_n^{>0}$, *the Gaussian Form Distribution* $\mathcal{D}_s([Q])$ *with* $s \geq \max\{\lambda_n(Q), \|B_Q^*\| \cdot \sqrt{\ln(2n+4)/\pi}\}$ *is* $\frac{n(n+1)}{2}$-*linear.*

Using $\mathcal{D}_s([Q])$ as distribution for the base set $[Q]$, we verified the correctness of Recover presented in the proof of Theorem 1 via a SAGEMATH implementation available at [9].

On Commutative Subgroups of $\mathrm{GL}(\mathbb{Z})$. If the secret unimodular matrix belongs to a commutative subgroup of $\mathrm{GL}(\mathbb{Z})$ (e.g. circulant matrices, powers of a matrix, ...), then it can be recovered in polynomial time from one single sample. More precisely, let $\mathcal{G}_c \subset \mathrm{GL}(\mathbb{Z})$ be a commutative group, and let $V \in \mathcal{G}_c$. Given a LIP instance $(Q, Q' = V^\mathsf{T} Q V)$, one is able to construct more LIP instances sharing the same secret unimodular matrix V (and simulate the calls to the oracle in to the oracle in Theorem 1) as follows. Sample unimodular matrices $U \in \mathcal{G}_c$ and compute

$$(\bar{Q} := U^\mathsf{T} Q U, \quad \bar{Q}' := U^\mathsf{T} Q' U = U^\mathsf{T} V^\mathsf{T} Q V U = V^\mathsf{T} U^\mathsf{T} Q U V = V^\mathsf{T} \bar{Q} V).$$

Hence, from one single call to the oracle, one can efficiently generate a long enough list of LIP instances sharing the same secret unimodular V and use Recover described in the proof of Theorem 1 to retrieve it.

4 Time/Samples Trade-Off Using Gröbner Basis

In this section we propose another approach for computing the secret unimodular matrix V from a list of m pairs $\mathcal{Q} = \{(Q_i, Q_i' = V^\mathsf{T} Q_i V)\}_{i=1,\dots,m}$ given by the randomized oracle $F_V^\$$ using Gröbner bases. This approach allows one to use fewer samples, i.e. take $m \leq d$, at the price of an increased computational complexity, and later allows us to target weak pseudorandomness specifically.

4.1   Algebraic Analysis

Naively, one may define n^2 variables $\{x_{i,j}\}_{i,j=1,...,n}$ representing the individual entries of V, and think of each sample of the form

$$Q' = \begin{bmatrix} x_{1,1} & \cdots & x_{n,1} \\ \vdots & \ddots & \vdots \\ x_{1,n} & \cdots & x_{n,n} \end{bmatrix} \cdot Q \cdot \begin{bmatrix} x_{1,1} & \cdots & x_{1,n} \\ \vdots & \ddots & \vdots \\ x_{n,1} & \cdots & x_{n,n} \end{bmatrix}$$

as giving $d = \frac{n(n+1)}{2}$ quadratic equations. However, notice the equations given are structured, as each only contains either n or $2n$ variables. Indeed, as noted already in the proof of Theorem 1 what we are given by the oracle $F_V^\$$ are inner product equations for the columns of V as in Equation (5). In particular, looking at $i = j$ each sample yields one norm equation $\|V_i\|_Q^2 = Q'_{i,i}$ per column, containing merely n variables.

Remark 4. Using the same observations in both the linearization approach and the algebraic approach using Gröbner basis computation is no coincidence. Algebraically, linearization is no more than the interreduction of a system of equations, i.e. reducing each polynomial of the system w.r.t. all others, whereas a Gröbner basis algorithm would also compute S-polynomials.

The main idea is the following. Instead of using all the equations given by the oracle $F_V^\$$, we focus on collecting norm equations to obtain m quadratic equations in n variables, one system per column of the secret unimodular matrix V. If these systems are sufficiently random, which we qualify in Assumption 2, each system will have two unique solutions $\pm V_i$ with overwhelming probability. We then use the inner product equations (from a single oracle query) to assemble these solutions into $\pm V$, which act equivalently on quadratic forms. Note also that the systems for different columns are disjoint in terms of variables, meaning the solutions for each column can be computed independently.

We require the following of our quadratic systems of equations.

Assumption 2. *For a quadratic form* $Q \in \mathcal{S}_n^{>0}$, *a unimodular matrix* V, *and* $\{Q_i\}_{i=1,...,m}$ *with* $m > n$ *sampled from the Gaussian Form Distribution* $\mathcal{D}_s([Q])$ *with* $s \geq \max\{\lambda_n(Q), \|B_Q^*\| \cdot \sqrt{\ln(2n+4)/\pi}\}$, *the system of norm equations obtained from* $\mathcal{Q} = \{(Q_i, V^T Q_i V)\}_{i=1,...,m}$ *forms a semi-regular sequence for each column of* V.

As the authors of [6] point out in their conclusion, this assumption (when the polynomials are viewed over $\mathbb{Q}$) is another form of Fröberg's conjecture [28], and it seems to hold experimentally.

Since computing each column is independent from all other column, we focus our analysis on the quadratic system of norm equations for one column. We have n as the number of variables, denote by $m > n$ the number of equations, and for each equation the total degree is $d_i = 2$. Under Assumption 2, the Hilbert series of the system is given by the following expression

$$S_{m,n}(z) = \frac{\prod_{i=1}^{m}(1 - z^2)}{(1 - z)^n} = \frac{(1 - z)^m(1 + z)^m}{(1 - z)^n} = (1 - z)^{m-n}(1 + z)^m$$

The computational complexity is by Lemma 1 exponential in i_{reg}, but is of course polynomial in m and n for any fixed i_{reg}. We note that the analysis in e.g. [6] is concerned with the behaviour of i_{reg} when the relationship between m and n is determined. We instead treat i_{reg} as fixed by the adversary depending on their computational power, and analyse how many equations are needed. The index of regularity i_{reg} is essentially determined by how many equations we have, descending towards 2 as m approaches n^2, and each sample gives precisely one norm equation for this column. We now analyse how many equations we need to reach the smallest possible $i_{\text{reg}} = 2$, where the Gröbner basis computation amounts only to producing S-polynomials of degree at most 2 and then using linear algebra on the resulting Macaulay matrix [34].

In order to achieve this, we need the coefficient c_2 in front of z^2 to be non-positive in $S_{m,n}(z)$. We therefore want

$$c_2 = \binom{m}{2} - \binom{m}{1}\binom{m-n}{1} + \binom{m-n}{2} \le 0$$

which simplifies to

$$\frac{n(n+1)}{2} \le m,$$

meaning we need $m = d$ equations to reach $i_{\text{reg}} = 2$, the same amount of samples we need for the linearization approach. The complexity of the Gröbner basis computation for a single column is then bounded by

$$O\left(2d\binom{n+1}{2}^{\omega}\right) = O\left(d^{1+\omega}\right) = O\left(n^{2+2\omega}\right).$$

By allowing the index of regularity i_{reg} to grow, we can reduce the number of equations (and thus samples) needed. A similar analysis for allowing $i_{\text{reg}} = 3$ requires that

$$c_3 = \binom{m}{3} - \binom{m}{2}\binom{m-n}{1} + \binom{m}{1}\binom{m-n}{2} - \binom{m-n}{3} \le 0$$

which simplifies to

$$\frac{n^2 + 3n + 2}{6} \le m,$$

while the complexity of Gröbner basis computation for a single column will be bounded by

$$O\left(3m\binom{n+2}{3}^{\omega}\right) = O\left(n^{2+3\omega}\right).$$

The following statement captures the approximate relation between the number of samples needed and the growth in complexity.

Proposition 5. *For any index of regularity $i \geq 2$, at least $m = O\left(\frac{n^2}{i^2}\right)$ oracle queries of $F_V^\$$ are required to compute the secret unimodular matrix V using Gröbner bases, with computational complexity bounded by $O(n^{2+i\omega})$.*

Proof. The number of samples for a fixed index of regularity is determined by

$$c_i = \sum_{k=1}^{i} (-1)^k \binom{m-n}{k} \binom{m}{i-k} = 0,$$

as given by the Binomial Theorem. Notice the highest degree term in n is $\frac{n^i}{i!}$, and that all degree-i terms that contain m cancel. The highest degree term in n that contains m is then $-\ell m n^{i-2}$ for a small positive rational constant ℓ depending only on i.

We rearrange the above equation by keeping all terms that contain only the variable n on the left hand side, and moving all other terms to the right hand side. We get an equation of the form

$$\frac{n^i}{i!} + O\left(n^{i-1}\right) \approx \ell m n^{i-2} \cdot O(1)$$

once we replace all the variables m inside the parentheses on the right hand side with their approximation n^2. Dividing both sides by ℓn^{i-2} we get $\frac{n^2}{\ell i!} \approx m$.

Let us consider the factor ℓ in its relation to i. The only terms of c_i that contribute to the coefficient in front of mn^{n-2} are terms with $k \in \{i, i-1, i-2\}$. The contribution of $k = i$ is

$$(-1)^i (-1)^{i-2} \frac{(-1-2-\cdots-(i-1))(i-1)}{i!} = -\frac{i(i-1)^2}{2i!},$$

the contribution of $k = i-1$ is

$$(-1)^{i-1}(-1)^{i-2} \frac{-1-2-\cdots-(i-2)}{(i-1)!} = \frac{i(i-1)(i-2)}{2i!},$$

and the contribution of $k = i-2$ is $-(-1)^{i-2}\frac{i(i-1)}{2i!}$. Observe the terms with i^3 in the numerator cancel, hence $\ell \approx \frac{i^2}{i!}$, and we get that $m \approx \frac{n^2}{i^2}$.

The complexity bound for a fixed i then follows from the bound given by Lemma 1

$$O\left(im\binom{n+i-1}{i}^\omega\right) = O\left(n^{2+i\omega}\right),$$

noting that $\binom{n+i-1}{i}$ is a polynomial of degree i in n.   □

Remark 5. We provide a table of approximate numbers of required samples for small values of i_{reg}, which shows the proposition holds even for small i_{reg}, not just asymptotically (Table 1).

Table 1. Approximate relationship between the number of queries of $F_V^\$$ needed to reach a desired index of regularity i_{reg} and n^2.

i_{reg}	2	3	4	5	6
$\frac{m}{n^2} \approx$	$\frac{1}{2}$	$\frac{1}{6}$	$\frac{1}{12}$	$\frac{1}{20}$	$\frac{1}{30}$

Finally, we describe our algorithm in the following theorem.

Theorem 2. *Let $Q \in \mathcal{S}_n^{>0}$, $i_0 \in \mathbb{N}$, and $\mathcal{D}_{\text{GL}_n^{\pm}(\mathbb{Z})}$ be a distribution over $\text{GL}_n^{\pm}(\mathbb{Z})$. Let $m \leq d$ be the number of oracle queries of $F_V^\$$ such that the systems of column norm equations have $i_{\text{reg}} \leq i_0$. Then the group action $(\text{GL}_n^{\pm}(\mathbb{Z}), [Q], \star)$ is not $(\mathcal{D}_s([Q]), \mathcal{D}_{\text{GL}_n^{\pm}(\mathbb{Z})}, t)$-weakly unpredictable for any $t \geq m$.*

Proof. We again show that $(\text{GL}_n^{\pm}(\mathbb{Z}), [Q], \star)$ is not a $(\mathcal{D}_{[Q]}, \mathcal{D}_{\text{GL}_n^{\pm}(\mathbb{Z})}, d)$-weakly unpredictable group action by providing a polynomial-time algorithm RecoverGB to invert the group action. Let $\mathcal{A}$ be an adversary able to make m queries to a randomized oracle $F_V^\$$ that, when queried, samples a $Q' \leftarrow \mathcal{D}_s([Q])$ and outputs $(Q', V^{\mathsf{T}}QV)$. The strategy of the adversary is the following.

By querying the oracle $F_V\$$, the adversary $\mathcal{A}$ is able to collect a list of m pairs $\mathcal{Q} := \{(Q_i, V^{\mathsf{T}}Q_iV)\}_{i=1,\ldots,m}$, and extracts the column norm equations as follows. The adversary keeps n lists, one for each column. When receiving a pair (Q, Q') from the oracle $F_V^\$$, they save the quadratic equation

$$\begin{bmatrix} x_1 & \cdots & x_n \end{bmatrix} \cdot Q \cdot \begin{bmatrix} x_1 \\ \vdots \\ x_n \end{bmatrix} - Q'_{i,i} = 0$$

to their i-th list. They only need to keep the inner product equations of the last sample to extract the complete solution.

The adversary $\mathcal{A}$ then runs RecoverGB that computes the reduced Gröbner basis w.r.t. the DRL monomial order of the ideal generated by each system of equations and obtains two solutions for each, which are exactly the i-th columns of V and $-V$, which we denote by $\pm V_i$.

To extract the matrix V, the algorithm RecoverGB then proceeds by guessing the solution $\tilde{V}_1$ for the first column. For all $i = 2, \ldots, n$ it then picks $\tilde{V}_i \in \{\pm V_i\}$ such that $\tilde{V}_1 Q \tilde{V}_i = Q'_{1,i}$, where (Q, Q') is the last sample that $\mathcal{A}$ kept. Depending on the guess $\tilde{V}_1$, the algorithm has computed either V or $-V$, allowing the adversary $\mathcal{A}$ to reproduce the group action of V. $\square$

4.2   Weak Pseudorandomness

When approaching weak pseudorandomness of LIGA alone, we can optimize the approach further both for the number of samples needed and the complexity estimate. Since the adversary is now not required to find the secret unimodular matrix V (or at least be able to reproduce its action on quadratic forms), it is enough for them to show that merely one system of norm equations describing one column has a solution. Furthermore, since breaking weak pseudorandomness is a decision problem, the adversary can consider solving the system of equations not over $\mathbb{Q}$ (or $\mathbb{Z}$) but a small finite field, namely $\mathbb{F}_2$ where they can use field equations $x_i^2 - x_i = 0$ of degree 2 for all $i = 1, \ldots, n$. Observe that the solution over $\mathbb{F}_2$ is unique, implying also there is no need to extract the final solution from column solutions.

Remark 6. An interesting consequence of this approach is how it positions LIGA as a cryptographic group action in relation to other hard computational problems, namely the $\mathcal{MQ}$ problem. Indeed, if the Gaussian Form Distribution $\mathcal{D}_s([Q])$ is wide enough [37, Lemmas 3.2 and 3.3], i.e. exceeds the Smoothing Bound, then by the Smoothing Lemma [29,37], the coefficients of the system of equations modulo 2 may be treated as uniformly random, since the two distributions are statistically close. It follows that if an adversary is able to solve $\mathcal{MQ}$ over $\mathbb{F}_2$ with n variables and m equations efficiently then they can also efficiently break weak pseudorandomness of the group action $(\mathrm{GL}_n^\pm(\mathbb{Z}), [Q], \star)$ using m samples for any $Q \in \mathcal{S}_n^{>0}$. More specifically, in this case the adversary is solving the Boolean $\mathcal{MQ}$ problem studied in detail in [7].

The approach is now twofold. We can compute over $\mathbb{Q}$ like in Sect. 4.1 and include the field equations into each of our column norm systems of equations which we reduce modulo 2. Since there are n field equations and all have degree 2, our analysis from above stands and we require $d - n = \frac{n(n-1)}{2}$ oracle queries of $F_V^\$$ to reach $i_{\mathrm{reg}} = 2$, as if we only had $n - 1$ variables. More generally, if reaching the index of regularity $i_{\mathrm{reg}} = i$ over $\mathbb{Q}$ requires m oracle queries, then solving the same system modulo 2 over in $\mathbb{Q}$ with the $\mathbb{F}_2$ field equations added requires $m - n$ oracle queries.

Alternatively, one may exclude the field equations from the m equations and instead compute over $\mathbb{F}_2$ directly. The field equations still need to be implied so as not to end up in the algebraic closure of $\mathbb{F}_2$, i.e. we are computing in the quotient ring $\mathbb{F}_2[x_1, \ldots, x_n]/\langle x_1^2 - x_1, \ldots, x_n^2 - x_n \rangle$. Following the analysis in [4, Cor. 7] and assuming the systems of equations remain semi-regular sequences in $\mathbb{F}_2$ as implied in Remark 6, the Hilbert series of our system of m equations and n variables is

$$T_{m,n}(z) = \frac{(1 + z)^n}{(1 + z^2)^m}$$

truncated after the first non-positive coefficient, which expands (around 0) to

$$T_{m,n}(z) = 1 + nz + \left(\frac{(n-1)n}{2} - m \right) z^2 + \left(\frac{(n-2)(n-1)n}{6} - mn \right) z^3 + O(z^4),$$

implying identical bounds for $i_{\mathrm{reg}} = 2, 3$ as in our analysis above, i.e. we need n fewer equations, courtesy of field equations. The Gröbner basis computation complexity estimate of $O(mi_{\mathrm{reg}}\binom{n}{i_{\mathrm{reg}}})$ given by [6, Prop. 9] then implies the bound of $O(n^{2+2\omega})$ (for one column) when $i_{\mathrm{reg}} = 2$, and $O(n^{2+i_{\mathrm{reg}}\omega})$ more generally.

Corollary 3. *Let $Q \in \mathcal{S}_n^{>0}$, $i_0 \in \mathbb{N}$, and $\mathcal{D}_{\mathrm{GL}_n^\pm(\mathbb{Z})}$ be a distribution over $\mathrm{GL}_n^\pm(\mathbb{Z})$, and let $s \geq \max\{\lambda_n(Q), \|B_Q^*\| \cdot \sqrt{\ln(2n+4)/\pi}\}$. Let $m \leq d - n$ be the number of oracle queries of $F_V^\$$ such that the systems of column norm equations modulo 2 have $i_{\mathrm{reg}} \leq i_0$. Then* LIGA *is not a $(\mathcal{D}_s([Q]), \mathcal{D}_{\mathrm{GL}_n^\pm(\mathbb{Z})}, t)$-weakly pseudorandom group action for any $t \geq m$.*

Proof. Following the reasoning in Remark 6, the parameter s is large enough by the Smoothing Bound [25, Lemma 2.6] so that the distribution $(\mathcal{D}_s([Q])$ mod 2), which returns the unimodular matrix U and the quadratic form $Q' = U^T Q U$ both with entries modulo 2, is within negligible statistical distance of the uniform distribution on respective sets modulo 2. The strategy of the adversary is therefore identical to the one presented in the proof of Theorem 2, except that they store equations modulo 2, and compute the Gröbner bases of the ideals generated by the column norm systems of equations in the quotient ring $\mathbb{F}_2[x_1, \ldots, x_n]/\langle x_1^2 - x_1, \ldots, x_n^2 - x_n \rangle$ instead of over $\mathbb{Q}$. □

4.3 Comparisons and Experimental Results

This section conducts a comparative analysis between the linearization (see proof of Theorem 1) and the Gröbner basis (see proof of Theorem 2) approaches to illustrate the trade-off between running time and required number of samples to recover the secret. We provide a proof-of-concept implementation (using the Sage Mathematics Software System SAGEMATH [45]) available at [9]. Our implementation of the Gröbner basis approach uses the MSOLVE library for solving polynomial systems [10].

By applying the Gröbner basis technique we can significantly reduce the number of samples required to break weak unpredictability, from $m = \frac{n(n+1)}{2}$ to $m \approx \frac{n^2}{i^2}$ for any constant index of regularity $i \geq 2$, while still ensuring a polynomial running time, whereas recovering the secret using linearization with fewer than $d = \frac{n(n+1)}{2}$ samples is not possible. However, the required time complexity of computing Gröbner bases to recover the secret with fewer samples is notably higher than that of the linearization approach in both a practical and asymptotic sense. Table 2 presents an asymptotic comparison between Gröbner basis and linearization techniques regarding the number of samples and runtime.

One could try to reduce the number of equations needed to recover the secret even lower at the cost of even higher complexity. For example, for $m = n \log_2(n)$ the complexity of Gröbner basis computation is known to be sub-exponential [4], however for smaller examples (e.g. $n = 32$) it can be done with index of regularity 3. This is because $\frac{n^2}{i^2}$ and $n \log_2(n)$ meet for small n with increasing i. Once n becomes larger, the index of regularity quickly grows as well (e.g. for $n = 64$ we require $i_{\mathrm{reg}} = 4$). Therefore, for cryptographically relevant sizes, the Gröbner basis approach is able to reduce the number of samples only by a small constant

Table 2. Asymptotic comparison between Gröbner basis and linearization regarding runtime. We consider Strassen's algorithm for the complexity exponent $\omega = \log_2(7)$ and present the base two logarithm of the running times. Note that, as the index of regularity (i_{reg}) increases, fewer samples are required to successfully recover the secret unimodular matrix.

n	16	32	64	128	256	512	1024
Recover	22.5	28.1	33.7	39.3	44.9	50.5	56.2
RecoverGB with $i_{\text{reg}} = 2$	30.5	38.1	45.7	53.3	60.9	68.5	76.2
RecoverGB with $i_{\text{reg}} = 3$	41.7	52.1	62.5	73.0	83.4	93.8	104.2
RecoverGB with $i_{\text{reg}} = 4$	52.9	66.2	79.4	92.6	105.8	119.1	132.3
RecoverGB with $i_{\text{reg}} = 5$	64.2	80.2	96.2	112.3	128.3	144.3	160.4

as shown in Proposition 5 (since we ideally want the index of regularity to be 2 or 3 as can be seen from Table 2).

We additionally compare the linearization and Gröbner basis approaches through timed experiments, as outlined in Table 3 and Fig. 1. All our experiments were conducted on a 2.3 GHz 8-Core Intel Core i9 machine with 16 GB of RAM. We emphasize that our implementation must be viewed as a proof-of-concept implementation and, therefore, is not optimized.

Table 3. The timings correspond with the average time (in seconds) of eight random LIP instances. In all the experiments, RecoverGB uses $m = n(n + 1)/2$ (which has $i_{\text{reg}} = 2$), and no parallelization. The row labeled Sampling corresponds with the timings of generating all the $m = n(n + 1)/2$ random instances of LIP with the same fixed secret U.

n	16	20	24	28	32	36	40
Sampling	13.63	34.68	84.84	504.83	1198.48	2321.70	4652.40
Recover	0.34	1.00	1.98	3.36	5.51	10.57	17.31
RecoverGB	2.04	5.64	13.40	31.59	67.72	130.52	252.16

5 New Hard Problems on Quadratic Forms

In this section, we introduce the following two new hard problems on quadratic forms. We make use of Theorem 1 to provide polynomial-time reductions from sLIP_Q to both problems, for any automorphism-free Q.

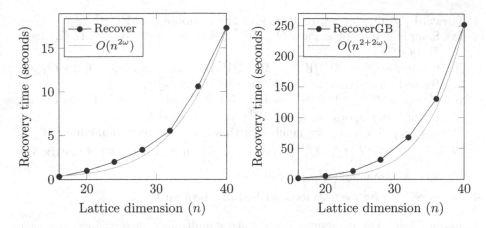

Fig. 1. In the above plots, we interpolate the first and the last measurements for Recover and RecoverGB from Table 3 with the corresponding asymptotic estimations $O(n^{2\omega})$ and $O(n^{2+2\omega})$ for $\omega = \log_2(7)$, and plot all table values. One can see that the experimental measurements fit the theoretical estimations well.

Definition 22 (Transpose Quadratic Form Problem (TQFP)). *Let $\mathcal{L}(B)$ be a full-rank n-dimensional lattice and $Q \in \mathcal{S}_n^{>0}$ be the quadratic form $Q = B^{\mathsf{T}}B$. Given $Q' \in [Q]$, the Transpose Quadratic Form Problem is to compute $\widehat{Q} \in [Q]$ such that $\widehat{Q} = UQU^{\mathsf{T}}$, where $U \in \mathrm{GL}_n(\mathbb{Z})$ satisfies $Q' = U^{\mathsf{T}}QU$.*

Definition 23 (Inverse Quadratic Form Problem (IQFP)). *Let $\mathcal{L}(B)$ be a full-rank n-dimensional lattice and $Q \in \mathcal{S}_n^{>0}$ be the quadratic form $Q = B^{\mathsf{T}}B$. Given $Q' \in [Q]$, the Inverse Quadratic Form Problem is to compute $\widehat{Q} \in [Q]$ such that $\widehat{Q} = U^{-\mathsf{T}}QU^{-1}$, where $U \in \mathrm{GL}_n(\mathbb{Z})$ satisfies $Q' = U^{\mathsf{T}}QU$.*

TQFP and IQFP accept as many solutions as the number of isomorphisms between Q and Q', up to the sign. For example, for the case of TQFP, the solution set is defined as $S_{Q'} := \{\widehat{Q}_V = (VU)^{\mathsf{T}}Q(VU) \colon V \in \mathrm{Aut}\,(Q)\}$. For the specific case of automorphism-free quadratic forms, the solution is unique ($|S_{Q'}| = 1$). Under Assumption 1, we give in Lemma 2 and Lemma 3 polynomial-time reductions from sLIP$_Q$ to TQFP and IQFP, respectively. We implemented and successfully tested these reductions in a SAGEMATH implementation available at [9].

Lemma 2 (From sLIP$_Q$ to TQFP). *Let $Q \in \mathcal{S}_n^{>0}$ be an automorphism-free quadratic form. Given an oracle $\mathcal{O}_{\mathsf{TQFP}}$ that solves TQFP in time T_0, there is an algorithm that solves sLIP$_Q$ in expected time $O\left(n^2(T_0 + T_1) + n^{2\omega}\right)$, where T_1 is the time complexity of one call to $\mathcal{D}_s\,([Q])$, for $s \geq \max\{\lambda_n(Q), \|B_Q^*\| \cdot \sqrt{\ln(2n + 4)/\pi}\}$.*

Proof. Fixing the same setup as Definition 22, we have Q and $Q' = V^{\mathsf{T}}QV$, where $Q' \in [Q]$. For simplicity, we assume that $\mathcal{O}_{\mathsf{TQFP}}$ always solves TQFP for isomorphic input Q, Q'. We give an algorithm which solves sLIP$_Q$ with a polynomial number of calls to $\mathcal{O}_{\mathsf{TQFP}}$ as follows. Let us set $d = \frac{n(n+1)}{2}$.

1. Forward (Q', Q) to $\mathcal{O}_{\mathsf{TQFP}}$ and receive the response $\widehat{Q} = VQV^\mathsf{T}$.
2. (a) Sample a quadratic form $\bar{Q} = W^\mathsf{T} QW$ along with $W \in \mathrm{GL}_n(\mathbb{Z})$ from $\mathcal{D}_s([Q])$.
   (b) Compute $Q'' = W\widehat{Q}W^\mathsf{T} = WVQV^\mathsf{T}W^\mathsf{T}$ and send (Q'', Q) to $\mathcal{O}_{\mathsf{TQFP}}$. Record its response as $\bar{Q} = V^\mathsf{T}W^\mathsf{T}QWV = V^\mathsf{T}\bar{Q}V$.
   (c) Compute $Q''' = WQ'W^\mathsf{T} = WV^\mathsf{T}QVW^\mathsf{T}$ and send (Q''', Q) to $\mathcal{O}_{\mathsf{TQFP}}$. Record its response as $\widehat{\bar{Q}} = VW^\mathsf{T}QWV^\mathsf{T} = V\bar{Q}V^\mathsf{T}$.
3. Repeat Step 2 a necessary number of times, for different unimodular W, to derive a set $\mathcal{Q} = \left\{ \left(Q_0^{(i)}, Q_1^{(i)} \right),\ i = 1, \ldots, d \right\}$ such that the $d \times d$ matrix $M_\mathcal{Q}$ whose rows are $\mathsf{unroll}\left(Q_0^{(i)} \right)$ is full rank.
4. Retrieve $V \leftarrow \mathsf{Recover}(\mathcal{Q})$ as described in Theorem 1.

Running Time. Let us assume both matrix multiplication and inversion take $O(n^\omega)$ integer operations. Step 1 costs one call to the oracle $\mathcal{O}_{\mathsf{TQFP}}$. Step 2 samples one random unimodular matrix, makes four matrix multiplications, and two queries to $\mathcal{O}_{\mathsf{TQFP}}$. Now, Step 2 must be repeated $O\left(\frac{n(n+1)}{2} \right)$ times to derive enough linear equations (Step 3). Then Steps 1 to 3 have complexity

$$O\left(T_0 + \frac{n(n+1)}{2} \left(2T_0 + T_1 + 4n^\omega \right) \right) = O\left(n^2(T_0 + T_1) + n^{2+\omega} \right).$$

Step 4 requires $O\left(n^{2\omega} \right)$ operations to retrieve V, which gives a total asymptotic time complexity of $O\left(n^2(T_0 + T_1) + n^{2\omega} \right)$.   □

Remark 7. Regarding Lemma 2, in practice one can reduce the number of calls to $\mathcal{O}_{\mathsf{TQFP}}$ by a factor of n by exploiting the following. Let $Q, Q', \widehat{Q} \in \mathcal{S}_n^{>0}$ be equivalent quadratic forms with $Q' = V^\mathsf{T}QV$ and $\widehat{Q} = VQV^\mathsf{T}$, for some unimodular matrix $V \in \mathrm{GL}_n(\mathbb{Z})$. Then, one can compute the quadratic forms

$$Q_1 := Q'QQ' = V^\mathsf{T}QVQV^\mathsf{T}QV, \qquad Q_0 := Q\widehat{Q}Q,$$

and have that (Q_0, Q_1) is such that $Q_1 = V^\mathsf{T}Q_0V$. Iteratively, one can define

$$Q_1^{(i)} := Q'(QQ')^i, \qquad Q_0^{(i)} := Q(\widehat{Q}Q)^i,$$

with $Q_1^{(i)} = V^\mathsf{T}Q_0^{(i)}V$, for $i \geq 0$. The Cayley-Hamilton theorem ensures that, for any square matrix M with n rows over a commutative ring, we have that $M^n \in \mathrm{Span}\{I_n, M, M^2, \ldots, M^{n-1}\}$ [2, §7.11]. Therefore, with the above approach, we can get a set $\mathcal{Q} = \{(Q_i, Q'_i = V^\mathsf{T}Q_iV)\}_{i=1}^p$ of size $p \leq n$ knowing $Q' = V^\mathsf{T}QV$ and $\widehat{Q} = VQV^\mathsf{T}$. Using this trick in Step 2 of the proof of Lemma 2, and assuming that p reaches n with high probability, one can reduce the number of calls to $\mathcal{O}_{\mathsf{TQFP}}$ by a factor of n. In this case, taking also into consideration the number of matrix multiplications, the total cost of the reduction in Lemma 2 would be $\widetilde{O}(n(T_0 + T_1) + n^{2\omega})$.[6] In our SAGEMATH implementation, we implemented and

---

[6] We have $\widetilde{O}(\cdot)$ instead of $O(\cdot)$ because of the increase of the integer coefficients size when applying this optimization trick.

tested the variant of the reduction in Lemma 2 that uses such optimization in Step 2.

Lemma 3 (From sLIP$_Q$ to IQFP). *Let $Q \in \mathcal{S}_n^{>0}$ be an automorphism-free quadratic form. Given an oracle $\mathcal{O}_{\mathsf{IQFP}}$ that solves IQFP in time T_0, there exists an algorithm that solves sLIP$_Q$ in expected time $O\left(n^2(T_0 + T_1) + n^{2\omega}\right)$, where T_1 is the time complexity of one call to $\mathcal{D}_s\left([Q]\right)$, for $s \geq \max\{\lambda_n(Q), \|B_Q^*\| \cdot \sqrt{\ln(2n+4)/\pi}\}$.*

Proof. Fixing the same setup as Definition 23, we have Q and $Q' = V^{\mathsf{T}}QV$, where $Q' \in [Q]$. For simplicity, we assume that $\mathcal{O}_{\mathsf{IQFP}}$ always solves IQFP, for a isomorphic input Q, Q'. We give an algorithm which solves sLIP$_Q$ with a polynomial number of calls to $\mathcal{O}_{\mathsf{IQFP}}$ as follows. Let us set $d = \frac{n(n+1)}{2}$.

1. Forward (Q', Q) to $\mathcal{O}_{\mathsf{IQFP}}$ and receive the response $\widehat{Q} = V^{-\mathsf{T}}QV^{-1}$.
2. (a) Sample a quadratic form $\bar{Q} = W^{\mathsf{T}}QW$ along with $W \in \mathrm{GL}_n(\mathbb{Z})$ from $\mathcal{D}_s\left([Q]\right)$.
   (b) Calculate $Z = W^{-1}$.
   (c) Compute $Q'' = Z^{\mathsf{T}}\widehat{Q}Z = Z^{\mathsf{T}}VQV^{\mathsf{T}}Z$ and send (Q'', Q) to $\mathcal{O}_{\mathsf{IQFP}}$. Record its response as $\widetilde{Q} = V^{\mathsf{T}}W^{\mathsf{T}}QWV = V^{\mathsf{T}}\bar{Q}V$.
3. Repeat Step 2 a necessary number of times, for different unimodular W, to derive a set $\mathcal{Q} = \left\{\left(Q_0^{(i)}, Q_1^{(i)}\right), i = 1, \ldots, d\right\}$ such that the $d \times d$ matrix $M_{\mathcal{Q}}$ whose rows are $\mathsf{unroll}\left(Q_0^{(i)}\right)$ is full rank.
4. Retrieve $V \leftarrow \mathsf{Recover}(\mathcal{Q})$ as described in Theorem 1.

Running Time. The cost analysis is analogous to Lemma 2, with the addition of a matrix inversion in Step 2. However, this is negligible on the total cost of the reduction, that is $O\left(n^2(T_0 + T_1) + n^{2\omega}\right)$.

□

To illustrate the above reductions from Lemma 2 and Lemma 3, we simulate the algorithms concerning TQFP and IQFP using a SAGEMATH library; our code is available at [9].

Remark 8. Lemma 2 and Lemma 3 can be generalized to the case of quadratic forms with a non-trivial automorphism group. However, in this case, the solutions to TQFP and IQFP are not unique, but there are as many solutions as the number of automorphisms divided by 2. Consider the case of a TQFP oracle $\mathcal{O}_{\mathsf{TQFP}}$ that returns one of the possible solutions uniformly at random. Then, the algorithm in Lemma 2 would allow retrieving the correct solution only when, for every query to the algorithm, it returns exactly the solution that we are looking for. Therefore, given that we require n correct solutions from $\mathcal{O}_{\mathsf{TQFP}}$, one must repeat on average the whole algorithm $(|\mathrm{Aut}(Q)|/2)^n$ times.

6 Open Problems

We believe that studying the Lattice Isomorphism Problem, as well as other computational problems related to isomorphisms or equivalence classes, in the group action framework is an important research direction which will help build a unified theoretical foundation for constructing cryptographic schemes. Below we list some research directions/open problems that arise from our work.

It would indeed be interesting to know the exact number of LIP samples sharing the same secret V that can be given to an adversary while still maintaining the weakly unpredictable nature of the group action. For example, one could to take into account the equation $\det(V) = \pm 1$. However, this should not be very useful since, for an indeterminate V, it is a polynomial in n^2 variables of total degree n (or $2n$, if one decides to square the equation to get rid of the sign ambiguity), and Gröbner basis computation is exponential in the degree of the system. Theorem 2 seems to imply a limit of $m = O(n)$ LIP samples at which solving a "random" system of quadratic equations is known to have complexity exponential in n [6], making it infeasible for the adversary to solve the system of equations using Gröbner basis computation.

Perhaps more relevant to cryptographers, one can ask: Which cryptographic constructions can be securely realized assuming one-wayness and the aforementioned limited version of weak unpredictability (and weak pseudorandomness) to $O(n)$ oracle calls to $F_V^\$$?

Another possible direction is to investigate whether an analogous result can be obtained also for group actions stemming from other equivalence problems, e.g. code equivalence or 3-tensor isomorphism. Recently, the authors of [22] studied the code equivalence problem using representation theory and linearization techniques. It will be interesting to study the impact of employing other algebraic methods such as Gröbner bases in this setting. More generally, it would be interesting to investigate whether other group actions also come with a similar limitation on the number of oracle queries allowed to an adversary, and characterize it in concrete terms such as a number of samples.

Acknowledgments. The authors thank Keita Xagawa, Victor Mateu, and Martin R. Albrecht for fruitful discussions on the topic. We also thank Elena Kirshanova and anonymous reviewers for the useful comments on an earlier version of this manuscript. Benjamin Benčina was supported by the EPSRC and the UK Government as part of the grant EP/S021817/1.

References

1. Alamati, N., De Feo, L., Montgomery, H., Patranabis, S.: Cryptographic group actions and applications. In: Moriai, S., Wang, H. (eds.) ASIACRYPT 2020, Part II. LNCS, vol. 12492, pp. 411–439. Springer, Heidelberg (2020). https://doi.org/10.1007/978-3-030-64834-3_14
2. Apostol, T.M.: Calculus, Multi-variable Calculus and Linear Algebra, vol. II. Blaisdell, Waltham (1969)

3. Bardet, M.: Étude des systèmes algébriques surdéterminés. Applications aux codes correcteurs et à la cryptographie. Ph.D. thesis, Université Pierre et Marie Curie - Paris VI (2004). https://theses.hal.science/tel-00449609

4. Bardet, M., Faugère, J.C., Salvy, B.: Complexity of Gröbner basis computation for Semi-regular Overdetermined sequences over $\mathbb{F}_2$ with solutions in $\mathbb{F}_2$. Research Report RR-5049, INRIA (2003). https://inria.hal.science/inria-00071534

5. Bardet, M., Faugère, J.C., Salvy, B.: On the complexity of Gröbner basis computation of semi-regular overdetermined algebraic equations. In: Proceedings of the International Conference on Polynomial System Solving Paris, November 2004 in Honor of Daniel Lazard, pp. 71–75. ICPSS (2004)

6. Bardet, M., Faugère, J.C., Salvy, B., Yang, B.: Asymptotic behaviour of the degree of regularity of semi-regular polynomial systems. In: 8th International Symposium on Effective Methods in Algebraic Geometry, pp. 1–17. MEGA (2005)

7. Bardet, M., Faugère, J.C., Salvy, B., Spaenlehauer, P.J.: On the complexity of solving quadratic Boolean systems. J. Complex. **29**(1), 53–75 (2011). https://doi.org/10.1016/j.jco.2012.07.001

8. Bennett, H., Ganju, A., Peetathawatchai, P., Stephens-Davidowitz, N.: Just how hard are rotations of $\mathbb{Z}^n$? algorithms and cryptography with the simplest lattice. In: Hazay, C., Stam, M. (eds.) EUROCRYPT 2023, Part V. LNCS, vol. 14008, pp. 252–281. Springer, Heidelberg (2023).https://doi.org/10.1007/978-3-031-30589-4_9

9. Benčina, B., Budroni, A., Chi-Domínguez, J.J., Kulkarni, M.: lip-properties. https://github.com/JJChiDguez/lip-properties.git

10. Berthomieu, J., Eder, C., Safey El Din, M.: msolve: a library for solving polynomial systems. In: Proceedings of the 2021 International Symposium on Symbolic and Algebraic Computation (ISSAC 2021), pp. 51–58. Association for Computing Machinery, Saint Petersburg (2021). https://doi.org/10.1145/3452143.3465545. Version 0.6.3

11. Beullens, W., Kleinjung, T., Vercauteren, F.: CSI-FiSh: efficient isogeny based signatures through class group computations. In: Galbraith, S.D., Moriai, S. (eds.) ASIACRYPT 2019, Part I. LNCS, vol. 11921, pp. 227–247. Springer, Heidelberg (2019). https://doi.org/10.1007/978-3-030-34578-5_9

12. Biasse, J.F., Micheli, G., Persichetti, E., Santini, P.: LESS is more: code-based signatures without syndromes. In: Nitaj, A., Youssef, A.M. (eds.) AFRICACRYPT 20. LNCS, vol. 12174, pp. 45–65. Springer, Heidelberg (2020). https://doi.org/10.1007/978-3-030-51938-4_3

13. Blanks, T.L., Miller, S.D.: Generating cryptographically-strong random lattice bases and recognizing rotations of $\mathbb{Z}^n$. In: Cheon, J.H., Tillich, J.P. (eds.) Post-Quantum Cryptography - 12th International Workshop, PQCrypto 2021, pp. 319–338. Springer, Heidelberg (2021). https://doi.org/10.1007/978-3-030-81293-5_17

14. Bläser, M., et al.: On digital signatures based on isomorphism problems: orom security, ring signatures, and applications. Cryptology ePrint Archive, Paper 2022/1184 (2022). https://eprint.iacr.org/2022/1184

15. Borin, G., Persichetti, E., Santini, P.: Zero-knowledge proofs from the action subgraph. Cryptology ePrint Archive, Paper 2023/718 (2023). https://eprint.iacr.org/2023/718

16. Brakerski, Z., Langlois, A., Peikert, C., Regev, O., Stehlé, D.: Classical hardness of learning with errors. In: Boneh, D., Roughgarden, T., Feigenbaum, J. (eds.) 45th ACM STOC, pp. 575–584. ACM Press (2013). https://doi.org/10.1145/2488608.2488680

17. Brassard, G., Yung, M.: One-way group actions. In: Menezes, A.J., Vanstone, S.A. (eds.) CRYPTO'90. LNCS, vol. 537, pp. 94–107. Springer, Heidelberg (1991). https://doi.org/10.1007/3-540-38424-3_7

18. Budroni, A., Chi-Domínguez, J.J., Kulkarni, M.: Lattice isomorphism as a group action and hard problems on quadratic forms. Cryptology ePrint Archive, Paper 2023/1093 - version 20230724:055703 (2023). https://eprint.iacr.org/archive/2023/1093/1690178223.pdf

19. Castryck, W., Lange, T., Martindale, C., Panny, L., Renes, J.: CSIDH: an efficient post-quantum commutative group action. In: Peyrin, T., Galbraith, S. (eds.) ASIACRYPT 2018, Part III. LNCS, vol. 11274, pp. 395–427. Springer, Heidelberg (2018). https://doi.org/10.1007/978-3-030-03332-3_15

20. Couveignes, J.M.: Hard homogeneous spaces. Cryptology ePrint Archive, Report 2006/291 (2006). https://eprint.iacr.org/2006/291

21. Cox, D.A., Little, J., O'Shea, D.: Ideals, varieties, and algorithms: an introduction to computational algebraic geometry and commutative algebra. In: Undergraduate Texts in Mathematics, 4th edn. Springer, Cham (2015). https://doi.org/10.1007/978-3-319-16721-3

22. D'Alconzo, G., Scala, A.J.D.: Representations of group actions and their applications in cryptography. Cryptology ePrint Archive, Paper 2023/1247 (2023). https://eprint.iacr.org/2023/1247

23. De Feo, L., et al.: SCALLOP: scaling the CSI-FiSh. In: Boldyreva, A., Kolesnikov, V. (eds.) PKC 2023, Part I. LNCS, vol. 13940, pp. 345–375. Springer, Heidelberg (2023). https://doi.org/10.1007/978-3-031-31368-4_13

24. Ducas, L., Postlethwaite, E.W., Pulles, L.N., van Woerden, W.P.J.: Hawk: module LIP makes lattice signatures fast, compact and simple. In: Agrawal, S., Lin, D. (eds.) ASIACRYPT 2022, Part IV. LNCS, vol. 13794, pp. 65–94. Springer, Heidelberg (2022). https://doi.org/10.1007/978-3-031-22972-5_3

25. Ducas, L., van Woerden, W.P.J.: On the lattice isomorphism problem, quadratic forms, remarkable lattices, and cryptography. In: Dunkelman and Dziembowski [26], pp. 643–646. https://doi.org/10.1007/978-3-031-07082-2_23

26. Dunkelman, O., Dziembowski, S. (eds.): EUROCRYPT 2022, Part III, LNCS, vol. 13277. Springer, Heidelberg (2022)

27. Felderhoff, J.: Hard Homogenous Spaces and Commutative Supersingular Isogeny based Diffie-Hellman (2019). https://api.semanticscholar.org/CorpusID:252082464

28. Fröberg, R.: An inequality for hilbert series of graded algebras. Math. Scand. **56**(2), 117–144 (1985)

29. Gentry, C., Peikert, C., Vaikuntanathan, V.: Trapdoors for hard lattices and new cryptographic constructions. In: Ladner, R.E., Dwork, C. (eds.) 40th ACM STOC, pp. 197–206. ACM Press (2008). https://doi.org/10.1145/1374376.1374407

30. Gentry, C., Szydlo, M.: Cryptanalysis of the revised NTRU signature scheme. In: Knudsen, L.R. (ed.) EUROCRYPT 2002. LNCS, vol. 2332, pp. 299–320. Springer, Heidelberg (2002). https://doi.org/10.1007/3-540-46035-7_20

31. Haviv, I., Regev, O.: On the lattice isomorphism problem. In: Chekuri, C. (ed.) 25th SODA, pp. 391–404. ACM-SIAM (2014). https://doi.org/10.1137/1.9781611973402.29

32. Ji, Z., Qiao, Y., Song, F., Yun, A.: General linear group action on tensors: a candidate for post-quantum cryptography. In: Hofheinz, D., Rosen, A. (eds.) TCC 2019, Part I. LNCS, vol. 11891, pp. 251–281. Springer, Heidelberg (2019). https://doi.org/10.1007/978-3-030-36030-6_11

33. Joux, A.: MPC in the head for isomorphisms and group actions. Cryptology ePrint Archive, Paper 2023/664 (2023). https://eprint.iacr.org/2023/664

34. Lazard, D.: Gröbner bases, Gaussian elimination and resolution of systems of algebraic equations. In: van Hulzen, J.A. (ed.) Computer Algebra. LNCS, vol. 162, pp. 146–156. Springer, Heidelberg (1983). https://doi.org/10.1007/3-540-12868-9_99
35. Machì, A.: Groups. Springer Milano (2012). https://doi.org/10.1007/978-88-470-2421-2
36. Micciancio, D., Goldwasser, S.: Cryptographic functions. In: Micciancio, D., Goldwasser, S. (eds.) Complexity of Lattice Problems. LNCS, vol. 671, pp. 143–194. Springer, Boston (2002). https://doi.org/10.1007/978-1-4615-0897-7_8
37. Micciancio, D., Regev, O.: Worst-case to average-case reductions based on Gaussian measures. SIAM J. Comput. **37**(1), 267–302 (2007). https://doi.org/10.1137/s0097539705447360
38. Naor, M., Reingold, O.: Number-theoretic constructions of efficient pseudo-random functions. In: 38th FOCS, pp. 458–467. IEEE Computer Society Press (1997). https://doi.org/10.1109/SFCS.1997.646134
39. NIST: Post-quantum cryptography: Digital signature schemes. https://csrc.nist.gov/projects/pqc-dig-sig
40. NIST: Post-quantum cryptography standardization. https://csrc.nist.gov/Projects/post-quantum-cryptography/selected-algorithms-2022
41. Rasslan, M.M.N., Youssef, A.M.: Cryptanalysis of a Public Key Encryption Scheme Using Ergodic Matrices. IEICE Trans. Fundam. Electron. Commun. Comput. Sci. **94-A**(2), 853–854 (2011).https://doi.org/10.1587/transfun.E94.A.853
42. Serre, J.P.: A Course in Arithmetic, Graduate Texts in Mathematics, vol. 7. Springer, New York (1973). https://doi.org/10.1007/978-1-4684-9884-4
43. Spaenlehauer, J.P.: Résolution de Systèmes Multi-homogènes et Déterminantiels. Ph.D. thesis, Université Pierre et Marie Curie (2012)
44. Tang, G., Duong, D.H., Joux, A., Plantard, T., Qiao, Y., Susilo, W.: Practical post-quantum signature schemes from isomorphism problems of trilinear forms. In: Dunkelman and Dziembowski [26], pp. 582–612.https://doi.org/10.1007/978-3-031-07082-2_21
45. The Sage Developers: SageMath, the Sage Mathematics Software System (Version 10.1) (2023). https://www.sagemath.org

A Subexponential Quantum Algorithm for the Semidirect Discrete Logarithm Problem

Christopher Battarbee[1,5]([✉]), Delaram Kahrobaei[1,2,3,4], Ludovic Perret[1], and Siamak F. Shahandashti[5]

[1] Sorbonne University, CNRS, LIP6, PolSys, Paris, France
`christopher.battarbee@lip6.fr`
[2] Departments of Computer Science and Mathematics, Queens College, City University of New York, New York, USA
[3] Initiative for the Theoretical Sciences, Graduate Center, City University of New York, New York, USA
[4] Department of Computer Science and Engineering, Tandon School of Engineering, New York University, New York, USA
[5] Department of Computer Science, University of York, York, UK

Abstract. *Group-based* cryptography is a relatively unexplored family in post-quantum cryptography, and the so-called Semidirect Discrete Logarithm Problem (SDLP) is one of its most central problems. However, the complexity of the general case of SDLP and its relationship to more well-known hardness problems, particularly with respect to its security against quantum adversaries, has not been well understood and was a significant open problem for researchers in this area. In this paper we give the first dedicated security analysis of the general case of SDLP. In particular, we provide a connection between SDLP and group actions, a context in which quantum subexponential algorithms are known to apply. We are therefore able to construct a subexponential quantum algorithm for solving SDLP, thereby classifying the complexity of SDLP and its relation to known computational problems.

1 Introduction

The goal of Post-Quantum Cryptography (PQC) is to design cryptosystems which are secure against classical and quantum adversaries. A topic of fundamental research for decades, the status of PQC drastically changed with the NIST PQC standardization process [11].

In July 2022, after five years and three rounds of selection, NIST selected a first set of PQC standards for Key-Encapsulation Mechanism (KEM) and Digital Signature Scheme (DSS) protocols, based on lattices and hash functions. The standardization process is still ongoing with a fourth round for KEM and a new NIST call for post-quantum DSS in 2023. Recent attacks [1,6,36] against round-3 multivariate signature schemes, Rainbow [6] and GeMSS [8], as well as

M.-J. Saarinen and D. Smith-Tone (Eds.): PQCrypto 2024, LNCS 14771, pp. 202–226, 2024.
https://doi.org/10.1007/978-3-031-62743-9_7

the cryptanalysis of round-4 isogeny based KEM SIKE [9,27], emphasise the need to continue the cryptanalysis effort in PQC as well as to increase the diversity in the potential post-quantum hard problems.

A relatively unexplored family of such problems come from *group-based* cryptography (see [23,24]). In particular we are interested in the so-called Semidirect Discrete Logarithm Problem (SDLP), which initially appears in the 2013 work of Habeeb et al. [17]. Roughly speaking, we generalise the standard notion of group exponentiation by employing products of the form $\phi^{x-1}(g) \cdot \ldots \cdot \phi(g) \cdot g$, where g is an element of a (semi)group, ϕ is an endomorphism and $x \in \mathbb{N}$ is a positive integer. Our task in SDLP is to recover the integer x given the pair g, ϕ and the value $\phi^{x-1}(g) \cdot \ldots \cdot \phi(g) \cdot g$. It turns out that products of this form have enough structure to be cryptographically useful, in a sense we will expand upon later - in particular, protocols based on SDLP are plausibly post-quantum, since there is no known reduction of SDLP to a Hidden Subgroup Problem.

By far the most studied such protocol is known as Semidirect Product Key Exchange (SDPKE), originally proposed in [17] (note that this is the same work in which SDLP first appears). It is a Diffie–Hellman-like key exchange protocol in which products of the form $\phi^{x-1}(g) \cdot \ldots \cdot \phi(g) \cdot g$ are exchanged between two parties in such a way as to allow both parties to recover the same shared key. Clearly, the security of SDPKE and the difficulty of SDLP are heavily related – in particular, an adversary able to solve SDLP is also able to break SDPKE.

There is therefore motivation to analyse the difficulty of SDLP. However, prior to this work the general-case complexity of SDLP and its relationship to more well-known hardness problems, particularly with respect to its security against quantum adversaries, has not been well understood and was a significant open problem for researchers in this area. In this paper, we provide the first dedicated analysis of SDLP, obtaining two key contributions. First, we demonstrate that a subset of all possible products of the form $\phi^{x-1}(g) \cdot \ldots \cdot \phi(g) \cdot g$ is a set upon which a finite abelian group acts; in other words, that SDPKE is, modulo some context-specific technicality, a variant of the group action-based key exchange schemes originally proposed by Couveignes [15]. In particular, solving SDLP can be translated into a problem with respect to a group action. This surprising connection provides a sharper classification of SDPKE than was previously known, and allows us to derive our second contribution, an application of known tools that gives a quantum algorithm for solving SDLP. The algorithm runs in subexponential time $2^{\mathcal{O}(\sqrt{\log p})}$, where p parameterises the size of the group action.

2   Related Work

Examples of concrete proposals for SDPKE can be found in [16,17,25,32,33]; respective cryptanalyses can be found in [4,5,7,21,29,31]. This body of work proceeds more or less chronologically, in that proposed platforms are a response to cryptanalysis addressing a weakness in an earlier version. A more detailed survey of the back-and-forth on this topic can be found in [3].

Despite the relationship between SDPKE and SDLP, none of the works discussed above provide an analysis of SDLP. Indeed, the general direction of research in this area has been either to achieve shared key recovery by exploiting some underlying linearity of a platform (semi)group, or to find examples of (semi)groups with sufficiently lax structure to render these attacks less powerful. In particular, none of the cryptanalyses in this area solve SDLP.

Recent Algorithms for SDLP. Since the preparation of this manuscript various works either related to it or advancing upon it have appeared. We detail them briefly below.

The authors of [2] derive a digital signature scheme whose security is based on the difficulty of SDLP in a certain p-group. Using similar techniques to that of this paper, they show that the resulting signature scheme admits quantum subexponential time forgeries.

Two papers dedicated to the analysis of SDLP, meanwhile, have appeared rather recently. The first is the work of [20], whose basic idea is use a clever recursion tool in the quotients of the underlying group to reduce some instance of SDLP to an instance of SDLP in an elementary abelian group. Moreover, an existing quantum algorithm due to [22] allows one to compute the necessary series of quotients; one is therefore done after showing that this abelian instance of SDLP is solved simply by solving a classical discrete logarithm problem in quantum polynomial time. The second of these papers is [28], which is more specifically tailored to the platform group proposed in [2] – again, however, it exploits the decomposition of that platform group into abelian constituents. Interestingly, [28] makes progress towards demonstrating the quantum equivalence of SDLP and the Computational Diffie-Hellman-like problem underpinning the security of SDPKE, highlighting the potential need for future vigilance against SDPKE attacks when considering the difficulty of SDLP.

All three of these works make reference to a pre-print of this paper, and indeed make use of insights and techniques first defined therein. Nevertheless, the chief novelty of this work in comparison with its peers is the generality of the method. As one might expect from the requirement of the groups in [20] to have some abelian quotient, the principal class of group admitting quantum polynomial algorithms for SDLP are the solvable groups (though the work does present a couple of other examples related to matrix groups over finite fields). Our algorithm is not restricted to this class of groups, and in fact is able to solve SDLP when the candidate group is replaced by a semigroup. On the other hand, in these solvable groups the method of [20] runs in quantum polynomial time - i.e. a significant speed-up of our general method. We therefore remark that in order to understand where SDLP fits in the general landscape of potentially post-quantum hard computational problems, it is important to consider both the current paper and the works discussed in this section.

Related Techniques. Ideas much closer to the spirit of our work appear in papers that, at first glance, appear unrelated to SDPKE and SDLP. Our results are achieved in part by careful synthesis of the techniques in the two papers of Childs et al. [12,13]: since the set of all products of the form $\phi^{x-1}(g) \cdot \ldots \cdot \phi(g) \cdot g$ admits some similarity to that of a monogenic semigroup, we can adapt some ideas from a quantum algorithm in [13] that solves the Semigroup Discrete Logarithm Problem. However, in our setting we are lacking some key structure that allows the direct application of [13]. The full algorithm is constructed by adapting ideas in [12], allowing us to show the important quantum algorithms of Kuperberg [26] and Regev [34] can be used to solve SDLP.

3   Organisation of the Paper and Main Results

The construction of the algorithm claimed in the title is, from a high-level perspective, achieved by two reduction proofs followed by an application of known algorithms. With this in mind, we make the following contributions.

Section 4. We start with preliminaries in which the necessary background is reviewed. In particular we give a brief discussion of the relevant algebraic objects, a short note on quantum computation, and a full description of SDPKE - including a discussion of appropriate asymptotic assumptions for the growth of the semigroups we work with, derived from currently proposed platforms. In particular we derive a notion of a parametrised family of semigroups called an 'easy' family of semigroups. The section finishes with a kind of glossary of computational problems.

Section 5. It will be immediately convenient to write $s(g, \phi, x)$ for $\phi^{x-1}(g) \cdot ... \cdot g$, not only for clarity of notation but to aid the crucial shift in perspective offered in this paper. Armed with this notation our first task is to study the set of possible exponents[1] $\{s(g, \phi, i) : i \in \mathbb{N}\}$. In Theorem 1 we deduce, borrowing from some standard ideas in semigroup theory, that this set is finite and has the form $\{g, ..., s(g, \phi, n), ..., s(g, \phi, n + r - 1)\}$ where the integers n, r are a function of the choice of (g, ϕ) (and may, when desirable, be written $r_{g,\phi}, n_{g,\phi}$ to highlight this point). The main result of this section is Theorem 3: an abelian group acts freely and transitively on the set $\{s(g, \phi, n), ..., s(g, \phi, n + r - 1)\}$. This set is called the cycle of g, ϕ and is denoted by the calligraphic letter $\mathcal{C}$. In particular, we show the following:

Theorem. *Fix* $(g, \phi) \in G \times End(G)$ *and let* n, r *be the index and period corresponding to* g, ϕ. *Moreover, let* $\mathcal{C}$ *be the corresponding cycle of size* r. *The abelian group* $\mathbb{Z}_r$ *acts freely and transitively on* $\mathcal{C}$.

where $\mathbb{Z}_r$ is the usual notion of a group of residues modulo r.

Section 6. If the set of exponents with respect to (g, ϕ) consisted entirely of the cycle we would immediately have a reduction to the Group Action Discrete Logarithm Problem (GADLP), also referred to as *Group Action DLog* in [30], or

---

[1] If (g, ϕ) is fixed we can think of $s(g, \phi, \cdot)$ as a function from $\mathbb{N}$ into G that generalises the usual group exponentiation map, in the sense that the usual exponentiation map is recovered if ϕ is the identity morphism. Within this intuition we shall feel comfortable referring to the values of s relative to some fixed (g, ϕ) as 'exponents'.

the *Parallelisation Problem* in [15]. Roughly speaking, since we know that an abelian group acts on the cycle, in this case the exponent x to be recovered is precisely the group element acting on g to give $s(g, \phi, x)$. This is not, however, generally the case, and to proceed it will be necessary to extract the pair n, r from the base values g, ϕ. In Theorem 4 we show that one can achieve this in efficient quantum time by using canonical quantum period-finding methods. We can therefore deduce in Theorem 5 that one can solve SDLP efficiently given access to a GADLP oracle; or, if $s(g, \phi, x)$ is not in the cycle of g, ϕ, by invoking a classical procedure exploiting the knowledge of n, r. Indeed, we show the following:

Theorem. *Let $\{G_p\}_p$ be an easy family of semigroups, and fix p. Algorithm 3 solves SDLP with respect to a pair $(g, \phi) \in G_p \times End(G_p)$ given access to a GADLP oracle for the group action $(\mathbb{Z}_{r_{g,\phi}}, \mathcal{C}_{g,\phi}, \circledast)$. The algorithm runs in time $\mathcal{O}((\log p)^4)$, makes at most a single query to the GADLP oracle, and succeeds with probability $\Omega(1)$.*

Clearly, many of the requisite notions in this statement have not yet been defined. Roughly speaking, an easy family of semigroups is a family of semigroups parameterised by p such that each of the functions taking p as an argument grows polynomially in p.

Section 7. In order to give a full description and complexity analysis of the algorithm it remains to examine the state of the art for solving GADLP. It is reasonably well-known (see [12,35]) that GADLP reduces to the Abelian Hidden Shift Problem if the action is free and transitive, though we provide a context-specific reduction in Theorem 6. There are two popular choices to solve this problem: an algorithm due to Kuperberg [26] and another due to Regev [34], each of which has trade-offs with respect to time and space complexity. Finally, the full algorithm is given in Theorem 9, though we are essentially assembling the components we have developed throughout the rest of the paper. This main result is the following:

Theorem. *Let $\{G_p\}_p$ be an easy family of semigroups, and fix p. For any pair $(g, \phi) \in G_p \times End(G_p)$, there is a quantum algorithm solving SDLP with respect to (g, ϕ) with time and query complexity $2^{\mathcal{O}(\sqrt{\log p})}$.*

which proves the claim of a quantum subexponential algorithm for SDLP given in the title.

4   Preliminaries

4.1   Notation

One need only be familiar with the standard $\mathcal{O}()$ and $\Omega()$ notations. Various bespoke notations are introduced throughout the course of the paper, but these will be defined in due course. We note also that all our logarithms are base-2.

4.2   Background Mathematics

We recall a number of group-theoretic notions used throughout this paper.

Recall that a group for which one is not guaranteed to have inverse with respect to the group operation is a *semigroup*. Writing the operation multipicatively, the semigroups G we are interested in all have an element 1 such that $1 \cdot g = g = g \cdot 1$ for each $g \in G$ - such a semigroup is also called a *monoid*. In this work we insist that we do not have a full group, and so write semigroups without meaning to refer to full groups.

We will deal with both abelian groups and non-abelian semigroups in this paper; that is, for a non-abelian semigroup G one cannot expect that $g \cdot h = h \cdot g$ for all $g, h \in G$. For the sake of clarity we will write abelian groups additively. In this case, the operation $g + h$ commutes, and we require an inverse for every element. Note also that the identity is written as 0 in this case.

Consider a function from G to itself, say ϕ. If ϕ preserves multiplication - that is, $\phi(g \cdot h) = \phi(g) \cdot \phi(h)$ for each $g, h \in G$ - we call it an *endomorphism*. Certainly we can compose these functions according to the usual notion, and indeed it is standard that the set of all endomorphisms under function composition defines a semigroup. Since we allow for (and in some cases require) that the endomorphisms are not invertible, we have a semigroup rather than a full group. In particular, every finite semigroup G immediately induces an *endomorphism semigroup*, denoted $End(G)$.

An important, and in this context frequently invoked source of semigroups come from *matrix algebras*. The set of square matrices of fixed size with entries in some ring R forms an R-module, since we can add matrices together and scale each entry of a matrix by some $r \in R$. The necessary distributivity properties are inherited from the properties of R. However, unlike in a usual R-module, we can also *multiply* elements just by defining multiplication to be the usual notion of matrix multiplication. The resulting matrix algebra is denoted $M_n(R)$, where $n \in \mathbb{N}$ is the fixed size of matrix, and R is the underlying ring. Indeed, consider a matrix algebra under only the multiplication operation. It is again clear that this object is a semigroup; we would have a full group if every matrix was invertible, but of course this is not true. The all-zero matrix, for example, has no multiplicative inverse. A matrix algebra considered only under its multiplication, therefore, is a useful source for concrete examples of semigroups.

It will be useful for us to build a new semigroup from an existing semigroup. One way of doing this is via a structure called the *holomorph*. Let G be a (semi)group and $End(G)$ its endomorphism semigroup. The holomorph $G \ltimes End(G)$ is the set $G \times End(G)$ equipped with multiplication

$$(g, \phi) \cdot (g', \phi') = (\phi'(g) \cdot g', \phi' \circ \phi)$$

where $\circ$ refers to function composition. In fact, the holomorph is itself a special case of the semidirect product, hence the 'semidirect' terminology found throughout this paper.

Group Actions. A key idea for us will be that of a group action, and in particular a commutative group action. Roughly speaking such an object allows one to map elements of a set to each other in a cryptographically useful fashion, but in a less structured manner than in more classical settings. More formally:

Definition 1 (Commutative Group Action). *Let G be a finite abelian group and X be a finite set. Consider a function from $G \times X \to X$, written by convention as $g \star x$, with the following properties:*

1. $1 \star x = x$
2. $(g + h) \star x = g \star (h \star x)$

The tuple $(G, X, \star)$ is a commutative group action. If only the identity fixes an arbitrary element of X the action is free, and if for any $x, y \in X$ there is a g such that $g \star x = y$ the action is transitive.

The group action defined in this paper is commutative, so we will sometimes just write 'group action' to mean a commutative group action. It will remain for us, however, to prove that this action is free and transitive. If the action is indeed free and transitive, it follows that for any $x \in X$, all $y \in X$ are such that there exists a unique $g \in G$ with $g \star x = y$. Borrowing notation from Couveignes [15], it will sometimes be convenient for us to write $\delta(y, x)$ to denote this value.

4.3 Quantum Computation

In order to present our quantum algorithm for SDLP (Sect. 6), the reader needs only be familiar with standard quantum tools, presented for example in [18]. We give a brief summary of the required notions below.

Recall that n qubits can be represented by the complex vector space H_{2^n}, where the basis states are exactly the n-fold tensor products of basis states of H_2. An ordered system of n qubits is called a *quantum register of length n*, and the basis states are sometimes written $\{|i\rangle : 0 \le i < 2^n\}$ by identifying i with its binary representation.

Recall also that we can create the uniform superposition efficiently with a Hadarmard gate. For an l-qubit register, the computational basis vector $|0\rangle$ is such that the Hadamard gate (written H_{2^l}) is such that

$$H_{2^l} |0\rangle = \frac{1}{\sqrt{2^l}} \sum_{i=0}^{2^l - 1} |i\rangle$$

Moreover, this transformation can be carried out efficiently, in time $\mathcal{O}(l)$.

4.4 Semidirect Product Key Exchange

We here define in full SDPKE. One verifies by induction that holomorph exponentiation takes the form

$$(g, \phi)^x = (\phi^{x-1}(g) \cdot \ldots \phi(g) \cdot g, \phi^x)$$

where ϕ^x denoted the endomorphism ϕ composed with itself x times. Note that this operation involves multiplying (semi)group elements, endomorphisms, and applying an endomorphism to a semigroup element. If all these operations are efficient, the holomorph exponentiation is efficient since one can apply standard square-and-multiply techniques.

The central idea of SDPKE is to use products of these form as a generalisation of Diffie–Helman Key-Exchange. Suppose N is the number of all possible distinct holomorph exponents - there are finitely many - then the protocol works as follows:

1. Suppose Alice and Bob agree on a public (semi)group G and hence the integer N, as well as a group element g and endomorphism of G, say ϕ.
2. Alice picks a secret integer x uniformly at random from $\{1, ..., N\}$, and calculates the holomorph exponent $(g, \phi)^x = (A, \phi^x)$. She sends **only** A to Bob.
3. Bob similarly calculates (B, ϕ^y) corresponding to a random, private integer y, and sends only B to Alice.
4. With her private automorphism ϕ^x Alice can now calculate her key as the group element $K_A = \phi^x(B) \cdot A$; Bob similarly calculates his key $K_B = \phi^y(A) \cdot B$.

We have

$$\phi^x(B) \cdot A = \phi^x(\phi^{y-1}(g) \cdot \ldots \cdot g) \cdot (\phi^{x-1}(g) \cdot \ldots \cdot g)$$
$$= (\phi^{x+y-1} \cdot \ldots \cdot \phi^x(g)) \cdot (\phi^{x-1}(g) \cdot \ldots \cdot g)$$
$$= (\phi^{x+y-1} \cdot \ldots \cdot \phi^y(g)) \cdot (\phi^{y-1}(g) \cdot \ldots \cdot g)$$
$$= \phi^y(A) \cdot B$$

so $K := K_A = K_B$. Note that $A \cdot B \neq K$ as a consequence of our insistence that the endomorphism ϕ is non-trivial - note that in the closed form derived in [17] when ϕ is a conjugation, we also require G to be non-commutative.

Writing these products in full will quickly become rather cumbersome. We therefore introduce some non-standard notation, which is useful both for convenience of exposition and the required shift in perspective we will introduce in this paper.

Definition 2. *Let G be a finite, non-commutative (semi)group, $g \in G$, and $\phi \in End(G)$. We define the following function:*

$$s : G \times End(G) \times \mathbb{N} \to G$$
$$(g, \phi, x) \mapsto \phi^{x-1}(g) \cdot \ldots \cdot \phi(g) \cdot g$$

Notice that when g, ϕ are fixed - as in the case of the key exchange - the function s is really only taking integer arguments, analogously to the standard notion of group exponentiation. Indeed, a passive adversary observing a round of SDPKE has access to the values $s(g, \phi, x)$ and $s(g, \phi, y)$ - in order to recover the shared key $s(g, \phi, x + y)$ one strategy they might adopt is to recover the private integers x, y from $s(g, \phi, x), s(g, \phi, y)$ to allow calculation of $s(g, \phi, x+y)$. In short, the security of SDPKE is clearly in some sense related to the Semidirect Discrete Logarithm Problem alluded to in the introduction. We shall have much more to say about this later on.

4.5 Efficiency Considerations

The works discussed in the introduction, as well as the contents of the more comprehensive survey [3], highlight that every extant proposal of a platform for SDPKE suggests for use some variety of matrix algebra. In particular, insofar as parameters are recommended, the convention is to fix a matrix size - usually 3 - and adjust the size of an underlying ring in order to increase security.

In other words, having defined SDPKE above relative to some semigroup G and its endomorphism semigroup $End(G)$, we can think of each such semigroup as one of a family of semigroups $\{G_p\}_p$, where the family $\{G_p\}_p$ is indexed by some set parameterising the underlying algebra (usually the primes). Note that this immediately induces a family of endomorphism semigroups $\{End(G_p)\}_p$, so we can talk about pairs (g, ϕ) from the set $G_p \times End(G_p)$ for each p.

Table 1 gives examples of platforms over 3×3 matrices, the size of the platform, and the variable that can be considered as the indexing variable[2].

Table 1. Growth of Proposed Platforms

Proposed Platform	Size of Platform	Indexing Variable
$M_3(G[R])$	$|R|^{9|G|}$	$|R|$
Certain classes of p-group	Polynomial in prime p	Prime p
$M_3(\mathbb{Z}_p)$	p^9	p

In each of these examples we have a family of semigroups indexed by some set P such that each semigroup G_p has size polynomial in p. We will give complexity estimates as a function of p - indeed, let us now see how the complexity of executing SDPKE grows with p. For a semigroup G, note that with respect to the holomorph $G \times End(G)$ we have $(g, \phi)^x = (s(g, \phi, x), \phi^x)$ by definition. By standard square-and-multiply techniques it therefore requires $\mathcal{O}(\log x)$ applications of the operation in the holomorph to compute $s(g, \phi, x)$.

In order to estimate the complexity of the holomorph operation we need to know the complexity of multiplication in G and that of applying the endomorphism ϕ. In this direction we note that another characteristic of the currently proposed platforms is that the endomorphisms suggested for use with SDPKE typically involve multiplication by one or more auxiliary matrices; that is, for a particular semigroup G_p, if $(g, \phi) \in G_p \times End(G_p)$ the group element $\phi(g)$ has the form $A \cdot g \cdot B$, where $A, B \in G$ are fixed. If the matrix size is fixed each application of ϕ therefore requires some constant number of operations in the underlying ring of the matrix semigroup, which we may assume has size polynomial in p. The complexity of this matrix multiplication will be dominated by the multiplication in the underlying ring. Since the size of the underlying ring

---

[2] Note here that $|R|$ is chosen as the parameter for reasons of efficiency of representation.

is also polynomial in p, each multiplication has complexity $\mathcal{O}((\log p)^2)$ (since $\mathcal{O}(\log poly(p)) = \mathcal{O}(\log p)$). We conclude that both multiplication of elements in G_p, and evaluation of $\phi(g)$, can be done in time $\mathcal{O}((\log p)^2)$.

With these observations in mind, we define the following:

Definition 3. *Let* P *some countable indexing set. A family of semigroups* $\{G_p\}_{p\in P}$ *is said to be easy if*

1. $|G_p|$ *grows monotonically and polynomially in* p
2. *For any* p, *any tuple* $(g, h, \phi) \in G_p \times G_p \times End(G_p)$ *is such that* $g \cdot h$ *and* $\phi(g)$ *can be evaluated in time* $\mathcal{O}((\log p)^2)$.

Many of the complexity results within the paper assume that we are dealing with an easy family of semigroups, basically in an attempt to model the behaviour of suggested examples of semigroup family.

4.6 Computational Problems

We have already alluded to some of the hard problems to be found in this paper. Here we give full definitions of all of them to serve as a kind of 'glossary' section.

Definition 4 (Semidirect Discrete Logarithm Problem). *Given a public (semi)group* G, *its public endomorphism semigroup* $End(G)$ *and a public pair* $(g, \phi) \in G \times End(G)$, *let* N *be the size of the set* $\{s(g, \phi, i) : i \in \mathbb{N}\}$. *Choose* x *from* $\{1, ..., N\}$ *uniformly at random, calculate* $s(g, \phi, x)$ *and create the pair* $((g, \phi), s(g, \phi, x))$. *The Semidirect Discrete Logarithm Problem (SDLP) with respect to* (g, ϕ) *is to recover the integer* x *given the pair* (g, ϕ) *and* $s(g, \phi, x)$.

We now give the computational problem that we seek to reduce to. This version of the problem is taken from [30], but can be found as the *vectorisation* problem, respectively, in [15].

Definition 5 (Group Action Discrete Logarithm). *Given a public commutative group action* $(G, X, \star)$, *sample* $g \in G$ *and* $x \in X$ *uniformly at random, compute* $y = g \star x$ *and create the pair* (x, y). *The Group Action Discrete Logarithm Problem (GADLP) with respect to* x *is to recover* g *given the pair* (x, y).

Remark 1. The idea of SDPKE is used in this paper to motivate the study of SDLP. However, as in the classical case, the security of SDPKE is not known to be precisely equivalent to SDLP, and indeed one can define group action-related and semidirect product-related problems in the style of the Computational Diffie-Hellman problem. Studying these problems is beyond the scope of this work.

Finally we give a seemingly unrelated problem requiring a small amount of introduction. Let $f, g : A \to S$ be injective functions, where S is a set and A is a finite abelian group. We say that f, g hide some $s \in A$ if one has $g(a) = f(a + s)$ for each $a \in A$.

Definition 6 (Abelian Hidden Shift Problem). *Given a public abelian group* A *and a set* S, *suppose two injective functions* f, g *hide some* $s \in A$. *The Abelian Hidden Shift Problem (AHSP) is to recover the group element* s.

5 Structure of the Exponents

All of the algorithms in this paper rely on the construction of a certain group action - recall that such an object consists of a group, a set, and a function (Sect. 4.2, Definition 1). As a general outline to our strategy, we first define and deduce properties of a particular set, from which the appropriate group and function will follow.

With this in mind, we make the following definition. For now we will dispense with our notion of an easy, parameterised family of semigroups, since the results presented in this section apply to any fixed semigroup. In fact, for compactness of exposition, for the remainder of this section by G we mean an arbitrary finite (semi)group, and by $End(G)$ we mean its associated endomorphism semigroup.

Definition 7. *For a pair $(g, \phi) \in G \times End(G)$, define*

$$\mathcal{X}_{g,\phi} := \{s(g, \phi, i) : i \in \mathbb{N}\}$$

We will often write $\mathcal{X}_{(g,\phi)}$ as $\mathcal{X}$ when clear from context. Certainly this object is neither a group nor a semigroup - numerous counterexamples can be found whereby multiplication of elements in this set are not contained in the set - but we can make some progress by borrowing from the standard theory of monogenic semigroups; presented, for example, in [19]. Since $\mathcal{X} \subset G$, $\mathcal{X}$ is finite — the set $\{x \in \mathbb{N} : \exists y \neq x \quad s(g, \phi, x) = s(g, \phi, y)\}$ must therefore be non-empty, or the set would be in bijection with the natural numbers, contradicting the fact that G is finite. We may therefore choose the smallest element of this set, say n. By definition of n the set $\{x \in \mathbb{N} : s(g, \phi, n) = s(g, \phi, n + x)\}$ must also be non-empty, so we may again pick its smallest element and call it r.

The structure of $\mathcal{X}$ is further restricted by the following result:

Lemma 1. *Let $(g, \phi) \in G \times End(G)$ and $x, y \in \mathbb{N}$, then*

$$\phi^x (s(g, \phi, y)) \cdot s(g, \phi, x) = s(g, \phi, x + y)$$

Proof. Note that $s(g, \phi, x+y) = \phi^{x+y-1}(g) \cdot \ldots \cdot g$. Since ϕ preserves multiplication, applying ϕ^x to $s(g, \phi, y)$ adds x to the exponent of each term. Multiplication on the right by $s(g, \phi, x)$ then completes the remaining terms of $s(g, \phi, x + y)$.   □

Remark 2. One can entirely symmetrically swap the roles of x and y in the above argument, which gives two ways of calculating $s(g, \phi, x+y)$. In essence, therefore, this result gives us a slightly more elegant proof of the correctness of SDPKE.

This method of inducing addition in the integer argument of s is sufficiently important that we will invoke a definition for it.

Definition 8. *Let $(g, \phi) \in G \times End(G)$ and define a function $f : \mathbb{N} \times \mathcal{X} \to \mathcal{X}$ by*

$$f(i, s(g, \phi, j)) = \phi^i(s(g, \phi, j)) \cdot s(g, \phi, i)$$

where $f(i, s(g, \phi, j))$ may also be written as $i * s(g, \phi, j)$.

Remark 3. Strictly speaking the $*$ operation depends on a choice of pair (g, ϕ) and so should be written $*_{g,\phi}$. However, since the remainder of the paper deals with SDLP when a choice of such a pair is fixed, we will suppress this detail.

Remark 4. If G is of the type discussed in Sect. 4.5 -i.e., $G = G_p$ is one of a family of easy semigroups - the value $i * s(g, \phi, j)$ can be computed in time $\mathcal{O}((\log i)(\log p)^2)$. provided $s(g, \phi, j)$ is already known. This is because to compute $\phi^i(s(g, \phi, j))$ requires the computation and evaluation of ϕ^i, the computation of $s(g, \phi, i)$, and some fixed number of multiplications in G - but we know from Sect. 4.5 that one can calculate $(g, \phi)^i = (s(g, \phi, i), \phi^i)$ in time $\mathcal{O}((\log i)(\log p)^2)$.

Thus far we have established that corresponding to any fixed pair $(g, \phi) \in G \times End(G)$ is a set $\mathcal{X}_{g,\phi} = \mathcal{X}$ and a pair of integers n, r. By Lemma 1 we know that $i * s(g, \phi, j) = s(g, \phi, i + j)$ for any $i, j \in \mathbb{N}$, so by definition of n, r we have

$$s(g, \phi, n + 2r) = r * s(g, \phi, n + r)$$
$$= r * s(g, \phi, n)$$
$$= s(g, \phi, n + r) = s(g, \phi, n)$$

We conclude, by extending this argument in the obvious way, that $s(g, \phi, n + qr) = s(g, \phi, n)$ for each $q \in \mathbb{N}$. In fact, we have the following:

Lemma 2. *Fix* $(g, \phi) \in G \times End(G)$ *and let* n, r *be the corresponding integer pair as above. One has that*

$$s(g, \phi, n + x + qr) = s(g, \phi, n + x)$$

for all $x, q \in \mathbb{N}$.

We will frequently invoke Lemma 2. Indeed, we immediately get that the set $\mathcal{X}$ cannot contain values other than $\{g, ..., s(g, \phi, n), ..., s(g, \phi, n + r - 1)\}$. If any of the values in $\{g, ..., s(g, \phi, n - 1)\}$ are equal we contradict the minimality of n, and if any of the values in $\{s(g, \phi, n), ..., s(g, \phi, n + r - 1)\}$ are equal we contradict the minimality of r. We have shown the following:

Theorem 1. *Fix* $(g, \phi) \in G \times End(G)$. *The set* $\mathcal{X} = \{s(g, \phi, i) : i \in \mathbb{N}\}$ *has size* $n + r - 1$ *for integers* n, r *dependent on* g, ϕ. *In particular*

$$\mathcal{X} = \{g, ..., s(g, \phi, n), ..., s(g, \phi, n + r - 1)\}.$$

We refer to the set $\{g, ..., s(g, \phi, n - 1)\}$ as the *tail*, written $\mathcal{T}_{g,\phi}$, of $\mathcal{X}_{g,\phi}$; and the set $\{s(g, \phi, n), ..., s(g, \phi, n + r - 1)\}$ as the *cycle*, written $\mathcal{C}_{g,\phi}$, of $\mathcal{X}_{g,\phi}$. The values $n_{g,\phi}$ and $r_{g,\phi}$ are called the *index* and *period* of the pair (g, ϕ). We shall feel free to omit the subscript at will when clear from context.

One can see that unique natural numbers correspond to each element in the tail, but infinitely many correspond to each element in the cycle. In fact, each element of the cycle corresponds to a unique residue class modulo r, shifted by the index n. This is a rather intuitive fact, but owing to its usefulness we will record it formally. In the following we assume the function mod returns the canonical positive residue.

Theorem 2. *Fix* $(g, \phi) \in G \times End(G)$ *and let* $x, y \in \mathbb{N}$. *We have*

$$s(g, \phi, n + x) = s(g, \phi, n + y)$$

if and only if $x \mod r = y \mod r$.

Proof. In the reverse direction, setting $x' = x \mod r$ and $y' = y \mod r$, we have by Lemma 2 that $s(g, \phi, n + x) = s(g, \phi, n + x')$ and $s(g, \phi, n + y) = s(g, \phi, n + y')$. By assumption $x' = y'$, and $0 \leq x', y' < r$. The claim follows since we know values in the range $\{s(g, \phi, n), ..., s(g, \phi, n + r - 1)\}$ are distinct by Theorem 1.

On the other hand, suppose $s(g, \phi, n + y) = s(g, \phi, n + x)$ but $x \not\equiv y \mod r$. Without loss of generality we can write $y = x' + u + qr$ for some $q \in \mathbb{N}, 0 < u < r$ and $x' = x \mod r$. By Lemma 2, since $s(g, \phi, n + y) = s(g, \phi, n + x)$ we must have

$$s(g, \phi, n + x') = s(g, \phi, n + x' + u)$$

where $s(g, \phi, n + x) = s(g, \phi, n + x')$ also by Lemma 2. There are now three cases to consider; we claim each of them gives a contradiction.

First, suppose $x'+u=r$, then $s(g, \phi, n+x')=s(g, \phi, n)$. Since $x'<r$ we contradict minimality of r. The case $x' + u < r$ gives a similar contradiction.

Finally, if $x' + u > r$, without loss of generality we can write $x' + u = r + v$ for some positive integer v, so we have $s(M, \phi, n + x') = s(M, \phi, n + v)$. Since $x' \neq v$ (else we contradict $u < r$), and both values are strictly less than r, we have a contradiction, since distinct integers of this form give distinct evaluations of s. □

5.1   A Group Action

It should be clear by now that we are interested in the argument of s in terms of residue classes modulo r. Recall that the group of residue classes modulo r is denoted $\mathbb{Z}_r$, and its elements are written as $[i]_r$. We conclude the section by constructing the action of $\mathbb{Z}_r$ on the cycle $\{s(g, \phi, n), ..., s(g, \phi, n+r-1)\}$, where we assume that the operator $\mod r$ returns the unique integer in $\{0, ..., r-1\}$ associated to its argument.

Theorem 3. *Fix* $(g, \phi) \in G \times End(G)$ *and let* n, r *be the index and period corresponding to* g, ϕ. *Moreover, let* C *be the corresponding cycle of size* r. *The abelian group* $\mathbb{Z}_r$ *acts freely and transitively on* C.

Proof. First note that Theorem 2 immediately gives that $j * s(g, \phi, i + n) = s(g, \phi, (i + j) \mod r + n)$ for any $j \in \mathbb{N}$. Our current definition of s is not defined for negative integer arguments; nevertheless, we can extend the range of the operator $*$ as follows. Let $* : \mathbb{Z} \times C \to C$ be defined by

$$j * s(g, \phi, i) = \phi^{j \mod r}(s(g, \phi, i + n)) \cdot s(g, \phi, j \mod r)$$

Since $j \mod r \geq 0$, as usual we have $j * s(g, \phi, i + n) = s(g, \phi, i + j \mod r + n)$; but since $s(g, \phi, i + n) \in C$, we know $0 \leq i < r$, so $i \mod r = i$. It follows that $j * s(g, \phi, i + n) = s(g, \phi, (i + j) \mod r + n)$.

In fact, fix some $i \in \mathbb{N}$, and let $[j]_r$ be a fixed element of $\mathbb{Z}_r$. By definition, every $k \in [j]_r$ is such that $k \mod r = j'$ for some $j' \in \{0, ..., r-1\}$; without loss of generality, $j' = j$. We may therefore define $\circledast : \mathbb{Z} \times \mathcal{C} \to \mathcal{C}$ by

$$[j]_r \circledast s(g, \phi, i + n) = s(g, \phi, (i + j) \mod r + n)$$

where j is the unique element of $[j]_r$ such that $k \mod r = j$ for each $k \in [j]_r$. We claim that $(\mathbb{Z}_r, \mathcal{C}, \circledast)$ is a free, transitive group action.

First, let us verify that a group action is indeed defined. Certainly $[0]_r$ fixes every element in $\mathcal{C}$, since $s(g, \phi, (i + 0) \mod r + n) = s(g, \phi, i + n)$ for each $i \in \{0, ..., r-1\}$. Moreover, one has

$$
\begin{aligned}
[k]_r \circledast ([j]_r \circledast s(g, \phi, i + n)) &= [k]_r \circledast s(g, \phi, (i + j) \mod r + n) \\
&= s(g, \phi, ((i + j) \mod r) + k \mod r + n) \\
&= s(g, \phi, (i + (j + k)) \mod r + n) \\
&= [j + k]_r \circledast s(g, \phi, i + n) \\
&= ([k]_r + [j]_r) \circledast s(g, \phi, i + n)
\end{aligned}
$$

It remains to check that the action is free and transitive. If $[j]_r \in \mathbb{Z}_r$ is such that $[j]_r$ fixes an arbitrary element of $\mathcal{C}$, say $s(g, \phi, i + n)$, then we have $s(g, \phi, (i + j) \mod r + n) = s(g, \phi, i + n)$. By Theorem 2, we must have $i + j \equiv i \mod r$, so $[j]_r = [0]_r$ and the action is free. Moreover, for arbitrary $s(g, \phi, i + n), s(g, \phi, j + n) \in \mathcal{C}$, $[k]_r = [j - i]_r \in \mathbb{Z}_r$ is such that $[k]_r \circledast s(g, \phi, i + n) = s(g, \phi, j + n)$, so the action is also transitive and we are done.

$\square$

We summarise the above by noting that for each $(g, \phi) \in G \times End(G)$ we have shown the existence of a free, transitive, commutative group action $(\mathbb{Z}_r, \mathcal{C}, \circledast)$, where r and $\mathcal{C}$ depend on the choice of pair (g, ϕ).

6   Group Action Discrete Logarithms

Now that we have established the group action, we recall the Group Action Discrete Logarithm Problem (GADLP) from the introduction. Roughly speaking, for a free transitive group action $(G, X, \star)$, and x, y sampled uniformly at random from the set X, we are tasked with recovering the unique G-element g such that $g \star x = y$. In this section we will show that one can construct a quantum reduction from SDLP to GADLP.

More precisely, we target the type of structure discussed in Sect. 4.5; that, is a set of finite semigroups $\{G_p\}_p$ indexed by some parameter p, such that the size of each G_p is polynomial in p - the so-called 'easy' families of semigroups. We know that multiplication in each G_p requires a number of operations bounded above by some constant independent of p, and that the complexity of these operations is bounded above by $\mathcal{O}((\log p)^2)$

With all this in mind let $\{G_p\}_p$ be such a family of semigroups. In the previous section we have shown that for a fixed p, to each pair $(g, \phi) \in G_p \times End(G_p)$ is associated a pair (n, r) and a set $\mathcal{C}$. In this section we seek to show there is an efficient quantum algorithm to solve SDLP with respect to an arbitrary choice of (g, ϕ), provided one has access to a GADLP oracle for the group action $(\mathbb{Z}_r, \mathcal{C}, \circledast)$.

Before giving this reduction there remains a significant obstacle to overcome: for an arbitrary pair (g, ϕ) we have only proved the existence of the corresponding values n, r, but we do not have a means of calculating them. In order to provide a reduction to a GADLP oracle, however, we need to specify the appropriate group action. We therefore require access to the values n, r - in the next section, we will provide a quantum method of recovering these integers. We note that assuming access to a quantum computer is, for our purposes, justified since the best-known algorithms for GADLP are quantum anyway.

6.1   Calculating the Index and Period

In order to reason on the complexity of our algorithm we will use the following worst-case indicator, defined as follows:

Definition 9. *Let $\{G_p\}_{p \in P}$ be an easy family of finite semigroups parameterised by some set P. Define the following function on P:*

$$N(p) = \max_{(g,\phi) \in G_p \times End(G_p)} |\mathcal{T}_{g,\phi} + \mathcal{C}_{g,\phi}|$$

The function $N(p)$ gives a bound on the size of $\mathcal{X}_{g,\phi}$ for any $(g, \phi) \in G_p \times End(G_p)$. Since a crude such bound is the size of an easy semigroup G_p, which is assumed polynomial in p, we have that $N(p)$ is at worst polynomial in p.

Our method of calculating the index and period borrows heavily from ideas in [13, Theorem 1], which is itself a slightly repurposed version of [14, Algorithm 5]. Indeed, after a certain point we will be able to quote methods of these algorithms verbatim - nevertheless, to cater to our specific context it remains incumbent upon us to justify the following.

Lemma 3. *Let $\{G_p\}_p$ be an easy family of semigroups, and for an arbitrary p fix a pair $(g, \phi) \in G_p \times End(G_p)$. For any $l \in \mathbb{N}$, one can construct the superposition*

$$\frac{1}{\sqrt{M}} \sum_{k=0}^{M-1} |k\rangle |s(g, \phi, k)\rangle$$

in time $\mathcal{O}((\log M)(\log p)^2)$, where $M = 2^l$.

Proof. When (g, ϕ) is fixed, notice that we can think of $s(g, \phi, i) : G \times End(G) \times \mathbb{N} \to G$ as a function $s_{g,\phi}(i) : \mathbb{N} \to G$. Since $N(p)$ is a bound on the size of $\mathcal{X}_{g,\phi}$, taking m to be smallest integer such that $2^m \geq N(p)$ (note that $m = \mathcal{O}(\log(N(p)))$), the set $\mathcal{X}_{g,\phi}$ has binary representation in the set $\{0,1\}^m$. By definition the integers $\{0, ..., M-1\}$ have binary representation in $\{0,1\}^l$, so we can think of the restriction of $s_{g,\phi}$ on $\{0, ..., M-1\}$ as a function from $\{0,1\}^l$ into $\{0,1\}^m$. There is therefore a Boolean circuit computing $s_{g,\phi}$; it is standard (say, by [18, Theorem 2.3.2]) that one can construct a circuit implementing $s_{g,\phi}$ using reversible gates. Call this circuit $Q_{s_{g,\phi}}$; since the reversible circuit does no worse than the classical circuit, we can assume a single application of $Q_{s_{g,\phi}}$ takes at worst the time complexity of calculating $s_{g,\phi}(M)$.

What is the time complexity of calculating $s_{g,\phi}(M)$? We know by definition that $(s_{g,\phi}(M), \phi^M) = (g, \phi)^M$, where the exponentiation refers to holomorph exponentiation. Recall that since we have assumed we are working in an easy family of semigroups, each multiplication in the holomorph involves one application of ϕ, followed by some fixed constant number of matrix multiplications independently of p. Calculating the holomorph exponentiation in the standard square-and-multiply fashion, therefore, we expect to perform $\mathcal{O}(\log M)$ holomorph multiplications. We know that evaluating ϕ takes time $\mathcal{O}((\log p)^2)$; since a fixed number of matrix multiplications follow, the total time for calculating $s(g, \phi, M)$ is $\mathcal{O}(\log M (\log p)^2)$.

If we can show a single application of $Q_{s_{g,\phi}}$ gives the desired superposition we are done. It is standard, however, that the uniform superposition of an M-bit quantum register, together with an ancillary m-bit register in the state $|0\rangle$, can be inputted into $Q_{s_{g,\phi}}$ to produce the desired superposition. Since preparing the appropriate uniform superposition can be done by applying a Hadamard gate in time $\mathcal{O}(\log M)$, we are done.   □

Armed with the ability to efficiently calculate the appropriate superposition, we will quickly find ourselves with exactly the kind of state arrived at in [14, Algorithm 5], thereby allowing us to recover the period r in Algorithm 1. A small adaptation of standard binary search techniques completes the task by using knowledge of r to recover the index n.

Algorithm 1. PeriodRecovery$(((g, \phi), M))$

Input: Pair $(g, \phi) \in G_p \times End(G_p)$, upper bound on size of superposition to create M
Output: Period r of (g, ϕ) or 'Fail'

1: $R_0 \leftarrow |0\rangle |0\rangle$
2: $R_1 \leftarrow$ Hadamard transform applied to first register
3: $R_2 \leftarrow$ appropriate quantum circuit applied to R_1
4: Measure second register leaving collapsed first register R_3
5: $R_4 \leftarrow$ QFT over $\mathbb{Z}_M$ applied to R_3
6: $R_5 \leftarrow$ measure R_4
7: $r \leftarrow$ continued fraction expansion of R_5/M
8: **if** $r * s(g, \phi, M) \neq s(g, \phi, M)$ **then**
9:     **return** 'Fail'
10: **else**
11:     **return** r
12: **end if**

Algorithm 2. BinarySearch$((g, \phi), start, end, r)$

Input: Pair (g, ϕ), integers $start, end$ where $start \leq end$, period r of g, ϕ
Output: Index n of (g, ϕ)

1: **if** $start = end$ **then**:
2:      **return** $start$
3: **end if**
4: $left \leftarrow start$
5: $right \leftarrow end$
6: $mid \leftarrow \lfloor (left + right)/2 \rfloor$
7: **if** $r * s(g, \phi, mid) \neq s(g, \phi, mid)$ **then**
8:      **return** BinarySearch$((g, \phi), mid + 1, right, r)$
9: **else**
10:     **return** BinarySearch$((g, \phi), left, mid, r)$
11: **end if**

Theorem 4. *Let $\{G_p\}_p$ be an easy family of semigroups, and fix p. For any pair $(g, \phi) \in G_p \times End(G_p)$:*

1. *For sufficiently large $M \in \mathbb{N}$, PeriodRecovery$((g, \phi), M)$ recovers the period r of (g, ϕ) in time $\mathcal{O}((\log p)^3)$, and with constant probability.*
2. *BinarySearch$((g, \phi), 1, M, r)$ returns the index n of g, ϕ in time $\mathcal{O}((\log p)^4)$.*

Proof. 1. Fix a pair $(g, \phi) \in G_p \times End(G_p)$ and let r be its period. Let $\ell \in \mathbb{N}$ be the smallest positive integer such that $2^\ell \geq (N(p)^2 + N(p))$, and $M = 2^\ell$. In steps 1–3 of Algorithm 1, we prepare the required superposition as described in Lemma 3.

In Step 4, we measure the second register. With probability n/M doing so will cause us to observe an element of the tail; that is, some $s(g, \phi, i)$ such that $i < n$. In this case, by the laws of partial observation, the first register is left in a superposition of integers corresponding to this value - but by definition there is only one of these, so the first register consists of a single computational basis state and the algorithm has failed. On the other hand, with probability $(M - n)/M$ measuring the second register gives an element of $\mathcal{C}$. Now, since $M \geq N(p)^2 + N(p)$, we observe an element of $\mathcal{C}$ with probability

$$\frac{M - n}{M} = 1 - \frac{n}{M} \geq 1 - \frac{n}{N(p)^2 + N(p)}$$

Since by definition one has $n \leq N(p)$, it follows that the relevant probability is better than $N(p)/(N(p) + 1) \geq 1/2$. In other words, we observe an element of the desired form with constant, positive probability. Provided such an element was observed, after measuring the second register, the superposition of corresponding integers in the first register is the following:

$$\frac{1}{\sqrt{s_r}} \sum_{j=0}^{s_r - 1} |x_0 + jr\rangle$$

To see this, note that the function s is periodic of period r, and by Theorem 1 each $s(g, \phi, i)$ such that $i \geq n$ can only assume one of the distinct values $s(g, \phi, n), ..., s(g, \phi, n + r - 1)$. In particular, the integers in $\{1, ..., M\}$ that give a specific value of the cycle under s are of the form $x_0 + jr$ for some $x_0 \in \{n, ..., n + r - 1\}$. The largest such integer, by definition, is $x_0 + s_r r$, where s_r is just the largest integer such that $x_0 + s_r r < M$. Note that the superposition is normalised by this factor so that the sum of the squares of the amplitudes is 1.

We now have exactly the same kind of state found in [14, Algorithm 5][3], so we may proceed exactly according to the remaining steps in this algorithm. In Step 5 we apply a Quantum Fourier Transform (QFT) over $\mathbb{Z}_M$ to the state, which can be done in time $\mathcal{O}((\log M)^2)$. In step 6 we measure the state R_4; it is shown in [14, Algorithm 5, Step 5] that with probability at least $4/\pi^2$, measuring the resulting state leaves one with the closest integer to one of the at most r multiples of M/r (note that M/r is not necessarily an integer) with probability better than $4/\pi^2$. Writing this closest integer as $\lfloor jM/r \rceil$ for some $j \in \mathbb{N}$, one checks that the fraction j/r is a distance of at most $1/2M$ from $(\lfloor jM/r \rceil)/M$; by [18, Theorem 8.4.3], j/r will appear as one of the convergents in the continued fraction expansion of $(\lfloor jM/r \rceil)/M$ provided $1/2M \leq 1/2r^2$. Certainly this holds, since $r < N(p) < M$. Provided we have observed an integer of the appropriate form, then, it remains to carry out a continued fraction expansion on $(\lfloor jM/r \rceil)/M$, which we can do with repeated application of the Euclidean algorithm.

Let us summarise the complexity of the algorithm. The dominating factors are the creating of the relevant superposition in time

$$\mathcal{O}((\log M)(\log p)^2) = \mathcal{O}((\log N(p)(\log p)^2 = \mathcal{O}((\log p)^3))$$

where the last equality follows from the easy property of the relevant semi-group family; that is, one has that $N(p)$ is at worst polynomial in p. Similarly, the application of QFT can be done in time $\mathcal{O}((\log p)^2)$, so we have the complexity estimate claimed at the outset. Note also that the algorithm succeeds provided an element of the cycle is observed after the first measurement, and that the second measurement gives an appropriate integer. Since both of these events occur with probability bounded below by a constant, the algorithm succeeds with probability $\Omega(1)$.

2. We prove correctness of the algorithm by proving that any values $start, end$ such that $start \leq n \leq end$ will return n, which we accomplish by strong induction on $k = start - end + 1$. To save on cumbersome notation we assume (g, ϕ) and r are fixed, and write

$$BinarySearch((g, \phi,), start, end, r) = BS(start, end)$$

First, suppose $k = 1$ and $start \leq n \leq end$. Either $n = start$ or $n = start + 1$, and we know that $mid = start$ after the floor function is applied. In the first case,

---

[3] This type of state also occurs in Shor's factoring algorithm.

$r * s(g, \phi, mid) = s(g, \phi, mid)$, so BS($start, mid$) is returned; but since $start = mid$, $start = n$ is returned. Otherwise, one has $r * s(g, \phi, mid) \neq s(g, \phi, mid)$ and BS($mid + 1, end$) is returned, and we are done since $mid + 1 = end = n$.

Now for some $k > 1$ suppose all positive integers $start', end'$ such that $start' \leq n \leq end'$ and $end' - start' + 1 < k$ have BS($start', end'$)$=n$. We should like to show that an arbitrary choice of $start, end$ with $start \leq n \leq end$ and $end - start + 1 = k$ enjoys this same property. To see that it does we can again consider the two cases.

The algorithm first calculates $mid = \lfloor (end - start)/2 \rfloor$. Suppose $r * s(g, \phi, mid) = s(g, \phi, mid)$, then BS($start, mid$) is run. Since n is the smallest integer such that $r * s(g, \phi, n) = s(g, \phi, n)$ and $n \geq start$ by assumption, we know $start \leq n \leq mid$. Moreover, $mid - start + 1 < end - start + 1 < k$. By inductive hypothesis BS($start, mid$) returns n.

The other case is similar; this time, if $r * s(g, \phi, mid) \neq s(g, \phi, mid)$ we know $n \geq mid + 1$ by definition of n. We also know that $end - (mid + 1) + 1 = end - mid < end - mid + 1 = k$, so the algorithm returns BS($mid + 1, end$)$=n$ by inductive hypothesis.

Notice that each time $BinarySearch$ is called the calculation of $r * s(g, \phi, mid)$ is required. We know already that $s(g, \phi, mid)$ can be calculated in time $\mathcal{O}(\log mid (\log p)^2) = \mathcal{O}((\log p)^3)$. Given ϕ^r, $s(g, \phi, r_{g,\phi})$ and $s(g, \phi, mid)$, the calculation of $r * s(g, \phi, mid)$ requires evaluating an endomorphism and a semigroup multiplication - we have argued already that this can be done in time $\mathcal{O}((\log p)^2)$. Recall that in the proof of Lemma 3, we showed that one can calculate the holomorph exponent $(g, \phi)^r = (s(g, \phi, r), \phi^r)$ in time $\mathcal{O}(\log r (\log p)^2)$, so the total calculation is done in time $\mathcal{O}((\log p)^3)$ since $r < M$. Clearly, BinarySearch will be called $\mathcal{O}(\log M) = \mathcal{O}(\log p)$ times, since the size of the interval to search halves at each iteration, and we conclude that $BinarySearch$ recovers the index in time $\mathcal{O}((\log p)^4)$. □

6.2 From SDLP to GADLP

Let us assemble the components developed so far in this section into a reduction of SDLP to GADLP.

Theorem 5. *Let $\{G_p\}_p$ be an easy family of semigroups, and fix p. Algorithm 3 solves SDLP with respect to a pair $(g, \phi) \in G_p \times End(G_p)$ given access to a GADLP oracle for the group action $(\mathbb{Z}_r, \mathcal{C}, \circledast)$. The algorithm runs in time $\mathcal{O}((\log p)^4)$, makes at most a single query to the GADLP oracle, and succeeds with probability $\Omega(1)$.*

Proof. Consider an instance of SDLP whereby we are given the pair (g, ϕ) and the value $s(g, \phi, x)$, for some x sampled uniformly at random from the set $\{1, .., n + r - 1\}$. We show that Algorithm 3 recovers x.

We start by applying Algorithms 1 and 2 to the pair (g, ϕ), recovering the pair n, r with constant probability. By Theorem 4, we can do so in time $\mathcal{O}((\log p)^4)$.

Algorithm 3. Solving SDLP with GADLP oracle

Input: $(g, \phi), s(g, \phi, x)$
Output: x

1:   $r \leftarrow$ PeriodRecovery($(g, \phi), M$) for sufficiently large M
2:   **if** $r =$ 'Fail' **then**
3:       **return** 'Fail'
4:   **end if**
5:   $n \leftarrow$ BinarySearch($(g, \phi), 1, M, r$)
6:   **if** $r * s(g, \phi, x) = s(g, \phi, x)$ **then**
7:       $d \leftarrow s(g, \phi, n)$
8:       $x' \leftarrow$ GADLP oracle applied to $d, s(g, \phi, x)$
9:       $x \leftarrow n + x'$
10: **else**
11:     $t \leftarrow$ BinarySearch2($s(g, \phi, x), 1, n, r$)
12:     $x \leftarrow n - t$
13: **end if**
14: **return** x

Now, $s(g, \phi, x)$ might be in tail or in the cycle - but with our knowledge of r we can check in Step 6 which is true by verifying whether $r * s(g, \phi, x) = s(g, \phi, x)$. As discussed in the proof of Theorem 4, we can perform this check in time $\mathcal{O}((\log p)^3)$.

There are now two cases to consider. First, suppose that the check in Step 6 is passed, then $s(g, \phi, x)$ is in the cycle, and we may proceed as follows. Compute $s(g, \phi, n)$ in time $\mathcal{O}((\log p)^3)$, and query the GADLP oracle on input $s(g, \phi, n), s(g, \phi, x)$ (Step 8) to recover the $\mathbb{Z}_r$ element $[y]_r$. Without loss of generality the smallest positive representative of this class, say x', is such that $n + x' = x$, so we recover x in Step 9.

Now suppose that $s(g, \phi, x)$ is in the tail. We run the algorithm BinarySearch2 to recover t, the smallest integer such that $t * s(g, \phi, x)$ is invariant under r. BinarySearch2 is precisely the same as Algorithm 2, except that in the verification step, we check if $r * (mid * s(g, \phi, x)) = mid * s(g, \phi, x)$. It is not hard to adapt the proof of correctness to show that BinarySearch2 does indeed return t in time $\mathcal{O}((\log p)^4)$. Moreover, by minimality of n and the additivity of $*$, we must have $x + t = n$, from which we recover $x = n - t$.

Finally, we note that the only probablistic step of this algorithm is the application of Algorithm 1, so we successfully recover x with the same success probability as Algorithm 1, and we are done. $\qquad\square$

In summary, we have an efficient quantum reduction from SDLP to GADLP: an efficient quantum procedure extracts the period r, and from there a classical procedure gives the index n. In order to recover x, it remains to either carry out an efficient classical procedure, or recover x with a single query to a GADLP oracle. Moreover, assuming the GADLP oracle always succeeds, the success probability

xx

is precisely that of Algorithm 1 - that is, bounded below by a positive constant independently of p.

Remark 5. The factor $\log p$ in the complexity estimate is really coming from the 'length' of a binary representation of G_p; that is, the number of bits required to represent G_p. In our case the size of G_p happens to be polynomial in p, and therefore the relevant 'length' is of order $\mathcal{O}(\log p)$. One might be used to seeing the complexity of similar period-finding routines, such as Shor's algorithm, presented as cubic in the length of a binary representation of the relevant parameters - see for example [18, Section 3.3.3]. In our case, the total complexity is quartic in the length of a binary representation, essentially because after the quantum part of the algorithm we still need to compute $\mathcal{O}(\log p)$ evaluations of the function s in order to compute the index. In a sense, then, we can think of this extra $\log p$ factor as the extra cost incurred from the slightly more complicated scenario inherent to the problem.

7 Quantum Algorithms for GADLP

Now that we have shown SDLP can be efficiently solved with access to an appropriate GADLP oracle it remains to examine the state of the art for GADLP. It is here that the Abelian Hidden Shift Problem (Definition 6) comes in to play. Roughly speaking, we are given two injective functions f, g from a group A to a set S that differ by a constant 'shift' value, and our task is to recover the shift value.

It is reasonably well-known (see [12,35]) that GADLP reduces to AHSP. In this section, we provide a context-specific proof of this fact, before discussing the best known algorithms for AHSP.

7.1 Group Actions to Hidden Shift

The following result is found more or less verbatim in, for example, [12]. We here give a context-specific reduction, for completeness.

Theorem 6. *Let $\{G_p\}_p$ be an easy family of semigroups and fix p. For some pair $(g, \phi) \in G_p \times End(G_p)$ let $(\mathbb{Z}_r, \mathcal{C}, \circledast)$ be the associated group action defined in Theorem 3. One can efficiently solve GADLP in $(\mathbb{Z}_r, \mathcal{C}, \circledast)$ given access to an AHSP oracle with respect to $\mathbb{Z}_r, \mathcal{C}$.*

Proof. Suppose we are given an instance of GADLP in $(\mathbb{Z}_r, \mathcal{C}, \circledast)$; that is, we are given a pair $(s(g, \phi, n + i), s(g, \phi, n + j)) \in \mathcal{C}$ for some $i, j \in \{1, ..., r\}$ and tasked with finding the unique $[k]_r \in \mathbb{Z}_r$ such that $[k]_r \circledast s(g, \phi, n + i) = s(g, \phi, n + j)$. Our strategy is to construct injective functions $f_A, f_B : \mathbb{Z}_r \to \mathcal{C}$ that hide $[k]_r$, and use the AHSP oracle to recover this value.

Set $f_A, f_B : \mathbb{Z}_r \to \mathcal{C}$ as $f_A([x]_r) = [x]_r * s(g, \phi, n+i)$ and $f_B([x]_r) = [x]_r * s(g, \phi, n+j)$. Then

$$\begin{aligned}
f_B([x]_r) &= [x]_r * s(g, \phi, n+j) \\
&= [x]_r * ([k]_r * s(g, \phi, n+i)) \\
&= ([x]_r + [k]_r) * s(g, \phi, n+i) \\
&= f_A([x]_r + [k]_r)
\end{aligned}$$

In other words, f_A, f_B hide $[k]_r$. To complete the setup of an instance of AHSP we require the functions to be injective, which follows from the action being free and transitive.   □

Note that we have in this case left out complexity estimates. This is because in order to give a full description of the functions f_A, f_B we need to compute the group $\mathbb{Z}_r$, which can be done efficiently with knowledge of r. However, since we have already described a method of recovering r, we will discuss the complexity in the full SDLP algorithm at the end of this section.

7.2 Hidden Shift Algorithms

We have finally arrived at the problem for which there are known quantum algorithms. The fastest known is of subexponential complexity, and is presented in [26, Proposition 6.1] as a special case of the Dihedral Hidden Subgroup Problem.

Theorem 7 (Kuperberg's Algorithm). *There is a quantum algorithm that solves* AHSP *with respect to* $\mathbb{Z}_r, \mathcal{C}$ *with time and query complexity* $2^{\mathcal{O}(\sqrt{\log r})}$.

Kuperberg's algorithm also requires quantum space $2^{\mathcal{O}(\log r)}$. For a slower but less space-expensive algorithm, we can also use a generalised version of an algorithm due to Regev [34]. The generalised version appears in [12, Theorem 5.2].

Theorem 8 (Regev's Algorithm). *There is a quantum algorithm that solves* AHSP *with respect to* $\mathbb{Z}_r, \mathcal{C}$ *with time and query complexity*

$$e^{\sqrt{2}+o(1)\sqrt{\ln r \ln \ln r}}$$

and space complexity $\mathcal{O}(poly(\log r))$.

We note that both Kuperberg's and Regev's algorithms succeed with constant probability.

7.3 Solving SDLP

We finish the section by stitching all the components together into an algorithm that solves SDLP. For brevity of exposition we include only complexity estimates for using Kuperberg's algorithm - but finding the bounds in the case of Regev's algorithm is very similar.

Theorem 9. *Let $\{G_p\}_p$ be an easy family of semigroups, and fix p. For any pair $(g, \phi) \in G_p \times End(G_p)$, there is a quantum algorithm solving* SDLP *with respect to (g, ϕ) with time and query complexity $2^{\mathcal{O}(\sqrt{\log p})}$.*

Proof. Let $(g, \phi) \in G_p \times End(G_p)$ and suppose we are given the value $s(g, \phi, x)$ for some x sampled uniformly from the set $\{1, ..., N\}$, where N is the size of $\mathcal{X}_{g,\phi}$. The following steps recover x:

1. Run Algorithms 1 and 2 on the pair (g, ϕ). By Theorem 4, with positive probability we recover the index and period of (g, ϕ), the pair (n, r), in time $\mathcal{O}((\log p)^4)$.
2. By Theorem 5, either we are done efficiently, or it remains to solve an instance of GADLP with respect to the group action $(\mathbb{Z}_r, \mathcal{C}, \circledast)$.
3. By Theorem 6, once we have computed the group action $(\mathbb{Z}_r, \mathcal{C}, \circledast)$ it remains to solve an instance of AHSP with respect to $\mathbb{Z}_r, \mathcal{C}$. This can be done with access to the index and period n, r.
4. Solve AHSP using Kuperberg's algorithm or Regev's algorithm.

In summary, the total quantum complexity of solving an SDLP instance for any pair in $G_p \times End(G_p)$ is either $\mathcal{O}((\log p)^4)$, or if a call to the GADLP oracle is required, $2^{\mathcal{O}(\sqrt{\log r})} = 2^{\mathcal{O}(\sqrt{\log p})}$ since G_p is from an easy family of semigroups. Depending on constants, we expect this latter term to dominate the complexity. Moreover, we note that since both our algorithm to extract the period and Kuperberg's algorithm succeed with constant probability, we expect our algorithm to succeed with constant probability also.   □

8   Conclusion

We have provided the first dedicated analysis of SDLP, showing a reduction to a well-studied problem. Perhaps the most surprising aspect of the work is the progress made by a simple rephrasing; we made quite significant progress through rather elementary methods, and we suspect much more can be made within this framework.

The reader may notice that we have shown that SDPKE shares a very similar structure to that of a commutative action-based key exchange; it is known that breaking all such protocols can be reduced to the Abelian Hidden Shift Problem. Indeed, this work shows the algebraic machinery of SDPKE is a step twoards a candidate for what Couveignes calls a *hard homogenous space*[4] [15], which was not known until now. In line with the naming conventions in this area we propose a renaming of SDPKE to SPDH, which stands for 'Semidirect Product Diffie–Hellman', and should be pronounced *spud*.

We would also like to stress the following sentiment. The purpose of this paper is not to claim a general purpose break of SDPKE (or, indeed, SPDH) - the

---

[4] Another major example of which arises from the theory of isogenies between elliptic curves - see, for example, [10].

algorithm presented is subexponential in complexity, which has been treated as tolerable in classical contexts. Instead, the point is to show a connection between SDLP and a known hardness problem, thereby providing insight on a problem about which little was known.

Acknowledgement. This work was in part supported by ONR Grant 62909-24-1-2002.

References

1. Baena, J., Briaud, P., Cabarcas, D., Perlner, R.A., Smith- Tone, D., Verbel, J.A.: Improving Support-Minors rank attacks: applications to GeMSS and Rainbow. IACR Cryptol. ePrint Arch., 1677 (2021). https://eprint.iacr.org/2021/1677
2. Battarbee, C., Kahrobaei, D., Perret, L., Shahandashti, S.F.: SPDH-sign: towards efficient, post-quantum group-based signatures. In: Johansson, T., Smith-Tone, D. (eds.) PQCrypto 2023, vol. 14154, pp. 113–138. Springer, Cham. https://doi.org/10.1007/978-3-031-40003-2_5
3. Battarbee, C., Kahrobaei, D., Shahandashti, S.F.: Semidirect product key exchange: the state of play. arXiv preprint arXiv:2202.05178 (2022)
4. Battarbee, C., Kahrobaei, D., Shahandashti, S.F.: Cryptanalysis of semidirect product key exchange using matrices over non-commutative rings. Math. Cryptol. **1**(2), 2–9 (2022)
5. Battarbee, C., Kahrobaei, D., Tailor, D., Shahandashti, S.F.: On the efficiency of a general attack against the MOBS cryptosystem. J. Math. Cryptol. **16**(1), 289–297 (2022)
6. Beullens, W.: Breaking rainbow takes a weekend on a laptop. IACR Cryptol. ePrint Arch. 214 (2022). https://eprint.iacr.org/2022/214
7. Brown, D.R., Koblitz, N., LeGrow, J.T.: Cryptanalysis of "MAKE". J. Math. Cryptol. **16**(1), 98–102 (2022)
8. Casanova, A., Faugere, J.C., Macario-Rat, G., Patarin, J., Perret, L., Ryckeghem, J.: GeMSS : a great multivariate short signature. PhD thesis. UPMC-Paris 6 Sorbonne Universités; INRIA Paris Research Centre, PolSys Team (2017)
9. Castryck, W., Decru, T.: An efficient key recovery attack on SIDH (preliminary version). Cryptology ePrint Archive, Paper 2022/975 (2022). https://eprint.iacr.org/2022/975
10. Castryck, W., Lange, T., Martindale, C., Panny, L., Renes, J.: CSIDH: an efficient post-quantum commutative group action. In: Peyrin, T., Galbraith, S. (eds.) ASIACRYPT 2018. LNCS, vol. 11274, pp. 395–427. Springer, Cham (2018). https://doi.org/10.1007/978-3-030-03332-3_15
11. Chen, L., et al.: Report on Post-Quantum Cryptography. Research report NISTIR 8105. NIST (2016). http://csrc.nist.gov/publications/drafts/nistir-8105/nistir_8105_draft.pdf
12. Childs, A., Jao, D., Soukharev, V.: Constructing elliptic curve isogenies in quantum subexponential time. J. Math. Cryptol. **8**(1), 1–29 (2014)
13. Childs, A.M., Ivanyos, G.: Quantum computation of discrete logarithms in semigroups. J. Math. Cryptol. **8**(4), 405–416 (2014)
14. Childs, A.M., Van Dam, W.: Quantum algorithms for algebraic problems. Rev. Mod. Phys. **82**(1), 1 (2010)
15. Couveignes, J.M.: Hard homogeneous spaces. Cryptology ePrint Archive (2006). https://eprint.iacr.org/2006/291.pdf
16. Grigoriev, D., Shpilrain, V.: Tropical cryptography II: extensions by homomorphisms. Commun. Algebra **47**(10), 4224–4229 (2019)

17. Habeeb, M., Kahrobaei, D., Koupparis, C., Shpilrain, V.: Public key exchange using semidirect product of (semi)groups. In: Jacobson, M., Locasto, M., Mohassel, P., Safavi-Naini, R. (eds.) ACNS 2013. LNCS, vol. 7954, pp. 475–486. Springer, Heidelberg (2013). https://doi.org/10.1007/978-3-642-38980-1_30
18. Hirvensalo, M.: Quantum Computing. Springer, Heidelberg (2003)
19. Howie, J.M.: Fundamentals of Semigroup Theory, vol. 12. Oxford University Press, Oxford (1995)
20. Imran, M., Ivanyos, G.: Efficient quantum algorithms for some instances of the semidirect discrete logarithm problem. arXiv preprint arXiv:2312.14028 (2023)
21. Isaac, S., Kahrobaei, D.: A closer look at the tropical cryptography. Int. J. Comput. Math. Comput. Syst. Theory 6(2), 137–142 (2021)
22. Ivanyos, G., Magniez, F., Santha, M.: Efficient quantum algorithms for some instances of the non-abelian hidden subgroup problem. In: Proceedings of the Thirteenth Annual ACM Symposium on Parallel Algorithms and Architectures, pp. 263–270 (2001)
23. Kahrobaei, D., Flores, R., Noce, M., Habeeb, M., Battarbee, C.: Applications of group theory in cryptography: post-quantum group-based cryptography. In: The Mathematical Surveys and Monographs series of the American Mathematical Society, forthcoming (2024)
24. Kahrobaei, D., Flores, R., Noce, M.: Group-based cryptography in the quantum era. In: The Notices of American Mathematical Society, to appear (2022). https://arxiv.org/abs/2202.05917
25. Kahrobaei, D., Shpilrain, V.: Using semidirect product of (semi)groups in public key cryptography. In: Beckmann, A., Bienvenu, L., Jonoska, N. (eds.) CiE 2016. LNCS, vol. 9709, pp. 132–141. Springer, Cham (2016). https://doi.org/10.1007/978-3-319-40189-8_14
26. Kuperberg, G.: A subexponential-time quantum algorithm for the dihedral hidden subgroup problem. SIAM J. Comput. 35(1), 170–188 (2005)
27. Maino, L., Martindale, C.: An attack on SIDH with arbitrary starting curve. Cryptology ePrint Archive, Paper 2022/1026 (2022). https://eprint.iacr.org/2022/1026
28. Mendelsohn, A., Dable-Heath, E., Ling, C.: A small serving of mash:(quantum) algorithms for SPDH-sign with small parameters. In: Cryptology ePrint Archive (2023)
29. Monico, C.: Remarks on MOBS and cryptosystems using semidirect products. arXiv preprint arXiv:2109.11426 (2021)
30. Montgomery, H., Zhandry, M.: Full quantum equivalence of group action DLog and CDH, and more. In: Agrawal, S., Lin, D. (eds.) ASIACRYPT 2022. LNCS, vol. 13791, pp. 3–32. Springer, Heidelberg (2022) isbn: 978-3-031-22962-6
31. Myasnikov, A., Roman'kov, V.: A linear decomposition attack. Groups Complex. Cryptol. 7(1), 81–94 (2015)
32. Rahman, N., Shpilrain, V.: MAKE: a matrix action key exchange. J. Math. Cryptol. 16(1), 64–72 (2022)
33. Rahman, N., Shpilrain, V.: MOBS: matrices over bit strings public key exchange (2021). https://eprint.iacr.org/2021/560
34. Regev, O.: A subexponential time algorithm for the dihedral hidden subgroup problem with polynomial space. arXiv preprint quant-ph/0406151 (2004)
35. Stolbunov, A.: Constructing public-key cryptographic schemes based on class group action on a set of isogenous elliptic curves. Adv. Math. Commun. 4(2), 215 (2010)
36. Tao, C., Petzoldt, A., Ding, J.: Efficient key recovery for all HFE signature variants. In: Malkin, T., Peikert, C. (eds.) CRYPTO 2021. LNCS, vol. 12825, pp. 70–93. Springer, Cham (2021). https://doi.org/10.1007/978-3-030-84242-0_4

On Digital Signatures Based on Group Actions: QROM Security and Ring Signatures

Markus Bläser[1(✉)], Zhili Chen[2(✉)], Dung Hoang Duong[3(✉)], Antoine Joux[4(✉)], Tuong Nguyen[3(✉)], Thomas Plantard[5(✉)], Youming Qiao[2(✉)], Willy Susilo[3(✉)], and Gang Tang[2(✉)]

[1] Department of Computer Science, Saarland University, Saarland Informatics Campus, Saarbrücken, Germany
mblaeser@cs.uni-saarland.de
[2] Centre for Quantum Software and Information, School of Computer Science, Faculty of Engineering and Information Technology, University of Technology Sydney, Ultimo, NSW, Australia
{zhili.chen,gang.tang-1}@student.uts.edu.au, Youming.Qiao@uts.edu.au
[3] Institute of Cybersecurity and Cryptology, School of Computing and Information Technology, University of Wollongong, Wollongong, NSW 2522, Australia
{hduong,wsusilo}@uow.edu.au, ntn807@uowmail.edu.au
[4] CISPA Helmholtz Center for Information Security, Saarbrücken, Germany
joux@cispa.de
[5] Nokia Bell Labs, Murray Hill, NJ, USA
thomas.plantard@nokia-bell-labs.com

Abstract. Group action based cryptography was formally proposed in the seminal paper of Brassard and Yung (Crypto 1990). Based on one-way group action, there is a well-known digital signature design based on the Goldreich–Micali–Widgerson (GMW) zero-knowledge protocol for the graph isomorphism problem and the Fiat–Shamir (FS) transformation. Recently, there is a revival of activities on group action based cryptography and the GMW-FS design, as witnessed by the schemes SeaSign (Eurocrypt 2019), CSI-FiSh (Asiacrypt 2019), LESS (Africacrypt 2020), ATFE (Eurocrypt 2022), and MEDS (Africacrypt 2023).

The contributions of this paper are two-fold: the first is about the GMW-FS design in general, and the second is on the ATFE-GMW-FS scheme.

First, we study the QROM security and ring signatures of the GMW-FS design. We distil properties of the underlying group action for the GMW-FS design to be secure in the quantum random oracle model (QROM). We also show that this design supports a (linkable) ring signature construction following the work of Beullens, Katsumata and Pintore (Asiacrypt 2020).

Second, we apply the above results to support the security of the ATFE-GMW-FS scheme in the QROM model. We then describe a linkable ring signature scheme based on it, and provide an implementation of the ring signature scheme. Preliminary experiments suggest that our scheme is competitive among existing post-quantum ring signatures.

M.-J. Saarinen and D. Smith-Tone (Eds.): PQCrypto 2024, LNCS 14771, pp. 227–261, 2024.
https://doi.org/10.1007/978-3-031-62743-9_8

1   Introduction

1.1   Background: Group Actions in Cryptography and the GMW-FS Digital Signature Design

Group Actions in (Post-quantum) Cryptography. The use of group actions in cryptography has a long tradition. Indeed, the discrete logarithm problem can be interpreted as a problem about cyclic group actions [30]. As far as we know, the first treatment of *abstract* group actions in cryptography goes back to Brassard and Yung [22], who proposed the notion of *one-way* group actions. When the groups are abelian (commutative), this was further developed by Couveignes [30]. Recently, two independent works [51] and [2] enriched this framework further by introducing the notion of (weakly) pseudorandom group actions, which generalises the celebrated Decisional Diffie–Hellman assumption [15,33].

Besides setting up frameworks, many cryptographic primitives can be realised, such as claw-free one-way functions and bit commitment [22], quantum-secure pseudorandom functions [51], and zero-knowledge identification protocols [30,51]. When the groups are abelian (commutative), more functions are possible, such as key exchange [30], smooth projective hashing, and dual-mode public-key encryption [2].

The GMW-FS Digital Signature Design. A major cryptographic application of group actions is the following digital signature design. In [43], Goldreich, Micali and Wigderson described a zero-knowledge proof protocol for the graph isomorphism (GI) problem. The Fiat–Shamir transformation FS [42] can be applied to it to yield a digital signature scheme. This construction has been observed by several researchers since the 1990's. However, this scheme based on graph isomorphism is not secure, because GI can be solved efficiently in practice [59,60], not to mention Babai's quasipolynomial-time algorithm [3].

Fortunately, the Goldreich–Micali–Wigderson (GMW) zero-knowledge proof protocol applies to *any* isomorphism problem. In fact, one way to formulate isomorphism problems is through group actions, and the hardness of an isomorphism problem naturally translates to the one-way assumption of the group action. This gives hope that, by choosing an appropriate group action (or isomorphism problem), such a construction could be secure. This was already carried out in two areas in the context of post-quantum cryptography, that is multivariate cryptography and isogeny-based cryptography. In multivariate cryptography, Patarin proposed using polynomial isomorphism problems to replace graph isomorphism [62]. In isogeny-based cryptography, Stolbunov applied this construction to the class group actions on elliptic curves [30,71]. However, these efforts met with some issues. For example, the parameters proposed by Patarin were too optimistic [21], and computational costs and uniform sampling for class group actions are tricky issues [26].

The Recent Revival of the GMW-FS Design. Recently, there has been a revival of the study of the GMW-FS design, which is attributed to two research directions.

The first direction is the study of elliptic curve isogenies, following Couveignes and Stolbunov. As mentioned above, the issues here are mostly due to the computational aspects of group actions. To remedy this, the commutative group action CSIDH based on supersingular curves over prime fields was introduced in [26]. This led to the schemes SeaSign [41] and CSI-FiSh [11], which greatly improve the situation by introducing both computational and protocol optimizations; see also the recent nice survey on this and more in [9].

The second direction may be viewed as a continuation of the polynomial isomorphism direction by Patarin [62]. Three schemes submitted to the most recent NIST call for post-quantum digital signatures [70] fall into this category, namely LESS [12] based on linear code monomial equivalence, ATFE [73] based on alternating trilinear form equivalence, and MEDS [28] based on matrix code equivalence[1]. Recent progress in complexity theory [45] shows that (1) linear code monomial equivalence reduces to matrix code equivalence in polynomial time [31,44], and (2) alternating trilinear form equivalence, isomorphism of quadratic polynomials with two secrets, cubic form equivalence, and matrix code equivalence are polynomial-time equivalent [45,46] (see also [67] for some of these equivalences).

The studies above are of particular interest in post-quantum cryptography. Since discrete logarithms can be solved efficiently on quantum computers [69], it is desirable to explore group actions suitable for post-quantum cryptography. As in the lattice case [66], the research into hidden subgroup problems is of particular relevance here, especially the hidden shift problems [27] and symmetric or general linear groups [47]. For the class group actions in the isogeny setting, even though the group action underlying CSIDH is commutative, the best quantum algorithms are still subexponential [17,63]. For the group actions underlying LESS, ATFE and MEDS, the groups are symmetric or general linear groups, so the previous negative evidence for standard techniques (such as coset sampling) in the hidden subgroup problem for graph isomorphisms [47] applies.

1.2   Our Contributions

Our contributions in this paper can be classified into two sets.

The first set of results is for the GMW-FS design based on abstract group actions. Briefly speaking, we first distil properties for group actions to be secure in the quantum random oracle model (QROM) based on the works [34,53,56]. We then present the linkable ring signature construction of Beullens, Katsumata and Pintore [10] with abstract group actions.

We then apply the results to a concrete setting, namely the digital signature scheme introduced in [73], which we refer to as the ATFE-GMW-FS scheme[2]. More specifically we demonstrate its QROM security, and implement the ring signature scheme above for ATFE-GMW-FS. Our preliminary experiments suggest that this

---

[1] Matrix code equivalence is also known as 3-tensor isomorphism in [45].

[2] Since the appearance of ATFE-GMW-FS, some nice cryptanalysis works were done, such as by Beullens [8], and by Ran, Samardjiska and Trimoska [65]. A submission to NIST's call for additional post-quantum digital signatures [70] is based on this scheme, and we refer the interested readers to [14] for its specifications.

230 M. Bläser et al.

scheme is competitive among existing post-quantum ring signatures. Finally, we show that the MPC-in-the-head paradigm for group actions [52] helps to reduce the signature sizes for the ATFE-GMW-FS scheme.

We now explain these in more detail.

Results for the GMW-FS Design. In the following, we always let G denote a group, S a set, and $\alpha : G \times S \to S$ a group action.

Security in the Quantum Random Oracle Model. The quantum random oracle model (QROM) was proposed by Boneh et al. [16] in 2011 and has received considerable attention since then. There are certain inherent difficulties to prove security in the QROM model, such as the adaptive programmability and rewinding [16]. Indeed, the QROM security of the Fiat–Shamir transformation was only recently shown after a series of works [34,53,56,77].

In this paper we make progress on the QROM security of the GMW-FS design based on the works [34,53,56,77]. Our results on this line can be informally summarised as follows. Recall that $\alpha : G \times S \to S$ is a group action. In the GMW-FS design, the protocol starts with some (chosen or randomly sampled) set element $s \in S$. For $s \in S$, the stabilizer group $\text{Stab}(s) := \{g \in G \mid \alpha(g, s) = s\}$.

1. The GMW-FS scheme is secure in the QROM model, if $\text{Stab}(s)$ is trivial, i.e. $|\text{Stab}(s)| = 1$ and α satisfies the C-one-way-$\mathcal{O}(s)$ assumption (see Definition 6 and Remark 1).
2. The GMW-FS scheme is secure in the QROM model, if the group action under ATFE satisfies the pseudorandom property as defined in [2,51] (see Definition 6), and the non-trivial automorphism hardness property (see Definition 8). In particular, in this setting the security proof is tight.

The GMW-FS-BKP Ring Signature Design. Ring signature, introduced by Rivest, Shamir and Tauman [68], is a special type of digital signature in which a signer can sign on behalf of a group chosen by him- or herself, while retaining anonymity within the group. In particular, ring signatures are formed without a complex setup procedure or the requirement for a group manager. They simply require users to be part of an existing public key infrastructure.

A linkable ring signature [55] is a variant of ring signatures in which any signatures produced by the same signer can be publicly linked. Linkable ring signatures are suitable in many different practical applications, such as privacy-preserving digital currency [72] and e-voting [74].

Beullens, Katsumata and Pintore [10] proposed an elegant way to construct efficient linkable ring signatures from group actions. Their focus was on commutative group actions, with instantiations in both isogeny and lattice settings. The advantage of their schemes is the scalability of signature sizes with the ring size, even compared to other logarithmic-size post-quantum ring signatures.

While [10] focussed on commutative group actions, their ring signature construction is readily applicable to general group actions. In fact, for our group action framework, the scheme becomes a bit simpler because [10] needs to work with rejection sampling due to certain stronger assumptions on the group actions.

We call this ring signature design the GMW-FS-BKP design, and describe its construction in Sect. 5. The linkability property requires extra discussions as it calls for an interesting property of pairs of group actions.

Comparisons with Some Previous Works. QROM securities and ring signature schemes have been shown for concrete schemes based on group actions. For example, the QROM security of CSI-FiSh (resp. MEDS, LESS) based on the perfect unique response was observed in [11] (resp. [12,28]), and the tight QROM security based on a lossy version of CSI-FiSh was shown in [36]. The ring signature scheme in [10] has been shown for the group actions underlying CSI-FiSh [10], LESS [4], and MEDS [28].

Indeed, we view our results for the GMW-FS design as mostly conceptual. Our aim is to make these results convenient for future uses. That is, we distil properties of group actions (pairs) that are key to the QROM security (Definition 8) or for linkable ring signatures (Definition 10). We hope that these will not only help with existing schemes, but also facilitate future schemes based on the GMW-FS design. Furthermore, to the best of our knowledge, the connection of the lossy approach for QROM security [53] with the pseudorandom group action assumption [2,51] and the non-trivial automorphism hardness assumption (Definition 8) was not stated explicitly before. Such results should benefit the LESS and MEDS schemes, which only discussed their QROM securities based on perfect unique response (but not the lossy scheme).

Results for the ATFE-GMW-FS Scheme. After working with the general GMW-FS design, we focus on the ATFE-GMW-FS scheme from [14,73], which demonstrates concrete uses of the results we obtained for abstract group actions.

The QROM Security of the ATFE-GMW-FS Scheme. The QROM security of the ATFE-GMW-FS scheme was briefly discussed in [73] but was left as an open problem. Based on the results from the first part, there are two approaches to show its QROM security: the first is based on the automorphism group order statistics, and the second is based on the pseudorandom group action assumption. The sEUF-CMA security in QROM of ATFE-GMW-FS scheme can be achieved by both two approaches.

For the first approach, we provide experimental results to support that, for those parameters proposed in [73], a random alternating trilinear form has the trivial automorphism group. This requires us to implement an algorithm for the automorphism group order computation.

For the second approach, the question of whether the group action under ATFE is pseudorandom or not is an open problem. In [73], some arguments were provided to support that it is. In particular, we do not need to modify the original ATFE-GMW-FS scheme in [73] to attain the security in QROM, i.e., as opposed to the lossy CSI-FiSh scheme [36]. We will discuss more about this in Sect. 1.3.

An Implementation of the ATFE-GMW-FS-BKP Ring Signature Scheme. We implement the ring signature protocol from [10] for ATFE-GMW-FS. Preliminary experimental results suggest that it's more balanced than Calamari and Falafl

in terms of signature size and signing time. We refer the reader to Sect. 6.2 and
Table 1 for the details. Here we give a brief summary and comparison with some
previous ring signature schemes.

Since we use the construction in [10], the signature size of our schemes only
depends on $\log R$, where R denotes the ring size. We see that our signature size
can be estimated as $0.8\log R + 19.7$KB, while the signature sizes of Calamari
and Falafl in [10] are estimated to be $\log R + 2.5$KB and $0.5\log R + 28.5$KB
respectively. For ring size $R = 8$, our signing time is 205ms which is twice Falafl's
90ms and much smaller than Calamari's 79 s. Meanwhile, our ring signature size
is 22.1KB, while Falafl and Calamari have the signature size of 30KB and 5.4KB
respectively. RAPTOR [57], and DualRing-LB [79] have shorter signature sizes
than ours when the ring size is small. However, their sizes are linearly dependent
on the number of ring users; therefore, the size significantly increases when the
number of participants rises. Regarding MRr-DSS [7], while it performs well for
low to medium users $(<= 2^7)$, our protocol can outperform it in this range. For
more comparisons with other ring signatures, please see Table 1. Finally, Fig. 1
reports the signing time of our protocol; there, n, M and K are the parameters
in the ATFE-GMW-FS-BKP scheme as defined in Sect. 6.2. Note that the signing
time is measured on a 2.4 GHz Quad-Core Intel Core i5 (Fig. 2).

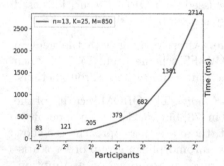

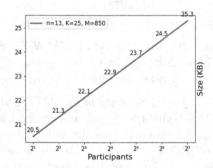

Fig. 1. Signature generation time   **Fig. 2.** Signature size

MPC-in-the-Head Paradigm. Another recent contribution to the GMW-FS
design is by Joux [52], who showed that the multiparty-computation (MPC)
in the head paradigm can be applied to a generic group action. This paradigm
allows for shorter signature sizes at the cost of longer computation time, and the
ATFE-GMW-FS scheme is a nice example of which such a tradeoff can bring benefits. Our calculation suggests that this has the effect of reducing the signature
size by about one-third (comparing Table 4 and Table 5).

Table 1. Comparison of the signature size (KB) between our schemes and others

	2^1	2^3	2^5	2^6	2^{10}	2^{12}	2^{15}	2^{21}	Hardness assumption	Secuirty level
	R									
MatRiCT [38]	18	19	/	31	/	59	/	148	MSIS, MLWE	128 bits
SMILE [58]	/	/	16	/	18	/	19	/	MSIS, MLWE	128 bits
MatRiCT$^+$ [37]	5.4	8.2	11	12.4	18	20.8	25	33.4	MSIS, MLWE	128 bits
RAPTOR [57]	2.5	10	/	81	/	5161	/	/	NTRU	100 bits
Calamari [10]	3.5	5.4	/	8.2	/	14	/	23	CSIDH-512	*
Falafl [10]	29	30	/	32	/	35	/	39	MSIS, MLWE	128 bits
DualRing-LB [79]	/	4.6	/	6	/	106.6	/	/	MSIS, MLWE	128 bits
MRr-DSS [7]	/	27	/	36	/	422	/	/	MinRank	128 bits
LESS [4]	/	10.8	/	13.7	/	19.7	/	28.6	Code Equiv.	128 bits
Ours	20.5	22.1	23.7	24.5	27.7	29.3	31.7	36.5	ATFE	128 bits

1.3   Discussions

Discussions on QROM Security. The QROM security for the GMW-FS design was shown based on perfect unique responses and lossy schemes. There is one further approach that could avoid analysing automorphism groups mathematically. In [34,56], a property called *quantum unique response* in [34] or collapsing sigma protocol in [56] is introduced, generalising the *collapsingness* which is introduced by Unruh [76] to the quantum setting. The definition of this property relies on a certain protocol and basically asks to distinguish between measuring or not measuring during the execution of the protocol. It is an interesting problem to study isomorphism problems from the point of this property, which would lead to another security proof under QROM.

Comparisons with Results from Isogeny Based Cryptography. First, the group action underlying our lossy identification scheme is the same action as the original ATFE-GMW-FS scheme, while the group action underlying the lossy CSI-FiSh [36] is the diagonal action of the class group on two elliptic curves following [71]. One reason is that for the pseudorandom group action assumption [51] (cf. Sect. 2.4) to be useful, it is necessary that the underlying group action is intransitive, but the class group action on the classes of elliptic curves is transitive, which is why two copies are needed there. This results in a doubling of the public-key size in lossy CSI-FiSh compared to the original CSI-FiSh, as opposed to our case where the public key size remains the same.

Second, we compare the GMW-FS-BKP design applied to ATFE here with that of the class group action [10]. The class group action leads to smaller signature sizes, but it suffers the problems of efficiently computing the group action and random sampling. The group action underlying ATFE allows for fast group action and random sampling, though the signature sizes are larger.

Concurrent Work. Recently, D'Alconzo and Gangemi [32] obtained a ring signature from ATFE by also following the construction in [10]. The comparison is summarized as follows. First of all, D'Alconzo and Gangemi used the fixed weight challenges. More specifically, they encode the challenge space as follows. For the challenge space $C_{M,K}$, they enumerate the strings inside and encode them into integers to record the position in this order to send instead of sending a string. In this way the cost for the challenge is $\log_2 \binom{M}{K}$. Our work considers the positions where the challenge is 0 for a string randomly sampled from the challenge space. Thus the cost is $K \log_2(M)$ for the challenge space $C_{M,K}$. However, we consider the different challenge space, that is, to divide M into K parts, and there exists one cha $= 0$ in each part. In this case, we have the cost $K \log_2(\frac{M}{K})$. Secondly, D'Alconzo and Gangemi defined a tag associated with a group action $\beta(g,s) = \alpha(g^{-1}, s)$ while our associated group action is $\beta(g,s) = \alpha(g^{-t}, s)$, see more details in Sect. 5. Last but not least, D'Alconzo and Gangemi do not provide implementations while in our work, we implemented the ring signature and compared it with other protocols.

2   Preliminaries

2.1   Notations

We collect some basic notation in this subsection. We use $\mathbb{F}_q$ to denote the finite field with q elements. The general linear group of degree n over $\mathbb{F}_q$ is denoted as $\mathrm{GL}(n,q)$. The base of the logarithm is 2 unless otherwise specified. For a finite set S, we use $s \xleftarrow{\$} S$ to denote that s is uniformly randomly sampled from S. Given a positive integer k, we denote by $[k]$ the set $\{1, \ldots, k\}$.

2.2 Σ-Protocol and Digital Signatures

Let $\mathcal{R} \subseteq \mathcal{X} \times \mathcal{W}$ be a binary relation, where $\mathcal{X}, \mathcal{W}, \mathcal{R}$ are recognizable finite sets. In other words, there is a polynomial time algorithm that can decide whether $(x,w) \in \mathcal{R}$ for $x \in \mathcal{X}$ and $w \in \mathcal{W}$. Given an instance generator Gen of a relation $\mathcal{R}$, the relation $\mathcal{R}$ is *hard* if for any poly-time quantum algorithm $\mathcal{A}$, the probability $\Pr[(x,w') \in \mathcal{R} \mid (x,w) \leftarrow \mathsf{Gen}(1^\lambda), w' \leftarrow \mathcal{A}(x)]$ is negligible.

Given a hard relation $\mathcal{R}$, the Σ-protocol for $\mathcal{R}$ is 3-move interactive protocol between a prover $\mathcal{P}$ and a verifier $\mathcal{V}$ in which the prover $\mathcal{P}$ who has the witness w for the statement x tries to convince the verifier $\mathcal{V}$ that he possesses a valid witness w without revealing anything more than the fact that he knows w. Formally, Σ-protocol is defined as follows.

Definition 1. *Let $\mathcal{R}$ be a hard binary relation. Let $\mathsf{ComSet}, \mathsf{ChSet}, \mathsf{ResSet}$ be the commitment space, challenge space and response space respectively. The Σ-protocol Σ for a relation $\mathcal{R}$ consists of three PPT algorithms $(\mathcal{P} = (\mathcal{P}_1, \mathcal{P}_2), \mathcal{V})$, where V is deterministic and we assume that $\mathcal{P}_1$ and $\mathcal{P}_2$ share the same state, working as the following:*

- *The prover $\mathcal{P}$ first computes a commitment $a \leftarrow \mathcal{P}_1(x,w)$ and sends a to the verifier $\mathcal{V}$.*

- *On input a commitment a, the $\mathcal{V}$ samples a random challenge c from the challenge space* ChSet *and sends to $\mathcal{P}$.*
- *$\mathcal{P}$ computes a response $r \leftarrow \mathcal{P}_2(x, w, a, c)$ and sends to the $\mathcal{V}$ who will run $\mathcal{V}(x, a, c, r)$ and outputs 1 if the transcript (a, c, r) is valid and 0 otherwise.*

We assume the readers are familiar with the following properties of Σ-protocols: identification from Σ-protocol, completeness, post-quantum 2-soundness, honest verifier zero knowledge (HVZK), α-bit min-entropy, perfect and computational unique response, and commitment recoverable. As most of them are classical, we collect them in the full version paper [13] for the readers' convenience, and only explain perfect and computational unique responses as they are key to the QROM security later.

Perfect Unique Response. A Σ-protocol has perfect unique response if for all pairs $(x, w) \in \mathcal{R}$, there is no two valid transcripts (a, c, r) and (a, c, r') of the same commitment a and challenge c but different responses $r \neq r'$, i.e. $\Pr[\mathcal{V}(x, a, c, r) = 1 \wedge \mathcal{V}(x, a, c, r') = 1 \wedge r \neq r'] = 0$.

Computationally Unique Response. A Σ-protocol has computationally unique response, if for any λ and any poly-time quantum adversary $\mathcal{A}$, the following probability is negligible, taken over the randomness of $(x, w) \leftarrow$ Gen(1^λ):

$$\Pr[\mathcal{V}(x, a, c, r) = 1 \wedge \mathcal{V}(x, a, c, r') = 1 \wedge r \neq r' \mid (a, c, r, r') \leftarrow \mathcal{A}(x)] \leq \mathsf{negl}(\lambda).$$

Definition 2. *A digital signature consists of the following polynomial-time (possibly probabilistic) algorithms.*

- Gen(1^λ): *On input a security parameter λ, generates a pair* (sk, pk) *of secret key* sk *and verification key* pk.
- Sign(sk, m): *On input a message m and the secret key* sk, *it generates a signature σ.*
- Ver(pk, m, σ): *On input the verification key* pk, *a message m and a signature σ, it returns 1 or 0.*

For correctness, it is required that for all message m and $\sigma \leftarrow$ Sign(sk, m), we always have that Ver(pk, m, σ) = 1.

Definition 3 (Security of Signature Schemes). *The signature scheme is said to be existentially unforgeable (i.e., EUF-CMA secure) if for any poly-time quantum adversaries $\mathcal{A}$, who can query some signatures of messages of his choices, the probability that $\mathcal{A}$ can sign a message whose signature hasn't been produced is negligible, i.e.,* $\Pr[\text{Verify}(pk, m, \sigma) = 1 \wedge m \notin \Sigma \mid (pk, sk) \leftarrow \text{Gen}(1^n), (\sigma, m) \leftarrow \mathcal{A}(pk)] \leq \mathsf{negl}(\lambda)$, *where Σ is the list of all messages that $\mathcal{A}$ has queried before.*

A stronger notion is *strongly unforgeable* (sEUF-CMA) that allows an adversary $\mathcal{A}$ to output a different signature of a message that has been queried before. The schemes presented in this paper satisfy this stronger notion of existential unforgeability.

Definition 4 (Strong Security of Signature Schemes). *The signature scheme is said to be strongly existentially unforgeable (i.e., sEUF-CMA secure) if for any poly-time quantum adversaries $\mathcal{A}$, who can query signatures of messages of his choices, the probability that $\mathcal{A}$ can sign a message that the corresponding message-signature pair hasn't been produced is negligible, i.e., $\Pr[\mathsf{Verify}(\mathsf{pk}, m, \sigma) = 1 \wedge (m, \sigma) \notin \Sigma | (\mathsf{pk}, \mathsf{sk}) \leftarrow \mathsf{Gen}(1^n), (\sigma, m) \leftarrow \mathcal{A}(\mathsf{pk})] \leq \mathsf{negl}(\lambda)$, where Σ is the list of all message-signature pairs that $\mathcal{A}$ has obtained before.*

Fiat-Shamir transformation. The Fiat-Shamir (FS) transformation [42] turns an identification protocol $\mathsf{ID} = (\mathsf{ID.Gen}, \mathcal{P} = (\mathcal{P}_1, \mathcal{P}_2), \mathcal{V})$ into a signature scheme $\mathsf{FS[ID]}$ as follows.

- $\mathsf{ID.Gen}(1^\lambda)$: On input a security parameter λ, run $(\mathsf{ID.sk}, \mathsf{ID.pk}) \leftarrow \mathsf{ID.Gen}(1^\lambda)$ and define the secret key $\mathsf{sk} := \mathsf{ID.sk}$ and verification key $\mathsf{pk} := \mathsf{ID.pk}$.
- $\mathsf{Sign}(\mathsf{sk}, M)$: On input the secret key sk and a message M, do the following:
  - Run $a \leftarrow \mathcal{P}_1(\mathsf{sk}, \mathsf{pk})$.
  - Compute $c := H(M\|a)$ where $H : \{0,1\}^* \to \mathsf{ChSet}$ is a secure hash function.
  - Run $r \leftarrow \mathcal{P}_2(\mathsf{sk}, \mathsf{pk}, a, c)$.
  - Return a signature $\sigma := (a, r)$.
- $\mathsf{Ver}(\mathsf{pk}, M, \sigma)$: On input a message M and a signature σ, do the following:
  - Compute $c := H(M\|a)$.
  - Return $\mathcal{V}(\mathsf{pk}, a, c, r)$.

Theorem 1 ([64]). *If an identification protocol is HVZK and satisfies special soundness, then FS[ID] has EUF-CMA security in the ROM model.*

2.3 Ring Signatures

In this section, we provide the definition of the ring signature. The definition and properties of linkable ring signatures are provided in the full version paper [13].

Definition 5 (Ring signature). *A ring signature scheme Π_{RS} consists of three PPT algorithms* $(\mathsf{RS.KeyGen}, \mathsf{RS.Sign}, \mathsf{RS.Verify})$ *where,*

- $\mathsf{RS.SetUp}(1^\lambda)$: *Given a security parameter λ, this algorithm outputs the corresponding public parameters* pp.
- $\mathsf{RS.KeyGen}(\mathsf{pp})$: *This algorithm generates, for a user i, a pair $(\mathsf{vk}_i, \mathsf{sk}_i)$ of the secret key sk_i and public key (verification key) vk_i.*
- $\mathsf{RS.Sign}(\mathsf{sk}_i, \mathsf{R}, \mathsf{M})$: *Given the secret key sk_i, a list of public keys $\mathsf{R} = \{\mathsf{vk}_1, \dots, \mathsf{vk}_N\}$ and a message M, it outputs a signature σ.*
- $\mathsf{RS.Verify}(\mathsf{R}, \mathsf{M}, \sigma)$: *Given a list of public key $\mathsf{R} = \{\mathsf{vk}_1, \dots, \mathsf{vk}_N\}$, a message M and a signature σ, this algorithm output 1 if this signature is valid or 0 otherwise.*

A ring signature needs to satisfy three properties: correctness, anonymity and unforgeability.

Correctness. A ring signature Π_{RS} is said to be correct if for any security parameter λ, polynomial $N = \text{poly}(\lambda)$, any message M, pp $\leftarrow$ RS.SetUp(1^λ), $(vk_1, sk_1), \ldots, (vk_N, sk_N) \leftarrow$ RS.KeyGen(pp), $\sigma \leftarrow$ RS.Sign(sk_i, R, M) with R := $\{vk_1, \ldots, vk_N\}$, it always holds that RS.Verify(R, M, σ) = 1.

Anonymity. A ring signature Π_{RS} is said to be anonymous if for every security parameter λ and polynomial $N = \text{poly}(\lambda)$, any PPT adversary $\mathcal{A}$ has at most negligible advantage in the following game:

(1) The challenger runs pp $\leftarrow$ RS.SetUp(1^λ) and generates key pairs $(vk_i, sk_i) \leftarrow$ RS.KeyGen(pp) for all $i \in [N]$ and samples $b \xleftarrow{\$} \{0,1\}$. Then it sends pp and the secret keys $\{sk_i\}_{i\in[N]}$ to $\mathcal{A}$.
(2) $\mathcal{A}$ computes a challenge (R, M, i_0, i_1), where R contains vk_{i_0} and vk_{i_1}, and sends it to the challenger.
(3) The challenger runs RS.Sign(sk_{i_b}, R, M) $\to \sigma$ and sends σ to $\mathcal{A}$.
(4) $\mathcal{A}$ outputs b'. If $b = b'$, then we say that $\mathcal{A}$ wins this game.

The advantage of $\mathcal{A}$ is

$$\text{Adv}_{RS}^{\text{Anon}}(\mathcal{A}) = |\Pr[\mathcal{A} \text{ wins}] - 1/2|.$$

Unforgeability. A ring signature Π_{RS} is said to be unforgeable if for every security parameter λ and polynomial $N = \text{poly}(\lambda)$, any PPT adversary $\mathcal{A}$ has at most negligible probability to win the following game:

(1) The challenger runs pp $\leftarrow$ RS.SetUp(1^λ) and generates key pairs $(vk_i, sk_i) \leftarrow$ RS.KeyGen(pp) for all $i \in [N]$. It sends the list of public keys VK = $\{vk_i\}_{i\in[N]}$ to $\mathcal{A}$ and prepares two empty list SL and CL.
(2) $\mathcal{A}$ can make polynomial times of signing queries and corrupting queries:
   - (sign, i, R, M):
     The challenger outputs the signature $\sigma \leftarrow$ RS.Sign(sk_i, R, M) to $\mathcal{A}$ and adds (i, R, M) to SL.
   - (corrupt, i) The challenger sends sk_i to $\mathcal{A}$ and adds vk_i to CL.
(3) We say $\mathcal{A}$ wins this game if $\mathcal{A}$ outputs (R', M', σ') such that $R' \subseteq$ VK $\setminus$ CL, $(\cdot, R', M') \notin$ SL, and RS.Verify(R', M', σ') = 1.

2.4 Abstract Group Actions in Cryptography

Let G be a group and S be a set. We use $*$ to denote the group multiplication. A group action is a function $\alpha : G \times S \to S$ satisfying certain natural axioms. There are several frameworks of group actions in cryptography [2,22,30,51], which are mostly the same but can be different in some details. In this paper, we use the following model.

Some Notation. Let $\alpha : G \times S \to S$ be a group action. For $s \in S$, its *orbit* under α is $\mathcal{O}(s) := \{t \in S \mid \exists g \in G, \alpha(g, s) = t\}$, and its *stabilizer group* under α is Stab(s) = $\{g \in G \mid \alpha(g, s) = s\}$. An element in Stab($s$) is called an *automorphism* of s. By the orbit-stabilizer theorem, $|\mathcal{O}(s)| \cdot |\text{Stab}(s)| = |G|$.

Computational Assumptions. We first make the following computational assumptions for using a group action in algorithms.

1. We work with group families $G = \{G_k\}_{k \in \mathbb{N}}$ and set families $S = \{S_k\}_{k \in \mathbb{N}}$.
2. For a fixed k, G_k and S_k are finite, where $|S_k| = A_k$ and $|G_k| = B_k$, and $\log A_k$ and $\log B_k$ are upper bounded by some polynomial in k.
3. The following tasks can be done in time polynomial in k: computing group product and inverse, deciding the equivalence of group elements, computing the group action function, and uniformly sampling group and set elements.

In the following, when k is clear from the context, we may just write G and S, and set $|S| = A$ and $|G| = B$.

We note that it is not necessary for a group action to satisfy all the above to be useful in cryptography. For example, the group action underlying CSIDH [26] cannot be efficiently computed for all group elements, though it can be modelled as a "restricted effective group action" as in [2].

Cryptographic Assumptions. We now list the following assumptions for a group action to be useful in cryptography. Let $\alpha : G \times S \to S$ be a group action. Given $s \in S$, we shall often use the fact that we can sample from $\mathcal{O}(s)$ uniformly. This is because we can uniformly sample $g \in G$ and return $\alpha(g, s)$.

1. One-way assumption: for $s \xleftarrow{\$} S$ and $t \xleftarrow{\$} \mathcal{O}(s)$, there is no probabilistic or quantum polynomial-time algorithm that returns g' such that $\alpha(g', s) = t$.
2. Pseudorandom assumption: there is no probabilistic or quantum polynomial-time algorithm that can distinguish the following two distributions with non-negligible probability:
   (a) The random distribution: $(s, t) \in S \times S$ where $s, t \xleftarrow{\$} S$.
   (b) The pseudorandom distribution: $(s, t) \in S \times S$ where $s \xleftarrow{\$} S, t \xleftarrow{\$} \mathcal{O}(s)$.

Those assumptions can be generalised to the following C-instance version.

Definition 6. *Let $\alpha : G \times S \to S$ be a group action.*

1. *We say that α satisfies the C-one-way assumption, if for $s_0 \xleftarrow{\$} S$, given s_0 and $s_1, \ldots, s_{C-1} \xleftarrow{\$} \mathcal{O}(s_0)$, there is no probabilistic or quantum polynomial-time algorithm that returns g', $i, j \in \{0, 1, \ldots, C - 1\}$, $i \neq j$, such that $\alpha(g', s_i) = s_j$, with non-negligible probability.*
2. *We say that α satisfies the C-pseudorandom assumption, if there is no probabilistic or quantum polynomial-time algorithm that can distinguish the following two distributions with non-negligible probability:*
   (a) *The random distribution: $(s_0, \ldots, s_{C-1}) \in S^C$ where $s_i \xleftarrow{\$} S$.*
   (b) *The pseudorandom distribution: $(s_0, \ldots, s_{C-1}) \in S^C$ where $s_0 \xleftarrow{\$} S$, and $s_1, \ldots, s_{C-1} \xleftarrow{\$} \mathcal{O}(s_0)$.*

Remark 1. These assumptions can also be restricted to the versions that work with a fixed s_0 rather than a random one. That is, in the above, replace $s_0 \xleftarrow{\$} S$ with a fixed choice $s_0 \in S$. We shall call these C-one-way-$\mathcal{O}(s_0)$ and C-pseudorandom-$\mathcal{O}(s_0)$ assumptions, respectively.

The GMW-FS Digital Signature Design. Let $\alpha : G \times S \to S$ be a group action. As mentioned in Sect. 1, we can obtain a digital signature by applying the Fiat-Shamir (FS) transformation to the Goldreich-Micali-Wigderson (GMW) zero-knowledge protocol instantiated with the group action α, assuming that the group action satisfies the C-one-way assumption. We call this digital signature the $\alpha(G, S)$-GMW-FS scheme.

For our purposes in this paper, the key is the GMW protocol instantiated with α with the C-one-way assumption. This protocol is easily interpreted as an identification protocol, and we shall refer it as the $\alpha(G, S)$-GMW protocol. Therefore, we describe the $\alpha(G, S)$-GMW protocol in detail.

In the $\alpha(G, S)$-GMW protocol, the public key consists of set elements $s_0, \ldots, s_{C-1}$ such that $s_0 \xleftarrow{\$} S$, and $s_1, \ldots, s_{C-1} \xleftarrow{\$} \mathcal{O}(s_0)$. The private keys consists of $g_0 = \mathrm{id}, g_1, \ldots, g_{C-1}$ such that $\alpha(g_i, s_0) = s_i$. In this protocol, the goal of the prover is to convince the verifier that, for every $i \neq j$, the prover knows some h such that $\alpha(h, s_i) = s_j$.

Define the relation $R := \{x = \{s_0, \ldots, s_{C-1}\}, w = \{g_1, \ldots, g_{C-1}\} \mid x \subseteq S, w \subseteq G, \alpha(g_i, s_1) = s_i, \forall i \in \{1, \ldots, C-1\}\}$. The protocol is described in Fig. 3, which will be repeated several times to attain the required security level.

It is known that $\alpha(G, S)$-GMW protocol in Fig. 3 has the following properties (see e.g. [73]): completeness, post-quantum 2-soundness, HVZK, min-entropy, and commitment recoverable. We provide some proof sketches for completeness in the full version paper [13].

The $\alpha(G, S)$-GMW-FS-$\mathcal{O}(s)$ Scheme. In Sect. 3, we will also discuss a variant of the $\alpha(G, S)$-GMW-FS scheme, following Remark 1. Briefly speaking, this variant restricts to an orbit of some specific $s \in S$ instead of working in the orbit of a random $s \xleftarrow{\$} S$. We call such a scheme the $\alpha(G, S)$-GMW-FS-$\mathcal{O}(s)$ scheme.

$\mathcal{P}(s_0, \ldots, s_{C-1}, g_0 = \mathrm{id}, g_1, \ldots, g_{C-1})$		$\mathcal{V}(s_0, \ldots, s_{C-1})$
$h \xleftarrow{\$} G$		
$t = \alpha(h, s_0)$	$\xrightarrow{\quad t \quad}$	
	$\xleftarrow{\quad c \quad}$	$c \xleftarrow{\$} \{0, \ldots, C-1\}$
Set $f := h * g_c^{-1}$	$\xrightarrow{\quad f \quad}$	Check if $\alpha(f, s_c) = t$?

Fig. 3. The $\alpha(G, S)$-GMW protocol.

2.5   Some Candidates of Group Actions for the GMW-FS Design

The Group Action Underlying ALTEQ [73]. Let $\mathbb{F}_q$ be the finite field of order q. A trilinear form $\phi : \mathbb{F}_q^n \times \mathbb{F}_q^n \times \mathbb{F}_q^n \to \mathbb{F}_q$ is *alternating*, if ϕ evaluates to 0 whenever two arguments are the same. We use $\mathrm{ATF}(n, q)$ to denote the set of all alternating trilinear forms defined over $\mathbb{F}_q^n$. Let A be an invertible matrix of size $n \times n$ over $\mathbb{F}_q$. Then A sends ϕ to another alternating trilinear form $\phi \circ A$, defined as $(\phi \circ A)(u, v, w) := \phi(A^{\mathrm{t}}(u), A^{\mathrm{t}}(v), A^{\mathrm{t}}(w))$.

The Group Action Underlying LESS [12]. For $1 \leq d \leq n$, let $\mathrm{M}(d \times n, \mathbb{F}_q)$ be the linear space of $d \times n$ matrices over $\mathbb{F}_q$. Let $\mathrm{Mon}(n, q)$ be the group of $n \times n$ monomial matrices over $\mathbb{F}_q$. The group $G = \mathrm{GL}(n, q) \times \mathrm{Mon}(n, q)$, the set $S = \mathrm{M}(d \times n, \mathbb{F}_q)$, and the action is defined as $(A, C) \in \mathrm{GL}(n, q) \times \mathrm{Mon}(n, q)$ sending $B \in \mathrm{M}(d \times n, q)$ to ABC^t.

The Group Action Underlying MEDS [28]. Let $n_1, n_2, n_3 \in \mathbb{N}$. The set S is $\mathbb{F}_q^{n_1} \otimes \mathbb{F}_q^{n_2} \otimes \mathbb{F}_q^{n_3}$. The group $G = \mathrm{GL}(n_1, q) \times \mathrm{GL}(n_2, q) \times \mathrm{GL}(n_3, q)$. The action is defined as $(A_1, A_2, A_3) \in G$ sending $u_1 \otimes u_2 \otimes u_3$ to $A_1(u_1) \otimes A_2(u_2) \otimes A_3(u_3)$, and then linearly extending this to the whole $\mathbb{F}_q^{n_1} \otimes \mathbb{F}_q^{n_2} \otimes \mathbb{F}_q^{n_3}$.

The Class Group Action Underlying CSIDH [26] *(such as for SeaSign* [41] *and CSIFiSh* [11]*).* Let E be an elliptic curve over $\mathbb{F}_p$, and let $O := \mathrm{End}_{\mathbb{F}_p}(E)$. The ideal class group $\mathrm{Cl}(O)$ acts on the set of $\mathbb{F}_p$-isomorphism classes of elliptic curves with $\mathbb{F}_p$-rational endomorphism ring O via a natural action. For details we refer the reader to [9,11,41]. Note that this action does not satisfy all the properties in Sect. 2.4; see [2].

Further Group Actions in Cryptography. We note that more isomorphism problems and group actions have been proposed for cryptographic uses, such as lattice isomorphism [35] and knot equivalence [39]. While these are interesting, we did not discuss these here due to space limitations.

3   QROM Security via Perfect Unique Responses

In this section, we show that the $\alpha(\mathsf{G}, \mathsf{S})$-GMW-FS scheme is secure in the quantum random oracle model (QROM) subject to a certain condition on the automorphism group of the alternating trilinear form in use.

    This section is organised as follows. In Sect. 3.1, we review some basics of the quantum random oracle model. In Sect. 3.2, we translate perfect and computational unique response properties of the $\alpha(\mathsf{G}, \mathsf{S})$-GMW protocol to certain properties about stabilizer groups. In Sect. 3.3, we formally state QROM security of the $\alpha(\mathsf{G}, \mathsf{S})$-GMW-FS-$\mathcal{O}(s_0)$ scheme in Theorem 2, with proof sketches in the full version paper [13].

3.1 Preliminaries on QROM

The random oracle model (ROM) was first proposed in 1993 by Bellare and Rogaway in [6] as a heuristic to provide security proofs in cryptography. Briefly speaking, in the ROM model, the hash function is modeled as by a random oracle. However, ROM is insufficient when considering quantum adversaries, which leads to the proposal of the *quantum* ROM (QROM) [16]. One main reason comes from that quantum adversaries can make queries at a superposition. For example, let $H : \mathcal{X} \to \mathcal{Y}$ be a hash function, a quantum adversary will make superposition queries to evaluate this function, that is, for input $\sum_x \beta_x |x\rangle$ return $\sum_x \beta_x |x\rangle |H(x)\rangle$. Security proof migration from ROM to QROM is not an easy task, due to several obstacles from some properties in the quantum setting, such as whether the query is a superposition, quantum no cloning, and quantum measurement cause collapse, etc. Indeed, there exist protocols that are secure in ROM but not in QROM [16,78].

Recently, thanks to a pair of breakthrough papers [34,56], the QROM security of the Fiat-Shamir transform is now much better understood. Based on these papers, we study the relation between the $\alpha(\mathsf{G}, \mathsf{S})$-GMW scheme and the *perfect unique response* property introduced by Unruh [75], so we can prove the security of the $\alpha(\mathsf{G}, \mathsf{S})$-GMW protocol in quantum ROM.

3.2 Perfect and Computationally Unique Responses of the $\alpha(\mathsf{G}, \mathsf{S})$-GMW Protocol

We require some extra properties such that the $\alpha(\mathsf{G}, \mathsf{S})$-GMW or $\alpha(\mathsf{G}, \mathsf{S})$-GMW-$\mathcal{O}(s_0)$ protocols meet the *perfect unique response* and *computationally unique response* properties, as recalled in Sect. 2.2.

Lemma 1 (Perfect Unique Response). *The* $\alpha(\mathsf{G}, \mathsf{S})$-*GMW-$\mathcal{O}(s_0)$ protocol supports perfect unique response if and only if* $\mathrm{Stab}(s_0)$ *is trivial.*

Proof. Assume that $\mathrm{Stab}(s_0)$ is trivial. If there are two valid transcripts (t, c, g_1) and (t, c, g_2) for the protocol in Fig. 3. Then we have $\alpha(g_1, t) = \alpha(g_2, t)$. It implies that $g_2 * g_1^{-1} \in \mathrm{Stab}(s_0)$ and thus $g_1 = g_2$.

Now assume that the $\alpha(\mathsf{G}, \mathsf{S})$-GMW-$\mathcal{O}(s_0)$ protocol satisfies the perfect unique response property. If $\mathrm{Stab}(s_0)$ is non-trivial, i.e., there exists a group element $h \neq \mathrm{id}$ such that $\alpha(h, s_0) = s_0$. Therefore, all the elements in $\{s_0, \ldots, s_{C-1}\}$ satisfy $\alpha(h, s_i) = s_i$. It follows that for the statement $\{s_0, \ldots, s_{C-1}\}$, any commitments $t \in S$, and any challenge $c \in \{0, 1, \ldots, C-1\}$, there are two different responses $g \in G$ and $h * g \in G$ such that (t, c, g) and $(t, c, h * g)$ are valid transcripts, which is a contradiction. □

Remark 2. For the $\alpha(\mathsf{G}, \mathsf{S})$-GMW, since s_0 is not fixed, in some cases, we can only say that the stabilizer group of a random $s_0 \leftarrow_R S$ is trivial with high probability. Such a property is known as the statistical unique response property. However, it is not known if statistical unique response is enough to prove the quantum proof of knowledge.

To illustrate the relation between the computationally unique response and group actions, we define the following algorithm problem.

Definition 7. *The $\alpha(G, S)$-stabilizer problem is the following.*

Input: *An element $s \in_R S$.*
Output: *Some $g \in G, g \neq \mathrm{id}$ such that $s = \alpha(g, s)$.*

The $\alpha(G, S)$-stabilizer problem is also known as the automorphism group problem in the literature (see e.g. the graph automorphism problem [54]).

Lemma 2 (Computationally Unique Response). *The $\alpha(G, S)$-GMW protocol in Fig. 3 supports computationally unique response if and only if no poly-time quantum algorithm can solve the $\alpha(G, S)$-stabilizer problem in Definition 7 with a non-negligible probability.*

Proof. Assume that the Σ-protocol supports computationally unique response. If there is a polynomial-time quantum adversary $\mathcal{A}$ such that for any statement $x = \{s_0, \ldots, s_{C-1}\} \subseteq S$, it can compute two valid transcripts (t, c, g_1) and (t, c, g_2), where $g_1 \neq g_2$, with a non-negligible probability. Then there is an algorithm $\mathcal{A}_1$ using $\mathcal{A}$ as subroutine such that for any $c \in \{0, 1, \ldots, C - 1\}$, it can produce an $h = g_2 * g_1^{-1}$ such that $\alpha(h, s_c) = s_c$ with a non-negligible probability.

Assume there is a polynomial-time quantum algorithm $\mathcal{A}_1$ such that, for any $s \in S$, it produces a stabilizer element h such that $\alpha(h, s) = s$ with a non-negligible probability. By the HVZK property, there exists a simulator $\mathcal{S}$ such that, for any $x = \{s_0, \ldots, s_{C-1}\} \subseteq S$, it produces a valid transcript (t, c, g). Then there is an adversary $\mathcal{A}$ using $\mathcal{A}_1$ and $\mathcal{S}$ as subroutines such that it firstly computes a valid transcript (t, c, g) by $\mathcal{S}$, and then computes h such that $\alpha(h, s_c) = s_c$ by $\mathcal{A}_1$. Thus, for any statement $\{s_0, \ldots, s_{C-1}\}$, $\mathcal{A}$ computes two transcripts (t, c, g) and $(t, c, h * g)$ with a non-negligible probability. $\square$

Remark 3. For a fixed $s_0 \in S$, we can define the $\alpha(G, S)$-stabilizer-$\mathcal{O}(s_0)$ problem by restricting the input to $s \in_R \mathcal{O}(s_0)$. Then the above proof can be applied to show the same result for $\alpha(G, S)$-GMW-$\mathcal{O}(s_0)$.

Based on the above, we define the following properties of group actions.

Definition 8. *Let $\alpha : G \times S \to S$ be a group action.*

1. *We say that α satisfies the (statistical) trivial stabiliser assumption, if for a random $s \in S$, $\mathrm{Stab}(s)$ is trivial.*
2. *We say that α satisfies the non-trivial automorphism hardness assumption, if no probabilistic or quantum polynomial-time algorithm can solve the $\alpha(G, S)$-stabilizer problem with non-negligible probability.*

3.3 QROM Security via Perfect Unique Response

Lemma 1 interprets the perfect unique response property as a property of group actions. Based on this, it is straightforward to adapt the results in [56] to give a security proof in QROM for $\alpha(\mathsf{G}, \mathsf{S})$-$GMW$-$FS$-$\mathcal{O}(s_0)$ signature scheme assuming the stabilizer group being trivial.

Theorem 2. *Suppose $s_0 \in S$ satisfies that $\mathrm{Stab}(s_0)$ is trivial, and assume the C-one-way-$\mathcal{O}(s_0)$ is hard. The $\alpha(\mathsf{G}, \mathsf{S})$-$GMW$-$FS$-$\mathcal{O}(s_0)$ signature based on the t repetitions of $\alpha(\mathsf{G}, \mathsf{S})$-$GMW$-$\mathcal{O}(s_0)$ protocol has existential unforgeability under chosen-message attack (EUF-CMA) security. More specifically, for any polynomial-time quantum adversary $\mathcal{A}$ querying the quantum random oracle Q_H times against EUF-CMA security of $\alpha(\mathsf{G}, \mathsf{S})$-$GMW$-$FS$-$\mathcal{O}(s_0)$ signature, there is a quantum adversary $\mathcal{B}$ for C-one-way-$\mathcal{O}(s_0)$ problem such that,*

$$\mathsf{Adv}_{\mathcal{A}}^{\alpha(\mathsf{G},\mathsf{S})\text{-}EUF\text{-}CMA} \leq O\left(Q_H^9 \cdot \left(\mathsf{Adv}_{\mathcal{B}}^{C\text{-}one\text{-}way\text{-}\mathcal{O}(s_0)} \right)^{\frac{1}{3}} \right).$$

For readers' convenience, we present the proof of Theorem 2 based on [56] in the full version paper [13].

Remark 4. The EUF-CMA security in QROM here can be strengthened to the sEUF-CMA security by assuming the computationally unique response property [53, Theorem 3.2]. Since we assume that the stabilizer group is trivial (perfect unique response) which implies the computationally unique response, $\alpha(\mathsf{G}, \mathsf{S})$-$GMW$-$FS$-$\mathcal{O}(s_0)$ signature here is sEUF-CMA secure.

Remark 5. The ATFE instantiation in Sect. 6 provides meaningful realization of Theorem 2 in a concrete group action setting. In fact, in Sect. 6.1, we experimentally verify that for a random alternating trilinear form, its stabilizer group is trivial, hence supporting the security of ATFE-GMW-FS signature in the QROM model; see Sect. 6.1 for more detail.

4 QROM Security via Lossy Schemes

4.1 Definitions and Previous Results

In this section, we recall the definition of lossy identification protocol [1,36] and a security result of its associated Fiat-Shamir signature in QROM from [53].

Definition 9. *An identification protocol ID is called lossy, denoted by $\mathsf{ID}_{\mathsf{ls}}$, if it has one additional PPT algorithm $\mathsf{LossyGen}$, called the lossy key generation that on inputs the security parameter outputs a lossy verification key pk. To be more precise, $\mathsf{LossyGen}(1^\lambda)$ generates $x_{\mathsf{ls}} \leftarrow \mathsf{LossyGen}(1^\lambda)$ such that there are no $w \in \mathcal{W}$ satisfying $(x_{\mathsf{ls}}, w) \in \mathcal{R}$.*

M. Bläser et al.

A lossy identification protocol is required to satisfy the following additional properties.

Indistinguishability of Lossy Statements. It is required that the lossy statements generated by $\mathsf{LossyGen}(1^\lambda)$ is indistinguishable with ones generated by $\mathsf{Gen}(1^\lambda)$, i.e., . for any PPT (or quantum PT) adversary $\mathcal{A}$, the advantage of $\mathcal{A}$ against the indistinguishability of lossy statements

$$\mathsf{Adv}_{\mathcal{A}}^{\mathsf{ls}}(\lambda) := |\Pr[\mathcal{A}(x_{\mathsf{ls}} = 1)|x_{\mathsf{ls}} \leftarrow \mathsf{LossyGen}(1^\lambda)]$$
$$- \Pr[\mathcal{A}(x) = 1|(x, w) \leftarrow \mathsf{Gen}(1^\lambda)]$$

is negligible.

Statistical Lossy Soundness. Consider following experiment $\mathsf{Exp}_{\mathsf{ID}, \mathcal{A}}^{\mathsf{ls}}(\lambda)$ between an adversary $\mathcal{A}$ and a challenger.

- The challenger runs $x_{\mathsf{ls}} \leftarrow \mathsf{LossyGen}(1^\lambda)$ and provides x_{ls} to the adversary $\mathcal{A}$.
- On input x_{ls}, the adversary $\mathcal{A}$ selects a commitment a and sends it to the challenger who responds with a random challenge c.
- On input (a, c), the adversary $\mathcal{A}$ outputs a response r.
- Return 1 if (a, c, r) is a valid transcript for x_{ls}, and 0 otherwise.

We say that the lossy identification protocol $\mathsf{ID}_{\mathsf{ls}}$ is ϵ_{ls}-lossy sound if for any unbounded (possibly quantum) adversary $\mathcal{A}$, the probability of winning the experiment $\mathsf{Exp}_{\mathsf{ID}, \mathcal{A}}^{\mathsf{ls}}(\lambda)$ is less than ϵ_{ls}, i.e.,

$$\Pr[\mathsf{Exp}_{\mathsf{ID}, \mathcal{A}}^{\mathsf{ls}}(\lambda) = 1] \le \epsilon_{\mathsf{ls}}.$$

Fiat-Shamir transformation applied to a lossy identification protocol yields a tightly secure signature in QROM [34,53,56].

Theorem 3 ([53, Theorem 3.1]). *Assume that the identification protocol* ID *is lossy, perfect HVZK, has* α *bits of min-entropy, and it is* ϵ_{ls}-*lossily sound. Then the signature scheme* FS[ID] *obtained from applying the Fiat-Shamir transformation to* ID *is such that for any quantum adversary* $\mathcal{A}$ *against the sEUF-CMA security that issues at most* Q_H *queries to the quantum random oracle, there exist a quantum adversary* $\mathcal{B}$ *against the lossiness and* $\mathcal{C}$ *against the computation unique response such that*

$$\mathsf{Adv}_{\mathcal{A}}^{sEUF\text{-}CMA}(\lambda) \le \mathsf{Adv}_{\mathcal{B}}^{\mathsf{ls}}(\lambda) + 2^{-\alpha+1} + 8(Q_H + 1)^2 \cdot \epsilon_{\mathsf{ls}} + \mathsf{Adv}_{\mathcal{C}}^{CUR}(\lambda),$$

and $\mathsf{Time}(\mathcal{B}) = \mathsf{Time}(\mathcal{C}) = \mathsf{Time}(\mathcal{D}) = \mathsf{Time}(\mathcal{A}) + Q_H \cong \mathsf{Time}(\mathcal{A})$.
In the classical setting, we can replace $8(Q_H + 1)^2$ *by* $(Q_H + 1)$.

4.2 Lossy Identification Protocol from Abstract Group Actions

In this section, we define a lossy identification protocol based on the K-pseudorandom assumption in Definition 6. The underlying sigma protocol is the $\alpha(\mathsf{G},\mathsf{S})$-GMW protocol in Fig. 3. Here, we consider a relation $\mathcal{R}$ consisting of statement-witness pairs (x,w) with $x = \{s_0, s_1, \ldots, s_{C-1}\} \subseteq S$ and $w = \{g_1, \ldots, g_{C-1}\} \subseteq G$, where $\alpha(g_i, s_0) = s_i$ for each $i \in [C-1]$.

The lossy identification scheme for the relation $\mathcal{R}$ defined as above with challenge space $\{0, 1, \cdots, C-1\}$ consists of five algorithms $(\mathsf{IGen}, \mathsf{LossyGen}, \mathcal{P}_1, \mathcal{P}_2, \mathcal{V})$ as follows. Note that the new addition is the $\mathsf{LossyGen}$ algorithm.

- Algorithm IGen randomly samples an element $s_0 \in S$ and group elements $g_1, \cdots, g_{C-1} \in_R G$. It outputs a statement $x = (s_0, s_1, \cdots, s_{C-1})$ with $s_i = \alpha(g_i, s_0)$ for $i = 1, \cdots, C-1$, and a witness $w = (g_1, \cdots, g_{C-1})$.
- Algorithm $\mathsf{LossyGen}$ randomly samples set elements $s_0, s_1, \cdots, s_{K-1} \in S$ and outputs a lossy statement $x_{\mathsf{ls}} = (s_0, s_1, \cdots, s_{C-1})$.
- On input a statement-witness pair (x, w), $\mathcal{P}_1$ samples a random group element $h \in_R G$ and outputs the commitment $t = \alpha(h, s_0)$.
- On input (x, w, t, c) where $c \in \{0, 1, \cdots, C-1\}$ is a challenge, $\mathcal{P}_2$ outputs a response $f = h * g_c$.
- On input (x, t, c, f), the verification algorithm $\mathcal{V}$ check whether $t = \alpha(f, s_c)$.

Security Analysis. Since the underlying protocol is the same as in Fig. 3, it is clear that our lossy identification protocol is complete, has α-bit min-entropy with $\alpha \approx \log_2 |\mathcal{O}|$, satisfies HVZK property and commitment recoverability. It remains to show that our protocol has indistinguishability of lossy statements, and to calculate the statistical lossy soundness.

Lemma 3. *Suppose $\alpha : G \times S \to S$ satisfies the C-pseudorandom assumption as in Definition 6. Then the lossy identification protocol satisfies the lossy statement indistinguishability.*

Proof. The lossy generator of our protocol just random samples C elements $s_0, s_1, \cdots, s_{C-1} \in_R S$. By the hardness assumption of the C-pseudorandom problem, lossy statements and real statements are indistinguishable. $\square$

The following lemma calculates the lossy soundness parameter ϵ_{ls}.

Lemma 4. *The lossy identification protocol satisfies statistical ϵ_{ls}-lossy soundness for $\epsilon_{\mathsf{ls}} = \frac{1}{C} \prod_{i=1}^{C-1} \frac{A-iB}{A} + \left(1 - \prod_{i=1}^{C-1} \frac{A-iB}{A}\right)$, where $B = |G|$, $A = |S|$.*

Proof. This proof is similar to the proof of [36, Lemma 3.3]. Let $\mathcal{X}$ be the set of the statements such that given a commitment $z \in_R S$, there is only one challenge c resulting in a valid transcript. Consider other commitment z with two valid transcripts (z, c_0, g_0) and (z, c_1, g_1) where these two transcripts satisfy following equations:

$$\alpha(g_0, s_{c_0}) = z$$
$$\alpha(g_1, s_{c_1}) = z.$$

It implies that $\alpha(g_0 * g_1^{-1}, s_{c_0}) = s_{c_1}$, i.e., s_{c_0} and s_{c_1} are in the same orbit. Therefore, if any two elements in the statement are not in the same orbit, the statement can't have two valid transcripts with different challenges.

The number of different statements in $\mathcal{X}$ is $A\prod_{i=1}^{C-1}(A-i|\mathcal{O}_i|) \geq A\prod_{i=1}^{C-1}(A-iB)$, where $|\mathcal{O}_i|$ is the size of $\mathcal{O}_i$ and $|\mathcal{O}_i| \leq B$. The number of all statements is A^C. Then we can have the probability that a statement is in $\mathcal{X}$ is $\Pr[x \in \mathcal{X} \mid x \leftarrow \mathsf{LossyGen}] \geq \prod_{i=1}^{C-1}\frac{A-iB}{A}$. We can obtain the probability that an adversary wins as follows:

$$
\begin{aligned}
\Pr[\mathcal{A}\ \text{wins}\ ] &= \Pr[\mathcal{A}\ \text{wins}\ \mid x \in \mathcal{X}]\Pr[x \in \mathcal{X}] + \Pr[\mathcal{A}\ \text{wins}\ \mid x \notin \mathcal{X}]\Pr[x \notin \mathcal{X}] \\
&\leq \Pr[\mathcal{A}\ \text{wins}\ \mid x \in \mathcal{X}]\Pr[x \in \mathcal{X}] + \Pr[x \notin \mathcal{X}] \\
&= \Pr[\mathcal{A}\ \text{wins}\ \mid x \in \mathcal{X}]\Pr[x \in \mathcal{X}] + (1 - \Pr[x \in \mathcal{X}]) \\
&= (\Pr[\mathcal{A}\ \text{wins}\ \mid x \in \mathcal{X}] - 1)\Pr[x \in \mathcal{X}] + 1 \\
&\leq (\Pr[\mathcal{A}\ \text{wins}\ \mid x \in \mathcal{X}] - 1)\prod_{i=1}^{C-1}\frac{A-iB}{A} + 1 \\
&= \Pr[\mathcal{A}\ \text{wins}\ \mid x \in \mathcal{X}]\prod_{i=1}^{C-1}\frac{A-iB}{A} + \left(1 - \prod_{i=1}^{C-1}\frac{A-iB}{A}\right).
\end{aligned}
$$

Note that the second inquality is due to $\Pr[\mathcal{A}\ \text{wins}\ \mid x \in \mathcal{X}] - 1 \leq 0$. This completes the proof.

Lemma 4 implies the following for a t-parallel repetition of the lossy identification protocol.

Corollary 1. *The lossy identification protocol in Fig. 3, that is run t parallel rounds with the same statement-witness pair, satisfies statistical ϵ_{ls}-lossy soundness for $\epsilon_{\mathsf{ls}} = \frac{1}{C^t}\prod_{i=1}^{C-1}\frac{A-iB}{A} + \left(1 - \prod_{i=1}^{C-1}\frac{A-iB}{A}\right)$, where $A = |S|$, $B = |G|$, and $|C|$ is the size of the challenge space.*

Remark 6. For our ATFE instantiation in Sect. 6, B is the order of the general linear group $\mathrm{GL}(n,q)$ and A is the size of $\mathrm{ATF}(n,q)$ which is far greater than B as the parameter n is large enough. Therefore, the error ϵ_{ls} is estimated to be $2^{-\lambda}$ where λ is the security level; see Sect. 6.1 for the detail.

4.3 Tightly Secure Signature Scheme in QROM from Abstract Group Actions

A digital signature scheme can be obtained by applying the Fiat-Shamir transformation to the t-fold parallel repetition of the lossy identification protocol in Sect. 4.2. We call this the $\alpha(\mathsf{G},\mathsf{S})$-GMW-FS-lossy scheme. Note that this result is essentially the same scheme as the $\alpha(\mathsf{G},\mathsf{S})$-GMW-FS scheme, as the additional LossyGen algorithm used for lossy key generation is only used for security analysis.

We now prove the QROM security of $\alpha(\mathsf{G},\mathsf{S})$-GMW-FS-lossy based on the C-pseudorandom assumption and the computational unique response assumption as in Lemma 2.

Theorem 4. *For any quantum adversary $\mathcal{A}$ against the sEUF-CMA security of $\alpha(\mathsf{G},\mathsf{S})$-GMW-FS-lossy that issues at most Q_H queries to the quantum random oracle, there exists a quantum adversary $\mathcal{B}$ against the C-pseudorandomness (Definition 6), a quantum adversary $\mathcal{C}$ against the $\alpha(\mathsf{G},\mathsf{S})$-stabilizer problem (Definition 7) such that*

$$\mathsf{Adv}_{\mathcal{A}}^{\alpha(\mathsf{G},\mathsf{S})\text{-}GMW\text{-}FS\text{-}lossy\text{-}sEUF\text{-}CMA}(\lambda)$$

$$\leq \quad \mathsf{Adv}_{\mathcal{B}}^{C\text{-}pseudorandom}(\lambda) + \frac{2}{|\mathcal{O}|}$$

$$+ 8(Q_H+1)^2 \cdot \left(\frac{1}{C^t} \prod_{i=1}^{C-1} \frac{A-iB}{A} + \left(1 - \prod_{i=1}^{C-1} \frac{A-iB}{A} \right) \right)$$

$$+ \mathsf{Adv}_{\mathcal{C}}^{\alpha(\mathsf{G},\mathsf{S})\text{-}Stab}(\lambda)$$

and $\mathsf{Time}(\mathcal{B}) = \mathsf{Time}(\mathcal{A}) + Q_H \cong \mathsf{Time}(\mathcal{A})$. *Here* $B = |G|$, $A = |S|$, *and* $|\mathcal{O}|$ *is the size of the orbit where elements of the statement* $x = (s_0, s_1, \cdots, s_{C-1})$ *are in.*

In the classical setting, we can replace $8(Q_H+1)^2$ *with* Q_H+1.

Proof. The proof initialises with Lemma 2 and Sect. 4.2 that the underlying sigma protocol has computational unique response, lossiness, lossy-soundness, perfect HVZK and at least $\log(|\mathcal{O}|)$ bits of min-entropy. The result now follows from Theorem 3.

5 Linkable Ring Signatures from Abstract Group Actions

In this section, we describe the construction of linkable ring signatures from abstract group actions. It follows the framework of Beullens, Katsumata and Pintore [10], so we call it the GMW-FS-BKP design. While [10] focussed on commutative group actions, their ring signature construction is readily applicable to general group actions. In fact, for our group action framework, the scheme becomes a bit simpler because [10] needs to work with rejection sampling. This has been observed and applied to LESS [4] and MEDS [28]. Therefore, here we will only briefly describe the main ideas, with a focus on presenting another assumption on group actions to achieve linkability.

The Beullens-Katsumata-Pintore Design. Briefly speaking, the GMW-FS-BKP ring signature is obtained by applying the Fiat-Shamir transformation to an OR-Sigma protocol, which is an interactive protocol in which a prover convinces a verifier that she knows the witness of one of given several inputs without revealing which one. Here, we describe the base OR-Sigma protocol for an abstract group action. Some optimization and the security proof are reproduced in the full version paper [13] for the readers' convenience.

Let $g_1, g_2, \ldots, g_N \xleftarrow{\$} G$ be the secret keys, and $s_1 = \alpha(g_1, s_0), \ldots, s_N = \alpha(g_N, s_0)$ be the public keys, Com be a commitment scheme. The base OR-Sigma protocol with *statement* $\{s_0, \ldots, s_N \in S\}$ and *witness* $\{g_I \in G, I \in [N]$ such that $\alpha(g_I, s_0) = s_I\}$, works as follows.

1. First, the prover, assumed to be the I-th user in the ring, random sample a group element $h \in G$, and apply it to $s_1, \ldots, s_N$ respectively. Specifically, $t_1 = \alpha(h, s_1), \ldots, t_N = \alpha(h, s_N)$. Then the prover samples $\text{bits}_i \overset{\$}{\leftarrow} \{0,1\}^\lambda$ and commits to t_i with $C_i = \text{Com}(t_i, \text{bits}_i)$. The prover further builds a Merkle tree[3] with the $(C_1, \ldots, C_N)$ as its leaves. The prover computes the root root of the Merkle tree and sends it to the verifier as the commitment.
2. When the verifier receives the commitment, it will randomly sample a challenge $c \overset{\$}{\leftarrow} \{0,1\}$ and respond to the prover.
3. If $c = 0$, then the prover computes $f = h * g_I$ and the authenticated path for C_I. The prover sends back a response $\text{rsp} = (f, \text{path}, \text{bits}_I)$. The verifier applies f to s_0 to get $\tilde{t}$ and computes $\tilde{C} = \text{Com}(\tilde{t}, \text{bits}_I)$. The verifier then get a root $\widetilde{\text{root}}$ by path and $\tilde{C}$. Finally the verifier checks whether $\widetilde{\text{root}} = \text{root}$.
4. If $c = 1$, then the prover sends $(h, \text{bits}_1, \ldots, \text{bits}_N)$ to the verifier. This information allows the verifier to rebuild a Merkle tree as in step 1, and then check that the roots are consistent.

A more formal description can be found in the full version paper [13].

The Linkable Property. Linkable ring signatures were first introduced by Liu and Wong [55] that allow public checking whether two ring signatures are 'linked', i.e., generated by one user. A typical approach to construct a linkable ring signature is to add a tag, which uniquely define the real signer, to a signature. The approach in [10] is to first construct a linkable OR sigma protocol and then apply Fiat-Shamir transformation to obtain a linkable ring signature.

Here we only briefly indicate how to construct a linkable OR sigma protocol. More details can be found in the full version paper [13].

For this, we add a tag $r_0 \in S$ associated with a group action $\beta : G \times S \to S$ into the relation. The group action β is defined as $\beta(g, s) = \alpha(g^{-t}, s)$ where t is an involution of G. This tag r_0 is used to track if some secret key is signed more than once. In addition, we restrict the initial public key s_0 is sampled from an orbit $\mathcal{O}(s_0)$ with a trivial automorphism group. By the discussions in Sect. 6.1, a randomly sampled form s_0 has a high probability to be in an orbit with the trivial automorphism group if we choose a proper parameter n and q, adding this restriction is reasonable. After adding the tag into the base OR sigma protocol, we can get a linkable OR sigma protocol and apply certain optimisation methods to it for more efficiency.

A linkable digital signature needs to satisfy linkability, linkable anonymity, and non-frameability, which can be translated to properties about group actions as done in [10, Definition 4.2] and also [4,28]. We refer the interested readers to the full version paper [13] with this submission for formal definitions of these notions. For example, the linkable anonymity is captured by the following property about group action pairs.

---

[3] Note that the Merkle tree used here is slightly modified. It is index-hiding Merkle tree, please see [10, Section 2.6].

Definition 10. *Let* $\alpha, \beta : G \times S \to S$ *be two group actions. We say that the* (α, β) *pair satisfies the* pseudorandom *assumption at* $(s_0, r_0) \in S \times S$, *if no probabilistic or quantum polynomial-time algorithms can distinguish the following two distributions with non-negligible probability:*

1. *The random distribution:* $(s_1, r_1) \in S \times S$, *where* $s_1, r_1 \xleftarrow{\$} S$.

2. *The pseudorandom distribution:* $(s_1, r_1) \in S \times S$, *where* $g \xleftarrow{\$} G$, *and* $s_1 = \alpha(g, s_0)$ *and* $r_1 = \beta(g, r_0)$.

Furthermore, if the group actions α and β also satisfy the trivial stabiliser assumption (Definition 8), then the linkability and non-frameability also follow. These together suffice to prove the security of the linkable GMW-FS-BKP design based on the action pair (α, β). We note that the above strategy was already used in MEDS [28] for the action underlying the matrix code equivalence problem.

Instantiations of Pseudorandom Group Action Pairs. Let $\alpha : G \times S \to S$ be a group action. There are some generic recipes in the literature about finding another action $\beta : G \times S \to S$ so that (α, β) is pseudorandom. In [10], β is constructed as $\beta(g, s) = \alpha(g^2, s)$. In [12,28], β is constructed as $\beta(g, s) = \alpha(g^{-1}, s)$. Note that here β is actually a right action (if α is a left action). It follows that the responses need to involve both gh and hg where h is a random group element and g is the secret.

We note that it is possible to do slightly better than the above, if we have an involution t of G, i.e. an anti-automorphism of order 2. This means that t is an automorphism, $g^t = g$, and $(g * h)^t = h^t * g^t$. We can then define $\beta(g, s) = \alpha(g^{-t}, s)$. In the case of $G = \mathrm{GL}(n, q)$ as of interest in ATFE (and MEDS), this t can be simply taken as the transpose of matrices. This gives a concrete linkable ring signature scheme based on ATFE-GMW-FS-BKP. Very recent work [24] shows that LESS-based group actions do not have pseudorandom group action pairs. This has no direct implications for MEDS and ATFE. Of course, further research is required to verify whether this instantiation does give a pseudorandom group action pair for MEDS and ATFE.

Remark 7. Note that our ring signature obtained from OR-Sigma protocol is proven securely only in ROM. As far as we are aware, whether it is secure in QROM is still an open problem.

6   Results for the ATFE-GMW-FS Scheme

We now apply the results obtained in Sects. 3, 4, and 5 to a concrete setting, namely the digital signature scheme introduced in [73], which we refer to as the ATFE-GMW-FS scheme.

For the QROM security, this requires us to examine the group action underlying the ATFE problem, to show that it satisfies the properties required for the QROM security. For the ring signature scheme, we provide an implementation of

250   M. Bläser et al.

the ring signature scheme based on ATFE-GMW-FS. These provide evidence for
the usefulness of the results obtained in the abstract group action framework.

Finally, we demonstrate that the MPC-in-the-head paradigm provided by
Joux [52] can be applied to ATFE-GMW-FS to further reduce the signature size
(at the cost of increasing the signing time).

6.1   The QROM Security of the ATFE-GMW-FS Scheme

Based on the results in Sects. 3, there are two approaches to show the QROM
security of the ATFE-GMW-FS scheme.

QROM Security via Perfect Unique Response. Let $\phi : \mathbb{F}_q^n \times \mathbb{F}_q^n \times \mathbb{F}_q^n \to \mathbb{F}_q$
be an alternating trilinear form. Recall that $\mathrm{Stab}(\phi) := \{A \in \mathrm{GL}(n,q) \mid \phi \circ A = \phi\}$.

By Lemma 1, the ATFE-GMW-FS-$\mathcal{O}(\phi)$ is secure in the quantum model, if
$\mathrm{Stab}(\phi)$ is trivial and assume the C-one-way-$\mathcal{O}(\phi)$, where ϕ is instantiated as
an alternating trilinear form. To decide whether $\mathrm{Stab}(\phi)$ is trivial or not is a
difficult algorithmic problem; see [73, Section 3.2] for a discussion. Still, we make
progress by running experiments for those n of interest in our context.

Basic Facts About $\mathrm{Stab}(\phi)$. First, note that if $3|q-1$, then $\mathrm{Stab}(\phi)$ cannot be
trivial. This is because $3|q-1$ implies the existence of $\lambda \in \mathbb{F}_q$, $\lambda \neq 1$, and $\lambda^3 = 1$.
Therefore $\lambda I_n \in \mathrm{Aut}(\phi)$. Second, for (a) $n = 7$ and (b) $n = 8$ and $\mathrm{char}(\mathbb{F}_q) \neq 3$,
there exist no alternating trilinear forms with trivial automorphism groups, by
classifications of alternating trilinear forms in these cases [29,48,61]. Third, for
$n = 9$ and $q = 2$, by the classification of alternating trilinear forms [49], there
exists a unique orbit of alternating trilinear forms with trivial automorphism
groups.

In general, because of the difference between the dimension of $\mathrm{GL}(n,q)$ (which
is n^2) and the dimension of $\mathrm{ATF}(n,q)$ (which is $\binom{n}{3}$), it is expected that for
$n \geq 10$ and $3 \nmid q - 1$, most alternating trilinear forms would have the trivial
automorphism group.

A Magma Program to Compute the Stabilizer Group Order. We implemented a
program in Magma [18] for computing automorphism group orders of alternating
trilinear forms as follows.

1. Enumerate every $v \in \mathbb{F}_q^n$ and compute the rank of $\phi(v, \cdot, \cdot)$ as an alternating
   bilinear form. Let $S \subseteq \mathbb{F}_q^n$ be the set of non-zero vectors such that $\phi(v, \cdot, \cdot)$ is
   of lowest rank.
2. Fix $u \in S$. Let X and Y be two $n \times n$ variable matrices. For every $v \in S$, set
   up a system of polynomial equations expressing the following:
   (a) $\phi \circ X = \phi$, and $\phi = \phi \circ Y$.
   (b) For any $a, b, c \in \mathbb{F}^n$, $\phi(X(a), X(b), c) = \phi(a, b, Y(c))$, and $\phi(X(a), b, c) = \phi(a, Y(b), Y(c))$.
   (c) $XY = I_n$, and $YX = I_n$.

(d) $X(u) = v$, and $Y(v) = u$.

The use the Gröbner basis algorithm implemented in Magma to compute the number of solutions to this system of polynomial equations. Let it be s_v.

3. Sum over s_v over $v \in S$ as the order of $\mathrm{Stab}(\phi)$.

This algorithm runs in time $q^n \cdot \mathsf{poly}(n, \log q)$. The use of Gröbner computations follows the practices of works in multivariate cryptography for solving polynomial isomorphism [19–21,40]. The reason for Step 1 is to limit the number of Gröbner basis computations, which are more costly compared to computing the ranks. This idea could be found, for example, in [23]. The way we set up the equations is from [73].

Report on the Results. Our experiment results are as follows.

- For $q = 2$ and $n = 9$, out of 100 samples there are three ones with trivial stabilizer groups. This is consistent with the fact that there exists exactly one orbit of alternating trilinear forms [49], so the probability of sampling one from this orbit is $|\mathrm{GL}(2,9)|/2^{84} \approx 3.6169\%$.
- For $q = 2$ and $n = 10, 11$, all 100 samples return trivial stabilizer groups.
- For $q = 3$ and $n = 10, 11$, all 10 samples return trivial stabilizer groups.

These suggest that for $n = 10$ and q satisfying $3 \nmid q - 1$, a random alternating trilinear form has the trivial automorphism group with good probability. This also implies that for larger n and q such that $3 \nmid q - 1$, a random alternating trilinear form has the trivial automorphism group with high probability, as the gap between the space dimension and the group dimension becomes larger as n increases. To the best of our knowledge, to give an estimation of this probability (depending on q and n) is an open problem.

QROM Security via Lossy Schemes. In the above, we presented evidence for the ATFE-GMW-FS scheme to satisfy the perfect unique response property for $n \geq 10$, supporting its QROM security by the results in Sect. 3. However, the reduction in this approach is not tight. Instead, the QROM security via the lossy scheme approach gives a tight reduction.

To apply the results in Sect. 4 to the ATFE-GMW-FS scheme, we need to examine whether the group action underlying ATFE is pseudorandom. In [73, Conjecture 1], the authors conjectured that this is indeed the case, and provided some supporting evidences, some of which traced back to [51]. Here we briefly explain that, a key argument in [73] is that there seem no easy-to-compute isomorphism invariants for ATFE, as such isomorphism invariants could be used to distinguish non-equivalent alternating trilinear forms.

If the above holds, then $B = |\mathrm{GL}(n, q)| \approx q^{n^2}$ and $A = |\mathrm{ATF}(n, q)| = q^{\binom{n}{3}}$, $A \gg B$ as the security parameter λ is large enough. Therefore, the lossy soundness $\epsilon_{ls} \approx \frac{1}{C^t} \approx \frac{1}{2^\lambda}$.

Lossy Schemes with Unbalanced Challenges. The unbalanced challenge technique is a classical technique that can be traced back to Fiat and Shamir's original paper [42]. The idea is to observe that, in the case of challenge 0, the response would be a random group element that can be expanded from a short seed, so sending the seed reduces the communication. As a result, the number of rounds needs to be increased. This is a standard technique that turns out to be useful in practice as witnessed in [5,14,28].

The parameters involved in the ATFE-GMW-FS scheme with unbalanced challenges are as follows. Let M be the round number, K be the number of non-zero challenges, and C the number of alternating trilinear forms in each round. To achieve λ-bit security, we should choose the proper M and K such that $\binom{M}{K} \cdot (C-1)^K \geq 2^\lambda$. Some care is then needed to demonstrate the lossy soundness in this setting.

Corollary 2. *The lossy identification protocol based on* ATFE *with the unbalanced challenge, satisfies statistical ϵ_{ls}-lossy soundness for*

$$\epsilon_{ls} = \frac{1}{\binom{M}{K}(C-1)^K} \prod_{i=1}^{C-1} \frac{A - iB}{A} + \left(1 - \prod_{i=1}^{C-1} \frac{A - iB}{A} \right),$$

where $A = |\text{ATF}(n, q)|$, $B = |\text{GL}(n, q)|$.

Proof. Since the size of the challenge space is $\binom{M}{K}(C-1)^K$, we have that $\Pr[\mathcal{A} \text{ wins} \mid x \in \mathcal{X}] \leq \frac{1}{\binom{M}{K}(C-1)^K}$. The result follows the proof for Lemma 4.   □

6.2 An Implementation of the **ATFE-GMW-FS-BKP** Ring Signature Scheme

We implement the GMW-FS-BKP ring signature design based on ATFE. Here, we report the formulas for calculating the parameters, and preliminary experiment results. Some comparisons with known ring signature schemes were presented in Sect. 1.2.

Some Formulas for Parameters. Recall that M is the round number, K is the number of non-zero challenges, R is the ring size, and C is the number of alternating trilinear forms in each round. To achieve the λ-bits security, we should choose the proper M and K such that $(\frac{M}{K})^K \geq 2^\lambda$. Here we use a trick that evenly divides M rounds into K sections with length of $\lceil \frac{M}{K} \rceil$. For each section, we can construct a seed tree of which the internal seeds are of the size at most $\lambda \cdot \lceil \log_2(\frac{M}{K}) \rceil$.

1. The public key, private key and signature size of (non-linkable) ring signature in terms of bits are as follows.

$$\text{Public Key Size} = (R+1) \cdot \binom{n}{3} \lceil \log_2 q \rceil,$$

$$\text{Private Key Size} = \binom{n}{3} \lceil \log_2 q \rceil + R \cdot n^2 \lceil \log_2 q \rceil,$$

$$\text{Signature Size} = K(\lambda \cdot \lceil \log_2 \left(\frac{M}{K}\right) \rceil + n^2 \lceil \log_2 q \rceil + 2\lambda \cdot \lceil \log_2 R \rceil + \lambda) + 3\lambda.$$

2. The public key, private key and signature size of linkable ring signature in terms of bits are as follows.

$$\text{Public Key Size} = (R+1) \cdot \binom{n}{3} \lceil \log_2 q \rceil,$$

$$\text{Private Key Size} = \binom{n}{3} \lceil \log_2 q \rceil + R \cdot n^2 \lceil \log_2 q \rceil,$$

$$\text{Signature Size} = K(\lambda \cdot \lceil \log_2 \left(\frac{M}{K}\right) \rceil + n^2 \lceil \log_2 q \rceil + 2\lambda \cdot \lceil \log_2 R \rceil + \lambda)$$
$$+ 3\lambda + \binom{n}{3} \lceil \log_2 q \rceil.$$

Concrete Parameters and Reports on the Performance. We provide the performance evaluation of our schemes in terms of signature size, as shown in Tables 2. Furthermore, Table 3 illustrates the signature generation time for our schemes. Our constructions are implemented and measured on a 2.4 GHz Quad-Core Intel Core i5.

Table 2. The signature size (KB) of the ring signature. The security meets the NIST level 1.

Parameters		Size in Bytes						
n	q		M	K	R				
					2^1	2^3	2^6	2^{12}	2^{21}
13	$4294967291 (\sim 2^{32})$		850	25	20.5	22.1	24.5	29.3	36.5

6.3 Signature Size Reduction by the MPC in the Head Paradigm

The multiparty computation (MPC) in the head paradigm was initially introduced in [50] as a means to enhance the theoretical and asymptotic constructions of zero-knowledge (ZK) protocols. Recently, Joux [52] proposed the application of MPC-in-the-head for creating signatures from isomorphism problems and group actions. By applying MPC-in-the-head, the identification scheme based on group action and additional primitive named *puncturable pseudo-random functions* (puncturable PRFs) are as follows.

Table 3. The signing time (ms) of the ring signature. The security meets the NIST level 1.

Parameters				Time in ms							
n	q	M	K	R							
				2^1	2^2	2^3	2^4	2^5	2^6	2^7	
13	$4294967291(\sim 2^{32})$	850	25	83	121	205	379	682	1381	2714	

Puncturable Pseudo-Random Functions. A puncturable PRF family F defined on $[N]$ refers to a PRF family that is indexed by a key K and has a domain of $[N]$. This family satisfies the following properties:

- For any given key K and index i, there exists a punctured key K_i^* along with an efficient algorithm $\mathcal{A}$ such that:

$$\forall j \in [N]\setminus\{i\} : \mathcal{A}(K_i^*, j) = F_K(j).$$

- Given the puncturable key K_i^*, the value of F_K at i should be computationally indistinguishable from a randomly chosen value.

Remark 8. The puncturable PRFs can be practically realized, and an elegant approach to achieve this is through the GGM tree construction. This method requires a length-doubling PRF, which, in practice, proves to be efficient and viable; see [25, page 14] for reference. Furthermore, it is feasible under the group action model [52].

Group Action Based Identification Scheme Using MPC-in-the-Head. Given an expander Expand and a puncturable PRF family F, where Expand sends the output of F into a group element. Note here we consider there are two set elements $s_0, s_1 \in S$ such that $\alpha(g, s_0) = s_1$ as the public keys. We have the identification scheme as follows.

- The prover randomly chooses a puncturable key K and lets $g^{(i)} =$ Expand$(F_K(i))$ such that $s^{(i)} = \alpha(g^{(i)}, s^{(i-1)})$ for $i \in [N]$. Note there $s^{(0)} = s_0$. Then the prover sends the hash value $h = H(s^{(1)}||s^{(2)}||\cdots||s^{(N)})$ as the commitment.
- The verifier randomly chooses an index $i^* \in [N]$ and sends back to the prover.
- The prover responses the puncturable key K_i^* and the offset map g^Δ such that $g^\Delta * g^{(N)} * g^{(N-1)} * \cdots * g^{(1)} = g$.
- The verifier can efficiently generate $g^{(j)}$ for $j \in [N]\setminus i^*$. Then the verifier computes all $s^{(i)}$ by forward computation from $s^{(0)}$ up to $s^{(i^*-1)}$ and by a backward computation from $s^{(N)}$ down to $s^{(i^*)}$. Finally he checks the commitment h.

This protocol has a soundness of $\frac{1}{2N}$. If we enlarge the public key size to C set elements then we have a soundness of $\frac{1}{N(C-1)}$.

Reducing the Signature Size. As mentioned above, the new identification scheme has a soundness of $\frac{1}{N(C-1)}$ if the public key consists of C set elements. Thus we need $\lambda = M \cdot \log_2(N(C-1))$ instead of $\lambda = M \cdot \log_2 C$ to achieve λ bit security. The new signature consists of a puncturable key and the round number of offset maps along with the challenge. The size (in terms of bit) of the signature is evaluated as follows:

$$3\lambda + M \cdot \lambda \cdot \log_2 N + M \cdot [\text{the bitsize of group elements}].$$

Of course it's possible to extend the $N(C-1)$ to $N(C-1)+1$ options. The extra option is actually revealing the unpuncturable key without revealing the offset map. Thus in this case, unbalanced challenge space is applied. We need $\lambda = \log_2(\binom{M}{K}(N(C-1))^K)$ to achieve λ bit security. By applying the unbalanced challenge, the size (in terms of bit) of the signature is evaluated as follows:

$$3\lambda + \lambda \cdot (M-K) + K \cdot [\text{the bitsize of group elements}].$$

Table 4. Parameters of 128-bit security from [14].

Parameters					Size in Bytes	
n	q	C	M	K	Public key	Signature
13	$2^{32} - 5$	7	84	22	8024	15896
		458	16	14	523968	9528

Table 5. Parameters of 128-bit security using the MPC-in-the-head paradigm with $N = 10$.

Parameters					Size in Bytes	
n	q	C	M	K	pubkey size	sig size
13	$2^{32} - 5$	7	94	13	8024	10132
		458	13	10	523968	6856

New Parameter Set Based on MPC-in-the-Head. For the optimisation by MPC-in-the-head, we consider the security level 128-bit as shown in Table 5. Here we set the N to be 10. Compared with the data in Table 4 as used in the current ALTEQ specification [14], we can see that the signature sizes in Table 5 are between 64% to 72% of the sizes in Table 4.

Acknowledgement. We thank the anonymous reviewers for their careful reading and helpful suggestions. Antoine Joux was partly supported by the European Union's H2020 Programme under grant agreement number ERC-669891. Youming Qiao was partly supported by ARC DP200100950 and LP220100332. Gang Tang was partly supported by ARC LP220100332, Sydney Quantum Academy, and EPSRC grant EP/V011324/1.

References

1. Abdalla, M., Fouque, P.-A., Lyubashevsky, V., Tibouchi, M.: Tightly-secure signatures from lossy identification schemes. In: Pointcheval, D., Johansson, T. (eds.) EUROCRYPT 2012. LNCS, vol. 7237, pp. 572–590. Springer, Heidelberg (2012). https://doi.org/10.1007/978-3-642-29011-4_34

2. Alamati, N., De Feo, L., Montgomery, H., Patranabis, S.: Cryptographic group actions and applications. In: Moriai, S., Wang, H. (eds.) ASIACRYPT 2020. LNCS, vol. 12492, pp. 411–439. Springer, Cham (2020). https://doi.org/10.1007/978-3-030-64834-3_14

3. Babai, L.: Graph isomorphism in quasipolynomial time [extended abstract]. In: Proceedings of the 48th Annual ACM SIGACT Symposium on Theory of Computing, STOC 2016, Cambridge, MA, USA, 18–21 June 2016, pp. 684–697 (2016)

4. Barenghi, A., Biasse, J.F., Ngo, T., Persichetti, E., Santini, P.: Advanced signature functionalities from the code equivalence problem. Int. J. Comput. Math. Comput. Syst. Theory 7(2), 112–128 (2022)

5. Barenghi, A., Biasse, J.-F., Persichetti, E., Santini, P.: LESS-FM: fine-tuning signatures from the code equivalence problem. In: Cheon, J.H., Tillich, J.-P. (eds.) PQCrypto 2021 2021. LNCS, vol. 12841, pp. 23–43. Springer, Cham (2021). https://doi.org/10.1007/978-3-030-81293-5_2

6. Bellare, M., Rogaway, P.: Random oracles are practical: a paradigm for designing efficient protocols. In: Proceedings of the 1st ACM Conference on Computer and Communications Security, pp. 62–73 (1993)

7. Bellini, E., Esser, A., Sanna, C., Verbel, J.: MR-DSS-smaller minrank-based (ring-) signatures. In: Cheon, J.H., Johansson, T. (eds.) PQCrypto 2022. LNCS, vol. 13512, pp. 144–169. Springer, Heidelberg (2022). https://doi.org/10.1007/978-3-031-17234-2_8

8. Beullens, W.: Graph-theoretic algorithms for the alternating trilinear form equivalence problem. In: Handschuh, H., Lysyanskaya, A. (eds.) CRYPTO 2023. LNCS, vol. 14083, pp. 101–126. Springer, Heidelberg (2023). https://doi.org/10.1007/978-3-031-38548-3_4

9. Beullens, W., Feo, L.D., Galbraith, S.D., Petit, C.: Proving knowledge of isogenies – a survey. Cryptology ePrint Archive, Paper 2023/671 (2023). https://eprint.iacr.org/2023/671

10. Beullens, W., Katsumata, S., Pintore, F.: Calamari and Falafl: logarithmic (linkable) ring signatures from isogenies and lattices. In: Moriai, S., Wang, H. (eds.) ASIACRYPT 2020. LNCS, vol. 12492, pp. 464–492. Springer, Cham (2020). https://doi.org/10.1007/978-3-030-64834-3_16

11. Beullens, W., Kleinjung, T., Vercauteren, F.: CSI-FiSh: efficient isogeny based signatures through class group computations. In: Galbraith, S.D., Moriai, S. (eds.) ASIACRYPT 2019. LNCS, vol. 11921, pp. 227–247. Springer, Cham (2019). https://doi.org/10.1007/978-3-030-34578-5_9

12. Biasse, J.-F., Micheli, G., Persichetti, E., Santini, P.: LESS is more: code-based signatures without syndromes. In: Nitaj, A., Youssef, A. (eds.) AFRICACRYPT 2020. LNCS, vol. 12174, pp. 45–65. Springer, Cham (2020). https://doi.org/10.1007/978-3-030-51938-4_3

13. Bläser, M., et al.: On digital signatures based on isomorphism problems: qrom security and ring signatures. Cryptology ePrint Archive, Paper 2022/1184 (2022). https://eprint.iacr.org/2022/1184

14. Bläser, M., et al.: The alteq signature scheme: algorithm specifications and supporting documentation (2023). https://pqcalteq.github.io/ALTEQ_spec_2023.09.18.pdf

15. Boneh, D.: The decision Diffie-Hellman problem. In: Algorithmic Number Theory, Third International Symposium, ANTS-III, Portland, Oregon, USA, 21–25 June 1998, Proceedings, pp. 48–63 (1998). https://doi.org/10.1007/BFb0054851

16. Boneh, D., Dagdelen, Ö., Fischlin, M., Lehmann, A., Schaffner, C., Zhandry, M.: Random oracles in a quantum world. In: Lee, D.H., Wang, X. (eds.) ASIACRYPT 2011. LNCS, vol. 7073, pp. 41–69. Springer, Heidelberg (2011). https://doi.org/10.1007/978-3-642-25385-0_3

17. Bonnetain, X., Schrottenloher, A.: Quantum security analysis of CSIDH. In: Canteaut, A., Ishai, Y. (eds.) EUROCRYPT 2020. LNCS, vol. 12106, pp. 493–522. Springer, Cham (2020). https://doi.org/10.1007/978-3-030-45724-2_17

18. Bosma, W., Cannon, J., Playoust, C.: The Magma algebra system. I. The user language. J. Symb. Comput. **24**(3-4), 235–265 (1997). https://doi.org/10.1006/jsco.1996.0125

19. Bouillaguet, C.: Etudes d'hypotheses algorithmiques et attaques de primitives cryptographiques. Ph.D. thesis, PhD thesis, Université Paris-Diderot–École Normale Supérieure (2011)

20. Bouillaguet, C., Faugère, J.-C., Fouque, P.-A., Perret, L.: Practical cryptanalysis of the identification scheme based on the isomorphism of polynomial with one secret problem. In: Catalano, D., Fazio, N., Gennaro, R., Nicolosi, A. (eds.) PKC 2011. LNCS, vol. 6571, pp. 473–493. Springer, Heidelberg (2011). https://doi.org/10.1007/978-3-642-19379-8_29

21. Bouillaguet, C., Fouque, P.-A., Véber, A.: Graph-theoretic algorithms for the "Isomorphism of Polynomials" problem. In: Johansson, T., Nguyen, P.Q. (eds.) EUROCRYPT 2013. LNCS, vol. 7881, pp. 211–227. Springer, Heidelberg (2013). https://doi.org/10.1007/978-3-642-38348-9_13

22. Brassard, G., Yung, M.: One-way group actions. In: Menezes, A.J., Vanstone, S.A. (eds.) CRYPTO 1990. LNCS, vol. 537, pp. 94–107. Springer, Heidelberg (1991). https://doi.org/10.1007/3-540-38424-3_7

23. Brooksbank, P.A., Li, Y., Qiao, Y., Wilson, J.B.: Improved algorithms for alternating matrix space isometry: From theory to practice. In: Grandoni, F., Herman, G., Sanders, P. (eds.) 28th Annual European Symposium on Algorithms, ESA 2020, Pisa, Italy (Virtual Conference), 7–9 September 2020. LIPIcs, vol. 173, pp. 26:1–26:15. Schloss Dagstuhl - Leibniz-Zentrum für Informatik (2020). https://doi.org/10.4230/LIPICS.ESA.2020.26

24. Budroni, A., Chi-Domínguez, J.J., D'Alconzo, G., Di Scala, A.J., Kulkarni, M.: Don't use it twice! solving relaxed linear code equivalence problems. Cryptology ePrint Archive, paper 2024/244 (2024)

25. Carozza, E., Couteau, G., Joux, A.: Short signatures from regular syndrome decoding in the head. In: Hazay, C., Stam, M. (eds.) EUROCRYPT 2023. LNCS, vol. 14008, pp. 532–563. Springer, Heidelberg (2023). https://doi.org/10.1007/978-3-031-30589-4_19

26. Castryck, W., Lange, T., Martindale, C., Panny, L., Renes, J.: CSIDH: an efficient post-quantum commutative group action. In: Peyrin, T., Galbraith, S. (eds.) ASIACRYPT 2018. LNCS, vol. 11274, pp. 395–427. Springer, Cham (2018). https://doi.org/10.1007/978-3-030-03332-3_15

27. Childs, A., Jao, D., Soukharev, V.: Constructing elliptic curve isogenies in quantum subexponential time. J. Math. Crypt. **8**(1), 1–29 (2014)

28. Chou, T., et al.: Take your meds: digital signatures from matrix code equivalence. In: El Mrabet, N., De Feo, L., Duquesne, S. (eds.) Progress in Cryptology - AFRICACRYPT 2023, vol. 14064, pp. 28–52. Springer, Heidelberg (2023). https:// doi.org/10.1007/978-3-031-37679-5_2

29. Cohen, A.M., Helminck, A.G.: Trilinear alternating forms on a vector space of dimension 7. Commun. Algebra **16**(1), 1–25 (1988)

30. Couveignes, J.M.: Hard homogeneous spaces. IACR Cryptology ePrint Archive (2006). http://eprint.iacr.org/2006/291

31. Couvreur, A., Debris-Alazard, T., Gaborit, P.: On the hardness of code equivalence problems in rank metric. arXiv preprint arXiv:2011.04611 (2020)

32. D'Alconzo, G., Gangemi, A.: Trifors: linkable trilinear forms ring signature. Cryptology ePrint Archive (2022)

33. Diffie, W., Hellman, M.: New directions in cryptography. IEEE Trans. Inf. Theory **22**(6), 644–654 (1976)

34. Don, J., Fehr, S., Majenz, C., Schaffner, C.: Security of the Fiat-Shamir transformation in the quantum random-oracle model. In: Boldyreva, A., Micciancio, D. (eds.) CRYPTO 2019. LNCS, vol. 11693, pp. 356–383. Springer, Cham (2019). https://doi.org/10.1007/978-3-030-26951-7_13

35. Ducas, L., van Woerden, W.: On the lattice isomorphism problem, quadratic forms, remarkable lattices, and cryptography. In: Dunkelman, O., Dziembowski, S. (eds.) EUROCRYPT 2022. LNCS, vol. 13277, pp. 643–673. Springer, Heidelberg (2022). https://doi.org/10.1007/978-3-031-07082-2_23

36. El Kaafarani, A., Katsumata, S., Pintore, F.: Lossy CSI-FiSh: efficient signature scheme with tight reduction to decisional CSIDH-512. In: Kiayias, A., Kohlweiss, M., Wallden, P., Zikas, V. (eds.) PKC 2020. LNCS, vol. 12111, pp. 157–186. Springer, Cham (2020). https://doi.org/10.1007/978-3-030-45388-6_6

37. Esgin, M.F., Steinfeld, R., Zhao, R.K.: Matrict+: more efficient post-quantum private blockchain payments. In: 2022 IEEE Symposium on Security and Privacy (SP), pp. 1281–1298. IEEE (2022)

38. Esgin, M.F., Zhao, R.K., Steinfeld, R., Liu, J.K., Liu, D.: Matrict: efficient, scalable and post-quantum blockchain confidential transactions protocol. In: Proceedings of the 2019 ACM SIGSAC Conference on Computer and Communications Security, pp. 567–584 (2019)

39. Farhi, E., Gosset, D., Hassidim, A., Lutomirski, A., Shor, P.: Quantum money from knots. In: Proceedings of the 3rd Innovations in Theoretical Computer Science Conference, pp. 276–289 (2012)

40. Faugère, J.-C., Perret, L.: Polynomial equivalence problems: algorithmic and theoretical aspects. In: Vaudenay, S. (ed.) EUROCRYPT 2006. LNCS, vol. 4004, pp. 30–47. Springer, Heidelberg (2006). https://doi.org/10.1007/11761679_3

41. De Feo, L., Galbraith, S.D.: SeaSign: compact isogeny signatures from class group actions. In: Ishai, Y., Rijmen, V. (eds.) EUROCRYPT 2019. LNCS, vol. 11478, pp. 759–789. Springer, Cham (2019). https://doi.org/10.1007/978-3-030-17659-4_26

42. Fiat, A., Shamir, A.: How to prove yourself: practical solutions to identification and signature problems. In: Odlyzko, A.M. (ed.) CRYPTO 1986. LNCS, vol. 263, pp. 186–194. Springer, Heidelberg (1987). https://doi.org/10.1007/3-540-47721-7_12

43. Goldreich, O., Micali, S., Wigderson, A.: Proofs that yield nothing but their validity for all languages in NP have zero-knowledge proof systems. J. ACM **38**(3), 691–729 (1991). https://doi.org/10.1145/116825.116852

44. Grochow, J.A., Qiao, Y.: On p-group isomorphism: search-to-decision, counting-to-decision, and nilpotency class reductions via tensors. In: 36th Computational

Complexity Conference, LIPIcs. Leibniz International Proceedings on Information, vol. 200, pp. 16–38. Schloss Dagstuhl. Leibniz-Zent. Inform., Wadern (2021). https://doi.org/10.4230/LIPIcs.CCC.2021.16

45. Grochow, J.A., Qiao, Y.: On the complexity of isomorphism problems for tensors, groups, and polynomials I: tensor isomorphism-completeness. In: Lee, J.R. (ed.) 12th Innovations in Theoretical Computer Science Conference, ITCS 2021, January 6-8, 2021, Virtual Conference. LIPIcs, vol. 185, pp. 31:1–31:19. Schloss Dagstuhl - Leibniz-Zentrum für Informatik (2021). https://doi.org/10.4230/LIPIcs.ITCS.2021.31

46. Grochow, J.A., Qiao, Y., Tang, G.: Average-case algorithms for testing isomorphism of polynomials, algebras, and multilinear forms. In: Bläser, M., Monmege, B. (eds.) 38th International Symposium on Theoretical Aspects of Computer Science, STACS 2021, March 16-19, 2021, Saarbrücken, Germany (Virtual Conference). LIPIcs, vol. 187, pp. 38:1–38:17. Schloss Dagstuhl - Leibniz-Zentrum für Informatik (2021)

47. Hallgren, S., Moore, C., Rötteler, M., Russell, A., Sen, P.: Limitations of quantum coset states for graph isomorphism. J. ACM **57**(6), 34:1–34:33 (2010). https://doi.org/10.1145/1857914.1857918

48. Hora, J., Pudlák, P.: Classification of 8-dimensional trilinear alternating forms over gf (2). Commun. Algebra **43**(8), 3459–3471 (2015)

49. Hora, J., Pudlák, P.: Classification of 9-dimensional trilinear alternating forms over gf (2). Finite Fields Appl. **70**, 101788 (2021)

50. Ishai, Y., Kushilevitz, E., Ostrovsky, R., Sahai, A.: Zero-knowledge from secure multiparty computation. In: STOC 2007—Proceedings of the 39th Annual ACM Symposium on Theory of Computing, pp. 21–30. ACM, New York (2007). https://doi.org/10.1145/1250790.1250794

51. Ji, Z., Qiao, Y., Song, F., Yun, A.: General linear group action on tensors: a candidate for post-quantum cryptography. In: Hofheinz, D., Rosen, A. (eds.) TCC 2019. LNCS, vol. 11891, pp. 251–281. Springer, Cham (2019). https://doi.org/10.1007/978-3-030-36030-6_11

52. Joux, A.: Mpc in the head for isomorphisms and group actions. Cryptology ePrint Archive, Paper 2023/664 (2023). https://eprint.iacr.org/2023/664

53. Kiltz, E., Lyubashevsky, V., Schaffner, C.: A concrete treatment of fiat-shamir signatures in the quantum random-oracle model. In: Nielsen, J.B., Rijmen, V. (eds.) EUROCRYPT 2018. LNCS, vol. 10822, pp. 552–586. Springer, Cham (2018). https://doi.org/10.1007/978-3-319-78372-7_18

54. Köbler, J., Schöning, U., Torán, J.: The Graph Isomorphism Problem. Basel Birkhüser (1993)

55. Liu, J.K., Wong, D.S.: Linkable ring signatures: security models and new schemes. In: Gervasi, O., Gavrilova, M.L., Kumar, V., Laganà, A., Lee, H.P., Mun, Y., Taniar, D., Tan, C.J.K. (eds.) ICCSA 2005. LNCS, vol. 3481, pp. 614–623. Springer, Heidelberg (2005). https://doi.org/10.1007/11424826_65

56. Liu, Q., Zhandry, M.: Revisiting post-quantum Fiat-Shamir. In: Boldyreva, A., Micciancio, D. (eds.) CRYPTO 2019. LNCS, vol. 11693, pp. 326–355. Springer, Cham (2019). https://doi.org/10.1007/978-3-030-26951-7_12

57. Lu, X., Au, M.H., Zhang, Z.: Raptor: a practical lattice-based (linkable) ring signature. In: Deng, R.H., Gauthier-Umaña, V., Ochoa, M., Yung, M. (eds.) ACNS 2019. LNCS, vol. 11464, pp. 110–130. Springer, Cham (2019). https://doi.org/10.1007/978-3-030-21568-2_6

58. Lyubashevsky, V., Nguyen, N.K., Seiler, G.: SMILE: set membership from ideal lattices with applications to ring signatures and confidential transactions. In: Malkin, T., Peikert, C. (eds.) CRYPTO 2021. LNCS, vol. 12826, pp. 611–640. Springer, Cham (2021). https://doi.org/10.1007/978-3-030-84245-1_21
59. McKay, B.D.: Practical graph isomorphism. Congr. Numer. pp. 45–87 (1980)
60. McKay, B.D., Piperno, A.: Practical graph isomorphism, II. J. Symb. Comput. **60**, 94–112 (2014)
61. Midoune, N., Noui, L.: Trilinear alternating forms on a vector space of dimension 8 over a finite field. Linear and Multilinear Algebra **61**(1), 15–21 (2013)
62. Patarin, J.: Hidden fields equations (HFE) and isomorphisms of polynomials (IP): two new families of asymmetric algorithms. In: Maurer, U. (ed.) EUROCRYPT 1996. LNCS, vol. 1070, pp. 33–48. Springer, Heidelberg (1996). https://doi.org/10.1007/3-540-68339-9_4
63. Peikert, C.: He gives C-sieves on the CSIDH. In: Canteaut, A., Ishai, Y. (eds.) EUROCRYPT 2020. LNCS, vol. 12106, pp. 463–492. Springer, Cham (2020). https://doi.org/10.1007/978-3-030-45724-2_16
64. Pointcheval, D., Stern, J.: Security arguments for digital signatures and blind signatures. J. Cryptol. **13**(3), 361–396 (2000)
65. Ran, L., Samardjiska, S., Trimoska, M.: Algebraic attack on the alternating trilinear form equivalence problem. In: Presented at CBCrypto 2023 (2023)
66. Regev, O.: Quantum computation and lattice problems. SIAM J. Comput. **33**(3), 738–760 (2004). https://doi.org/10.1137/S0097539703440678
67. Reijnders, K., Samardjiska, S., Trimoska, M.: Hardness estimates of the code equivalence problem in the rank metric. Des. Codes Cryptogr. 1–30 (2024)
68. Rivest, R.L., Shamir, A., Tauman, Y.: How to leak a secret. In: Boyd, C. (ed.) ASIACRYPT 2001. LNCS, vol. 2248, pp. 552–565. Springer, Heidelberg (2001). https://doi.org/10.1007/3-540-45682-1_32
69. Shor, P.W.: Polynomial-time algorithms for prime factorization and discrete logarithms on a quantum computer. SIAM J. Comput. **26**(5), 1484–1509 (1997). https://doi.org/10.1137/S0097539795293172
70. of Standards, N.I., Technology: Call for additional digital signature schemes for the post-quantum cryptography standardization process (2022). https://csrc.nist.gov/csrc/media/Projects/pqc-dig-sig/documents/call-for-proposals-dig-sig-sept-2022.pdf
71. Stolbunov, A.: Cryptographic schemes based on isogenies. Ph.D. thesis, Norwegian University of Science and Technology (2012)
72. Sun, S.-F., Au, M.H., Liu, J.K., Yuen, T.H.: RingCT 2.0: a compact accumulator-based (linkable ring signature) protocol for blockchain cryptocurrency monero. In: Foley, S.N., Gollmann, D., Snekkenes, E. (eds.) ESORICS 2017. LNCS, vol. 10493, pp. 456–474. Springer, Cham (2017). https://doi.org/10.1007/978-3-319-66399-9_25
73. Tang, G., Duong, D.H., Joux, A., Plantard, T., Qiao, Y., Susilo, W.: Practical post-quantum signature schemes from isomorphism problems of trilinear forms. In: Dunkelman, O., Dziembowski, S. (eds.) EUROCRYPT 2022. LNCS, vol. 13277, pp. 582–612. Springer, Heidelberg (2022). https://doi.org/10.1007/978-3-031-07082-2_21
74. Tsang, P.P., Wei, V.K.: Short linkable ring signatures for E-Voting, E-Cash and attestation. In: Deng, R.H., Bao, F., Pang, H.H., Zhou, J. (eds.) ISPEC 2005. LNCS, vol. 3439, pp. 48–60. Springer, Heidelberg (2005). https://doi.org/10.1007/978-3-540-31979-5_5

75. Unruh, D.: Quantum proofs of knowledge. In: Pointcheval, D., Johansson, T. (eds.) EUROCRYPT 2012. LNCS, vol. 7237, pp. 135–152. Springer, Heidelberg (2012). https://doi.org/10.1007/978-3-642-29011-4_10

76. Unruh, D.: Computationally binding quantum commitments. In: Fischlin, M., Coron, J.-S. (eds.) EUROCRYPT 2016. LNCS, vol. 9666, pp. 497–527. Springer, Heidelberg (2016). https://doi.org/10.1007/978-3-662-49896-5_18

77. Unruh, D.: Post-quantum security of fiat-shamir. In: Takagi, T., Peyrin, T. (eds.) ASIACRYPT 2017. LNCS, vol. 10624, pp. 65–95. Springer, Cham (2017). https://doi.org/10.1007/978-3-319-70694-8_3

78. Yamakawa, T., Zhandry, M.: Classical vs quantum random oracles. In: Canteaut, A., Standaert, F.-X. (eds.) EUROCRYPT 2021. LNCS, vol. 12697, pp. 568–597. Springer, Cham (2021). https://doi.org/10.1007/978-3-030-77886-6_20

79. Yuen, T.H., Esgin, M.F., Liu, J.K., Au, M.H., Ding, Z.: *DualRing*: generic construction of ring signatures with efficient instantiations. In: Malkin, T., Peikert, C. (eds.) CRYPTO 2021. LNCS, vol. 12825, pp. 251–281. Springer, Cham (2021). https://doi.org/10.1007/978-3-030-84242-0_10

Lattice-Based Cryptography

Phoenix: Hash-and-Sign with Aborts
from Lattice Gadgets

Corentin Jeudy[1,2]([✉])[iD], Adeline Roux-Langlois[3][iD], and Olivier Sanders[1][iD]

[1] Orange Labs, Applied Crypto Group, Cesson-Sévigné, France
{corentin.jeudy,olivier.sanders}@orange.com
[2] University of Rennes, CNRS, IRISA, Rennes, France
[3] Normandie University, UNICAEN, ENSICAEN, CNRS, GREYC,
14000 Caen, France
adeline.roux-langlois@cnrs.fr

Abstract. Preimage sampling is a fundamental tool in lattice-based cryptography, and its performance directly impacts that of the cryptographic mechanisms relying on it. In 2012, Micciancio and Peikert proposed a new way of generating trapdoors (and an associated preimage sampling procedure) with very interesting features. Unfortunately, in some applications such as digital signatures, the performance may not be as competitive as other approaches like Fiat-Shamir with Aborts. In an effort to improve preimage sampling for Micciancio-Peikert (MP) trapdoors, Lyubashevsky and Wichs (LW) introduced a new sampler which leverages rejection sampling but suffers from strong parameter requirements that hampered performance. As a consequence it seemed to be restricted to theoretical applications and has not been, to our knowledge, considered for real-world applications.

Our first contribution is to revisit the LW sampler by proposing an improved analysis which yields much more compact parameters. This leads to gains on the preimage size of about 60% over the LW sampler, and up to 25% compared to the original MP sampling technique. It thus sheds a new light on the LW sampler, opening promising perspectives for the efficiency of advanced lattice-based constructions relying on such mechanisms. To provide further improvements, we show that it perfectly combines with the approximate trapdoors approach by Chen, Genise and Mukherjee, but with a smaller preimage error.

Building upon those results, we introduce a hash-and-sign signature scheme called Phoenix. The scheme is based on the M-LWE and M-SIS assumptions and features attractive public key and signature sizes which are even smaller than those of the most recent gadget-based construction EAGLE of Yu, Jia and Wang (Crypto'23). Moreover, Phoenix is designed to support a broad variety of distributions (uniform, spherical Gaussian, etc.) which can facilitate implementation, in particular in constrained environments.

Keywords: Lattice-Based Cryptography · Trapdoors · Preimage Sampling · Signature

M.-J. Saarinen and D. Smith-Tone (Eds.): PQCrypto 2024, LNCS 14771, pp. 265–299, 2024.
https://doi.org/10.1007/978-3-031-62743-9_9

1   Introduction

Lattice-based cryptography has proven to be a relatively stable and extensively studied candidate to provide post-quantum secure primitives, and has now shifted towards proposing concretely efficient constructions. The NIST standardization [38] perfectly reflects this trend as they recently released the first round of standards, which is dominated by lattice-based constructions [9,17,46], and are moving to practical deployment discussions. Although they provide a first set of solutions for initiating the post-quantum transition, NIST recently called for additional digital signatures [39]. The lattice-based candidates to this new competition, along with some recent publications, e.g., [48], show that there is still room for improvement in this area in terms of optimizing bandwidth, ease of implementation, side-channel protection, etc.

If we set aside schemes designed with very specific applications in mind, e.g., [7,26,32], lattice-based signature schemes usually follow one of two main paradigms. The first one, called the *hash-and-sign* paradigm, was instantiated by Gentry, Peikert and Vaikuntanathan [24] (later abbreviated GPV) with lattice preimage sampleable trapdoor functions. In such schemes, the signing key consists of a trapdoor for a publicly computable function which allows one to efficiently find short preimages. Signatures are then preimages of seemingly random (and possibly message-dependent) syndromes. Only the signer is able to compute such preimages, but everyone is able to compute the image to ensure they represent valid signatures. Several schemes rely on variants of the above, e.g., [18,19,24,35], and were successfully pushed towards concrete practicality [20,46,48] using an additional assumption. Trapdoor preimage sampleable functions also represent the most widely used building block in the design of more advanced forms of signatures such as group signatures [33,44], blind signatures [1,7,43], signatures with efficient protocols [26,30], etc. In their general use, trapdoor preimage sampling can however be quite computationally intensive, and most solutions are designed to only support Gaussian-distributed preimages.

An alternative, called the *Fiat-Shamir with Aborts* (FSwA) paradigm, was proposed by Lyubashevsky [31], building signatures on Schnorr-like proofs made non-interactive with the Fiat-Shamir transform. This framework avoids the use of trapdoors, and uses rejection sampling to control the distribution of signatures while making them independent of the signing key. Even though most applications yield Gaussian-distributed signatures, it is possible to tweak the rejection sampling step to get other distributions that can be more suitable depending on the context. Efficient instantiations of this signature paradigm were proposed, such as qTESLA [3] and Dilithium [17].

Interestingly, in [34], Lyubashevsky and Wichs show that these two approaches may be combined in the case of Micciancio-Peikert trapdoors [35].

1.1   Micciancio-Peikert Sampler

In [35], Micciancio and Peikert propose a preimage sampling algorithm (later called MP sampler) for matrices $\mathbf{A_H} = [\mathbf{A}|\mathbf{HG} - \mathbf{AR}]$, where $\mathbf{R}$ constitutes the trapdoor. More precisely, $\mathbf{A}$ is a uniform matrix in $R_q^{d \times 2d}$, $\mathbf{H}$ is a tag matrix in $GL_d(R_q)$, $\mathbf{G} \in R^{d \times kd}$ (with $k = \log_b q$) is the base-b gadget matrix, and $\mathbf{R}$ is a short matrix over the ring R, e.g., power-of-two cyclotomic ring. Their algorithm uses the knowledge of $\mathbf{R}$ to sample $\mathbf{v} \in R^{(2+k)d}$ according to a spherical discrete Gaussian of parameter s such that $\mathbf{A_H v} = \mathbf{u} \bmod q$ for an input syndrome $\mathbf{u}$. The technique first relies on the observation that if $\mathbf{z}$ is a Gaussian with width $s_\mathbf{G}$ such that $\mathbf{HGz} = \mathbf{u}$, then the vector $\mathbf{v}' = [(\mathbf{Rz})^T | \mathbf{z}^T]^T$ is a valid candidate. This naive approach leaks information on the trapdoor $\mathbf{R}$, which is why the authors perturb this solution $\mathbf{v}'$ into $\mathbf{v} = \mathbf{p} + \mathbf{v}'$, for some suitable perturbation vector $\mathbf{p}$, while adjusting $\mathbf{z}$ to verify $\mathbf{HGz} = \mathbf{u} - \mathbf{A_H p}$. By carefully choosing the covariance of the Gaussian $\mathbf{p}$, one can indeed ensure that $\mathbf{v}$ follows a spherical Gaussian distribution of width s, which in turn does not leak information on the trapdoor.

Although the approach above perfectly fulfils the security expectations of preimage sampling, it remains unsatisfactory in a number of aspects. First, the information on $\mathbf{R}$ in $\mathbf{v}' = [(\mathbf{Rz})^T | \mathbf{z}^T]^T$ that needs to be hidden only affects the first component. One would expect to only have to perturb the first part to ensure security. Additionally, the sampler is quite rigid as it requires sampling perturbations $\mathbf{p}$ from highly non-spherical Gaussian, and is limited to Gaussian preimages.

1.2 Lyubashevsky-Wichs Sampler

To address these problems, Lyubashevsky and Wichs [34] break the symmetry between $\mathbf{v}_1 = \mathbf{p}_1 + \mathbf{Rz}$ and $\mathbf{v}_2 = \mathbf{p}_2 + \mathbf{z}$ by setting $\mathbf{p} = [\mathbf{p}_1^T | \mathbf{0}]^T$ and $\mathbf{z} = \mathbf{G}^{-1}(\mathbf{u} - \mathbf{Ap}_1)$ where $\mathbf{G}^{-1}(\cdot)$ is the base-b decomposition. Directly outputting $\mathbf{v}_1 = \mathbf{p}_1 + \mathbf{Rz}$ and $\mathbf{v}_2 = \mathbf{z}$ again leaks information on $\mathbf{R}$ because of $\mathbf{v}_1$ and they thus need to adjust this approach. By identifying $\mathbf{Ap}_1$, $\mathbf{z}$ and $\mathbf{v}_1$ with (respectively) the commitment, the challenge and the response of a zero-knowledge proof of knowledge of $\mathbf{R}$, this problem is very similar to the one of Fiat-Shamir signatures in [31]. They then resort to the same workaround, namely rejection sampling: before outputting $\mathbf{v}_1 = \mathbf{p}_1 + \mathbf{Rz}$ and $\mathbf{v}_2 = \mathbf{z}$, one performs rejection sampling on $\mathbf{v}_1$ to make its distribution independent of $\mathbf{R}$ and $\mathbf{z}$. We later refer to this sampling method as the LW sampler.

However, to thoroughly show that the preimages do not leak information on $\mathbf{R}$, they provide a simulation result which suffers from parameter constraints that make it less efficient than the MP sampler in terms of preimage size. More concretely, they show that the output distribution of the preimages is statistically close to a distribution that does not depend on the trapdoor $\mathbf{R}$ for an arbitrary (potentially adversarial) syndrome $\mathbf{u}$. Because they deal with an arbitrary $\mathbf{u}$, nothing can be assumed about its distribution which in turn places strong restrictions on the parameters to compensate. Indeed, in their result, they need to assume that $\mathbf{Av}_1$ (and $\mathbf{Ap}_1$) is *statistically* close to uniform requiring the parameters to be large enough to use a regularity lemma. This requirement in turn prevents them from using a computational instantiation of MP trapdoors. Since computational MP trapdoors lead to much smaller preimages, they are usually more compact than the ones generated by the LW sampler. Concretely, the size of a GPV signature [24] with the LW sampler are about $80 - 90\%$ larger than the ones using the MP sampler, as described in Sect. 4. This looks like a paradox as one would intuitively expect the method from [34] to combine the best of trapdoor-based signatures and Fiat-Shamir with aborts signatures.

1.3 Our Contributions

The goal of our paper is to revisit the LW approach [34] so as to achieve its full potential. Our first result is a reassessment of the original security analysis showing that we can significantly alleviate the requirements identified in [34], at least in the most common applications of preimage sampling. It entails important gains in performance of around 60%, resulting in shorter preimages than the one obtained with the original MP method [35] by 25%, thus solving the apparent paradox mentioned above.

In a second step, we leverage the works on approximate trapdoors initiated by Chen, Genise and Mukherjee [11] to further reduce the size of the preimages. Our approach allows to reduce the sampling error, thus yielding either higher security guarantees or better compactness.

Finally, we illustrate the potential of the sampler by designing a hash-and-sign signature scheme, which we call Phoenix. The latter showcases interesting features including small keys and signatures, but also an implementation-friendly design that in particular supports a variety of signature distributions.

We now give more details on these contributions. For the sake of genericity, the contributions in this paper are described over structured lattices but we note that they also apply to standard ones.

Contribution 1: Re-Assessing the Lyubashevsky-Wichs Sampler. Our first contribution is a more specific analysis of the LW sampler to get rid of the restrictive requirements mentioned above and thus obtain more compact preimages. Intuitively, our new analysis stems from the observation that the initial assumption of [34], namely the fact that the syndrome can be fully controlled by the adversary, is too strong in general. Indeed, in many common situations, the syndrome follows a prescribed distribution, which can be leveraged to simulate preimages in the proof.

For GPV signatures [24] for example, the syndrome $\mathbf{u}$ is the hash output of the message $\mathcal{H}(\mathbf{m})$ where $\mathcal{H}$ is modelled as a random oracle. This means that the syndromes we expect are uniformly distributed and cannot be controlled by the adversary. This allows us to remove this constraint on $\mathbf{Av}_1$ being statistically close to uniform, as we can, at a high level, use the randomness of $\mathbf{u}$ to achieve the same conclusion. As we show in our paper, removing this constraint removes the need for a large perturbation (either in norm or dimension) and thus leads to improved performances. In the meantime, our result avoids placing restrictions on the underlying algebraic ring R nor the working modulus q, making it suitable for a larger variety of settings and applications.

Compared to the original Micciancio-Peikert sampler, the size of v_1 increases, but v_2 is now in base b which is much smaller (even minimal when $b = 2$ for example). Concretely, the total bit-size of v for a GPV signature built upon our improved simulation result is reduced by respectively 60% compared to the original[1] LW sampler, and by 25% compared to the MP sampling method. The estimates are detailed in Tables 2, 3 and 4. Along with these estimates, we also analyze the impact of the gadget base b. We show that the intuition of increasing b to reduce the signature size, that was true for the MP sampler (as well as the original LW sampler), should be re-assessed when the sampler changes. More precisely, we explain why the MP sampler and the previous version of the LW sampler perform better with higher bases, and why our new analysis and parameter constraints show that the base leading to the smallest signatures is $b = 2$.

Contribution 2: Leveraging Approximate Trapdoors. At this stage, we have shown that the revisited LW sampler can outperform the MP one but the resulting signature size is still far from competitive compared to, e.g., the future NIST standard Dilithium [17]. To fully reinstate LW samplers, we thus need to find other means of reducing this size.

As the LW approach inherently leads to signatures where most elements are very small (since $\|v_2\|_\infty < b$), the remaining target to improve performance is essentially the dimension of those signatures. Thanks to our new analysis above, we have already managed to reduce the one of $\mathbf{A}$, and hence of v_1. When it comes to v_2, the situation is more complex as the dimension seems to be dictated by the one of the gadget matrix $\mathbf{G}$. Fortunately, a study initiated by Chen, Genise and Mukherjee [11] improved the performance of gadget-based constructions through the notion of approximate trapdoors. The idea is to drop the low-order gadget entries and only consider a partial gadget $\mathbf{G}_H = \mathbf{I}_d \otimes \mathbf{g}_H^T$ with $\mathbf{g}_H = [b^\ell | \ldots | b^{k-1}]^T$. It not only reduces the dimension of v_2 (and hence the number of elements in the signature), but it also reduces the public and secret key sizes. Additionally, having a secret key $\mathbf{R}$ with fewer columns allows us to reduce $\|\mathbf{Rz}\|_2$ which defines the quality of our sampler, thus reducing the size of v_1 as well.

The removed low-order entries however introduce an error on the preimage which must be taken into account in the security assessment. Intuitively, the more entries are dropped, the larger the error, and in turn the less secure it gets. Reducing the error is thus critical as it leads to better security, or enables to drop more entries to further improve performance. In this regard, we note that our revisited LW sampler lends itself well to approximate trapdoors since v_2 is binary and not gaussian. This leads to a sampling error that is smaller than the one from [11] and (almost) as small as that of the recent gadget construction of Yu, Jia and Wang [48].

Contribution 3: Phoenix, a New Hash-and-Sign Scheme. Plugging the previous contributions in the GPV framework leads to a new hash-and-sign

---

[1] By "original", we mean the LW sampler with the parameters resulting from the original analysis in [34].

signature scheme, which we call Phoenix, which allows to assess the benefits of the LW sampler for concrete applications. The performances of Phoenix are summarized in Table 1.

One of the most surprising features of Phoenix is arguably its relatively small signatures sizes |sig|. Given the initial performance of the LW sampler, this was clearly unexpected. An interesting byproduct of having an extremely short v_2 is also that we can apply public key compression as is done in e.g. Dilithium [17]. This cuts the public key size |pk| in half at almost no cost on the security, allowing us to reach smaller public keys than [48] as well. We give a detailed comparison with the other M-LWE-based signatures Dilithium [17], Haetae [12], Raccoon [42], EAGLE [48] and G+G [15] in Sect. 6.4 and Table 6.

Table 1. Performance in bytes of Phoenix for NIST-II, NIST-III and NIST-V security.

NIST-II			NIST-III			NIST-V		
|sk|	|pk|	|sig|	|sk|	|pk|	|sig|	|sk|	|pk|	|sig|
512	1184	2190	648	1490	2897	972	2219	4468

Finally, the scheme also benefits from interesting features due to the nature of the LW sampler. The latter can be instantiated with a variety of distributions that are more suited for easy and secure implementations. In particular, Phoenix only involves spherical Gaussians over R which removes the need for complex Gaussian samplers as in previous hash-and-sign schemes (FFO sampler for [46], hybrid sampler for [20], perturbation samplers for [11,48]). This makes Phoenix easier to protect against side-channel attacks. We also provide a version of Phoenix which uses uniform distributions over hypercubes to avoid floating points altogether, but we defer it to the full version [27] due to space limitations.

Our scheme thus combines the benefits of Fiat-Shamir with Aborts schemes and of hash-and-sign schemes, as was originally expected from the LW sampler. This work shows that said sampler is not only of theoretical interest but may have concrete applications that could benefit from its nice performance and implementation features.

1.4   Organization

We start by recalling some notations and standard notions in Sect. 2. Then, we provide our new preimage sampling analysis in Sect. 3, and discuss its performance with respect to the gadget base b in Sect. 4. We provide in Sect. 5 an approximate version of the sampler and propose Phoenix as a concrete hash-and-sign signature based on the latter in Sect. 6. Certain missing proofs are deferred to the full version [27] due to space limitations.

2   Preliminaries

In this paper, for two integers $a \leq b$, we define $[a, b] = \{k \in \mathbb{Z} : a \leq k \leq b\}$. When $a = 1$, we simply use $[b]$ instead of $[1, b]$. Further, q is a positive integer, and we define $\mathbb{Z}_q = \mathbb{Z}/q\mathbb{Z}$. We may identify the latter with the set of representatives $(-q/2, q/2] \cap \mathbb{Z} = [-\lfloor (q-1)/2 \rfloor, \lceil (q-1)/2 \rceil]$. Vectors are written in bold lowercase letters $\mathbf{a}$ and matrices in bold uppercase letters $\mathbf{A}$. The transpose of a matrix $\mathbf{A}$ is denoted by $\mathbf{A}^T$. The identity matrix of dimension d is denoted by $\mathbf{I}_d$. We use $\|\cdot\|_p$ to denote the ℓ_p norm of $\mathbb{R}^d$, i.e., $\|\mathbf{a}\|_p = (\sum_{i \in [d]} |a_i|^p)^{1/p}$ for any positive integer p, and $\|\mathbf{a}\|_\infty = \max_{i \in [d]} |a_i|$. We also define the spectral norm of a matrix $\mathbf{A}$ by $\|\mathbf{A}\|_2 = \max_{\mathbf{x} \neq \mathbf{0}} \|\mathbf{A}\mathbf{x}\|_2 / \|\mathbf{x}\|_2$.

2.1   Lattices

A full-rank *lattice* $\mathcal{L}$ of rank d is a discrete subgroup of $(\mathbb{R}^d, +)$. The *dual lattice* of $\mathcal{L}$ is defined by $\mathcal{L}^* = \{\mathbf{x} \in \operatorname{Span}_{\mathbb{R}}(\mathcal{L}) : \forall \mathbf{y} \in \mathcal{L}, \mathbf{x}^T\mathbf{y} \in \mathbb{Z}\}$. For d, m, q positive integers, we consider the family of q-ary lattices $\{\mathcal{L}_q^\perp(\mathbf{A}); \mathbf{A} \in \mathbb{Z}_q^{d \times m}\}$, where $\mathcal{L}_q^\perp(\mathbf{A}) = \{\mathbf{x} \in \mathbb{Z}^m : \mathbf{A}\mathbf{x} = \mathbf{0} \bmod q\mathbb{Z}\}$. For any $\mathbf{A} \in \mathbb{Z}_q^{d \times m}$ and $\mathbf{u} \in \mathbb{Z}_q^d$, we define $\mathcal{L}_q^\mathbf{u}(\mathbf{A}) = \{\mathbf{x} \in \mathbb{Z}^m : \mathbf{A}\mathbf{x} = \mathbf{u} \bmod q\mathbb{Z}\}$ which is a coset of $\mathcal{L}_q^\perp(\mathbf{A})$.

2.2   Probabilities

For a finite set S, we define $U(S)$ to be the uniform probability distribution over S. We use $x \hookleftarrow P$ to describe the action of sampling $x \in S$ according to the probability distribution P. In contrast, we use $x \sim P$ to mean that the random variable x follows P. The *statistical distance* between two discrete distributions P, Q over a countable set S is defined as $\Delta(P, Q) = \frac{1}{2}\sum_{x \in S} |P(x) - Q(x)|$. Later, $\mathcal{D}_s, \mathcal{D}_t$ denote arbitrary distributions called source and target distributions respectively. Let P, Q be two discrete distributions such that the support of P, denoted by S is a subset of that of Q. The Rényi divergence of order $a \in (1, +\infty]$ from P to Q is defined by $RD_a(P\|Q) = (\sum_{\mathbf{x} \in S} P(\mathbf{x})^a / Q(\mathbf{x})^{a-1})^{1/(a-1)}$. We also use the smooth Rényi divergence from P to Q, parameterized by $\varepsilon \geq 0$, defined in [14] as $RD_\infty^\varepsilon(P\|Q) = \inf\{M > 0 : \mathbb{P}_{\mathbf{x} \sim P}[M \cdot Q(\mathbf{x}) \geq P(\mathbf{x})] \geq 1 - \varepsilon\}$. It essentially allows one to use the infinite-order Rényi divergence and its properties, while discarding a fraction ε of the problematic points. In particular, we can now define the divergence even when $\operatorname{Supp}(P) \not\subseteq \operatorname{Supp}(Q)$ as it allows for discarding the points in $\operatorname{Supp}(P) \setminus \operatorname{Supp}(Q)$ that would lead to an undefined quantity for $RD_\infty(P\|Q)$. We insist that it is a different notion and thus does not have the exact same properties. In particular, it is not log-positive in the sense that $RD_\infty^\varepsilon(\mathcal{P}\|\mathcal{Q})$ is not always above 1. We refer to [14] for more details on this notion and its implications in rejection sampling.

For a center $\mathbf{c} \in \mathbb{R}^d$ and positive definite $\mathbf{S} \in \mathbb{R}^{d \times d}$, we define the Gaussian function $\rho_{\sqrt{\mathbf{S}}, \mathbf{c}} : \mathbf{x} \in \mathbb{R}^d \mapsto \exp(-\pi(\mathbf{x} - \mathbf{c})^T \mathbf{S}^{-1}(\mathbf{x} - \mathbf{c}))$. For a countable set $A \subseteq \mathbb{R}^d$, we define the *discrete Gaussian distribution* $\mathcal{D}_{A, \sqrt{\mathbf{S}}, \mathbf{c}}$ of support A, covariance $\mathbf{S}$ and center $\mathbf{c}$ by its density $\mathcal{D}_{A, \sqrt{\mathbf{S}}, \mathbf{c}} : \mathbf{x} \in A \mapsto \rho_{\sqrt{\mathbf{S}}, \mathbf{c}}(\mathbf{x}) / \rho_{\sqrt{\mathbf{S}}, \mathbf{c}}(A)$, where $\rho_{\sqrt{\mathbf{S}},\mathbf{c}}(A) = \sum_{\mathbf{x} \in A} \rho_{\sqrt{\mathbf{S}},\mathbf{c}}(\mathbf{x})$. When $\mathbf{c} = \mathbf{0}$, we omit it from the notations. When $\mathbf{S} = s^2 \mathbf{I}_d$, we use s as subscript instead of $\sqrt{\mathbf{S}}$. As coined by Micciancio and Regev [36], we define the *smoothing parameter* of a lattice $\mathcal{L}$, parameterized by $\varepsilon > 0$, by $\eta_\varepsilon(\mathcal{L}) = \inf\{s > 0 : \rho_{1/s}(\mathcal{L}^*) \le 1 + \varepsilon\}$.

We also give the standard tail bounds for the discrete Gaussian distribution from [4,40]. Notice that when $\mathbf{c} = \mathbf{0}$, the smoothing requirement $s \ge \eta_\varepsilon(\mathcal{L})$ in the following is not needed.

Lemma 2.1 ([4, Lem. 1.5][40, Cor. 5.3]). *Let $\mathcal{L} \subset \mathbb{R}^d$ be a lattice of rank d, and $s > 0$. It holds that for $c \ge 1$, $\mathbb{P}_{\mathbf{x} \sim \mathcal{D}_{\mathcal{L},s}}[\|\mathbf{x}\|_2 > cs\sqrt{d/2\pi}] < (c\sqrt{e}e^{-c^2/2})^d$. Additionally, for $t \ge 0$, we have $\mathbb{P}_{\mathbf{x} \sim \mathcal{D}_{\mathcal{L},s}}[\|\mathbf{x}\|_\infty > ts/\sqrt{2\pi}] < 2de^{-t^2/2}$.*

Finally, we give the rejection sampling results from [14, Lem. 2.2, Lem. 4.1], which we slightly specify to our context.

Lemma 2.2 (Adapted from [14, Lem. 2.2, Lem. 4.1]). *Let d, m be positive integers. Let $\mathscr{D}_s, \mathscr{D}_t, \mathscr{D}_r, \mathscr{D}_z$ be distributions on $\mathbb{R}^d, \mathbb{R}^d, \mathbb{R}^{d \times m}, \mathbb{R}^m$ respectively. Let $\mathbf{R}$ be drawn from $\mathscr{D}_r$. Then, let $Y \subseteq \mathbb{R}^d$ be the support of the distribution of $\mathbf{R} \cdot \mathscr{D}_z$. We assume they are such that $Supp(\mathscr{D}_t) \subseteq Supp(\mathscr{D}_s^{+\mathbf{Rz}})$ for all $\mathbf{Rz} \in Y$, where $\mathscr{D}_s^{+\mathbf{Rz}}$ is the distribution corresponding to sampling $\mathbf{p}$ from $\mathscr{D}_s$ and outputting $\mathbf{p} + \mathbf{Rz}$. Let $M > 1$ and $\varepsilon \in [0, 1/2]$ such that $\max_{\mathbf{Rz} \in Y} RD_\infty^\varepsilon(\mathscr{D}_t \| \mathscr{D}_s^{+\mathbf{Rz}}) \le M$. We then define two distributions*

$$\boxed{\begin{array}{ll} \mathcal{P}_1 & \textit{Sample } \mathbf{z} \hookleftarrow \mathscr{D}_z, \mathbf{p} \hookleftarrow \mathscr{D}_s \textit{ and set } \mathbf{v} \leftarrow \mathbf{p} + \mathbf{Rz}. \textit{ Then sample a continuous} \\ & u \hookleftarrow U([0,1]). \textit{ If } u > \min(1, \mathscr{D}_t(\mathbf{v})/(M \cdot \mathscr{D}_s(\mathbf{p}))), \textit{ restart, otherwise output} \\ & (\mathbf{v}, \mathbf{z}). \end{array}}$$

$$\boxed{\begin{array}{ll} \mathcal{P}_2 & \textit{Sample } \mathbf{z} \hookleftarrow \mathscr{D}_z, \mathbf{v} \hookleftarrow \mathscr{D}_t. \textit{ Then sample a continuous } u \hookleftarrow U([0,1]). \textit{ If } u > \\ & 1/M, \textit{ restart, otherwise output } (\mathbf{v}, \mathbf{z}). \end{array}}$$

Then, $\Delta(\mathcal{P}_1, \mathcal{P}_2) \le \varepsilon$ and for all $a \in (1, +\infty]$, $RD_a(\mathcal{P}_1 \| \mathcal{P}_2) \le 1/(1-\varepsilon)^{a/(a-1)}$.

To perform rejection sampling in the Gaussian case, we use the following bound on the smooth Rényi divergence between shifted Gaussians.

Lemma 2.3 ([14, Lem. C.2]). *Let d be a positive integer, $\mathbf{y}$ in $\mathbb{R}^d$, $\varepsilon \in (0,1)$, and $s > 0$. Then, $RD_\infty^\varepsilon(\mathcal{D}_{\mathbb{Z}^d, s} \| \mathcal{D}_{\mathbb{Z}^d, s, \mathbf{y}}) \le \exp(\pi \frac{\|\mathbf{y}\|_2^2}{s^2} + 2\frac{\|\mathbf{y}\|_2}{s}\sqrt{\pi \ln \varepsilon^{-1}})$. For $M > 1$, the bound is less than M if $s > \|\mathbf{y}\|_2 \cdot \frac{\sqrt{\pi}}{\ln M}(\sqrt{\ln \varepsilon^{-1} + \ln M} + \sqrt{\ln \varepsilon^{-1}})$.*

2.3 Algebraic Number Theory

We now give the necessary background in algebraic number theory. A number field $K = \mathbb{Q}(\zeta)$ is an extension field of $\mathbb{Q}$ of finite degree n obtained by adjoining an algebraic number ζ. The unique monic polynomial $f \in \mathbb{Q}[X]$ of smallest degree that vanishes at ζ is called the minimal polynomial of K. Its degree is the degree of K. The set of algebraic integers in K defines a ring R called the ring of integers of K, sometimes denoted by $\mathcal{O}_K$. We also define $R_q = R/qR$ for any modulus $q \ge 2$. Although most of our result apply to general number fields, the rest of the paper focuses on cyclotomic fields. For $\nu \not\equiv 2 \bmod 4$, the cyclotomic field of conductor ν is $K = \mathbb{Q}(\zeta_\nu)$ where ζ_ν is a primitive ν-th root of unity. Its degree is $n = \varphi(\nu)$, where φ is the Euler totient function, and its ring of integers is $R = \mathbb{Z}[\zeta_\nu] \cong \mathbb{Z}[X]/\langle \Phi_\nu \rangle$ where Φ_ν is the ν-th cyclotomic polynomial. A particularly popular case is when $\nu = 2^{\mu+1}$, which we call power-of-two cyclotomic field, as it results in $n = 2^\mu$ and $\Phi_\nu = X^n + 1$.

Embeddings. Field and ring elements can be naturally embedded into $\mathbb{R}^n$ by their coefficient vector when seen as polynomials in ζ or X. We call τ the coefficient embedding of R, i.e., for all $r = \sum_{i \in [0,n-1]} r_i \zeta^i \in R$, $\tau(r) = [r_0 | \ldots | r_{n-1}]^T$. One can extend τ to vectors of R^d by concatenating the coefficient embeddings of each vector entry. For an integer η, we define $S_\eta = \tau^{-1}([-\eta, \eta]^n)$ We also define the usual norms $\|\cdot\|_p$ over R by $\|r\|_p := \|\tau(r)\|_p$. The conjugate of an element r is defined by $r^* = r(\zeta^{-1}) = \sum_{i \in [0,n-1]} r_i \zeta^{-i}$. For a matrix $\mathbf{R} = [r_{i,j}] \in R^{d \times k}$, $\mathbf{R}^* = [r_{j,i}^*] \in R^{k \times d}$.

Multiplication Matrices. For all $r, s \in R$, $\tau(rs) = M_\tau(r)\tau(s)$, where $M_\tau(r)$ is the multiplication matrix of $\mathbb{R}^{n \times n}$ associated to r with respect to τ. In the field of minimal polynomial $f = X^n + \sum_{i \in [0,n-1]} f_i X^i$, we have $M_\tau(r) = \sum_{i \in [0,n-1]} r_i \mathbf{C}^i$ where $\mathbf{C}$ the companion matrix of f. We naturally extend M_τ to matrices $\mathbf{A} = [a_{i,j}]_{i,j} \in R^{d \times m}$ entrywise by $M_\tau(\mathbf{A}) = [M_\tau(a_{i,j})]_{i,j} \in \mathbb{R}^{nd \times nm}$. It also holds that $M_\tau(\mathbf{A}^*) = M_\tau(\mathbf{A})^T$. Then, we define $\|\mathbf{A}\|_2$ as $\|M_\tau(\mathbf{A})\|_2$.

Lattices. For any $\mathbf{A} \in R_q^{d \times m}$, we define $\mathcal{L}_q^\perp(\mathbf{A}) = \{\mathbf{x} \in R^m : \mathbf{A}\mathbf{x} = \mathbf{0} \bmod qR\}$. For any $\mathbf{u} \in R_q^d$, we similarly define $\mathcal{L}_q^\mathbf{u}(\mathbf{A}) = \{\mathbf{x} \in R^m : \mathbf{A}\mathbf{x} = \mathbf{u} \bmod qR\}$.

Gaussians. For a positive definite matrix $\mathbf{S} \in \mathbb{R}^{nd \times nd}$, we define the discrete Gaussian distribution over R^d by $\tau^{-1}(\mathcal{D}_{\tau(R^d), \sqrt{\mathbf{S}}})$, which we denote by $\mathcal{D}_{R^d, \sqrt{\mathbf{S}}}$. Since $\tau(R^d) = \mathbb{Z}^{nd}$ in cyclotomic fields, the distribution corresponds to sampling an integer vector according to $\mathcal{D}_{\mathbb{Z}^{nd}, \sqrt{\mathbf{S}}}$ which thus defines a vector of R^d via τ^{-1}.

2.4   Hardness Assumptions

We now recall the relevant hardness assumptions for our work, namely the (resp. *Inhomogeneous*) *Module Short Integer Solution* M-SIS (resp. M-ISIS) and *Module Learning With Errors* M-LWE problems [29]. We consider the problems in their Hermite Normal Form, i.e., we specify the identity in the M-SIS and M-ISIS matrix, and we use the same distribution for the M-LWE secret and error. We also consider a version of M-ISIS and M-SIS which imposes an infinity norm constraint on the solution for our signature scheme Phoenix.

Definition 2.1 (M-ISIS and M-SIS). *Let K be a number field of degree n and R its ring of integers. Let d, m, q be positive integers and $\beta, \beta_\infty > 0$ with*

$m > d$. The Module Inhomogeneous Short Integer Solution problem in Hermite Normal Form M-ISIS$_{n,d,m,q,\beta,\beta_\infty}$ asks to find $\mathbf{x} \in \mathcal{L}_q^{\mathbf{u}}([\mathbf{I}_d|\mathbf{A}'])$ such that $\|\mathbf{x}\|_2 \leq \beta$ and $\|\mathbf{x}\|_\infty \leq \beta_\infty$, given $\mathbf{A}' \hookleftarrow U(R_q^{d \times m-d})$ and $\mathbf{u} \hookleftarrow U(R_q^d)$. When $\mathbf{u} = \mathbf{0}$ we call it M-SIS and expect $\mathbf{x}$ to be non-zero as well. When only considering the Euclidean norm, we remove the subscript β_∞.

We now present the M-LWE problem in its variant with multiple secrets which we use throughout the paper.

Definition 2.2 (M-LWE). *Let K be a number field of degree n and R its ring of integers. Let d, m, k, q be positive integers and $\mathscr{D}_r$ a distribution on R. The decision Module Learning With Errors problem M-LWE$_{n,d,m,q,\mathscr{D}_r}^k$ asks to distinguish between the following distributions: (1) $(\mathbf{A}', [\mathbf{I}_m|\mathbf{A}']\mathbf{R} \bmod qR)$, where $\mathbf{A}' \sim U(R_q^{m \times d})$ and $\mathbf{R} \sim \mathcal{D}_r^{d+m \times k}$, and (2) $(\mathbf{A}', \mathbf{B})$, where $\mathbf{A}' \sim U(R_q^{m \times d})$ and $\mathbf{B} \sim U(R_q^{m \times k})$. The search variant asks to find $\mathbf{R}$ given a sample from (1).*

For a problem $P \in \{$M-SIS, M-ISIS, M-LWE$\}$ where the parameters are clear from the context, we define the hardness bound $\varepsilon_P = \sup_{\mathcal{A} \text{ PPT}} \mathrm{Adv}_P[\mathcal{A}]$. In the case of M-LWE, this is a distinguishing advantage.

3   Revisiting Trapdoor Sampling

We here focus on the trapdoor preimage sampling procedure proposed by Lyubashevsky and Wichs [34] for Micciancio-Peikert trapdoors [35] (which we late abbreviate MP trapdoors). We start by recalling the structure of MP trapdoors and describe the LW sampler from [34] which suffers from very restrictive constraints on the parameters, as explained in Sect. 1. We provide an improved analysis of the LW sampler which gets rid of those parameter constraints, leading to a performance improvement of about 60% over the sampler analysis from [34], and of around 25% over the MP sampler. Our result places however moderate constraints on the applications, albeit easily met in practice as we discuss.

3.1   Micciancio-Peikert Preimage Sampling

The notion of trapdoors introduced by Micciancio and Peikert [35] is very versatile and has been extensively used in cryptographic constructions, including many advanced lattice-based primitives. These trapdoors involve matrices $\mathbf{A_H}$ of the form $\mathbf{A_H} = [\mathbf{A}|\mathbf{HG} - \mathbf{AR}] \bmod qR \in R_q^{d \times d(2+k)}$, where $\mathbf{H} \in R_q^{d \times d}$ is an invertible tag matrix, $\mathbf{G} \in R^{d \times dk}$ a primitive gadget matrix, and $\mathbf{R} \in R^{2d \times dk}$ a short matrix corresponding to the trapdoor. In what follows, we consider the gadget matrix of [35] in base $b \geq 2$, i.e., $\mathbf{G} = \mathbf{I}_d \otimes [1|b|\ldots|b^{k-1}] \in \mathbb{Z}^{d \times dk} \subseteq R^{d \times dk}$ where[2] $k = \lceil \log_b(\lceil (q-1)/2 \rceil + 1) \rceil$, but any other gadget matrix would work, as long as it enables to easily compute short preimages.

---

[2] See Remark 3.2 for details on the definition of k.

The sampling algorithm relies on the link between such matrices $\mathbf{A_H}$ and the gadget matrix $\mathbf{G}$, that is $\mathbf{A_H}[\mathbf{R}^T|\mathbf{I}_{dk}]^T = \mathbf{GH} \bmod qR$. Thence, if $\mathbf{z}$ is a short vector in $\mathcal{L}_q^u(\mathbf{HG})$, then $\mathbf{v} = [(\mathbf{Rz})^T|\mathbf{z}^T]^T$ is a short vector in $\mathcal{L}_q^u(\mathbf{A_H})$, i.e., verifying $\mathbf{A_H}\mathbf{v} = \mathbf{u} \bmod qR$, that is $\mathbf{v}$ is a preimage of $\mathbf{u}$ by $\mathbf{A_H}$. Unfortunately, $\mathbf{v}$ leaks information about the trapdoor $\mathbf{R}$ which is undesirable in cryptographic applications as $\mathbf{R}$ usually corresponds to the long-term secret key. To circumvent this issue, the authors use the Gaussian convolution theorem [41, Thm. 3.1] to perturb $\mathbf{v}$ in order to make the final samples independent of $\mathbf{R}$. In more details, they sample a (highly) non-spherical Gaussian perturbation $\mathbf{p} = [\mathbf{p}_1^T|\mathbf{p}_2^T]^T \sim \mathcal{D}_{R^{d(2+k)},\sqrt{\mathbf{S}}}$ with $\mathbf{S} = M_\tau \left(s^2\mathbf{I}_{d(2+k)} - s_\mathbf{G}^2 \begin{bmatrix} \mathbf{RR}^* & \mathbf{R} \\ \mathbf{R}^* & \mathbf{I}_{dk} \end{bmatrix} \right)$, and then compensate this perturbation by sampling $\mathbf{z} \sim \mathcal{D}_{\mathcal{L}_q^x(\mathbf{G}),s_\mathbf{G}}$ with $\mathbf{x} = \mathbf{H}^{-1}(\mathbf{u} - \mathbf{A_H}\mathbf{p}) \bmod qR$. The output sample is then $\mathbf{v}' = [(\mathbf{p}_1 + \mathbf{Rz})^T|(\mathbf{p}_2 + \mathbf{z})^T]^T$. By the convolution theorem, $\mathbf{v}'$ is statistically close to a Gaussian distribution over $\mathcal{L}_q^u(\mathbf{A_H})$ with parameter s, which no longer depends on $\mathbf{R}$.

Therefore, from the security standpoint, the approach above perfectly addresses the problem of preimage sampling for cryptographic applications. However, if we reconsider the unperturbed vector $\mathbf{v} = [(\mathbf{Rz})^T|\mathbf{z}^T]^T$, we note that the convolution is now applied to both parts in the same way. This does not seem optimal as the bottom section of $\mathbf{v}$ is independent of $\mathbf{R}$ and as $\mathbf{Rz}$ is always larger than $\mathbf{z}$. Unfortunately, this seems inherent to the approach stated in [41, Sec. 1.3] which only considers covariance matrices of the form $s^2\mathbf{I} - \mathbf{S}_1$ for some covariance matrix $\mathbf{S}_1$. Ideally, we would like to select a perturbation that only affects the top component, typically $\mathbf{p} = [\mathbf{p}_1^T|\mathbf{0}]^T \sim \mathcal{D}_{R^{d(2+k)},\sqrt{\mathbf{S}}}$, with $\mathbf{S} = M_\tau \left(\begin{bmatrix} s^2\mathbf{I}_{2d} - s_\mathbf{G}^2\mathbf{RR}^* & \mathbf{0} \\ \mathbf{0} & \mathbf{0} \end{bmatrix} \right)$. However, when sampling $\mathbf{z}$ and outputting $\mathbf{p} + [\mathbf{R}^T|\mathbf{I}_{dk}]^T\mathbf{z}$, we end up with a joint probability of covariance (up to applying M_τ)

$$\begin{bmatrix} s^2\mathbf{I}_{2d} - s_\mathbf{G}^2\mathbf{RR}^* & \mathbf{0} \\ \mathbf{0} & \mathbf{0} \end{bmatrix} + s_\mathbf{G}^2 \begin{bmatrix} \mathbf{RR}^* & \mathbf{R} \\ \mathbf{R}^* & \mathbf{I}_{dk} \end{bmatrix} = \begin{bmatrix} s^2\mathbf{I}_{2d} & s_\mathbf{G}^2\mathbf{R} \\ s_\mathbf{G}^2\mathbf{R}^* & s_\mathbf{G}^2\mathbf{I}_{dk} \end{bmatrix},$$

which again leaks information about $\mathbf{R}$. This highlights the need to hide both $\mathbf{Rz}$ and $\mathbf{z}$ to rely on the convolution technique. Intuitively, the first component $\mathbf{v}_1 = \mathbf{p}_1 + \mathbf{Rz}$ can be seen as a Gaussian distribution with a secret center $\mathbf{Rz}$. Looking at its marginal distribution, one could use standard techniques to hide this secret center, namely convolution when $\mathbf{z}$ is Gaussian or noise flooding (based on either the statistical distance or the Rényi divergence) if $\mathbf{z}$ is non-Gaussian. However, giving $\mathbf{v}_2 = \mathbf{z}$ provides side information on this secret center which explains why $\mathbf{z}$ also has to be perturbed for the convolution technique to be meaningful. We therefore need a middle way between this efficient, but insecure, approach and the one from [35] that does not seem optimal for the type of asymmetric vectors we have to perturb.

From the implementation standpoint, the MP approach also leads to some specific problems. It indeed requires the sampling of a perturbation vector $\mathbf{p}$ from a (highly) non-spherical Gaussian distribution. Such a perturbation sampling is rather costly and represents the most part of the computation time of preimage sampling. The gadget sampling step (sampling $\mathbf{z} \hookleftarrow \mathcal{D}_{\mathcal{L}_q^\times(\mathbf{G}),s_\mathbf{G}}$) also requires the sampling of non-spherical Gaussian perturbations when q is not a power of the gadget base b. The latter case has been considered in several works [23, 49] which show how to leverage specific structures in the basis of $\mathcal{L}_q^\perp(\mathbf{G})$ to enable more efficient sampling over $\mathcal{L}_q^\perp(\mathbf{G})$. Unfortunately, this does not work for the perturbation $\mathbf{p}$ and the covariance matrix $\mathbf{S}$ we consider because $\mathbf{R}$ is random. Another downside is that this convolution method is seemingly limited to Gaussian distributions, which limits the possible preimage distributions.

3.2   A More Flexible Preimage Sampler

To circumvent these shortcomings, Lyubashevsky and Wichs [34] proposed a more flexible preimage sampling procedure which only perturbs the top part.

3.2.1   Description.
The approach from [34] can be seen as combining the features of tag-friendly gadget-based preimage sampling with rejection sampling that is extensively used in Fiat-Shamir with Aborts (FSwA) signatures. Let $\mathbf{G}^{-1}(\cdot)$ be the entry-wise base-b decomposition of vectors of R_q^d. As we explain below in Remark 3.2, we consider a centered representation of $\mathbb{Z}_q$ which results in a signed base-b decomposition. Hence, $\mathbf{G}^{-1}$ maps to vectors of S_{b-1}^{dk}. The intuition is to sample a perturbation $\mathbf{p}_1 \in R^m$ from a source distribution $\mathcal{D}_s$. Further, instead of using Gaussian $\mathbf{G}$-sampling, we simply use $\mathbf{G}^{-1}$ and obtain $\mathbf{v}_2 = \mathbf{G}^{-1}(\mathbf{H}^{-1}(\mathbf{u} - \mathbf{A}\mathbf{p}_1))$. Then, we can define $\mathbf{v}_1 = \mathbf{p}_1 + \mathbf{R}\mathbf{v}_2$ so that the relation $\mathbf{A}_\mathbf{H}\mathbf{v} = \mathbf{u}$ is verified, and apply rejection sampling to make $\mathbf{v}_1$ independent of $\mathbf{R}\mathbf{v}_2$ and in turn $\mathbf{R}$. This setting is reminiscent of lattice-based zero-knowledge arguments or Lyubashevsky's signature scheme [31], where $\mathbf{R}$ is the witness, $\mathbf{p}_1$ is the mask, $\mathbf{A}\mathbf{p}_1$ is a commitment to the mask, $\mathbf{v}_2$ is the challenge, and $\mathbf{v}_1$ is the response to the challenge. We slightly modify the presentation of the sampler from [34] by taking the matrix $\mathbf{A}$ in Hermite Normal Form. Concretely, throughout the rest of the paper, $\mathbf{A} = [\mathbf{I}_d|\mathbf{A}']$ for a matrix $\mathbf{A}'$ of dimension $d \times (m - d)$.

Algorithm 3.1: SamplePreRej($\mathbf{R}; \mathbf{A}', \mathbf{H}, \mathbf{u}, \mathcal{D}_s, \mathcal{D}_t$)

Input (offline phase): Matrix $\mathbf{A}' \in R_q^{d \times (m-d)}$, Source distribution $\mathcal{D}_s$ over R^m.
Input (online phase): Trapdoor $\mathbf{R} \in R^{m \times dk}$, Tag $\mathbf{H} \in GL_d(R_q)$, Syndrome $\mathbf{u} \in R_q^d$, Target distribution $\mathcal{D}_t$ over R^m such that rejection sampling can be performed with respect to the source distribution $\mathcal{D}_s$.

    Offline phase
1. $\mathbf{p}_1 \hookleftarrow \mathcal{D}_s$.
2. $\mathbf{w} \leftarrow [\mathbf{I}_d|\mathbf{A}']\mathbf{p}_1 \bmod qR$.
    Online phase
3. $\mathbf{x} \leftarrow \mathbf{H}^{-1}(\mathbf{u} - \mathbf{w}) \bmod qR$. $\triangleright$ Syndrome correction
4. $\mathbf{v}_2 \leftarrow \mathbf{G}^{-1}(\mathbf{x}) \in S_{b-1}^{dk}$. $\triangleright$ Deterministic
5. $\mathbf{v}_1 \leftarrow \mathbf{p}_1 + \mathbf{R}\mathbf{v}_2$.
6. Sample a continuous $u \hookleftarrow U([0,1])$.

7. **if** $u > \min\left(1, \frac{\mathscr{D}_t(\mathbf{v}_1)}{M \cdot \mathscr{D}_s(\mathbf{p}_1)}\right)$ **then** go back to 1.   ▷ Rejection

Output: $\mathbf{v} = \begin{bmatrix} \mathbf{v}_1 \\ \mathbf{v}_2 \end{bmatrix}$.

3.2.2 Current Limitations. At first glance, the approach from [34] seems to fully achieve what we wanted to do in Sect. 3.1, namely to completely break the symmetry between $\mathbf{v}_1$ and $\mathbf{v}_2$ to reduce the size of $\mathbf{v}_2$. However, in practice, the choice of parameters and suitable distributions $\mathscr{D}_s, \mathscr{D}_t$ is conditioned by the security requirements coming from the simulation result of [34, Thm. 3.1]. Unfortunately, the latter is too restrictive in most cases, which explains why it does not lead to improvements on the preimage size, as we explain below.

Concretely, in [34, Thm. 3.1], it is shown that the output distribution of SamplePreRej is statistically close to some ideal distribution that does not depend on the trapdoor $\mathbf{R}$ for an arbitrary (potentially adversarial) syndrome $\mathbf{u}$. It means that a preimage $\mathbf{v}$ of $\mathbf{u}$ can be simulated without resorting to the trapdoor $\mathbf{R}$, and thus does not leak information on $\mathbf{R}$. There are however some challenges to overcome in order to prove this result. The first one is to identify this ideal distribution that must additionally be close to the one of actual preimages. If we focus on the $\mathbf{v}_2$ component of these preimages, we indeed note that the SamplePreRej algorithm above generates them as $\mathbf{G}^{-1}(\mathbf{H}^{-1}(\mathbf{u} - \mathbf{w}))$ where $\mathbf{w} = \mathbf{A}\mathbf{p}_1$. If $\mathbf{w}$ is non-uniform, then so is $\mathbf{H}^{-1}(\mathbf{u} - \mathbf{w})$, which makes the distribution of $\mathbf{v}_2$ complex to define when $\mathbf{u}$ is arbitrary.

It therefore seems necessary to assume that $\mathbf{A}\mathbf{p}_1$ is close to uniform, but at this stage one could still wonder whether a computational argument is sufficient. Unfortunately we here face a second challenge which is due to the very nature of the perturbation $\mathbf{p}_1$. Indeed, $\mathbf{p}_1$ does not only affect the syndrome (through $\mathbf{A}\mathbf{p}_1$) but also the preimage as it is eventually added to its upper component to form $\mathbf{v}_1$. In a computational argument, one would end up with an intermediate game where $\mathbf{A}\mathbf{p}_1$ would be replaced by some random vector $\mathbf{r}$, but then how to generate $\mathbf{v}_1$? The syndrome would indeed be $\mathbf{u} + \mathbf{r}$, which seems impossible to invert without resorting to the trapdoor since the reduction does not control $\mathbf{u}$.

This is why the authors of [34] need to assume that $\mathbf{A}\mathbf{p}_1$ is *statistically* close to uniform requiring $\mathbf{p}_1$ to have a high entropy in order to use a regularity lemma, which in turn leads to large parameters (either in the dimension m of $\mathbf{p}_1$, or in the size of its entries). This in particular prevents them from using a (much more efficient) computational instantiation of MP trapdoors where $m = 2d$. This results in significant performance losses which cancel out the benefits of having smaller $\mathbf{v}_2$. In addition, regularity lemmas generally require the modulus q to be prime and with low splitting in the ring R, which may be undesirable for concrete applications.

We give concrete parameter and performance estimates in Table 3 following the original result and parameter selection from [34, Sec 3.2] in the Gaussian case, i.e., when $\mathscr{D}_s = \mathscr{D}_t = \mathcal{D}_{R^m,s}$ is a spherical discrete Gaussian of width s. Their simulation result leads to choosing $m = dk = d\lceil \log_b q \rceil$ and

$s = \alpha \cdot (b-1)\sqrt{ndk}(\sqrt{ndk} + \sqrt{ndk} + t)$, for a constant factor $\alpha \approx 8$. Overall it yields a signature of around 20 KB whereas the original MP sampler yields signature of approximately 10.2 KB.

3.3 Improved Simulatability of Preimages

We now explain how to get rid of these requirements when the syndrome follows a prescribed uniform distribution. This is for example the case for GPV signatures [24], where the syndrome $\mathbf{u}$ is the hash output $\mathcal{H}(\mathbf{m})$ of the message $\mathbf{m}$, where $\mathcal{H}$ is modelled as a random oracle. With this assumption, we can drastically change the proof strategy. Indeed, we first note that we no longer have to study the distribution of $\mathbf{v}$ conditioned on some arbitrary $\mathbf{u}$ as we can now consider the joint distribution of $\mathbf{v}$ and $\mathbf{u}$. Put differently, we can now manipulate these two vectors as long as their joint distribution is correct, which offers a lot more flexibility in the proof. In particular, this allows to circumvent the challenges faced in the proof of [34] because we can now leverage the randomness of $\mathbf{u}$ to compensate the one introduced by the computational assumption. More precisely, this allows us to specify the expected distribution of $\mathbf{v}_2$ as $\mathbf{H}^{-1}(\mathbf{u} - \mathbf{Ap}_1)$ is now uniform because $\mathbf{u}$ is uniform and independent of $\mathbf{Ap}_1$.

This alleviates the restriction on $\mathbf{Ap}_1$ being statistically uniform, while still being able to simulate the pairs $(\mathbf{v}, \mathbf{u})$ without resorting to the trapdoor $\mathbf{R}$. Note that $\mathbf{p}_1$ still needs to have a sufficient entropy so as to hide $\mathbf{Rv}_2$, which is given by the rejection sampling condition. This trapdoor-independence property of the preimages is necessary for cryptographic applications, e.g., signatures, as an adversary can usually have access to many such preimages (and syndromes) for a single key. As a consequence, we no longer need a large perturbation (either in norm or dimension), which leads to improved performances, as illustrated by the tables in Sect. 4.

We provide our new simulation result in Theorem 3.1, which we instantiate for Gaussian distributions in Corollary 3.1. Due to space limitations, we only provide the proof of Theorem 5.1 dealing with the approximate version which generalizes Theorem 3.1.

Theorem 3.1. *Let K be a number field, and R its ring of integers. Let d, q, b be positive integers with $b \geq 2$, and let $k = \lceil \log_b(\lceil (q-1)/2 \rceil + 1) \rceil$. Let $\mathcal{D}_r, \mathcal{D}_s, \mathcal{D}_t$ be three distributions over $R^{2d \times dk}$, R^{2d} and R^{2d} respectively. Let $\mathbf{A}' \sim U(R_q^{d \times d})$, $\mathbf{R} \sim \mathcal{D}_r$, $\mathbf{H} \in GL_d(R_q)$ and $\mathbf{A} = [\mathbf{I}_d | \mathbf{A}'] \in R_q^{d \times 2d}$. Then, let $Y \subseteq R^{2d}$ be the support of the distribution of $\mathbf{R} \cdot \mathbf{G}^{-1}(U(R_q^d))$. Let $M > 1, \varepsilon \in [0, 1/2]$ such that $\max_{\mathbf{Rv}_2 \in Y} RD_\infty^\varepsilon(\mathcal{D}_t \| \mathcal{D}_s^{+\mathbf{Rv}_2}) \leq M$. We then define two distributions*

$\mathcal{P}_1$ | $\mathbf{u} \hookleftarrow U(R_q^d)$, and $\mathbf{v} \leftarrow \mathsf{SamplePreRej}(\mathbf{R}; \mathbf{A}', \mathbf{H}, \mathbf{u}, \mathcal{D}_s, \mathcal{D}_t)$.
Output: $(\mathbf{v}, \mathbf{u})$.

$\mathcal{P}_2$
1. $\mathbf{v}_1 \hookleftarrow \mathcal{D}_t$, $\mathbf{v}_2 \hookleftarrow \mathbf{G}^{-1}(U(R_q^d))$.
2. $\mathbf{v} \leftarrow [\mathbf{v}_1^T | \mathbf{v}_2^T]^T$.
3. $\mathbf{u} \leftarrow [\mathbf{A}|\mathbf{HG} - \mathbf{AR}]\mathbf{v} \bmod qR$.
4. With probability $1 - 1/M$ go back to 1.
Output: $(\mathbf{v}, \mathbf{u})$.

Then, $\Delta(\mathcal{P}_1, \mathcal{P}_2) \leq \varepsilon$ *and for all* $a \in (1, +\infty]$, $RD_a(\mathcal{P}_1 \| \mathcal{P}_2) \leq 1/(1 - \varepsilon)^{a/(a-1)}$.

Theorem 3.1 also provides the simulation in Rényi divergence because, as noted for example in [45], it usually leads to tighter constructions. One can indeed take a much larger ε for (almost) the same security guarantees, which in turn relaxes the constraints on other parameters.

Because our new analysis does not require any regularity result to argue that $\mathbf{A}\mathbf{p}_1$ is statistically uniform, we do not need to place any restrictions on the modulus q, nor the field K. Typically, regularity lemmas in the module setting are usually restricted to monogenic fields and/or to prime modulus with low splitting, i.e., such that the ideal qR factors into a small number of distinct prime ideals. Our simulation avoids these constraints altogether. Additionally, the result specifies to the integers by choosing the field $K = \mathbb{Q}$, and thus the ring $R = \mathbb{Z}$, of degree $n = 1$.

Remark 3.1. Our proof strategy would still work if the syndrome $\mathbf{u}$ is statistically uniform and not necessarily a hash output. This is for example the case in the recent signature with efficient protocols of [26] where they simulate one signature query $\mathbf{v}$ along with the public key syndrome $\mathbf{u}$.

Remark 3.2. Note that when working with centered modular arithmetic, the gadget needs to invert possibly negative elements. For $w \in (-q/2, q/2] \cap \mathbb{Z}$, the gadget inversion thus takes the base-b decomposition of $|w|$ and multiplies all coefficients by the sign of w. Additionally, the elements have magnitude at most $\lceil (q-1)/2 \rceil$ and not $q-1$. The base-b decomposition thus requires k entries where $b^k - 1 \geq \lceil (q-1)/2 \rceil$ which indeed leads to $k = \lceil \log_b(\lceil (q-1)/2 \rceil + 1) \rceil$ instead of $k = \lceil \log_b q \rceil$. This almost never differs for large bases and moduli except for rare corner cases, but when $b = 2$ for example this saves one dimension in the gadget length and thus d columns for $\mathbf{R}$.

3.3.1 Gaussian Instantiation.

We instantiate Theorem 3.1 with a Gaussian distribution on $\mathbf{v}_1$ for a fair comparison with previous results. We thus choose $\mathcal{D}_r = U(S_1^{2d \times dk})$ for the trapdoor distribution, and we select $\mathcal{D}_s = \mathcal{D}_t = \mathcal{D}_{R^{2d}, s}$ for the source and target distributions. For convenience, we write SamplePreRej$(\mathbf{R}; \mathbf{A}', \mathbf{H}, \mathbf{u}, s)$ instead of specifying $\mathcal{D}_s$ and $\mathcal{D}_t$.

In order to set s, we need to derive a bound T on $\|\mathbf{R}\mathbf{v}_2\|_2$ to use Lemma 2.3. For that, we bound it by $\|\mathbf{R}\|_2 \|\mathbf{v}_2\|_2$, and apply the standard bound $\|\mathbf{R}\|_2 \leq \sqrt{2nd} + \sqrt{ndk} + t =: B$. We simply note that as the matrix is structured, this bound, which could be proven by [47] in the unstructured case, is only verified empirically as in several works using lattice gadgets, e.g., [5,32]. To thoroughly match the conditions of the rejection sampling, we need to enforce this spectral bound on $\|\mathbf{R}\|_2$ before the sampling procedure. Since $\mathbf{R}$ represents the secret key, this bound should be enforced during key generation[3]. As it is verified with non-negligible probability, typically overwhelming or constant depending on t, this

---

[3] It is also the case for the original MP sampler as it may happen (albeit with negligible probability) that the sampler fails if $\mathbf{R}$ has norm larger than the bound used to set the Gaussian width s.

only discards a small fraction of all the possible keys. Note that such rejections based on the quality of keys has become quite common in other lattice designs, e.g., [20,46]. We therefore actually apply Theorem 3.1 on $\mathscr{D}_r = \text{``}U(S_1^{2d \times dk})$ conditioned on $\|\mathbf{R}\|_2 \leq B\text{''}$. We then choose a repetition rate $M > 1$ and a loss ε, which both define the minimal slack $\alpha > 0$ so that $s = \alpha T$. This leads to the following corollary, which will be more convenient to use later. The proof is given in the full version [27], but essentially follows from Theorem 3.1 combined with [14, Lem. C.2].

Corollary 3.1. *Let R be the power-of-two cyclotomic ring of degree n. Let d, q, b be positive integers with $b \geq 2$, and define the gadget dimension $k = \lceil \log_b(\lceil (q-1)/2 \rceil + 1) \rceil$. Let $t > 0$, and $T = (b-1)\sqrt{ndk}(\sqrt{2nd} + \sqrt{ndk} + t)$. Let $M > 1$, $\varepsilon \in (0, 1/2]$ and define $\alpha = \frac{\sqrt{\pi}}{\ln M}(\sqrt{\ln \varepsilon^{-1} + \ln M} + \sqrt{\ln \varepsilon^{-1}})$. Finally $s = \alpha T$. Let $\mathbf{A}' \sim U(R_q^{d \times d})$, $\mathbf{R} \sim U(S_1^{2d \times dk})$ conditioned on $\|\mathbf{R}\|_2 \leq \sqrt{2nd} + \sqrt{ndk} + t$, and $\mathbf{H} \in GL_d(R_q)$. We define $\mathcal{P}_1$ and $\mathcal{P}_2$ the same way as in Theorem 3.1 but where $\mathscr{D}_s, \mathscr{D}_t$ are replaced with $\mathcal{D}_{R^{2d},s}$. Then, it holds that $\Delta(\mathcal{P}_1, \mathcal{P}_2) \leq \varepsilon$ and $RD_a(\mathcal{P}_1 \| \mathcal{P}_2) \leq 1/(1-\varepsilon)^{a/(a-1)}$ for all $a \in (1, +\infty]$.*

In this specific instantiation of [34] and Theorem 3.1 with Gaussian distributions, we only reach widths s which are larger than the ones from [35]. Indeed, in the latter, $\mathbf{v}_1$ was distributed according to a discrete Gaussian of width $s = \Theta(b\|\mathbf{R}\|_2) = \Theta(b(\sqrt{2nd} + \sqrt{ndk}))$, while here we obtain a width $s = \Theta(b\sqrt{ndk}(\sqrt{2nd} + \sqrt{ndk}))$. However, in the meantime, we drastically reduce the size of $\mathbf{v}_2$, which largely compensate for the increase in size of $\mathbf{v}_1$ for typical parameters, as shown in Sect. 4.

4   Optimal Gadget Base and Sampler Performances

In the computational instantiation of MP trapdoors, the gadget base b is an important parameter to optimize over. Since the base defines the length of the gadget matrix $dk = d \lceil \log_b(\lceil (q-1)/2 \rceil + 1) \rceil$, choosing a larger base results in lower dimensional vectors, at the expense of a larger norm. As the norm only impacts the bitsize logarithmically while the dimension impacts it linearly, one could think that the optimal choice for b is around $\sqrt{q}$, thus resulting in $k = 2$, smaller preimages and in turn smaller signatures. The goal of this section is to show that the optimal base actually depends on the preimage sampler. We illustrate our discussion with the instructive example of GPV signatures [24]. Other applications would need a similar assessment. We compare signatures generated using the original sampler of [35] (thereafter called MP signatures) with those generated using the original sampler (recalled in Algorithm 3.1) of [34] (called LW signatures) and those resulting from our new simulation result in Corollary 3.1 (later called LW* signatures). In the process, we demonstrate interesting improvement factors on the size of preimages resulting from our new analysis. This represents a step towards concrete practicality of constructions based on MP trapdoors.

GPV Signature. We briefly describe the signature framework from [24] with MP trapdoors. The secret key $\mathbf{R}$ is drawn from $U(S_1^{m \times dk})$, and the public key is composed of $\mathbf{A} = [\mathbf{I}_d | \mathbf{A}'] \in R_q^{d \times m}$ and $\mathbf{B} = \mathbf{AR} \bmod qR$. As described before, the signature of a message $\mathbf{m} \in \{0,1\}^*$ consists of a short preimage $\mathbf{v} = [\mathbf{v}_1^T | \mathbf{v}_2^T]^T \in R^{m+dk}$ satisfying $[\mathbf{A} | \mathbf{G} - \mathbf{B}]\mathbf{v} = \mathcal{H}(\mathbf{m}) \bmod qR$. Since the matrix $\mathbf{A}$ has $\mathbf{I}_d$ as its first block, we can use similar tricks as for example [20,22,46] to reduce the signature size. The GPV signature now consists of $(\mathbf{v}_{1,2}, \mathbf{v}_2)$, where $\mathbf{v}_1 = [\mathbf{v}_{1,1}^T | \mathbf{v}_{1,2}^T]^T$, because $\mathbf{v}_{1,1}$ is determined by the verification equation as $\mathbf{v}_{1,1} = \mathcal{H}(\mathbf{m}) - \mathbf{A}'\mathbf{v}_{1,2} - (\mathbf{G} - \mathbf{B})\mathbf{v}_2 \bmod qR$. Below, the signature size is thus computed as $|\mathsf{sig}| = |\mathbf{v}_{1,2}| + |\mathbf{v}_2|$. The bitsize of Gaussian vectors is estimated by the entropy bound, which can be achieved using the rANS encoding as discussed in [22]. More precisely, for a discrete Gaussian vector of dimension N and width s, the entropy bound is close to $N/2 \cdot (1 + \log_2 s^2) = N(1/2 + \log_2 s)$.

Choosing the Gadget Base. The main difficulty when determining the optimal base for a given sampler is that b impacts both the bitsize evaluation of the signature and the hardness of the underlying computational assumptions. As the latter in turn affects the parameters (and hence the bitsize), this may lead to some counterintuitive situations.

For a given base, the minimal Gaussian parameter needed for MP signatures $\mathbf{v}$ is[4] $s \approx \alpha_1 b \|\mathbf{R}\|_2$, with α_1 linked to the randomized rounding parameter and where $\|\mathbf{R}\|_2$ can be bounded heuristically by $\sqrt{2nd} + \sqrt{ndk} + t$ for a slack $t \approx 7$ which thus depends on b as $\sqrt{1/\ln(b)}$. The bitsize of a signature is thus

$$|\mathsf{sig}_{\mathsf{MP}}| \approx nd(1/2 + \log_2(\alpha_1 b \|\mathbf{R}\|_2)) + nd \log_b(q)(1/2 + \log_2(\alpha_1 b \|\mathbf{R}\|_2)). \quad (1)$$

For the sampler from Algorithm 3.1, the Gaussian parameter for $\mathbf{v}_1$ is given by $s \approx \alpha_2 b \|\mathbf{R}\|_2 \sqrt{ndk}$ where α_2 defines the repetition rate M. As mentioned in Sect. 3.2.2, the dimension m for LW signatures is chosen to be $m = dk$ instead of $m = 2d$ for LW* signatures. The corresponding bitsizes are thus given by

$$|\mathsf{sig}_{\mathsf{LW}}| \approx nd(\log_b(q) - 1)(1/2 + \log_2(\alpha_2 b \|\mathbf{R}\|_2 \sqrt{ndk})) + nd \log_2 q \quad (2)$$

$$|\mathsf{sig}_{\mathsf{LW}^*}| \approx nd(1/2 + \log_2(\alpha_2 b \|\mathbf{R}\|_2 \sqrt{ndk})) + nd \log_2 q. \quad (3)$$

We already see that the size of $\mathbf{v}_2$, for both LW and LW*, is $nd \log_2 q$, independently of the choice of b. This is because we can equivalently send $\mathbf{x} \in R_q^d$ instead of $\mathbf{v}_2 = \mathbf{G}^{-1}(\mathbf{x})$. For those two schemes, the dependency in b thence only comes from the first component $\mathbf{v}_{1,2}$.

In the case of LW*, the situation is simple according to Eq. 3: the bitsize increases with b despite the $1/\ln(b)$ dependency due to k, which pleads for a

---

[4] For ease of exposition, we simplify the formulas in this paragraph but we stress that the final estimates in Tables 2, 3 and 4 are computed with the exact parameter settings.

small base b, i.e., $b = 2$. Conversely, the bitsize of LW signatures essentially benefits from large bases b. The same holds true for MP signatures. In the latter two cases, the optimal base therefore seems to be $b = \lceil \sqrt{q} \rceil$ if we consider this sole metric.

We must now evaluate the impact of the base b on the on the underlying computational assumptions. We indeed recall that, in the security proof, one needs to simulate signatures and program the random oracle responses accordingly. To do so, we use the simulation result from Corollary 3.1 (or its equivalent for the original sampling procedure for MP signatures). After that, we simulate the public key and we thus need to consider parameters that ensure the M-LWE$_{n,d,d,q,U(S_1)}$ problem is hard. The security proof is then concluded by a reduction to M-SIS$_{n,d,d(2+k),q,\beta}$ where $\beta \geq \|\mathbf{v} - \mathbf{v}^*\|_2$ for two preimages $\mathbf{v}, \mathbf{v}^*$. It yields $\beta = 2s\sqrt{nd(2+k)}$ for MP signatures, $\beta = 2\sqrt{ndk(s^2 + (b-1)^2)}$ for LW signatures, and $\beta = 2\sqrt{nd(2s^2 + k(b-1)^2)}$ for LW* signatures.

For MP signatures, the bound β is dominated by the bottom part $\mathbf{v}_2$ as $k \geq 2$. It thus makes sense to increase b in order to reduce the dimension of dk and thus have balanced contributions of $\mathbf{v}_1$ and $\mathbf{v}_2$ to the M-SIS bound β. On the contrary, for LW* signatures, $\mathbf{v}_1$ and $\mathbf{v}_2$ have essentially the same dimension but the specificity of this sampler leads to a strong asymmetry between them. This re-balances the contributions of $\mathbf{v}_1$ and $\mathbf{v}_2$ in the bound β which is actually already dominated by the former for $b = 2$. In this case, increasing b will only enlarge the gap between the contributions of $\mathbf{v}_1$ and $\mathbf{v}_2$ to the M-SIS bound and thus decrease the security. In parallel, using too large bases such as $b = \sqrt{q}$ impacts the M-SIS bound too drastically, as noted in e.g. [11], and parameters need to be increased to compensate the security accordingly. In particular, one has to ensure that the infinity norm of the M-SIS solution is smaller than q to avoid trivial solutions.

Estimates. This intricate situation is reflected by the estimated performance of a GPV signature that we describe below, for different samplers and parameter constraints. We aim to achieve $\lambda = 128$ bits of security for the GPV signature using the security assessment methodology described in Appendix A. For all the estimates, we fix when necessary the randomized rounding factor $r = 5$, the spectral norm slack $t = 7$, $Q = 2^{40}$ as the maximal number of emitted signatures per key. We then choose the repetition rate $M \approx 11$ which leads to $\alpha \approx 8$ for $\varepsilon = 1/Q$. We then find the appropriate rank d and modulus q to achieve the security target while minimizing the signature size.

To highlight the importance of the gadget base, we give the performance of MP, LW and LW* signatures for several choices of bases. The estimates are given in Tables 2, 3, and 4. The values of $\lambda_{\text{M-LWE}}$ and $\lambda_{\text{M-SIS}}$ correspond to the reached security of M-LWE$_{n,m-d,d,q,U(S_1)}$ and M-SIS$_{n,d,m+dk,q,\beta}$ respectively. When the base is said to be $q^{1/k}$, we actually consider $b = \lceil q^{1/k} \rceil$ to have an integer base for which the gadget dimension is dk. The rows with the value of b giving the smallest size (for $n = 256$) are highlighted in the tables. The goal of Tables 2, 3, and 4 is to highlight the role of b according to each sampler. Different trade-offs

Table 2. Parameter and size estimates of MP signatures using different bases b. The sizes are expressed in KB. The ring degree is $n = 256$.

	$\lambda_{\text{M-LWE}}$	$\lambda_{\text{M-SIS}}$	q	d	s	$|\mathbf{v}_{1,2}|$	$|\mathbf{v}_2|$	$|\text{sig}_{\text{MP}}|$
$b = 2$	239	146	$\approx 2^{15.2}$	5	2596	1.85	27.75	29.60
$b = 4$	233	150	$\approx 2^{15.6}$	5	3461	1.92	15.32	17.24
$b = q^{1/5}$	216	147	$\approx 2^{16.8}$	5	7661	2.09	10.47	12.56
$b = q^{1/3}$	181	131	$\approx 2^{19.7}$	5	56804	**2.54**	**7.64**	**10.18**
$b = q^{1/2}$	194	154	$\approx 2^{26.7}$	7	6616938	5.07	10.13	15.20

Table 3. Parameter and size estimates of LW signatures (with the parameter constraints of [34]). The sizes are expressed in KB. The ring degree is $n = 256$. The parameter selection is dictated by the regularity condition of [34], which explains the high M-LWE hardness only reported here for completeness. We also note that we extrapolated the result of [34] which is only presented for $b = 2$. In particular, the parameters we give for $b = q^{1/3}$ and $b = q^{1/2}$ do not perfectly meet the regularity condition from their paper, namely $ndk \log_2 s > 3nd \log_2 q + 4\lambda$. For low values of k, one would need to increase s but it would also lead to increasing q to compensate the security loss.

	$\lambda_{\text{M-LWE}}$	$\lambda_{\text{M-SIS}}$	q	d	s	$|\mathbf{v}_{1,2}|$	$|\mathbf{v}_2|$	$|\text{sig}_{\text{LW}}|$
$b = 2$	> 1000	131	$\approx 2^{23.6}$	6	572109	80.96	4.50	86.46
$b = 4$	> 1000	130	$\approx 2^{23.8}$	6	901768	41.83	4.50	46.33
$b = q^{1/5}$	597	130	$\approx 2^{27.3}$	6	5586865	17.19	5.25	22.44
$b = q^{1/3}$	428	133	$\approx 2^{30.6}$	7	105308864	**11.88**	**6.78**	**18.66**
$b = q^{1/2}$	161	138	$\approx 2^{40.5}$	9	96061795597	10.40	11.53	21.93

Table 4. Parameter and size estimates of LW* signatures (this work) using different bases b. The sizes are expressed in KB. The ring degree is $n = 256$.

	$\lambda_{\text{M-LWE}}$	$\lambda_{\text{M-SIS}}$	q	d	s	$|\mathbf{v}_{1,2}|$	$|\mathbf{v}_2|$	$|\text{sig}_{\text{LW*}}|$
$b = 2$	195	157	$\approx 2^{22.5}$	6	362140	**3.56**	**4.31**	**7.87**
$b = 4$	188	151	$\approx 2^{23.2}$	6	645772	3.71	4.50	8.21
$b = q^{1/5}$	167	134	$\approx 2^{25.6}$	6	3576993	4.18	4.87	9.05
$b = q^{1/3}$	167	137	$\approx 2^{30.3}$	7	90206170	5.89	6.78	12.67
$b = q^{1/2}$	162	138	$\approx 2^{40.3}$	9	90202905475	10.37	11.53	21.90

in the parameter selection (e.g., changing n) are likely to be possible but we believe they will not change the overall trend.

These estimates show that the choice of the base is far from anecdotal, with a 3–4 ratio for the signature size between the best option and the worst one. They also show that there is no generic choice as $b = 2$ is optimal in our case (LW*) whereas it corresponds to the worst case for both MP and LW. When plugged into other signature designs [5,6,19,32,33,44], the conclusions may differ as the relative contributions of $\mathbf{v}_1$ and $\mathbf{v}_2$ to the M-SIS bound may evolve compared to the case of GPV signature.

Besides this sole consideration of optimal base, these tables clearly show the benefits of the LW* sampler as it yields signatures that are about 60% smaller than those produced with the LW sampler and 25% smaller when compared with the MP sampler. It thus shows that one can indeed leverage rejection sampling to improve MP sampling, which solves the apparent paradox of the original LW sampler.

5   Approximate Rejection Sampler

In Sects. 3 and 4, we revisited the original LW sampler, showing that it could outperform the MP sampler thanks to our new analysis. However, when plugged into the GPV framework, one still ends up with signature sizes that are much larger than the state-of-the-art.

Fortunately, a study initiated by Chen, Genise and Mukherjee [11] improves the performance of gadget-based constructions through the notion of approximate trapdoors. The idea is to drop the low-order gadget entries and only consider a partial gadget $\mathbf{G}_H = \mathbf{I}_d \otimes \mathbf{g}_H^T$, with $\mathbf{g}_H = [b^\ell|\dots|b^{k-1}]^T$, which reduces the signature dimension and the number of columns in the trapdoor $\mathbf{R}$. Obviously, this introduces an error in the preimage which depends on ℓ but also on the specificities of the sampler. In [11], which is based on the MP sampler, the authors generate normally (see Sect. 3.1) $\mathbf{z} \sim \mathcal{D}_{\mathcal{L}_q^\mathbf{x}(\mathbf{G}),s_\mathbf{G}}$ for the full gadget matrix $\mathbf{G}$ and some appropriate vector $\mathbf{x}$ and then drop the component $\mathbf{z}_L$ of $\mathbf{z}$ corresponding to $\mathbf{G}_L = \mathbf{I}_d \otimes \mathbf{g}_L^T$, with $\mathbf{g}_L = [1|\dots|b^{\ell-1}]^T$. This leads to a Gaussian error $\mathbf{e} = \mathbf{G}_L\mathbf{z}_L$ whose infinity norm is likely to be larger than $b^\ell - 1$, which does not seem optimal.

Conversely, in the case of the LW* sampler, $\mathbf{z}$ is exactly $\mathbf{G}^{-1}(\mathbf{w})$ for some syndrome $\mathbf{w}$. Put differently, $\mathbf{z}$ is simply the signed base-b decomposition of $\mathbf{w}$. Applying the approximate trapdoor approach in our case then essentially consists in discarding the lower-order entries $\mathbf{z}_L$ of this decomposition, which leads to an error $\mathbf{e} = \mathbf{G}_L\mathbf{z}_L$, with $\|\mathbf{e}\|_\infty < b^\ell$. Actually, we show afterwards that this error is (almost) uniform over a subset of $S_{b^\ell-1}$, which also improves the bound on $\|\mathbf{e}\|_2$. This smaller error, having a behaviour similar to the one in [48], allows for dropping more entries than in [11], leading to better performance. In our scheme in Sect. 6, we can in particular drop $\ell = k - 1$ entries, yielding a gadget of length 1 as in [48].

The formal description of our approximate sampler is provided in Algorithm 5.1.

Algorithm 5.1: Approx.SamplePreRej($\mathbf{R}; \mathbf{A}', \mathbf{u}, \mathscr{D}_s, \mathscr{D}_t$)

Input: Trapdoor $\mathbf{R} \in R^{2d \times d(k-\ell)}$, Matrix $\mathbf{A}' \in R_q^{d \times d}$, Syndrome $\mathbf{u} \in R_q^d$, Source and target distributions $\mathscr{D}_s$ and $\mathscr{D}_t$ over R^{2d} such that rejection sampling can be performed.

1. $\mathbf{p}_1 \hookleftarrow \mathscr{D}_s$.
2. $\mathbf{w} \leftarrow \mathbf{u} - [\mathbf{I}_d | \mathbf{A}'] \mathbf{p}_1 \bmod qR$.   ▷ Syndrome correction
3. $\mathbf{z} \leftarrow \mathbf{G}^{-1}(\mathbf{w}) \in S_{b-1}^{dk}$.   ▷ Deterministic.
4. Parse $\mathbf{z}$ into $\mathbf{z}_L \in S_{b-1}^{d\ell}$ and $\mathbf{z}_H \in S_{b-1}^{d(k-\ell)}$ so that $\mathbf{Gz} = \mathbf{G}_L \mathbf{z}_L + \mathbf{G}_H \mathbf{z}_H$.
5. $\mathbf{v}_1' \leftarrow \mathbf{p}_1 + \mathbf{R}\mathbf{z}_H$.
6. $u \hookleftarrow U([0,1])$ ▷ Continuous
7. **if** $u > \min(1, \mathscr{D}_t(\mathbf{v}_1')/(M\mathscr{D}_s(\mathbf{p}_1)))$, go back to 1.
8. **else** $\mathbf{v}_1 \leftarrow \mathbf{v}_1' + \begin{bmatrix} \mathbf{G}_L \mathbf{z}_L \\ \mathbf{0} \end{bmatrix}$
9. $\mathbf{v}_2 \leftarrow \mathbf{z}_H$

Output: $\mathbf{v} = \begin{bmatrix} \mathbf{v}_1 \\ \mathbf{v}_2 \end{bmatrix}$.

The simulatability of preimages is provided in Theorem 5.1, which we prove below. Note that setting $\ell = 0$ in Algorithm 5.1 and Theorem 5.1 gives exactly Algorithm 3.1 and Theorem 3.1. We slightly abuse notations and denote by $\mathbf{G}_H^{-1}$ (resp. $\mathbf{G}_L^{-1}$) the map that from $\mathbf{w}$ computes $\mathbf{z} = \mathbf{G}^{-1}(\mathbf{w})$ and outputs the vector $\mathbf{z}_H$ (resp. $\mathbf{z}_L$) defined above. We nevertheless recall that $\mathbf{G}_L \mathbf{G}_L^{-1}(\mathbf{w}) = \mathbf{w}$ only holds for some vectors $\mathbf{w}$ and not in general. We also note that $\mathbf{G}_H^{-1}(R_q^d) \subset S_{b-1}^{d(k-\ell)}$ but equality does not hold simply by a counting argument.

Theorem 5.1. *Let K be a number field and R its ring of integers. Let d, q, b be positive integers with $b \geq 2$. We define $k = \lceil \log_b(\lceil (q-1)/2 \rceil + 1) \rceil$ and let $\ell \in [0, k-1]$. Let $\mathscr{D}_r, \mathscr{D}_s, \mathscr{D}_t$ be three distributions over $R^{2d \times d(k-\ell)}$, R^{2d} and R^{2d} respectively. Let $\mathbf{A}' \sim U(R_q^{d \times d})$, $\mathbf{R} \sim \mathscr{D}_r$ and $\mathbf{A} = [\mathbf{I}_d | \mathbf{A}'] \in R_q^{d \times 2d}$. Then, let $Y \subseteq R^{2d}$ be the support of the distribution of $\mathbf{R} \cdot \mathbf{G}_H^{-1}(U(R_q^d))$. Let $M > 1, \varepsilon \in [0, 1/2]$ such that $\max_{\mathbf{R}\mathbf{z}_H \in Y} RD_\infty^\varepsilon(\mathscr{D}_t \| \mathscr{D}_s^{+\mathbf{R}\mathbf{z}_H}) \leq M$. We also define the error distribution $\mathscr{D}_e = \mathbf{G}_L \mathbf{G}_L^{-1}(U(R_q^d))$ over $S_{b^\ell - 1}^d$. We then define two distributions*

$\mathcal{P}_1$ | $\mathbf{u} \hookleftarrow U(R_q^d)$, *and* $\mathbf{v} \leftarrow$ Approx.SamplePreRej$(\mathbf{R}; \mathbf{A}', \mathbf{u}, \mathscr{D}_s, \mathscr{D}_t)$.
| | ***Output:*** $(\mathbf{v}, \mathbf{u})$.

$\mathcal{P}_2$ | *1.* $\mathbf{v}_1' \hookleftarrow \mathscr{D}_t$, $\mathbf{v}_2 \hookleftarrow \mathbf{G}_H^{-1}(U(R_q^d))$, $\mathbf{e} \hookleftarrow \mathscr{D}_e$.
| | *2.* $\mathbf{v} \leftarrow [\mathbf{v}_1'^T + [\mathbf{e}^T|\mathbf{0}]|\mathbf{v}_2^T]^T$.
| | *3.* $\mathbf{u} \leftarrow [\mathbf{A}|\mathbf{G}_H - \mathbf{AR}]\mathbf{v} \bmod qR$.
| | *4. With probability* $1 - 1/M$ *go back to 1.*
| | ***Output:*** $(\mathbf{v}, \mathbf{u})$.

Then, $\Delta(\mathcal{P}_0, \mathcal{P}_1) \leq \varepsilon$ and for all $a \in (1, +\infty]$, $RD_a(\mathcal{P}_0 \| \mathcal{P}_1) \leq 1/(1-\varepsilon)^{a/(a-1)}$.

Proof. We define the following hybrid distributions from $\mathcal{H}_1$ to $\mathcal{H}_6$, where $\mathcal{H}_1 = \mathcal{P}_1$ and $\mathcal{H}_6 = \mathcal{P}_2$.

$\mathcal{H}_1$

$\mathbf{u} \hookleftarrow U(R_q^d)$, $\mathbf{p}_1 \hookleftarrow \mathscr{D}_s$, $\mathbf{w} \leftarrow \mathbf{u} - \mathbf{A}\mathbf{p}_1 \bmod qR$, $\mathbf{z} \leftarrow \mathbf{G}^{-1}(\mathbf{w})$, $\mathbf{v}_1' \leftarrow \mathbf{p}_1 + \mathbf{R}\mathbf{z}_H$. Then $u \hookleftarrow U([0,1])$ and restart if $u > \min(1, \mathscr{D}_t(\mathbf{v}_1')/(M \cdot \mathscr{D}_s(\mathbf{p}_1)))$. Otherwise define $\mathbf{v} \leftarrow [\mathbf{v}_1'^T + [(\mathbf{G}_L\mathbf{z}_L)^T|\mathbf{0}]|\mathbf{z}_H^T]^T$.
Output: $(\mathbf{v}, \mathbf{u})$.

$\mathcal{H}_2$

$\mathbf{w} \hookleftarrow U(R_q^d)$, $\mathbf{p}_1 \hookleftarrow \mathscr{D}_s$, $\mathbf{u} \leftarrow \mathbf{w} + \mathbf{A}\mathbf{p}_1 \bmod qR$, $\mathbf{z} \leftarrow \mathbf{G}^{-1}(\mathbf{w})$, $\mathbf{v}_1' \leftarrow \mathbf{p}_1 + \mathbf{R}\mathbf{z}_H$. Then $u \hookleftarrow U([0,1])$ and restart if $u > \min(1, \mathscr{D}_t(\mathbf{v}_1')/(M \cdot \mathscr{D}_s(\mathbf{p}_1)))$. Otherwise define $\mathbf{v} \leftarrow [\mathbf{v}_1'^T + [(\mathbf{G}_L\mathbf{z}_L)^T|\mathbf{0}]|\mathbf{z}_H^T]^T$.
Output: $(\mathbf{v}, \mathbf{u})$.

$\mathcal{H}_3$

$\mathbf{z} \hookleftarrow \mathbf{G}^{-1}(U(R_q^d))$, $\mathbf{w} \leftarrow \mathbf{G}\mathbf{z} \bmod qR$, $\mathbf{p}_1 \hookleftarrow \mathscr{D}_s$, $\mathbf{u} \leftarrow \mathbf{w} + \mathbf{A}\mathbf{p}_1 \bmod qR$, $\mathbf{v}_1' \leftarrow \mathbf{p}_1 + \mathbf{R}\mathbf{z}_H$. Then $u \hookleftarrow U([0,1])$ and restart if $u > \min(1, \mathscr{D}_t(\mathbf{v}_1')/(M \cdot \mathscr{D}_s(\mathbf{p}_1)))$. Otherwise define $\mathbf{v} \leftarrow [\mathbf{v}_1'^T + [(\mathbf{G}_L\mathbf{z}_L)^T|\mathbf{0}]|\mathbf{z}_H^T]^T$.
Output: $(\mathbf{v}, \mathbf{u})$.

$\mathcal{H}_4$

$\mathbf{e} \hookleftarrow \mathscr{D}_e$, $\mathbf{z}_H \leftarrow \mathbf{G}_H^{-1}(U(R_q^d))$, $\mathbf{w} \leftarrow \mathbf{e} + \mathbf{G}_H\mathbf{z}_H \bmod qR$, $\mathbf{p}_1 \hookleftarrow \mathscr{D}_s$, $\mathbf{u} \leftarrow \mathbf{w} + \mathbf{A}\mathbf{p}_1 \bmod qR$, $\mathbf{v}_1' \leftarrow \mathbf{p}_1 + \mathbf{R}\mathbf{z}_H$. Then $u \hookleftarrow U([0,1])$ and restart if $u > \min(1, \mathscr{D}_t(\mathbf{v}_1')/(M \cdot \mathscr{D}_s(\mathbf{p}_1)))$. Otherwise define $\mathbf{v} \leftarrow [\mathbf{v}_1'^T + [\mathbf{e}^T|\mathbf{0}]|\mathbf{z}_H^T]^T$.
Output: $(\mathbf{v}, \mathbf{u})$.

$\mathcal{H}_5$

$\mathbf{e} \hookleftarrow \mathscr{D}_e$, $\mathbf{z}_H \leftarrow \mathbf{G}_H^{-1}(U(R_q^d))$, $\mathbf{p}_1 \hookleftarrow \mathscr{D}_s$, $\mathbf{v}_1' \leftarrow \mathbf{p}_1 + \mathbf{R}\mathbf{z}_H$. Then $u \hookleftarrow U([0,1])$ and restart if $u > \min(1, \mathscr{D}_t(\mathbf{v}_1')/(M \cdot \mathscr{D}_s(\mathbf{p}_1)))$. Otherwise define $\mathbf{v} \leftarrow [\mathbf{v}_1'^T + [\mathbf{e}^T|\mathbf{0}]|\mathbf{z}_H^T]^T$, and $\mathbf{u} \leftarrow [\mathbf{A}|\mathbf{G}_H - \mathbf{A}\mathbf{R}]\mathbf{v} \bmod qR$.
Output: $(\mathbf{v}, \mathbf{u})$.

$\mathcal{H}_6$

$\mathbf{e} \hookleftarrow \mathscr{D}_e$, $\mathbf{z}_H \leftarrow \mathbf{G}_H^{-1}(U(R_q^d))$, $\mathbf{v}_1' \hookleftarrow \mathscr{D}_t$. Then $u \hookleftarrow U([0,1])$ and restart if $u > 1 - 1/M$. Otherwise define $\mathbf{v} \leftarrow [\mathbf{v}_1'^T + [\mathbf{e}^T|\mathbf{0}]|\mathbf{z}_H^T]^T$, and $\mathbf{u} \leftarrow [\mathbf{A}|\mathbf{G}_H - \mathbf{A}\mathbf{R}]\mathbf{v} \bmod qR$.
Output: $(\mathbf{v}, \mathbf{u})$.

Let us now show that these distributions are statistically close to each other.

<u>$\mathcal{H}_1$ - $\mathcal{H}_2$:</u> Here we just change the sampling order of $\mathbf{u}$ and $\mathbf{w}$. In $\mathcal{H}_2$ the vector $\mathbf{w}$ is uniform and independent of $\mathbf{A}\mathbf{p}_1$ implying that $\mathbf{u}$ is also uniform, as in $\mathcal{H}_1$. Hence $\mathcal{H}_1$ and $\mathcal{H}_2$ are identically distributed.

<u>$\mathcal{H}_2$ - $\mathcal{H}_3$:</u> We now change the way $\mathbf{w}$ is generated. Notice that, for correctness, once $\mathbf{w}$ is fixed then so is $\mathbf{z}$ and vice-versa. In $\mathcal{H}_2$, $\mathbf{w}$ is uniform over R_q^d which means that $\mathbf{z}$ follows exactly $\mathbf{G}^{-1}(U(R_q^d))$ as in $\mathcal{H}_3$. Also, $\mathbf{w}$ is coherently set in $\mathcal{H}_3$. Thence, $\mathcal{H}_2$ and $\mathcal{H}_3$ are identically distributed as well.

<u>$\mathcal{H}_3$ - $\mathcal{H}_4$:</u> $\mathcal{H}_4$ simply separates the sampling of low-order and high-order parts compared to $\mathcal{H}_3$. When $\mathbf{z}$ is drawn from $\mathbf{G}^{-1}(U(R_q^d))$, the corresponding $\mathbf{z}_L$ and $\mathbf{z}_H$ are independent. So $\mathbf{z}_H \sim \mathbf{G}_H^{-1}(U(R_q^d))$ and $\mathbf{z}_L \sim \mathbf{G}_L^{-1}(U(R_q^d))$. As such, $\mathbf{z}_H$ is identically distributed in $\mathcal{H}_4$ as in $\mathcal{H}_3$ by definition of $\mathbf{G}_H^{-1}$ which samples a whole vector and drops the low-order entries. Since $\mathbf{z}_L$ is not directly used but only as $\mathbf{e} = \mathbf{G}_L\mathbf{z}_L$, and because $\mathbf{z}_L \sim \mathbf{G}_L^{-1}(U(R_q^d))$ in both $\mathcal{H}_3$ and $\mathcal{H}_4$, it holds that $\mathbf{e} \sim \mathbf{G}_L\mathbf{G}_L^{-1}(U(R_q^d)) = \mathscr{D}_e$ in both hybrids. The way $\mathbf{z}_L$ is sampled,

recomposing the low-order entries gives $\mathbf{e} \in S_\gamma^d$ where $\gamma = \sum_{i=0}^{\ell-1}(b-1)b^i = b^\ell - 1$, as desired. This shows that $\mathcal{H}_3$ and $\mathcal{H}_4$ are identically distributed.

$\mathcal{H}_4$ - $\mathcal{H}_5$: $\mathcal{H}_5$ is merely a re-writing of $\mathcal{H}_4$. Indeed, in $\mathcal{H}_5$, $\mathbf{w}$ only acts as an intermediate vector to define $\mathbf{u}$. Defining $\mathbf{R}' = [\mathbf{R}^T|\mathbf{I}_{m_2}]^T$, we have $[\mathbf{A}|\mathbf{G}_H - \mathbf{A}\mathbf{R}]\mathbf{R}' = \mathbf{G}_H \bmod qR$. In $\mathcal{H}_4$, this yields

$$\mathbf{u} = \mathbf{G}_H \mathbf{z}_H + \mathbf{e} + \mathbf{A}\mathbf{p}_1 \bmod qR = [\mathbf{A}|\mathbf{G}_H - \mathbf{A}\mathbf{R}]\mathbf{R}'\mathbf{z}_H + \mathbf{A}\mathbf{p}_1 + \mathbf{e} \bmod qR$$
$$= [\mathbf{A}|\mathbf{G}_H - \mathbf{A}\mathbf{R}]\mathbf{v} \bmod qR,$$

as $\mathbf{v} = [\mathbf{p}_1^T + [\mathbf{e}^T|\mathbf{0}]|\mathbf{0}]^T + \mathbf{R}'\mathbf{z}_H$. Again, $\mathcal{H}_4$ and $\mathcal{H}_5$ are identical.

$\mathcal{H}_5$ - $\mathcal{H}_6$: We now change the way $\mathbf{v}_1'$ is generated by using the rejection sampling result. In $\mathcal{H}_5$, $\mathbf{R}\mathbf{z}_H$ is distributed according to $\mathbf{R} \cdot \mathbf{G}_H^{-1}(U(R_q^d))$ with support Y as defined in the theorem statement. By our assumptions on Y, $\mathcal{D}_s$, $\mathcal{D}_t$, the rejection sampling result from Lemma 2.2 yields that

$$\Delta((\mathbf{v}_1', \mathbf{z}_H)_{\mathcal{H}_5}, (\mathbf{v}_1', \mathbf{z}_H)_{\mathcal{H}_6}) \le \varepsilon \text{ and } RD_a((\mathbf{v}_1', \mathbf{z}_H)_{\mathcal{H}_5}\|(\mathbf{v}_1', \mathbf{z}_H)_{\mathcal{H}_6}) \le \frac{1}{(1-\varepsilon)^{\frac{a}{a-1}}},$$

for all $a > 1$. By the data processing inequality of the statistical distance and Rényi divergence, it holds $\Delta(\mathcal{H}_5, \mathcal{H}_6) \le \varepsilon$, and $RD_a(\mathcal{H}_5\|\mathcal{H}_6) \le 1/(1-\varepsilon)^{a/(a-1)}$. Since $\mathcal{H}_1 = \mathcal{P}_1$ and $\mathcal{H}_6 = \mathcal{P}_2$, combining the above gives the result. $\square$

The study carried in Sect. 4 leads to the same conclusions for the approximate samplers, although the analysis is slightly more complex as one can optimize over the number of dropped entries ℓ as well. Because the sampling error $\mathbf{e}$ is smaller in our case, we can drop more entries and thus increase the performance gap between the approximate MP sampler and ours. In particular, we observe an improvement in the signature size of around $30 - 35\%$ over the former, for the same estimation methodology as Sect. 4. The signature sizes are now more attractive, but we push the performance in Sect. 6 by providing a new hash-and-sign scheme based on our approach.

6   A New Hash-and-Sign Scheme: Phoenix

In our quest to test the limits of the LW sampler, we plug our approximate LW* sampler described above in the GPV framework to build a new signature scheme which we call Phoenix. The optimal base for our approximate sampler is also $b = 2$ and we thus we express everything in base 2 directly. Also, we choose the modulus to be $q = 2^{k+1} - 1$ so that the representatives of $\mathbb{Z}_q$ are taken in the centered interval $[-(q-1)/2, (q-1)/2] = [-(2^k-1), 2^k-1]$. The resulting gadget dimension is $\lceil \log_2(\lceil (q-1)/2 \rceil + 1) \rceil = k$. We start by presenting in Sect. 6.1 the public key compression technique we apply for Phoenix, before giving the full description of the scheme in Sect. 6.2. We then detail the security analysis in Sect. 6.3 and give concrete instantiations in Sect. 6.4.

6.1 Adding Public Key Compression

The approximate sampler already enables a significant compression of both the public key and the signature. However, in the context of hash-and-sign signatures following the GPV framework, the public key[5] is $\mathbf{B} = [\mathbf{I}_d | \mathbf{A}']\mathbf{R} \bmod qR \in R_q^{d \times d(k-\ell)}$ which remains quite large for typical parameters. Fortunately, the features of our sampler allow us to use standard techniques for public key compression, like the one used in [13,17] for example. As this is a standard trick, we only sketch the idea and explain the impact it has on the construction.

Let ℓ' be a positive integer in $[0, k-1]$. Once the public key $\mathbf{B}$ has been generated, we interpret it in R as a matrix over $S_{(q-1)/2}$. We then write it as $\mathbf{B} = \mathbf{B}_L + \mathbf{B}_H$ to separate the low-order and high-order bits, with $\mathbf{B}_L \in S_{2^{\ell'}-1}^{d \times d(k-\ell)}$ and $\mathbf{B}_H \in 2^{\ell'} S_\gamma^{d \times d(k-\ell)}$ for $\gamma = \left\lfloor 2^{-\ell'} \frac{q-1}{2} \right\rfloor = 2^{k-\ell'} - 1$. The public key now only consists of the matrix $\mathbf{B}_H$ (or $2^{-\ell'}\mathbf{B}_H$) which can be stored using $nd^2(k-\ell)(1+k-\ell')$ bits, thus saving ℓ' bits per coefficients.

The discarded low-order bits then introduce a new error $\mathbf{e}_{\mathsf{pk}} = \mathbf{B}_L\mathbf{v}_2 = \mathbf{B}_L\mathbf{z}_H$ in the signature. This error can be combined with the sampling error $\mathbf{e}$ during preimage sampling.

The reason why this compression technique is particularly interesting in our situation, as opposed to EAGLE [48] for example, is because $\mathbf{z}_H$ is ternary and not Gaussian. As such, the error $\mathbf{e}_{\mathsf{pk}}$ remains moderate compared to $\mathbf{e}$ if $\ell' \leq \ell$, as detailed below.

6.2 Description

We give an instantiation of Phoenix based on discrete Gaussian distributions. We also defer in the full version of the paper [27] another version of the scheme using only uniform distributions.

Algorithm 6.1: Phoenix.Setup

Input: Security parameter λ.

1. Choose positive integers d, k.
2. $q \leftarrow 2^{k+1} - 1$.
3. Choose $\ell, \ell' \in [0, k-1]$.
4. $\mathbf{G} = \mathbf{I}_d \otimes [1 \cdots 2^{k-1}] \in R_q^{d \times dk}$.
5. $\mathbf{G}_H = \mathbf{I}_d \otimes [2^\ell \cdots 2^{k-1}] \in R_q^{d \times d(k-\ell)}$.
6. $\mathbf{G}_L = \mathbf{I}_d \otimes [1 \cdots 2^{\ell-1}] \in R_q^{d \times d\ell}$.
7. $\varepsilon \leftarrow 1/4Q$ ▷ Rejection sampling loss
8. Choose $M > 1$.   ▷ Repetition rate
9. $\alpha \leftarrow \frac{\sqrt{\pi}}{\ln M}(\sqrt{\ln \varepsilon^{-1} + \ln M} + \sqrt{\ln \varepsilon^{-1}})$.   ▷ Rejection sampling slack
10. $s \leftarrow \alpha\sqrt{nd(k-\ell)}(\sqrt{2nd} + \sqrt{nd(k-\ell)})$.   ▷ Gaussian width
11. $\mathbf{A}' \hookleftarrow U(R_q^{d \times d})$.

Output: $\mathsf{pp} = (\mathbf{A}'; \mathbf{G}, \mathbf{G}_L, \mathbf{G}_H; \lambda, n, q, d, k, \ell, s, M)$.

---

[5] The other public key matrix $\mathbf{A}'$ is generated using a public seed of 256 bits.

Algorithm 6.2: Phoenix.KeyGen

Input: Public parameters pp as in Algorithm 6.1.

1. $\mathbf{R} \hookleftarrow U(S_1^{2d \times d(k-\ell)})$ such that $\|\mathbf{R}\|_2 \leq \sqrt{2nd} + \sqrt{nd(k-\ell)}$.
2. $\mathbf{B} \leftarrow [\mathbf{I}_d | \mathbf{A}'] \mathbf{R} \bmod qR \in R_q^{d \times d(k-\ell)}$
3. Parse $\mathbf{B}$ as $\mathbf{B}_L + \mathbf{B}_H$ with $\mathbf{B}_L \in S_{2^{\ell'}-1}^{d \times d(k-\ell)}$ and $\mathbf{B}_H \in 2^{\ell'} S_{2^{k-\ell'}-1}^{d \times d(k-\ell)}$.

Output: pk $= \mathbf{B}_H$, and sk $= \mathbf{R}$.   ▷ pp stored with pk for simplicity

---
Algorithm 6.3: Phoenix.Sign

Input: Secret key sk, Message $\mathbf{m} \in \{0,1\}^*$, Public key pk.

1. salt $\hookleftarrow U(\{0,1\}^{320})$.
2. $(\widetilde{\mathbf{v}_1}, \mathbf{v}_2) \leftarrow$ Approx.SamplePreRej$(\mathbf{R}; \mathbf{A}', \mathcal{H}(\mathbf{m}, \text{salt}), s)$.   ▷ Algorithm 5.1
3. $\mathbf{e}_{\text{pk}} \leftarrow (([\mathbf{I}_d|\mathbf{A}']\mathbf{R} \bmod qR) - \mathbf{B}_H)\mathbf{v}_2$.   ▷ Recomputing $\mathbf{B}_L$, and $\mathbf{B}_{L\mathbf{z}_H}$
4. Parse $\widetilde{\mathbf{v}_1}$ as $[\widetilde{\mathbf{v}_{1,1}}^T | \mathbf{v}_{1,2}^T]^T$ with $\widetilde{\mathbf{v}_{1,1}}, \mathbf{v}_{1,2} \in R^d$.
5. $\mathbf{v}_{1,1} \leftarrow \widetilde{\mathbf{v}_{1,1}} - \mathbf{e}_{\text{pk}}$.
6. $\gamma_1 \leftarrow (\|\mathbf{v}_{1,1}\|_2 \leq B_{1,1}) \wedge (\|\mathbf{v}_{1,2}\|_2 \leq B_{1,2})$.
7. $\gamma_2 \leftarrow (\|\mathbf{v}_{1,1}\|_\infty \leq B_{1,1}^\infty) \wedge (\|\mathbf{v}_{1,2}\|_\infty \leq B_{1,2}^\infty) \wedge (\|\mathbf{v}_2\|_\infty \leq 1)$.
8. if $\gamma_1 \wedge \gamma_2 = 0$, restart.

Output: sig $= (\text{salt}, \mathbf{v}_{1,2}, \mathbf{v}_2)$.

Algorithm 6.4: Phoenix.Verify

Input: Public key pk, Message $\mathbf{m} \in \{0,1\}^*$, Signature sig.

1. $\mathbf{v}_{1,1} \leftarrow \mathcal{H}(\mathbf{m}, \text{salt}) - \mathbf{A}'\mathbf{v}_{1,2} - (\mathbf{G}_H - \mathbf{B}_H)\mathbf{v}_2 \bmod qR \in R^d$.
2. $\gamma_1 \leftarrow (\|\mathbf{v}_{1,1}\|_2 \leq B_{1,1}) \wedge (\|\mathbf{v}_{1,2}\|_2 \leq B_{1,2})$.
3. $\gamma_2 \leftarrow (\|\mathbf{v}_{1,1}\|_\infty \leq B_{1,1}^\infty) \wedge (\|\mathbf{v}_{1,2}\|_\infty \leq B_{1,2}^\infty) \wedge (\|\mathbf{v}_2\|_\infty \leq 1)$.

Output: $\gamma_1 \wedge \gamma_2$.   ▷ 1 if valid, 0 otherwise

Preimage Error Distribution. Let us define a modified error distribution $\mathscr{D}_e^+$ where we sample $\mathbf{e} \hookleftarrow \mathscr{D}_e$ and output $\mathbf{e}^+$ corresponding to $\mathbf{e}$ but where the coefficient embeddings of $\mathbf{e}^+$ are the magnitude of that of $\mathbf{e}$. We observe that $\mathscr{D}_e^+$ is almost the uniform distribution over $\tau^{-1}(\{0, \ldots, 2^\ell - 1\}^{nd})$ because of the form of q. This means that the Euclidean norm of $\mathbf{e}$ will be distributed the same way as that of $\mathbf{e}^+$. The variance of $U(\{0, \ldots, 2^\ell - 1\})$ is exactly $(2^{2\ell} - 1)/12$ and the norm can be bounded on average by $\sqrt{(2^\ell - 1))(2^{\ell+1} - 1)/6}\sqrt{nd}$ by the central limit theorem.

Verification Bounds. We now explain how the verification bounds are set. First, the ones on $\mathbf{v}_{1,2}$ are simply taken from Lemma 2.1 by adjusting the slack to avoid too many repetitions. As such we set $B_{1,2} = 1.048 \cdot s\sqrt{nd/2\pi}$ and $B_{1,2}^\infty = \lfloor 4.6s/\sqrt{2\pi} \rfloor$.

Choosing appropriate bounds is more complex for $\mathbf{v}_{1,1}$ because the value recovered by the verifier is $\mathbf{v}_{1,1}' + \mathbf{e} - \mathbf{e}_{\text{pk}}$ which contains the error terms. Bounding each term separately overshoots the actual norm of $\mathbf{v}_{1,1}$. We thus give a more fine-grained analysis based on the following observations. We first notice that the coefficients of $e_{pk} = B_L v_2$ behave in a similar fashion to the drift of lazy random walks with adaptive steps whose magnitude are at most $2^{\ell'} - 1$, up to a slack factor μ depending on the conductor of the cyclotomic field[6]. As such, we can approach the bounds on $v_{1,1} - e_{pk}$ by the Gaussian tail bound with the appropriate variance. Then, $\|e\|_2$ can be evaluated as described above which also behaves like the Gaussian tail bound, and $\|e\|_\infty$ is very likely to be close to the worst-case bound $2^\ell - 1$. Using these Gaussian approximations, we set

$$B_{1,1} = 1.04 \sqrt{\frac{s^2}{2\pi} + \frac{(2^\ell - 1)(2^{\ell+1} - 1)}{6} + \mu^2 \frac{2^{\ell'}(2^{\ell'} - 1)}{6} \frac{nd(k - \ell)}{2}} \sqrt{nd}$$

$$B_{1,1}^\infty = \left\lfloor 3.8 \cdot \sqrt{\frac{s^2}{2\pi} + \mu^2 \frac{2^{\ell'}(2^{\ell'} - 1)}{6} \frac{nd(k - \ell)}{2}} \right\rfloor + (2^\ell - 1).$$

which are verified empirically and only entail a small degradation of the average number of repetition M. The term in $nd(k-\ell)/2$ stems from the contribution of e_{pk}, and naturally comes from average number of steps in the lazy random walk due to the Hamming weight of $\tau(v_2)$. As a result, choosing $\ell' \approx \ell$ would not be optimal because it would essentially make e_{pk} larger than e as e_{pk} grows faster with ℓ' than e does with ℓ. For common parameters (see Sect. 6.4), where ℓ is close to k[7], choosing $\ell' \approx (k+1)/2$ seems to be the best option as it halves the public key size while incurring (almost) no security loss. This is because for such parameters e_{pk} is overpowered by the preimage error e.

Remark 6.1. Phoenix shares with [22] the goal of moving the bulk of the preimage in $v_{1,1}$ which is not transmitted. Our treatment is howbeit very different from the twisted norm approach of the latter work. This gives further evidence of the benefits of the asymmetry in concrete lattice-based cryptography.

6.3 Security Analysis

Our scheme follows the GPV framework. One can thus use the simulation result of Theorem 5.1 adapted to Phoenix, which we provide here. Due to space limitations, the proof is deferred to the full version [27] but follows from [14, Lem. C.2] as well.

Corollary 6.1. *Let d, k be positive integers, define $q = 2^{k+1} - 1$ and let $\ell \in [0, k-1]$. Let $T = \sqrt{nd(k - \ell)}(\sqrt{2nd} + \sqrt{nd(k - \ell)})$. Let $M > 1$, $\varepsilon \in (0, 1/2]$ and define $\alpha = \frac{\sqrt{\pi}}{\ln M}(\sqrt{\ln \varepsilon^{-1} + \ln M} + \sqrt{\ln \varepsilon^{-1}})$. Finally $s = \alpha T$. Let $A' \sim U(R_q^{d \times d})$,*

---

[6] This slack comes from the multiplication $M_\tau(B_L)\tau(v_2)$ in the coefficient embedding. Later we choose 3-smooth conductors yielding $\mu = \sqrt{2}$, and $\mu = 1$ for power-of-two conductors.

[7] Choosing $\ell = k-2$ or $\ell = k-1$ is possible as opposed to the approach in [11] because e is smaller by a factor of $\sqrt{3}\omega(\sqrt{\log_2 nd})$.

$\mathbf{R} \sim U(S_1^{2d \times d(k-\ell)})$ conditioned on $\|\mathbf{R}\|_2 \leq \sqrt{2nd} + \sqrt{nd(k-\ell)}$. We define $\mathcal{P}_1$ and $\mathcal{P}_2$ the same way as in Theorem 5.1 but where $\mathscr{D}_s, \mathscr{D}_t$ are replaced with $\mathcal{D}_{R^{2d},s}$. Then, it holds that $\Delta(\mathcal{P}_1, \mathcal{P}_2) \leq \varepsilon$ and $RD_a(\mathcal{P}_1 \| \mathcal{P}_2) \leq 1/(1-\varepsilon)^{a/(a-1)}$ for all $a \in (1, +\infty]$.

We can now formally state the strong EUF-CMA security of Phoenix for uncompressed public key and then discuss the slight differences stemming from key compression. Compared to the original GPV security result [24], we note that we rely on a version of M-SIS which adds a norm check in the infinity norm of the candidate solutions. Nevertheless, as it still follows the GPV framework [24], it is also secure in the QROM [8].

Theorem 6.1 ([24] adapted). *Phoenix is strongly EUF-CMA-secure in the random oracle model under* M-LWE$_{n,d,d,q,U(S_1)}$ *and* M-SIS$_{n,d,d(2+k-\ell),q,\beta,\beta_\infty}$, *where* $\beta = 2\sqrt{B_{1,1}^2 + B_{1,2}^2 + nd(k-\ell)}$ *and* $\beta_\infty = 2\max(B_{1,1}^\infty, B_{1,2}^\infty, 1) = 2B_{1,1}^\infty$. *More precisely, the advantage of* $\mathcal{A}$ *attacking the unforgeability of Phoenix is bounded by* $Adv[\mathcal{A}] \lesssim (\varepsilon_{\text{M-SIS}} + d(k-\ell)\varepsilon_{\text{M-LWE}})/(1-\varepsilon)^Q$.

As our scheme features key compression, we can use the M-LWE assumption in the security reduction but the public key will not be uniform over R_q but only over the high-order bits. This would give a skewed M-SIS assumption over the instance $[\mathbf{I}_d | \mathbf{A}' | \mathbf{G}_H - \mathbf{B}_H]$ where the third block only has high-order bits. Since solving M-SIS involves discarding columns as described in Appendix A to find an optimal subdimension between nd and $2nd$, this skewed assumption could be estimated by M-SIS$_{n,d,2d,q,\beta',\beta'_\infty}$ where the bounds are set by taking $\mathbf{v}_2 = \mathbf{0}$. In all cases, this will not affect our concrete parameters that we directly derive from the M-ISIS instance corresponding to our signature, as explained below.

6.4 Concrete Parameters

We now suggest parameter sets to instantiate Phoenix in Table 5. Although our scheme is presented over modules of rank d, working over rings offers better key compression. We thus give parameters in the ring setting. As all our tools hold for general number fields, we can use cyclotomic fields of composite conductors. This has been done in MITAKA [20] to achieve fine-grained security levels where they consider 3-smooth conductors. In this case, it incurs a loss of $\sqrt{2}$ in the quality of our sampler similarly to [20] due to the spectral bound on $\mathbf{R}$, which we take into account in our parameter selection. An alternative would be to choose a power-of-two cyclotomic ring of smaller degree and a larger rank d so that nd matches the dimension we suggest, the parameters scaling with nd. Although it would deteriorate the key sizes, it can be acceptable in applications where the public key is not sent often.

The concrete security is assessed as described in Appendix A. At a high-level, the key recovery is evaluated via the M-LWE assumption. The complexity of the forgery is lower-bounded by Theorem 6.1. However, it is best approximated via the inhomogeneous variant M-ISIS as is done in most hash-and-sign schemes

Table 5. Suggested parameter sets for Phoenix. Sizes are in bytes. The public key includes 32 bytes for the seed that expands to $\mathbf{A}'$. The size of Gaussian vectors is estimated by the entropy bound which can be achieved via the rANS encoding (see [22]). The bit security is the estimated core-SVP hardness (classical C, quantum Q).

	Phoenix-II	Phoenix-III	Phoenix-V
Security	NIST-II	NIST-III	NIST-V
Conductor	2^{11}	$2^4 3^5$	$2^3 3^6$
n	1024	1296	1944
d	1	1	1
(k, ℓ, ℓ')	(16,15,8)	(17,16,9)	(18,17,10)
q	$2^{17} - 1$	$2^{18} - 1$	$2^{19} - 1$
(M, ε, α)	$(20, 2^{-66}, 8.13)$	$(20, 2^{-66}, 8.13)$	$(20, 2^{-66}, 8.13)$
s	20105	35986	53978
$B_{1,1}$	688341.2	1541069.0	3705333.9
$B_{1,2}$	268983.0	541623.4	995025.8
$B_{1,1}^{\infty}$	64537	127114	238760
$B_{1,2}^{\infty}$	36895	66037	99056
|sk| (B)	512	648	972
|pk| (B)	1184	1490	2219
|sig| (B)	2190	2897	4468
Key Recovery (C/Q)	162/143	203/179	312/275
Forgery (C/Q)	125/110	161/142	257/226

[20,46,48]. We follow the same approach and estimate it using the Approx-CVP attack carried by the nearest-colattice algorithm [21]. We see that the forgery security for Phoenix-III, estimated through M-ISIS in Euclidean norm, falls a few bits short of NIST-III level. Our estimate is however rather pessimistic because we discard the infinity norm bound and the asymmetry between $\mathbf{v}_{1,1}$ and $\mathbf{v}_{1,2}$. Our cryptanalysis thus underestimates the actual complexity of the forgery. As pointed out in Appendix A, we believe that a thorough cryptanalysis would place the cost of the forgery above the NIST-III requirement, and also yield a better security for Phoenix-II and Phoenix-V. We however leave this cryptanalysis for future work.

Table 6 details the performance and the security levels of Phoenix and the main M-LWE-based signature schemes, namely Dilithium [17], Haetae [12], Raccoon [42], EAGLE [48], and G+G [15]. We nevertheless stress that comparing these schemes directly has some limits as all of them, except EAGLE, follows the Fiat-Shamir approach which is fundamentally different from the hash-and-sign one. Our goal here is not to discuss in depth the comparative advantages of each approach but we note that the current state-of-the-art tends to show that schemes based on Fiat-Shamir are easier to implement as they support "simple" distributions, such as the uniform or the spherical Gaussian ones, but they rely on rewinding/forking lemma techniques which makes security in the QROM harder to prove, at least for the proposed parameters [25,28]. On the contrary, security of hash-and-sign constructions in the QROM is better understood [8] but these constructions require distributions that are harder to implement. In this regard, Phoenix illustrates the benefits of the LW* sampler as it combines the nice features of these two approaches and thus constitutes an interesting alternative for those that do not want to choose between them.

We also note for completeness that other hash-and-sign schemes based on NTRU such as Falcon [46], MITAKA [20], or ROBIN [48] usually achieve a smaller bandwidth (signature + public key) than the schemes from Table 6, but at the expense of an extra assumption. Designs based on M-LWE may be preferred to those based on NTRU in specific use cases, e.g., with stretched parameters. Such schemes also carry a certain complexity of implementation due to complex Gaussian samplers (FFO sampler for [46], hybrid sampler for [20], perturbation samplers for [48], mask sampler for [15]).

Table 6. Security (strong EUF-CMA versions, randomized signing) and performance comparisons between Dilithium [17], Haetae [12], Raccoon [42], EAGLE [48], G+G [15] and Phoenix. * Does not include the Gaussian perturbation sampling material.

	$|sk|$ (B)	$|pk|$ (B)	$|sig|$ (B)	λ (C/Q)
Dilithium-2	2544	1312	2420	121/110
Haetae-120	1376	992	1463	97/85
Raccoon-128	14800	2256	11524	133/114
G+G-120	480*	1472	1677	121/106
Phoenix-II	512	1184	2190	125/110
Dilithium-3	4016	1952	3293	176/159
Haetae-180	2080	1472	2337	149/131
Raccoon-192	18840	3160	14554	193/166
EAGLE-1024	512*	1952	3052	176/160
G+G-180	640*	1952	2143	178/156
Phoenix-III	648	1490	2897	161/142
Dilithium-5	4880	2592	4595	252/229
Haetae-260	2720	2080	2908	214/188
Raccoon-256	26016	4064	20330	284/243
G+G-260	768*	2336	2804	219/193
Phoenix-V	972	2219	4468	257/226

Conclusion

Introduced in 2015, the LW sampler is an intriguing tool that combines ideas from different lattice techniques such as rejection sampling and MP trapdoors. When considered as an abstract tool, it suffers from a high complexity stemming from the need to assume the worst case in the security analysis. In this work, we completely revisited this sampler by showing that one can considerably alleviate the requirements placed on it when plugged in concrete constructions such as digital signatures. In the latter case, it not only results in much better parameters (compared to the original paper [34]) but also in an interesting middle way between Fiat-Shamir and hash-and-sign approaches. It indeed borrows the nice features of both approaches and can thus be seen as an interesting alternative that has been overlooked so far. Beyond the sole digital signature use-case, we hope that our work will incite to investigate other practical applications of the LW sampler that could benefit from its unique characteristics.

Acknowledgments. This work has received a French government support managed by the National Research Agency in the ASTRID program, under the national project AMIRAL with reference ANR-21-ASTR-0016, and in the MobiS5 project with reference ANR-18-CE-39-0019-02 MobiS5. We warmly thank Vadim Lyubashevsky for helpful discussions on the Lyubashevsky-Wichs sampler, as well Nicholas Genise for interesting discussions on approximate trapdoors.

A   Concrete Security Analysis

In this section we recall the methodology we use to estimate the bit security of the forgery and key recovery attacks in Sect. 4 and for Phoenix in Sect. 6.4. All our estimates use the Core-SVP model where the cost of the attack is given by the cost of running once the self-dual BKZ lattice reduction [37] with block size B. The cost is then modeled by the best known cost for lattice sieving, i.e., $2^{0.292B}$ for the classical security and $2^{0.257B}$ for the quantum security.

Under the Gaussian Heuristic and the Geometric Series Assumption, the BKZ algorithm with blocksize B would find a vector $\mathbf{v}$ in a N-dimensional lattice $\mathcal{L}$ with $\|\mathbf{v}\|_2 \leq \delta_B^N \mathrm{Vol}(\mathcal{L})^{1/N}$, where $\delta_B \approx ((\pi B)^{1/B} B/(2\pi e)))^{1/(2(B-1))}$, by [10].

A.1   Key Recovery: M-LWE

In all the schemes derived from the samplers in Sect. 4, the public key is given by $\mathbf{A}' \in R_q^{d\times m_1-d}$ and $\mathbf{B} = [\mathbf{I}_d|\mathbf{A}']\mathbf{R} \bmod qR$ and the secret key by $\mathbf{R} \sim U(S_1^{m_1\times m_2})$. Except for the LW signature, all our schemes use $m_1 = 2d$. Key recovery thus corresponds to an instance of search M-LWE$_{n,d,m_1-d,q,U(S_1)}$ with m_2 uniform ternary secrets. We use the lattice estimator [2] on the instance LWE$_{nd,n(m_1-d),q,U(\{-1,0,1\})}$ to determine the minimal BKZ block size B among all the evaluated attacks. We discard the structure of the underlying ring and simply extend the dimensions by the ring degree n by considering the matrix

$M_\tau(\mathbf{A}')$. To account for the m_2 secrets, we consider the final cost to be that of running m_2 times BKZ which gives a cost of $m_2 2^{\nu B}$ for $\nu \in \{0.292, 0.257\}$.

In the case of Phoenix, we apply public key compression which means that the adversary only has access to the high-order bits of $\mathbf{B}$. At a high-level, the key recovery consists in solving $d(k - \ell)$ instances of M-LWE to recover $\mathbf{R}$ from $\mathbf{B}_H \bmod q$. Since $\mathbf{B}_H$ contains less information on $\mathbf{R}$ than the full matrix $\mathbf{B} = [\mathbf{I}_d | \mathbf{A}']\mathbf{R} \bmod qR$, we lower bound the complexity of key recovery by assessing the cost of recovering $\mathbf{R}$ given $\mathbf{B}$ as described above.

A.2 Forgery: M-SIS or M-ISIS

The complexity of the forgery can be estimated either by the security proof which relies on the M-SIS assumption, or by the M-ISIS assumption. In Sect. 4, we use the former approach on the M-SIS$_{n,d,m,q,\beta,\beta_\infty}$ assumption where the infinity norm $\beta_\infty < q$ is discarded except for ensuring that q-vectors are not solutions. For Phoenix, we aim for a tighter security assessment using the M-ISIS$_{n,d,m,q,\beta',\beta'_\infty}$ assumption. Both approaches are detailed below.

A.2.1 Solving M-SIS. To estimate the security of M-SIS$_{n,d,m,q,\beta,\beta_\infty}$, we find the cost of finding $\mathbf{v} \in \mathcal{L}_q^\perp([\mathbf{I}_d | \mathbf{A}' | \mathbf{B}'])$ such that $\|\mathbf{v}\|_2 \leq \beta$ and $\|\mathbf{v}\|_\infty \leq \beta_\infty$, given $\mathbf{A}' \sim U(R_q^{d \times m_1 - d})$ and $\mathbf{B}' \sim U(R_q^{d \times m_2})$ (with $m = m_1 + m_2$). We again look at the unstructured problem SIS$_{nd,nm,q,\beta,\beta_\infty}$. For that, we first check that $\min(\beta, \beta_\infty) < q$ to avoid trivial solutions. Then, a standard optimization consists in finding a solution in a lattice of smaller dimension $nd \leq m^* \leq nm$ and completing the solution with zeros. We then use BKZ in block size B such that $\beta \geq \min_{nd \leq m^* \leq nm} \delta_B^{m^*} q^{nd/m^*}$. More precisely, for a fixed β, we find m^* that maximizes $\delta_B = \beta^{1/m^*} q^{-nd/m^{*2}}$ and then determine the block size B.

A.2.2 Direct Forgery: M-ISIS. In Phoenix, we estimate the forgery security via the M-ISIS assumption. A forgery consists of a vector $\mathbf{v} = [\mathbf{v}_{1,1}^T | \mathbf{v}_{1,2}^T | \mathbf{v}_2^T]^T$ such that $[\mathbf{I}_d | \mathbf{A}' | \mathbf{G}_H - \mathbf{B}_H]\mathbf{v} = \mathbf{u} \bmod qR$ for a seemingly random and non-adversarial syndrome $\mathbf{u} = \mathcal{H}(\mathsf{salt}, \mathbf{m})$. Since the adversary must provide the salt as part of the signature, the best strategy is to select an arbitrary message and salt, compute $\mathbf{u} = \mathcal{H}(\mathsf{salt}, \mathbf{m})$ and find $\mathbf{v}$. Additionally, as $\mathbf{v}_2$ has very strict bounds (ternary), it is unlikely to have such small coefficients for $\mathbf{v}_2$ by solving M-ISIS on $([\mathbf{I}_d | \mathbf{A}' | \mathbf{G}_H - \mathbf{B}_H], \mathbf{u})$, unless they are set to zero. To hope for a valid forgery, one would thus fix a value for $\mathbf{v}_2 \in S_1^{d(k-\ell)}$ and solve the M-ISIS instance $([\mathbf{I}_d | \mathbf{A}'], \mathbf{u}' = \mathbf{u} - (\mathbf{G}_H - \mathbf{B}_H)\mathbf{v}_2)$ with norm bounds set from the signature verification from Algorithm 6.4. Setting $\mathbf{v}_2 = \mathbf{0}$ would discard these columns which is done in the concrete attack below anyway. Due to the asymmetry of our preimages, the solution returned by the adversary should also have a specific form. In particular $\mathbf{v}_{1,1}, \mathbf{v}_{1,2}$ are bounded both in Euclidean and infinity norms. This makes the fine-grained cryptanalysis difficult as current lattice reduction algorithms focus mostly on the Euclidean norm. Our approach is therefore once again to underestimate the actual cost of the attack by discarding the infinity norm and also the asymmetry of the solution. We believe that a thorough cryptanalysis would show that the forgery is more complex than the approach we describe here. More precisely, we simply evaluate the complexity of finding $\mathbf{v}_1$ such that $[\mathbf{I}_d | \mathbf{A}'] \mathbf{v}_1 = \mathbf{u}'$ mod q and $\|\mathbf{v}_1\|_2 \leq \beta = \sqrt{B_{1,1}^2 + B_{1,2}^2}$. We note that if β is close to or larger than $q\sqrt{nd/12}$, this M-ISIS instance becomes trivial but not the forgery because of our infinity norm checks.

If $\beta < q\sqrt{nd/12}$, a solution can be found using the Approximate CVP attack using the nearest-colattice algorithm of Espitau and Kirchner [21]. Given $(M_\tau([\mathbf{I}_d | \mathbf{A}']), \tau(\mathbf{u}')) \in \mathbb{Z}_q^{N \times D} \times \mathbb{Z}_q^N$, where $N = nd$ and $D = 2nd$, the algorithm can compute a solution within Euclidean norm β with BKZ of block size B such that $\beta \geq \min_{k^* \leq D - N} \delta_B^{D-k^*} q^{N/(D-k^*)}$. Again, for a fixed β, we find k^* which maximizes $\delta_B = \beta^{1/(D-k^*)} q^{-N/(D-k^*)^2}$ and then find the block size B.

Although our modulus is not particularly small with respect to the dimension and the M-ISIS bound, we also ran the estimator recently proposed by Ducas, Espitau and Postlethwaite [16] as a sanity check to make sure it does not lead to a more efficient attack than the previously described approach. Their tool unfortunately suffers from large memory requirements when computing the intersection of the hypercube and ball if the parameters are too large. We also leave this cryptanalysis to future work. The preimage and key compression can easily be reduced, and as a result the M-ISIS bound, to avoid these vulnerable parameter regimes at the expense of slightly larger signatures and/or keys. For example, if one were to take more conservative to achieve a smaller ratio β/q, we could still get signatures of 2412 bytes and a public key of 2592 bytes. Nevertheless, we again insist on the fact that our scheme also places infinity norm bounds which may invalidate the attack or make it much more complex.

References

1. Agrawal, S., Kirshanova, E., Stehlé, D., Yadav, A.: Practical. Round-Optimal Lattice-Based Blind Signatures. In: CCS (2022). https://doi.org/10.1145/3548606.3560650
2. Albrecht, M.R., Player, R., Scott, S.: On the concrete hardness of learning with errors. J. Math, Cryptol. 9(3), 169–203 (2015)
3. Alkim, E., Barreto, P.S.L.M., Bindel, N., Krämer, J., Longa, P., Ricardini, J.E.: The lattice-based digital signature scheme qTESLA. In: Conti, M., Zhou, J., Casalicchio, E., Spognardi, A. (eds.) ACNS 2020. LNCS, vol. 12146, pp. 441–460. Springer, Cham (2020). https://doi.org/10.1007/978-3-030-57808-4_22
4. Banaszczyk, W.: New Bounds in Some Transference Theorems in the Geometry of Numbers. Math, Ann (1993)
5. Bert, P., Eberhart, G., Prabel, L., Roux-Langlois, A., Sabt, M.: Implementation of lattice trapdoors on modules and applications. In: Cheon, J.H., Tillich, J.-P. (eds.) PQCrypto 2021 2021. LNCS, vol. 12841, pp. 195–214. Springer, Cham (2021). https://doi.org/10.1007/978-3-030-81293-5_11

6. Bert, P., Fouque, P.-A., Roux-Langlois, A., Sabt, M.: Practical implementation of ring-SIS/LWE based signature and IBE. In: Lange, T., Steinwandt, R. (eds.) PQCrypto 2018. LNCS, vol. 10786, pp. 271–291. Springer, Cham (2018). https://doi.org/10.1007/978-3-319-79063-3_13
7. Beullens, W., Lyubashevsky, V., Nguyen, N.K., Seiler, G.: Lattice-based blind signatures: short, efficient, and round-optimal. IACR Cryptol. ePrint Arch. p. 77 (2023)
8. Boneh, D., Dagdelen, Ö., Fischlin, M., Lehmann, A., Schaffner, C., Zhandry, M.: Random oracles in a quantum world. In: Lee, D.H., Wang, X. (eds.) ASIACRYPT 2011. LNCS, vol. 7073, pp. 41–69. Springer, Heidelberg (2011). https://doi.org/10.1007/978-3-642-25385-0_3
9. Bos, J.W., et al.: CRYSTALS - Kyber: a CCA-secure module-lattice-based KEM. In: EuroS&P (2018). https://doi.org/10.1109/EuroSP.2018.00032
10. Chen, Y.: Réduction de Réseau et Sécurité Concrète du Chiffrement Complètement Homomorphe. Ph.D. thesis, Paris 7 (2013)
11. Chen, Y., Genise, N., Mukherjee, P.: Approximate trapdoors for lattices and smaller hash-and-sign signatures. In: Galbraith, S.D., Moriai, S. (eds.) ASIACRYPT 2019. LNCS, vol. 11923, pp. 3–32. Springer, Cham (2019). https://doi.org/10.1007/978-3-030-34618-8_1
12. Cheon, J.H., et al.: HAETAE: Shorter lattice-based fiat-shamir signatures. IACR Cryptol. ePrint Arch. p. 624 (2023)
13. Le Dévéhat, A., Shizuya, H., Hasegawa, S.: On the higher-bit version of approximate inhomogeneous short integer solution problem. In: Conti, M., Stevens, M., Krenn, S. (eds.) CANS 2021. LNCS, vol. 13099, pp. 253–272. Springer, Cham (2021). https://doi.org/10.1007/978-3-030-92548-2_14
14. Devevey, J., Fawzi, O., Passelègue, A., Stehlé, D.: On rejection sampling in lyubashevsky's signature scheme. In: ASIACRYPT (2022). https://doi.org/10.1007/978-3-031-22972-5_2
15. Devevey, J., Passelègue, A., Stehlé, D.: G+G: A fiat-shamir lattice signature based on convolved gaussians. In: ASIACRYPT (2023). https://doi.org/10.1007/978-981-99-8739-9_2
16. Ducas, L., Espitau, T., Postlethwaite, E.W.: Finding short integer solutions when the modulus is small. In: CRYPTO (2023). https://doi.org/10.1007/978-3-031-38548-3_6
17. Ducas, L., et al.: CRYSTALS-dilithium: a lattice-based digital signature scheme. IACR Trans. Cryptographic Hardware Embed. Syst. **2018**, 238–268 (2018). https://doi.org/10.13154/tches.v2018.i1.238-268
18. Ducas, L., Lyubashevsky, V., Prest, T.: Efficient identity-based encryption over NTRU lattices. In: Sarkar, P., Iwata, T. (eds.) ASIACRYPT 2014. LNCS, vol. 8874, pp. 22–41. Springer, Heidelberg (2014). https://doi.org/10.1007/978-3-662-45608-8_2
19. Ducas, L., Micciancio, D.: Improved short lattice signatures in the standard model. In: Garay, J.A., Gennaro, R. (eds.) CRYPTO 2014. LNCS, vol. 8616, pp. 335–352. Springer, Heidelberg (2014). https://doi.org/10.1007/978-3-662-44371-2_19
20. Espitau, T., et al: A simpler, parallelizable. maskable variant of falcon. In: EUROCRYPT (2022). https://doi.org/10.1007/978-3-031-07082-2_9
21. Espitau, T., Kirchner, P.: The nearest-colattice algorithm: time-approxmation tradeoff for approx-CVP. In: ANTS XIV (2020)
22. Espitau, T., Tibouchi, M., Wallet, A., Yu, Y.: Shorter hash-and-sign lattice-based signatures. In: CRYPTO (2022). https://doi.org/10.1007/978-3-031-15979-4_9

23. Genise, N., Micciancio, D.: Faster gaussian sampling for trapdoor lattices with arbitrary modulus. In: Nielsen, J.B., Rijmen, V. (eds.) EUROCRYPT 2018. LNCS, vol. 10820, pp. 174–203. Springer, Cham (2018). https://doi.org/10.1007/978-3-319-78381-9_7

24. Gentry, C., Peikert, C., Vaikuntanathan, V.: Trapdoors for hard lattices and new cryptographic constructions. In: STOC (2008). https://doi.org/10.1145/1374376.1374407

25. Jackson, K., Miller, C., Wang, D.: Evaluating the security of CRYSTALS-dilithium in the quantum random oracle model. IACR Cryptol. ePrint Arch, pp. 1968 (2023)

26. Jeudy, C., Roux-Langlois, A., Sanders, O.: Lattice signature with efficient protocols. application to anonymous credentials. In: CRYPTO (2023). https://doi.org/10.1007/978-3-031-38545-2_12

27. Jeudy, C., Roux-Langlois, A., Sanders, O.: Phoenix: hash-and-sign with aborts from lattice gadgets. IACR Cryptol. ePrint Arch, pp. 446 (2023)

28. Kiltz, E., Lyubashevsky, V., Schaffner, C.: A concrete treatment of fiat-shamir signatures in the quantum random-oracle mode. In: EUROCRYPT (2018). https://doi.org/10.1007/978-3-319-78372-7_18

29. Langlois, A., Stehlé, D.: Worst-case to average-case reductions for module lattices. Des. Codes Crypt. **75**(3), 565–599 (2014). https://doi.org/10.1007/s10623-014-9938-4

30. Libert, B., Ling, S., Mouhartem, F., Nguyen, K., Wang, H.: Signature schemes with efficient protocols and dynamic group signatures from lattice assumptions. In: Cheon, J.H., Takagi, T. (eds.) ASIACRYPT 2016. LNCS, vol. 10032, pp. 373–403. Springer, Heidelberg (2016). https://doi.org/10.1007/978-3-662-53890-6_13

31. Lyubashevsky, V.: Lattice signatures without trapdoors. In: Pointcheval, D., Johansson, T. (eds.) EUROCRYPT 2012. LNCS, vol. 7237, pp. 738–755. Springer, Heidelberg (2012). https://doi.org/10.1007/978-3-642-29011-4_43

32. Lyubashevsky, V., Nguyen, N.K., Plançon, M.: Lattice-based zero-knowledge proofs and applications: shorter, simpler, and more general. In: CRYPTO (2022). https://doi.org/10.1007/978-3-031-15979-4_3

33. Lyubashevsky, V., Nguyen, N.K., Plançon, M., Seiler, G.: Shorter Lattice-Based Group Signatures via "Almost Free" Encryption and Other Optimizations. In: ASIACRYPT (2021). https://doi.org/10.1007/978-3-030-92068-5_8

34. Lyubashevsky, V., Wichs, D.: Simple lattice trapdoor sampling from a broad class of distributions. In: PKC (2015). https://doi.org/10.1007/978-3-662-46447-2_32

35. Micciancio, D., Peikert, C.: Trapdoors for lattices: simpler, tighter, faster. smaller. In: EUROCRYPT (2012). https://doi.org/10.1007/978-3-642-29011-4_41

36. Micciancio, D., Regev, O.: Worst-case to average-case reductions based on gaussian measures. SIAM J. Comput. (2007). https://doi.org/10.1137/S0097539705447360

37. Micciancio, D., Walter, M.: Practical, predictable lattice basis reduction. In: EUROCRYPT (2016). https://doi.org/10.1007/978-3-662-49890-3_31

38. NIST: Post-Quantum Cryptography Standardization. https://csrc.nist.gov/Projects/Post-Quantum-Cryptography/Post-Quantum-Cryptography-Standardization

39. NIST: Post-quantum cryptography: standardization of additional digital signature schemes. https://csrc.nist.gov/Projects/pqc-dig-sig/standardization

40. Peikert, C.: Limits on the hardness of lattice problems in l_p norms. Comput. Complex. (2008). https://doi.org/10.1007/s00037-008-0251-3

41. Peikert, C.: An efficient and parallel gaussian sampler for lattices. In: CRYPTO (2010). https://doi.org/10.1007/978-3-642-14623-7_5

42. del Pino, R., et al.: Raccoon: a side-channel secure signature scheme. https://github.com/masksign/raccoon/blob/main/doc/raccoon.pdf

43. del Pino, R., Katsumata, S.: A new framework for more efficient round-optimal lattice-based (partially) blind signature via trapdoor sampling. In: CRYPTO (2022). https://doi.org/10.1007/978-3-031-15979-4_11

44. del Pino, R., Lyubashevsky, V., Seiler, G.: Lattice-based group signatures and zero-knowledge proofs of automorphism stability. In: CCS (2018). https://doi.org/10.1145/3243734.3243852

45. Prest, T.: Sharper bounds in lattice-based cryptography using the Rényi divergence. In: ASIACRYPT (2017). https://doi.org/10.1007/978-3-319-70694-8_13

46. Prest, T., et al.: FALCON. Tech. rep. (2020). https://csrc.nist.gov/Projects/post-quantum-cryptography/selected-algorithms-2022

47. Vershynin, R.: Introduction to the non-asymptotic analysis of random matrices. In: Compressed Sensing (2012). https://doi.org/10.1017/cbo9780511794308.006

48. Yu, Y., Jia, H., Wang, X.: Compact lattice gadget and its applications to hash-and-sign signatures. In: CRYPTO (2023). https://doi.org/10.1007/978-3-031-38554-4_13

49. Zhang, S., Yu, Y.: Towards a simpler lattice gadget toolkit. In: PKC (2022). https://doi.org/10.1007/978-3-030-97121-2_18

Efficient Identity-Based Encryption
with Tight Adaptive Anonymity
from RLWE

Toi Tomita$^{(\boxtimes)}$ and Junji Shikata

Yokohama National University, Kanagawa, Japan
{tomita-toi-sk,shikata-junji-rb}@ynu.ac.jp

Abstract. In this paper, we propose an efficient identity-based encryption (IBE) scheme based on the ring learning with errors (RLWE) assumption in the (quantum) random oracle model. Our IBE scheme is (asymptotically) as efficient as the most practical lattice-based IBE scheme proposed by Ducal et al. (ASIACRYPT 2014). Furthermore, our scheme is adaptively and anonymously secure, and its security reduction is tight. We design our IBE scheme by instantiating the framework of Gentry et al. (STOC 2008) using the compact preimage sampling proposed by Yu et al. (CRYPTO 2023). The tightness of our IBE scheme is obtained by combining the proof technique of Katsumata et al. (ASIACRYPT 2018) with the results for ideal lattices developed by Mera et al. (PKC 2022).

1 Introduction

1.1 Background

Identity-based encryption (IBE), introduced by Shamir [46], is a generalization of public key encryption (PKE). Unlike traditional PKE, IBE allows senders to encrypt messages using a master public key mpk and an arbitrary string id, such as the recipient's username or email address. With this functionality, IBEs do not require a Public Key Infrastructure (PKI). In addition, when communicating with multiple users, an IBE only needs one mpk, whereas a PKE requires as many public keys as there are users. Because of these advantages, IBE has been discussed in the context of several practical applications [5,15,20,27,38,49,54]. The first IBE schemes were proposed in 2001 [11,19]. Since then, they have been improved from various perspectives [8,9,21,50]. However, these traditional constructions are vulnerable to quantum attacks due to Shor's algorithm [47].

Lattice-based cryptography is a desirable alternative to traditional number-theoretic cryptography due to its security against quantum computers, algorithmic simplicity, and versatility in constructing various advanced schemes. For the standard encryption and signature, lattice-based constructions are the most practical of the post-quantum cryptosystems. In 2022, the National Institute of Standards and Technology (NIST) announced that the first four post-quantum algorithms would be standardized [12,22,44]. These schemes are as efficient as the classical ones.

M.-J. Saarinen and D. Smith-Tone (Eds.): PQCrypto 2024, LNCS 14771, pp. 300–321, 2024.
https://doi.org/10.1007/978-3-031-62743-9_10

Gentry et al. proposed the first lattice-based IBE scheme (GPV-IBE) [25]. The security of the scheme is based on the learning with errors (LWE) assumption [45] in the random oracle model (ROM). Since then, there have been several studies on lattice-based IBEs from different perspectives, including extending to the quantum ROM (QROM) [32,33,53], removing the random oracle [1,2,13,16,31,51], and adding security properties [3,4,24,30,42]. However, these constructions only indicate improvements on the theoretical side. In particular, these IBE schemes still suffer from inefficiencies when instantiated on ideal lattices and in the ROM. On the practical side, Ducas et al. [23] proposed the first practical lattice-based IBE scheme (DLP-IBE) based on NTRU lattices, and McCarthy et al. [39] then improved its performance through a series of software optimizations. Subsequently, Bert et al. [6,7] provided efficient implementations based on ideal/module lattices.

The most efficient lattice-based IBE scheme is the DLP-IBE [23]. However, even this scheme faces several efficiency challenges. One of these is the tightness of the security reduction. The efficiency of cryptographic schemes depends on the tightness of the security reduction. In general, we say that the security of a cryptographic scheme under a given computational assumption is tight if breaking the scheme's security is as hard as solving the assumption. More precisely, suppose that we have proved that if there is an adversary who can break the security of the scheme with advantage ϵ and running time T, we can break the underlying assumption with advantage ϵ' and running time T'. We then obtain the inequality $\epsilon/T \leq L \cdot \epsilon'/T'$, where L is the reduction loss of the scheme. The scheme is tightly secure if $L = O(1)$. If the scheme is not tightly secure, we need to set the parameters larger to ensure the concrete security of the scheme. Unfortunately, the security of the DLP-IBE is not tight because the reduction loss depends on a polynomial in the number of random oracle queries made by the adversary. From the above, the natural question is:

Can we construct a tightly-secure IBE scheme that is as efficient as the DLP-IBE?

1.2 Our Contributions

In this paper, we answer the above questions in the affirmative. Namely, we propose an IBE scheme that is (asymptotically) as efficient as the DLP-IBE scheme and tightly secure under the ring-LWE (RLWE) assumption in the (Q)ROM. Furthermore, our proposed IBE scheme also satisfies anonymity, by ensuring that the ciphertext does not reveal any information about the identity as well as the message. Table 1 compares the efficiency and security of our proposed IBE scheme and those of the other lattice-based IBE schemes in the (Q)ROM.

Technical Overview. Here, we briefly summarize the spirit of our construction and security proof. Our proposed scheme is a GPV-IBE [25] instantiated by Yu et al.'s compact preimage sampling [52]. Hence, we first briefly describe the GPV-IBE.

Table 1. Efficiency and security comparison of adaptively and anonymously secure lattice-based IBE schemes in the (Q)ROM. The columns $|\mathsf{mpk}|$, $|\mathsf{sk}|$, and $|\mathsf{ct}|$ indicate the size of a master public key, a secret key, and a ciphertext, respectively. n and q are the parameters of the underlying assumption. Q_H and Q_id are the numbers of (quantum) random oracle and secret key queries, respectively. ϵ is the advantage of the scheme. [†] Its security losses are based on the results of previous works [25,34] because the security proof is omitted in their paper.

Scheme	$|\mathsf{mpk}|$	$|\mathsf{sk}|$	$|\mathsf{ct}|$	Assumption	Security loss	(Q)ROM?
[25]	$O(n^2 \log^2 q)$	$O(n \log^2 q)$	$O(n \log^2 q)$	LWE	$O(Q_\mathsf{H})$	ROM
[53]	$O(n^2 \log^2 q)$	$O(n \log^2 q)$	$O(n \log^2 q)$	LWE	$O\left(\frac{(Q_\mathsf{H}+Q_\mathsf{id})^4}{\epsilon}\right)$	QROM
[23]	$O(n \log q)$	$O(n \log q)$	$O(n \log q)$	NTRU	$O(Q_\mathsf{H})$	ROM
[33]	$O(n^2 \log^2 q)$	$O(n \log^2 q)$	$O(n \log^2 q)$	LWE	$O(1)$	(Q)ROM
[33]	$O(n \log^2 q)$	$O(n \log^2 q)$	$O(n \log^2 q)$	RLWE	$O(1)$	QROM
[23] + [34]	$O(n \log q)$	$O(n \log q)$	$O(n \log q)$	NTRU	$O(Q_\mathsf{H}^2)$	QROM
[29][†]	$O(n \log^2 q)$	$O(n \log^2 q)$	$O(n \log^2 q)$	RLWE	$O(Q_\mathsf{H})$	ROM
[29][†] + [34]	$O(n \log^2 q)$	$O(n \log^2 q)$	$O(n \log^2 q)$	RLWE	$O(Q_\mathsf{H}^2)$	QROM
Ours	$O(n \log q)$	$O(n \log q)$	$O(n \log q)$	RLWE	$O(1)$	(Q)ROM

GPV-IBE and its tight security proof by Katsumata et al. [32,33]. In the GPV-IBE, a master public key is a fat matrix $\mathbf{A} \in \mathbb{Z}_q^{n \times m}$ and a master secret key is its trapdoor $\mathsf{td}_\mathbf{A}$, which enables one to sample a short preimage $\mathbf{z} \in \mathbb{Z}_q^m$ such that $\mathbf{Az} = \mathbf{u}$ given an arbitrary vector $\mathbf{u} \in \mathbb{Z}_q^n$. A secret key sk_id for an identity $\mathsf{id} \in \{0,1\}^*$ is a short vector $\mathbf{z}_\mathsf{id} \in \mathbb{Z}_q^m$ such that $\mathbf{Az}_\mathsf{id} = \mathbf{u}_\mathsf{id}$, where $\mathbf{u}_\mathsf{id} = \mathsf{H}(\mathsf{id})$ for a hash function $\mathsf{H} : \{0,1\}^* \to \mathbb{Z}_q^n$. A ciphertext for a message $\mathsf{M} \in \{0,1\}$ and an identity id consists of $\mathbf{c} = \mathbf{A}^\top \mathbf{s} + \mathbf{e} \in \mathbb{Z}_q^m$ and $c = \mathbf{u}_\mathsf{id}^\top \mathbf{s} + e + \mathsf{M} \cdot \lfloor q/2 \rfloor \in \mathbb{Z}_q$ and , where $\mathbf{s} \in \mathbb{Z}_q^n$ is a uniform random vector, $\mathbf{e}$ and e are small noise term.

Katsumata et al. showed that GPV-IBE has tight security in the (Q)ROM. We outline the security proof in the ROM. To answer a random oracle query on id, the reduction algorithm chooses a random short vector $\mathbf{z}_\mathsf{id}$ and sets $\mathbf{u}_\mathsf{id} = \mathbf{Az}_\mathsf{id}$. If $\mathbf{z}_\mathsf{id}$ has sufficient entropy, $\mathbf{u}_\mathsf{id}$ is uniformly distributed over $\mathbb{Z}_q^n$. Using this fact, the reduction algorithm returns $\mathbf{u}_\mathsf{id}$ for the random oracle query and $\mathbf{z}_\mathsf{id}$ for the secret key query. Note that the reduction algorithm knows a secret key $\mathbf{z}_{\mathsf{id}^*}$ for a target identity id^*. Thus, the reduction algorithm can simulate the challenge ciphertext by generating $\mathbf{c}^* = \mathbf{A}^\top \mathbf{s} + \mathbf{e} \in \mathbb{Z}_q^m$ and $c^* = \mathbf{z}_{\mathsf{id}^*}^\top \mathbf{c}^* + \mathsf{M} \cdot \lfloor q/2 \rfloor \in \mathbb{Z}_q$. It is important to note that we no longer need the LWE instance $(\mathbf{u}_{\mathsf{id}^*}, \mathbf{u}_{\mathsf{id}^*}^\top \mathbf{s} + e)$ to simulate the challenge ciphertext. The actual proof uses the noise re-randomization technique by Katsumata and Yamada [31] to simulate the distribution of c^* (especially the noise term e).

Compact scheme using Yu et al.'s approximate preimage sampling. At the heart of the GPV-IBE is the preimage sampling technique, which is also a source of inefficiency. This is because the width of the matrix A must be $m = O(n \log q)$ to realize preimage sampling. To improve the practicality, Chen et al. [17] introduced the relaxed notion of preimage sampling, called approximate preimage sampling. With approximate preimage sampling, instead of sampling an exact preimage $\mathbf{z}$ such that $\mathbf{A}\mathbf{z} = \mathbf{u}$, sample an approximate preimage $\mathbf{z}'$ such that $\mathbf{A}\mathbf{z}' = \mathbf{u} + \tilde{\mathbf{z}}$, where $\tilde{\mathbf{z}} \in \mathbb{Z}_q^n$ is a short error vector. Recently, Yu, Jia, and Wang [52] developed a compact framework for approximate preimage sampling that uses a nearly square matrix instead of the short and fat one used in [17].

To construct an efficient IBE scheme, we instantiate the GPV-IBE using Yu et al.'s approximate preimage sampling. Very recently and concurrently, Izabachène et al. [28][1] and Jia et al. [29] proposed compact IBE schemes by using the approximate preimage sampling. The design idea of our scheme is similar to their schemes. Namely, to encrypt a message M under an identity id, we use a short random vector $\mathbf{s} \in \mathbb{Z}_q^n$ instead of a uniform random vector. This is to keep the error term $\mathbf{z}'^{\top}\mathbf{s}$ that appears during decryption small, where $\mathbf{z}'$ is an approximate preimage vector.

To prove the tight security of our scheme, we use the security proof of Katsumata et al. [32,33]. Mostly, their proof technique can be applied, but there is one part where it cannot. This is the part that simulates the c^* of the challenge ciphertext. In their proof, they use a secret key $\mathbf{z}_{\mathsf{id}^*}$, which is an exact preimage vector, and the noise re-randomization technique of Katsumata and Yamada [31] to approximately simulate c^*. In our scheme, $\mathbf{z}_{\mathsf{id}^*}$ is an approximate preimage vector rather than an exact preimage vector. Then, when we try to simulate c^*, we have

$$
\begin{aligned}
c^* &= \mathbf{z}_{\mathsf{id}^*}^{\top}\mathbf{c}^* + \mathsf{M} \cdot \lfloor q/2 \rceil \\
&= \mathbf{z}_{\mathsf{id}^*}^{\top}(\mathbf{A}^{\top}\mathbf{s} + \mathbf{e}) + \mathsf{M} \cdot \lfloor q/2 \rceil \\
&= (\mathbf{A}\mathbf{z}_{\mathsf{id}^*})^{\top}\mathbf{s} + \mathbf{z}_{\mathsf{id}^*}^{\top}\mathbf{e} + \mathsf{M} \cdot \lfloor q/2 \rceil \\
&= \mathbf{u}_{\mathsf{id}^*}^{\top}\mathbf{s} + \tilde{\mathbf{z}}^{\top}\mathbf{s} + \mathbf{z}_{\mathsf{id}^*}^{\top}\mathbf{e} + \mathsf{M} \cdot \lfloor q/2 \rceil,
\end{aligned}
$$

where $\tilde{\mathbf{z}}$ is an approximate error. Unfortunately, the noise re-randomization technique cannot account for this additional error term $\tilde{\mathbf{z}}^{\top}\mathbf{s}$, which appears by evaluating $\mathbf{A}\mathbf{z}_{\mathsf{id}^*}$. Therefore, we must use a different approach to complete the proof.

Solution: Multi-hint Extended (R)LWE [40]. To overcome the above problem, we use the multi-hint extended (R)LWE assumption, introduced by Mera et al. [40], instead of the noise re-randomization technique. Roughly speaking, this assumption says that the (R)LWE assumption holds even if some hints of the secret $\mathbf{s}$ and the noise $\mathbf{e}$ are given. Mera et al. [40] shows a reduction from the (R)LWE problem to this variant. This allows us to exactly simulate c^* by using an approximate preimage vector $\mathbf{z}_{\mathsf{id}^*}$ and some hints without the noise re-randomization. Therefore, we can complete the proof.

Finally, we note that the above proof naturally fits in the ideal lattices and the QROM setting similar to [32,33]. Thus, the proof in the classical ROM can be almost automatically converted into the one in the QROM.

Organization. This paper is organized as follows. In Sect. 2, we review some preliminaries. In Sect. 3, we present our IBE scheme. In Sect. 4, we show a secu-

---

[1] Their proposed scheme is *selectively* secure in the *standard model*.

rity proof of our IBE scheme in the ROM. In Sect. 5, we provide security proof of our IBE scheme in the QROM.

2   Preliminaries

Notations. Let λ denote the security parameter throughout the paper. For integers $a, b \in \mathbb{N}$ such that $a \leq b$, let $[a, b] := \{a, a + 1, \cdots, b\}$ and $[a] := \{1, 2, \cdots, a\}$. For a finite set $\mathcal{S}$, let $\mathcal{U}(\mathcal{S})$ be the uniform distribution over $\mathcal{S}$ and let $s \leftarrow_\$ \mathcal{S}$ denote the operation of sampling a from $\mathcal{S}$ uniformly at random. For a probability distribution $\mathcal{X}$, let $x \leftarrow_\$ \mathcal{X}$ denote the operation of sampling x according to $\mathcal{X}$. For two random variables X and Y over $\mathcal{S}$, the statistical distance $\Delta(X, Y)$ between X and Y is defined as $\Delta(X, Y) := \sum_{s \in \mathcal{S}} \Pr[X = s] - \Pr[Y = s]$. We say that the two distributions X and Y are statistically close when $\Delta(X, Y)$ is negligible in the security parameter λ.

2.1   Linear Algebra and Lattices

A vector is denoted by a bold lowercase letter and in column form. For a vector $\mathbf{x} \in \mathbb{R}^n$, let $\|\mathbf{x}\|$ and $\|\mathbf{x}\|_\infty$ be the ℓ_2-norm and ℓ_∞-norm of $\mathbf{x}$, respectively. A matrix is denoted by a bold uppercase letter. For a matrix $\mathbf{X} \in \mathbb{R}^{n \times m}$, let $\tilde{\mathbf{X}}$ denote the Gram-Schmidt orthogonalization of $\mathbf{X}$. The largest singular value of $\mathbf{X}$ is denote by $s_1(\mathbf{X}) = \max_{\mathbf{y} \neq \mathbf{0}} \|\mathbf{X}\mathbf{y}\| / \|\mathbf{y}\|$.

We write $\mathbf{\Sigma} \succ 0$, when a symmetric matrix $\mathbf{\Sigma} \in \mathbb{R}^{m \times m}$ is positive definite, i.e., $\mathbf{x}^\top \mathbf{\Sigma} \mathbf{x} > 0$ for all non-zero vector $\mathbf{x} \in \mathbb{R}^m \setminus \{\mathbf{0}\}$. We write $\mathbf{\Sigma}_1 \succ \mathbf{\Sigma}_2$ if $\mathbf{\Sigma}_1 - \mathbf{\Sigma}_2 \succ 0$. For any scalar s, we write $\mathbf{\Sigma} \succ s$ if $\mathbf{\Sigma} - s \cdot \mathbf{I}_m \succ 0$, where $\mathbf{I}_m \in \mathbb{R}^{m \times m}$ is the m-by-m identity matrix. We use $\sqrt{\mathbf{\Sigma}}$ to denote any square root of $\mathbf{\Sigma}$ when the context permits it.

Given $\mathbf{B} = (\mathbf{b}_1 \| \cdots \| \mathbf{b}_n) \in \mathbb{R}^{m \times n}$ with all $\mathbf{b}_i$'s linearly independent, the lattice generated by $\mathbf{B}$ is $\Lambda(\mathbf{B}) = \{\mathbf{B}\mathbf{z} \mid \mathbf{z} \in \mathbb{Z}^n\}$. The dimension of $\Lambda(\mathbf{B})$ is n, and $\mathbf{B}$ is called a basis. For a lattice Λ, let $\Lambda^* = \{\mathbf{y} \in \text{span}(\Lambda) \mid \mathbf{x}^\top \mathbf{y} \in \mathbb{Z}, \forall \mathbf{x} \in \Lambda\}$ be the dual lattice of Λ.

In lattice-based cryptography, the q-ary lattice is special interest and defined by some $\mathbf{B} \in \mathbb{Z}_q^{n \times m}$ as

$$\Lambda_q^\perp(\mathbf{B}) := \{\mathbf{x} \in \mathbb{Z}^m \mid \mathbf{B}\mathbf{x} = \mathbf{0} \bmod q\}.$$

For any $\mathbf{u} \in \mathbb{Z}_q^n$ and $\mathbf{x} \in \mathbb{Z}^m$ such that $\mathbf{B}\mathbf{x} = \mathbf{u} \bmod q$, the *shifted lattice* is the set

$$\Lambda_\mathbf{u}^\perp(\mathbf{B}) = \{\mathbf{z} \in \mathbb{Z}^m \mid \mathbf{A}\mathbf{z} = \mathbf{u} \bmod q\} = \Lambda_q^\perp(\mathbf{B}) + \mathbf{x}.$$

2.2   Ideal Lattices

In this paper, we shall denote with $\mathcal{R}$ a polynomial ring $\mathcal{R} = \mathbb{Z}[X]/\Phi$, where Φ is an irreducible polynomial. For the sake of simplicity, Φ will be equal to

$X^n + 1$, where n is a power of 2. We shall use a standard notation $\mathcal{R}_q$ to denote $\mathcal{R}/q\mathcal{R} = \mathbb{Z}_q[X]/\Phi$. The modulus q is chosen such that polynomial Φ of degree n factors into n distinct linear polynomials over $\mathbb{Z}_q$, i.e., $\Phi = \prod_{i \in [n]} \phi_i$, where each ϕ_i is linear. Therefore, by Chinese remainder theorem (CRT), the ring $\mathcal{R}_q$ factors into n ideals and can be written as $\mathcal{R}_q \cong \prod_{i \in [n]} \mathcal{R}_q/\phi_i$. Since each $\mathcal{R}_q/\phi_i$ is isomorphic to $\mathbb{Z}_q$, this gives an isomorphism between $\mathcal{R}_q$ and $\mathbb{Z}_q^n$.

For a polynomial $a = \sum_{i=0}^{n-1} a_i X^i \in \mathcal{R}$, let $\mathsf{coeff}(a) = (a_0, a_1, \ldots, a_{n-1})^\top \in \mathbb{Z}^n$ be its coefficient vector and the anti-circulant matrix

$$\mathsf{Rot}(a) := \begin{pmatrix} a_0 & -a_{n-1} & \cdots & -a_1 \\ a_1 & a_0 & \cdots & -a_2 \\ \vdots & \vdots & \ddots & \vdots \\ a_{n-1} & a_{n-2} & \cdots & a_0 \end{pmatrix}$$
$$= \left(\mathsf{coeff}(a), \mathsf{coeff}(aX), \ldots, \mathsf{coeff}(aX^{n-1}) \right) \in \mathbb{Z}^{n \times n}$$

be its matrix form. Let $\bar{a} = a(X^{-1})$ for $a \in \mathcal{R}$, then $\bar{a} = a_0 - \sum_{i=1}^{n-1} a_{n-i} X^i$. More generally, let $\sigma_k(a) = a(X^k)$ for $k \in \mathbb{Z}_n^*$. Then, for two polynomials $a, b \in \mathcal{R}$, the following properties hold:

- $\mathsf{Rot}(a) + \mathsf{Rot}(b) = \mathsf{Rot}(a + b)$,
- $\mathsf{Rot}(a) \cdot \mathsf{Rot}(b) = \mathsf{Rot}(ab)$,
- $\mathsf{Rot}(\bar{a}) = \mathsf{Rot}(a)^\top$.

In the rest of the paper, we identify a with $\mathsf{coeff}(a)$ when the context is clear.

2.3 Gaussian

The Gaussian function $\rho : \mathbb{R}^m \to (0, 1]$ is defined as $\rho(\mathbf{x}) = \exp(-\pi \mathbf{x}^\top \mathbf{x})$. Applying a linear transformation given by an invertible matrix $\mathbf{B}$ yields

$$\rho_{\mathbf{B}}(\mathbf{x}) = \rho(\mathbf{B}^{-1}\mathbf{x}) = \exp(-\pi \mathbf{x}^\top \Sigma^{-1} \mathbf{x}),$$

where $\Sigma = \mathbf{B}\mathbf{B}^\top$. Since $\rho_{\mathbf{B}}$ is exactly determined by Σ, we also write it as $\rho_{\sqrt{\Sigma}}$. For a lattice Λ and $\mathbf{c} \in \mathrm{span}(\Lambda)$, the discrete Gaussian distribution $\mathcal{D}_{\Lambda + \mathbf{c}, \sqrt{\Sigma}}$ is defined as

$$\mathcal{D}_{\Lambda + \mathbf{c}, \sqrt{\Sigma}}(\mathbf{x}) := \frac{\rho_{\sqrt{\Sigma}}(\mathbf{x})}{\sum_{\mathbf{y} \in \Lambda + \mathbf{c}} \rho_{\sqrt{\Sigma}}(\mathbf{y})}$$

for any $\mathbf{x} \in \Lambda + \mathbf{c}$. If $\Lambda = \mathbb{Z}^n$ and $\mathbf{c} = \mathbf{0}$, we shall write just $\mathcal{D}_{\sqrt{\Sigma}}$, and is $\Sigma = \sigma \mathbf{I}_n$ for a positive real $\sigma \in \mathbb{R}$, we write $\mathcal{D}_\sigma$.

For a lattice Λ and a positive real $\epsilon \in (0, 1)$, let

$$\eta_\epsilon(\Lambda) := \min\left\{ s > 0 \mid \rho(s \cdot \Lambda^*) \leq 1 + \epsilon \right\}$$

be the smoothing parameter with respect to Λ and ϵ. We write $\sqrt{\Sigma} \geq \eta_\epsilon(\Lambda)$ if $\rho_{\sqrt{\Sigma^{-1}}}(\Lambda^*) \leq 1 + \epsilon$.

We have the following useful facts on a discrete Gaussian distribution.

Lemma 2.1 ([35]). *We have* $\Pr_{\mathbf{x} \leftarrow\$ \mathcal{D}_\sigma}[\|\mathbf{x}\|_\infty > \sqrt{\lambda}\sigma] \leq 2\exp(-\lambda/2)$.

Lemma 2.2 ([37]). *Let q, k, and m be positive integers such that $q \geq 2$ and $k < m \leq \mathsf{poly}(\lambda)$. Let $\mathbf{A} = (\mathbf{I}_k\|\bar{\mathbf{A}}) \in \mathcal{R}_q^{k\times m}$, where $\bar{\mathbf{A}} \in \mathcal{R}_q^{k\times(m-k)}$ is sampled uniformly at random. Then, with probability $1 - 2^{-\Omega(n)}$ over the choice of $\bar{\mathbf{A}}$, the distribution of $\mathbf{A}\mathbf{z} \bmod q$, where $\mathbf{z} \leftarrow\$ \mathcal{D}_\sigma^m$ with $\sigma \geq 2nq^{k/m+2/(nm)}$ is within statistical distance $2^{-\Omega(n)}$ of the uniform distribution over $\mathcal{R}_q^2$.*

2.4   Ring Learning with Errors

The security of our IBE scheme is reduced to the ring learning with errors (RLWE) assumption, introduced by [36], and the multi-hint extended RLWE (mheRLWE) assumption, introduced by [40].

Definition 2.1 (RLWE [36]). *For integers n, m, and $q > 2$, an error distribution χ over $\mathcal{R}$, and an algorithm $\mathcal{A}$, the advantage for the RLWE problem $\mathsf{RLWE}_{q,m,\chi}$ of $\mathcal{A}$ is defined as follows:*

$$\mathsf{Adv}_{\mathcal{A}}^{\mathsf{RLWE}_{q,m,\chi}}(\lambda) := |\Pr[\mathcal{A}(\mathbf{a}, \mathbf{a}s + \mathbf{e} \bmod q) = 1] - \Pr[\mathcal{A}(\mathbf{a}, \mathbf{b}) = 1]|,$$

where $\mathbf{a}, \mathbf{b} \leftarrow\$ \mathcal{R}_q^m$, $s \leftarrow\$ \chi$, and $\mathbf{e} \leftarrow\$ \chi^m$. We say that the RLWE assumption holds if $\mathsf{Adv}_{\mathcal{A}}^{\mathsf{RLWE}_{q,m,\chi}}(\lambda) = \mathsf{negl}(\lambda)$ for any quantum polynomial time (QPT) algorithm $\mathcal{A}$.

As shown in [14,43], the RLWE assumption $\mathsf{RLWE}_{q,m,\chi}$ with any (not necessarily prime) modulus q and some β-bounded error distribution[2] χ is implied by the worst-case hardness of the approximate shortest vector problem in an ideal lattice with approximation factor $\approx q/\beta$.

Definition 2.2 (mheRLWE [40]). *Let n, m, and l be positive integers. For $i \in [l]$, let $\mu_i \in \mathcal{R}$ and $\boldsymbol{\nu}_i \in \mathcal{R}^m$ be arbitrary such that $\|\mu_i\|_\infty, \|\boldsymbol{\nu}_i\|_\infty \leq C$ for some $C > 0$, and fixed by the adversary in advance. For integers n, m, and $q > 2$, a distribution χ over $\mathcal{R}$, and an algorithm $\mathcal{A}$, the advantage for the mheRLWE problem $\mathsf{mheRLWE}_{q,m,\chi,l,C}$ of $\mathcal{A}$ is defined as follows:*

$$\begin{aligned} \mathsf{Adv}_{\mathcal{A}}^{\mathsf{mheRLWE}_{q,m,\chi,l,C}}(\lambda) := \big| &\Pr[\mathcal{A}(\mathbf{a}, \mathbf{a}s + \mathbf{e} \bmod q, \mathsf{Hint}) = 1] \\ &- \Pr[\mathcal{A}(\mathbf{a}, \mathbf{b}, \mathsf{Hint}) = 1]\big|, \end{aligned}$$

where $\mathbf{a}, \mathbf{b} \leftarrow\$ \mathcal{R}_q^m$, $s, g_1, \ldots, g_l \leftarrow\$ \chi$, $\mathbf{e}, \mathbf{h}_1, \ldots, \mathbf{h}_l \leftarrow\$ \chi^m$, and

$$\mathsf{Hint} = \big\{ \mu_i, \mu_i s + g_i, \boldsymbol{\nu}_i, \boldsymbol{\nu}_i \circ \mathbf{e} + \mathbf{h}_i \big\}_{j\in[l]},$$

and $\circ$ denotes the component-wise product. We say that the mheRLWE assumption holds if $\mathsf{Adv}_{\mathcal{A}}^{\mathsf{mheRLWE}_{q,m,\chi,l,C}}(\lambda) = \mathsf{negl}(\lambda)$ for any QPT algorithm $\mathcal{A}$.

---

[2] A distribution χ over $\mathcal{R}$ is β-bounded if $\Pr_{e \leftarrow\$ \chi}[\|e\|_\infty \leq \beta] = 1$.

Lemma 2.3 ([40]). *For any QPT algorithm $\mathcal{A}$, positive integers n, q, m, and l, and positive reals σ, δ, C, ϵ satisfying $\sigma\sqrt{1-(\sqrt{2+l}\sigma nC)^2/\delta^2} > \eta_\epsilon(\mathbb{Z}^{n+nl})$, there exists a QPT algorithm $\mathcal{B}$ such that*

$$\mathsf{Adv}_{\mathcal{A}}^{\mathsf{mheRLWE}_{q,m,\mathcal{D}_\delta,l,C}}(\lambda) \leq \mathsf{Adv}_{\mathcal{B}}^{\mathsf{RLWE}_{q,m,\mathcal{D}_\sigma}}(\lambda) + \mathsf{negl}(\lambda).$$

2.5 Approximate Trapdoor for Ideal Lattices

Here, we introduce the approximate trapdoor for ideal lattices.

Definition 2.3 (Approximate Trapdoor). *Let m and Q be positive integers. A string $\mathsf{td_a}$ is called an (α, β)-approximate trapdoor for a vector $\mathbf{a} \in \mathcal{R}_Q^m$ if there is a PPT algorithm $\mathsf{AppSampPre}$ that given $\mathbf{a}$, $\mathsf{td_a}$, a polynomial $u \in \mathcal{R}_Q$, and an auxiliary information aux, outputs $\mathbf{z} \in \mathcal{R}^m$ such that $\|\mathbf{z}\| \leq \beta$ and there is a vector $\tilde{z} \in \mathcal{R}$ satisfying $\|\tilde{z}\| \leq \alpha$ and $\mathbf{a}^\top \mathbf{z} = u + \tilde{z} \bmod Q$.*

Yu et al. [52] proposed the compact approximate trapdoor for (ideal) lattices. In the following lemma, we summarise their results on the compact approximate trapdoor.

Lemma 2.4 ([52]). *Let m, p, q, and Q be positive integers with $m > n$ and $Q = pq$. Let $\mathbf{a} \in \mathcal{R}_Q^m$ and $\mathsf{td_a} \in \mathcal{R}^m$ be vectors such that $\mathbf{a}^\top \mathsf{td_a} = p \bmod Q$ and $\mathsf{aux} = \sigma$ be a positive real satisfying $\sigma^2 \geq \eta_\epsilon(\mathbb{Z}^n)^2(q^2+1)(s_1(\mathsf{Rot}(\mathsf{td_a}))^2+1)$. Then, there exists a PPT algorithm $\mathsf{AppSampPre}$ such that:*

1. $\mathsf{td_a}$ *is* $(\sqrt{n(p^2-1)/12}, \sqrt{nm}\sigma)$-*approximate trapdoor.*
2. *The following two distributions are statistically indistinguishable:*

$$\left\{(\mathbf{a}, \mathbf{z}, u, \tilde{z}) : \begin{array}{l} u \leftarrow_\$ \mathcal{R}_Q, \mathbf{z} \leftarrow_\$ \mathsf{AppSampPre}(\mathbf{a}, \mathsf{td_a}, u, \sigma), \\ \tilde{z} := u - \mathbf{a}^\top \mathbf{z} \bmod Q \end{array}\right\},$$

$$\left\{(\mathbf{a}, \mathbf{z}, u, \tilde{z}) : \mathbf{z} \leftarrow_\$ \mathcal{D}_\sigma^m, \tilde{z} \leftarrow_\$ \mathcal{R}_p, u := \mathbf{a}^\top \mathbf{z} + \tilde{z} \bmod Q\right\}.$$

2.6 Identity-Based Encryption

Syntax. We use the standard syntax of identity-based encryption (IBE) [11,33]. Let $\mathcal{ID}$ and $\mathcal{M}$ be the scheme's identity and message space, respectively. An IBE scheme Π consists of the following four PPT algorithms.

- $\mathsf{Setup}(1^\lambda) \to (\mathsf{msk}, \mathsf{mpk})$: It takes as input a security parameter 1^λ and outputs a master secret key msk and a master public key mpk.
- $\mathsf{KGen}(\mathsf{msk}, \mathsf{mpk}, \mathsf{id}) \to \mathsf{sk}$: It takes as input the master secret key msk, the master public key mpk, and an identity $\mathsf{id} \in \mathcal{ID}$ and outputs a secret key $\mathsf{sk_{id}}$. We assume that id is implicitly included in $\mathsf{sk_{id}}$.
- $\mathsf{Enc}(\mathsf{mpk}, \mathsf{id}, \mathsf{M}) \to \mathsf{ct}$: It takes as input the master public key mpk, an identity id, and a message $\mathsf{M} \in \mathcal{M}$ and outputs a ciphertext ct.
- $\mathsf{Dec}(\mathsf{sk_{id}}, \mathsf{ct}) \to \mathsf{M}$: It takes as input a secret key $\mathsf{sk_{id}}$ and a ciphertext ct and outputs a message M.

Correctness. We require correctness: that is, for all $\lambda \in \mathbb{N}$, all $\text{id} \in \mathcal{ID}$, and all $\text{M} \in \mathcal{M}$, it holds that

$$\Pr\left[\text{Dec}(\text{KGen}(\text{msk}, \text{mpk}, \text{id}), \text{Enc}(\text{mpk}, \text{id}, \text{M})) = \text{M}\right] = 1 - \text{negl}(\lambda),$$

where $(\text{mpk}, \text{msk}) \leftarrow_\$ \text{Setup}(1^\lambda)$ and the probability is taken over the randomness used in $\text{Setup}(1^\lambda)$, $\text{KGen}(\text{msk}, \text{mpk}, \text{id})$, and $\text{Enc}(\text{mpk}, \text{id}, \text{M})$.

Security. Let Π be an IBE scheme. The security notion is defined via a game between an adversary $\mathcal{A}$ and the challenger Chal.

Setup: At the outset of the game, Chal runs $\text{Setup}(1^\lambda) \to (\text{msk}, \text{mpk})$ and gives mpk to $\mathcal{A}$. Chal also picks a random coin $\text{coin} \leftarrow_\$ \{0,1\}$ and keeps it secretly. After the mpk is given, $\mathcal{A}$ can adaptively make the following two types of queries to Chal.

Key Queries: If $\mathcal{A}$ submits $\text{id} \in \mathcal{ID}$ to Chal, Chal runs $\text{KGen}(\text{msk}, \text{mpk}, \text{id}) \to \text{sk}_{\text{id}}$ and returns it.

Challenge Query: If $\mathcal{A}$ submits a message $\text{M}^* \in \mathcal{M}$ and an identity $\text{id}^* \in \mathcal{ID}$ to Chal, Chal proceeds as follows. If $\text{coin} = 0$, it runs $\text{Enc}(\text{mpk}, \text{id}^*, \text{M}^*) \to \text{ct}^*$ and gives the challenge ciphertext ct^* to $\mathcal{A}$. If $\text{coin} = 1$, it chooses the challenge ciphertext ct^* from a ciphertext space uniformly at random and gives it to $\mathcal{A}$. $\mathcal{A}$ can only make a challenge query once during the game. We prohibit $\mathcal{A}$ from making a challenge query for an identity id^* such that it has already made a key query for the same $\text{id} = \text{id}^*$ and vice versa.

Guess: Finally, $\mathcal{A}$ outputs a guess $\widehat{\text{coin}}$ for coin. The advantage of $\mathcal{A}$ is defined as

$$\text{Adv}^{\text{IBE}}_{\mathcal{A},\Pi}(\lambda) := |\Pr[\widehat{\text{coin}} = \text{coin}] - 1/2|.$$

We say that an IBE scheme Π is *adaptively anonymous* if the advantage of any PPT $\mathcal{A}$ is negligible in the above game.

3 Our IBE Scheme

In this section, we propose our IBE scheme Π.

Parameters. Our IBE scheme Π uses the following parameters. Let n, p, q, and $Q = pq$ be positive integers. Let δ be a positive real that will serve as a discrete Gaussian parameter. Let α and β be positive reals. Let the message space $\mathcal{M}$ of Π be $\{0,1\}^n \subset \mathcal{R}$ and the identity space of Π be $\{0,1\}^{\ell_{\text{id}}}$, where $\ell_{\text{id}} = \ell_{\text{id}}(\lambda)$ denotes the identity-length. Let $\text{H} : \{0,1\}^{\ell_{\text{id}}} \to \mathcal{R}_Q$ be a hash function treated as a (quantum) random oracle during security proofs. Let $\text{Expand} : \{0,1\}^{256} \to \mathcal{R}_Q$ be a function that maps a seed to an element in $\mathcal{R}_Q$.

Let ω_1 and ω_{-1} be positive integers such that $\omega_1 + \omega_{-1} \leq n$. Let

$$T(n, \omega_1, \omega_{-1}) := \left\{ v \in \mathcal{R} \mid v \text{ has } \begin{array}{l} \omega_1 \text{ coefficients equal to } 1; \\ \omega_{-1} \text{ coefficients equal to } -1; \\ n - \omega_1 - \omega_{-1} \text{ coefficients equal to } 0. \end{array} \right\}.$$

Let α be the parameter controlling the quality of the trapdoor such that

$$\sqrt{s_1(\mathsf{Rot}(f\bar{f} + g\bar{g}))} \leq \alpha \|(f, g)\| = \alpha\sqrt{2(\omega_1 + \omega_{-1})},$$

where $f, g \in T(n, \omega_1, \omega_{-1})$ is the trapdoor. Let $\sigma \geq r\alpha\sqrt{2(\omega_1 + \omega_{-1})(1 + q^2)}$ be the width for approximate preimages, where $r = \eta_\epsilon(\mathbb{Z}^n)$. Let β be the acceptance bound of $\|(z_0 + \tilde{z}, \gamma z_1, \gamma z_2)\|$, where (z_0, z_1, z_2) is the approximate preimage, $\tilde{z}$ is the approximate error, and $\gamma = \frac{\sqrt{\sigma^2 + (p^2 - 1)/12}}{\sigma}$ such that $\|z_0 + \tilde{z}\| \approx \gamma\|z_1\| \approx \gamma\|z_2\|$.

3.1 Construction

Our IBE scheme $\Pi = (\mathsf{Setup}, \mathsf{KGen}, \mathsf{Enc}, \mathsf{Dec})$ is given as follows.

$\mathsf{Setup}(1^\lambda) \rightarrow (\mathsf{msk}, \mathsf{mpk})$:

```
1 :   seed_a ←$ {0,1}^256, ā := Expand(seed_a)
2 :   f_1,...,f_5,g_1,...,g_5 ←$ U(T(n,ω_1,ω_{-1}))
3 :   for i = 1,...5 do
4 :      for j = 1,...5 do
5 :         Find k ∈ Z*_n minimizing s_1 (Rot(f_i f̄_i + σ_k(g_j) σ_k(g_j)‾))
6 :         (f,g) := (f_i, σ_k(g_j))
7 :         if √(s_1(Rot(f f̄ + g ḡ))) ≤ α√(2(ω_1 + ω_{-1})) then
8 :            b := p - (af + g) mod Q
9 :               return (msk, mpk) := ((f,g), (seed_a, b))
10:         endif
11:      endfor
12:   endfor
13:   Restart
```

$\mathsf{KGen}(\mathsf{msk}, \mathsf{mpk}, \mathsf{id} \in \mathcal{ID}) \to \mathsf{sk}_{\mathsf{id}}$:

---

1 : $\bar{a} := \mathsf{Expand}(\mathsf{seed}_a)$, $u_{\mathsf{id}} := \mathsf{H}(\mathsf{id})$

2 : $\mathbf{a} := (1, \bar{a}, b)^{\top}$, $\mathsf{td}_{\mathbf{a}} := (-g, -f, 1)^{\top}$

3 : $\mathbf{z} := (z_0, z_1, z_2)^{\top} \leftarrow_{\$} \mathsf{AppSampPre}(\mathbf{a}, \mathsf{td}_{\mathbf{a}}, u_{\mathsf{id}}, \sigma)$

4 : $\tilde{z} := u_{\mathsf{id}} - \mathbf{a}^{\top}\mathbf{z} \bmod Q$

5 :   **if** $\|(z_0 + \tilde{z}, \gamma z_1, \gamma z_2)\| > \beta$ **then**

6 :   Restart

7 :   **endif**

8 : $\mathbf{z}_{\mathsf{id}} := (z_1, z_2)^{\top} \in \mathcal{R}^2$

9 :   **return** $\mathsf{sk}_{\mathsf{id}} := \mathbf{z}_{\mathsf{id}}$

$\mathsf{Enc}(\mathsf{mpk}, \mathsf{id} \in \mathcal{ID}, \mathsf{M} \in \mathcal{M}) \to \mathsf{ct}$:

---

1 : $\bar{a} := \mathsf{Expand}(\mathsf{seed}_a)$, $u_{\mathsf{id}} := \mathsf{H}(\mathsf{id})$, $\mathbf{a}' := (a, b)^{\top} \in \mathcal{R}_Q^2$

2 : $s, e_0, e_1, e_2 \leftarrow_{\$} \mathcal{D}_{\delta}$, $\mathbf{e}' \leftarrow_{\$} \mathcal{D}_{\delta}^2$

3 : $e_u := e_0 + e_1 + e_2$

4 : $c_u := u_{\mathsf{id}}s + e_u + \mathsf{M}\lfloor Q/2 \rceil \bmod Q$

5 : $\mathbf{c} := \mathbf{a}'s + \mathbf{e}' \bmod Q \in \mathcal{R}_Q^2$

6 :   **return** $\mathsf{ct} := (c_u, \mathbf{c})$

$\mathsf{Dec}(\mathsf{mpk}, \mathsf{sk}_{\mathsf{id}}, \mathsf{ct}) \to \mathsf{M}'$:

---

1 : $d \leftarrow c_u - \mathbf{c}^{\top}\mathbf{z}_{\mathsf{id}} \bmod Q$

2 :   **return** $\mathsf{M}' := \lfloor \mathsf{coeff}(d) \cdot 2/Q \rceil \bmod 2$

3.2   Correctness

Here, we show the correctness of the above IBE scheme Π. Suppose that the ciphertext $\mathsf{ct} = (\mathbf{c}, c_u)$ and the secret key $\mathsf{sk}_{\mathsf{id}} = \mathbf{z}_{\mathsf{id}}$ are correctly generated. When the Dec algorithm operates as specified, we have

$$
\begin{aligned}
d &= c_u - \mathbf{c}^{\top}\mathbf{z}_{\mathsf{id}} \\
&= u_{\mathsf{id}}s + e_u + \mathsf{M}\lfloor Q/2 \rceil - (\mathbf{a}'s + \mathbf{e}')^{\top}\mathbf{z}_{\mathsf{id}} \\
&= u_{\mathsf{id}}s + e_u + \mathsf{M}\lfloor Q/2 \rceil - s\mathbf{a}'^{\top}\mathbf{z}_{\mathsf{id}} - \mathbf{e}'^{\top}\mathbf{z}_{\mathsf{id}} \\
&= u_{\mathsf{id}}s + e_u + \mathsf{M}\lfloor Q/2 \rceil - s(u_{\mathsf{id}} - \tilde{z} - z_0) - \mathbf{e}'^{\top}\mathbf{z}_{\mathsf{id}} \\
&= \mathsf{M}\lfloor Q/2 \rceil + \underbrace{e_u + s(\tilde{z} + z_0) - \mathbf{e}'^{\top}\mathbf{z}_{\mathsf{id}}}_{\text{noise}}.
\end{aligned}
$$

Here, we use the fact that $\mathbf{a}'^{\top}\mathbf{z}_{\mathsf{id}} = az_1 + bz_2 = u_{\mathsf{id}} - z_0 - \tilde{z} \bmod Q$ holds. For the correctness, we need $\|\text{noise}\|_{\infty} \le Q/4$. By Lemma 2.1, $\|s\|_{\infty} \le \sqrt{\lambda}\delta$, $\|\mathbf{e}'\|_{\infty} \le \sqrt{\lambda}\delta$, and $\|e_u\|_{\infty} \le \sqrt{3\lambda}\delta$ hold. Also, by construction, $\|(z_0 + \tilde{z}, z_1, z_2)\| \le \|(z_0 +$

$\tilde{z}, \gamma z_1, \gamma z_2)\| \leq \beta$ holds. Thus, the ℓ_∞-norm of noise is bounded by

$$
\begin{aligned}
\|\mathsf{noise}\|_\infty &= \|e_u + s(\tilde{z} + z_0) - \mathbf{e}'^\top \mathbf{z}_{\mathsf{id}}\|_\infty \\
&\leq \|e_u\|_\infty + \|s(\tilde{z} + z_0) - \mathbf{e}'^\top \mathbf{z}_{\mathsf{id}}\|_\infty \\
&\leq \|e_u\|_\infty + \|(s, -\mathbf{e}'^\top)\|_\infty \cdot \|(\tilde{z} + z_0, z_1, z_2)\| \\
&\leq \sqrt{3\lambda}\delta + \sqrt{\lambda}\delta\beta \\
&\leq \sqrt{\lambda}\delta(\sqrt{3} + \beta).
\end{aligned}
$$

We will set the parameters below so that the upper bound is less than $Q/4$.

3.3 Parameter Conditions

We set the parameters of the scheme Π to satisfy the following conditions:

- $Q/4 > \sqrt{\lambda}\delta(\sqrt{3} + \beta)$ for correctness.
- $\sigma \geq 2nQ^{2/3+2/3n}$ for Lemma 2.2.
- $\sigma \geq \sqrt{2(\omega_1 + \omega_{-1})(1 + q^2)}$ for Lemma 2.4.
- $\beta \geq \sqrt{n(p^2-1)/12} + \sqrt{3}n\sigma$ for KGen to run correctly.
- $\sigma > \left(1 - (\sqrt{2 + l}\sigma n C)^2/\delta^2\right)^{-1/2} \eta_\epsilon(\mathbb{Z}^{n+nQ_{\mathsf{H}}})$ for Lemma 2.3, where Q_{H} is the maximum number of random oracle queries.
- The $\mathsf{RLWE}_{Q,1,\chi}$ assumption holds, where $\chi = \mathcal{U}(\mathcal{T}(n, \omega_1, \omega_{-1}))$.

4   Security Proof in the Random Oracle Model

In this section, we prove the following theorem.

Theorem 4.1. *Let* $\chi = \mathcal{U}(\mathcal{T}(n, \omega_1, \omega_{-1}))$ *be a distribution. If the* $\mathsf{RLWE}_{Q,1,\chi}$ *and* $\mathsf{mheRLWE}_{Q,2,\mathcal{D}_\delta,Q_{\mathsf{H}},C}$ *assumptions hold, our IBE scheme* Π *in Sect. 3.1 achieves adaptively anonymous in the random oracle model. In particular, for any classical PPT adversary* $\mathcal{A}$ *making at most* Q_{H} *random oracle queries to* H *and* Q_{id} *secret key queries, there exist two classical PPT reduction algorithms* $\mathcal{B}_1$ *and* $\mathcal{B}_2$ *such that*

$$
\mathsf{Adv}_{\mathcal{A},\Pi}^{\mathsf{IBE}}(\lambda) \leq \mathsf{Adv}_{\mathcal{B}_1}^{\mathsf{RLWE}_{Q,1,\chi}}(\lambda) + \mathsf{Adv}_{\mathcal{B}_2}^{\mathsf{mheRLWE}_{Q,2,\mathcal{D}_\delta,Q_{\mathsf{H}},C}}(\lambda) + \mathsf{negl}(\lambda).
$$

Proof. Let $\mathcal{A}$ be a classical PPT adversary attacking the adaptively anonymous security of Π. Without loss of generality, we make some simplifying assumptions about $\mathcal{A}$. First, we assume that whenever $\mathcal{A}$ queries a secret key or asks for a challenge ciphertext, the corresponding id has already been queried to the random oracle H. Second, we assume that $\mathcal{A}$ makes the same query to the same random oracle at most once. Third, we assume that $\mathcal{A}$ does not repeat secret key queries for the same identity more than once.

We show the security of Π via the following games. In each game, we define E_i as the event that $\mathcal{A}$ wins in Game$_i$.

Game$_0$: This is the real security game. At the beginning of the game, the challenger Chal runs $(\mathsf{mpk}, \mathsf{msk}) \leftarrow_\$ \mathsf{Setup}(1^\lambda)$ and gives mpk to $\mathcal{A}$. Chal then samples coin $\leftarrow_\$ \{0, 1\}$ and keeps it secret. During the game, $\mathcal{A}$ can make many random oracle and secret key queries and one challenge query. For each query, Chal behaves as follows:

 - When $\mathcal{A}$ makes a random oracle query to H on id, Chal samples a random polynomial $u_{\mathsf{id}} \leftarrow_\$ \mathcal{R}_Q$ and locally stores the tuple $(\mathsf{id}, u_{\mathsf{id}}, \perp)$, and returns u_{id} to $\mathcal{A}$.
 - When $\mathcal{A}$ makes a secret key query for id, Chal returns $\mathsf{sk}_{\mathsf{id}} := \mathbf{z}_{\mathsf{id}} = (z_1, z_2)$, where $(z_0, z_1, z_2)^\top \leftarrow_\$ \mathsf{AppSampPre}(\mathbf{a}, \mathsf{td}_\mathbf{a}, u_{\mathsf{id}}, \sigma)$.
 - When $\mathcal{A}$ makes the challenge query for the challenge identity id^* and a message M^*, Chal returns $\mathsf{ct}^* = (c_u^*, \mathbf{c}^*) \leftarrow_\$ \mathsf{Enc}(\mathsf{mpk}, \mathsf{id}^*, \mathsf{M}^*)$ if coin $= 0$ and $\mathsf{ct}^* \leftarrow_\$ \mathcal{R}_Q^3$ if coin $= 1$.

At the end of the game, $\mathcal{A}$ outputs a guess $\widehat{\mathsf{coin}}$ for coin. Finally, Chal outputs $\widehat{\mathsf{coin}}$.

By definition, we have

$$\left| \Pr[\mathsf{E}_0] - \frac{1}{2} \right| = \left| \Pr[\widehat{\mathsf{coin}} = \mathsf{coin}] - \frac{1}{2} \right| = \mathsf{Adv}_{\mathcal{A},\Pi}^{\mathsf{IBE}}(\lambda).$$

Game$_1$: This game changes the way random oracle queries to H are answered. At the beginning of the game, for $i \in [Q_\mathsf{H}]$, Chal samples $\mathbf{z}_i \leftarrow_\$ \mathcal{D}_\sigma^3$ and $\tilde{z}_i \leftarrow_\$ \mathcal{R}_p$ and computes $u_i := \mathbf{a}^\top \mathbf{z}_i + \tilde{z}_i \bmod Q$. To answer the i-th random oracle queries for id_i, Then, it locally stores $\{ (u_i, \mathbf{z}_i, \tilde{z}_i) \}_{i \in [Q_\mathsf{H}]}$. For the i-th random oracle query to H on id, Chal retrieves the tuple $(u_i, \mathbf{z}_i, \tilde{z}_i)$ from local storage, returns $u_{\mathsf{id}} := u_i$, and locally stores $(\mathsf{id}, u_{\mathsf{id}}, (\mathbf{z}_i, \tilde{z}_i))$.

Based on our choice of parameters, we can apply Lemma 2.4, which ensures that all u_{id} are statistically close to uniform as in Game$_0$. Thus, the statistical distance between the view of $\mathcal{A}$ in Game$_0$ and Game$_1$ is $Q_\mathsf{H} \cdot \mathsf{negl}(\lambda) = \mathsf{negl}(\lambda)$. Therefore, we have

$$|\Pr[\mathsf{E}_0] - \Pr[\mathsf{E}_0]| = \mathsf{negl}(\lambda).$$

Game$_2$: This game changes the way secret key queries are answered. In particular, Chal does not use the trapdoor $\mathsf{td}_\mathbf{a}$ to create them. When $\mathcal{A}$ queries a secret key for id, Chal retrieves the unique tuple $(\mathsf{id}, u_{\mathsf{id}}, (\mathbf{z} = (z_0, z_1, z_2)^\top, \tilde{z}))$ from local storage and returns $\mathsf{sk}_{\mathsf{id}} := \mathbf{z}_{\mathsf{id}} = (z_1, z_2)^\top$.

Based on our choice of parameters, we can apply Lemma 2.4, which ensures that $\mathbf{z}$ in Game$_1$ sampled by the AppSampPre algorithms distribute statistically close to $\mathcal{D}_\sigma^3$ conditioned on u_{id}. Since $\mathcal{A}$ obtains at most Q_{id} secret keys, we have

$$|\Pr[\mathsf{E}_1] - \Pr[\mathsf{E}_2]| = Q_{\mathsf{id}} \cdot \mathsf{negl}(\lambda) = \mathsf{negl}(\lambda).$$

Game$_3$: This game changes the way the master public key is generated. Chal samples $b \leftarrow_\$ \mathcal{R}_Q$ uniformly at random instead of setting $b = p - (af + g) \bmod Q$ and does not sample a trapdoor $\mathsf{td}_\mathbf{a} = (-g, -f, 1)^\top$. Since Chal did not use a trapdoor $\mathsf{td}_\mathbf{a}$ to answer $\mathcal{A}$'s secret key queries in Game_2, it can answer all $\mathcal{A}$'s secret key queries similarly.

The $\mathsf{RLWE}_{Q,1,\chi}$ assumption ensures that Game_2 and Game_3 are computationally indistinguishable. To show this, we use $\mathcal{A}$ to construct an RLWE adversary $\mathcal{B}_1$ as follows: $\mathcal{B}_1$ is given a problem instance of RLWE as (a, b'), where $b' = af + g$ or $b' = v$ and $f, g \leftarrow_\$ \mathcal{U}(\mathcal{T}(n, \omega_1, \omega_{-1}))$, $v \leftarrow_\$ \mathcal{R}_Q$. Then, $\mathcal{B}_1$ gives $\mathsf{mpk} = (a, b := p - b')$ to $\mathcal{A}$. During the game, $\mathcal{B}_1$ behaves as Chal in Game_2 upon random oracle queries, secret key queries, and a challenge query. At the end of the game, $\mathcal{A}$ outputs $\widehat{\mathsf{coin}}$. Finally, $\mathcal{B}_1$ returns 1 if $\widehat{\mathsf{coin}} = \mathsf{coin}$ and 0 otherwise. It can be seen that if (a, b') is a valid RLWE sample (i.e., $b' = af + g$), the view of $\mathcal{A}$ corresponds to Game_2. Otherwise (i.e., $v \leftarrow_\$ \mathcal{R}_Q$), it corresponds to Game_3. We therefore conclude that assuming the hardness of $\mathsf{RLWE}_{Q,1,\chi}$ problem, we have

$$|\Pr[\mathsf{E}_2] - \Pr[\mathsf{E}_3]| = \mathsf{negl}(\lambda).$$

Game_4: This game changes the way the challenge ciphertext is created when $\mathsf{coin} = 0$. Recall that in the previous games, Chal created a valid challenge ciphertext ct^* as in the real scheme when $\mathsf{coin} = 0$. In this game, to create ct^* for identity id^* and message M^*, Chal first retrieves the unique tuple $(\mathsf{id}^*, u_{\mathsf{id}^*}, (\mathbf{z}^* = (z_0^*, z_1^*, z_2^*)^\top, \tilde{z}^*))$ from local storage and sets $\mathbf{z}_{\mathsf{id}^*} = (z_1^*, z_2^*)^\top$. Chal the computes

$$\mathbf{c}^* := \mathbf{a}'s + \mathbf{e}' \bmod Q,$$
$$c_u^* := (\mathbf{c}^* - \mathbf{e}')^\top \mathbf{z}_{\mathsf{id}^*} + e_u - s(z_0^* + \tilde{z}^*) + \mathsf{M}^* \lfloor Q/2 \rceil \bmod Q.$$

where $s, e_0, e_1, e_2 \leftarrow_\$ \mathcal{D}_\delta$, $\mathbf{e}' \leftarrow_\$ \mathcal{D}_\delta^2$, and $e_u := e_0 + e_1 + e_2$. This change is conceptual because

$$
\begin{aligned}
c_u^* &= (\mathbf{c}^* - \mathbf{e}')^\top \mathbf{z}_{\mathsf{id}^*} + e_u - s(z_0^* + \tilde{z}^*) + \mathsf{M}^* \lfloor Q/2 \rceil \\
&= s\mathbf{a}'^\top \mathbf{z}_{\mathsf{id}^*} + e_u - s(z_0^* + \tilde{z}^*) + \mathsf{M}^* \lfloor Q/2 \rceil \\
&= s(u_{\mathsf{id}^*} + z_0^* + \tilde{z}^*) + e_u - s(z_0^* + \tilde{z}^*) + \mathsf{M}^* \lfloor Q/2 \rceil \\
&= u^* s + e_u + \mathsf{M}^* \lfloor Q/2 \rceil.
\end{aligned}
$$

Therefore, we have

$$\Pr[\mathsf{E}_3] = \Pr[\mathsf{E}_4].$$

Game_5: This game further changes the way the challenge ciphertext is created when $\mathsf{coin} = 0$. If $\mathsf{coin} = 0$, to create the challenge ciphertext, Chal first samples $\mathbf{c}^* \leftarrow_\$ \mathcal{R}_Q^2$ and computes c_u^* as in Game_4.

The $\mathsf{mheRLWE}_{Q,2,\mathcal{D}_\delta,Q_\mathsf{H},C}$ assumption ensures that Game_4 and Game_5 are computationally indistinguishable. To show this, we use $\mathcal{A}$ to construct an mheRLWE adversary $\mathcal{B}_2$ as follows: $\mathcal{B}_2$ declares $\{\mu_i, \boldsymbol{\nu}_i\}_{i \in [Q_\mathsf{H}]}$ to the mheRLWE challenger in advance, where $\mu_i = z_{0,i} + \tilde{z}$, $\boldsymbol{\nu}_i = (z_{1,i}, z_{2,i})^\top$, $z_{0,i}, z_{1,i}, z_{2,i} \leftarrow_\$ \mathcal{D}_\sigma$, and $\tilde{z}_i \leftarrow_\$ \mathcal{R}_p$. $\mathcal{B}_2$ receives $(\mathbf{a}', \mathbf{c}^*, \mathsf{Hint})$, where $\mathbf{c}^* =$

$\mathbf{a}'s + \mathbf{e}' \bmod Q$ or $\mathbf{c}^* \leftarrow_\$ \mathcal{R}_Q^2$, Hint $= \{\mu_i, \mu_i s + e_{0,i}, \boldsymbol{\nu}_i, \boldsymbol{\nu}_i \circ \mathbf{e}' + \mathbf{e}_i\}_{i \in [Q_H]}$, $e_{0,i} \leftarrow_\$ \mathcal{D}_\delta$, and $\mathbf{e}_i \leftarrow_\$ \mathcal{D}_\delta^2$. Then, $\mathcal{B}_2$ gives mpk $= \mathbf{a}'$ to $\mathcal{A}$. During the game, $\mathcal{B}_2$ behaves as Chal in Game$_4$. Upon $\mathcal{A}$'s challenge query, $\mathcal{B}_2$ behaves in the same way as in Game$_4$. At the end of the game, $\mathcal{A}$ outputs coin. Finally, $\mathcal{B}_2$ returns 1 if $\widetilde{\text{coin}}$ = coin and 0 otherwise. If $\mathbf{c}^*$ is a valid mheRLWE sample, then the view of $\mathcal{A}$ corresponds to Game$_4$. Otherwise, it corresponds to Game$_5$. Thus, we complete the reduction, and we have

$$|\Pr[\mathsf{E}_4] - \Pr[\mathsf{E}_5]| = \mathsf{negl}(\lambda).$$

Game$_6$: This game changes the way the challenge ciphertext is created again. Regardless of the value coin, Chal samples $c_u^* \leftarrow_\$ \mathcal{R}_Q$. Thus, we have

$$\Pr[\mathsf{E}_6] = 0.$$

We show that Game$_5$ and Game$_6$ are statistically indistinguishable. Based on our choice of parameters, we can apply Lemma 2.2, which ensures that $\mathbf{c}^{*\top}\mathbf{z}_{\mathsf{id}^*}$ is statistically close to uniform. Therefore, the statistical distance between the view of $\mathcal{A}$ in Game$_5$ and Game$_6$ is $\mathsf{negl}(\lambda)$ and we have

$$|\Pr[\mathsf{E}_5] - \Pr[\mathsf{E}_6]| = \mathsf{negl}(\lambda).$$

Therefore, by combining everything, the theorem is proven. □

5   Security Proof in the Quantum Random Oracle Model

In this section, we provide the security proof of our scheme in the quantum random oracle model (QROM). To do this, we recall the foundations of the QROM with reference to [33,48]. We refer to [41] for more details.

5.1   Preliminaries on the QROM

Quantum Computation. Let $|0\rangle := (1,0)^\top$ and $|1\rangle := (0,1)^\top$ denote the state of 1 qubit. Let $|\psi\rangle = \sum_{x \in \{0,1\}^n} \alpha_x |x\rangle \in \mathbb{C}^{2^n}$ denote the state of n qubits, where $\alpha_x \in \mathbb{C}$ satisfying $\sum_{x \in \{0,1\}^n} |\alpha_x|^2 = 1$ and $|x\rangle = |x_1 x_2 \cdots x_n\rangle = |x_1\rangle \otimes \cdots \otimes |x_n\rangle$ for $x_1, \ldots, x_n \in \{0,1\}$ is an orthonormal basis on $\mathbb{C}^{2^n}$ called the computational basis. If we measure the state $|\psi\rangle$ in the computational basis, the classical bit $x \in \{0,1\}^n$ is observed with probability $|\alpha_x|^2$ and the state becomes $|x\rangle$.

An arbitrary evolution of quantum state from $|\psi\rangle$ to $|\psi'\rangle$ is described by a unitary matrix $\mathbf{U}$, where $|\psi'\rangle = \mathbf{U}|\psi\rangle$. In short, a quantum algorithm is described by quantum evolutions that consist of evolutions with unitary matrices and measurements. The running time of a quantum algorithm $\mathcal{A}$ is defined as the number of universal gates and measurements required to execute $\mathcal{A}$. If $\mathcal{A}$ is a quantum oracle algorithm, we assume that $\mathcal{A}$ runs in a unit of time. Any efficient classical computation can be achieved by a quantum computation efficiently. In particular, for any function f that is classically computable, there exists a unitary matrix $\mathbf{U}_f$ such that $\mathbf{U}_f|x,y\rangle = |x, f(x) \oplus y\rangle$, and the number of universal gates to express $\mathbf{U}_f$ is linear in the size of a classical circuit that computes f.

QROM. The notion of the QROM was introduced by Boneh et al. [10] as an extension of the (classical) random oracle model (ROM) in a quantum world. In the case of the ROM, the QROM is an idealized model, where a hash function is idealized to be an oracle that simulates a random function. On the other hand, as opposed to the ROM, the hash function in the QROM is a quantumly accessible oracle. In security proofs in the QROM, a random function $H : X \rightarrow Y$ is uniformly chosen at the beginning, and an adversary can make queries on a quantum state $\sum_{x,y} \alpha_{x,y} |x\rangle |y\rangle$ to the oracle and receive $\sum_{x,y} \alpha_{x,y} |x\rangle |H(x) \oplus y\rangle$.

Let $\mathcal{A}^{|H\rangle}$ denote a quantum algorithm that can quantumly access the oracle $|H\rangle$. As shown by Zhandry [53], quantum random oracles can be simulated by a family of $2Q_H$-wise independent hash functions for an adversary that quantumly accesses the random oracle at most Q_H times.

Lemma 5.1 ([53]). *Any quantum algorithm $\mathcal{A}$ making quantum queries to random oracles can be efficiently simulated by a quantum algorithm $\mathcal{B}$, which has the same output distribution but makes no queries.*

5.2 Security Proof

Theorem 5.1. *Let $\chi = \mathcal{U}(\mathcal{T}(n, \omega_1, \omega_{-1}))$ be a distribution. If the $\mathsf{RLWE}_{Q,1,\chi}$ and $\mathsf{mheRLWE}_{Q,2,\mathcal{D}_\delta,Q_H,C}$ assumptions hold, our IBE scheme Π in Sect. 3.1 achieves adaptively anonymous in the quantum random oracle model. In particular, for any quantum PPT adversary $\mathcal{A}$ making at most Q_H random oracle queries to H and Q_{id} secret key queries, there exist two quantum polynomial time reduction algorithms $\mathcal{B}_1$ and $\mathcal{B}_2$ such that*

$$\mathsf{Adv}_{\mathcal{A},\Pi}^{\mathsf{IBE}}(\lambda) \leq \mathsf{Adv}_{\mathcal{B}_1}^{\mathsf{RLWE}_{Q,1,\chi}}(\lambda) + \mathsf{Adv}_{\mathcal{B}_2}^{\mathsf{mheRLWE}_{Q,2,\mathcal{D}_\delta,Q_H,C}}(\lambda) + \mathsf{negl}(\lambda).$$

Proof. We show the security of Π via the following games. In each game, we define E_i as the event that $\mathcal{A}$ wins in Game_i. Let $\mathsf{Samp}(\sigma, p; r)$ be a PPT algorithm that, given a Gaussian parameter σ, a positive integer p, and a random coin $r \in \{0,1\}^{\ell_r}$, outputs $(\mathbf{z}, \tilde{z})$, where $\mathbf{z}$ sampled from a distribution statistically close to $\mathcal{D}_\sigma^3$ and $\tilde{z}$ sampled from $\mathcal{U}(\mathcal{R}_p)$.

Game_0: This is the actual security game. At the beginning of the game, the challenge Chal chooses a random function $H : \{0,1\}^{\ell_{\mathsf{id}}} \rightarrow \mathcal{R}_Q$. Then, it generates $(\mathsf{msk}, \mathsf{mpk}) \leftarrow_\$ \mathsf{Setup}(1^\lambda)$ and gives mpk to the adversary $\mathcal{A}$. Then, it samples $\mathsf{coin} \leftarrow_\$ \{0,1\}$ and keeps it secret. During the game, $\mathcal{A}$ can make many (quantum) random oracle and secret key queries and one challenge query. These queries are handled as follows:

  – When $\mathcal{A}$ makes a (quantum) random oracle query on a quantum state $\sum_{\mathsf{id},y} \alpha_{\mathsf{id},y} |\mathsf{id}\rangle |y\rangle$, Chal returns $\sum_{\mathsf{id},y} \alpha_{\mathsf{id},y} |\mathsf{id}\rangle |H(\mathsf{id}) \oplus y\rangle$.
  – When $\mathcal{A}$ makes a secret key query for id, Chal returns $\mathsf{sk}_{\mathsf{id}} := \mathbf{z}_{\mathsf{id}} = (z_1, z_2)$, where $(z_0, z_1, z_2)^\top \leftarrow_\$ \mathsf{AppSampPre}(\mathbf{a}, \mathsf{td}_\mathbf{a}, u_{\mathsf{id}}, \sigma)$.
  – When $\mathcal{A}$ makes a challenge query for id^* and a message M^*, Chal returns $\mathsf{ct}^* \leftarrow_\$ \mathsf{Enc}(\mathsf{mpk}, \mathsf{id}^*, M^*)$ if $\mathsf{coin} = 0$ and $\mathsf{ct}^* \leftarrow_\$ \mathcal{R}_Q^3$ if $\mathsf{coin} = 1$.

At the end of the game, $\mathcal{A}$ outputs a guess $\widehat{\text{coin}}$ for coin. Finally, Chal outputs coin.

By definition, we have

$$\left|\Pr[\mathsf{E}_0] - \frac{1}{2}\right| = \left|\Pr[\widehat{\text{coin}} = \text{coin}] - \frac{1}{2}\right| = \mathsf{Adv}^{\mathsf{IBE}}_{\mathcal{A},\Pi}(\lambda).$$

Game$_1$: This game changes the way the random oracle H is simulated. First, Chal picks a $2Q_H$-wise independent hash function $\mathsf{h}_{2Q_H} : \{0,1\}^{\ell_{\text{id}}} \rightarrow \{0,1\}^{\ell_r}$. Then, we define $\mathsf{H}(\text{id}) := \mathbf{a}^\top \mathbf{z} + \tilde{z} \bmod Q$, where $(\mathbf{z}, \tilde{z}) := \mathsf{Samp}(\sigma, p; \mathsf{h}_{2Q_H}(\text{id}))$, and use this H throughout the game.

For any fixed id, the distribution of H(id) is identical, and its statistical distance from the uniform distribution is $\mathsf{negl}(\lambda)$ due to Lemma 2.4. Note that in this game, we only change the distribution of u_{id} for each identity, and the way we create secret keys is unchanged. Then, due to Lemma 5.1, we have

$$|\Pr[\mathsf{E}_0] - \Pr[\mathsf{E}_1]| = \mathsf{negl}(\lambda).$$

Game$_2$: This game changes the way secret key queries are answered. By the end of this game, Chal will no longer require the trapdoor $\mathsf{td}_{\mathbf{a}}$ to generate the secret keys. When $\mathcal{A}$ queries a secret key for id, Chal returns $\mathsf{sk}_{\text{id}} := \mathbf{z}_{\text{id}} = (z_1, z_2)$, where $(\mathbf{z} = (z_0, z_1, z_2), \tilde{z}) := \mathsf{Samp}(\sigma, p; \mathsf{h}_{2Q_H}(\text{id}))$.

By following the same argument in Game$_2$ of the proof of Theorem 4.1, we have

$$|\Pr[\mathsf{E}_1] - \Pr[\mathsf{E}_2]| = Q_{\text{id}} \cdot \mathsf{negl}(\lambda) = \mathsf{negl}(\lambda).$$

Game$_3$: This game changes the way the master public key is generated. Chal samples $b \leftarrow_\$ \mathcal{R}_Q$ uniformly at random instead of setting $b = p - (af + g) \bmod Q$ and does not sample a trapdoor $\mathsf{td}_{\mathbf{a}} = (-g, -f, 1)^\top$. Since Chal did not use a trapdoor $\mathsf{td}_{\mathbf{a}}$ to answer $\mathcal{A}$'s secret key queries in Game$_2$, it can answer all $\mathcal{A}$'s secret key queries similarly.

By following the same argument in Game$_3$ of the proof of Theorem 4.1, we have

$$|\Pr[\mathsf{E}_2] - \Pr[\mathsf{E}_3]| = \mathsf{negl}(\lambda)$$

when the RLWE$_{Q,1,\chi}$ assumption holds.

Game$_4$: This game changes the way the challenge ciphertext is created when coin $= 0$. Recall that in the previous games, Chal created a valid challenge ciphertext ct^* as in the real scheme when coin $= 0$. In this game, to create ct^* for identity id* and message M*, Chal first retrieves the unique tuple $(\text{id}^*, u_{\text{id}^*}, (\mathbf{z}^* = (z_0^*, z_1^*, z_2^*)^\top, \tilde{z}^*))$ from local storage and sets $\mathbf{z}_{\text{id}^*} = (z_1^*, z_2^*)^\top$. Chal the computes

$$\mathbf{c}^* := \mathbf{a}'s + \mathbf{e}' \bmod Q,$$

$$c_u^* := (\mathbf{c}^* - \mathbf{e}')^\top \mathbf{z}_{\text{id}^*} + e_u - s(z_0^* + \tilde{z}^*) + \mathsf{M}^* \lfloor Q/2 \rceil \bmod Q.$$

where $s, e_0, e_1, e_2 \leftarrow_\$ \mathcal{D}_\delta$, $\mathbf{e}' \leftarrow_\$ \mathcal{D}_\delta^2$, and $e_u := e_0 + e_1 + e_2$.

By following the same argument in Game_4 of the proof of Theorem 4.1, we have

$$\Pr[\mathsf{E}_3] = \Pr[\mathsf{E}_4].$$

Game_5: This game further changes the way the challenge ciphertext is created when $\mathsf{coin} = 0$. If $\mathsf{coin} = 0$, to create the challenge ciphertext, Chal first samples $\mathbf{c}^* \leftarrow_\$ \mathcal{R}_Q^2$ and computes c_u^* as in Game_4.

By following the same argument in Game_5 of the proof of Theorem 4.1, we have

$$|\Pr[\mathsf{E}_4] - \Pr[\mathsf{E}_5]| = \mathsf{negl}(\lambda)$$

when the $\mathsf{mheRLWE}_{Q,2,\mathcal{D}_\delta,Q_{\mathsf{H}},C}$ assumption holds.

Game_6: This game further changes the way the challenge ciphertext is created again. Regardless of the value coin, Chal samples $c_u^* \leftarrow_\$ \mathcal{R}_Q$. Thus, we have

$$\Pr[\mathsf{E}_6] = 0.$$

By following the same argument in Game_6 of the proof of Theorem 4.1, we have

$$|\Pr[\mathsf{E}_5] - \Pr[\mathsf{E}_6]| = \mathsf{negl}(\lambda).$$

Therefore, by combining everything, the theorem is proven. □

Acknowledgements. This research was in part conducted under a contract of "Research and development on new generation cryptography for secure wireless communication services" among "Research and Development for Expansion of Radio Wave Resources (JPJ000254)", which was supported by the Ministry of Internal Affairs and Communications, Japan. This work was in part supported by JSPS KAKENHI Grant Numbers JP22H03590 and JP21H03395.

References

1. Abla, P., Liu, F.-H., Wang, H., Wang, Z.: Ring-based identity based encryption – asymptotically shorter MPK and tighter security. In: Nissim, K., Waters, B. (eds.) TCC 2021. LNCS, vol. 13044, pp. 157–187. Springer, Cham (2021). https://doi.org/10.1007/978-3-030-90456-2_6

2. Agrawal, S., Boneh, D., Boyen, X.: Efficient lattice (H)IBE in the standard model. In: Gilbert [26], pp. 553–572 (2010). https://doi.org/10.1007/978-3-642-13190-5_28

3. Agrawal, S., Boneh, D., Boyen, X.: Lattice basis delegation in fixed dimension and shorter-ciphertext hierarchical IBE. In: Rabin, T. (ed.) CRYPTO 2010. LNCS, vol. 6223, pp. 98–115. Springer, Heidelberg (2010). https://doi.org/10.1007/978-3-642-14623-7_6

4. Alperin-Sheriff, J., Peikert, C.: Circular and KDM security for identity-based encryption. In: Fischlin, M., Buchmann, J., Manulis, M. (eds.) PKC 2012. LNCS, vol. 7293, pp. 334–352. Springer, Heidelberg (2012). https://doi.org/10.1007/978-3-642-30057-8_20

5. Asokan, N., Kostiainen, K., Ginzboorg, P., Ott, J., Luo, C.: Applicability of identity-based cryptography for disruption-tolerant networking. In: Proceedings of the 1st International MobiSys Workshop on Mobile Opportunistic Networking, pp. 52–56 (2007)

6. Bert, P., Eberhart, G., Prabel, L., Roux-Langlois, A., Sabt, M.: Implementation of lattice trapdoors on modules and applications. In: Cheon, J.H., Tillich, J.-P. (eds.) PQCrypto 2021 2021. LNCS, vol. 12841, pp. 195–214. Springer, Cham (2021). https://doi.org/10.1007/978-3-030-81293-5_11

7. Bert, P., Fouque, P.-A., Roux-Langlois, A., Sabt, M.: Practical implementation of ring-SIS/LWE based signature and IBE. In: Lange, T., Steinwandt, R. (eds.) PQCrypto 2018. LNCS, vol. 10786, pp. 271–291. Springer, Cham (2018). https://doi.org/10.1007/978-3-319-79063-3_13

8. Blazy, O., Kiltz, E., Pan, J.: (Hierarchical) Identity-based encryption from affine message authentication. In: Garay, J.A., Gennaro, R. (eds.) CRYPTO 2014. LNCS, vol. 8616, pp. 408–425. Springer, Heidelberg (2014). https://doi.org/10.1007/978-3-662-44371-2_23

9. Boldyreva, A., Goyal, V., Kumar, V.: Identity-based encryption with efficient revocation. In: Ning, P., Syverson, P.F., Jha, S. (eds.) ACM CCS 2008, pp. 417–426. ACM Press (2008).https://doi.org/10.1145/1455770.1455823

10. Boneh, D., Dagdelen, Ö., Fischlin, M., Lehmann, A., Schaffner, C., Zhandry, M.: Random oracles in a quantum world. In: Lee, D.H., Wang, X. (eds.) ASIACRYPT 2011. LNCS, vol. 7073, pp. 41–69. Springer, Heidelberg (2011). https://doi.org/10.1007/978-3-642-25385-0_3

11. Boneh, D., Franklin, M.: Identity-based encryption from the weil pairing. In: Kilian, J. (ed.) CRYPTO 2001. LNCS, vol. 2139, pp. 213–229. Springer, Heidelberg (2001). https://doi.org/10.1007/3-540-44647-8_13

12. Bos, J., et al.: CRYSTALS-kyber: a CCA-secure module-lattice-based KEM. In: 2018 IEEE European Symposium on Security and Privacy (EuroS&P), pp. 353–367. IEEE (2018)

13. Boyen, X., Li, Q.: Towards tightly secure lattice short signature and id-based encryption. In: Cheon, J.H., Takagi, T. (eds.) ASIACRYPT 2016. LNCS, vol. 10032, pp. 404–434. Springer, Heidelberg (2016). https://doi.org/10.1007/978-3-662-53890-6_14

14. Brakerski, Z., Langlois, A., Peikert, C., Regev, O., Stehlé, D.: Classical hardness of learning with errors. In: Boneh, D., Roughgarden, T., Feigenbaum, J. (eds.) 45th ACM STOC, pp. 575–584. ACM Press (2013). https://doi.org/10.1145/2488608.2488680

15. Butler, K.R., Ryu, S., Traynor, P., McDaniel, P.D.: Leveraging identity-based cryptography for node ID assignment in structured p2p systems. IEEE Trans. Parallel Distrib. Syst. **20**(12), 1803–1815 (2008)

16. Cash, D., Hofheinz, D., Kiltz, E., Peikert, C.: Bonsai trees, or how to delegate a lattice basis. In: Gilbert, H. (ed.) EUROCRYPT 2010. LNCS, vol. 6110, pp. 523–552. Springer, Heidelberg (2010). https://doi.org/10.1007/978-3-642-13190-5_27

17. Chen, Y., Genise, N., Mukherjee, P.: Approximate trapdoors for lattices and smaller hash-and-sign signatures. In: Galbraith, S.D., Moriai, S. (eds.) ASIACRYPT 2019. LNCS, vol. 11923, pp. 3–32. Springer, Cham (2019). https://doi.org/10.1007/978-3-030-34618-8_1

18. Cheon, J.H., Takagi, T. (eds.): ASIACRYPT 2016. LNCS, vol. 10032. Springer, Heidelberg (2016). https://doi.org/10.1007/978-3-662-53890-6
19. Cocks, C.: An identity based encryption scheme based on quadratic residues. In: Honary, B. (ed.) Cryptography and Coding 2001. LNCS, vol. 2260, pp. 360–363. Springer, Heidelberg (2001). https://doi.org/10.1007/3-540-45325-3_32
20. Da Silva, E., Dos Santos, A.L., Albini, L.C.P., Lima, M.N.: Identity-based key management in mobile ad hoc networks: techniques and applications. IEEE Wirel. Commun. **15**(5), 46–52 (2008)
21. Döttling, N., Garg, S.: Identity-based encryption from the Diffie-Hellman assumption. In: Katz, J., Shacham, H. (eds.) CRYPTO 2017. LNCS, vol. 10401, pp. 537–569. Springer, Cham (2017). https://doi.org/10.1007/978-3-319-63688-7_18
22. Ducas, L., et al.: CRYSTALS-Dilithium: a lattice-based digital signature scheme. IACR Trans. Cryptographic Hardware Embedded Syst. 2018(1), 238–268 (2018)
23. Ducas, L., Lyubashevsky, V., Prest, T.: Efficient identity-based encryption over NTRU lattices. In: Sarkar, P., Iwata, T. (eds.) ASIACRYPT 2014. LNCS, vol. 8874, pp. 22–41. Springer, Heidelberg (2014). https://doi.org/10.1007/978-3-662-45608-8_2
24. Emura, K., Katsumata, S., Watanabe, Y.: Identity-based encryption with security against the KGC: a formal model and its instantiation from lattices. In: Sako, K., Schneider, S., Ryan, P.Y.A. (eds.) ESORICS 2019. LNCS, vol. 11736, pp. 113–133. Springer, Cham (2019). https://doi.org/10.1007/978-3-030-29962-0_6
25. Gentry, C., Peikert, C., Vaikuntanathan, V.: Trapdoors for hard lattices and new cryptographic constructions. In: Ladner, R.E., Dwork, C. (eds.) 40th ACM STOC, pp. 197–206. ACM Press (2008).https://doi.org/10.1145/1374376.1374407
26. Gilbert, H. (ed.): EUROCRYPT 2010. LNCS, vol. 6110. Springer, Heidelberg (2010). https://doi.org/10.1007/978-3-642-13190-5
27. Han, J., Susilo, W., Mu, Y.: Identity-based data storage in cloud computing. Futur. Gener. Comput. Syst. **29**(3), 673–681 (2013)
28. Izabachène, M., Prabel, L., Roux-Langlois, A.: Identity-based encryption from lattices using approximate trapdoors. In: Simpson, L., Baee, M.A.R. (eds.) ACISP 23. LNCS, vol. 13915, pp. 270–290. Springer, Heidelberg (2023).https://doi.org/10.1007/978-3-031-35486-1_13
29. Jia, H., Hu, Y., Tang, C., Wang, L.: Towards compact identity-based encryption on ideal lattices. Cryptology ePrint Archive (2024)
30. Katsumata, S., Matsuda, T., Takayasu, A.: Lattice-based revocable (Hierarchical) IBE with decryption key exposure resistance. In: Lin, D., Sako, K. (eds.) PKC 2019. LNCS, vol. 11443, pp. 441–471. Springer, Cham (2019). https://doi.org/10.1007/978-3-030-17259-6_15
31. Katsumata, S., Yamada, S.: Partitioning via non-linear polynomial functions: more compact IBEs from ideal lattices and bilinear maps. In: Cheon, J.H., Takagi, T. (eds.) ASIACRYPT 2016. LNCS, vol. 10032, pp. 682–712. Springer, Heidelberg (2016). https://doi.org/10.1007/978-3-662-53890-6_23
32. Katsumata, S., Yamada, S., Yamakawa, T.: Tighter security proofs for GPV-IBE in the quantum random oracle model. In: Peyrin, T., Galbraith, S. (eds.) ASIACRYPT 2018. LNCS, vol. 11273, pp. 253–282. Springer, Cham (2018). https://doi.org/10.1007/978-3-030-03329-3_9
33. Katsumata, S., Yamada, S., Yamakawa, T.: Tighter security proofs for GPV-IBE in the quantum random oracle model. J. Cryptology **34**(1), 1–46 (2021). https://doi.org/10.1007/s00145-020-09371-y

34. Liu, Y., Jiang, H., Zhao, Y.: Tighter post-quantum proof for plain FDH, PFDH and GPV-IBE. Cryptology ePrint Archive, Report 2022/1441 (2022). https://eprint.iacr.org/2022/1441

35. Lyubashevsky, V.: Lattice signatures without trapdoors. In: Pointcheval, D., Johansson, T. (eds.) EUROCRYPT 2012. LNCS, vol. 7237, pp. 738–755. Springer, Heidelberg (2012). https://doi.org/10.1007/978-3-642-29011-4_43

36. Lyubashevsky, V., Peikert, C., Regev, O.: On ideal lattices and learning with errors over rings. In: Gilbert, H. (ed.) EUROCRYPT 2010. LNCS, vol. 6110, pp. 1–23. Springer, Heidelberg (2010). https://doi.org/10.1007/978-3-642-13190-5_1

37. Lyubashevsky, V., Peikert, C., Regev, O.: A toolkit for ring-LWE cryptography. In: Johansson, T., Nguyen, P.Q. (eds.) EUROCRYPT 2013. LNCS, vol. 7881, pp. 35–54. Springer, Heidelberg (2013). https://doi.org/10.1007/978-3-642-38348-9_3

38. Markmann, T., Schmidt, T.C., Wählisch, M.: Federated end-to-end authentication for the constrained internet of things using IBC and ECC. ACM SIGCOMM Comput. Commun. Rev. **45**(4), 603–604 (2015)

39. Ducas, L., Lyubashevsky, V., Prest, T.: Efficient identity-based encryption over NTRU lattices. In: Sarkar, P., Iwata, T. (eds.) ASIACRYPT 2014. LNCS, vol. 8874, pp. 22–41. Springer, Heidelberg (2014). https://doi.org/10.1007/978-3-662-45608-8_2

40. Mera, J.M.B., Karmakar, A., Marc, T., Soleimanian, A.: Efficient lattice-based inner-product functional encryption. In: Hanaoka, G., Shikata, J., Watanabe, Y. (eds.) PKC 2022, Part II. LNCS, vol. 13178, pp. 163–193. Springer, Heidelberg (2022).https://doi.org/10.1007/978-3-030-97131-1_6

41. Nielsen, M.A., Chuang, I.L.: Quantum Computation and Quantum Information. Cambridge University Press, Cambridge (2010)

42. Nishimaki, R., Yamakawa, T.: Leakage-resilient identity-based encryption in bounded retrieval model with nearly optimal leakage-ratio. In: Lin, D., Sako, K. (eds.) PKC 2019. LNCS, vol. 11442, pp. 466–495. Springer, Cham (2019). https://doi.org/10.1007/978-3-030-17253-4_16

43. Peikert, C., Regev, O., Stephens-Davidowitz, N.: Pseudorandomness of ring-LWE for any ring and modulus. In: Hatami, H., McKenzie, P., King, V. (eds.) 49th ACM STOC, pp. 461–473. ACM Press (2017).https://doi.org/10.1145/3055399.3055489

44. Prest, T., et al.: Falcon. Post-Quantum Cryptography Project of NIST (2020)

45. Regev, O.: On lattices, learning with errors, random linear codes, and cryptography. In: STOC, pp. 84–93. ACM Press (2005)

46. Shamir, A.: Identity-based cryptosystems and signature schemes. In: Blakley, G.R., Chaum, D. (eds.) CRYPTO'84. LNCS, vol. 196, pp. 47–53. Springer, Heidelberg (Aug (1984)

47. Shor, P.W.: Polynomial-time algorithms for prime factorization and discrete logarithms on a quantum computer. SIAM Rev. **41**(2), 303–332 (1999)

48. Takayasu, A.: Adaptively secure lattice-based revocable IBE in the QROM: compact parameters, tight security, and anonymity. Des. Codes Crypt. **89**(8), 1965–1992 (2021)

49. Tan, C.C., Wang, H., Zhong, S., Li, Q.: Body sensor network security: an identity-based cryptography approach. In: Proceedings of the first ACM conference on Wireless network security, pp. 148–153 (2008)

50. Waters, B.: Dual system encryption: realizing fully secure IBE and HIBE under simple assumptions. In: Halevi, S. (ed.) CRYPTO 2009. LNCS, vol. 5677, pp. 619–636. Springer, Heidelberg (2009). https://doi.org/10.1007/978-3-642-03356-8_36

51. Yamada, S.: Asymptotically compact adaptively secure lattice IBEs and verifiable random functions via generalized partitioning techniques. In: Katz, J., Shacham, H. (eds.) CRYPTO 2017. LNCS, vol. 10403, pp. 161–193. Springer, Cham (2017). https://doi.org/10.1007/978-3-319-63697-9_6

52. Yu, Y., Jia, H., Wang, X.: Compact lattice gadget and its applications to hash-and-sign signatures. In: Handschuh, H., Lysyanskaya, A. (eds.) CRYPTO 2023, Part V. LNCS, vol. 14085, pp. 390–420. Springer, Heidelberg (2023).https://doi.org/10.1007/978-3-031-38554-4_13

53. Zhandry, M.: Secure identity-based encryption in the quantum random oracle model. In: Safavi-Naini, R., Canetti, R. (eds.) CRYPTO 2012. LNCS, vol. 7417, pp. 758–775. Springer, Heidelberg (2012). https://doi.org/10.1007/978-3-642-32009-5_44

54. Zhong, S., Chen, T.: An efficient identity-based protocol for private matching. Int. J. Commun Syst 24(4), 543–552 (2011)

An Improved Practical Key Mismatch Attack Against NTRU

Zhen Liu[1], Vishakha[2], Jintai Ding[3(✉)], Chi Cheng[4], and Yanbin Pan[5(✉)]

[1] School of Cyber Science and Technology, Hubei Key Laboratory of Applied
Mathematics, Hubei University, Wuhan 430062, China
liuzhen@hubu.edu.cn
[2] University of Cincinnati, Cincinnati, OH, USA
sharmav4@mail.uc.edu
[3] Tsinghua University, Haidian, Beijing, China
jintai.ding@gmail.com
[4] China University of Geosciences, Wuhan 430074, China
chengchi@cug.edu.cn
[5] Key Laboratory of Mathematics Mechanization, NCMIS, Academy of Mathematics
and Systems Science, Chinese Academy of Sciences, Beijing 100190, China
panyanbin@amss.ac.cn

Abstract. NTRU is a very famous lattice-based public key cryptosystem, whose security has undergone analysis for the past two decades. Hoffstein, Pipher and Silverman firstly proposed a key recovery attack against the original NTRU with a key mismatch oracle that helps to determine whether the ciphertext can be decrypted correctly or not. However, some additional assumptions are needed to make their attack work. In this paper, we present a key mismatch attack against NTRU that eliminates these assumptions. Using polynomials with coefficients satisfying a fixed ℓ_1 norm to construct ciphertexts, we can keep recovering the coefficients of consecutive positions until the private key is fully recovered. In our experiment, we always succeeded to recover the private keys of NTRUEncrypt and NTRU-HPS with the recommended parameters, which were submitted to the NIST Post-Quantum Cryptography Standardization. Above all, regrading NTRU, our attack has the minimum number of queries to the oracle so far, which is also closest to the theoretical lower bound on the minimum average number of queries analyzed in Qin et al.'s work at Asiacrypt 2021.

Keywords: NTRU · key mismatch attack · key recovery · decryption
failure

1 Introduction

Since the cryptosystems based on number-theoretic problems such as the integer factorization problem and the discrete logarithm problem are threatened by Shor's quantum algorithm [30,31], post quantum cryptography (PQC) has been developing rapidly in recent years. Lattice-based cryptography is one of the most promising PQC, as shown by the large number of lattice based submissions to

© The Author(s), under exclusive license to Springer Nature Switzerland AG 2024
M.-J. Saarinen and D. Smith-Tone (Eds.): PQCrypto 2024, LNCS 14771, pp. 322–342, 2024.
https://doi.org/10.1007/978-3-031-62743-9_11

the recent NIST post-quantum competition [1]. Among them, the LWE problem with its variants and the NTRU problem are widely used to build cryptosystems.

NTRU, introduced by Hoffstein, Pipher and Silverman in 1996 [16], has been regarded as a compelling cryptosystem due to its high efficiency and low memory requirement. Over the past two decades, efforts have been dedicated to enhancing this cryptosystem. The NTRU algorithm was standardized by IEEE 1363 [32] in 2008 and ANSI X9.98 [3] in 2010, both adopting parameters from [14] in 2008. Besides, several padding versions of NTRU were proposed to strength the scheme [19,23].

In 2017, three main variants of NTRU algorithms were submitted to the NIST Post-Quantum Cryptography Standardization process, including NTRUEncrypt [7], NTRU-prime [5] and NTRU-HRSS [20]. In the Round 3 finalists of the NIST PQC competition, the latest variants of NTRU [1] cryptosystem, containing NTRU-HPS and NTRU-HRSS, is a merger of NTRUEncrypt and NTRU-HRSS from the Round 1 submissions.

Key recovery attacks on lattice-based cryptosystems have been extensively studied, with a variety of approaches based on different oracles. Among these attacks, a notable approach relies on (1) the reuse of a pair of public and private keys and (2) assessing whether decryption results match or not, leading to ongoing research efforts. When a user reuses her public key, a adversary can potentially recover her secret key. This is achieved by sending special ciphertexts and observing whether the shared key derived by the user matches the adversary's guesses or not. Under this scenario, an oracle named key mismatch oracle (KMO) is utilized to execute such attacks by verifying if the shared keys match. This type of attack is commonly referred to as key mismatch attacks. Furthermore, a related attack termed a reaction attack can be viewed as a variant of the key mismatch attack, enabling attackers to ascertain the correctness of ciphertext decryption.

The key mismatch attack can be directly applied to the lattice based cryptosystems with the CPA security, when the pair of the public key and private key is reused. As for the CCA security version, this kind of attack recently becomes more feasible with the use of side channel information [28]. For example, Xagawa et al. [33] successfully presented a fault injection attack to implement a KMO at Asiacrypt2021.

An accurate estimate of the number of queries to the KMO gives a better understanding on the security of the cryptosystems. Besides, the number of queries to the KMO will influence the efficiency of the key mismatch attack. Actually, a series of such attacks against lattice-based cryptosystems have been successively proposed and improved to reduce the number of queries. For the LWE-based cryptosystems, the idea of key mismatch attack on lattice-based key exchange is first proposed by Ding et al. [9] against the one-pass case of the protocol in [10]. As for Newhope KEM [2], Bauer et al. first [4] proposed a key mismatch attack against it at CT-RSA 2019, and it was further analyzed and improved by Qin et al. [25] at ESORICS 2019. Later, at ACISP 2020, Okada et al. [24] improved the method in [25] to further reduce the number of queries.

With a similar analysis, Qin et al. [26] gave a key mismatch attack on Kyber [6]. In [12], a key mismatch attack requiring up to 8 queries for each coefficient was proposed against LAC [21]. At Asiacrypt2021, Qin et al. gave a systematic approach to find a lower bound of queries to the oracle needed for such attacks on lattice-based NIST Candidate KEMs [27]. Recently, at PQCrypto 2023, Guo and Mårtensson [13] proposed two-positional key mismatch attacks against Kyber and Saber [11], breaking the bounds in [27]. Later, at Asiaccs 2024, Shao et al. [29] introduced pairwise-parallel key mismatch attacks on Kyber and other lwe-based KEMs using a multi-value key mismatch oracle, effectively reducing the number of required queries. For the lwe technology route, it's apparent that there's substantial effort put into updating and even breaking the lower bound given by Qin et al. [27].

When it comes to NTRU-based cryptosystems, the related research progresses slowly. Hoffstein, Pipher and Silverman [17] firstly proposed a reaction attack against the original NTRU. However, the feasibility of their attack heavily relies on a strong assumption that the upper (lower) wrapping failure only occurs at one coefficient. Although Hoffstein, Pipher and Silverman also pointed out that the general case that both upper and lower wrapping failures at one or more coefficients should be considered, they did not present how to perform such an attack, but just "leave for the reader the necessary alterations". In 2003, Howgrave et al. successfully gave a reaction attack against the padded NTRUs [18] that employ a large number of queries to the oracle, which makes the attack infeasible in practice as stated in [22]. In 2019, Ding et al. proposed a key mismatch attack on the original NTRU scheme with a linear number of queries [8]. In 2021, Zhang et al. successfully mounted a key mismatch attack against NTRU-HRSS based on searching for the optimum binary recovery tree [34], which has the minimum number of queries proposed by Qin et al.'s work [27] with a success rate of 93.6%.

Contributions. In this paper, we propose a key mismatch attack against NTRU to recover the private key, which features high efficiency. The main contributions of the paper include:

– Our attack gets rid of the assumptions used in Hoffstein et al.'s attack [17]. Instead of using the statistical information to separately analyze the positions of 1, -1 or 0 of the private key in [17], our attack can recover consecutive coefficients one position by one position. More precisely, the attacker first determines the smallest n such that $c_i = c + n * p * x^i$ causes a decryption failure, for some $i \in [N]$, where c is a ciphertext that can be decrypted correctly and N is the number of coefficients of the private key. For the polynomial t with coefficients having a fixed ℓ_1 norm satisfying $\sum_{j=0}^{N-1} |t_j| = n$, the attacker constructs N ciphertexts $c_i' = c + p * x^i * t$, $i \in [N]$. If there exists a ciphertext c_i' that causes a decryption failure, $\|t * f\|_\infty$ must be n, indicating the correlation between t and f. Therefore, by employing different t such that the corresponding c_i' causes a decryption failure, for some $i \in [N]$, the attacker can first recover a consecutive coefficient sequence of the private key. This sequence has a number of nonzero elements equal to $\min\{n, 2d_f+1\}$, where $2d_f+1$ represents the number of nonzero coefficients of the private key. If $n \geq 2d_f+1$, the private key has been recovered. Otherwise, the attacker has recovered a consecutive sequence of coefficients whose length has an expectation about $\frac{3}{2}n$ according to our theoretical analysis. Then the attacker selects a long enough subsequence of it to continue the recovery process until the number of nonzero elements in the newly recovered sequence is up to n. Finally, the private key is expected to be recovered by repeating this process.

- Our attack has the number of queries to the KMO closest to the lower bound on the minimum average number of queries stated in [27]. More precisely, considering $c = 0$, the value of n can be directly determined to be $\lceil \frac{q}{2p} \rceil$ and the whole attack becomes concise. Since all c'_i will cause decryption failures at the same time, we actually only need to consider one ciphertext that has the form of $c' = p * t$. Then every coefficient of the private key will be recovered after at most 2 queries to the KMO. Due to the condition that the private key is sampled from the fixed-weight spaces, the accurate number of queries needed for our attack is $2N - d_f - 1$. In addition, comparing with the number of queries in Ding et al.'s work [8], the number of queries to the KMO in our attack against NTRU is minimum at present, which is also closest to the lower bound proposed by Qin et al.'s work at Asiacrypt2021.
- Our attack can be applied to any valid ciphertext, making it difficult to be easily detected. As long as the ciphertext can be decrypted correctly, we can use this to construct new ciphertexts and complete the key mismatch attack.

Since NTRUEncrypt and NTRU-HPS are similar to the original NTRU, we use the parameters selected in them to implement our attack for $c = 0$. The experiments show that our attacks succeeded to recover the whole private key with a success rate of 100%. Hence, we give an improved practical key mismatch attack against NTRU without any assumption on the decryption failure, and the number of queries to the KMO in our attack almost reaches the theoretical lower bounds analyzed at Asiacrypt 2021 [27] at the same time.

Roadmap. The remainder of the paper is organized as follows. In Sect. 2, we recall the original NTRU encryption scheme. In Sect. 3, we give our practical key mismatch attack against NTRU and implement our attack. In addition, we describe our theoretical analysis about the length of recovered coefficient sequence whose number of nonzero elements is fixed. In Sect. 4, we propose our key mismatch attack against NTRU with the general ciphertext. Finally, we give a conclusion in Sect. 5.

2   Overview of NTRU

2.1   Notations

Let $\mathcal{R}$ denote the ring $\mathbb{Z}[x]/(x^N - 1)$, where N is a prime. All polynomials and vectors in this paper are in bold. Let $+$ and $*$ denote addition and multiplication in $\mathcal{R}$, respectively. Let $\cdot$ denote multiplication in the real field $\mathbb{R}$. For integers p, q, assume that $\gcd(p, q) = 1$ and $p \ll q$. Let $\mathcal{R}_q$ be the ring $\mathbb{Z}_q[x]/(x^N - 1)$ and $\mathcal{R}_p$ be the ring $\mathbb{Z}_p[x]/(x^N - 1)$. We also use $[N]$ to denote the set $\{0, 1, \cdots, N - 1\}$. For a real number y, $\lceil y \rceil$ represents the smallest integer larger than y. Denote the ℓ_∞ norm by $\|\cdot\|_\infty$ and the Euclidean norm by $\|.\|$. For two real valued functions f and g, we write $f(x) = O(g(x))$ if and only if there exists a positive real number M and a real number x_0 such that $|f(x)| \leq Mg(x)$, for all $x \geq x_0$.

For positive integers d_1, d_2, we set the notation:

$$\mathcal{T}_{(d_1, d_2)} = \left\{ \begin{array}{c} \text{trinary polynomials of } \mathcal{R} \text{ with } d_1 \text{ entries} \\ \text{equal to 1 and } d_2 \text{ entries equal to } -1 \end{array} \right\}.$$

Definition 1. A polynomial $a(x) = a_0 + a_1 x + \cdots + a_{N-1} x^{N-1} \in \mathcal{R}$ is identified with its vector of coefficients $\boldsymbol{a} = (a_0, a_1, \cdots, a_{N-1})$. The maximum and minimum coefficients of polynomial or vector are denoted by

$$a_{max} = \max_{0 \leq i \leq N-1} \{a_i\} \quad and \quad a_{min} = \min_{0 \leq i \leq N-1} \{a_i\}.$$

The width of a polynomial $a(x)$ is the difference between its maximum and minimum coefficients

$$Width(a(x)) = a_{max} - a_{min}.$$

Definition 2. For $\boldsymbol{a} \in \mathcal{R}$, we define a consecutive coefficient sequence of length M $(1 \leq M \leq N)$ in polynomial $\boldsymbol{a}$ as $a_{i \bmod N}, a_{(i+1) \bmod N}, \cdots, a_{(i+M-1) \bmod N}$, for $i \in [N]$.

Definition 3. For an integer $z \in \mathbb{Z}$, we define the sign of z as

$$sign(z) = \left\{ \begin{array}{ll} 1 & z > 0 \\ -1 & z < 0 \\ 0 & z = 0 \end{array} \right.$$

2.2 Presentation of the Scheme

We now briefly present the basic NTRU encryption scheme, for more details see [16]. The polynomials used in NTRU are selected from four sets $\mathcal{L}_f, \mathcal{L}_g, \mathcal{L}_s, \mathcal{L}_m$, where $\mathcal{L}_f = \{\boldsymbol{f} : \boldsymbol{f} \in \mathcal{T}_{(d_f+1, d_f)}\}$, $\mathcal{L}_g = \{\boldsymbol{g} : \boldsymbol{g} \in \mathcal{T}_{(d_g, d_g)}\}$, $\mathcal{L}_s = \{\boldsymbol{s} : \boldsymbol{s} \in \mathcal{T}_{(d_s, d_s)}\}$, and $\mathcal{L}_m = \{\boldsymbol{m} \in \mathcal{R} : \text{every coefficient of } \boldsymbol{m} \text{ lies between } -\frac{p-1}{2} \text{ and } \frac{p-1}{2}\}$.

- **KeyGen(1^κ):** On input security parameter κ, the key generation algorithm KenGen first chooses $\boldsymbol{f} \in \mathcal{L}_f$, such that $\boldsymbol{f}$ has inverse $\boldsymbol{f}_q^{-1}$ in R_q and $\boldsymbol{f}_p^{-1}$ in R_p, $\boldsymbol{g} \in \mathcal{L}_g$, then computes $\boldsymbol{h} = p * \boldsymbol{g} * \boldsymbol{f}_q^{-1} \bmod q$ and outputs public key $\boldsymbol{pk} = \boldsymbol{h}$ and private key $\boldsymbol{sk} = (\boldsymbol{f}, \boldsymbol{g})$.

- **Enc**(pk, m): On input the public key pk and a message $m \in \mathcal{L}_m$, the encryption algorithm Enc chooses $s \in \mathcal{L}_s$ and outputs the ciphertext $c = h * s + m \bmod q$.

- **Dec**(sk, c): On input the private key sk and the ciphertext c, the decryption algorithm Dec computes $a = c * f \bmod q$, and places the coefficient of a in the interval $(-\frac{q}{2}, \frac{q}{2}]$. Outputs $m = a * f_p^{-1} \bmod p$.

2.3 Decryption Failure

When decrypting a ciphertext c, one calculates

$$a = c * f \bmod q = p * g * s + m * f \bmod q.$$

Since the polynomials f, g, s and m are small, for appropriate parameters, the coefficients of polynomial $p * g * s + m * f$ lie in $(-\frac{q}{2}, \frac{q}{2}]$. This means a is equal to $p * g * s + m * f$. Then we have

$$a * f_p^{-1} \bmod p = p * g * s * f_p^{-1} + m * f * f_p^{-1} \bmod p = m \bmod p.$$

Hence decryption works if $a = p * g * s + m * f$. A wrap failure occurs if $\|p * g * s + m * f\|_\infty \geq \frac{q}{2}$ and a gap failure occurs if the width of $p * g * s + m * f$ is greater than or equal to q. Since a gap failure must be a warp failure, we call both of them a decryption failure.

2.4 Hoffstein et al.'s Key Mismatch Attack

As Hoffstein et al.'s attack described in [17], the attacker has access to a weaken decryption oracle, which only tells whether a ciphertext can be decrypted correctly or not, rather than providing the decryption result.

Now, we briefly outline their attack. For more details, see [17]. Let c be a valid ciphertext that can be decrypted correctly, and $c_i = c + n * p * x^i$ be the modified ciphertext, $\forall i \in [N]$. Recall that $a = c * f \bmod q = p * g * s + m * f$, one has $c_i * f = a + n * p * x^i * f \bmod q$. When $a_{max} + n \cdot p \leq \frac{q}{2}$ and $a_{min} - n \cdot p > -\frac{q}{2}$, c_i can be decrypted to obtain the original message m. So for large values of n, there exists some c_i that can cause decryption failures. During their attack, they first find the smallest n for which there exists c_i causing decryption failures, for some $i \in [N]$, i.e., $a_{max} + (n-1) \cdot p \leq \frac{q}{2} < a_{max} + n \cdot p$ or $a_{min} - n \cdot p \leq -\frac{q}{2} < a_{min} - (n-1) \cdot p$.

They assume that the maximum coefficient of a only occurs at one coefficient, $a_{max} + a_{min} > p$ and $a_{max} - a_i \geq p$ ($\forall a_i \neq a_{max}$). Then one has $a_{max} + n \cdot p > \frac{q}{2}$, $a_{min} - n \cdot p > -\frac{q}{2}$, and $a_i + n \cdot p \leq \frac{q}{2}$ ($\forall a_i \neq a_{max}$). For convenience, let u denote the position of this maximum coefficient. If c_i causes decryption failure, only at the u-th coefficient of c_i the upper warp failure occurs, which indicates that the $(u-i)$-th coefficient of f must be 1. Therefore, they record $i_1, i_2, \cdots, i_s$ that be the i's for which c_i causes decryption failure, which implies that

$f_{(u-i_1) \bmod N} = \cdots = f_{(u-i_s) \bmod N} = 1$. Although u is unknown, they can recover a shifted version of the positions of 1 in $\boldsymbol{f}$.

With a similar analysis, if assuming $\boldsymbol{a}$ to take the minimum coefficient only at one coefficient, e.g., the v-th coefficient, $a_{max} + a_{min} < -p$ and $a_i - a_{min} > p$ ($\forall a_i \neq a_{min}$). When $\boldsymbol{c}_i$ causes decryption failure, we know only at the v-th coefficient of $\boldsymbol{c}_i$ causes the lower warp failure. The attacker finally finds $f_{(v-j_1) \bmod N} = \cdots = f_{(v-j_k) \bmod N} = -1$, for some $j_1, j_2, \cdots, j_k$, i.e., a shifted version of the positions of -1 in $\boldsymbol{f}$.

Therefore, the attacker needs to collect and distinguish some ciphertexts $\boldsymbol{c}$ to meet above assumptions respectively. Then sets $F = x^{i_1} + \cdots + x^{i_s}$ and $G = x^{j_1} + \cdots + x^{j_k}$ to check N polynomials $F - x^k G$ for $k \in [N]$, until finding a shifted version of $\boldsymbol{f}$.

3 Our Practical Key Mismatch Attack Against NTRU

In this section, we will illustrate how our attack can recover the private key of NTRU under the key mismatch attack scenario, where the attacker has access to a KMO to detect decryption failures. Then, we provide a theoretical analysis regarding the length of the recovered sequence with a fixed number of nonzero elements. Finally, we present our experimental results.

3.1 Key Observation

In our analysis, we have observed that for the ciphertext $\boldsymbol{c} = \boldsymbol{0}$, we can construct different polynomials $\boldsymbol{t} \in \mathcal{R}$ that meet the condition $\sum_{j=0}^{N-1} |t_j| = \lceil \frac{q}{2p} \rceil$, maintaining a fixed ℓ_1 norm. For each $\boldsymbol{t}$, we can construct a ciphertext $\boldsymbol{c}' = \boldsymbol{c} + p*\boldsymbol{t} = p*\boldsymbol{t}$. According to the following Lemma 1, for some $\boldsymbol{t}$ that $\boldsymbol{c}'$ causes a decryption failure, there is a strong relation between the coefficients of $\boldsymbol{t}$ and $\boldsymbol{f}$.

Lemma 1. *Using a polynomial $\boldsymbol{t}$ that satisfies $\sum_{j=0}^{N-1} |t_j| = \lceil \frac{q}{2p} \rceil$, one can construct a ciphertext $\boldsymbol{c}' = p * \boldsymbol{t}$. If $\boldsymbol{c}'$ causes a decryption failure, then $\|\boldsymbol{t} * \boldsymbol{f}\|_\infty = \lceil \frac{q}{2p} \rceil$.*

Proof. To decrypt $\boldsymbol{c}'$, we have

$$\boldsymbol{c}' * \boldsymbol{f} \bmod q = p * \boldsymbol{t} * \boldsymbol{f} \bmod q.$$

If $\boldsymbol{c}' * \boldsymbol{f} \bmod q = p * \boldsymbol{t} * \boldsymbol{f}$, then every coefficient of $p * \boldsymbol{t} * \boldsymbol{f}$ lies in $(-\frac{q}{2}, \frac{q}{2}]$ and the decrypted result of $\boldsymbol{c}'$ matches the decrypted result of $\boldsymbol{c} = \boldsymbol{0}$. Otherwise, we say a decryption failure occurs. Since the attacker has access to a KMO, an occurrence of mismatch means an occurrence of decryption failure.

As $\boldsymbol{t} * \boldsymbol{f}$ can be computed by the matrix multiplication as

$$\boldsymbol{t} * \boldsymbol{f} = (t_0, t_1, \cdots, t_{N-1}) \begin{pmatrix} f_0 & f_1 & \cdots & f_{N-1} \\ f_{N-1} & f_0 & \cdots & f_{N-2} \\ \vdots & \vdots & & \vdots \\ f_2 & f_3 & \cdots & f_1 \\ f_1 & f_2 & \cdots & f_0 \end{pmatrix},$$

the $(i-1)th$ coefficient of $t * f$ is

$$t_{N-1} \cdot f_{i \bmod N} + t_{N-2} \cdot f_{(i+1) \bmod N} + \cdots + t_1 \cdot f_{(i+N-2) \bmod N} + t_0 \cdot f_{(i+N-1) \bmod N},$$

for $1 \le i \le N$, which means the $(i-1)th$ coefficient of $t * f$ is determined by two consecutive coefficient sequences

$$t_{N-1}, t_{N-2}, \cdots, t_0$$

and

$$f_{i \bmod N}, f_{(i+1) \bmod N}, \cdots, f_{(i+N-1) \bmod N}$$

of t and f, respectively.

Since f has coefficients in $\{0, 1, -1\}$ and $\sum_{j=0}^{N-1} |t_j| = \lceil \frac{q}{2p} \rceil$, we know that $\|t * f\|_\infty \le \lceil \frac{q}{2p} \rceil$. Thus, if c' causes a decryption failure, then $\|t * f\|_\infty = \lceil \frac{q}{2p} \rceil$.

From Lemma 1, the nonzero coefficient of t will leak the information about the corresponding coefficient of f. Furthermore, if we construct the polynomial t with nonzero coefficients at consecutive positions, the matching result of c' and $c = 0$ will reveal information about the corresponding consecutive coefficients of f.

Another observation we have made is that the recovered consecutive coefficients can be used to construct new polynomials t. These new polynomials, t, can then be used to recover the coefficient of the next position of f. Ultimately, the whole private key f will be recovered by fully utilizing these various t.

Here, we give a simplified framework of our key recovery process. The specific construction of t to recover consecutive coefficients of f will be discussed in the next section.

1. Use $c' = p * t$ to recover the consecutive coefficients one by one position until the number of nonzero elements reaches $\min\{\lceil \frac{q}{2p} \rceil, 2d_f + 1\}$.
2. (if needed) Choose a long enough consecutive subsequence from step 1, to recover the remaining coefficients.

The whole procedure is like this,

$$\overbrace{f_{i \bmod N}, \cdots, \underbrace{f_{(i+M'-1) \bmod N}, \cdots, f_{(i+M-1) \bmod N}}, \cdots, f_{(i+M''-1) \bmod N}}, \cdots$$

the number of nonzero elements is $\min\{\lceil \frac{q}{2p} \rceil, 2d_f + 1\}$

3.2 Finding a Consecutive Sequence with a Fixed Number of Nonzero Elements

To reiterate, the idea in this section is to use the recovered consecutive coefficient sequence to recover the coefficient of the next position, and then use the newly recovered coefficient sequence for the recovery of the next position, until the recovered coefficients satisfy the condition that the number of nonzero elements is equal to $\min\{\lceil \frac{q}{2p} \rceil, 2d_f + 1\}$.

Since the polynomial f is trinary, there must exist $i \in [N]$ with $f_{i \bmod N} \neq 0$. For simplicity's sake, let's assume $f_{i \bmod N} = 1$ to start the recovery. We use the notation $f' = (f'_0, f'_1, \cdots, f'_{N-1})$ to denote the private key recovered by our attack, and let $f'_{i \bmod N} = f_{i \bmod N} = 1$.

We first start with a simple case to explain how to recover the coefficient sequence $f'_{i \bmod N}, f'_{(i+1) \bmod N}$. To determine the next coefficient $f'_{(i+1) \bmod N}$, the attacker will obey the following policies. Specifically speaking, the attacker first prepares two polynomials t, whose coefficients are reversed signs only in one position. For example, one set

$$t = (0, 0, \cdots, 0, \lceil \frac{q}{2p} \rceil - |f'_{i \bmod N}|, f'_{i \bmod N}),$$

and

$$t = (0, 0, \cdots, 0, -(\lceil \frac{q}{2p} \rceil - |f'_{i \bmod N}|), f'_{i \bmod N}).$$

Then, there will be two different ciphertexts constructed by two different t. If the first choice of t causes a decryption failure, the attacker sets $f'_{(i+1) \bmod N} = 1$. Otherwise, the attacker will use the second t to see if a decryption failure occurs or not. If so, the attacker sets $f'_{(i+1) \bmod N} = -1$. What we need to emphasize is that the attacker will only set $f'_{(i+1) \bmod N} = 0$ when neither of the two choices for t can cause decryption failure.

In the same way, the attacker can recover consecutive coefficients as long as possible. Without loss of generality, suppose the attacker has recovered consecutive coefficients $f'_{i \bmod N}, f'_{(i+1) \bmod N}, \cdots, f'_{(i+k-1) \bmod N}$, for some integer $k \geq 1$. First, we will explain how the attacker can recover the next coefficient $f'_{(i+k) \bmod N}$, and then demonstrate that the recovered coefficient sequence $f'_{i \bmod N}, f'_{(i+1) \bmod N}, \cdots, f'_{(i+k) \bmod N}$ is indeed in f or $-f$.

The attacker can use these coefficients to construct t, which will be employed to decide the next coefficient $f'_{(i+k) \bmod N}$. To be more precise, the attacker first sets

$$t = (0, \cdots, 0, \underbrace{\lceil \frac{q}{2p} \rceil - \sum_{j=0}^{k-1} |f'_{(i+j) \bmod N}|, f'_{(i+k-1) \bmod N}, f'_{(i+k-2) \bmod N}, \cdots, f'_{i \bmod N}}_{k+1}),$$

If c' causes a decryption failure, the attacker will set $f'_{(i+k) \bmod N} = 1$ and turn to recover $f'_{(i+k+1) \bmod N}$. Otherwise, the attacker sets

$$t = (0, \cdots, 0, \underbrace{-(\lceil \frac{q}{2p} \rceil - \sum_{j=0}^{k-1} |f'_{(i+j) \bmod N}|), f'_{(i+k-1) \bmod N}, f'_{(i+k-2) \bmod N}, \cdots, f'_{i \bmod N}}_{k+1}),$$

to see if c' causes a decryption failure or not. When the failure occurs, the attacker will set $f'_{(i+k) \bmod N} = -1$ and proceed to the next step of recovering $f'_{(i+k+1) \bmod N}$. Only if both two choices of t cannot cause a decryption failure, the attacker sets $f'_{(i+k) \bmod N} = 0$.

Regardless of the two choices of t in the determination about $f'_{(i+k) \bmod N}$, every coefficient of $t * f$ has the form of

$$z_0 \cdot t_{N-1} + z_1 \cdot t_{N-2} + \cdots + z_{k-1} \cdot t_{N-k} + z_k \cdot t_{N-k-1},$$

for $z_j \in \{-1, 0, 1\}$, $0 \le j \le k$. Further, it can be written as

$$z_0 \cdot f'_{i \bmod N} + z_1 \cdot f'_{(i+1) \bmod N} + \cdots + z_{k-1} \cdot f'_{(i+k-1) \bmod N} + z_k \cdot t_{N-k-1} \quad (3.1)$$

for $z_j \in \{-1, 0, 1\}$, $0 \le j \le k$, $t_{N-k-1} \in \{\lceil \frac{q}{2p} \rceil - \sum_{j=0}^{k-1} |f'_{(i+j) \bmod N}|, -(\lceil \frac{q}{2p} \rceil - \sum_{j=0}^{k-1} |f'_{(i+j) \bmod N}|)\}$.

Recall that if there exist coefficients of $p * t * f$ fall outside $(-\frac{q}{2}, \frac{q}{2}]$, a decryption failure about c' occurs. It is possible for the coefficients of the polynomial $p * t * f$ to attain maximum or minimum values at multiple locations. We are only concerned with whether the decryption error about c' results in the maximum coefficient exceeding the upper bound or the minimum coefficient exceeding the lower bound. To give a comprehensive analysis, we divide the decryption failure c' into three categories: 1) overflow in the upper bound: the maximum coefficient of $p * t * f$ falls on the right side of the range $(-\frac{q}{2}, \frac{q}{2}]$ and the minimum coefficient of $p * t * f$ still lies in $(-\frac{q}{2}, \frac{q}{2}]$. 2) overflow in the lower bound: the maximum coefficient of $p * t * f$ lies in the range $(-\frac{q}{2}, \frac{q}{2}]$ and the minimum coefficient of $p * t * f$ falls on the left side of the range $(-\frac{q}{2}, \frac{q}{2}]$. 3) overflow on both sides: both the maximum coefficient and minimum coefficient of $p * t * f$ fall outside the range $(-\frac{q}{2}, \frac{q}{2}]$.

Now, by analyzing the maximum coefficient and minimum coefficient of $t * f$, we prove that $f'_{i \bmod N}, \cdots, f'_{(i+k-1) \bmod N}, f'_{(i+k) \bmod N}$ is a part of an equivalent private key, i.e., $f'_{i \bmod N}, \cdots, f'_{(i+k) \bmod N}$ is in f or $-f$, for integer $k \ge 1$.

Case 1: Suppose the recovered sequence $f'_{i \bmod N}, f'_{(i+1) \bmod N}, \cdots, f'_{(i+k-1) \bmod N}$ $\in \{1, -1\}$, $k \ge 1$.

- (overflow in the upper bound) : According to Lemma 1, in this category, the maximum coefficient of $t * f$ is $\lceil \frac{q}{2p} \rceil$ and the minimum coefficient of $t * f$ is greater than $-\lceil \frac{q}{2p} \rceil$. If the first choice of t causes a decryption failure, which indicates that there must exist $z_j = f'_{(i+j) \bmod N}$, for $0 \le j \le k - 1$, and $z_k = 1$ by Eq. 3.1. Therefore, the recovered coefficient sequence $f'_{i \bmod N}, \cdots, f'_{(i+k-1) \bmod N}, f'_{(i+k) \bmod N} = 1$ is in f. Similarly, if the second choice of t causes a decryption failure, the recovered sequence $f'_{i \bmod N}, \cdots, f'_{(i+k-1) \bmod N}, f'_{(i+k) \bmod N} = -1$ is in f. As for the rest, the recovered sequence $f'_{i \bmod N}, \cdots, f'_{(i+k-1) \bmod N}, f'_{(i+k) \bmod N} = 0$ is in f.
- (overflow in the lower bound) : i.e., the maximum coefficient of $t * f$ is smaller than $\lceil \frac{q}{2p} \rceil$ and the minimum coefficient of $t * f$ is equal to $-\lceil \frac{q}{2p} \rceil$. If the first choice of t causes a decryption failure, which indicates that there must exist $z_j = -f'_{(i+j) \bmod N}$, for $0 \le j \le k - 1$, and $z_k = -1$. Therefore, the recovered sequence $f'_{i \bmod N}, f'_{(i+1) \bmod N}, \cdots, f'_{(i+k-1) \bmod N}, f'_{(i+k) \bmod N} = 1$ is in $-f$. Similarly, if the second choice of t causes a decryption failure, the recovered

sequence $f'_{i \bmod N}, \cdots, f'_{(i+k-1) \bmod N}, f'_{(i+k) \bmod N} = -1$ is in $-\boldsymbol{f}$. As for the rest, the recovered $f'_{i \bmod N}, \cdots, f'_{(i+k-1) \bmod N}, f'_{(i+k) \bmod N} = 0$ is in $-\boldsymbol{f}$.

- (overflow on both sides) : i.e., both the absolute values of minimum coefficient and the maximum coefficient of $\boldsymbol{t} * \boldsymbol{f}$ are equal to $\lceil \frac{q}{2p} \rceil$. According to the policy of the recovery, the recovered sequence $f'_{i \bmod N}, \cdots, f'_{(i+k) \bmod N}$ is actually in $\boldsymbol{f}$ or $-\boldsymbol{f}$.

Case 2: Considering that $f'_{(i+k-1) \bmod N} = 0$ is the first zero coefficient among $f'_{i \bmod N}, f'_{(i+1) \bmod N}, \cdots, f'_{(i+k-1) \bmod N}.$

- (overflow in the upper bound) : If the first choice of $\boldsymbol{t}$ causes a decryption failure, there must exist $z_j = f'_{(i+j) \bmod N}$, for $0 \le j \le k-2$, and $z_k = 1$ by Eq. 3.1. Since $f'_{(i+k-1) \bmod N} = 0$, it seems that the value of z_{k-1} can be nonzero. However, if z_{k-1} is nonzero, it means during the step of recovering $f'_{(i+k-1) \bmod N}$, the value of $f'_{(i+k-1) \bmod N}$ can be nonzero, which doesn't fit with our strategy. Therefore, $z_{k-1} = f'_{(i+k-1) \bmod N} = 0$, and the recovered sequence $f'_{i \bmod N}, f'_{(i+1) \bmod N}, \cdots, f'_{(i+k-1) \bmod N}, 1$ is in $\boldsymbol{f}$. Similarly, if the second choice of $\boldsymbol{t}$ causes a decryption failure, the recovered sequence $f'_{i \bmod N}, \cdots, f'_{(i+k-1) \bmod N}, -1$ is in $\boldsymbol{f}$. As for the rest, the recovered sequence $f'_{i \bmod N}, \cdots, f'_{(i+k-1) \bmod N}, 0$ is in $\boldsymbol{f}$.
- (overflow in the lower bound) : The recovered sequence $f'_{i \bmod N}, f'_{(i+1) \bmod N}, \cdots, f'_{(i+k) \bmod N}$ is actually in $-\boldsymbol{f}$.
- (overflow on both sides) : The recovered sequence $f'_{i \bmod N}, \cdots, f'_{(i+k) \bmod N}$ is actually in $\boldsymbol{f}$ or $-\boldsymbol{f}$.

Case 3: For the rest of the case that $f'_{i \bmod N}, \cdots, f'_{(i+k-1) \bmod N}$ involving more than one zero elements, we can conclude that the recovered sequence $f'_{i \bmod N}, \cdots, f'_{(i+k) \bmod N}$ is actually in $\boldsymbol{f}$ or $-\boldsymbol{f}$ with the restriction on the deducing of zero coefficients.

To summarize, once the attacker has determined the current value of the coefficient, he will extend the recovered sequence and turn to recover the coefficient of the next position by using Algorithm 1. Since $\boldsymbol{f}$ has $2d_f + 1$ nonzero coefficients, the process continues to recover the consecutive coefficients until the number of nonzero coefficients in it reaches $\min\{\lceil \frac{q}{2p} \rceil, 2d_f + 1\}$, as shown in Algorithm 2. Moreover, this recovered sequence is in $\boldsymbol{f}$ or $-\boldsymbol{f}$ regardless of the category of the decryption failure.

Remark 1. Using above results, we have to point out that when the attacker has recovered $f'_{i \bmod N}, f'_{(i+1) \bmod N}, \cdots, f'_{(i+k-1) \bmod N}$, for integer $k \ge 1$, to determine $f'_{(i+k) \bmod N}$, it's possible that both two choices of $\boldsymbol{t}$ will cause decryption failures. In order to reduce the number of queries to the KMO, one can choose one of the two choices of $\boldsymbol{t}$ and only if this choice of $\boldsymbol{t}$ cannot cause a decryption failure, then the attacker uses the other choice of $\boldsymbol{t}$ to test. For convenience, we always first determine if the next position can be 1. In fact, we can also ensure the existence of -1 first, and the different sequence can be recovered from difference choice at every step.

Algorithm 1. Recover the next position

Input: $f'_{i \bmod N}, \cdots, f'_{(i+l) \bmod N}$ with $l \geq 0$
Output: $f'_{(i+l+1) \bmod N}$

1: set $t = (0, \cdots, 0, \lceil \frac{q}{2p} \rceil - \sum_{j=0}^{l} |f'_{(i+j) \bmod N}|, f'_{(i+l) \bmod N}, \cdots, f'_{i \bmod N})$;

2: **if** $c' = p * t$ causes a decryption failure **then**
3: $\quad f'_{(i+l+1) \bmod N} = 1$;
4: **else**
5: $\quad$ set $t = (0, \cdots, 0, -(\lceil \frac{q}{2p} \rceil - \sum_{j=0}^{l} |f'_{(i+j) \bmod N}|), f'_{(i+l) \bmod N}, \cdots, f'_{i \bmod N})$;
6: $\quad$ **if** $c' = p * t$ causes a decryption failure **then**
7: $\qquad f'_{(i+l+1) \bmod N} = -1$;
8: $\quad$ **else**
9: $\qquad f'_{(i+l+1) \bmod N} = 0$;
10: $\quad$ **end if**
11: **end if**
12: **return** $f'_{(i+l+1) \bmod N}$

Algorithm 2. Recover a consecutive coefficient sequence

Input: $\lceil \frac{q}{2p} \rceil$, d_f
Output: a consecutive coefficient sequence with $\min\{\lceil \frac{q}{2p} \rceil, 2d_f + 1\}$ nonzero elements.

1: set $f'_{i \bmod N} = 1$;
2: set $s = 1$;
3: set $l = 0$;
4: **while** $s < \min\{\lceil \frac{q}{2p} \rceil, 2d_f + 1\}$ **do**
5: $\quad f'_{(i+l+1) \bmod N} = $ Algorithm $1(f'_{i \bmod N}, \cdots, f'_{(i+l) \bmod N})$;
6: $\quad l = l + 1$;
7: $\quad$ **if** $f'_{(i+l) \bmod N} \neq 0$ **then**
8: $\qquad s = s + 1$
9: $\quad$ **end if**
10: **end while**
11: **return** $f'_{i \bmod N}, f'_{(i+1) \bmod N}, \cdots, f'_{(i+l) \bmod N}$

3.3 Recovering the Private Key

After that, the remaining problem is to decide whether the recovered sequence by Sect. 3.2 is a valid private key or not. If not, what should be done further to recover the private key. For convenience, we denote the length of this consecutive sequence by M.

When $\lceil \frac{q}{2p} \rceil \geq (2d_f + 1)$, no matter which kind of decryption failure occurs, we must have $M = N$, which means the recovered coefficient sequence by Sect. 3.2 is in f or $-f$ of length N. It's notable that this consecutive sequence of length N can be seen as an equivalent private key.

When $\lceil \frac{q}{2p} \rceil < (2d_f + 1)$, more work is needed. We describe a way to recover the private key, that is,

1. The attacker first recovers a consecutive sequence of length M by Algorithm 2, for $\lceil \frac{q}{2p} \rceil \leq M \leq N - (2d_f + 1 - \lceil \frac{q}{2p} \rceil)$.

$$\underbrace{f'_{i \bmod N}, f'_{(i+1) \bmod N} \cdots, f'_{(i+M-1) \bmod N}}_{\text{the number of nonzero elements is } \lceil \frac{q}{2p} \rceil} \cdot$$

2. The attacker selects a long enough subsequence, for $M' \geq 1$.

$$\underbrace{f'_{(i+M'-1) \bmod N}, f'_{(i+M') \bmod N} \cdots, f'_{(i+M-1) \bmod N}}_{\text{the number of nonzero elements is smaller than } \lceil \frac{q}{2p} \rceil} \cdot$$

3. The attacker continues to recover the next position of this subsequence by Algorithm 1 until the number of nonzero elements in this extended sequence is up to $\lceil \frac{q}{2p} \rceil$.

$$\underbrace{f'_{(i+M'-1) \bmod N}, \cdots, f'_{(i+M-1) \bmod N} \cdots, f'_{(i+M''-1) \bmod N}}_{\text{the number of nonzero elements is } \lceil \frac{q}{2p} \rceil} \cdot$$

4. The attacker obtains a longer consecutive sequence of length M''.

$$f_{i \bmod N}, \cdots, f_{(i+M'-1) \bmod N}, \cdots, f_{(i+M-1) \bmod N}, \cdots, f_{(i+M''-1) \bmod N} \cdot$$

5. If $M'' = N$, then the recovery process can terminate. Otherwise the attacker moves to step 2 to repeat the process.

Number of Queries. It can be seen that the number of queries to the KMO is at most 2 to determine each coefficient. Since the number of 1s in f is $d_f + 1$, the whole number of queries to the oracle to recover the private key is $2N - d_f - 1$.

3.4 The Expectation of M

Since $\lceil \frac{q}{2p} \rceil \geq (2d_f + 1)$, we have $M = N$. In this section, we evaluate M as $\lceil \frac{q}{2p} \rceil < (2d_f + 1)$.

Before illustrating our analysis, we first review the negative hypergeometric distribution. To be more precise, there are N_1 elements, of which K_1 are defined as "failures" and the rest are "successes". Elements are drawn one after the other, without replacements, until r_1 "successes" are encountered. Then, the drawing stops and the number k_1 of "failures" is counted. The distribution of k_1 is called negative hypergeometric distribution. Moreover, one has $\Pr[k_1 = y] = \frac{\binom{y+r_1-1}{y} \cdot \binom{N_1-r_1-y}{K_1-y}}{\binom{N_1}{K_1}}$, where $y = 0, 1, \cdots, K_1$. Note that the expectation of k_1 is $\frac{r_1 \cdot K_1}{N_1 - K_1 + 1}$.

Recall that $f = (f_0, f_1, \cdots, f_{N-1})$ is sampled from $\mathcal{T}_{(d_f+1,d_f)}$. If we view the value of -1 or 1 as "success", and 0 as "failure", then $f_0, f_1, \cdots, f_{N-1}$ can be viewed as N elements, of which $N - 2d_f - 1$ are "failures" and the rest are "successes".

Considering a consecutive sequence in f with a fixed number of nonzero elements, and the last element in this sequence is nonzero. Although the length of this sequence denoted by M_1 is unknown, we know the number of zero elements in this sequence follows the negative hypergeometric distribution, which has the expectation $\frac{n_1 \cdot (N - 2d_f - 1)}{N - (N - 2d_f - 1) + 1} = \frac{n_1 \cdot (N - 2d_f - 1)}{2d_f + 2}$, where the number of nonzero elements is denoted by n_1. Therefore, the expectation of M_1 is $n_1 + \frac{n_1 \cdot (N - 2d_f - 1)}{2d_f + 2} = \frac{n_1(N+1)}{2d_f + 2}$.

As the consecutive sequence $f'_{i \bmod N} \neq 0, f'_{(i+1) \bmod N}, \cdots, f'_{(i+M-1) \bmod N}$ of length M recovered by Sect. 3.2 is in f or $-f$, where the number of nonzero elements in it is $\lceil \frac{q}{2p} \rceil$. It is notable that if we reversed the sequence, we have $f'_{(i+M-1) \bmod N}, \cdots, f'_{(i+1) \bmod N}, f'_{i \bmod N} \neq 0$. To evaluate M, we have $M_1 = M$ and $n_1 = \lceil \frac{q}{2p} \rceil$. Moreover, the expectation of M is $\frac{\lceil \frac{q}{2p} \rceil \cdot (N+1)}{2d_f + 2}$.

3.5 Experimental Results

We implemented the NTRU cryptosystem in C++ using Shoup's NTL library version 11.4.3 with the parameters chosen in NTRUEncrypt and NTRU-HPS for the NIST PQC competition. Our attack ran on a MacOS Montery system with a 1.4GHZ Inter Core i5 processor.

The parameter sets in NTRUEncrypt and NTRU-HPS follow the original NTRU's use of fixed weight sample spaces. To be more precise, In NTRUEncrypt, f has the form of $f = 1 + p * F$, and $g \in \mathcal{T}_{(d_g, d_g)}$. In NTRU-HPS, f is a nonzero trinary polynomial with degree at most $N - 2$, and g is a nonzero trinary polynomial with degree at most $N - 2$ with a fixed weight, that is, g has d_g coefficients equal to 1 and d_g coefficients equal to -1. Either in NTRUEncrypt or in NTRU-HPS, the polynomial g is trinary with a fixed weight. Hence the attack is aimed at recovering g.

The difference is that the attacker reconstructs the modified ciphertext c' as $c' = c + h * t = h * t$. To decrypt c', if $c' * f \bmod q = p * g * t$, the decryptions of $c = 0$ and c' match. Otherwise, c' causes a decryption failure. Thus the attacker can recover the polynomial g in the light of the attack described in Sect. 3, and the number of queries to the KMO to recover g is about $2N - dg$.

For a comparison with the previous work, we compute the lower bound on the minimum average number of queries needed for such attacks in light of the theoretic work in [27]. Besides, we follow the strategies described in Ding et al.'s work to implement their attack and obtain the number of queries to the KMO. Since every coefficient recovered by Ding et al.'s work needs at least two queries to the oracle, the whole number of queries in their work is about $2N$. We list the experimental results in Table 1.

Note that when $N = 443$ and $N = 821$, we have $M = N$, which means that the process at Sect. 3.2 can directly recover the private key. As for $N = 743$, we know $342 \leq M \leq 591$. In the experiment, the value of M mainly lies in the range

Table 1. The number of queries to the KMO needed for NTRUEncrypt and NTRU-HPS. Q and Q_D denote the corresponding number of queries in our attack and Ding et al.'s attack respectively. E denotes the lower bound on the minimum average number of queries from Qin et al.'s work.

instance	N	q	p	d_g	E	Q_D	Q	Success Rate	Running Time(second)
NTRUEncrypt	443	2048	3	143	739	878	**742**	100%	48.75
NTRUEncrypt	743	2048	3	247	1239	1473	**1238**	100%	315.80
NTRU-HPS	821	4096	3	255	1369	1633	**1387**	100%	455.38

$[508, 520]$. In theory, we can use $\frac{\lceil \frac{q}{2p} \rceil \cdot (N+1)}{2d_g+1}$ to evaluate M, which is about 515. Moreover, the size of M gives the reason why our experiments have a success rate 100% in Table 1 as the private key is generated randomly.

It can also be seen that the experimental results agree with our theoretical analysis. Compared with the results of Ding et al., the number of queries in our attack is reduced by about 16%, as $\frac{d_g}{N}$ is chosen to approximate $\frac{1}{3}$. Moreover, the number of queries in our attack is closest to the lower bound on the minimum average number of queries proposed in [27].

4   Our Key Mismatch Attack Against NTRU with the General Ciphertext

One may argue that the situation $\boldsymbol{c} = \boldsymbol{0}$ can be easily detected. Therefore, in this section, we show how to complete the recovery when $\boldsymbol{c} \neq \boldsymbol{0}$. Compared with the method described in Sect. 3, the main difference is that for a general ciphertext $\boldsymbol{c}$ that can be decrypted correctly, the ℓ_1 norm of $\boldsymbol{t}$ is needed to be first determined. We follow the strategies outlined below.

1. Use $\boldsymbol{c}_i = \boldsymbol{c} + n * p * x^i$ to find the smallest positive integer n that causes decryption failures among $\boldsymbol{c}_i$, for $i \in [N]$.
2. Use $\boldsymbol{c}'_i = \boldsymbol{c} + p * \boldsymbol{t} * x^i$ to recover the consecutive sequence until the number of nonzero elements reaches $\min\{n, 2d_f + 1\}$, where $\sum_{j=0}^{N-1} |t_j| = n$.
3. (if needed) Choose a long enough consecutive subsequence from step 2, to recover the remaining coefficients.

Notice that the original message $\boldsymbol{m}$ can be recovered correctly by $\boldsymbol{c}_i$ only if $\boldsymbol{c}_i * \boldsymbol{f} \bmod q$ equals $\boldsymbol{a} + n * p * x^i * \boldsymbol{f}$, where $\boldsymbol{c} * \boldsymbol{f} \bmod q = p * \boldsymbol{g} * \boldsymbol{s} + \boldsymbol{m} * \boldsymbol{f} = \boldsymbol{a}$, otherwise a decryption failure occurs.

Let a_{max} be the maximum coefficient of $\boldsymbol{a}$ and a_{min} be the minimum coefficient of $\boldsymbol{a}$. For any ciphertext $\boldsymbol{c}$ that can be decrypted correctly, we have that $a_{max} + n \cdot p$ or $a_{min} - n \cdot p$ falls outside the range $(-\frac{q}{2}, \frac{q}{2}]$ by the choice of n. For any positive integer n_1 less than n, we have $a_{max} + n_1 \cdot p$ and $a_{min} - n_1 \cdot p$ lie in $(-\frac{q}{2}, \frac{q}{2}]$.

Borrowing from the categories ideas and naming strategies in Sect. 3, we also divide all the decryption failures about c_i into three categories.

- overflow in the upper bound: $a_{max} + n \cdot p > \frac{q}{2}$ and $a_{min} - n \cdot p > -\frac{q}{2}$.
- overflow in the lower bound: $a_{min} - n \cdot p \leq -\frac{q}{2}$ and $a_{max} + n \cdot p \leq \frac{q}{2}$.
- overflow on both sides: $a_{max} + n \cdot p > q/2$ and $a_{min} - n \cdot p \leq -q/2$.

As shown in Sect. 2, Hoffstein et al.'s attack works well in the situation that only one coefficient in the decryption result of c_i mismatches the original message m, which also means that only one coefficient of $a + n * p * x^i * f$ falls outside the range $(-\frac{q}{2}, \frac{q}{2}]$, for some $i \in [N]$. We have to point out that the decryption failure restriction regarding c_i in their work can be switched to either overflowing in the upper bound or overflowing in the lower bound. However, overflowing in the upper bound or overflowing in the lower bound includes more scenarios, such as multiple coefficients of c_i exceeding the upper(lower) bound.

Our observation about the relation between t and f helps us handle all possible cases for the decryption failure.

Lemma 2. *Let c be a ciphertext that can be decrypted correctly and n be the smallest positive integer such that there exists a $c_i = c + n * p * x^i$ causing a decryption failure, for some $i \in [N]$. Using the polynomial t that satisfies $\sum_{j=0}^{N-1} |t_j| = n$, one can construct N ciphertexts $c'_i = c + p * x^i * t$, $i \in [N]$. If there exists a c'_i that causes a decryption failure, for some $i \in [N]$, then $\|t * f\|_\infty = n$.*

Proof. To decrypt c'_i, we have

$$c'_i * f \bmod q = p * g * s + m * f + p * x^i * t * f \bmod q = a + p * x^i * t * f \bmod q.$$

If $c'_i * f \bmod q = a + p * x^i * t * f$, then the decryption of c'_i will be the original message m. Otherwise, we say a decryption failure occurs.

Let $a_{max}^{(i)}$ be the maximum coefficient of $a + p * x^i * t * f$, and $a_{min}^{(i)}$ be the minimum coefficient of $a + p * x^i * t * f$. Let $(tf)_{max}$ be the maximum coefficient of $t * f$, and $(tf)_{min}$ be the minimum coefficient of $t * f$. Let $a'_{max} = \max_{i \in [N]} \{a_{max}^{(i)}\} = a_{max} + p \cdot (tf)_{max}$, and $a'_{min} = \min_{i \in [N]} \{a_{min}^{(i)}\} = a_{min} + p \cdot (tf)_{min}$.

Since f has coefficients in $\{0, 1, -1\}$, we know that $\|t * f\|_\infty \leq n$. Furthermore, we get $a'_{max} \leq a_{max} + n \cdot p$ and $a'_{min} \geq a_{min} - n \cdot p$. Now suppose there exists c'_i that causes a decryption failure, for some $i \in [N]$, we have $a'_{max} > \frac{q}{2}$ or $a'_{min} \leq -\frac{q}{2}$. Besides, we have $a_{max} + n \cdot p > \frac{q}{2}$ or $a_{min} - n \cdot p \leq -\frac{q}{2}$.

- In the case of overflowing in the upper bound, $a_{max} + n \cdot p > \frac{q}{2}$ and $a_{min} - n \cdot p > -\frac{q}{2}$. Since $a'_{min} \geq a_{min} - n \cdot p > -\frac{q}{2}$, we have $a'_{max} > \frac{q}{2}$. If $(tf)_{max} < n$, then $a'_{max} = a_{max} + p \cdot (tf)_{max} \leq \frac{q}{2}$ according to the smallest choice of n, which is contrary to the fact that $a'_{max} > \frac{q}{2}$. Thus, $(tf)_{max} = n$ and $\|t * f\|_\infty = n$.
- In the case of overflowing in the lower bound, $a_{min} - n \cdot p \leq -\frac{q}{2}$ and $a_{max} + n \cdot p \leq \frac{q}{2}$. Since $a'_{max} \leq a_{max} + n \cdot p \leq \frac{q}{2}$, we have $a'_{min} \leq -\frac{q}{2}$. If $(tf)_{min} > -n$, then $a'_{min} = a_{min} + p \cdot (tf)_{min} > -\frac{q}{2}$. This is a contradiction. Therefore, $(tf)_{min} = -n$ and $\|t * f\|_\infty = n$.

– In the case of overflowing on both sides, $a_{max} + n \cdot p > q/2$ and $a_{min} - n \cdot p \leq -q/2$. If $\|t * f\|_\infty < n$, then $a'_{max} = a_{max} + p \cdot (tf)_u \leq q/2$ and $a'_{min} = a_{min} + p \cdot (tf)_{min} > -q/2$. This contradicts the assumption that there exists decryption failures for some c'_i. Therefore, $\|t * f\|_\infty = n$.

Now, we give the details about our recovery process.

Step 1: We first specify the procedure of finding n by the binary search in Algorithm 3.

Algorithm 3. Compute the value of n by binary search

Input: a ciphertext c
Output: the value of n
1: **set** $begin = 1$, $end = \lceil \frac{q}{2p} \rceil$;
2: **while** $begin <= end$ **do**
3:       $middle = (begin + end)/2$;
4:       **for** $i \in [N]$ **do**
5:             **if** $c + middle * p * x^i$ causes a decryption failure **then**
6:                   break;
7:             **end if**
8:       **end for**
9:       **if** $i < N$ **then**
10:           $end = middle - 1$;
11:     **else**
12:           $begin = middle + 1$;
13:     **end if**
14: **end while**
15: $n = begin$;
16: **return** n

Remark 2. As in [15], for a trinary polynomial f, we assume that the coefficients of f are independent random variables taking the value 1 with probability $\frac{d_f+1}{N}$, -1 with probability $\frac{d_f}{N}$ and 0 with probability $\frac{N-2d_f-1}{N}$, the same holds for g, s. Since the number of nonzero coefficients in the message m, such as [7,15], can not exceed $N - d_m$, we assume that the coefficient of m is chosen as ± 1 with the probability $\frac{N-d_m}{N}$ and 0 with the probability $\frac{d_m}{N}$. With central limit theorem, we know every coefficient of $a = p * g * s + m * f$ has the normal distribution with mean 0 and variance

$$\sigma^2 = \frac{4p^2 d_s d_g + (2d_f + 1) \cdot (N - d_m)}{N}.$$

According to three sigma rule, it's obvious that the value of n is larger than $(q/2 - 3 * \sigma)/p$ with overwhelming probability.

Step 2: Given the ciphertext c and the corresponding n in Algorithm 3, the attacker can recover the consecutive sequence of length M, where the number of nonzero elements in the sequence is equal to $\min\{n, 2d_f + 1\}$. We summarize this procedure in Algorithm 4. With a similar analysis in Sect. 3, it can be easily verified that no matter which kind of decryption failures occurs, the recovered sequence is in f or $-f$.

Algorithm 4. Recover a consecutive sequence of length M in f or $-f$

Input: the ciphertext c

Output: a consecutive sequence of length M in f or $-f$ with $\min\{n, 2d_f+1\}$ nonzero elements.

1: Initialize $t = (0, 0, \cdots, 0)$;
2: $t_{N-1} \in \{1, -1\}$;
3: $j = N - 1$;
4: $s = 1$;   // s: the sum of nonzero coefficients of t
5: **while** $s < \min\{n, 2d_f + 1\}$ **do**
6:      $j = j - 1$;
7:      $t_j = (n - \sum_{k=j+1}^{N-1} |t_k|)$;
8:      **if** $\exists\, i \in [N]$ that $c + p * x^i * t$ causes a decryption failure **then**
9:         $t_j = sign(t_j)$;
10:         $s = s + 1$;
11:      **else**
12:         $t_j = -t_j$;
13:         **if** $\exists\, i \in [N]$ that $c + p * x^i * t$ causes a decryption failure **then**
14:            $t_j = sign(t_j)$;
15:            $s = s + 1$;
16:         **else**
17:            $t_j = 0$;
18:         **end if**
19:      **end if**
20: **end while**
21: **return** $t_{N-1}, t_{N-2}, \cdots, t_j$

Step 3: When $n \geq 2d_f + 1$, the length of the recovered sequence by Algorithm 4 is N. That is, this sequence is actually an equivalent private key. When $n < 2d_f + 1$, the attacker first recovers a sequence of length M by Algorithm 4. To further lengthen the length of this recovered sequence, the attacker selects a long enough subsequence of it whose number of nonzero elements is smaller than n, and uses the same idea to recover more coefficients. The recovery process moves on until the length of the recovered sequence reaches N.

Remark 3. When $n < 2d_f + 1$, the attacker can recover a coefficient sequence of length M consisting of n nonzero elements by Algorithm 4, for $n \leq M \leq N - (2d_f + 1 - n)$. As the analysis in Sect. 3.4, we know the expectation of M is $\frac{n \cdot (N+1)}{2d_f + 2}$. Note that the value $\frac{2d_f + 1}{N}$ is always chosen to approximate $\frac{2}{3}$, the expectation of M is about $\frac{3}{2}n$.

Remark 4. We have to point out that when $c = 0$, one can easily get $n = \lceil \frac{q}{2p} \rceil$. Since all c_i' will cause decryption failures at the same time, the ciphertext in the form of $c' = p * t$ will be utilized to complete the recovery process. Therefore, $c = 0$ in Sect. 3 is a special case of this Section.

To find the value of n, the attacker queries the oracle in $O(\log(\frac{q}{2p})N)$ times using the binary search in the worst case. In Algorithm 4, the attacker needs $2N$ ciphertexts in the worst case to determine one coefficient of the private key. Therefore, the private key is expected to be recovered with $O(N^2)$ queries to the KMO in the worst case.

For the general ciphertext, we also experimented the parameter sets $N = 443$ to verify our idea. For $N = 443$, our attack can always recover the private key within 6 h, with the total number of queries to KMO being approximately three hundred thousand. This result is also consistent with the theoretical analysis.

Our experimental results aim to validate the theoretical analysis of the attack's correctness, rather than focusing on program execution efficiency. Therefore, the implementation is not optimized and the running time can be further optimized for improvement. We simply implemented our attack using C++ with the NTL library and present the results for reference.

5   Conclusion

In this paper, we present an explicit practical key mismatch attack against NTRU with no additional assumptions on the decryption failure. By constructing different ciphertexts that cause decryption failures, the attacker can successfully recover the private key. More impressive is that the number of queries to the KMO in our attack is currently closest to the lower bound on the minimum average number of queries in Qin et al.'s work at Asiacrypt 2021 [27].

Acknowledgement. The authors would like to thank the anonymous reviewers for their helpful comments. Zhen Liu was supported in part by the National Natural Science Foundation of China(No. 12201193) and the Innovation Group Project of the Natural Science Foundation of Hubei Province of China(No. 2023AFA021). Chi Cheng was supported in part by the National Natural Science Foundation of China(No. 62172374) and Open Research Project of The Hubei Key Laboratory of Intelligent Geo-Information Processing (KLIGIP-2022-B06, KLIGIP-2021-B07).Yanbin Pan was supported in part by the National Key Research and Development Project (No. 2018YFA0704705), the National Natural Science Foundation of China (Nos. 62372445, 62032009, 12226006) and the Innovation Program for Quantum Science and Technology(No.2021ZD0302902).

References

1. NIST post-quantum cryptography project. https://csrc.nist.gov/Projects/Post-Quantum-Cryptography/Round-3-Submissions
2. Alkim, E., et al.: NewHope (2017). NewHope_2017_12_21. pdf

3. ANSI, X.: 98: Lattice-based polynomial public key establishment algorithm for the financial services industry. Tech. rep., Technical report, ANSI (2010)
4. Bauer, A., Gilbert, H., Renault, G., Rossi, M.: Assessment of the key-reuse resilience of NewHope. In: Matsui, M. (ed.) CT-RSA 2019. LNCS, vol. 11405, pp. 272–292. Springer, Cham (2019). https://doi.org/10.1007/978-3-030-12612-4_14
5. Bernstein, D.J., Chuengsatiansup, C., Lange, T., van Vredendaal, C.: NTRU prime: reducing attack surface at low cost. In: Adams, C., Camenisch, J. (eds.) SAC 2017. LNCS, vol. 10719, pp. 235–260. Springer, Cham (2018). https://doi.org/10.1007/978-3-319-72565-9_12
6. Bos, J., et al.: Crystals-kyber: a CCA-secure module-lattice-based KEM. In: 2018 IEEE European Symposium on Security and Privacy (EuroS&P), pp. 353–367. IEEE (2018)
7. Chen, C., Hoffstein, J., Whyte, W., Zhang, Z.: NTRUEncrypt. Tech. rep. (2019). https://csrc.nist.gov/projects/post-quantum-cryptography/round-1-submissions
8. Ding, J., Deaton, J., Schmidt, K., Zhang, Z., et al.: A simple and efficient key reuse attack on NTRU cryptosystem. Cryptology ePrint Archive (2019)
9. Ding, J., Fluhrer, S., Rv, S.: Complete attack on RLWE key exchange with reused keys, without signal leakage. In: Susilo, W., Yang, G. (eds.) ACISP 2018. LNCS, vol. 10946, pp. 467–486. Springer, Cham (2018). https://doi.org/10.1007/978-3-319-93638-3_27
10. Ding, J., Xie, X., Lin, X.: A simple provably secure key exchange scheme based on the learning with errors problem. Cryptology ePrint Archive (2012)
11. D'Anvers, J., Karmakar, A., Roy, S., Vercauteren, F.: Saber: Mod-LWR based KEM algorithm specification and supporting documentation. Tech. rep. (2019). https://csrc.nist.gov/projects/post-quantum-cryptography/round-1-submissions
12. Greuet, A., Montoya, S., Renault, G.: Attack on LAC key exchange in misuse situation. In: Krenn, S., Shulman, H., Vaudenay, S. (eds.) CANS 2020. LNCS, vol. 12579, pp. 549–569. Springer, Cham (2020). https://doi.org/10.1007/978-3-030-65411-5_27
13. Guo, Q., Mårtensson, E.: Do not bound to a single position: near-optimal multi-positional mismatch attacks against kyber and saber. In: Johansson, T., Smith-Tone, D. (eds.) Post-Quantum Cryptography. PQCrypto 2023. LNCS, vol. 14154. Springer, Cham (2023). https://doi.org/10.1007/978-3-031-40003-2_11
14. Hirschhorn, P.S., Hoffstein, J., Howgrave-Graham, N., Whyte, W.: Choosing NTRUEncrypt parameters in light of combined lattice reduction and MITM approaches. In: Abdalla, M., Pointcheval, D., Fouque, P.-A., Vergnaud, D. (eds.) ACNS 2009. LNCS, vol. 5536, pp. 437–455. Springer, Heidelberg (2009). https://doi.org/10.1007/978-3-642-01957-9_27
15. Hoffstein, J., Pipher, J., Schanck, J.M., Silverman, J.H., Whyte, W., Zhang, Z.: Choosing parameters for NTRUEncrypt. In: Handschuh, H. (ed.) CT-RSA 2017. LNCS, vol. 10159, pp. 3–18. Springer, Cham (2017). https://doi.org/10.1007/978-3-319-52153-4_1
16. Hoffstein, J., Pipher, J., Silverman, J.H.: NTRU: a ring-based public key cryptosystem. In: Buhler, J.P. (ed.) ANTS 1998. LNCS, vol. 1423, pp. 267–288. Springer, Heidelberg (1998). https://doi.org/10.1007/BFb0054868
17. Hoffstein, J., Silverman, J.H.: Reaction attacks against the NTRU public key cryptosystem (2000). https://ntru.org/resources.shtml
18. Howgrave-Graham, N., et al.: The impact of decryption failures on the security of NTRU encryption. In: Boneh, D. (ed.) CRYPTO 2003. LNCS, vol. 2729, pp. 226–246. Springer, Heidelberg (2003). https://doi.org/10.1007/978-3-540-45146-4_14

19. Howgrave-Graham, N., Silverman, J.H., Singer, A., Whyte, W., Cryptosystems, N.: NAEP: provable security in the presence of decryption failures. IACR Cryptology ePrint Archive **2003**, 172 (2003)

20. Hülsing, A., Rijneveld, J., Schanck, J., Schwabe, P.: High-speed key encapsulation from NTRU. In: Fischer, W., Homma, N. (eds.) CHES 2017. LNCS, vol. 10529, pp. 232–252. Springer, Cham (2017). https://doi.org/10.1007/978-3-319-66787-4_12

21. Lu, X., et al.: Lac: Practical ring-LWE based public-key encryption with byte-level modulus. Cryptology ePrint Archive (2018)

22. Mol, P., Yung, M.: Recovering NTRU secret key from inversion oracles, pp. 18–36 (2008)

23. Nguyen, P.Q., Pointcheval, D.: Analysis and improvements of NTRU encryption paddings. In: Yung, M. (ed.) CRYPTO 2002. LNCS, vol. 2442, pp. 210–225. Springer, Heidelberg (2002). https://doi.org/10.1007/3-540-45708-9_14

24. Okada, S., Wang, Y., Takagi, T.: Improving key mismatch attack on NewHope with fewer queries. In: Liu, J.K., Cui, H. (eds.) ACISP 2020. LNCS, vol. 12248, pp. 505–524. Springer, Cham (2020). https://doi.org/10.1007/978-3-030-55304-3_26

25. Qin, Y., Cheng, C., Ding, J.: A complete and optimized key mismatch attack on NIST candidate NewHope. In: Sako, K., Schneider, S., Ryan, P.Y.A. (eds.) ESORICS 2019. LNCS, vol. 11736, pp. 504–520. Springer, Cham (2019). https://doi.org/10.1007/978-3-030-29962-0_24

26. Qin, Y., Cheng, C., Ding, J.: An efficient key mismatch attack on the NIST second round candidate kyber. Cryptology ePrint Archive (2019)

27. Qin, Y., Cheng, C., Zhang, X., Pan, Y., Hu, L., Ding, J.: A systematic approach and analysis of key mismatch attacks on lattice-based NIST candidate KEMs. In: Tibouchi, M., Wang, H. (eds.) ASIACRYPT 2021. LNCS, vol. 13093, pp. 92–121. Springer, Cham (2021). https://doi.org/10.1007/978-3-030-92068-5_4

28. Ravi, P., Roy, S.S., Chattopadhyay, A., Bhasin, S.: Generic side-channel attacks on CCA-secure lattice-based PKE and KEMS. In: IACR Transactions on Cryptographic Hardware and Embedded Systems, pp. 307–335 (2020)

29. Shao, M., Liu, Y., Zhou, Y.: Pairwise and parallel: enhancing the key mismatch attacks on kyber and beyond. Cryptology ePrint Archive (2023)

30. Shor, P.W.: Algorithms for quantum computation: discrete logarithms and factoring. In: Foundations of Computer Science, 1994 Proceedings of the 35th Annual Symposium on, pp. 124–134. IEEE (1994)

31. Shor, P.W.: Polynomial-time algorithms for prime factorization and discrete logarithms on a quantum computer. SIAM Rev. **41**(2), 303–332 (1999)

32. Whyte, W., Howgrave-Graham, N., Hoffstein, J., Pipher, J., Silverman, J., Hirschhorn, P.: Ieee p1363. 1: Draft standard for public-key cryptographic techniques based on hard problems over lattices. Tech. rep., Technical report, IEEE (2008)

33. Xagawa, K., Ito, A., Ueno, R., Takahashi, J., Homma, N.: Fault-injection attacks against NIST's post-quantum cryptography round 3 KEM candidates. In: Tibouchi, M., Wang, H. (eds.) ASIACRYPT 2021. LNCS, vol. 13091, pp. 33–61. Springer, Cham (2021). https://doi.org/10.1007/978-3-030-92075-3_2

34. Zhang, X., Cheng, C., Ding, R.: Small leaks sink a great ship: an evaluation of key reuse resilience of PQC third round finalist NTRU-HRSS. In: Gao, D., Li, Q., Guan, X., Liao, X. (eds.) ICICS 2021. LNCS, vol. 12919, pp. 283–300. Springer, Cham (2021). https://doi.org/10.1007/978-3-030-88052-1_17

Improved Provable Reduction of NTRU and Hypercubic Lattices

Henry Bambury[1,2]([✉]) and Phong Q. Nguyen[1]

[1] DIENS, École Normale Supérieure, PSL University, CNRS, Inria, Paris, France
[2] DGA, Paris, France
henry.bambury@m4x.org

Abstract. Lattice-based cryptography typically uses lattices with special properties to improve efficiency. We show how blockwise reduction can exploit lattices with special geometric properties, effectively reducing the required blocksize to solve the shortest vector problem to half of the lattice's rank, and in the case of the hypercubic lattice $\mathbb{Z}^n$, further relaxing the approximation factor of blocks to $\sqrt{2}$. We study both provable algorithms and the heuristic well-known primal attack, in the case where the lattice has a first minimum that is almost as short as that of the hypercubic lattice $\mathbb{Z}^n$. Remarkably, these near-hypercubic lattices cover Falcon and most concrete instances of the NTRU cryptosystem: this is the first provable result showing that breaking NTRU lattices can be reduced to finding shortest lattice vectors in halved dimension, thereby providing a positive response to a conjecture of Gama, Howgrave-Graham and Nguyen at Eurocrypt 2006.

Keywords: Lattices · Cryptanalysis · NTRU · ZLIP

1 Introduction

Lattice-based cryptography has emerged as the main alternative to classical public key cryptography based on factoring and discrete logarithm: it can provide resistance to quantum computers and offer new functionalities such as fully-homomorphic encryption. However, for efficiency reasons, the lattices used in concrete cryptosystems are usually not random lattices: they have special properties, to improve keysize and/or speed up operations and/or enable extra operations. For instance, all the lattices used in NIST's new post-quantum standards are special: module lattices for Kyber [7] and Dilithium [18], and NTRU lattices for Falcon [24]. Recently, even hypercubic lattices [46], which are simply rotations of $\mathbb{Z}^n$, have been proposed in [8,19,22] as the basis of concrete cryptosystems, with Hawk [19] being submitted to the new NIST call for post-quantum signatures.

Accordingly, it is crucial to understand if these special properties make the underlying lattice problems easier to solve, and if so, by how much. In the case of module lattices, this remains very much an open problem, except for the case of ideal lattices, for which better algorithms have been found [9,15,41]. For

M.-J. Saarinen and D. Smith-Tone (Eds.): PQCrypto 2024, LNCS 14771, pp. 343–370, 2024.
https://doi.org/10.1007/978-3-031-62743-9_12

NTRU lattices, it is also an open problem: in fact, Gama, Howgrave-Graham and Nguyen [26] conjectured at Eurocrypt 2006 that the reduction of a $2n$-dimensional NTRU lattice could be reduced to that of an αn-dimensional lattice for some $\alpha < 2$. The hypercubic lattice $\mathbb{Z}^n$ was first studied by Szydlo [46] twenty years ago, but it was only shown very recently to be significantly easier to reduce than generic lattices: one can recover an orthonormal basis of $\mathbb{Z}^n$ in time $2^{n/2+o(n)}$ using the algorithm of Bennett, Ganju, Peetathawatchai and Stephens-Davidowitz[1] [8], or, as shown by Ducas [17] by using polynomially many calls to an oracle for the shortest vector problem (SVP) in dimension $n/2$, which also leads to an asymptotic running time of $2^{n/2+o(n)}$. In other words, solving SVP for $\mathbb{Z}^n$ can be reduced to solving SVP in dimension $n/2$.

Our Results. We introduce a new blockwise reduction algorithm, which is a variant of Ducas's algorithm [17], itself a variant of Gama-Nguyen's slide reduction [27]. The differences with Ducas's approach are twofold.

First, our algorithm is more general, as it is not restricted to $\mathbb{Z}^n$: it also applies to any lattice L such that the product of its first minimum with that of its dual lattice is small, namely $\lambda_1(L)\lambda_1(L^\times) < 1 - \frac{1}{\mathrm{poly}(n)}$, where $\lambda_1(\cdot)$ and $L^\times$ denote respectively the first minimum and the dual lattice. This condition is typically not satisfied for a generic lattice: Minkowski's inequality only implies that $\lambda_1(L)\lambda_1(L^\times) = O(n)$. But it turns out to be satisfied by most instantiations of NTRU, because the symplectic property of NTRU uncovered by Gama *et al.* [26] implies that $\lambda_1(L)\lambda_1(L^\times) = \lambda_1(L)^2/q$ where q is the small modulus of the NTRU cryptosystem, and also equal to $\mathrm{vol}(L)^{2/\mathrm{rank}(L)}$. In the recent NTRU-HPS submission [12] to NIST, we have $\lambda_1(L)^2/q < 1/2$ for all three parameter sets proposed, due to the absence of decryption failures. For the original NTRU [31] from the 90 s and for Falcon [24], this does not hold but can be taken care of by a mild heuristic assumption on the projection of secret vectors over random subspaces related to lattice reduction: similar yet stronger assumptions were made and checked in the context of lattice enumeration [29]. Thus, we show that for the NTRU-HPS submission [12], one can provably find a non-zero lattice vector at least as short as the secret key, by solving the shortest vector problem in a lattice of halved dimension. This is the first rigorous result showing that an NTRU lattice can be solved by working with SVP oracles in a smaller dimension than what is required for a generic lattice. It should not be confused with heuristic security estimates where the blocksize required to break the underlying system is heuristically estimated to be a fraction of the lattice dimension.

Second, our algorithm improves that of Ducas in the case of $\mathbb{Z}^n$. Ducas required an exact or nearly-exact algorithm for SVP in dimension $n/2$, whereas our algorithm can tolerate an approximate-SVP algorithm in dimension $n/2$ with an approximation factor essentially $\sqrt{2}$. Intuitively, a factor $\sqrt{2}$ should make the problem easier, and the SVP challenges [43] suggest that the problem is easier in practice. Eisenbrand and Venzin [23] note that the best sieving algorithms

---

[1] Note that the *semi-stable* variant of their algorithm [8, Cor. 5.5] also applies to NTRU lattices.

give a provable $2^{0.802n+o(n)}$-runtime algorithm for $O(1)$ approximations of the shortest vector, although the constant is larger than $\sqrt{2}$. There is currently no theoretical evidence that approximating SVP to within $\sqrt{2}$ is easier than solving exact SVP, but if ever it is strictly easier, such as solvable in time $2^{\alpha n+o(n)}$ for some $\alpha < 1$, we would immediately obtain an exponentially faster algorithm for the $\mathbb{Z}^n$-Lattice Isomorphism Problem ($\mathbb{Z}$-LIP), running in time $2^{\alpha n/2+o(n)}$.

Finally, we compare the performances of our provable algorithms with heuristic estimates provided by the so-called primal attack [6]. In the case of $\mathbb{Z}^n$, this was done by [19], where the authors state without giving many details that a blocksize of $n/2 + o(n)$ is heuristically sufficient to recover a shortest vector. We show more generally that for any n-dimensional lattice L such that $\lambda_1(L) = O(\text{vol}(L)^{1/n})$, the primal attack heuristically recovers a shortest lattice vector using a blocksize $n/2 + \Theta(n/\log n)$: this result applies to both $\mathbb{Z}^n$ and NTRU lattices. For these lattices, there are actually multiple shortest vectors, even a linear number: somewhat surprisingly, we show that the heuristic asymptotical blocksize required by the primal attack remains $n/2 + \Theta(n/\log n)$, even though in practice, it is somewhat easier. This means there is not much difference between the best theoretical algorithm and the best heuristic algorithm, and that the result depends essentially on the existence of one unusually short lattice vector.

Technical Overview. Our algorithm differs from Ducas's algorithm in two main aspects. First, we distinguish the primal and the dual lattice. Second, we change the termination condition: instead of densifying a certain sublattice until it becomes hypercubic, we check whether our current primal and dual sublattices include a shortest vector.

Ducas's analysis [17] is based on a surprising upper bound $\sqrt{1 - 1/n}$ on the first minimum of projections of $\mathbb{Z}^n$ over certain subspaces. This upper bound is tight when the subspace is a hyperplane corresponding to the dual root lattice $A_{n-1}^\times$. However, we show that the upper bound can be improved for certain lower-dimensional subspaces, which might be of independent interest, and allows us to relax the SVP oracle to an approximate-SVP oracle with factor essentially $\sqrt{2}$. More precisely, it is well-known that the expectation of the squared norm of the projection of a unit vector onto a k-dimensional random subspace of $\mathbb{R}^n$ is k/n. We show that the expectation of the squared norm of the projection of a random element of a fixed orthonormal basis of $\mathbb{R}^n$ onto a fixed k-dimensional subspace is also k/n. This allows us to replace the bound $\sqrt{1 - 1/n}$ by essentially $\sqrt{1/2}$ when $k \approx n/2$.

Our analysis of the primal attack [6] differs a bit from the literature [5,16]. In the primal attack, it is crucial to estimate the projection of a short vector onto random subspaces related to lattice reduction. Previous work [5,16] restricted to a short vector from LWE, whose coordinates are independent Gaussians. However, we argue that this model does not match $\mathbb{Z}^n$ nor NTRU. So instead of the χ^2 distribution, we rely on the Beta distribution related to classical sphere statistics. And we heuristically extend the analysis to the case of linearly many short vectors.

Roadmap. Section 2 provides background. In Sect. 3, we present our new block-wise reduction algorithm for near-hypercubic lattices. In Sect. 4, we study the heuristic primal attack on those same lattices, and analyse which blocksize is required.

2 Preliminaries

General Notations. Vectors are written in bold lowercase $\mathbf{v}$. The Euclidean norm of a vector $\mathbf{v} \in \mathbb{R}^n$ is denoted $\|\mathbf{v}\|$. The associated scalar product of $\mathbf{a} \in \mathbb{R}^n$ and $\mathbf{b} \in \mathbb{R}^n$ is written $\langle \mathbf{a}, \mathbf{b} \rangle$. Throughout this paper, we use row representation of matrices. For a set of vectors $V \subseteq \mathbb{R}^n$, we write $\mathrm{span}(V)$ the real vector space generated by V. We write $V^\perp$ or $\mathrm{span}(V)^\perp$ for the set of vectors $\mathbf{w} \in \mathbb{R}^n$ such that $\langle \mathbf{w}, \mathbf{v} \rangle = 0$ for all $\mathbf{v}$ in V. π_V denotes the orthogonal projection onto $\mathrm{span}(V)$. We use the standard asymptotic notations $o(\cdot), O(\cdot), \Theta(\cdot)$ and $\omega(\cdot)$. As n goes to infinity, we use the notation $a_n \sim b_n$ as shorthand for $a_n = b_n + o(b_n)$. We use $\ll$ slightly differently to how it might usually be used: $a_n \ll b_n$ if there exists a polynomial P of constant degree such that for any large enough n, $a_n < b_n - \frac{1}{P(n)}$.

Probabilities. We denote the expectation of a random variable by $\mathbb{E}(\cdot)$, and probabilities by $\mathbb{P}(\cdot)$. As proved in [25], the squared norm of the projection of a unit vector of $\mathbb{R}^n$ onto a random k-dimensional subspace of $\mathbb{R}^n$ follows the *Beta distribution* $B(k/2, (n-k)/2)$. In particular, the expected squared norm of this projection is k/n. The cumulative distribution function of $B(a, b)$ is the *regularised incomplete beta function* $I_x(a, b)$. Asymptotic expansions of the regularised incomplete beta function rely on the *complementary error function* $\mathrm{erfc}(z) := \frac{2}{\sqrt{\pi}} \int_z^\infty e^{-t^2} dt$. When z goes to infinity, $\mathrm{erfc}(z) \sim \pi^{-1/2} z^{-1} e^{-z^2}$ (Fig. 1).

Lattices. A *lattice* L is a discrete subgroup of $\mathbb{R}^m$. Alternatively, we can define a lattice as the set $\mathcal{L}(\mathbf{b}_1, \ldots, \mathbf{b}_n) = \{\sum_{i=1}^n x_i \mathbf{b}_i : x_i \in \mathbb{Z}\}$ of all integer combinations of n linearly independent vectors $\mathbf{b}_1, \ldots, \mathbf{b}_n \in \mathbb{R}^m$. This sequence of vectors is known as a *basis* of the lattice L. All the bases of L have the same number n of elements, called the dimension or rank of L, and the n-dimensional volume of the parallelepiped $\{\sum_{i=1}^n a_i \mathbf{b}_i : a_i \in [0, 1)\}$ they generate. We call this volume the volume, or determinant, of L, and denote it by $\mathrm{vol}(L)$. The lattice L is said to be *full-rank* if $n = m$. We denote by $\lambda_1(L)$ the first minimum of L, defined as the norm of a shortest nonzero vector of L.

Orthogonalisation. For a basis $B = (\mathbf{b}_1, \ldots, \mathbf{b}_n)$ of a lattice L, and an index $1 \leq i \leq n$, we denote by π_i the orthogonal projection on $\mathrm{span}(\mathbf{b}_1, \ldots, \mathbf{b}_{i-1})^\perp$. The *Gram-Schmidt orthogonalisation* (GSO) of the basis B is defined as the orthogonal sequence of vectors $B^\star = (\mathbf{b}_1^\star, \ldots, \mathbf{b}_n^\star)$, where $\mathbf{b}_i^\star := \pi_i(\mathbf{b}_i)$. The

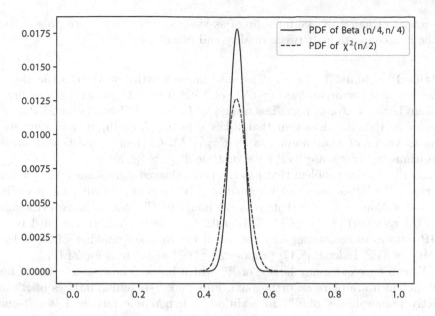

Fig. 1. Comparing the χ^2 and *Beta* distributions for $n = 1000$

projection of a lattice is not always a lattice, but for all $i \in \{1, \ldots, n\}$, $\pi_i(L)$ is a lattice of dimension $n + 1 - i$ generated by the basis $\pi_i(\mathbf{b}_i), \ldots, \pi_i(\mathbf{b}_n)$, such that $\mathrm{vol}(\pi_i(L)) = \prod_{j=i}^{n} \|\mathbf{b}_j^\star\|$.

Duality. For any lattice L, its *dual lattice* $L^\times$ is defined by

$$L^\times := \{\mathbf{w} \in \mathrm{span}(L) : \langle \mathbf{w}, \mathbf{v} \rangle \in \mathbb{Z} \text{ for all } \mathbf{v} \in L\}.$$

If L has rank $n > 0$, then $L^\times$ also, and $\mathrm{vol}(L) = \mathrm{vol}(L^\times)^{-1}$. If $B = (\mathbf{b}_1, \ldots, \mathbf{b}_n)$ is a basis of L, then there is a unique *dual basis* $(\mathbf{d}_1, \ldots, \mathbf{d}_n)$ of $L^\times$ such that $\langle \mathbf{b}_i, \mathbf{d}_j \rangle = \delta_{i,j}$ (Kronecker symbol) for all i, j. Duality is related to GSO as $\langle \mathbf{b}_i^\star / \|\mathbf{b}_i^\star\|^2, \mathbf{b}_i \rangle = 1$ implies that

$$\frac{\mathbf{b}_i^\star}{\|\mathbf{b}_i^\star\|^2} \in \mathcal{L}(\mathbf{b}_1, \ldots, \mathbf{b}_i)^\times.$$

In particular, $\mathbf{d}_n = \mathbf{b}_n^\star / \|\mathbf{b}_n^\star\|^2$ and $\|\mathbf{d}_n\| = \|\mathbf{b}_n^\star\|^{-1}$.

Primitivity. A sublattice L' of L is called *primitive* if $L' = \mathrm{span}(L') \cap L$ or equivalently L/L' is torsion free. In this case, $L = L' \oplus L/L'$. Equivalently, a sublattice of L is primitive if its bases can be completed into a basis of L. We will make heavy use of the following identity: if L' is a primitive sublattice of L, then

$$L/L' = \pi_{L'^\perp}(L) = (L^\times \cap \mathrm{span}(L')^\perp)^\times.$$

We refer to Chap. 1 of [38] for a proof as well as a more complete presentation of the interconnections between duality and primitivity.

Lattice Problems. Let $\gamma \geq 1$. The most famous lattice problem is the *approximate shortest vector problem* (γ-SVP or SVP if $\gamma = 1$), which asks to find a nonzero lattice vector of norm less than $\gamma\lambda_1(L)$. A γ-SVP-oracle (or SVP-oracle when $\gamma = 1$) is an algorithm that takes a lattice L as input, and outputs a nonzero vector of L of norm less than $\gamma\lambda_1(L)$. Currently, the fastest known algorithms for worst-case SVP have runtime $2^{n+o(n)}$ ([1,3]).

Another lattice problem that has recently achieved significant cryptographic interest is the *lattice isomorphism problem* (LIP), and in particular its specialisation to rotations of $\mathbb{Z}^n$ ($\mathbb{Z}$LIP): given the image of $\mathbb{Z}^n$ under a linear orthogonal map (or rotation) $O \in \mathcal{O}_n(\mathbb{R})$, $\mathbb{Z}$LIP asks to recover O. It is not hard to see $\mathbb{Z}$LIP reduces to recovering unit vectors of the rotation, making $\mathbb{Z}$LIP at least as easy as SVP. Indeed, [8,17] propose $2^{n/2+o(n)}$ algorithms for $\mathbb{Z}$LIP.

We call *hypercubic* any lattice of $\mathbb{R}^n$ which has a $\mathbb{Z}$-basis consisting of unit vectors which are pairwise orthogonal. Full rank hypercubic lattices of $\mathbb{R}^n$ are exactly isomorphisms of $\mathbb{Z}^n$. In addition, a hypercubic lattice Λ is self-dual: $\Lambda = \Lambda^\times$.

Lattice Reduction. The celebrated LLL algorithm [36] solves 2^n-SVP in polynomial time. Blockwise algorithms such as BKZ [14,45] and its variants [2,27,39] approximate SVP within better factors, using polynomially many calls to an exact (or near-exact) SVP oracle in rank less than an input parameter called the *blocksize*. Following [2,27,39], we call γ-SVP-reduction any algorithm which outputs a basis whose first vector solves γ-SVP. Similarly, we call γ-DVSP-reduction (where D stands for dual) any algorithm which outputs a basis whose last Gram-Schmidt vector solves γ-SVP in the dual lattice. Given a γ-SVP-oracle, it is possible to γ-SVP-reduce or γ-DSVP-reduce in polynomial time (see [28,39]).

Reduced Bases. Lattice reduction algorithms aim to transform an input basis into a "high quality" basis. There are many ways to quantify the quality of bases produced by lattice reduction algorithms. One popular way is to consider the Gram-Schmidt norms $\|\mathbf{b}_1^\star\|, \ldots, \|\mathbf{b}_n^\star\|$. Intuitively speaking, a good basis is one in which this sequence does not decay too fast. In practice, it turns out that the Gram-Schmidt coefficients of bases produced by the main reduction algorithms (such as LLL or BKZ) have a certain "typical shape", assuming the input basis is sufficiently random. This property was thoroughly investigated in [28,40]. This typical shape is often used to estimate the running time of various algorithms. In particular, many theoretical asymptotic analyses (as introduced by Schnorr [44]) assume for simplicity that this shape is given by $\|\mathbf{b}_i^\star\|/\|\mathbf{b}_{i+1}^\star\| = q$ where q depends on the reduction algorithm; although less precise, this approximation called the *geometric series assumption (GSA)* is close to the shape observed in practice. It is heuristically[2] estimated [13,14,37] that the BKZ algorithm with blocksize β, given as input a basis of an n-rank lattice L outputs a basis whose first vector has norm approximately equal to $\delta_\beta^n \mathrm{vol}(L)^{1/n}$, where $\delta_\beta = \left(\frac{\beta}{2\pi e}(\pi\beta)^{1/\beta}\right)^{\frac{1}{2(\beta-1)}}$. Combining this with the GSA and the fact that $\mathrm{vol}(L) = \prod_{i=1}^{n}\|\mathbf{b}_i^\star\|$ gives estimates of the Gram-Schmidt norms: for $1 \leq i \leq n$,

$$\|\mathbf{b}_i^\star\| \approx \delta_\beta^{n-\frac{2n}{n-1}(i-1)}\mathrm{vol}(L)^{1/n}.$$

Such a heuristic model is widely used in security estimates of lattice-based NIST submissions.

The Primal Attack. Parameters of lattice-based cryptosystems are chosen after careful study of known attacks. The most important attack that people consider today is called the *primal attack*, which runs the BKZ blockwise reduction [14,45] with a sufficiently high blocksize. Building upon [14,28], the authors of [6] proposed to heuristically estimate the blocksize required by this attack to recover a short vector $\mathbf{s}$ in a rank n lattice L, by comparing the expected norm of $\pi_{n-\beta+1}(\mathbf{s})$ to the expected value of $\|\mathbf{b}_{n-\beta+1}^\star\|$. Using the GSA, as soon as

$$\sqrt{\frac{\beta}{n}}\|\mathbf{s}\| < \delta_\beta^{2\beta-n-1}\mathrm{vol}(L)^{1/n} \tag{1}$$

holds, the projection $\pi_{n-\beta+1}(\mathbf{s})$ is either 0 and then $\mathbf{s}$ lives in the subspace generated by the first $n - \beta$ vectors of the reduced basis, or it has a high chance of being shorter than $\|\mathbf{b}_{n-\beta+1}^\star\|$, making it such that the SVP oracle on the last block of size β will recover it. Albrecht, Göpfert, Virdia and Wunderer [5] and Dachman-Soled, Ducas, Gong, Rossi [16] refine and experimentally confirm this framework in the case of LWE. It should be stressed that the analysis of the primal attack remains very much heuristic.

The Original NTRU Cryptosystem. The NTRU cryptosystem [31], proposed by Hoffstein, Pipher and Silverman, works in the ring $\mathcal{R} = \mathbb{Z}[X]/(X^n - 1)$. An element $f = \sum_{i=0}^{n-1} f_i x^i = [f_0, f_1, \ldots, f_{n-1}] \in \mathcal{R}$ is seen as a polynomial or a row vector. To select keys, one uses the set $\mathcal{L}(d_1, d_2)$ of polynomials $F \in \mathcal{R}$ such that d_1 coefficients are equal to 1, d_2 coefficients are equal to -1, and the rest are zero. There are two small coprime moduli $p < q$, such as $q = 128$ and $p = 3$.

Historically, the secret keys were $f \in \mathcal{L}(d_f, d_f - 1)$ and $g \in \mathcal{L}(d_g, d_g)$ for some integers d_f and d_g significantly smaller than n, but other NTRU instantiations [12,30,32] use different parameters for $\mathcal{L}$, such as binary polynomials $\mathcal{L}(d, 0)$. To illustrate, we focus on the NTRU-HPS parameters of NTRU's NIST submission [12], one of the seven finalists: f is a random polynomial in $\{0, \pm 1\}^n$, and $g \in \mathcal{L}(d_g, d_g)$ where $2d_g = q/8 - 2$. With high probability, f is invertible mod

---

[2] By replacing Hermite's constant by a Gaussian heuristic estimate.

q. The public key $h \in \mathcal{R}$ is defined as $h = g/f \mod q$. Thus, in the ring $\mathcal{R}/q\mathcal{R}$ which we represent by $\mathbb{Z}_q^n$, we have $f * h = g$. In this article, there is no need to know how NTRU encryption or signature works. The polynomial h defines the so-called NTRU lattice Λ_h, formed by all pairs of polynomials $(u, v) \in \mathcal{R}^2$ such that $v * h \equiv u \mod q$. Here, we follow the definition of [33], but other papers may use a variant of Λ_h, using a permutation of the coordinates. Λ_h is generated by the rows of the following lower-triangular matrix, which is its Hermite normal form:

$$\begin{pmatrix} qI_n & 0 \\ H & I_n \end{pmatrix},$$

where H is the circulant matrix for the polynomial $h \equiv g/f = \sum_{i=0}^{n-1} h_i x^i$:

$$H = \begin{pmatrix} h_0 & h_1 & \cdots & h_{n-1} \\ h_{n-1} & h_0 & \ddots & \vdots \\ \vdots & \ddots & \ddots & h_1 \\ h_1 & \cdots & h_{n-1} & h_0 \end{pmatrix}.$$

The lattice Λ_h contains by definition the following set of n secret short vectors $\mathcal{S}_h = \{(x^i * g, x^i * f), 0 \le i \le n-1\}$ formed by the secret vector (g, f) and its $n-1$ rotations.

NTRU Variants. Variants of the original NTRU [31] choose to use different polynomial rings $\mathcal{R} = \mathbb{Z}[X]/P(X)$, for a unitary degree n polynomial $P \in \mathbb{Z}[X]$. Without giving an exhaustive list, examples of cryptosystems that use such variants include NTRU Prime [10], NTRU+ [34], as well as the Falcon signature scheme [24]. In these cases, the public key $h \in \mathcal{R}/q\mathcal{R}$ is also defined as $h = g/f \mod q$, where $(f, g) \in \mathcal{R}^2$ is the secret key. In the most general case, the NTRU lattice is obtained by embedding the rank 2 $\mathcal{R}$-module that we call the *NTRU module*

$$M_h := \{(u, v) \in \mathcal{R}^2 : hu \equiv v \mod q\mathcal{R}\}$$

into $\mathbb{C}^{2n}$ via an embedding map $\sigma : \mathcal{R} \to \mathbb{C}^n$. The secret key is usually of small norm after embedding, that is $\|(\sigma(g), \sigma(f))\|$ is small. Most commonly, as is the case in the aforementioned cryptosystems, σ is simply the *coefficient embedding*. It has the advantage of being simple as it is easy to implement, as its image is integral. Other embeddings can also be of cryptanalytic interest. Most notably, the *canonical embedding* is obtained by evaluating a polynomial of $\mathcal{R}$ at all complex roots of P. This embedding is more complicated to deal with on a computer, but is a ring homomorphism and therefore behaves well with multiplication, which is usually not the case with the coefficient embedding. In particular if P is irreducible, then $\mathcal{R}$ is the ring of integers of a number field and the *canonical embedding* coincides with the *Minkowski embedding*.

3 Blockwise Reduction of Near-Hypercubic Lattices

In this section, we describe our reduction algorithm, and specialise its analysis to NTRU and hypercubic lattices.

3.1 Provable Algorithm

Algorithm 1. Primal/dual reduction with blocksize of halved dimension

Input: A basis $B = (\mathbf{b}_1, \ldots, \mathbf{b}_n)$ of a lattice $\Lambda \subseteq \mathbb{Z}^m$, together with two upper bounds r and $r^\times$ such that $\lambda_1(L) \leq r$ and $\lambda_1(L^\times) \leq r^\times$. L (resp. N) is the sublattice spanned by the first $\lfloor n/2 \rfloor$ (resp. $\lfloor n/2 \rfloor + 1$) vectors of B, *i.e.* $L = \mathcal{L}(\mathbf{b}_1, \ldots, \mathbf{b}_{\lfloor n/2 \rfloor})$. Keep in mind that L and N are updated naturally as B evolves.

Output: A short non-zero vector in Λ of norm $\leq r$ or a short non-zero vector in the dual $\Lambda^\times$ of norm $\leq r^\times$, or a basis B such that $\mathrm{vol}(L)$ is guaranteed to be small.

1: LLL-reduce B.
2: **while** $\mathrm{vol}(L)$ strictly decreases **do**
3:   $\mathbf{e} \leftarrow$ SVP-oracle(L) to check for short primal lattice vectors.
4:   **if** $\|\mathbf{e}\| \leq r$ **then**
5:     Return $\mathbf{e}$.
6:   **else**
7:     SVP-reduce(Λ/L) to reduce the second half of B modulo its first half.
8:   **end if**
9:   $\mathbf{e}' \leftarrow$ SVP-oracle($\Lambda^\times \cap \mathrm{span}(N)^\perp$) to check for short dual lattice vectors.
10:   **if** $\|\mathbf{e}'\| \leq r^\times$ **then**
11:     Return $\mathbf{e}'$.
12:   **else**
13:     SVP-reduce($N^\times$) to dual-reduce the first half of B: this is DSVP-reduction of the lattice N.
14:   **end if**
15: **end while**
16: Return B.

Algorithm 1 can be viewed as a variant of Gama-Nguyen's slide algorithm [27] and Ducas' algorithm [17, Algorithm 1]. However, in differs in a few ways, mainly:

- It is not specialised to $\mathbb{Z}^n$.
- The termination conditions are different: instead of uniquely focusing on the reduction task, our algorithm can also check for the presence of short vectors in the lattice Λ or its dual $\Lambda^\times$. Indeed, the tests at Lines 4 and 10 are parametrised by values r and $r^\times$, which will be specified in the case of NTRU lattices and hypercubic lattices. If the user knows that Λ and/or $\Lambda^\times$ contains a short vector of a prescribed length, then he can change the values of r and $r^\times$ accordingly, for example by setting $r = \lambda_1(\Lambda)$ and/or $r^\times = \lambda_1(\Lambda^\times)$ when the first minima are known.

- Lines 3 and 9 add an extra call to the SVP oracle, which provides a way to prematurely abort if the objective is to find a vector of Λ and/or $\Lambda^\times$ of norm less than a fixed value. This is especially useful in the case of NTRU and hypercubic lattices where the first minimum is well-known.
- Unlike [17,27], our algorithm assumes no requirement on the parity of n.

We make an important remark on Algorithm 1, which explains why we view this reduction as a primal/dual reduction: Steps 9-14 are dual to Steps 3-8, in the sense that they are exactly Steps 3-8 if we replace the lattice Λ by its dual $\Lambda^\times$, and the sublattice L by $\Lambda^\times \cap \operatorname{span}(N)^\perp$.

The efficiency of the algorithm is based on the following key elementary result:

Lemma 1. *Assume that $\Lambda \subseteq \mathbb{Z}^m$. During a loop iteration, the sublattice L (at the beginning of a loop iteration) is transformed into L', after Step 14. Then:*

$$\frac{\operatorname{vol}(L')}{\operatorname{vol}(L)} = \lambda_1(\Lambda/L)\lambda_1(N^\times), \tag{2}$$

where N is from Step 13. Furthermore, if the exact reduction oracles of Steps 7 and 13 are replaced by approximate-reduction with factor respectively γ and γ', then:

$$\frac{\operatorname{vol}(L')}{\operatorname{vol}(L)} \leq \gamma\gamma'\lambda_1(\Lambda/L)\lambda_1(N^\times). \tag{3}$$

Proof. The sublattice L can only be changed by Step 13, which cannot change the sublattice N. Since $\operatorname{vol}(N) = \operatorname{vol}(L)\|\mathbf{b}_{k+1}^\star\|$, we are interested in $\|\mathbf{b}_{k+1}^\star\|$, which can only be changed by Steps 7 and 13. After Step 7, we have $\|\mathbf{b}_{k+1}^\star\| = \lambda_1(\Lambda/L)$. After Step 13, we have $1/\|\mathbf{b}_{k+1}^\star\| = \lambda_1(N^\times)$. So $\|\mathbf{b}_{k+1}^\star\|$ changes from $\lambda_1(\Lambda/L)$ to $1/\lambda_1(N^\times)$, which proves (2). The inequality (3) follows from the definition of approximate reduction.

□

Theorem 1. *Let $\Lambda \subseteq \mathbb{Z}^m$ be a rank n lattice. Assume that $\lambda_1(\Lambda)\lambda_1(\Lambda^\times) < 1-\varepsilon$ for some $\varepsilon = \frac{1}{\operatorname{poly}(n)}$. Then Alg. 1 returns a non-zero vector of Λ with norm $\leq r$, or a non-zero vector of its dual $\Lambda^\times$ with norm $\leq r^\times$. The number of loop iterations from Step 3 till Step 14 is polynomial in the size of the input basis B and $1/\varepsilon$. The number of SVP oracle queries is linear in the number of loop iterations, and the dimension of the lattice in each oracle query is $\leq \lfloor n/2 \rfloor + 1$.*

Proof. $\Lambda \subseteq \mathbb{Z}^m$ implies that $\operatorname{vol}(L)^2 \in \mathbb{Z}$. $\log \operatorname{vol}(L)$ is polynomially bounded by the size of the input basis B, and can only decrease with LLL reduction (Step 1). This means that the number of times $\operatorname{vol}(L)$ decreases by $1 - \varepsilon$ is polynomially bounded by the size of the input basis B and $1/\varepsilon$.

If $\|\mathbf{e}\| > r \geq \lambda_1(\Lambda)$, there exists $\mathbf{u} \in \Lambda$ such that $\|\mathbf{u}\| = \lambda_1(\Lambda)$ and $\mathbf{u} \notin L$, therefore $\lambda_1(\Lambda/L) \leq \|\mathbf{u}\| = \lambda_1(L)$. Similarly, if $\|\mathbf{e}'\| > r^\times \geq \lambda_1(\Lambda^\times)$, then

$\lambda_1(N^\times) \leq \lambda_1(\Lambda^\times)$. Thus, if both $\|e\| > r$ and $\|e'\| > r^\times$, then using our assumption, $\lambda_1(\Lambda/L)\lambda_1(N^\times) \leq \lambda_1(\Lambda)\lambda_1(\Lambda^\times) < 1-\varepsilon$. This implies by Lem. 1 that $\mathrm{vol}(L)$ decreases by at least $1-\varepsilon$, which can only happen polynomially many times.

Thus, we will find, within polynomially many iterations, some $e \in L \subseteq \Lambda$ such that $\|e\| \leq r$ or some $e \in N^\times \subseteq \Lambda^\times$ such that $\|e'\| \leq r^\times$.

By definition, each loop iteration makes four calls to an SVP oracle, and the underlying lattice has rank $\in \{\lfloor n/2 \rfloor, n - \lfloor n/2 \rfloor, n - \lfloor n/2 \rfloor - 1, \lfloor n/2 \rfloor + 1\}$.

$\square$

3.2   Application to NTRU and Falcon

In 2006, Gama, Howgrave-Graham and Nguyen [26] showed that coordinate embedding NTRU lattices from the ring $\mathbb{Z}[X]/(X^n - 1)$ are proportional to symplectic lattices, which is a special case of isodual lattices, *i.e.* there is an isometry between the lattice and its dual. We derive the following property of NTRU lattices:

Theorem 2. *Let $\mathcal{R}$ be $\mathbb{Z}[X]/(X^n - 1)$ or $\mathbb{Z}[X]/(X^n + 1)$. Let $(f, g) \in \mathcal{R}^2$ be an NTRU secret key corresponding to parameters (q, n) and a lattice Λ obtained from the coefficient embedding. Then there is an explicit bijection $\phi : \Lambda \to q\Lambda^\times$ which preserves the Euclidean norm, and which can be computed in polynomial time (in both directions). In particular,*

$$\lambda_1(\Lambda^\times) = \frac{\lambda_1(\Lambda)}{q},$$

where $\lambda_1(\Lambda)^2 \leq \|\mathbf{f}\|^2 + \|\mathbf{g}\|^2$, where $(\mathbf{f}, \mathbf{g})$ is the coefficient embedding of (f, g).

Proof. Using row notation, it is not hard to show that Λ and $\Lambda^\times$ are respectively generated by the bases B_Λ and $B_{\Lambda^\times}$, where

$$B_\Lambda = \begin{pmatrix} qI_n & 0 \\ H & I_n \end{pmatrix} \text{ and } B_{\Lambda^\times} = \begin{pmatrix} \frac{1}{q}I_n & -\frac{1}{q}H^T \\ 0 & I_n \end{pmatrix},$$

where H is circulant (resp. anti-circulant) in the coefficients of $h \in \mathcal{R}$ the public key corresponding to (f, g) if $\mathcal{R} = \mathbb{Z}[X]/(X^n - 1)$ (resp. $\mathcal{R} = \mathbb{Z}[X]/(X^n + 1)$). We claim that

$$\phi : \begin{cases} \Lambda & \to q\Lambda^\times \\ (\mathbf{u}, \mathbf{v}) & \mapsto (\tilde{\mathbf{v}}, -\tilde{\mathbf{u}}) \end{cases}$$

is the desired isometry, where $\tilde{\mathbf{u}}$ is $\mathbf{u}$ in reverse order. Indeed, because of the circulant or anti-circulant nature of H, the i-th row of h is exactly the same as the $(n + 1 - i)$-th row of H^T in reverse order. The structure of $B_{\Lambda^\times}$ relatively to B_Λ allows us to conclude that ϕ is a suitable candidate. This map ϕ can clearly be computed in polynomial time, in both directions. Finally, the inequality $\lambda_1(\Lambda)^2 \leq \|\mathbf{f}\|^2 + \|\mathbf{g}\|^2$ follows from the fact that (g, f) is a lattice vector.

$\square$

Thus, we can upper bound $\lambda_1(\Lambda^\times)\lambda_1(\Lambda)$ by $\frac{1}{q}(\|\mathbf{f}\|^2 + \|\mathbf{g}\|^2)$. Table 1 gives the explicit value of this upper bound for three types of NTRU lattices: the ones of the NTRU submission to NIST [12], the original NTRU cryptosystem [31], and the NIST signature standard Falcon [24]. These three types differ from the distribution used for f and g:

- For the first two, f and g have ternary coefficients $\in \{0, \pm 1\}$ but the number of ± 1 differ for each type.
- For Falcon however, f and g no longer have ternary coefficients: instead, its coefficients follow a discrete Gaussian distribution. We used publicly-available key generation software to compute the typical value of $\|\mathbf{f}\|^2 + \|\mathbf{g}\|^2$.

In addition, all of these examples use the coefficient embedding version of NTRU. The first two use the ring $\mathbb{Z}[X]/(X^n - 1)$, and the third uses $\mathbb{Z}[X]/(X^n + 1)$, both of which fall into the scope of Theorem 2.

Table 1. NTRU parameters: the two filled-in columns determine whether Theorem 1 applies, theoretically or heuristically. The last column illustrates by how much we can relax the SVP-reduction used Steps 7 and 13 of Algorithm 1. When $\|(\mathbf{f}, \mathbf{g})\|^2$ is not fixed by the specifications, we take the experimental median over 1000 instances.

Upper bound on $\lambda_1(L)\lambda_1(L^\times)$ for various NTRU parameters						
Lattice	N	q	$\|(\mathbf{f}, \mathbf{g})\|^2$	$\lambda_1(L)\lambda_1(L^\times)$	$\frac{1}{2}\lambda_1(L)\lambda_1(L^\times)$	Approx factor
NIST-1 [12]	509	2048	593	.2897	.1449	2.628
NIST-2 [12]	677	2048	705	.3444	.1722	2.410
NIST-3 [12]	821	2048	1057	.2581	.1291	1.969
Original toy [31]	107	64	53	.8281	.4141	1.554
	167	128	161	1.258	.6289	1.261
Original [31]	263	128	147	1.148	.5742	1.320
	503	256	575	2.246	1.123	N/A
Falcon-512 [24]	512	12889	16481	1.341	.6706	1.251
Falcon-1024 [24]	1024	12889	16487	1.342	.6708	1.250

In Table 1, the green colour indicates that the upper bound is $< 1 - \varepsilon$ for some constant $\varepsilon > 0$, which makes Theorem 1 applicable: this is the case for all parameter sets of NTRU submission to NIST [12], and for the toy parameter set of the original NTRU [31]. If we run Algorithm 1 with input $r^2 = \|\mathbf{f}\|^2 + \|\mathbf{g}\|^2$ and $r^\times = \frac{1}{q}\sqrt{\|\mathbf{f}\|^2 + \|\mathbf{g}\|^2}$ (where the exact value may be replaced by a good upper bound): this will return a nonzero vector in the primal lattice at least as short as the secret key, using only an SVP oracle in halved dimension. Indeed, if ever a dual vector is returned, the isometry of Theorem 2 allows to transform the short dual vector into a short primal vector. Bare in mind that it is believed that the secret-key vectors are the shortest vectors of the NTRU lattice, but this has not been proved.

We explain the situation of the NTRU submission to NIST [12]. To avoid decryption failures, the generation of $\mathbf{f}$ and $\mathbf{g}$ is such that $\|\mathbf{f}\|^2 + \|\mathbf{g}\|^2 \leq q/2$. In fact, we have $\|\mathbf{f}\|^2 \leq N$ and $\|\mathbf{g}\|^2 = q/8 - 2$. Thus:

$$\lambda_1(\Lambda^\times)\lambda_1(\Lambda) \leq \frac{1}{q}(\|\mathbf{f}\|^2 + \|\mathbf{g}\|^2) \leq \frac{1}{2}.$$

On the other hand, the historical parameters of NTRU allowed decryption failures, which increased $\|\mathbf{f}\|$ and $\|\mathbf{g}\|$.

The red colour in Tab. 1 shows that the bound is not satisfied. However, there is a way to get around this issue, under a mild assumption, except for the largest parameter of original NTRU [31]. Indeed, Theorem 1 uses an upper bound on $\lambda_1(\Lambda)\lambda_1(\Lambda^\times)$ to actually upper bound $\lambda_1(\Lambda/L)$ and $\lambda_1(N^\times)$, knowing that none of the n short vectors $\mathbf{s}_1, \ldots, \mathbf{s}_n$ related to the secret key, obtained by coefficient embedding of the $(x^i * f, x^i * g)$, belong to the sublattice L (and similarly for the dual, with respect to $N^\times$). It follows that $\lambda_1(\Lambda/L) \leq \min_{1 \leq i \leq n} \|\pi(\mathbf{s}_i)\|$, where π denotes the orthogonal projection over $\mathrm{span}(L)^\perp$. If $\mathrm{span}(L)^\perp$ was a random subspace, the expectation of $\|\pi(\mathbf{s}_i)\|^2$ would be $\|\mathbf{s}_i\|^2 \frac{1}{n} \dim \mathrm{span}(L)^\perp \approx \|\mathbf{s}_i\|^2 \frac{1}{2}$. This suggests to make the mild assumption that:

$$\lambda_1(\Lambda/L)\lambda_1(N^\times) \leq \frac{\lambda_1(\Lambda)\lambda_1(\Lambda^\times)}{2}.$$

If this assumption holds at each loop iteration, then the conclusions of Theorem 1 still hold: we will obtain a nonzero vector in the primal lattice at least as short as the secret key. The second to last column of Table 1 therefore shows an upper bound of $\frac{1}{2}\lambda_1(\Lambda)\lambda_1(\Lambda^\times)$: it turns out that the upper bound is now always $\ll 1$, except for the largest parameter of original NTRU [31]. If this product is $\ll 1$, then we can heuristically relax the SVP-reductions used in Steps 7 and 13 of Algorithm 1 to approximate-SVP-reductions with approximation factor $\ll \sqrt{\frac{2}{\lambda_1(\Lambda)\lambda_1(\Lambda^\times)}}$. The rightmost column of Table 1 provides explicit values of the best approximation factors.

To summarise, Algorithm 1 provably returns a nonzero lattice vector at least as short as the secret key for all parameter sets of NTRU submission to NIST [12], using only an SVP oracle in halved dimension. And it succeeds heuristically under a mild assumption, for Falcon [24] and all parameter sets of original NTRU [31] except for one. This gives a positive answer to the conjecture of Gama et al. [26]: the reduction of a $2n$-dimensional NTRU lattice can be reduced to that of a n-dimensional lattice[3]. In addition, half of the oracle calls of our algorithm still work with approximate reduction, up to constant approximation factors that increase as $\lambda_1(\Lambda)\lambda_1(\Lambda^\times)$ decreases.

We provide an additional result regarding the isodual nature of the NTRU modules, which we believe can be of independent cryptanalytic interest.

---

[3] In this sentence *reduction* and *reduced* have different meanings.

Theorem 3. *Any NTRU module is isomorphic to its dual module. Additionally, the canonical embedding NTRU lattice is isometric up to a scalar factor to its dual lattice.*

Proof. Let $\mathcal{R} = \mathbb{Z}[X]/P(X)$ for some unitary degree n polynomial $P \in \mathbb{Z}[X]$. Let $h \in \mathcal{R}$ and M_h be a NTRU module as defined in Sect. 2:

$$M_h := \{(u, v) \in \mathcal{R}^2 : hu \equiv v \mod q\mathcal{R}\}.$$

The dual module $M_h^{\times}$ is defined as the set of module homomorphisms from M_h to $\mathcal{R}$. We have

$$M_h^{\times} = \{(\alpha, \beta) \in (\mathbb{Q}[X]/P(X))^2 : \forall (u, v) \in M_h, \alpha u + \beta v \in \mathcal{R}\}.$$

Let $(\alpha, \beta) \in M_h^{\times}$. Observe that $(0, q) \in M_h$. Therefore $q\beta \in \mathcal{R}$, and there exists $\beta' \in \mathcal{R}$ such that $\beta = \frac{1}{q}\beta'$. Now observe that $(1, h) \in M_h$. This gives $\alpha + \frac{1}{q}\beta'h \in \mathcal{R}$, from which we deduce that there also exists $\alpha' \in \mathcal{R}$ such that $\alpha = \frac{1}{q}\alpha'$, and $\frac{1}{q}(\alpha' + \beta'h) \in \mathcal{R}$. Let

$$L_h := \{(x, y) \in \mathcal{R}^2 : hy \equiv -x \mod q\mathcal{R}\},$$

then $(\alpha', \beta') \in L_h$, therefore $qM_h^{\times} \subseteq L_h$. But clearly L_h and M_h are isomorphic via the map $\psi : (x, y) \mapsto (y, -x)$, so by examining the index of $qM_h^{\times}$ in M_h we can conclude that M_h and $M_h^{\times}$ are isomorphic via the map $\frac{1}{q}\psi$. Because the canonical embedding is a ring homomorphism, the second part of the statement follows directly from the shape of the isomorphism.

$\square$

Theorem 3 essentially says that any NTRU lattice can be turned in a symplectic version of itself by a simple change of embedding. Note that this isn't a generalisation of Theorem 2.

3.3   Reducing Hypercubic Lattices with Approximate-SVP Oracles

In this subsection, we specialise Algorithm 1 to the case of $\mathbb{Z}^n$, and allow to relax the exact-SVP oracle into an approximate-SVP oracle: Ducas [17] was only able to relax his oracle for an approximation factor very close to 1, while we allow an approximation factor close to $\sqrt{2}$. Our improvement also leads to a speculative improvement over the $2^{n/2}$ running time, if approximating SVP to within a factor $\sqrt{2}$ is exponentially faster than solving SVP.

We first present our specialised algorithm: Algorithm 2 is basically Algorithm 1 with $r = r^{\times} = 1$ and approximate oracles instead of exact oracles, with a different termination: since we want to obtain an orthonormal basis, we don't stop once a unit vector has been found, we reduce the dimension of Λ by projection, and keep iterating Algorithm 1 until the rank becomes trivial.

Algorithm 2. An algorithm for ℤLIP with approximate-SVP oracles in dimension $n/2$.

Input: An approximation factor $\gamma \in [1, \sqrt{2 - 2/n})$. A basis B of $\Lambda \simeq \mathbb{Z}^n$. L (resp. N) is the lattice spanned by the first $\lfloor n/2 \rfloor$ (resp. $\lfloor n/2 \rfloor + 1$) vectors of B.
Output: O an orthonormal basis of Λ.
1: $O = \{\}$
2: LLL-reduce B
3: **while** $\dim(B) > 0$ **do**
4:    **if** γ-SVP-oracle(L) returns a vector $\mathbf{e}$ such that $\|\mathbf{e}\| = 1$ **then**
5:       $O \leftarrow O \cup \{\mathbf{e}\}$.
6:       $B \leftarrow \mathrm{LLL}(\pi_{\mathbf{e}^\perp}(B))$ (update L and N accordingly).
7:    **else**
8:       γ-SVP-reduction-oracle(Λ/L) to reduce the second half of B modulo its first half.
9:    **end if**
10:   **if** γ-SVP-oracle($(\Lambda^\times/N)^\times$) returns a vector $\mathbf{e}'$ such that $\|\mathbf{e}'\| = 1$ **then**
11:      $O \leftarrow O \cup \{\mathbf{e}'\}$.
12:      $B \leftarrow \mathrm{LLL}(\pi_{\mathbf{e}'^\perp}(B))$ (update L and N accordingly).
13:   **else**
14:      γ-SVP-reduction-oracle($N^\times$) to dual-reduce the first half of B.
15:   **end if**
16: **end while**
17: Return O.

The main result in this subsection is the following:

Theorem 4. *Given as input a basis B of $\Lambda \simeq \mathbb{Z}^n$ and given access to a γ-SVP approximation oracle in dimension $\lfloor n/2 \rfloor + 1$ where $\gamma \in \left[1, \sqrt{2 - \frac{2}{n}}\right)$, Algorithm 2 returns an orthonormal basis of Λ in polynomial time.*

We briefly compare Algorithm 2 with Ducas's algorithm [17]. Ducas's algorithm restricts to a hypercubic lattice of odd dimension: the algorithm keeps reducing until the "half-sublattice" L (the sublattice generated by the first half of the current basis) generates a hypercubic lattice. Instead, Algorithm 2 checks using an approximate SVP oracle whether the "half-sublattice" L or its dual counterpart contains a unit vector: if not, the first minimum of L is > 1, which allows us to better upper bound the first minimum of Λ/L or its dual counterpart, compared to [17, Lem. 4]. If ever a unit vector is discovered, we can decrement the lattice rank by projection, which also means that our algorithm must not be sensitive to the parity of the rank. The key to our improvement is the following technical result on random projections, which might be of independent interest.

Projecting an Orthonormal Basis. It is well-known that the expectation of the squared norm of the projection of a unit vector onto a k-dimensional random subspace of $\mathbb{R}^n$ is $\frac{k}{n}$. The following elementary lemma shows that the expectation of the squared norm of the projection of a random element of a fixed orthonormal basis of $\mathbb{R}^n$ onto a fixed k-dimensional subspace is also $\frac{k}{n}$.

Lemma 2. *Let* $(\mathbf{e}_1, \ldots, \mathbf{e}_n)$ *be an orthonormal basis of* $\mathbb{R}^n$. *Let* π *be the orthogonal projection over a* k-*dimensional subspace* F *of* $\mathbb{R}^n$. *Then:*

$$\sum_{i=1}^{n} \|\pi(\mathbf{e}_i)\|^2 = k.$$

Proof. Let $(\mathbf{f}_1, \ldots, \mathbf{f}_k)$ be an orthonormal basis of F. Then for each $1 \leq i \leq n$:

$$\|\pi(\mathbf{e}_i)\|^2 = \sum_{j=1}^{k} \langle \mathbf{e}_i, \mathbf{f}_j \rangle^2.$$

Therefore:

$$\sum_{i=1}^{n} \|\pi(\mathbf{e}_i)\|^2 = \sum_{i=1}^{n} \sum_{j=1}^{k} \langle \mathbf{e}_i, \mathbf{f}_j \rangle^2 = \sum_{j=1}^{k} \sum_{i=1}^{n} \langle \mathbf{e}_i, \mathbf{f}_j \rangle^2 = \sum_{j=1}^{k} 1 = k,$$

because each $\mathbf{f}_j$ is a unit vector and $(\mathbf{e}_1, \ldots, \mathbf{e}_n)$ is an orthonormal basis of $\mathbb{R}^n$. □

The previous lemma allows us to upper bound the first minimum of the projection of a hypercubic lattice, as follows:

Corollary 1. *Let* L *be a primitive sublattice of rank* $1 \leq k < n$ *of a full-rank hypercubic lattice* Λ *of* $\mathbb{R}^n$ *such that* $\lambda_1(L) \geq \sqrt{2}$. *Then* $\lambda_1(\Lambda/L)^2 \leq 1 - \frac{k}{n}$.

Proof. L is primitive so Λ/L is a lattice and $\lambda_1(\Lambda/L)$ is well-defined. Let π be the orthogonal projection onto the $(n-k)$-dimensional subspace $L^\perp$. We know that Λ has an orthonormal basis $(\mathbf{e}_1, \ldots, \mathbf{e}_n)$: this is also an orthonormal basis of $\mathbb{R}^n$ so the lemma shows that

$$\sum_{i=1}^{n} \|\pi(\mathbf{e}_i)\|^2 = n - k$$

Furthermore, note that all the $\pi(\mathbf{e}_i)$'s are nonzero: if $\pi(\mathbf{e}_i) = 0$ for some i, then $\mathbf{e}_i \in L$ because L is primitive, then $\lambda_1(L) \leq 1$, which contradicts $\lambda_1(L) \geq \sqrt{2}$. Therefore there exists an integer $i \in \{1, \ldots, n\}$ such that $0 < \|\pi(\mathbf{e}_i)\|^2 \leq \frac{n-k}{n}$. Hence $\lambda_1(\Lambda/L)^2 \leq 1 - \frac{k}{n}$. □

In other words, under certain conditions over L, we can decrease Ducas [17]'s upper bound $\sqrt{1 - 1/n}$ to $\sqrt{1 - k/n}$, which is better as soon $k \geq 2$: we note that for $k = 1$, Ducas [17]'s upper bound is actually tight for L spanned by the all-one vector $(1, 1, \ldots, 1)$, which means that Λ/L is the dual root lattice $A_{n-1}^\times$. We are now ready for the proof of Theorem 4, which is very similar to that of Theorem 1: we simply combine Lemma 2 with (3) of Lemma 1.

Proof (of Theorem 4). $\Lambda \simeq \mathbb{Z}^n$ implies that $\operatorname{vol}(L)^2 \in \mathbb{Z}$. Because $\operatorname{vol}(\Lambda) = 1$ and well-known properties of LLL reduction, Step 2 guarantees $\log \operatorname{vol}(L) = O(n^2)$. This means that the number of times $\operatorname{vol}(L)$ decreases by a factor $1 - \varepsilon$ (without changing Λ) is $O(n^2/\varepsilon)$.

We have $n = 2k$ or $n = 2k + 1$ where $k = \lfloor n/2 \rfloor$. We let L be the primitive lattice spanned by $(\mathbf{b}_1, \ldots, \mathbf{b}_k)$.

Consider Step. 4. if $\|\mathbf{e}\| < \sqrt{2}$, then $\|\mathbf{e}\| = 1$ because Λ has no vector of norm in the interval $(1, \sqrt{2})$. So we recovered a shortest vector $\mathbf{e}$ of Λ, and Step. 6 iterates the algorithm, by projecting Λ over the hyperplane orthogonal to $\mathbf{e}$: this is a hypercubic lattice of rank $n - 1$, and we have to recompute an LLL-reduced basis.

Otherwise, $\|\mathbf{e}\| \geq \sqrt{2}$. We deduce that $\lambda_1(L) > 1$, as otherwise $\lambda_1(L) = 1$ because $\lambda_1(\Lambda) = 1$, which would contradict $\|\mathbf{e}\| \leq \gamma$. But $\lambda_1(L) > 1$ implies that $\lambda_1(L) \geq \sqrt{2}$ because Λ has no vector of norm in the interval $(1, \sqrt{2})$. So Corollary 1 shows that $\lambda_1(\Lambda/L)^2 \leq 1 - \frac{k}{n}$.

The remaining steps are the dual counter part. So if $\|\mathbf{e}'\| \geq \sqrt{2}$ in Step. 10, we deduce similarly by applying Corollary 1 to the sublattice $\Lambda^\times \cap \operatorname{span}(N)^\perp$ of rank $n - (k+1)$, that $\lambda_1(N^\times)^2 = \lambda_1(\Lambda^\times/(\Lambda^\times \cap \operatorname{span}(N)^\perp))^2 \leq 1 - \frac{n-(k+1)}{n}$. We thus have proved:

$$\lambda_1(\Lambda/L)\lambda_1(N^\times) \leq \sqrt{1 - \frac{k}{n}}\sqrt{1 - \frac{n-(k+1)}{n}} = \frac{\sqrt{(n-k)(k+1)}}{n}.$$

If $n = 2k$, then:

$$\frac{\sqrt{(n-k)(k+1)}}{n} = \frac{1}{2}\sqrt{1 + \frac{2}{n}} = \frac{1}{2}\left(1 + \frac{1}{n} - \frac{1}{2n^2} + O\left(\frac{1}{n^3}\right)\right).$$

Otherwise, $n = 2k + 1$ and:

$$\frac{\sqrt{(n-k)(k+1)}}{n} = \frac{k+1}{n} = \frac{1}{2}\left(1 + \frac{1}{n}\right).$$

Since $\gamma^2 < 2 - \frac{2}{n}$, (3) of Lemma 1 implies that, unless we find a unit vector, $\operatorname{vol}(L)$ decreases by at least $\left(1 - \frac{1}{n}\right)\left(1 + \frac{1}{n}\right) = 1 - \frac{1}{n^2}$. Thus, within polynomially many iterations, we will find a unit vector $\mathbf{e}$ or $\mathbf{e}'$. Since there are only n unit vectors, we find all of them within polynomially many iterations.

$\square$

A consequence of Theorem 4 is the following speculative Corollary, that would break the $n/2$ barrier for $\mathbb{Z}$LIP as long as $\sqrt{2}$-approx SVP is exponentially easier than its exact counterpart.

Corollary 2. *Let $\alpha < 1$ be a constant. If there exists an algorithm for approx-SVP with approximation factor $\sqrt{2 - 2/n}$ that runs in time $2^{\alpha n + o(n)}$, then there also exists an algorithm for $\mathbb{Z}$LIP that runs in time $2^{\alpha n/2 + o(n)}$.*

Aside from being visibly easier in practice, γ-approx SVP has been shown to be exponentially easier than exact SVP for some larger constant approximation factors (Th. 3.2 of [23]), this gives some evidence as to why the premise of Corollary 2 might be true.

4   The Primal Attack on Near-Hypercubic Lattices

In this section, we derive the asymptotic behaviour of the heuristic minimal blocksizes required to break lattice problems such as ZLIP and NTRU. We then tweak the primal attack framework to incorporate the fact that special lattices like the hypercubic and NTRU lattice have not just one, but many shortest vectors. In both cases, the quantity $\mathrm{vol}(L)^{1/n}/\lambda_1(L)$ is a constant, whereas we would expect it to be $\Theta(n^{-1/2})$ for a generic lattice. Our results using the primal attack approach could be considered folklore, but we think it profitable to write them down clearly. They nicely complement Sect. 3, because they provide an opportunity to compare the best known provable and heuristic reduction algorithms for ZLIP and NTRU.

4.1   Using a Single Short Vector

Proposition 1. *Let $c = \Theta(1)$ be a positive constant. If $\beta = \omega(1)$ satisfies the equation:*

$$\sqrt{\frac{\beta}{n}} = \delta_\beta^{2\beta-n-1}\sqrt{c},$$

then

$$\beta = \frac{n}{2} - \frac{\log(2c)}{4}\frac{n}{\log n} + o\left(\frac{n}{\log n}\right).$$

Proof. All equivalents denote asymptotics as n goes to infinity. Let $0 < \beta < n$ be a solution to the equation for which $\beta = \omega(1)$. Because

$$\frac{\beta}{n} = \left(\frac{\beta}{2\pi e}(\pi\beta)^{\frac{1}{\beta}}\right)^{\frac{2\beta-n-1}{\beta-1}} c \sim \left(\frac{\beta}{2\pi e}\right)^{\frac{2\beta-n-1}{\beta-1}} c,$$

we obtain

$$\left(\frac{\beta}{n}\right)^{\beta-1} \sim \left(\frac{\beta}{2\pi e}\right)^{2\beta-n-1} c^{\beta-1}.$$

It is clear from $\beta = \omega(1)$ and the above expression that $\beta = n/2 + o(n)$. In what follows we write $\beta = (1/2 - \varepsilon)n$, where $\varepsilon = o(1)$. We get

$$(1/2 - \varepsilon)^{(1/2-\varepsilon)n-1} \sim \left(\frac{(1/2-\varepsilon)n}{2\pi e}\right)^{-2\varepsilon n-1} c^{(1/2-\varepsilon)n-1},$$

and by taking the log of the ratio, we must have

$$((1/2-\varepsilon)n - 1)(\log(1/2-\varepsilon) - \log c) + (2\varepsilon n + 1)\log\left(\frac{(1/2-\varepsilon)n}{2\pi e}\right) \longrightarrow 0.$$

The dominating terms of the expression above are $2\varepsilon n\log(n)$ and $-\frac{n}{2}\log(2c)$ so they must cancel out, leaving us with $\varepsilon = \frac{\log(2c)}{4\log(n)} + o(\log(n)^{-1})$. $\square$

Remark 1. We pay no concern to β having to be an integer. We choose to replace the inequality in Eq. 1 by an equality as we are interested in the largest value of β such that the inequality still holds.

Corollary 3. *Let L be a rank n lattice and $\mathbf{s}$ a short vector of L for which $\|\mathbf{s}\|/\text{vol}(L)^{1/n} =: c^{-1/2} = O(1)$. The primal attack framework heuristically predicts that applying BKZ with blocksize $\beta = n(1/2 - \log(2c)/4\log n + o(1/\log n))$ recovers a vector of norm $\|\mathbf{s}\|$ or less with high probability. In particular, this condition holds for hypercubic and NTRU lattices.*

Proof. The main point follows directly from Proposition 1. In the case of hypercubic lattices, $\text{vol}(L) = \|\mathbf{s}\| = 1$. For NTRU lattices, $\text{vol}(L)^{1/n} = \sqrt{q} = \Theta(\sqrt{n})$, and $\|\mathbf{s}\| = \Theta(\sqrt{n})$, where $\mathbf{s} = (\mathbf{g}, \mathbf{f})$ is the secret key and q is the NTRU modulus. $\quad\square$

The authors of the Hawk signature specifications [11,19] use the primal attack to heuristically evaluate the security of their scheme. They obtain from Eq. 1 that the optimal blocksize for secret key recovery is $n/2 + o(n)$. Corollary 3 helps with understanding the hidden contribution.

Remark 2. In the case of NTRU, the Gram-Schmidt norms after reduction behave differently to the GSA because of the presence of q-vectors, and this could influence our primal attack heuristic analysis (See [4] for a more precise discussion of the difference in shape). Because we can always choose to randomise the input bases, it is sound to presume GSA behaviour.

4.2   Using Many Short Vectors

Hypercubic and NTRU lattices have multiple shortest vectors. The primal attack framework as described by Eq. 1 does not take this into account, as it only relies on the expected value of the norm of the projection of a single vector. We only need one projection to be smaller than the expected Gram-Schmidt norm $\|\mathbf{b}_{n-\beta+1}^\star\|$ for the SVP oracle on the last BKZ block of size β to recover said projection. And because the squared norms of the projections onto random subspaces follow Beta distributions, we can estimate the expected value of the minimal projection and slightly lower the blocksize. See Fig. 2 for an illustration. For smaller dimensions, we observe how considering more short vectors improves the double-intersection phenomenon described in [5].

The *Leaky-LWE estimator* has an option to account for the presence of multiple shortest vectors, however this option is not discussed in detail in [16]. Our new framework (although the same in spirit), addresses this issue differently, offering asymptotic insights as well as specifically isolating the impact of this condition on the blocksize.

In the literature on the primal attack, authors have never used any special property of the Beta distribution other than its mean. The authors of [16] use a probabilistic model in which the squared norms of the projections are approximated using a χ^2 distribution. Even though the χ^2 and the Beta distributions

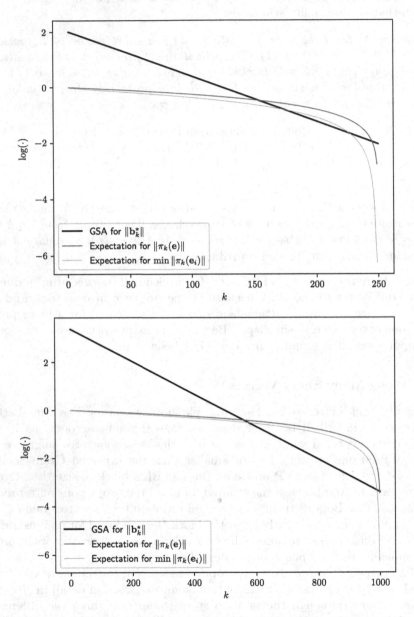

Fig. 2. Comparing the expected norms of randomised Gram-Schmidt vectors of a basis of $\mathbb{Z}^n$ after BKZ reduction with blocksize $n/2$ with the expected projection norms of one and n unit vectors. $n = 250$ above and $n = 1000$ below.

are very good approximations of each other in the small-β context, the difference might become more noticeable for larger blocksizes, so to correct this we choose to work with Beta distributions instead.

We want to emphasise that our framework is not intended for practical use or to supplant existing work. Instead, its purpose is to enhance our comprehension of the components involved in the primary attack. When compared to [16] it simplifies the situation greatly by not taking into account lifting probabilities, or even more precise Gram-Schmidt norm estimates. It also ignores possible fluctuations in the value of $\|\mathbf{b}^\star_{n-\beta+1}\|$. Estimations for hypercubic lattices obtained by both frameworks are compared in Fig. 4.

To estimate the expectation of the minimal norm of the projections, we use the following heuristic.

Heuristic 1. *Let $0 < k < n$. If a lattice L of rank n contains N vectors $\mathbf{s}_1, \ldots, \mathbf{s}_N$ of equal norm r, then the random variables defined by the squared norms of their projections onto a random dimension k subspace of $\mathbb{R}^n$ are independent.*

Heuristic 1 is very close to heuristics used in the study of the dual attack [20]. We argue that when N is not too large (we only use $N \leq n$), this heuristic is reasonable for our purposes. See Fig. 3 for a comparison of the average minimal squared norms of the projections of shortest vectors onto random subspaces in the cases of a random set of unit vectors, an orthonormal basis of $\mathbb{R}^n$, and a circulant set of n vectors.

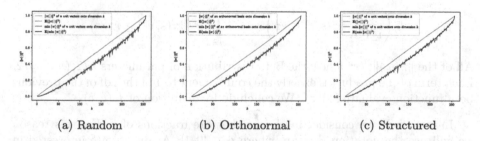

(a) Random   (b) Orthonormal   (c) Structured

Fig. 3. Comparing average/minimal norms of projections π of sets of n unit vectors onto random k-dimensional subspaces of $\mathbb{R}^n$. $n = 256$, and k ranges from 0 to n. Theoretical expected values are plotted in black. The sets considered are random on the sphere (3a), orthonormal basis (3b) and structured: all cyclic permutations of a normalised NTRU-like secret vector (3c). Each point correspond to a single random choice of vectors as well as a single random choice of subspace.

Lemma 3. *Let $0 < k < n$. Let $\mathbf{s}_1, \ldots, \mathbf{s}_N$ be vectors of norm r in a lattice that satisfies Heuristic 1. Then*

$$\mathbb{E}\left(\min_{1 \leq i \leq N} \|\pi(\mathbf{s}_i)\|^2\right) = r^2 \int_0^1 \left(1 - I_x\left(\frac{k}{2}, \frac{n-k}{2}\right)\right)^N dx,$$

where π is the projection onto a random dimension k subspace of $\mathbb{R}^n$, and I is the regularised incomplete beta function.

Proof. All of the $\|\pi(\mathbf{s}_i)\|^2/r^2$ follow the Beta distribution $B(k/2, (n-k)/2)$. Let f denote its probability density function (pdf), and F the associated cumulative distribution function (cdf). Then by independence, the pdf $f_{\min}$ of $\min_{1 \le i \le N} \|\pi(\mathbf{s}_i)\|^2/r^2$ satisfies $f_{\min}(x) = N(1 - F(x))^{N-1} f(x)$. It follows that

$$\mathbb{E}\left(\min_{1 \le i \le N} \|\pi(\mathbf{s}_i)\|^2/r^2\right) = \int_0^1 x f_{\min}(x) dx = \int_0^1 (1 - F(x))^N dx,$$

where we used integration by parts. We conclude using the fact that the cdf of the beta function is equal to the regularised incomplete beta function. $\qquad\square$

While Lemma 3 can be quite practical, we prefer to work with a slightly different quantity that is easier to manipulate.

Lemma 4. *Let $\tau > 0$. Let $0 < k < n$ and π a projection onto a random dimension k subspace of $\mathbb{R}^n$. Let $\mathbf{s}_1, \ldots, \mathbf{s}_N$ be vectors of norm r in a lattice that satisfies Heuristic 1. Then*

$$\mathbb{P}\left(\min_{1 \le i \le N} \|\pi(\mathbf{s}_i)\| < r\tau\right) = 1 - \left(1 - I_{\tau^2}\left(\frac{k}{2}, \frac{n-k}{2}\right)\right)^N$$

Proof. By independence,

$$\mathbb{P}\left(\min_{1 \le i \le N} \|\pi(\mathbf{s}_i)\| < r\tau\right) = 1 - \prod_{i=1}^N \mathbb{P}\left(\|\pi(\mathbf{s}_i)\|^2 \ge r^2 \tau^2\right).$$

All of the $\|\pi(\mathbf{s}_i)\|^2/r^2$ follow the Beta distribution of parameters $k/2, (n-k)/2$. Each term of the product is exactly the complement to 1 of the cdf of the previous beta function evaluated at τ^2. We conclude by definition of $I_x(a,b)$. $\qquad\square$

In our study we consider blocksizes that are fractions of n. For this reason we will use the notation $\beta = \alpha n$, where $\alpha \in [0,1]$. Again, we are interested in asymptotic behaviours as n goes to infinity, which means we do not care if β is not integral. In order to get anything meaningful from Lemma 4, we need a precise estimate of $I_x\left(\frac{\alpha n}{2}, \frac{(1-\alpha)n}{2}\right)$. For this we use a result by Temme [47].

Lemma 5 (Derived from [47], Sect. 3). *Let $\varepsilon > 0$, $x \in (0,1)$ and $\alpha \in (\varepsilon, 1 - \varepsilon)$. Then*

$$I_x\left(\frac{\alpha n}{2}, \frac{(1-\alpha)n}{2}\right) = \frac{1}{2}\mathrm{erfc}\left(-\frac{\eta\sqrt{n}}{2}\right) + o\left(\mathrm{erfc}\left(-\frac{\eta\sqrt{n}}{2}\right)\right),$$

where $\eta = \mathrm{sign}(x - \alpha)\sqrt{-2\alpha \log\left(\frac{x}{\alpha}\right) - 2(1-\alpha)\log\left(\frac{1-x}{1-\alpha}\right)}$, and $\mathrm{erfc} = 1 - \mathrm{erf}$ is the complementary error function.

Proof. We are in the second case studied by [47], where $a = \frac{\alpha n}{2}$ and $b = \frac{(1-\alpha)n}{2}$ are such that $a + b = \frac{n}{2} \to \infty$, and both ratios $\frac{a}{b} = \frac{\alpha}{1-\alpha}$ and $\frac{b}{a} = \frac{1-\alpha}{\alpha}$ are bounded away from 0. The Lemma follows directly from Eq. (3.9) in [47].

$\square$

Lemma 5 begs the question: how big can η get? By deriving the asymptotic behaviour of η, we can deduce the asymptotic blocksize required by our variant of the primal attack.

Proposition 2. *Let $0 < p < 1$ be a fixed constant probability. Let $0 < \varepsilon < 1$ and $\varepsilon < \alpha < 1 - \varepsilon$ be a function of n. Let $\pi_{n-\alpha n+1}$ be a projection onto a random dimension αn subspace of $\mathbb{R}^n$. Let $\mathbf{s}_1, \ldots, \mathbf{s}_N$ be $\Theta(n)$ vectors of norm r in a lattice L that satisfies Heuristic 1. Suppose also that $c := \mathrm{vol}(L)^{1/n}/r = \Theta(1)$. Then if the asymptotic identity*

$$\mathbb{P}\left(\min_{1 \leq i \leq N} \|\pi_{n-\alpha n+1}(\mathbf{s}_i)\| < \delta_{\alpha n}^{(2\alpha-1)n-1}\sqrt{c} \right) = p + o(1) \tag{4}$$

holds, then

$$\beta := \alpha n = \frac{n}{2} - \frac{\log(2c)}{4}\frac{n}{\log(n)} + o\left(\frac{n}{\log n}\right).$$

Proof. By Lemma 4 with $\tau = \delta_{\alpha n}^{(2\alpha-1)n-1}\sqrt{c}$,

$$\mathbb{P}\left(\min_{1 \leq i \leq N} \|\pi_{n-\alpha n+1}(\mathbf{s}_i)\| < \delta_{\alpha n}^{(2\alpha-1)n-1}\sqrt{c} \right) = 1 - \left(1 - I_x\left(\frac{\alpha n}{2}, \frac{(1-\alpha)n}{2} \right) \right)^N,$$

where $x = \delta_{\alpha n}^{2((2\alpha-1)n-1)}c$ therefore it would suffice to prove that

$$\log\left(1 - I_x\left(\frac{\alpha n}{2}, \frac{(1-\alpha)n}{2} \right) \right) \sim \frac{\log p}{N}. \tag{5}$$

Letting $\eta = \mathrm{sign}(x - \alpha)\sqrt{-2\alpha \log\left(\frac{x}{\alpha}\right) - 2(1-\alpha)\log\left(\frac{1-x}{1-\alpha}\right)}$ as in Lemma 5 and combining the result of this same Lemma with Eq. 5, we get

$$-\frac{\log p}{n} \sim I_x\left(\frac{\alpha n}{2}, \frac{(1-\alpha)n}{2} \right) \sim \frac{1}{2}\mathrm{erfc}\left(-\frac{\eta\sqrt{n}}{2} \right).$$

This yields $x < \alpha$ and $\eta^2 \sim 4\frac{\log n}{n}$ (we used that $N = \Theta(n)$) and the following estimate for large u: $\mathrm{erfc}(u) \sim \pi^{-1/2}u^{-1}e^{-u^2}$. See also [42] for an alternative method). To conclude we look for the most important terms inside of η^2. Looking at

$$4\frac{\log n}{n} \sim 2\alpha \log \alpha + 2(1-\alpha)\log(1-\alpha) - 2\alpha \log x - 2(1-\alpha)\log(1-x), \tag{6}$$

we deduce that $\alpha = \frac{1}{2} - \frac{\xi}{\log n}$, where $\xi = O(1)$. By carefully taking care of the little o terms, x can be expressed using

$$\frac{x}{c} = \delta_{\alpha n}^{2((2\alpha-1)n-1)}c = \left(\frac{\alpha n}{2\pi e}(\alpha n \pi)^{1/(\alpha n)}\right)^{\frac{-2\xi n/\log n-1}{\alpha n-1}} \sim \left(\frac{n}{4\pi e}\right)^{-4\frac{\xi}{\log n}} \sim e^{-4\xi}.$$

We can now compute the largest contribution K to the right hand side of Eq. 6:

$$K = \log\left(\frac{e^{4\xi}}{4c(1 - ce^{-4\xi})}\right) = \log\left(\frac{(e^{4\xi} - 2c)^2 + 4c(e^{4\xi} - c)}{4c(e^{4\xi} - c)}\right).$$

We must have $K + o(K) = 4\frac{\log n}{n}$, therefore the constant term must be 0, and thus $\xi = \frac{\log(2c)}{4} + o(1)$, which concludes our proof. □

Corollary 4. *Let L be a rank n lattice for which Heuristic 1 holds with vectors $s_1, \ldots, s_N$ of norm r such that $N = \Theta(n)$ and $r/\mathrm{vol}(L)^{1/n} := c^{-1/2} = O(1)$. The primal attack framework predicts that applying BKZ reduction with blocksize $\beta = n(1/2 - \log(2c)/4\log n + o(1/\log n))$ recovers a vector of norm at most r with high probability. In particular if the heuristic holds for hypercubic and NTRU lattices, then so does this result.*

Proof. The main point follows directly from Proposition 2. For a hypercubic lattice Λ, $\mathrm{vol}(\Lambda) = \|s\| = 1$. For a NTRU lattice L, $\mathrm{vol}(L)^{1/n} = \sqrt{q} = \Theta(\sqrt{n})$, and $\|s\| = \Theta(n)$, where $s = (g, f)$ is the secret key and q is the NTRU modulus. □

4.3 Discussion and Illustration

The results of Proposition 1 and Proposition 2 are identical. If we focus uniquely on the primal attack[4], this means that asymptotically, having n short vectors does not offer any advantage over having just one. In fact, we conjecture that for k a constant, if we had a polynomial number N of independent (in the sense of Heuristic 1) equally short vectors, then the following k terms of the expansion of the predicted blocksize assuming the presence of these N vectors would match precisely with the next k terms (of the form $a_i n \log^{-i}(n)$) derived in the case of a solitary short vector. Indeed, the estimates of Proposition 1 and Proposition 2 are not very good in practice, because the convergence rate is very weak (notice that the term in the erfc function is a $\Theta(\sqrt{\log n})$). This means that the asymptotic regime will only kick in for huge values of n, beyond cryptographic relevance. However, this does not prove that the presence of more short vectors is useless with regards to the primal attack. In fact, the structure of Eq. 1 indicates that having strictly more short vectors is directly advantageous.

---

[4] Dense sublattice attacks can asymptotically outperform generic lattice reduction for NTRU with overstretched parameters [21,35], but this is outside the scope of our study.

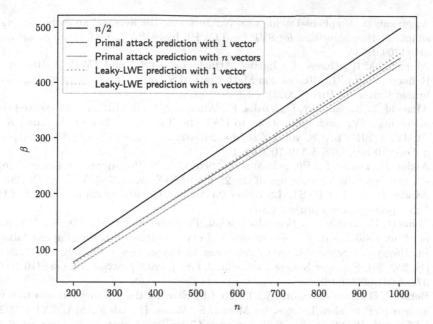

Fig. 4. Blocksizes required to recover unit vectors in dimension n hypercubic lattices. The predictions in dotted lines were generated using the sage script provided in [19]. Our model does not assume progressive-BKZ execution.

Practical Alternative. Due to the reasons mentioned above, for practical application of our framework, we recommend directly solving the modified primal attack equation obtained from combining Eq. 1 and Lemma 3 numerically. The results for hypercubic lattices are plotted in Fig. 4, and compared with the predictions of [16]. In the observed range of dimensions, the heuristic blocksize gain is consistently between 11 and 13, compared to simply evaluating the asymptotic formula. Surprisingly, our naive predictions end up being very close to the more precise predictions of [16]. We provide a proof of concept sage script at https://github.com/htmb-bot/NTRU-and-Hypercubic.

Acknowledgements. This project has received funding from the European Research Council (ERC) under the European Union's Horizon 2020 research and innovation programme (grant agreement No 885394). We would like to thank Huck Bennett, Léo Ducas, Noah Stephens-Davidowitz and Wessel van Woerden for insightful discussions.

References

1. Aggarwal, D., Dadush, D., Stephens-Davidowitz, N.: Solving the closest vector problem in 2^n time - the discrete gaussian strikes again!. In: Proceedings of the IEEE 56th FOCS, pp. 563–582 (2015)
2. Aggarwal, D., Li, J., Nguyen, P.Q., Stephens-Davidowitz, N.: Slide reduction, revisited—filling the gaps in SVP approximation. In: Micciancio, D., Ristenpart, T. (eds.) CRYPTO 2020. LNCS, vol. 12171, pp. 274–295. Springer, Cham (2020). https://doi.org/10.1007/978-3-030-56880-1_10

3. Aggarwal, D., Stephens-Davidowitz, N.: Just take the average! an embarrassingly simple 2^n-time algorithm for SVP (and CVP). In: SOSA (2018). http://arxiv.org/abs/1709.01535

4. Albrecht, M.R., Ducas, L.: Lattice Attacks on NTRU and LWE: A History of Refinements, pp. 15–40. London Mathematical Society Lecture Note Series, Cambridge University Press (2021)

5. Albrecht, M.R., Göpfert, F., Virdia, F., Wunderer, T.: Revisiting the expected cost of solving uSVP and applications to LWE. In: Takagi, T., Peyrin, T. (eds.) ASIACRYPT 2017. LNCS, vol. 10624, pp. 297–322. Springer, Cham (2017). https://doi.org/10.1007/978-3-319-70694-8_11

6. Alkim, E., Ducas, L., Pöppelmann, T., Schwabe, P.: Post-quantum key exchange - A new hope. In: Proceedings of the 25th USENIX, pp. 327–343. USENIX (2016)

7. Avanzi, R., et al.: CRYSTALS-Kyber (version 2.0) – submission to round 2 of the NIST post-quantum project (2019)

8. Bennett, H., Ganju, A., Peetathawatchai, P., Stephens-Davidowitz, N.: Just how hard are rotations of $\mathbb{Z}^n$? algorithms and cryptography with the simplest lattice. In: Hazay, C., Stam, M. (eds.) Advances in Cryptology – EUROCRYPT 2023, pp. 252–281. Springer Nature Switzerland, Cham (2023). https://doi.org/10.1007/978-3-031-30589-4_9

9. Bernard, O., Roux-Langlois, A.: Twisted-PHS: using the product formula to solve approx-SVP in ideal lattices. In: Moriai, S., Wang, H. (eds.) ASIACRYPT 2020. LNCS, vol. 12492, pp. 349–380. Springer, Cham (2020). https://doi.org/10.1007/978-3-030-64834-3_12

10. Bernstein, D.J., Chuengsatiansup, C., Lange, T., van Vredendaal, C.: NTRU prime: reducing attack surface at low cost. Cryptology ePrint Archive, Paper 2016/461 (2016)

11. Bos, J.W., et al.: Hawk signature specification document (2023)

12. Chen, C., et al.: NTRU algorithm specifications and supporting documentation (2020)

13. Chen, Y.: Réduction de réseau et sécurité concrète du chiffrement complètement homomorphe. Ph.D. thesis, Univ. Paris (2013)

14. Chen, Y., Nguyen, P.Q.: BKZ 2.0: better lattice security estimates. In: Lee, D.H., Wang, X. (eds.) ASIACRYPT 2011. LNCS, vol. 7073, pp. 1–20. Springer, Heidelberg (2011). https://doi.org/10.1007/978-3-642-25385-0_1

15. Cramer, R., Ducas, L., Wesolowski, B.: Short Stickelberger class relations and application to ideal-SVP. In: Coron, J.-S., Nielsen, J.B. (eds.) EUROCRYPT 2017. LNCS, vol. 10210, pp. 324–348. Springer, Cham (2017). https://doi.org/10.1007/978-3-319-56620-7_12

16. Dachman-Soled, D., Ducas, L., Gong, H., Rossi, M.: LWE with side information: attacks and concrete security estimation. In: Micciancio, D., Ristenpart, T. (eds.) CRYPTO 2020. LNCS, vol. 12171, pp. 329–358. Springer, Cham (2020). https://doi.org/10.1007/978-3-030-56880-1_12

17. Ducas, L.: Provable lattice reduction of $\mathbb{Z}^n$ with blocksize $n/2$. Designs, Codes and Cryptography (2023)

18. Ducas, L., et al.: CRYSTALS-Dilithium – submission to round 2 of the NIST post-quantum project (2019)

19. Ducas, L., Postlethwaite, E.W., Pulles, L.N., van Woerden, W.P.J.: Hawk: Module LIP makes lattice signatures fast, compact and simple. In: Agrawal, S., Lin, D. (eds.) Advances in Cryptology - Proceeding ASIACRYPT 2022. Lecture Notes in Computer Science, vol. 13794, pp. 65–94. Springer, Cham (2022). https://doi.org/10.1007/978-3-031-22972-5_3

20. Ducas, L., Pulles, L.N.: Does the dual-sieve attack on learning with errors even work? In: Handschuh, H., Lysyanskaya, A. (eds.) Advances in Cryptology – CRYPTO 2023, pp. 37–69. Springer Nature Switzerland, Cham (2023). https://doi.org/10.1007/978-3-031-38548-3_2

21. Ducas, L., van Woerden, W.: NTRU fatigue: how stretched is overstretched? In: Tibouchi, M., Wang, H. (eds.) ASIACRYPT 2021. LNCS, vol. 13093, pp. 3–32. Springer, Cham (2021). https://doi.org/10.1007/978-3-030-92068-5_1

22. Ducas, L., van Woerden, W.: On the lattice isomorphism problem, quadratic forms, remarkable lattices, and cryptography. In: Dunkelman, O., Dziembowski, S. (eds.) Advances in Cryptology - Proc. EUROCRYPT 2022. Lecture Notes in Computer Science, vol. 13277, pp. 643–673. Springer, Cham (2022). https://doi.org/10.1007/978-3-031-07082-2_23

23. Eisenbrand, F., Venzin, M.: Approximate CVP_p in time $2^{0.802n}$. J. Comput. Syst. Sci. **124**, 129–139 (2022)

24. Fouque, P.A., et al.: Falcon: fast-fourier lattice-based compact signatures over NTRU (2019)

25. Frankl, P., Maehara, H.: Some geometric applications of the beta distribution. Ann. Inst. Stat. Math. **42**, 463–474 (1990)

26. Gama, N., Howgrave-Graham, N., Nguyen, P.Q.: Symplectic lattice reduction and NTRU. In: Vaudenay, S. (ed.) EUROCRYPT 2006. LNCS, vol. 4004, pp. 233–253. Springer, Heidelberg (2006). https://doi.org/10.1007/11761679_15

27. Gama, N., Nguyen, P.Q.: Finding short lattice vectors within Mordell's inequality. In: Proceedings of the 40th ACM Symposium on Theory of Computing (STOC) (2008)

28. Gama, N., Nguyen, P.Q.: Predicting lattice reduction. In: Smart, N. (ed.) EURO-CRYPT 2008. LNCS, vol. 4965, pp. 31–51. Springer, Heidelberg (2008). https://doi.org/10.1007/978-3-540-78967-3_3

29. Gama, N., Nguyen, P.Q., Regev, O.: Lattice enumeration using extreme pruning. In: Gilbert, H. (ed.) EUROCRYPT 2010. LNCS, vol. 6110, pp. 257–278. Springer, Heidelberg (2010). https://doi.org/10.1007/978-3-642-13190-5_13

30. Hirschhorn, P.S., Hoffstein, J., Howgrave-Graham, N., Whyte, W.: Choosing NTRUEncrypt parameters in light of combined lattice reduction and MITM approaches. In: Abdalla, M., Pointcheval, D., Fouque, P.-A., Vergnaud, D. (eds.) ACNS 2009. LNCS, vol. 5536, pp. 437–455. Springer, Heidelberg (2009). https://doi.org/10.1007/978-3-642-01957-9_27

31. Hoffstein, J., Pipher, J., Silverman, J.H.: NTRU: a ring-based public key cryptosystem. In: Buhler, J.P. (ed.) ANTS 1998. LNCS, vol. 1423, pp. 267–288. Springer, Heidelberg (1998). https://doi.org/10.1007/BFb0054868

32. Hoffstein, J., Pipher, J., Schanck, J.M., Silverman, J.H., Whyte, W., Zhang, Z.: Choosing parameters for NTRUEncrypt. In: Handschuh, H. (ed.) CT-RSA 2017. LNCS, vol. 10159, pp. 3–18. Springer, Cham (2017). https://doi.org/10.1007/978-3-319-52153-4_1

33. Howgrave-Graham, N.: A hybrid lattice-reduction and meet-in-the-middle attack against NTRU. In: Menezes, A. (ed.) CRYPTO 2007. LNCS, vol. 4622, pp. 150–169. Springer, Heidelberg (2007). https://doi.org/10.1007/978-3-540-74143-5_9

34. Kim, J., Park, J.H.: NTRU+: compact construction of NTRU using simple encoding method. IEEE Trans. Inform. Forensics Secur. **18**, 4760–4774 (2023)

35. Kirchner, P., Fouque, P.-A.: Revisiting lattice attacks on overstretched NTRU parameters. In: Coron, J.-S., Nielsen, J.B. (eds.) EUROCRYPT 2017. LNCS, vol. 10210, pp. 3–26. Springer, Cham (2017). https://doi.org/10.1007/978-3-319-56620-7_1

36. Lenstra, A.K., Lenstra, H.W., Jr., Lovász, L.: Factoring polynomials with rational coefficients. Mathematische Ann. **261**, 513–534 (1982)
37. Li, J., Nguyen, P.Q.: A complete analysis of the BKZ lattice reduction algorithm. Cryptology ePrint Archive, Paper 2020/1237 (2020)
38. Martinet, J.: Perfect Lattices in Euclidean Spaces. Springer, Heidelberg (2003). https://doi.org/10.1007/978-3-662-05167-2
39. Micciancio, D., Walter, M.: Practical, predictable lattice basis reduction. In: Fischlin, M., Coron, J.-S. (eds.) EUROCRYPT 2016. LNCS, vol. 9665, pp. 820–849. Springer, Heidelberg (2016). https://doi.org/10.1007/978-3-662-49890-3_31
40. Nguyen, P.Q., Stehlé, D.: LLL on the average. In: Hess, F., Pauli, S., Pohst, M. (eds.) ANTS 2006. LNCS, vol. 4076, pp. 238–256. Springer, Heidelberg (2006). https://doi.org/10.1007/11792086_18
41. Pellet-Mary, A., Hanrot, G., Stehlé, D.: Approx-SVP in ideal lattices with preprocessing. In: Ishai, Y., Rijmen, V. (eds.) EUROCRYPT 2019. LNCS, vol. 11477, pp. 685–716. Springer, Cham (2019). https://doi.org/10.1007/978-3-030-17656-3_24
42. Philip, J.R.: The Function inverfc θ. Aust. J. Phys. **13**, 13–20 (1960)
43. Schneider, M., Gama, N.: SVP challenge. http://www.latticechallenge.org/svp-challenge/
44. Schnorr, C.P.: Lattice reduction by random sampling and birthday methods. In: Alt, H., Habib, M. (eds.) STACS 2003. LNCS, vol. 2607, pp. 145–156. Springer, Heidelberg (2003). https://doi.org/10.1007/3-540-36494-3_14
45. Schnorr, C.P., Euchner, M.: Lattice basis reduction: improved practical algorithms and solving subset sum problems. Math. Prog. **66**, 181–199 (1994)
46. Szydlo, M.: Hypercubic lattice reduction and analysis of GGH and NTRU signatures. In: Biham, E. (ed.) EUROCRYPT 2003. LNCS, vol. 2656, pp. 433–448. Springer, Heidelberg (2003). https://doi.org/10.1007/3-540-39200-9_27
47. Temme, N.: Asymptotic inversion of the incomplete beta function. J. Comput. Appl. Math. **41**(1), 145–157 (1992)

Compact Encryption Based on Module-NTRU Problems

Shi Bai[1]([✉]), Hansraj Jangir[1]([✉]), Hao Lin[2]([✉]), Tran Ngo[1]([✉]),
Weiqiang Wen[3]([✉]), and Jinwei Zheng[3]([✉])

[1] Florida Atlantic University, Boca Raton, USA
{shih.bai,ngotbtran}@gmail.com, hjangir2020@fau.edu
[2] Delft University of Technology, Delft, Netherlands
baronlin001@gmail.com
[3] LTCI, Telecom Paris, Institut Polytechnique de Paris, Palaiseau, France
{weiqiang.wen,jinwei.zheng}@telecom-paris.fr

Abstract. The Module-NTRU problem, introduced by Cheon, Kim, Kim, Son (IACR ePrint 2019/1468), and Chuengsatiansup, Prest, Stehlé, Wallet, Xagawa (ASIACCS '20), generalizes the versatile NTRU assumption. One of its main advantages lies in its ability to offer greater flexibility on parameters, such as the underlying ring dimension. In this work, we present several lattice-based encryption schemes, which are IND-CPA (or OW-CPA) secure in the standard model based on the Module-NTRU and Module-LWE problems. Leveraging the Fujisaki-Okamoto transformations, one can obtain IND-CCA secure key encapsulation schemes. Our first encryption scheme is based on the Module-NTRU assumption, which uses the determinant of the secret matrix over the underlying ring for the decryption. Our second scheme is analogue to the Module-LWE encryption scheme, but uses only a matrix as the public key, based on a vectorial variant of the Module-NTRU problem. In the end, we conduct comprehensive analysis of known attacks and propose concrete parameters for the instantiations. In particular, our ciphertext size is about 614 (resp. 1228) bytes for NIST Level 1 (resp. Level 5) security and small decryption failure, placing it on par with the most recent schemes such as the one proposed by Zhang, Feng and Yan (ASIACRYPT '23). We also present several competitive parameters for NIST Level 3, which has a ciphertext size of 921 bytes. Moreover, our schemes do not require specific codes for plaintext encoding and decoding.

Keywords: Lattice-based cryptography · Encryption · Encapsulation · Module-NTRU problem

1 Introduction

As quantum technology progresses, current public key cryptosystems, such as RSA, become vulnerable due to Shor's algorithm [Sho97]. Cryptosystems built from lattices have attracted considerable research interests as they are believed

© The Author(s), under exclusive license to Springer Nature Switzerland AG 2024
M.-J. Saarinen and D. Smith-Tone (Eds.): PQCrypto 2024, LNCS 14771, pp. 371–405, 2024.
https://doi.org/10.1007/978-3-031-62743-9_13

to be quantum-resistant. As evidence, many promising candidates in the recent NIST Post-Quantum Cryptography Standardization (PQC) process [NIS16] are grounded in lattice-based approaches, including three standardized schemes Kyber [SAB+22], Dilithium [LDK+22] and Falcon [PFH+22].

Lattice-based cryptosystem have their security relying on the presumed intractability of computational problems on high-dimensional Euclidean lattices. Fundamental average-case problems in lattice-based cryptography include the Short Integer Solution problem (SIS) [Ajt96, MR04], the Learning with Errors problem (LWE) [Reg05] and the NTRU problem [HPS98, HHP+03].

For efficiency, many practical lattice-based cryptosystems are based on assumptions on structured lattices such as the Ring-LWE [LPR10, SSTX09], Ring-SIS [Mic02, PR07] and NTRU. Notably, all of the aforementioned schemes Kyber, Falcon and Dilithium used such algebraic structures over some underlying rings. Several popular choices of the underlying rings include: (1) ring $R = \mathbb{Z}[x]/(x^n \pm 1)$ for power of two n, which is used in Kyber [SAB+22], Falcon [PFH+22] and Dilithium [LDK+22]. (2) $R = \mathbb{Z}[x]/(x^p - 1)$ and $R = \mathbb{Z}[x]/(x^p - x - 1)$ for prime p, which is used in NTRU [CDH+20] and NTRU Prime [BCLv17, BBC+20] respectively. (3) $R = \mathbb{Z}[x]/(x^n - x^{n/2} + 1)$, namely the NTTRU ring used in [LS19, DHK+23]. Our work focuses on this research area, using the module structure, to construct encryption schemes based on Module-NTRU problems.

1.1   Previous and Related Work

Introduced in the pioneering work of Hoffstein, Pipher and Silverman [HPS98], the NTRU problem asks: input a polynomial h in ring $R_q = \mathbb{Z}_q[x]/(P(x))$, find two polynomials $f, g \in R_q$ with small magnitudes such that $h \equiv g/f \pmod{q}$ given the promise that such polynomials exist. Usually, the polynomials f, g are related to the secret keys of the cryptosystem. Since its invention, the NTRU problem has been widely used in cryptographic constructions such as encryption, signature and many others [HHP+03, DDLL13, DLP14]. Notably, the presumed hardness of the NTRU problem underlies the security of Falcon [PFH+22], a selected algorithm in the NIST PQC standardization process; NTRU [CDH+20], a Round 3 finalist; and NTRU Prime [BCLv17, BBC+20], an alternate Round 3 candidate. It is therefore evident that NTRU is an attractive foundation that plays an important role in constructing post-quantum schemes.

As discussed, there are several popular choices for the underlying rings in lattice-based cryptography with algebraic structure. For a native support of the number theoretic transform (NTT), it is often preferred to use power-of-two cyclotomic rings [LZ22, LS19, DHK+23]. This is the case used in the NIST's standardized schemes such as Falcon. From a practical point of view, a drawback of this option is that powers of two are sparse and therefore the security levels/parameters are widely separated. More specifically, considering a scenario where the cryptosystem's security level needs to be increased slightly. It is possible that the updated instantiation requires the ring dimension to be doubled. Indeed, this problem has been stressed in [LPR13]: *"powers of two are sparsely distributed, and the desired concrete security level for an application may call for a ring dimension much smaller than the next-largest power of two"*. This could result in a severe loss in efficiency and overkill in term of the obtained security level. This can be reflected in the choice of parameters in Falcon [PFH+22]. With ring dimension $n = 512$, `Falcon-512` has a signature size of 666 bytes with a classic forgery security of 120 bits. The other parameter doubles the ring dimension to $n = 1024$, which has a signature size of 1280 bytes with a classic forgery security of 277 bits. Thus for power-of-two rings, there is a potential discontinuity in the parameter search for the intermediate levels.

An ingenious solution to address this problem is to use algebraically structured lattices of larger module rank and smaller ring dimensions. For the case of LWE, the Module Learning with Errors problem (Module-LWE) has been proposed [BGV12,LS15] to address such issue by interpolating between LWE and Ring-LWE. As a by-product, a smaller ring dimension n may also offer a wider range for the choices of modulus q, as an NTT-friendly ring typically requires some divisibility condition between the two. An additional benefit is that the lattice is less algebraically structured, thus potentially leveraging against future algebraic attacks. Yet, it has been shown that the Module-LWE problem reduces to the Ring-LWE problem with an appropriate change of parameters [AD17].

Recently, a module variant of the NTRU problem known as the Module-NTRU assumption (MNTRU) [CKKS19,CPS+20], has been proposed. The MNTRU problem constructs the public key $\mathbf{h} \equiv \mathbf{F}^{-1} \cdot \mathbf{g} \pmod{q}$, where $\mathbf{h}, \mathbf{g}$ are vectors in R_q^k and $\mathbf{F}$ is an invertible matrix of dimension k over R_q. Analogue to NTRU, the elements in $\mathbf{F}, \mathbf{g}$ are small for the problem to be well-defined. When $k = 1$, the Module-NTRU problem reduces to the NTRU problem. The work [CKKS19,CPS+20] constructed trapdoors and hash-and-sign signatures using the MNTRU assumption.

In comparison to the Module-LWE problem, (relative) less is known about the average-case hardness of the Module-NTRU problem. The difficulty of showing such a reduction may stem from the difficulty of proving the average-case hardness of NTRU itself. For parameters in the statistical regime, it has been shown that [SS11]: when the support of f, g are sufficiently large, the distribution of $h \equiv f/g \pmod{q}$ is statistically close to the uniform distribution over the set of invertible elements. A similar argument (i.e., uniformity of the key) can be used for the Module-NTRU case, as shown in [CPS+20]. On the pseudo-randomness side, Pellet-Mary and Stehlé [PS21] demonstrated an efficient reduction from the worst-case approximate shortest vector problem over ideal lattices to the decisional NTRU problem (see also [FPS22] for progress on this). Note that, the practical parameters of NTRU do not satisfy the full conditions in these reductions. Yet, the NTRU assumption with conventional parameters remains essentially unbroken after several decades of cryptanalysis.

Another interesting approach is to consider alternative rings, rather than power-of-two cyclotomics. There are generally two approaches in this category: using more diversified rings with Karatsuba/Toom-Cook multiplication, and using NTT-friendly rings (but not necessarily power-of-two) with NTT multiplication. The NIST PQC submissions NTRU [CDH+20] and NTRU

374   S. Bai et al.

Prime [BCLv17, BBC+20] are examples of the first type which used the rings $R = \mathbb{Z}[x]/(x^p - 1)$ and $R = \mathbb{Z}[x]/(x^p - x - 1)$ for prime p, respectively. This approach does not restrict to NTT-friendly rings/modulus and thus greatly expands the range of choices for the parameters. A second approach is to explore a wider choice of NTT-friendly rings. The NTTRU ring [LS19, DHK+23] used such approach over the ring $R = \mathbb{Z}[x]/(x^n - x^{n/2} + 1)$, where n is a product of power-of-two and power-of-three. This also considerably expands the parameter selection ranges. For a summary of the NTT-friendly rings, we refer to the survey [LZ22].

Given the above discussion, it appears that there is a dilemma between the choice of the best flexibility on parameters and the best NTT-friendly feature of the rings/modulus for NTRU. This is also observed in [LS19] which states that: *"One of the possible reasons that NTT-based NTRU has not been proposed as a candidate is that NTT is most efficient over rings whose dimension is a power of 2 – i.e. rings of the form $\mathbb{Z}[x]/(x^d \pm 1)$ where d is a power of 2"*. Indeed, based on the current cryptanalysis [APS15], an NTRU-based encryption requires the ring dimension to be about $700 - 800$ for the NIST Level 1 security. Our work aims to tackle this problem, using the module lattices of higher rank, to construct compact encryption scheme based on Module-NTRU problems.

A recent work on NTRU-based encryption provided a different solution [ZFY23], using an interesting encoding/decoding technique from [ADPS16, PG14]. They proposed to embed the message into higher bits of the ciphertext as $c = hr + e + p^{-1}m \pmod{q}$ where p denotes the plaintext modulus. Instead of using the usual $p = 2$, they choose to use $p = 1 - x^{n/k}$ corresponding to a repetition code. With such two changes, the decryption failure can be neatly managed and they were able to achieve NIST Level 1 security using ring dimension $n = 512$.

1.2 Contributions

In this work, we present two lattice-based encryption schemes that aim to leverage the Module-NTRU problem [CKKS19, CPS+20] and its variants for better flexibility on the parameter choices. Our first encryption scheme, based on the Module-NTRU problem, uses the determinant of the secret matrix in decryption. Our second scheme is conceptually similar to a Module-LWE based encryption, which is based on a vectorial variant of the Module-NTRU assumption. Our second scheme offers competitive ciphertext and public key size which is on par with the most recent schemes such as [ZFY23], while the ciphertext and public key size of our first scheme is larger due to a larger modulus.

Following the key generation of Module-NTRU [CKKS19, CPS+20], our first scheme (Sect. 3) begins with sampling a small invertible matrix $\mathbf{F}$ in $R_q^{k \times k}$ and a small vector $\mathbf{g} \in R_q^k$. The public key $\mathbf{h}$ is computed from $\mathbf{h} := \mathbf{F}^{-1}\mathbf{g} \pmod{q}$ and secret key is set to be $\det(\mathbf{F})$. A message m is encrypted as $c := p\mathbf{h}^T\mathbf{r} + pe + m \pmod{q}$ where $\mathbf{r}, e$ are some small randomness. The receiver recovers the plaintext m by computing $c \cdot \det(\mathbf{F}) \pmod{p}$. To see the decryption works, one uses the fact that $\mathbf{adj_F} \cdot \mathbf{F} = \det(\mathbf{F}) \cdot \mathbf{I}$ and note that decryption is $c \cdot \det(\mathbf{F}) = p(\mathbf{g}^T \cdot \mathbf{adj(F)}^T \cdot \mathbf{r} + \varphi \cdot m) + m \pmod{q}$ for some small φ. Therefore, the decryption works as long as the components $\mathbf{g}, \mathbf{r}, \mathbf{adj_F}, \varphi$ are small. We show that the scheme is IND-CPA (resp. OW-CPA) secure from the decisional Module-NTRU and decisional (resp. search) Module-LWE problems.

The idea of using the determinant in the construction has already been used in [CPS+20] to complete the trapdoor. But it appears to be the first time of being used in the decryption procedure directly. Note that a nice feature of this scheme is that the ciphertext c is a single ring element in R_q (instead of a vector), while the security boils down to the module rank (times ring dimension). On the other hand, the decryption error is multiplicative w.r.t the module rank due to matrix $\mathbf{adj_F}$ and thus could lead to a larger modulus. This motivates our second encryption scheme, whose decryption noise is additively w.r.t module rank.

Our second encryption scheme (Sect. 4) is analogue to a Module-LWE based encryption, and is based on a vectorial variant of the Module-NTRU assumption. This scheme begins with sampling two small vectors $\mathbf{f} = \{f_i\}_i, \mathbf{g} = \{g_i\}_i \in R_q^k$. The public key $\mathbf{H} = \{h_{ij}\}_{ij}$ is constructed in the following way: first sample uniform $h_{ij} \leftarrow_\$ R_q$ for $j > 1$ and set $h_{i1} := (g_i - \sum_{j=2}^{k} h_{ij} f_j)/f_1 \pmod q$ for $1 \leq i \leq n$. The secret key is $\mathbf{f} \in R_q^k$ and public key is $\mathbf{H} \in R_q^{k \times k}$. Note that the construction implies $\mathbf{H}\mathbf{f} = \mathbf{g} \pmod q$, which has a similar form as the NTRU key but with a matrix $\mathbf{H}$. The message $\mathbf{m} = (0, \cdots, 0, m)$ is encrypted as $\mathbf{c} := p\mathbf{H}^T \mathbf{r} + p\mathbf{e} + \mathbf{m} \pmod q$, where $\mathbf{r}, \mathbf{e}$ are some small random vectors. The receiver can recover the plaintext by computing $\mathbf{c}^T \mathbf{f} \pmod p$. To see the decryption works, one checks that $\mathbf{c}^T \mathbf{f} = p\mathbf{r}^T \mathbf{g} + p\mathbf{e}^T \mathbf{f} + \mathbf{m}^T \mathbf{f} \pmod q$. So the decryption is correct as long as the vectors $\mathbf{g}, \mathbf{f}, \mathbf{r}, \mathbf{e}$ are small. The decryption error is increased additively w.r.t the module rank k.

We prove that the schemes in Sect. 3 and 4 are IND-CPA (resp. OW-CPA) secure from the decisional Module-NTRU and decisional (resp. search) Module-LWE problems. By employing standard Fujisaki-Okamoto transformations, our IND-CPA PKE scheme (or OW-CPA PKE) scheme can be turned into IND-CCA secure KEM schemes in the ROM (or QROM) model.

In Sect. 5, we propose concrete parameters and security analysis for the instantiations of both schemes. To further leverage the flexibility for choosing parameters, we consider two NTT-friendly rings: cyclotomic power-of-two rings of the form $R_q = \mathbb{Z}_q[x]/(x^n + 1)$ and NTTRU rings [LS19] of the form $R_q = \mathbb{Z}_q[x]/(x^n - x^{n/2} + 1)$. The modulus q and ring dimension n are chosen such that all the parameters are NTT-friendly. The instantiation of these schemes appears to be competitive with the current state of the art. In particular, the second scheme offers a ciphertext size of 614 (resp. 1228) bytes for NIST Level 1 (resp. Level 5) security and admits a small decryption failure, placing it on par with the most recent NTRU-based scheme such as [ZFY23]. Moreover, it leads smallest parameters for NIST Level 3 security (ciphertext 921 bytes), which does not seem to be commonly available in the previous NTT-friendly setup. A quick comparison to existing schemes is given in Table 1, where our full parameters are presented in Sect. 5.

Table 1. Comparison to the parameters of existing work including schemes: Kyber [SAB+22], NEV [ZFY23], NTRU [CDH+20], Streamlined NTRU Prime [BBC+20] and NTTRU [LS19]. The schemes are listed in alphabetical order, and roughly categorized in three groups in terms of the BKZ-β & Estimate size. For Kyber [SAB+22], we take the estimates from their Table 4. For NTTRU, we use the parameters presented in [LS19,DHK+23]. For NTRU [CDH+20], we cited the three schemes "ntru-hrss-701", "ntru-hps-2048677" and "ntru-hps-4096821". For NTRU Prime [BBC+20], we listed their three streamlined schemes "sntrup653", "sntrup857" and "sntrup1013".

	Dim.	Rank	q	Dec. δ	CT	PK	BKZ-β	Estimate
Kyber-512	256	2	3329	2^{-139}	768	800	$(406, 413)$	$(107, 151)$
NEV-512	512	2	769	2^{-138}	614	614	413	141
NEV'-512	512	2	769	2^{-200}	614	614	426	145
ntru-hps-2048677	677	2	2048	0	931	931	$(483, 496)$	$(144, 205)$
ntru-hrss-701	701	2	8192	0	1138	1138	$(448, 470)$	$(134, 195)$
sntrup653	653	2	4621	0	897	994	n/a	$(117, 219)$
I in Table 2a	**256**	**3**	**769**	$\mathbf{2^{-131}}$	**614**	**646**	**404**	**144**
Kyber-768	256	3	3329	2^{-164}	1088	1184	$(626, 637)$	$(166, 215)$
ntru-hps-4096821	821	2	4096	0	1230	1230	612	$(178, 253)$
NTTRU	768	2	7681	2^{-1217}	1248	1248	n/a	183
sntrup857	857	2	5167	0	1184	1322	n/a	$(159, 300)$
II(b) in Table 2a	**256**	**4**	**1153**	$\mathbf{2^{-129}}$	**921**	**953**	**638**	**210**
Kyber-1024	256	4	3329	2^{-174}	1568	1568	$(878, 894)$	$(232, 287)$
NEV-1024	1024	2	769	2^{-152}	1228	1228	929	281
NEV'-1024	1024	2	769	2^{-200}	1228	1228	953	292
sntrup1013	1013	2	7177	0	1455	1623	n/a	$(190, 384)$
III(b) in Table 2a	**256**	**5**	**769**	$\mathbf{2^{-131}}$	**1228**	**1260**	**895**	**282**

1.3 Discussion and Comparison

In Table 1, we compare our parameters to the state-of-the art parameters for lattice-based encryption schemes, including Kyber, NEV, NTRU, NTRU Prime and NTTRU. We describe the notations in the table. The column "Dim." denotes the underlying ring dimension used by the scheme and the column "Rank" denotes the module rank. For problems defined over a ring NTRU, we denote rank equals 2. The column "q" denotes the ciphertext modulus. The column "Dec. δ" denotes the decryption failure probability, and we write 0 if the system is designed to be deterministically correct. The columns "CT" and "PK" record the ciphertext and public key size in bytes, respectively. The column "BKZ-β" records the BKZ blocksize required to break the scheme, and the last column "Estimate" denotes the cryptanalysis estimate given by the scheme: as different schemes derive their parameters using different approaches, with different models

of computation, strategies used in lattice attacks, quantum-versus-classic estimates (note that the NIST defines the security level in either quantum gates
or classic gates). In addition, these estimates are sometimes presented using the
core-SVP approach, which is potentially more conservative than counting the
estimated gates. It would be inconclusive to compare their precise security in
our table given the current status. Thus we decided to cite a range of estimates
(instead of a fixed value) given in their original paper. For example, the BKZ-β
range $(406, 413)$ for Kyber-512 is from the [SAB+22], where the 406 is derived
using the Core-SVP approach and the 413 is derived using the refined estimate
described in [SAB+22, Table 4]. For certain schemes such as NTRU [CDH+20],
one could see that the range given is a large interval – this is because different
sieving models or core-estimate has been used. As a summary, we prefer to pre-
serve the authors' own estimation, rather than re-estimating them, because we
believe the authors understand their own methods better. Therefore, the column
"Estimate" should not be solely considered as the NIST security levels. For comparison purposes, it is perhaps better to use the column BKZ-β, which can be
observed to more stable across different schemes.

In this table, we select several parameters from our schemes in Table 2a that
are most competitive. In particular, they admit a ciphertext size of 614, 921,
and 1228 bytes, which roughly correspond to NIST security Level 1, 3 and 5. All
the schemes admit a small decryption failure $\approx 2^{-128}$. Additionally, their size is
comparable to the most recent NTRU-based schemes such as [ZFY23]. Moreover,
our scheme does not require any specific encoding and decoding, although it is
possible to add such features for further improvement.

Finally, we discuss and compare a few recent work that follows a similar line
of research as our work. First, the NTTRU ring [LS19, DHK+23] was proposed
for the same purpose, which enables better flexibility on the parameters and
is NTT-friendly. Our work aims to achieve the same goal and our schemes are
compatible with such rings. In fact, our parameters in Sect. 5 are instantiated
for both power-of-two and NTTRU rings. Moreover, our work partly answers an
open question given in [LS19], that is: *"And unlike schemes based on generalized
LWE (like Kyber) that are able to use a public key consisting of a matrix of
smaller-degree power-of-2 rings without increasing the public key size, this approach does not work for NTRU."* Indeed, the public key **H** in our second scheme
of Subsect. 4.1 is (partly) truly random. Thus one can use a random seed to
generate the first $k - 1$ column of the public key matrix **H** and then send the
last column which is a vector of k ring elements. Secondly, we note that the
work [CPS+20, Section 5] has also proposed an encryption scheme based on the
Module-NTRU problem. This scheme is somewhat similar to our first scheme
in Sect. 3. Note that its public key has the form of $\mathbf{H} = p\mathbf{F}^{-1}\mathbf{G} \pmod q$ where
the public key is matrix **H** while our public is a vector. Thus our decryption
procedure is simpler. Finally, the work [ZFY23] finds some NIST Level 1 security parameters using ring dimension $n = 512$, using some encoding/decoding
technique. Comparably, our scheme does not require any encoding/decoding and
our parameters are on par with the parameters proposed in [ZFY23].

2 Preliminaries

We give the notations and definitions used in this paper. Let q be a positive integer modulus. Let $\mathbb{Z}_q$ denote the set of all integers modulo q. We use balanced representation where the set $\mathbb{Z}_q$ is $(-\frac{q}{2}, \frac{q}{2}]$ when q is even and $[-\lfloor\frac{q}{2}\rfloor, \lfloor\frac{q}{2}\rfloor]$ when q is odd. We let R and R_q denote the quotient rings $\mathbb{Z}[x]/(P(x))$ and $\mathbb{Z}_q[x]/(P(x))$ respectively for some polynomial $P(x)$. An element f in R or R_q is written as $f = \sum_{i=0}^{n-1} f_i x^i$ where f_i's are the coefficients.

We represent vectors with bold lowercase letters. By default, a vector is in column form unless mentioned otherwise. A vector $\mathbf{v}$ of length n has entries $(v_1, \ldots, v_n)^T$. Given a vector $\mathbf{v}$, we denote by $\mathbf{v}^T$ its transposed row vector. A zero vector is denoted as $\mathbf{0}$. The coefficient vector of a ring element f is denoted as $\mathbf{f}$. Abusing notation, we sometimes identify a ring element in R (or R_q) with its coefficient vector, which will be made clear from the context. The ℓ_∞ and ℓ_2 norm of a ring element f is defined to be the corresponding norm of its coefficient vector. We denote matrices with bold uppercase letters such as $\mathbf{A}$. The i-th row of a matrix $\mathbf{A}$ is denoted as $\mathbf{A}_i$. The element in the i-th row and j-th column of a matrix $\mathbf{A}$ is denoted as $\mathbf{A}_{ij}$. For $i \leq j$, the submatrix consisting of the i-th row to the j-th row (inclusive) of a matrix $\mathbf{A}$ is denoted as $\mathbf{A}_{i:j}$.

Let f be a function where $f : \mathbb{N} \to (0, 1]$. We say f is negligible (e.g., negl) if for all positive polynomials $p(\cdot)$ there exists a positive integer N such that $f(n) < \frac{1}{p(n)}$ for all $n > N$. We say a function $g(n)$ is overwhelming if $1 - g(n)$ is negligible. These functions are usually defined w.r.t the security parameter λ.

For $n \geq 1$ and $r > 0$, we let $V_n(r)$ denote the volume of the n-dim ball of radius r. We let v_n denote the volume of an n-dimensional unit ball where $v_n \approx (2\pi e/n)^{n/2}/\sqrt{n\pi}$. For integer $n \geq 1$ denote by $[n]$ the set $\{0, \ldots, n-1\}$. We denote by $\log_b$ the logarithm of base b and log the natural logarithm.

2.1 Probability Distribution

Given a distribution D, we let $\mathrm{Supp}(D)$ denote its support. Let S be a finite set. We denote U_S the uniform distribution on S. For example, U_{R_q} denotes the uniform distribution on the set $\mathbb{Z}_q[x]/(P(x))$. Let D be a distribution over S. We denote by $x \leftarrow_\$ D$ the process of sampling $x \in X$ according to the distribution D. By notation abuse, we identify the random variable associated to the output of the sampling algorithm. When the distribution D is uniform, we use the shortcut notation $x \leftarrow_\$ S$. In this work, we often consider sampling the coefficients of a polynomial f from certain distribution D. We use $f \leftarrow_\$ D$ to denote that the coefficients of f are sampled independently from D. We say a distribution D is B-bounded for a real number $B > 0$ if the $\Pr_{s \leftarrow_\$ D}[\|\mathbf{x}\| \leq B]$ is overwhelming for some norm $\|\cdot\|$ that will be made clear in the context. Let $f : X \to \mathbb{R}$ be a non-negative function, then for all countable $Y \subseteq X$, we define $f(Y) = \sum_{y \in Y} f(y) \in [0, +\infty]$.

We will use several standard distributions in this work. The centered binomial distribution with parameter $\eta \in \mathbb{Z}$ is defined as $\mathcal{B}_\eta = \{\sum_{i=0}^{\eta-1}(a_i - b_i), \forall a_i, b_i \leftarrow_\$$

$\{0,1\}\}$. Its density $\mathcal{B}_\eta(x) = \binom{2\eta}{\eta+x}/2^{2\eta}$ where $x \in [-\eta, \eta]$. The ternary distribution $\mathcal{T}_\sigma$ where $\sigma \in (0, 1/2)$ has support $\{-1, 0, 1\}$, and density $\Pr[X = -1] = \Pr[X = 1] = \sigma$ and $\Pr[X = 0] = 1 - 2\sigma$. For any vector $\mathbf{c} \in \mathbb{R}^n$ and any real $\sigma > 0$, the spherical Gaussian function with deviation parameter σ and center $\mathbf{c}$ is $\rho_{\sigma,\mathbf{c}}(\mathbf{x}) = \exp(-\pi\|\mathbf{x} - \mathbf{c}\|^2/\sigma^2)$. The spherical Gaussian distribution has density $D_{\sigma,\mathbf{c}}(\mathbf{x}) = \rho_{\sigma,\mathbf{c}}(\mathbf{x})/\sigma^n$. When $\mathbf{c} = 0$, we may omit the subscript $\mathbf{c}$.

To quantify similarities between distributions, we consider the notion of statistical distance and Rényi divergence.

Definition 2.1. *Let P, Q be two discrete probability distributions with density p, q. The statistical distance between P and Q is defined as*

$$\Delta(P, Q) = \frac{1}{2} \sum_{x \in \mathrm{Supp}(P) \cup \mathrm{Supp}(Q)} |p(x) - q(x)|.$$

Definition 2.2. *Let P, Q be two discrete probability distributions and $\mathrm{Supp}(P) \subseteq \mathrm{Supp}(Q)$. Let $a \in (1, +\infty)$. We define the Rényi divergence of order a by*

$$R_a(P\|Q) = \left(\sum_{x \in \mathrm{Supp}(P)} \frac{P(x)^a}{Q(x)^{a-1}} \right)^{\frac{1}{a-1}}.$$

We will use the following preservation and data processing properties.

Lemma 2.3 (Lemma 2.9, [BLL+15]). *Let P, Q be two discrete probability distributions and $\mathrm{Supp}(P) \subseteq \mathrm{Supp}(Q)$. Let $a \in [1, +\infty]$. The following holds:*

- *Data Processing Inequality: $R_a(P^f\|Q^f) \leq R_a(P\|Q)$ for any function f, where P^f denotes the induced distribution of $f(y)$ where $y \leftarrow_\$ P$ (resp. Q^f).*
- *Probability Preservation: Let $E \subseteq \mathrm{Supp}(Q)$ be an event. If $a \in (1, +\infty)$, then $Q(E) \geq P(E)^{\frac{a}{a-1}}/R_a(P\|Q)$.*
- *Multiplicativity: Let P and Q be two distributions over a pair of random variables (Y_1, Y_2). For $i \in \{1, 2\}$, let P_i (resp. Q_i) denote the marginal distribution of Y_i under P (resp. Q), and let $P_{2|1}(\cdot|y_1)$ (resp. $Q_{2|1}(\cdot|y_1)$) denote the conditional distribution of Y_2 given that $Y_1 = y_1$. If Y_1 and Y_2 are independent, then $R_a(P\|Q) = R_a(P_1\|Q_1) \cdot R_a(P_2\|Q_2)$. This extends to the cases of more than two random variables.*

We will also use a lemma on the summation of two discrete Gaussians.

Lemma 2.4 (Theorem 3.1, [Pei10]). *Let n be the security parameter. Let $\alpha, \beta, \gamma > 0$ be reals and c be an integer such that $\alpha \geq \omega(\sqrt{\log n})$, $\gamma = \sqrt{\alpha^2 + c^2\beta^2}$, $\alpha\beta c/\gamma \geq \sqrt{2}\cdot\omega(\sqrt{\log n})$. Consider the following probabilistic experiment:*

Choose $x_2 \leftarrow_\$ D_\beta$, then choose $x_1 \leftarrow_\$ c \cdot x_2 + D_\alpha$.

Then the marginal distribution of x_1 is statistically close to D_γ.

2.2 Lattices

A lattice $\mathcal{L}$ is an additive discrete subgroup of $\mathbb{Q}^m$. It can be represented as the set of all integer linear combinations $\sum_{i=1}^n x_i \mathbf{b}_i$ of some $\mathbb{Q}$-basis $\mathbf{B} = (\mathbf{b}_i)_{1 \le i \le n}$ of $\mathbb{Q}^m$. Equivalently, the lattice $\mathcal{L}$ generated by $\mathbf{B}$ is defined as $\mathcal{L}(\mathbf{B}) = \{\mathbf{B}\mathbf{x} \mid \forall \mathbf{x} \in \mathbb{Z}^n\}$. The matrix $\mathbf{B}$ is called a basis of $\mathcal{L}(\mathbf{B})$. Denote n to be the rank of the lattice $\mathcal{L}$. A lattice has full rank if $m = n$. For any basis $\mathbf{B}$ of $\mathcal{L}(\mathbf{B})$, the determinant $\det(\mathcal{L}(\mathbf{B}))$ is defined as $\sqrt{\det(\mathbf{B}^T \mathbf{B})}$ and is independent of the choice of the basis. For a lattice $\mathcal{L}$ and any $i \le n$, the ith successive minimum $\lambda_i(\mathcal{L})$ is the smallest radius r such that $\mathcal{L}$ contains i linearly independent vectors of ℓ_2-norm at most r. The spherical discrete Gaussian distribution over a lattice $\mathcal{L} \subseteq \mathbb{R}^n$, with standard deviation $s > 0$ and center $\mathbf{c}$ is defined as $D_{\mathcal{L},s,\mathbf{c}} = \rho_{s,\mathbf{c}}(\mathbf{x})/\rho_{s,\mathbf{c}}(\mathcal{L}), \forall \mathbf{x} \in \mathcal{L}$. When the center is $\mathbf{0}$, we omit the subscript $\mathbf{c}$.

Let $\mathcal{S}$ be a measurable set in the span of $\mathcal{L}$. The Gaussian Heuristic states that the number of lattice points in $\mathcal{S}$ is $|\mathcal{L} \cap \mathcal{S}| \approx \mathrm{Vol}(\mathcal{S})/\mathrm{Vol}(\mathcal{L})$. When $\mathcal{S}$ is an n-dimensional ball of radius r, the latter quantity is about $(v_n \cdot r^n)/\mathrm{Vol}(\mathcal{L})$. Taking $v_n \cdot r^n \approx \mathrm{Vol}(\mathcal{L})$, we see that $\lambda_1(\mathcal{L})$ is about $\mathrm{GH}(\mathcal{L}) := v_n^{-1/n} \cdot \mathrm{Vol}(\mathcal{L})^{1/n} \approx \sqrt{n/(2\pi e)} \cdot \mathrm{Vol}(\mathcal{L})^{1/n}$. Thus λ_1 of a random n-dim lattice $\mathcal{L}$ is roughly $\mathrm{GH}(\mathcal{L})$.

2.3 Public-Key Encryption and Encapsulation

A public-key encryption (PKE) scheme Π_{PKE} with a plaintext space $\mathcal{M}$ consists of three probabilistic polynomial time (PPT) algorithms (KeyGen, Enc, Dec) with the following properties:

- KeyGen(1^λ): on input a security parameter λ, it outputs a pair of public and secret keys (pk, sk), denoted as $(pk, sk) \leftarrow_\$ \mathsf{KeyGen}(1^\lambda)$.
- Enc(pk, m): given the public key pk and a plaintext $m \in \mathcal{M}$ as input, it produces a ciphertext $c = \mathsf{Enc}(pk, m) \in \mathcal{C}$. If necessary, we make the used randomness explicit by writing $c = \mathsf{Enc}(pk, m; r)$.
- Dec(sk, c): given the secret key sk and a ciphertext c as input, it outputs a plaintext m' or a special symbol $\perp \notin \mathcal{M}$ to indicate that c is not a valid ciphertext. This is written as $m' = \mathsf{Dec}(sk, c)$.

We say that a PKE scheme Π_{PKE} has a (worst-case) correctness error δ [HHK17], if for any message $m \in \mathcal{M}$, the probability that $\mathsf{Dec}(sk, \mathsf{Enc}(pk, m)) \ne m$ is at most δ, where $(pk, sk) \leftarrow_\$ \mathsf{KeyGen}(\lambda)$ and the probability is taken over the randomness of KeyGen and Enc. Similarly, a PKE scheme Π_{PKE} has an (average-case) correctness error if the above probability is further averaged over the randomness of message space. We say that a PKE scheme Π_{PKE} is (weakly) γ-spread [DFMS22] if the min-entropy of a ciphertext is bounded, e.g., $-\log \mathbb{E}[\max_{m \in \mathcal{M}, c \in \mathcal{C}} \Pr[c = \mathsf{Enc}(pk, m)]] \ge \gamma$, where the probability is taken over the randomness of Enc and the expected value is taken over the randomness of KeyGen. Now we define the one-way security (OW-CPA) and indistinguishability under chosen plaintext attack (IND-CPA) of a PKE scheme.

Definition 2.5 (OW-CPA PKE). *The* OW-CPA *security game is given in Fig. 1. In the game, the adversary is given a ciphertext c^* of a random plaintext m^* and then it returns candidate m' to the challenger. We say that a PKE scheme Π_{PKE} is* OW-CPA *secure if for any* PPT *adversary $\mathcal{A}$, the advantage* $\text{Adv}_{\Pi_{\text{PKE}}}^{\text{OW-CPA}}(\mathcal{A}) := \Pr[m' = m^*]$ *in the security game is negligible. The advantage is taken over the randomness of (pk, sk), messages and the encryption random coin. The* OW-CPA *is defined for random messages and the adversary has to reconstruct the entire message.*

Definition 2.6 (IND-CPA PKE). *The* IND-CPA *security game is given in Fig. 1. In the game, the adversary offers two distinct chosen plaintexts m_0, m_1 to the challenger. The challenger selects a random bit b and sends the challenge ciphertext c of the message m_b. Finally, the adversary outputs a guessed bit b'. We say that a PKE scheme Π_{PKE} is* IND-CPA *secure if for any* PPT *adversary $\mathcal{A} = (\mathcal{A}_1, \mathcal{A}_2)$, the advantage* $\text{Adv}_{\Pi_{\text{PKE}}}^{\text{IND-CPA}}(\mathcal{A}) := |\Pr[b = b'] - 1/2|$ *in the security game is negligible. The advantage is taken over the randomness of (pk, sk), challenge bit and the encryption random coin.*

PKE OW-CPA
1 : $(pk, sk) \leftarrow\!\!\$\ \text{KeyGen}(1^\lambda)$
2 : $m^* \leftarrow\!\!\$\ \mathcal{M}$
3 : $c^* = \text{Enc}(pk, m^*)$
4 : $m' = \mathcal{A}(pk, c^*)$
5 : **return** $[m' = m^*]$

PKE IND-CPA
1 : $(pk, sk) \leftarrow\!\!\$\ \text{KeyGen}(1^\lambda)$
2 : $(m_0, m_1) = \mathcal{A}_1(pk)$
3 : $b \leftarrow\!\!\$\ \{0, 1\}$
4 : $c^* = \text{Enc}(pk, m_b)$
5 : $b' = \mathcal{A}_2(pk, c^*)$
6 : **return** $[b = b']$

Fig. 1. OW-CPA and IND-CPA Game for PKE.

A key encapsulation mechanism (KEM) scheme Π_{KEM} with session key space $\mathcal{K}$ consists of three algorithms (KeyGen, Encap, Decap) with the following syntax:

- KeyGen(1^λ): given a security parameter λ as input, it generates a pair of public and secret keys (pk, sk), denoted as $(pk, sk) \leftarrow\!\!\$\ \text{KeyGen}(1^\lambda)$.
- Encap(pk): given the public key pk as input, it generates a ciphertext c and a session key $k \in \mathcal{K}$, denoted as $(c, k) = \text{Encap}(pk)$. If necessary, we make the used randomness explicit by writing $(c, k) = \text{Encap}(pk; r)$.
- Decap(sk, c): given the secret key sk and a ciphertext c as input, it outputs a session key k' or a special symbol $\perp \notin \mathcal{K}$ to indicate that c is not a valid ciphertext, denoted as $k' = \text{Decap}(sk, c)$.

A KEM scheme Π_{KEM} is δ-correct if the probability that $\text{Decap}(sk, c) \neq k$ where $(c, k) = \text{Encap}(pk)$ is at most δ, where the probability is taken over the random coins used in KeyGen and Encap.

Definition 2.7 (IND-CCA KEM). *We say that a KEM scheme Π_{KEM} is IND-CCA secure if for any PPT adversary $\mathcal{A}$, its advantage $\text{Adv}_{\Pi_{\text{KEM}}}^{\text{IND-CCA}}(\mathcal{A}) := |\Pr[b' = b] - \frac{1}{2}|$ in the IND-CCA security game in Fig. 2 is negligible, where the probability is taken over the randomness in KeyGen and Encap.*

KEM IND-CCA	Oracle $\mathcal{O}_{\text{Decap}}(c)$
1 : $(pk, sk) \leftarrow_\$ \text{KeyGen}(1^\lambda)$	1 : **if** $c = c^*$ **then**
2 : $(c^*, k_0) = \text{Encap}(pk)$	2 : **return** $\perp$
3 : $k_1 \leftarrow_\$ \mathcal{K}$	3 : **return** $\text{Decap}(sk, c)$
4 : $b \leftarrow_\$ \{0, 1\}$	
5 : $b' = \mathcal{A}^{\mathcal{O}_{\text{Decap}}(\cdot)}(pk, c^*, k_b)$	
6 : **return** $[b' = b]$	

Fig. 2. IND-CCA Game for KEM.

Fujisaki-Okamoto Transform. A PKE scheme $\Pi_{\text{KEM}} = (\text{KeyGen}, \text{Encap}, \text{Decap})$ with message space $\mathcal{M}$ can be turned into a IND-CCA KEM using the Fujisaki-Okamoto (FO) transform in the random oracle model. Let H be a hash functions $H : \{0, 1\}^* \mapsto \mathcal{R} \times \mathcal{K}$, where $\mathcal{R}, \mathcal{K}$ denotes the randomness and key space. We demonstrate the Fujisaki-Okamoto transform in Fig. 3.

Algorithm $\text{Encaps}(pk)$:	Algorithm $\text{Decaps}(sk, c)$:
1 : $m \leftarrow \mathcal{M}$	1 : $m' := \text{Dec}(sk, c)$
2 : $(r, K) := H(m)$	2 : $(r', K') := H(m')$
3 : $c := \text{Enc}(pk, m; r)$	3 : **if** $m' = \perp$ **or** $c \neq \text{Enc}(pk, m'; r')$ **then**
4 : **return** (K, c)	4 : **return** $\perp$
	5 : **else**
	6 : **return** K'

Fig. 3. The Fujisaki-Okamoto Transform

Theorem 2.8 (IND-CPA PKE to IND-CCA KEM under ROM [HHK17]). *Let Π_{PKE} be a δ-correct public-key encryption scheme satisfying γ-spreadness. For any adversary $\mathcal{A}$, making at most q_D decapsulation, q_H hash* *queries, against the* IND-CCA *security of* KEM, *there exists an adversary* $\mathcal{B}$ *against the* IND-CPA *security of* PKE *such that*

$$\mathsf{Adv}_{\mathsf{KEM}}^{\mathsf{IND-CCA}}(\mathcal{A}) \leq 3\mathsf{Adv}_{\mathsf{PKE}}^{\mathsf{IND-CPA}}(\mathcal{B}) + 2q_{\mathsf{H}}/\mathcal{M} + q_{\mathsf{H}}\delta + q_{\mathsf{D}}2^{-\gamma},$$

and the running-time of $\mathcal{B}$ *is about that of* $\mathcal{A}$.

Theorem 2.9 (OW-CPA PKE to IND-CCA KEM under QROM [DFMS22]). *Let* Π_{PKE} *be a* δ-*correct public-key encryption scheme satisfying* γ-*spreadness. For any quantum adversary* $\mathcal{A}$, *making at most* q_{D} *decapsulation,* q_{H} *(quantum) hash queries, against the* IND-CCA *security of* KEM, *there exists an adversary* $\mathcal{B}$ *against the* OW-CPA *security of* PKE *such that*

$$\mathsf{Adv}_{\mathsf{KEM}}^{\mathsf{IND-CCA}}(\mathcal{A}) \leq 2q\sqrt{\mathsf{Adv}_{\mathsf{PKE}}^{\mathsf{OW-CPA}}(\mathcal{B})} + 24q^2\sqrt{\delta} + 24q\sqrt{q \cdot q_{\mathsf{D}}}2^{-\gamma/4},$$

where $q := 2(q_{\mathsf{H}} + q_{\mathsf{D}})$ *and* $\mathrm{Time}(\mathcal{B}) \approx \mathrm{Time}(\mathcal{A}) + O(q_{\mathsf{H}} \cdot q_{\mathsf{D}} \cdot \mathrm{Time}(\mathsf{Enc}) + q^2)$.

2.4 Computational Problems

LWE and NTRU are two fundamental average-case problems used in lattice-based cryptography. We recall their definitions as follows.

The Module-LWE (MLWE) problem introduced in [LS15] can be considered as a balanced solution that interpolates the parameters used in-between Ring-LWE and LWE. Our schemes reduce from the security of MLWE problems. We recall the definition of MLWE.

Definition 2.10 (MLWE$_{R_q,k,\mathbf{s},\chi_e}$ distribution). *Let* R_q *be a quotient polynomial ring,* k *be a positive integer,* $\mathbf{s} \in \mathcal{R}_q^k$ *and* χ_e *be a distribution on* R_q, *the* MLWE$_{R_q,k,\mathbf{s},\chi_e}$ *distribution is defined as:* $\{(\mathbf{a}, \langle \mathbf{a}, \mathbf{s} \rangle + e) \mid \mathbf{a} \leftarrow\!\!{\$}\ R_q^k, e \leftarrow\!\!{\$}\ \chi_e\}$.

Definition 2.11 (Search and decisional MLWE$_{R_q,k,\chi_s,\chi_e}$ problems). *Let* R_q, k *be defined as above and* χ_s, χ_e *be two distributions on* R_q. *The search version* MLWE$_{R_q,k,\chi_s,\chi_e}$ *problem asks to recover the secret* $\mathbf{s}$ *given arbitrarily many samples from the distribution* MLWE$_{R_q,k,\mathbf{s},\chi_e}$, *where* $\mathbf{s} \leftarrow\!\!{\$}\ \chi_s^k$. *the decisional version* MLWE$_{R_q,k,\chi_s,\chi_e}$ *problem asks to distinguish between arbitrarily many independent samples from the distribution* MLWE$_{R_q,k,\mathbf{s},\chi_e}$, *where* $\mathbf{s} \leftarrow\!\!{\$}\ \chi_s^k$. *and the same number of independent uniform samples on* R_q^{k+1}.

The MLWE assumption states that there is no PPT algorithm that can solve decisional (or search) version MLWE$_{R_q,k,\chi_s,\chi_e}$ problem with a non-negligible advantage. Furthermore, there exist reductions between the Ring-LWE and Module-LWE problems [LS15, AD17] with the same entropy but slightly different noise rate, which gives theoretical confidence for the MLWE assumption.

As an analogue generalization of NTRU, the Module-NTRU (MNTRU) problem is introduced in [CKKS19, CPS+20], which also enables a greater flexibility on the parameter choices. It has been used in various constructions such as trapdoors, signatures and identity-based encryption in [CKKS19, CPS+20, BBJ+22].

Definition 2.12 (MNTRU$_{R_q,k,\chi_{\mathbf{F}},\chi_{\mathbf{g}}}$ **distribution**). *Let R_q be a ring, k be a positive integer and $\chi_{\mathbf{F}}, \chi_{\mathbf{g}}$ be distributions defined over $R_q^{k \times k}$ and R_q^k. The* MNTRU$_{R_q,k,\chi_{\mathbf{F}},\chi_{\mathbf{g}}}$ *distribution is defined as follows:*

$$\{\mathbf{h} = \mathbf{F}^{-1}\mathbf{g} \mid \mathbf{F} \leftarrow\!\!\$\ \chi_{\mathbf{F}}, \mathbf{F} \ invertible, \ \mathbf{g} \leftarrow\!\!\$\ \chi_{\mathbf{g}}\}.$$

The MNTRU *distribution is the induced distribution of the product $\mathbf{F}^{-1}\mathbf{g}$, when $\mathbf{F}, \mathbf{g}$ are sampled from $\chi_{\mathbf{F}}, \chi_{\mathbf{g}}$ and $\mathbf{F}$ being invertible in R_q.*

Analogue to the NTRU problem, we often require the two distributions $\chi_{\mathbf{F}}, \chi_{\mathbf{g}}$ to have small magnitude. Example distributions include centered binomial distributions, uniform distributions with small support and discrete Gaussian with small deviation. In our work, we will use the following decisional problem.

Definition 2.13 (Decision MNTRU$_{R_q,k,\chi_{\mathbf{F}},\chi_{\mathbf{g}}}$ **problem).** *Let $R_q, k, \chi_{\mathbf{F}}, \chi_{\mathbf{g}}$ be defined as above. The decision* MNTRU$_{R_q,k,\chi_{\mathbf{F}},\chi_{\mathbf{g}}}$ *problem asks to distinguish between arbitrarily many independent samples from the distribution* MNTRU$_{R_q,k,\chi_{\mathbf{F}},\chi_{\mathbf{g}}}$ *and the same number of independent uniform samples on R_q^k.*

The above MNTRU$_{R_q,k,\chi_{\mathbf{F}},\chi_{\mathbf{g}}}$ assumption states that there is no PPT algorithm that can solve the decision MNTRU$_{R_q,k,\chi_{\mathbf{F}},\chi_{\mathbf{g}}}$ problem with non-negligible advantage over a random guess. The search version of the MNTRU$_{R_q,k,\chi_{\mathbf{F}},\chi_{\mathbf{g}}}$ can be defined similarly which asks to recover small $\mathbf{F}, \mathbf{g}$ given $\mathbf{h}$ with non-negligible advantage.

In Sect. 4, we will use a variant of the MNTRU problem, which we denote as the v-Module-NTRU (v-MNTRU) problem. A similar assumption has been used in constructing signatures in [BBJ+22]. The v-MNTRU problem begins with a secret vector $\mathbf{f} \in R_q^k$ and a ring element g, and then computes $\mathbf{h}$. For such reason, it can be considered as a vectorial version of the MNTRU problem. To obtain a vector $\mathbf{h}$, one can first sample $\mathbf{h}_i \in R_q$ uniformly for $i > 1$ and then compute the first entry $\mathbf{h}_1$ via some equation. Furthermore, our construction uses k such polynomials $\mathbf{h}$, leading to a matrix $\mathbf{H} \in R_q^{k \times k}$. This gives the following definition.

Definition 2.14 (v-MNTRU$_{R_q,k,\chi_f,\chi_g}$ distribution). *Let R_q, k be defined as above, χ_f, χ_g be distributions on R_q, an v-MNTRU$_{R_q,k,\chi_f,\chi_g}$ sampler is a polynomial-time algorithm that samples entries of $\mathbf{f}, \mathbf{g}$ from χ_f, χ_g, polynomials $\mathbf{h}_i \in R_q, \forall i \leq k-1$, and then completes the full $\mathbf{h}$ in $\langle \mathbf{h}, \mathbf{f} \rangle = \mathbf{g} \pmod{q}$. Moreover, we use k such samples, e.g., the sampler outputs a matrix $\mathbf{H} \in R_q^{k \times k}$ such that $\mathbf{Hf} = \mathbf{g} \pmod{q}$. The v-MNTRU$_{R_q,k,\chi_f,\chi_g}$ distribution is the induced distribution $\mathbf{H}$ from an v-MNTRU$_{R_q,k,\chi_f,\chi_g}$ sampler.*

We will use the decision version of the v-MNTRU$_{R_q,k,\chi_f,\chi_g}$ problem.

Definition 2.15 (Decision v-MNTRU$_{R_q,k,\chi_f,\chi_g}$ problem). *Let R_q, k, χ_f, χ_g be defined as above. The decisional v-MNTRU$_{R_q,k,\chi_f,\chi_g}$ problem is to distinguish the v-MNTRU$_{R_q,k,\chi_f,\chi_g}$ distribution from the uniform distribution on $R_q^{k \times k}$ given the same number of samples.*

The computational v-MNTRU$_{R_q,k,\chi_f,\chi_g}$ assumption states that there is no PPT algorithm that can solve the decisional v-MNTRU$_{R_q,k,\chi_f,\chi_g}$ problem with a non-negligible advantage over a random guess. The search version of the v-MNTRU$_{R_q,k,\chi_f,\chi_g}$ problem can be defined to recover a small $\mathbf{f},\mathbf{g}$ given $\mathbf{H}$.

One can reduce from the one sample v-MNTRU problem to the k sample variant, assuming a worst-case oracle by rerandomizing $\mathbf{h}_i + r_i$ for some small r_i's. However, we are not aware of any reduction for the average-case. The main obstacle appears to arise from the need of a careful rerandomization of the public keys $\mathbf{h}$, which is known to be nontrivial already for the original NTRU case. A recent [PS21] showed a reduction of the NTRU problem, using some rerandomization process. We left such possible extension for future work. Similarly, one can reduce from the MNTRU problem to the v-MNTRU problem assuming a worst-case oracle on the inhomogeneous MNTRU problem and by rewinding the oracle. Furthermore, the v-MNTRU problem can be compared to the low-density Ring-SIS problem [Lyu12] except that the last entry of $\mathbf{h}$ being pseudorandom instead of truly uniform.

3   Encryption Based on Module-NTRU

In this section, we describe a public-key encryption scheme based on the Module-NTRU problem. In this scheme, we use the determinant of the secret matrix to decrypt. Let $R = \mathbb{Z}[x]/(P(x))$ be a quotient ring where $P(x)$ has degree n. Let k be a positive integer where $k+1$ denotes the module rank, q be a prime denoting the ciphertext modulus, p be a small prime denoting the plaintext modulus. Let $\chi_f, \chi_g, \chi_r, \chi_e$ be distributions over R_q which are somewhat small.

3.1   Encryption Schemes

The IND-CPA PKE scheme $\Pi_{\text{IND}}^{\text{MNTRU}}$ consists of the following algorithms.

- KeyGen$(R, q, p, k, \chi_f, \chi_g)$: The key generation algorithm samples an invertible matrix $\{\mathbf{F}_{ij}\}_{i,j\in[k]} \leftarrow\!\!{}_\$ \chi_f^{k\times k}$ where $\mathbf{F}$ has the following form:

$$\mathbf{F} = \begin{bmatrix} p\,f_{11}+1, & p\,f_{12}, & p\,f_{13}, & \cdots, & p\,f_{1k} \\ f_{21}, & p\,f_{22}+1, & p\,f_{23}, & \cdots, & p\,f_{2k} \\ f_{31}, & f_{32}, & p\,f_{33}+1, & \cdots, & p\,f_{3k} \\ \vdots & \vdots & \vdots & \ddots & \vdots \\ f_{k1}, & f_{k2}, & f_{k3}, & \cdots, & p\,f_{kk}+1 \end{bmatrix}. \tag{1}$$

  It also samples a vector $\mathbf{g} = (g_1, \ldots, g_k) \leftarrow\!\!{}_\$ \chi_g^k$. The secret key is $\det(\mathbf{F})$, and the public key is $\mathbf{h} := \mathbf{F}^{-1}\mathbf{g} \pmod{q}$. Such key generation procedure is the same as those used in [CKKS19, CPS+20].
- Enc$(\mathbf{h}, m)$: Input a plaintext polynomial $m \in R_p$, the sender samples a small random vector $\mathbf{r} \leftarrow\!\!{}_\$ \chi_r^k$ and a small element $e \leftarrow\!\!{}_\$ \chi_e$. The ciphertext is $c := p\,\mathbf{h}^T\mathbf{r} + p\,e + m \pmod{q}$.

```
┌─────────────────────────────────────────────────────────────────────┐
│ KeyGen(R, q, p, k, χ_f, χ_g) :                                        │
├─────────────────────────────────────────────────────────────────────┤
│  1 :   Sample {f_{ij}}_{i,j∈[k]} ←$ χ_f^{k,k} and set F by Equation (1)│
│        until F invertible                                             │
│  2 :   Sample g = (g_i)_{i∈[k]} ←$ χ_g^k                              │
│  3 :   Compute h = F^{-1} g   (mod q)                                 │
│  4 :   return pk := h and sk := det(F)                                │
│                                                                       │
│ Enc(h, m) :                                                           │
├─────────────────────────────────────────────────────────────────────┤
│  5 :   Sample r = (r_i)_{i∈[k]} ←$ χ_r^k                              │
│  6 :   Compute c = p h^T r + m   (mod q)              // OW-CPA        │
│  7 :   Sample e ←$ χ_e and compute                   // IND-CPA        │
│            c = p h^T r + p e + m   (mod q)           // IND-CPA        │
│  8 :   return c                                                       │
│                                                                       │
│ Dec(det(F), c) :                                                      │
├─────────────────────────────────────────────────────────────────────┤
│  8 :   return c · det(F)   (mod p)                                    │
└─────────────────────────────────────────────────────────────────────┘
```

Fig. 4. Encryption schemes (IND/OW-CPA) based on MNTRU.

– Dec(det(F), c): Input a ciphertext c, the receiver computes $c \cdot \det(F)$ (mod p).

The algorithms are presented in Fig. 4. We observe that matrix F in Equation (1) has determinant $\sum_{\sigma \in S_k} \text{sgn}(\sigma) F_{1,\sigma(1)} \cdots F_{n,\sigma(n)}$ where S_k is the symmetric group of k elements. So the determinant has the form $p\varphi + 1$ for some polynomial φ. We now show the error bound and correctness of the OW-CPA encryption scheme for the case of $k = 2$, which is the case we used in the instantiation. Let adj_F be the adjugate of F where,

$$\text{adj}_F = \begin{bmatrix} p f_{22} + 1 & -p f_{12} \\ -f_{21} & p f_{11} + 1 \end{bmatrix}. \tag{2}$$

Using $\text{adj}_F \cdot F = \det(F) \cdot I$ and $h = F^{-1} \cdot g$, we can write the decryption as

$$c \cdot \det(F) = (p h^T r + m) \cdot \det(F) = p g^T \det(F) F^{-T} r + m \det(F)$$
$$= p (g^T \cdot \text{adj}(F)^T \cdot r + \varphi \cdot m) + m \quad (\text{mod } q).$$

Now denote $g = (g_1, g_2)^T$, $r = (r_1, r_2)^T$ and note $\varphi = p(p f_{11} f_{22} - f_{12} f_{21} + f_{11} + f_{22})$. The term $d_1 := g^T \cdot \text{adj}(F)^T \cdot r$ is,

$$d_1 = p (g_1 f_{22} - g_2 f_{12}) r_1 + (p g_2 f_{11} - g_1 f_{21}) r_2 + g_1 r_1 + g_2 r_2.$$

The term $d_2 := \varphi \cdot m$ is

$$d_2 = (p f_{11} f_{22} + f_{11} + f_{12} - f_{12} f_{21}) \cdot m.$$

Overall the decryption is $d := p(d_1 + d_2) + m$. If $\|d\|_\infty \leq \lfloor q/p \rfloor$, then $c \cdot \det(\mathbf{F})$ (mod q) equals d in R and hence $m = d$ (mod p). So the decryption is correct as long as we set the parameters $\chi_f, \chi_g, \chi_r, \chi_e$ such that the errors are small.

Remark 3.1. Note that the scheme has ciphertext of the form $p\mathbf{h}^T\mathbf{r} + pe + m$ (mod q) which is similar to a conventional NTRU-based encryption, where the message is embedded in lower-bits. It is possible to embed m into higher-bits and then use a repetition code as suggested by the recent work [ZFY23]. For instance, one can choose the plaintext modulus $p = 2x^{n-1}$ and hence $p^{-1} = \frac{q-1}{2}x^{n/2+1}$ over the NTTRU rings [LS19]. We leave such improvement for future work.

3.2   Security Proof

In this section, we provide the IND-CPA and OW-CPA security proofs for the two encryption schemes. We provide several proofs in different flavors. In Theorem 3.2 and 3.3, we directly show the IND-CPA (resp. OW-CPA) from the decisional MNTRU and decisional (resp. search) MLWE problems. In Theorem 3.11, we show the OW-CPA from the decisional MNTRU and decisional MLWE problems by bridging some intermediate problems.

Theorem 3.2 (IND-CPA security). *Let R_q be a quotient polynomial ring where q is a prime, k be a positive integer, λ be the security parameter. Let $\chi_f, \chi_g, \chi_r, \chi_e$ be somewhat small distributions over R_q. The $\Pi_{\text{IND}}^{\text{MNTRU}}(\chi_f, \chi_g, \chi_r, \chi_e)$ scheme described in Fig. 4 is provably IND-CPA secure in the standard model under the Decisional $\text{MNTRU}_{R_q,k,\chi_f,\chi_g}$ and Decision $\text{MLWE}_{R_q,k,\chi_r,\chi_e}$ problems.*

Proof. We prove it via a sequence of games, where G_0 is the genuine IND-CPA game and G_2 is a random one. We show that G_0 and G_2 are indistinguishable. Let $\mathcal{A}$ be an IND-CPA adversary as in Fig. 1 which can break the IND-CPA security of the PKE with advantage ϵ. Let F_i be the event that $\mathcal{A}$ correctly guesses $b = b'$ in game G_i for $i \leq 2$. By definition, the adversary's advantage in G_i is $|\Pr[F_i] - 1/2|$. We describe the sequence of games. For convenience, we omit p as q is a prime.

Game G_0: This is the genuine IND-CPA game shown in Fig. 1. In this game, a challenger $\mathcal{C}$ first generates a pair genuine keys (pk, sk) and sends pk to $\mathcal{A}$. By given assumption, we have $|\Pr[F_0] - 1/2| = \epsilon$.

Game G_1: This game is similar to game G_0 except that the challenger $\mathcal{C}$ modifies the KeyGen algorithm by sampling $\mathbf{h} \leftarrow_\$ R_q^k$ uniformly, and returns this as the public key to the adversary. Using the decisional $\text{MNTRU}_{R_q,k,\chi_f,\chi_g}$ assumption, we see $|\Pr[F_1] - \Pr[F_0]| \leq \text{negl}(\lambda)$.

Game G_2: This game is similar to game G_1 except that the challenger $\mathcal{C}$ modifies the challenge phase as follows: Upon receiving two challenge plaintexts $(m_0, m_1) \in R_q^2$ from the adversary $\mathcal{A}$, the challenger first chooses a random $b \leftarrow_\$ \{0,1\}$ and $u \leftarrow_\$ R_q$, then compute $c = u + m_b$. Then it returns the challenge ciphertext c to the adversary. Using the decisional $\text{MLWE}_{R_q,k,\chi_r,\chi_e}$

assumption, G_2 and G_1 are indistinguishable in the adversary's view. We have $|\Pr[F_2] - \Pr[F_1]| \leq \mathsf{negl}(\lambda)$.

In G_2, the ciphertext c statistically hides the information of m_b. Combining the three games, we obtain that $\epsilon = |\Pr[F_0] - 1/2| \leq \mathsf{negl}(\lambda)$. □

In many NTRU-based encryption schemes, it is common to use the message randomness as the error in the encryption process to control the error growth, thus leading to a more efficient scheme. This is the purpose of the second scheme $\Pi_{\mathsf{OW}}^{\mathsf{MNTRU}}$, marked with OW-CPA in Fig. 4. In this scheme, the randomness $\mathbf{e}$ used in the encryption is discarded. We prove its OW-CPA security. The main idea is that the message m follows the error distribution from MLWE.

Theorem 3.3 (OW-CPA security). *Let R_q, k be defined as above, and $\chi_f, \chi_g, \chi_r, \chi_r', \chi_e$ be somewhat small distributions over R_q. The $\Pi_{\mathsf{OW}}^{\mathsf{MNTRU}}(\chi_f, \chi_g, \chi_r, \chi_e)$ scheme described in Fig. 4 is provably OW-CPA secure in the standard model under the Decisional $\mathsf{MNTRU}_{R_q,k,\chi_f,\chi_g}$ and the Search $\mathsf{MLWE}_{R_q,k,\chi_r',\chi_e}$ problems.*

Proof. We sketch the proof. Let $\mathcal{A}$ be an adversary, who can break the OW-CPA security of the $\Pi_{\mathsf{OW}}^{\mathsf{MNTRU}}(\chi_f, \chi_g, \chi_r, \chi_e)$ scheme. We construct an algorithm $\mathcal{B}$ against the Search $\mathsf{MLWE}_{R_q,k,\chi_r',\chi_e}$. Algorithm $\mathcal{B}$ queries MLWE samples $(\mathbf{a}, b)$ from the search $\mathsf{MLWE}_{R_q,k,\chi_r',\chi_e}$ oracle where $\mathbf{a} \leftarrow\!\!\$\ R_q^k$. For KeyGen, it simulates the public key $\mathbf{h}$ by setting $\mathbf{h} = \mathbf{a}/p \pmod q$. Using the Decisional $\mathsf{MNTRU}_{R_q,k,\chi_f,\chi_g}$ assumption and p is a prime, the public key $\mathbf{h}$ is a legitimate public key to the adversary.

A single successful run of the OW-CPA adversary is not sufficient to break the MLWE problem as the secret is a k-dim vector over R_q. But it does form one equation in k unknown: one needs to invoke the oracle at least k times to get k such linear equations. Therefore, Algorithm $\mathcal{B}$ keeps querying MLWE samples $\{(\mathbf{a}_i, b_i)\}_i$. For each such sample, it calls the OW-CPA adversary $\mathcal{A}$ to get such an equation. If the obtained linear system is non-singular, one can recover the secret by linear algebra. We bound the probability of seeing a non-singular matrix of dimension k over R_q in Lemma 3.7.

Moreover, the OW-CPA adversary $\mathcal{A}$ is seeing samples with the same secret thus one needs to re-randomize the MLWE secret. We can set the ciphertext $c_i = b_i + p \cdot \mathbf{h}_i^T \cdot \mathbf{s}_i' \pmod q$ for some random known $\mathbf{s}_i'$. We conclude the proof by re-randomizing the MLWE secret using a Rényi divergence argument in Lemma 3.5 where we show the relation between χ_r' and χ_r. □

Remark 3.4. The above proof is somewhat similar to the reduction from the search sspRLWE to the search RLWE problem presented in [ZFY23, Theorem 5]: as both reductions invoke the oracle several times on the same secret, although they were used in different context. In their reduction, it seems that they assumed a worst-case RLWE oracle so there is no need to re-randomize the secret. In our model, the advantage of the OW-CPA adversary is averaged over the randomness of the encryption randomness, which corresponds to the MLWE secrets.

In the following, we use a lemma of [BGM+16, Corollary 1] but swapping the two distributions in the divergence computation. This also follows from a more general result [LSS14, Lemma 4.2].

Lemma 3.5 (Randomization of small secrets). *Let m, B, q be positive integers and λ be the security parameter. Let $D_{\mathbb{Z},\sigma}$ denote the discrete Gaussian over $\mathbb{Z}$ with deviation σ where $\sigma < q$. Let $s \in \mathbb{Z}_q$ where $|s| \leq B < q$. The divergence $R_2((D_{\mathbb{Z},\sigma})^m \| (s + D_{\mathbb{Z},\sigma})^m)$ is polynomial in λ when $\sigma = \Omega(B\sqrt{m/\log\lambda})$.*

Proof. The proof follows directly from [BGM+16, Corollary 1], by swapping the two distributions. We show the divergence between two continuous Gaussian distributions, and then take the scaling and rounding. Let D_σ denote the continuous Gaussian with deviation σ. Then

$$R_2(D_\sigma \| s + D_\sigma) = \frac{1}{\sigma} \int_{-\infty}^{\infty} e^{(-\pi/\sigma^2)\cdot(2x^2 - (x-s)^2)} \mathrm{d}x$$

$$= \frac{1}{\sigma} e^{2\pi(s/\sigma)^2} \int_{-\infty}^{\infty} e^{(-\pi/\sigma^2)\cdot(x+s)^2} \mathrm{d}x = e^{2\pi(s/\sigma)^2}.$$

Finally, we use the multiplicativity in Lemma 2.3 on m independent samples.

Remark 3.6. We use Lemma 3.5 in the OW-CPA proof where we use the probability preservation property of Lemma 2.3 to complete the proof. Thus the number m refers to the secret vector dimension $n \cdot k$. We consider the bound B in Lemma 3.5 to be a constant (e.g., MLWE secrets follow a binomial distribution). This implies that the increment on the secret size in the reduction is $O(\sqrt{n/\log n})$ as k is a small constant. Finally, as many previous work, the parameters used in the reduction are not tied with the concrete parameters. Instead, they are derived using concrete lattice and hybrid cryptanalysis as detailed in Sect. 5.

In the next lemma, we consider the density of non-singular matrices of dimension $k \times k$ whose entries are in R_q, which may be of independent interest. More specifically, we focus on the cases where the polynomial $P(x)$ in $R_q = \mathbb{Z}[x]/(P(x))$ splits into many factors of small and equal degree.

Lemma 3.7 (Density of non-singular matrices). *Let $R_q = \mathbb{Z}[x]/(P(x))$ be a quotient polynomial ring of degree n. Let $P(x) \equiv \prod_{i=1}^{l} \Phi_i(x) \pmod{q}$ be the complete factorization of $P(x)$ into l irreducible factors in R_q. Suppose that the factors are distinct and have equal degree $d = n/l$, then the density of non-singular $k \times k$ matrices is*

$$\prod_{i=1}^{k}\left(1 - q^{-d\cdot i}\right)^{l} \tag{3}$$

Proof. We sketch the proof. Let $\mathrm{GL}_k(S)$ denote the general linear group of degree k over a ring S. The cardinality of $\mathrm{GL}_k(\mathbb{F}_{q^d})$ is $\prod_{i=0}^{k-1}(q^{d\cdot k} - q^{d\cdot i})$. Given the equal degree factorization of distinct factors, we have $R_q \cong \bigoplus_{i=1}^{l}\mathbb{F}_{q^d}$, which induces an isomorphism between $\mathrm{GL}_k(R_q)$ and $\bigoplus_{i=1}^{l} \mathrm{GL}_k(\mathbb{F}_{q^d})$. Thus the density is $\prod_{i=0}^{k-1}(q^{d\cdot k} - q^{d\cdot i})^l / q^{nk^2}$.

Remark 3.8. In our application, the degree d is usually tiny, e.g., $d \leq 4$ and thus l is close to n. The rank k is also a tiny constant, e.g. $k \leq 4$ in all of our instantiations. Using that $q > n$, the density of Equation (3) can be roughly lower bounded by $1 - l/q^d$, which is a constant w.r.t to n.

OW-CPA from Decisional MLWE.

OW-CPA from Decisional MLWE. The above proof of OW-CPA reduces from the search MLWE problem, which involves multiple uses of the adversary oracle. This could lead to some tightness losses. An alternative approach is to reduce from the decisional MLWE problem by adopting a method used in [ZFY23]. This involves introducing an intermediate computational problem named sspMLWE (i.e. subset sum parity MLWE), for which we can tightly reduce the security from the sspMLWE problem.

Definition 3.9 (sspMLWE problem). *Let R_q be a quotient polynomial ring, k, m be positive integers, χ_r, χ_e be distributions over R. Let $\mathrm{MLWE}_{R_q,k,\chi_s,\chi_e}$ be the MLWE distribution and $(\mathbf{A}, \mathbf{b} = \mathbf{A} \cdot \mathbf{s} + \mathbf{e}) \in R_q^{m \times k} \times R_q^m$ be samples from the $\mathrm{MLWE}_{R_q,k,\chi_s,\chi_e}$ distribution. The $\mathrm{sspMLWE}_{R_q,k,\chi_s,\chi_e,v}$ problem asks to recover $v \cdot e_m \pmod 2 \in R_2$ for some fixed ring element $v \in R$, where e_m denotes the last ring element of $\mathbf{e}$.*

The sspMLWE problem can be seen as a module extension of the sspRLWE problem defined in [ZFY23]. In this work, we take $v = 1$ and omit it. We first prove the hardness of the sspMLWE problem from the decisional MLWE problem.

Theorem 3.10. *Let R_q be a quotient polynomial ring of degree n, k be a positive integer and χ_r be a distribution over R. Let α, β, γ be three positive reals satisfying $\alpha \geq \omega(\sqrt{\log n})$, $\gamma = \sqrt{\alpha^2 + 4\beta^2}$, $2\alpha\beta/\gamma \geq \sqrt{2} \cdot \omega(\sqrt{\log n})$ and $\gamma\sqrt{n} < q/2$. Let D_β, D_γ be two discrete Gaussian distributions with parameter β and γ, respectively. If there is a PPT algorithm $\mathcal{A}$ solving the $\mathrm{sspMLWE}_{R_q,k,\chi_r,D_\gamma}$ problem, then there is a PPT algorithm $\mathcal{B}$ solving the decisional $\mathrm{MLWE}_{R_q,k,\chi_r,D_\beta}$.*

Proof. We give the description of $\mathcal{B}$. Input a set of MLWE samples $(\mathbf{A}, \mathbf{b}) \in R_q^{m \times k} \times R_q^m$, adversary $\mathcal{B}$ first divides the samples into two parts: the first part consists of the first $m - 1$ samples denoted as $(\mathbf{A}_1, \mathbf{b}_1) \in R_q^{(m-1) \times k} \times R_q^{(m-1)}$, and the second part consisting of the last sample denoted as $(\mathbf{a}_m, b_m) \in R_q^k \times R_q$.

First, the adversary $\mathcal{B}$ samples a vector $\mathbf{e}_1' \in R_q^{m-1}$ from the distribution $D_{\alpha'}^{m-1}$ where $\alpha' = \sqrt{\gamma^2 - \beta^2}$, and sets $(\mathbf{A}_1', \mathbf{b}_1') = (\mathbf{A}_1, \mathbf{b}_1 + \mathbf{e}_1')$. Secondly, it samples an element $e_m' \in R_q$ from the distribution D_α and sets $(\mathbf{a}_m', b_m') = (2\mathbf{a}_m, 2b_m + e_m')$. It then invokes algorithm $\mathcal{A}$ with input $(\mathbf{A}', \mathbf{b}')$, and obtains a $w \in R_2$ from $\mathcal{A}$. Finally, $\mathcal{B}$ returns 1 if $w = e_m' \pmod 2$, otherwise returns 0.

We analyze the behavior of algorithm $\mathcal{B}$. For genuine MLWE samples $(\mathbf{A}, \mathbf{b})$, their errors are sampled from D_β. Using Lemma 2.4, we see that distribution of $\hat{\mathbf{e}}_1 := \mathbf{e}_1 + \mathbf{e}_1'$ is statistically close to D_γ, and distribution of $\hat{e}_m := 2e_m + e_m'$

is also statistically close to D_γ due to our parameter choice. Since $\gamma\sqrt{n} < q/2$, we have $\|\hat{e}_m\|_\infty < q/2$ except with negligible probability using a standard Gaussian tail bound. Hence $(\mathbf{A}', \mathbf{b}')$ is statistically close to the $\mathsf{sspMLWE}_{R_q,k,\chi_r,D_\gamma}$ distribution. On the other hand, if $(\mathbf{A}, \mathbf{b})$ is truly uniform, then $(\mathbf{A}', \mathbf{b}')$ is also uniform. So the probability for any $\mathcal{A}$ output $w \in R_2$ such that $w = e'_m \pmod{2}$ is negligible. This completes the proof.

We will use Theorem 3.10 in both the proof of Theorem 3.11 of this section and the proof of Theorem 4.4 in Sect. 4. Now we prove the OW-CPA security from the $\mathsf{sspMLWE}$ problem, taking the number of samples $m = 1$.

Theorem 3.11 (OW-CPA security from sspMLWE). *Let R_q, k, q and distributions be defined similarly as above. The $\Pi_{\mathsf{OW}}^{\mathsf{MNTRU}}(\chi_f, \chi_g, \chi_r, \chi_e)$ scheme described in Fig. 4 is provably OW-CPA secure in the standard model under the decisional $\mathsf{MNTRU}_{R_q,k,\chi_f,\chi_g}$ and the $\mathsf{sspMLWE}_{R_q,k,\chi_r,U(\{0,1\})}$ problems.*

Proof. The security follows from fact that the ciphertext c contains a valid $\mathsf{sspMLWE}$ instance of the form $p h r + e$. We sketch the proof. First, under the decisional $\mathsf{MNTRU}_{R_q,k,\chi_f,\chi_g}$ assumption, the public key $\mathbf{h}$ is indistinguishable from a uniform one. Since q is a prime, from the adversary's view, (ph, c) is a genuine $\mathsf{sspMLWE}_{R_q,k,\chi_r,U(\{0,1\})}$ instance. Hence if an adversary can win the OW-CPA game with non-negligible advantage, it would break the $\mathsf{sspMLWE}$ problem with non-negligible advantage.

The parameters required in the reduction, like many previous work in this area, do not exactly match our concrete parameters used in the instantiations, which are derived by concrete cryptanalysis instead.

IND-CCA KEM via FO. By combining our IND-CPA (resp. OW-CPA) PKE scheme with the standard FO transformation, one can obtain IND-CCA secure KEM schemes. The correctness of these KEM schemes directly follows from the PKE schemes. To conclude, we have the following theorem for the KEM schemes by combining Theorem 2.8 and Theorem 3.2. For the OW-CPA PKE scheme, we have a similar result, by using 2.9 and Theorem 3.2, and either Theorem 3.3 or Theorem 3.11.

Theorem 3.12. *Let R_q be a quotient polynomial ring, k be a positive integer, q be a prime. Let $\chi_f, \chi_g, \chi_r, \chi'_r, \chi_e, \chi'_e$ be somewhat small distributions defined as above. The KEM scheme by combining the FO transformation in Fig. 3 and the IND-CPA PKE scheme (OW-CPA PKE scheme) in Fig. 4 is provably IND-CCA secure in the ROM (QROM) under the Decisional $\mathsf{MNTRU}_{R_q,k,\chi_f,\chi_g}$ and the Decision $\mathsf{MLWE}_{R_q,k,\chi_r,\chi_e}$ (Search $\mathsf{MLWE}_{R_q,k,\chi'_r,\chi_e}$ or $\mathsf{sspMLWE}_{R_q,k,\chi_r,\chi'_e}$) problems.*

4   Encryption Based on Vectorial Module-NTRU

The encryption scheme in Sect. 3 uses the secret matrix's determinant for decryption, whose size can be increased geometrically with the module rank. For the decryption to work, a smaller rank k and a larger modulus q are therefore needed.

This somehow limits the concrete parameters. In this section, we describe a second encryption scheme based on the v-MNTRU problem introduced in Sect. 2, where the decryption noise is increased additively with the module rank.

4.1   Encryption Schemes

Let $R, k, q, p, \chi_f, \chi_g, \chi_e, \chi_r$ be defined similarly as in Sect. 3. The IND-CPA PKE scheme $\Pi_{\text{IND}}^{\text{v-MNTRU}}$ consists of the following algorithms.

- KeyGen$(R, p, q, k, \chi_f, \chi_g)$: The key generation algorithm samples polynomials $f_i \leftarrow\!\!\$ \ \chi_f, g_i \leftarrow\!\!\$ \ \chi_g$ for $i \in [k]$, where $\mathbf{f}_i$'s are invertible. It sets $\mathbf{f} = (f_1, \ldots, f_{k-1}, pf_k + 1)$, and $\mathbf{g} = (g_i)_i$. Then it generates $\mathbf{H} = \{h_{ij}\}_{ij}$ where $h_{ij} \leftarrow\!\!\$ \ R_q$ for $j > 1$ and $h_{i1} := (g_i - \sum_{j=2}^{k} h_{ij} f_j)/f_1 \pmod q$ for all $1 \leq i \leq n$. The secret key is $\mathbf{f} \in R_q^k$ and public key is $\mathbf{H} \in R_q^{k \times k}$. Note that $\mathbf{H}\mathbf{f} = \mathbf{g} \pmod q$.
- Enc$(\mathbf{H}, m)$: Input a plaintext polynomial $m \in R_p$, the sender samples small random vectors $\mathbf{r} = (r_i)_i \leftarrow\!\!\$ \ \chi_r^k$ and $\mathbf{e} = (e_i)_i \leftarrow\!\!\$ \ \chi_e^k$. Denote $\mathbf{m} = (0, \cdots, 0, m)$. The ciphertext is $\mathbf{c} := p\mathbf{H}^T \mathbf{r} + p\mathbf{e} + \mathbf{m} \pmod q$.
- Dec$(\mathbf{f}, c)$: Input a ciphertext $\mathbf{c}$, the receiver computes $\mathbf{c}^T \mathbf{f} \pmod p$.

The algorithms are presented in Fig. 5. Compared to the first scheme in Sect. 3, here we use a matrix $\mathbf{H}$ for the public key and a vector secret $\mathbf{f}$ for the decryption. It is clear that the decryption noise is linear in the rank k. This scheme resembles a Module-LWE based encryption. However, there are two main differences. First, the public key matrix in an Module-LWE encryption is truly uniform while the $\mathbf{H}$ here is pseudorandom (like the standard NTRU problem). Second, ciphertext $\mathbf{c}$ has rank k, while a Module-LWE based encryption has rank $k + 1$ for the ciphertext. Also for this reason, the message m is embedded into a vector $\mathbf{m}$.

The correctness can be derived as long as the $\mathbf{f}, \mathbf{g}, \mathbf{e}, \mathbf{r}$ are sufficiently small. We consider the magnitude of the decryption error distribution: the distribution of the decryption error for several popular distributions and over the rings $R_q = \mathbb{Z}[x]/(x^n \pm 1)$ is studied in Lemma 4.1. These distributions are widely used in instantiations, though our concrete parameters are obtained using a SageMath script as described in Sect. 5.

Lemma 4.1 (Distribution of decryption error). *Let $R_q = \mathbb{Z}[x]/(x^n \pm 1)$, k be a positive integer, q be a prime. Let χ_f, χ_e be distributions with expected value 0 and variance v_1^2 and v_2^2 respectively. Assuming that $f_i, g_i \leftarrow\!\!\$ \ \chi_f$ and $r_i, e_i, m \leftarrow\!\!\$ \ \chi_e$, where f_i, g_i, r_i, e_i, m are denoted in the PKE schemes in Fig. 5. The distribution of decryption error roughly follows a spherical Gaussian with deviation $\sigma \approx pv_1 v_2 \sqrt{n(2k + p^2)}$, using the central limit theorem.*

KeyGen$(R, q, k, \chi_f, \chi_g)$:

1 :   Sample $\mathbf{g} := (g_i)_i \leftarrow_{\$} \chi_g^k, \mathbf{f} = (f_1, \ldots, f_{k-1}, pf_k + 1)$ where $f_i \leftarrow_{\$} \chi_f$

2 :   Sample $h_{ij} \leftarrow_{\$} R_q, \forall j > 1$ and set $h_{i1} := (g_i - \sum_{j>1} h_{ij} f_j)/f_1$

3 :   **return** pk $:= \mathbf{H} = \{h_{ij}\}_{ij}$ and sk $:= \mathbf{f}$

Enc$(\mathbf{H}, m)$:

4 :   Sample $\mathbf{r} = (r_i)_{i=1}^k \leftarrow_{\$} \chi_r^k, \mathbf{e} = (e_i)_{i=1}^k \leftarrow_{\$} \chi_e^k$ // IND-CPA

5 :   Sample $\mathbf{r} = (r_i)_{i=1}^k \leftarrow_{\$} \chi_r^k, \mathbf{e} = (e_1, \cdots, e_{k-1}, 0), e_i \leftarrow_{\$} \chi_e$ // OW-CPA

6 :   Set $\mathbf{m} = (0, \cdots, 0, m)$

7 :   Compute $\mathbf{c} := p\mathbf{H}^T \mathbf{r} + p\mathbf{e} + \mathbf{m}$ $(\bmod\ q)$

8 :   **return** $\mathbf{c}$

Dec$(\mathbf{f}, \mathbf{c})$:

7 :   **return** $\mathbf{c}^T \mathbf{f}$ $(\bmod\ p)$

Fig. 5. Encryption schemes (IND/OW-CPA) based on v-MNTRU.

Proof. The decryption equals:

$$\mathbf{c}^T \mathbf{f} \quad (\bmod\ q) = p\mathbf{r}^T \mathbf{g} + p\mathbf{e}^T \mathbf{f} + \mathbf{m}^T \mathbf{f} =$$

$$p\left(\sum_{i=1}^{k} r_i g_i + \sum_{i=1}^{k-1} e_i f_i + e_k(pf_k + 1) + mf_k\right) + m. \tag{4}$$

Denote $\epsilon = \sum_{i=1}^{k} r_i g_i + \sum_{i=1}^{k-1} e_i f_i + e_k(pf_k + 1) + mf_k$. If $\|p \cdot \epsilon + m\|_\infty < q$, then one can compute $(\mathbf{c}^T \mathbf{f} \bmod q) \pmod p$ to recover the message m correctly. This means $\|\epsilon\|_\infty < \lfloor q/p \rfloor$. We consider the terms in ϵ.

The first term $\sum_{i=1}^{k} r_i g_i$ consists of a summation of convolution of two polynomials. It boils down to check the statistics of $r_i g_i$. This is a convolution of two polynomials of degree n. We consider the distribution of one coordinate in $r_i g_i$, whose expected value is 0 and variance is $nv_1^2 v_2^2$. With a summation of k independent terms, the variance is $knv_1^2 v_2^2$. Similarly, the term $\sum_{i=1}^{k-1} e_i f_i + mf_k$ has expected value 0, and variance $knv_1^2 v_2^2$. The term $pe_k f_k$ has variance $p^2 nv_1^2 v_2^2$. We omit the small terms consisting of only e_k and m. Thus the marginal distribution of a coordinate of $p \cdot \epsilon$ has expected value 0 and variance $\approx p^2 v_1^2 v_2^2 n(2k + p^2)$. Finally, we use the central limit theorem to conclude that the marginal distribution of a coordinate follows approximately a centered Gaussian with deviation $\sigma \approx pv_1 v_2 \sqrt{n(2k + p^2)}$. The deviation has $O(\sqrt{n})$ as p, k are tiny constants.

Now we show that the joint probability density of ϵ is spherical by studying its covariance. We consider the ring $R_q = \mathbb{Z}[x]/(x^n - 1)$ here and the other ring $\mathbb{Z}[x]/(x^n + 1)$ follows similarly. First, we look at the convolution of the form $c(x) = a(x) \cdot b(x) \pmod{x^n - 1}$. Let $a(x) = \sum_{i=0}^{n-1} a_i x^i$, $b(x) = \sum_{i=0}^{n-1} b_i x^i$ and $c_k = \sum_{i=0}^{n-1} a_i b_{k-j}$. All the indices took values modulo n implicitly. We abuse notation and denote random variables by c_k as well. We show that $\mathrm{Cov}(c_0, c_1) = 0$ and its easy to see this is true for $\mathrm{Cov}(c_i, c_j)$ where $i \neq j$. We check that $\mathrm{Cov}(c_0, c_1) = \mathbb{E}(c_0 c_1) - \mathbb{E}(c_0)\mathbb{E}(c_1) = \mathbb{E}(c_0 c_1)$, where c_0 and c_1 are random variables induced from $\sum_{i+j \equiv 0} a_i b_j$ and $\sum_{l+m \equiv 1} a_l b_m$ respectively. Now we write $\mathbb{E}(c_0 c_1) = \mathbb{E}((\sum_{i+j \equiv 0} a_i b_j) \cdot (\sum_{l+m \equiv 1} a_l b_m))$. Exchanging the expected value with summation, we obtain $\sum_{i=0}^{n-1} \sum_{l=0}^{n-1} \mathbb{E}(a_i b_{n-i} a_l b_{1-l})$. For any fixed index i of outer summation, observe that the inner summation admits a similar pattern, that is, precisely two terms contain repeated random variables (i.e. the given a_i and b_{n-i}). The rest $n - 2$ terms consists of independent variables. Thus for these $n - 2$ terms, we have $\mathbb{E}(a_i b_{n-i} a_l b_{1-l}) = 0$. For the two terms with repeated variables, we have $\mathbb{E}(a_i b_{n-i} a_i b_{1-i}) = \mathbb{E}(a_i^2)\mathbb{E}(b_{n-i})\mathbb{E}(b_{1-i}) = 0$ and $\mathbb{E}(a_i b_{n-i} a_{i+1} b_{n-i}) = 0$.

In the concrete parameters, we used similar distributions as described in Lemma 4.1. For example, the χ_f and χ_e are usually centered binomial distribution $\mathcal{B}_\eta$ or ternary distribution $\mathcal{T}_\sigma$. However, the message m is often binary uniform thus its expected value is not zero. In such case, the covariance matrix is not isotropic anymore (due to the term $m \cdot f_k$ in Equation (4)) – but the impact should be minor as this is a single polynomial term. Indeed, a similar analysis shows that the off-diagonal entries of the covariance matrix has $O(v_1^2 n/4)$ which is independent of k. Note that it is also possible to conduct a similar analysis for the schemes described in Subsect. 3.1. We omit such details as in the concrete instantiation since we used a script to compute the precise density function.

4.2   Security Proof

In this subsection, we provide the IND-CPA and OW-CPA security proofs for the encryption schemes described in this section.

Theorem 4.2 (IND-CPA security). *Let R_q be a quotient polynomial ring, k be a positive integer, q be a prime. Let $\chi_f, \chi_g, \chi_r, \chi_e$ be somewhat small distributions defined as above. The $\Pi_{\mathrm{IND}}^{v\text{-}\mathrm{MNTRU}}(\chi_f, \chi_g, \chi_r, \chi_e)$ scheme described in Fig. 5 is provably IND-CPA secure in the standard model under the Decisional $v\text{-}\mathrm{MNTRU}_{R_q, k, \chi_f, \chi_g}$ and the Decisional $\mathrm{MLWE}_{R_q, k, \chi_r, \chi_e}$ problems.*

Proof. The IND-CPA security essentially follows from fact that the ciphertext $\mathbf{c}$ contains a valid LWE instance of the form $p(\mathbf{H}^T \mathbf{r} + \mathbf{e})$. The proof is the same as Theorem 3.2 so we sketch it. For convenience, we omit p as q is a prime. On receiving a decisional $\mathrm{MLWE}_{R_q, k, \chi_r, \chi_e}$ (or uniform) problem, for every k samples of the form $(\mathbf{A}, \mathbf{b})$, the simulator sets $\mathbf{A}$ as the public key and sends to the adversary. Under the Decisional $v\text{-}\mathrm{MNTRU}_{R_q, k, \chi_f, \chi_g}$ assumption, such change is computationally indistinguishable from the adversary's view. On receiving the challenge messages $\{\mathbf{m}_0, \mathbf{m}_1\}$, the simulator sends the $\mathbf{u} + \mathbf{m}_i$ of randomly chosen $\mathbf{m}_i$ and $\mathbf{u}$.

Similarly, one can drop some randomness in **e** used in the encryption scheme for efficiency. This is demonstrated in Fig. 5 (lines marked by OW-CPA). In this OW-CPA variant, the last entry of the randomness **e** used in the encryption becomes zero. We prove its OW-CPA security.

Theorem 4.3 (OW-CPA security). *Let R_q be a quotient polynomial ring, k be a positive integer, q be a prime. Let $\chi_f, \chi_g, \chi_r, \chi_e$ be somewhat small distributions defined as above. The $\Pi_{\mathrm{OW}}^{v\text{-MNTRU}}(\chi_f, \chi_g, \chi_r, \chi_e)$ scheme described in Fig. 5 is provably OW-CPA secure in the standard model under the Decisional $v\text{-MNTRU}_{R_q,k,\chi_f,\chi_g}$ and the Search $\mathsf{MLWE}_{R_q,k,\chi_r',\chi_e}$ problems.*

Proof. We sketch the proof. Let $\mathcal{A}$ be an adversary, who can break the OW-CPA security of the $\Pi_{\mathrm{OW}}^{v\text{-MNTRU}}(\chi_f, \chi_g, \chi_r, \chi_e)$ scheme. The simulator queries samples from the search $\mathsf{MLWE}_{R_q,k,\chi_r',\chi_e}$ problem and processes them in batches of k such samples of the form $(\mathbf{A}, \mathbf{b})$, where $\mathbf{A} \in R_q^{k \times k}$. For KeyGen, it simulates the public key $\mathbf{H}$ by setting the first $k-1$ rows of $\mathbf{H}^T$ from the first $k-1$ rows of $\mathbf{A}$ (e.g., $(\mathbf{H}^T)_i = \mathbf{A}_i, \forall i \leq k-1$) and sets the last row $(\mathbf{H}^T)_k = \mathbf{A}_k/p \pmod{q}$. Using the Decisional $v\text{-MNTRU}_{R_q,k,\chi_f,\chi_g}$ and p is a prime, the public key $\mathbf{H}$ is a legitimate public key of the $\Pi_{\mathrm{OW}}^{v\text{-MNTRU}}$ scheme to the adversary. For Enc, it construct the first $k-1$ entries of the ciphertext $\mathbf{c}$ by setting $\mathbf{c}_i = p \cdot (\mathbf{b}_i + (\mathbf{H}^T)_{1:k-1} \cdot \mathbf{s}') \pmod{q}, \forall i \leq k-1$, where $\mathbf{s}'$ is some small random vector to re-randomize the MLWE secret. It sets the last entry of the ciphertext $\mathbf{c}_k = \mathbf{b}_k + \langle (\mathbf{H}^T)_k, \mathbf{s}' \rangle \pmod{q}$. Note that in an OW-CPA game, the message m is chosen randomly, which fits the definition of an MLWE error. It sends the simulated ciphertext to the OW-CPA adversary. A single successful run of the OW-CPA adversary only recovers the last entry m in the message vector $\mathbf{m}$. Equivalently, it essentially only extracts some information about the last entry of the error in an MLWE instance. One needs to invoke the oracle at least k times. Given that the obtained system is non-singular, one can recover the secret by linear algebra. We use the bound from Lemma 3.7 for the density. In the end, we apply Lemma 3.5 and use the probability preservation property of Lemma 2.3 to complete the proof.

OW-CPA from Decisional MLWE. Similar to Sect. 3.2, we can also tightly reduce the security of scheme from the sspMLWE problem and thus from the decisional MLWE problem. We obtain the following theorem:

Theorem 4.4 (OW-CPA under sspMLWE). *Let R_q be a quotient polynomial ring, k be a positive integer, q be a prime. Let $\chi_f, \chi_g, \chi_r, \chi_e$ be somewhat small distributions defined as above. The $\Pi_{\mathrm{OW}}^{v\text{-MNTRU}}(\chi_f, \chi_g, \chi_r, \chi_e)$ scheme described in Fig. 5 is provably OW-CPA secure in the standard model under the Decisional $v\text{-MNTRU}_{R_q,k,\chi_f,\chi_g}$ and the $\mathsf{sspMLWE}_{R_q,k,m,\chi_r,U(\{0,1\})}$ problems.*

IND-CCA KEM via FO. Similarly, the two PKE schemes in this section can also be transformed into two KEM schemes through FO transformation. And we obtain the following theorem:

Theorem 4.5. *Let R_q be a quotient polynomial ring, k be a positive integer, q be a prime, λ be the security parameter. Let $\chi_f, \chi_g, \chi_r, \chi_e$ be somewhat small distributions defined as above. The KEM scheme by combining the FO transformation in Fig. 3 and the IND-CPA PKE scheme (OW-CPA PKE scheme) in Fig. 5 is provably IND-CCA secure in the ROM (QROM) under the Decisional v-MNTRU$_{R_q,k,\chi_f,\chi_g}$ and the Decisional MLWE$_{R_q,k,\chi_r,\chi_e}$ (Search MLWE$_{R_q,k,\chi'_r,\chi_e}$ or sspMLWE$_{R_q,k,m,\chi_r,U(\{0,1\})}$) problems.*

5   Parameters and Security Analysis

In this section we present the parameters and security analysis for concrete instantiations. We focus on two underlying rings: power-of-two rings of the form $R_q = \mathbb{Z}_q[x]/(x^n + 1)$ where n is a power of two and NTTRU rings [LS19] of the form $R_q = \mathbb{Z}_q[x]/(x^n - x^{n/2} + 1)$. Both rings are number theoretical transform compatible with appropriate modulus, and have been used widely in lattice-based cryptography. For the scheme presented in Subsect. 4.1, we give concrete parameters for both the OW-CPA and IND-CPA encryption schemes over both rings. For the scheme presented in Subsect. 3.1, we give concrete parameters for the OW-CPA encryption scheme mainly over NTTRU rings.

5.1   Concrete Security Estimate

We discuss known attacks against the Module-NTRU problems and its variants. A standard method to evaluate the security of the NTRU problem is the lattice reduction on NTRU lattices [CS97]. Given a (ring) NTRU public key $h = g/f$ (mod q), the NTRU lattice is defined by $\Lambda_q(h) := \{(x,y) \in R^2 \mid h \cdot x - y = 0$ (mod q)}. The coefficient vector of (f,g) is an unusual short vector compared to the Gaussian heuristic estimate defined in Sect. 2. This naturally extends to the module case [CKKS19, CPS+20]. Let $\mathbf{h} = \{h_i\}_i \in R_q^k$ be the public key of the encryption scheme in Subsect. 3.1. The Module-NTRU lattice of rank $k + 1$ associated to $\mathbf{h}$ is defined as

$$\Lambda_q(\mathbf{h}) := \{(x_i)_i \in R^{k+1} : \sum_{i=1}^{k} h_i x_i - x_{k+1} = 0 \pmod{q}\}.$$

Now let $\mathbf{H}_i$ denote the multiplication matrices associated to the h_i's. The coefficient vector of the secret $(f_1, \ldots, f_k, g)$ is an unusual short vector in the lattice $\Lambda_q(\mathbf{h})$ with $\mathbb{Z}$-basis

$$\begin{bmatrix} \mathbf{H}_1 \cdots \mathbf{H}_k & \mathbf{I} \\ q\mathbf{I} & \mathbf{0} \\ & \ddots & \vdots \\ \mathbf{0} \cdots q\mathbf{I} & \mathbf{0} \end{bmatrix}.$$

This lattice has rank $(k+1)n$ and determinant q^{kn}. For the ciphertext security, one could consider a lattice similar to the Module-LWE. We omit the details.

Concrete security in lattice reduction can be estimated using standard methods [AGVW17, GJ21, MAT22, DP23]. We used the `Lattice Estimator` [APS15] which implemented these estimates. We describe the approach we used for the security estimate. For each plausible parameters, we search for candidate moduli q based on the decryption failure criterion and then check the set of estimates consisting of "`primal usvp`", "`primal bdd`", "`primal hybrid`", "`dual`", "`dual hybrid`" implemented in the `Lattice Estimator`. These estimate functions are called with default parameters. We also used some homebrewed code to double-check the security for lattice reduction attacks.

We omit the algebraic attacks [AG11] as the number of samples given is limited. Also note that all the parameters have $n \cdot k$ (ring dimension times module rank) $\ll q^{2.484}$ [Dv21], thus we do not consider the overstretched case.

Hybrid attacks. Our parameters are similar to many previous work for NTRU-based encryption [ZFY23, BBC+20, CDH+20], where the secrets are chosen to be ternary or sparse (and sometimes binomial $\mathcal{B}_2$). This poses the question of whether they are secure under potential combinatorial attacks. In particular, the hybrid lattice and meet-in-the-middle approaches [How07] are the most popular evaluation for such range of parameters: the general idea is to partly reduce the lattice using a lattice reduction with intermediate blocksizes, enumerate part of the secret vectors, and then use a nearest neighborhood algorithm to recover the full secret. We also evaluate the security w.r.t such hybrid attacks in details. We adapted a `SageMath` script[1] from Léo Ducas, which credited Thomas Wunderer, for estimating the hybrid attacks. We have made two main changes: First, in order to reflect the recent advances in lattice reduction algorithms [AGVW17, GJ21, MAT22, DP23], we leverage the `Lattice Estimator` [APS15] inside the hybrid attack to estimate its partial lattice reduction time. Second, compared to [How07], we use a more conservative approach by exhaustively searching all possible length for the meet-in-the-middle region (instead of estimating it using a BKZ simulator). Such method should be more conservative and result in some safe margins. We see that the code tends to return a larger dimension for the partial lattice reduction – this is due to improved running-time in the lattice reduction estimates – which reduces the meet-in-the-middle region as a result of running-time re-balancing (between lattice reduction and meet-in-the-middle).

NTT-friendly parameters. We choose the parameters such that the ring dimension n and modulus q are NTT-friendly. Let $R_q = \mathbb{Z}[x]/(P(x))$ be the ring and we choose modulus q such that $P(x)$ factorize into l irreducible factors of degree d in R_q where we restrict $d \leq 4$. For more discussions on the NTT friendly parameters, we refer to work [LS19, LZ22]. Note that these parameters also satisfy the conditions used in Lemma 3.7 for the security reduction, such that the density of non-singular matrices is overwhelming.

Decryption failure estimate. Given a targeted failure probability, one can estimate a candidate modulus q conditioned on the input probability. We used a `SageMath` script modified from the `Python` script from Kyber [SAB+22]. We

---

[1] https://github.com/lducas/LatRedHybrid.

modified the script such that it supports a higher precision and also NTTRU rings of the form $R_q = \mathbb{Z}_q[x]/(x^n - x^{n/2} + 1)$. For the NTTRU ring, calculation of the density function for the product of polynomials used an approach described in [LS19]. We set our targeted decryption failure probability to be $\approx 2^{-128}$ with some very small margins. For each scheme described in Subsect. 3.1 and 4.1, we build the concrete probability density function by applying convolution/addition/scaling from the input distributions, according to the precise form of the error terms. As most previous work, we ignore the dependency between coefficients (note that some analysis considering the dependency has also been discussed in Subsect. 4.1).

Recovering the determinant. The encryption scheme of Subsect. 3.1 used the determinant of the secret matrix $\mathbf{F}$ to decrypt. In the previous paragraphs, we have considered the security of recovering $\mathbf{F}$. However, it is tempting to recover the determinant $\det(\mathbf{F})$ instead. To do this, consider the identity $\mathbf{h}^T \cdot \det(\mathbf{F}) = \mathbf{g}^T \cdot \mathbf{adj}(\mathbf{F})^T$. Note $\mathbf{h}^T \cdot \det(\mathbf{F})$ is a vector of length k. We look at a single coordinate of it, i.e. its j-th coordinate is $(\mathbf{h}^T)_j \cdot \det(\mathbf{F}) = (\mathbf{g}^T \cdot \mathbf{adj}(\mathbf{F})^T)_j$. This looks like an ring-NTRU instance where the public key is $(\mathbf{h}^T)_j$ with secrets $\det(\mathbf{F}) \in R_q$ and $(\mathbf{g}^T \cdot \mathbf{adj}(\mathbf{F})^T)_j \in R_q$. We assume that the solution $\det(\mathbf{F})$ is unique among different indices j, thus it is sufficient to break any such instance (for a conservative estimate). In the parameter selection of Table 4, we have considered the security of such attacks. Notice that now the secrets $\det(\mathbf{F})$ and $\mathbf{g}^T \cdot \mathbf{adj}(\mathbf{F})^T$ have a larger size compared to the original secrets $\mathbf{F}, \mathbf{g}$. We can estimate their size as above, e.g., by modeling the distribution of product/convolution of random variables.

5.2   Parameters

We now propose concrete parameters for our OW-CPA and IND-CPA encryption schemes described in Subsects. 3.1 and 4.1.

We first explain the notations used, which are common in all the tables in this section. The rows "Ring dimension n" denotes the underlying ring dimension for R and "Module rank $(k + 1)$" denotes the rank of the Module-NTRU where k follows the same notation as used in Subsects. 3.1 and 4.1. The row "Modulus q" denotes the ciphertext modulus. The rows "Key dist." denotes the secret key distribution χ_f, χ_g for generating entries of $\mathbf{f}, \mathbf{g}$ and "Enc dist." denotes the encryption randomness distribution χ_r, χ_e. For our parameters, we choose to use the same distribution on the secret key $\mathbf{f}$ and $\mathbf{g}$. But sometimes the distributions χ_r and χ_e of the encryption randomness could be different. The notations for these distributions are specified in the "Preliminaries" section. The row "Dec. failure" denotes the decryption failure probability, computed using the script mentioned previously. The "Blocksize" is the smallest blocksize found over all the attacks described before, including using the Lattice Estimator and our modified script for hybrid attacks. The last two rows show the public key and ciphertext size in bytes.

The columns I, II and III roughly correspond to NIST security Levels 1, 3 and 5, as one can see from their bit security and BKZ blocksizes. For a fixed security level, we sometimes present two set of parameters (e.g., II (a) and II (b) in Table 2a). This usually occur if the first set of parameters admits a much smaller decryption failure – which leaves some room for optimization. Finally, we describe the schemes in the three tables of this section:

– In Table 2, we present the parameters for the schemes in Subsect. 4.1 over power-of-two rings. More precisely, the parameters for the OW-CPA scheme $\Pi_{\text{OW}}^{\text{v-MNTRU}}$ is given in Table 2a, and the parameters for the IND-CPA scheme $\Pi_{\text{IND}}^{\text{v-MNTRU}}$ is given in Table 2b. These parameters are mostly competitive with the current state of the art parameters.

Table 2. Parameters for the OW/IND-CPA schemes of Sect. 4 based on the v-MNTRU problem over Power-of-two rings.

	I	II (a)	II (b)	III (a)	III (b)
Ring dimension n	256	256	256	256	256
Module rank $(k+1)$	3	4	4	5	5
Modulus q	769	1153	769	1153	769
Key dist. χ_f, χ_g	$\mathcal{B}_1, \mathcal{B}_1$	$\mathcal{T}_{5/16}, \mathcal{T}_{5/16}$	$\mathcal{B}_1, \mathcal{B}_1$	$\mathcal{B}_1, \mathcal{B}_1$	$\mathcal{T}_{1/5}, \mathcal{T}_{1/5}$
Enc. dist. χ_r, χ_e	$\mathcal{B}_1, \mathcal{B}_1$	$\mathcal{T}_{5/16}, \mathcal{T}_{5/16}$	$\mathcal{T}_{1/6}, \mathcal{B}_1$	$\mathcal{B}_1, \mathcal{B}_1$	$\mathcal{T}_{1/6}, \mathcal{B}_1$
Dec. failure	2^{-131}	2^{-154}	2^{-129}	2^{-180}	2^{-131}
Blocksize	404	646	638	883	895
Bit security	144	212	210	278	282
Public key (bytes)	646	1009	953	1334	1260
Ciphertext (bytes)	614	977	921	1302	1228

(a) Parameters for OW-CPA $\Pi_{\text{OW}}^{\text{v-MNTRU}}$ over Power-of-two rings.

	I	II	III
Ring dimension n	256	256	256
Module rank $(k+1)$	3	4	5
Modulus q	1409	1409	1409
Key dist. χ_f, χ_g	$\mathcal{T}_{5/16}, \mathcal{T}_{5/16}$	$\mathcal{B}_1, \mathcal{B}_1$	$\mathcal{T}_{1/5}, \mathcal{T}_{1/5}$
Enc. dist. χ_r, χ_e	$\mathcal{T}_{5/16}, \mathcal{B}_1$	$\mathcal{B}_1, \mathcal{B}_1$	$\mathcal{B}_1, \mathcal{B}_1$
Dec. failure	2^{-127}	2^{-133}	2^{-138}
Blocksize	380	614	836
Bit security	137	203	265
Public key (bytes)	702	1037	1371
Ciphertext (bytes)	670	1005	1339

(b) Parameters for IND-CPA $\Pi_{\text{IND}}^{\text{v-MNTRU}}$ over power-of-two rings.

Table 3. Parameters for the OW/IND-CPA schemes of Sect. 4 based on the v-MNTRU problem over NTTRU rings.

	I	II (a)	II (b)	III
Ring dimension n	256	384	384	324
Module rank $(k+1)$	3	3	3	4
Modulus q	1153	2017	1153	1297
Key dist. χ_f, χ_g	$\mathcal{T}_{5/16}, \mathcal{T}_{5/16}$	$\mathcal{B}_2, \mathcal{B}_2$	$\mathcal{B}_1, \mathcal{B}_1$	$\mathcal{B}_1, \mathcal{B}_1$
Enc. dist. χ_r, χ_e	$\mathcal{B}_1, \mathcal{B}_1$	$\mathcal{T}_{5/16}, \mathcal{T}_{5/16}$	$\mathcal{T}_{1/5}, \mathcal{B}_1$	$\mathcal{B}_1, \mathcal{B}_1$
Dec. failure	2^{-139}	2^{-153}	2^{-130}	2^{-134}
Blocksize	380	595	613	811
Bit security	137	197	203	260
Public key (bytes)	683	1086	1009	1289
Ciphertext (bytes)	651	1054	977	1257

(a) Parameters for OW-CPA $\Pi_{\text{IND}}^{\text{v-MNTRU}}$ over NTTRU rings.

	I (a)	I (b)	II	III
Ring dimension n	288	288	384	324
Module rank $(k+1)$	3	3	3	4
Modulus q	2017	1297	2017	2269
Key dist. χ_f, χ_g	$\mathcal{B}_1, \mathcal{B}_1$	$\mathcal{T}_{1/6}, \mathcal{T}_{1/6}$	$\mathcal{B}_1, \mathcal{B}_1$	$\mathcal{T}_{5/16}, \mathcal{T}_{5/16}$
Enc. dist. χ_r, χ_e	$\mathcal{B}_1, \mathcal{B}_1$	$\mathcal{B}_1, \mathcal{T}_{1/6}$	$\mathcal{B}_1, \mathcal{B}_1$	$\mathcal{T}_{5/16}, \mathcal{B}_1$
Dec. failure	2^{-187}	2^{-138}	2^{-142}	2^{-130}
Blocksize	411	410	586	777
Bit security	146	146	195	250
Public key (bytes)	823	777	1086	1387
Ciphertext (bytes)	791	745	1054	1355

(b) Parameters for IND-CPA $\Pi_{\text{IND}}^{\text{v-MNTRU}}$ over NTTRU rings.

- In Table 3, we present the parameters for the schemes in Subsect. 4.1 over the *NTTRU* rings. We give the parameters for the OW-CPA scheme $\Pi_{\text{OW}}^{\text{v-MNTRU}}$ in Table 3a, and the parameters for the IND-CPA scheme $\Pi_{\text{IND}}^{\text{v-MNTRU}}$ in Table 2b.
- In Table 4, we present the parameters for the OW-CPA scheme in Subsect. 3.1 over both *power-of-two* and *NTTRU* rings. It also appears that the NTTRU ring provides more flexibility in choosing parameters for this scheme. Similarly, one can see the ring dimension is not necessarily a power-of-two for these parameters.

We discuss how the public key and ciphertext size are derived. The ciphertext of the scheme in Subsect. 4.1 (i.e., Tables 2 and 3) is a vector $\mathbf{c} \in R_q^k$ consists of k ring elements. Its public key is a matrix $\mathbf{H} \in R_q^{k \times k}$ which is truly random except

Table 4. Parameters for the OW-CPA scheme (Sect. 3) based on the MNTRU problem over NTTRU and Power-of-two rings.

	I_{nttru}	II_{nttru}	II_{pow2}	III_{nttru}
Ring dimension n	384	512	512	768
Module rank $(k+1)$	3	3	3	3
Modulus q	30817	52609	57089	118081
Key dist. χ_f, χ_g	$\mathcal{T}_{1/6}, \mathcal{T}_{1/6}$	$\mathcal{T}_{1/6}, \mathcal{T}_{1/6}$	$\mathcal{B}_1, \mathcal{B}_1$	$\mathcal{B}_1, \mathcal{B}_1$
Enc. dist. χ_r, χ_e	$\mathcal{T}_{1/6}, \mathcal{T}_{1/6}$	$\mathcal{B}_1, \mathcal{B}_1$	$\mathcal{B}_1, \mathcal{B}_1$	$\mathcal{B}_1, \mathcal{B}_1$
Dec. failure	2^{-127}	2^{-145}	2^{-175}	2^{-145}
Blocksize	397	556	551	854
Bit security	142	187	186	272
Public key (bytes)	1432	2008	2023	3235
Ciphertext (bytes)	716	1004	1012	1618

the first column. Therefore, it is sufficient to send the first column consisting k ring elements plus a 32-bytes random seed. The ciphertext of the scheme in Subsect. 3.1 (i.e., Tables 4) consists of a single ring element in R_q. However, its public key $\mathbf{h} \in R_q^k$ is pseudorandom and cannot be expanded by a random seed.

In the end, we highlight several parameter set which could be interesting. First, the parameters I, II (b) and III in Table 2a are most competitive with the current state of the part. In particular, it offers a ciphertext size of 614, 921 and 1228 bytes for NIST Level 1, 3 and 5 security which all admit small decryption failure rate. If the NTTRU ring is preferred, one can uses the parameters in Table 3a, whose ciphertext size are 651, 977 and 1257 bytes for NIST Level 1, 3 and 5 security. These ciphertext sizes are quite close to the power-of-two rings cases.

Acknowledgments. The authors would like to express their gratitude to the anonymous reviewer for suggesting the attack of recovering the determinant in Sect. 5.

This research was funded in part by the U.S. National Science Foundation under Grant No. 2044855 & 2122229. The authors would like to acknowledge the use of the services provided by Research Computing at Florida Atlantic University.

References

AD17. Albrecht, M.R., Deo, A.: Large modulus ring-LWE ≥ module-LWE, in Takagi and Peyrin [TP17], pp. 267–296 (2017)

ADPS16. Alkim, E., Ducas, L., Pöppelmann, T., Schwabe, P.: Newhope without reconciliation, Cryptology ePrint Archive, Paper 2016/1157 (2016). https://eprint.iacr.org/2016/1157

AG11. Arora, S., Ge, R.: New algorithms for learning in presence of errors. In: Aceto, L., Henzinger, M., Sgall, J. (eds.) ICALP 2011. LNCS, vol. 6755, pp. 403–415. Springer, Heidelberg (2011). https://doi.org/10.1007/978-3-642-22006-7_34

AGVW17. Albrecht, M.R., Göpfert, F., Virdia, F., Wunderer, T.: Revisiting the expected cost of solving uSVP and applications to LWE, in Takagi and Peyrin [TP17], pp. 297–322 (2017)

Ajt96. Ajtai, M.: Generating hard instances of lattice problems (extended abstract). In: 28th ACM STOC, ACM Press, pp. 99–108 (1996)

APS15. Albrecht, M.R., Player, R., Scott, S.: On the concrete hardness of learning with errors. J. Math. Cryptol. **9**(3), 169–203 (2015)

BBC+20. Bernstein, D.J., et al.: NTRU Prime, Tech. report, National Institute of Standards and Technology (2020). https://csrc.nist.gov/projects/post-quantum-cryptography/post-quantum-cryptography-standardization/round-3-submissions

BBJ+22. Bai, S., Beard, A., Johnson, F., Vidhanalage, S.K.B., Ngo, T.: Fiat-shamir signatures based on module-NTRU. In: ACISP 22 (Khoa Nguyen, Guomin Yang, Fuchun Guo, and Willy Susilo, eds.), LNCS, vol. 13494, pp. 289–308. Springer, Heidelberg (2022). https://doi.org/10.1007/978-3-031-22301-3_15

BCLv17. Bernstein, D.J., Chuengsatiansup, C., Lange, T., van Vredendaal, C.: NTRU Prime: reducing attack surface at low cost. In: Adams, C., Camenisch, J. (eds.) SAC 2017. LNCS, vol. 10719, pp. 235–260. Springer, Cham (2018). https://doi.org/10.1007/978-3-319-72565-9_12

BGM+16. Bogdanov, A., Guo, S., Masny, D., Richelson, S., Rosen, A.: On the hardness of learning with rounding over small modulus. In: Kushilevitz, E., Malkin, T. (eds.) TCC 2016. LNCS, vol. 9562, pp. 209–224. Springer, Heidelberg (2016). https://doi.org/10.1007/978-3-662-49096-9_9

BGV12. Brakerski, Z., Gentry, C., Vaikuntanathan, V.: (leveled) fully homomorphic encryption without bootstrapping. In: Proceedings of the 3rd Innovations in Theoretical Computer Science Conference (New York, NY, USA), ITCS '12, Association for Computing Machinery, pp. 309–325 (2012)

BLL+15. Bai, S., Lepoint, T., Roux-Langlois, A., Sakzad, A., Stehlé, D., Steinfeld, R.: Improved security proofs in lattice-based cryptography: using the Rényi divergence rather than the statistical distance. J. Cryptol. **31**(2), 610–640 (2017). https://doi.org/10.1007/s00145-017-9265-9

CDH+20. Chen, C., et al.: NTRU, Tech. report, National Institute of Standards and Technology (2020). https://csrc.nist.gov/projects/post-quantum-cryptography/post-quantum-cryptography-standardization/round-3-submissions

CKKS19. Cheon, J.H., Kim, D., Kim, T., Son, Y.: A new trapdoor over module-NTRU lattice and its application to ID-based encryption, Cryptology ePrint Archive, Report 2019/1468 (2019). https://eprint.iacr.org/2019/1468

CPS+20. Chuengsatiansup, C., Prest, T., Stehlé, D., Wallet, A., Xagawa, K.: Mod-Falcon: compact signatures based on module-NTRU lattices, ASIACCS 20 (Hung-Min Sun, Shiuh-Pyng Shieh, Guofei Gu, and Giuseppe Ateniese, eds.), ACM Press, pp. 853–866 (2020)

CS97.   Coppersmith, D., Shamir, A.: Lattice attacks on NTRU. In: Fumy, W. (ed.) EUROCRYPT 1997. LNCS, vol. 1233, pp. 52–61. Springer, Heidelberg (1997). https://doi.org/10.1007/3-540-69053-0_5

DDLL13. Ducas, L., Durmus, A., Lepoint, T., Lyubashevsky, V.: Lattice signatures and bimodal gaussians. In: Canetti, R., Garay, J.A. (eds.) CRYPTO 2013. LNCS, vol. 8042, pp. 40–56. Springer, Heidelberg (2013). https://doi.org/10.1007/978-3-642-40041-4_3

DFMS22. Don, J., Fehr, S., Majenz, C., Schaffner, C.: Online-extractability in the quantum random-oracle model, EUROCRYPT 2022, Part III (Orr Dunkelman and Stefan Dziembowski, eds.), LNCS, vol. 13277, pp. 677–706. Springer, Heidelberg (2022). https://doi.org/10.1007/978-3-031-07082-2_24

DHK+23. Duman, J., Hövelmanns, K., Kiltz, E., Lyubashevsky, V., Seiler, G., Unruh, D.: A thorough treatment of highly-efficient NTRU instantiations, PKC 2023, Part I (Alexandra Boldyreva and Vladimir Kolesnikov, eds.), LNCS, vol. 13940, pp. 65–94. Springer, Heidelberg (2023). https://doi.org/10.1007/978-3-031-31368-4_3

DLP14. Ducas, L., Lyubashevsky, V., Prest, T.: Efficient identity-based encryption over NTRU lattices. In: Sarkar, P., Iwata, T. (eds.) ASIACRYPT 2014. LNCS, vol. 8874, pp. 22–41. Springer, Heidelberg (2014). https://doi.org/10.1007/978-3-662-45608-8_2

DP23. Ducas, L., Pulles, L.: Does the dual-sieve attack on learning with errors even work? Cryptology ePrint Archive, Paper 2023/302 (2023). https://eprint.iacr.org/2023/302

Dv21. Ducas, L., van Woerden, W.: NTRU Fatigue: how stretched is overstretched? In: Tibouchi, M., Wang, H. (eds.) ASIACRYPT 2021. LNCS, vol. 13093, pp. 3–32. Springer, Cham (2021). https://doi.org/10.1007/978-3-030-92068-5_1

FPS22. Felderhoff, J., Pellet-Mary, A., Stehlé, D.: On module unique-SVP and NTRU, ASIACRYPT 2022, Part III (Shweta Agrawal and Dongdai Lin, eds.), LNCS, vol. 13793, pp. 709–740. Springer, Heidelberg (2022). https://doi.org/10.1007/978-3-031-22969-5_24

GJ21. Guo, Q., Johansson, T.: Faster dual lattice attacks for solving LWE with applications to CRYSTALS, in Tibouchi and Wang [TW21], pp. 33–62 (2021)

HHK17. Hofheinz, D., Hövelmanns, K., Kiltz, E.: A modular analysis of the Fujisaki-Okamoto transformation. In: Kalai, Y., Reyzin, L. (eds.) TCC 2017. LNCS, vol. 10677, pp. 341–371. Springer, Cham (2017). https://doi.org/10.1007/978-3-319-70500-2_12

HHP+03. Hoffstein, J., Howgrave-Graham, N., Pipher, J., Silverman, J.H., Whyte, W.: NTRUSign: digital signatures using the NTRU lattice. In: Joye, M. (ed.) CT-RSA 2003. LNCS, vol. 2612, pp. 122–140. Springer, Heidelberg (2003). https://doi.org/10.1007/3-540-36563-X_9

How07. Howgrave-Graham, N.: A hybrid lattice-reduction and meet-in-the-middle attack against NTRU. In: Menezes, A. (ed.) CRYPTO 2007. LNCS, vol. 4622, pp. 150–169. Springer, Heidelberg (2007). https://doi.org/10.1007/978-3-540-74143-5_9

HPS98. Hoffstein, J., Pipher, J., Silverman, J.H.: NTRU: a ring-based public key cryptosystem. In: Buhler, J.P. (ed.) ANTS 1998. LNCS, vol. 1423, pp. 267–288. Springer, Heidelberg (1998). https://doi.org/10.1007/BFb0054868

LDK+22. Lyubashevsky, V., et al.: CRYSTALS-DILITHIUM, Tech. report, National Institute of Standards and Technology (2022). https://csrc.nist.gov/Projects/post-quantum-cryptography/selected-algorithms-2022

LPR10. Lyubashevsky, V., Peikert, C., Regev, O.: On Ideal Lattices and Learning with Errors over Rings. In: Gilbert, H. (ed.) EUROCRYPT 2010. LNCS, vol. 6110, pp. 1–23. Springer, Heidelberg (2010). https://doi.org/10.1007/978-3-642-13190-5_1

LPR13. Lyubashevsky, V., Peikert, C., Regev, O.: A toolkit for ring-LWE cryptography. In: Johansson, T., Nguyen, P.Q. (eds.) EUROCRYPT 2013. LNCS, vol. 7881, pp. 35–54. Springer, Heidelberg (2013). https://doi.org/10.1007/978-3-642-38348-9_3

LS15. Langlois, A., Stehlé, D.: Worst-case to average-case reductions for module lattices. Des. Codes Cryptography **75**(3), 565–599 (2015)

LS19. Lyubashevsky, V., Seiler, G.: NTTRU: Truly fast NTRU using NTT, IACR TCHES **2019**(3), 180–201 (2019). https://tches.iacr.org/index.php/TCHES/article/view/8293

LSS14. Langlois, A., Stehlé, D., Steinfeld, R.: GGHLite: more efficient multilinear maps from ideal lattices. In: Nguyen, P.Q., Oswald, E. (eds.) EUROCRYPT 2014. LNCS, vol. 8441, pp. 239–256. Springer, Heidelberg (2014). https://doi.org/10.1007/978-3-642-55220-5_14

Lyu12. Lyubashevsky, V.: Lattice signatures without trapdoors. In: Pointcheval, D., Johansson, T. (eds.) EUROCRYPT 2012. LNCS, vol. 7237, pp. 738–755. Springer, Heidelberg (2012). https://doi.org/10.1007/978-3-642-29011-4_43

LZ22. Liang, Z., Zhao, Y.: Number theoretic transform and its applications in lattice-based cryptosystems: a survey (2022)

MAT22. MATZOV: Report on the security of LWE: improved dual lattice attack (2022)

Mic02. Micciancio, D.: Generalized compact knapsacks, cyclic lattices, and efficient one-way functions from worst-case complexity assumptions. In: 43rd FOCS, IEEE Computer Society Press, pp. 356–365 (2002)

MR04. Micciancio, D., Regev, O.: Worst-case to average-case reductions based on Gaussian measures. In: 45th FOCS, IEEE Computer Society Press, pp. 372–381 (2004)

NIS16. NIST: National institute of standards and technology's Post-Quantum Cryptography Standardization (2016). https://csrc.nist.gov/projects/post-quantum-cryptography

Pei10. Peikert, C.: An efficient and parallel gaussian sampler for lattices. In: Rabin, T. (ed.) CRYPTO 2010. LNCS, vol. 6223, pp. 80–97. Springer, Heidelberg (2010). https://doi.org/10.1007/978-3-642-14623-7_5

PFH+22. Prest, T., et al.: FALCON, Tech. report, National Institute of Standards and Technology (2022). https://csrc.nist.gov/Projects/post-quantum-cryptography/selected-algorithms-2022

PG14. Pöppelmann, T., Güneysu, T.: Towards practical lattice-based public-key encryption on reconfigurable hardware. In: Lange, T., Lauter, K., Lisoněk, P. (eds.) SAC 2013. LNCS, vol. 8282, pp. 68–85. Springer, Heidelberg (2014). https://doi.org/10.1007/978-3-662-43414-7_4

PR07. Peikert, C., Rosen, A.: Lattices that admit logarithmic worst-case to average-case connection factors. In: 39th ACM STOC (David S. Johnson and Uriel Feige, eds.), ACM Press, pp. 478–487 (2007)

PS21. Wang, Y., Wang, M.: On the hardness of NTRU problems. Front. Comput. Sci. **16**(6), 1–10 (2022). https://doi.org/10.1007/s11704-021-1073-6

Reg05. Regev, O.: On lattices, learning with errors, random linear codes, and cryptography. In: 37th ACM STOC (Harold N. Gabow and Ronald Fagin, eds.), ACM Press, pp. 84–93 (2005)

SAB+22. Schwabe, P., et al.: CRYSTALS-KYBER, Tech. report, National Institute of Standards and Technology (2022). https://csrc.nist.gov/Projects/post-quantum-cryptography/selected-algorithms-2022

Sho97. Shor, P.W.: Polynomial-time algorithms for prime factorization and discrete logarithms on a quantum computer. SIAM J. Comput. **26**(5), 1484–1509 (1997)

SS11. Stehlé, D., Steinfeld, R.: Making NTRU as secure as worst-case problems over ideal lattices. In: Paterson, K.G. (ed.) EUROCRYPT 2011. LNCS, vol. 6632, pp. 27–47. Springer, Heidelberg (2011). https://doi.org/10.1007/978-3-642-20465-4_4

SSTX09. Stehlé, D., Steinfeld, R., Tanaka, K., Xagawa, K.: Efficient public key encryption based on ideal lattices. In: Matsui, M. (ed.) ASIACRYPT 2009. LNCS, vol. 5912, pp. 617–635. Springer, Heidelberg (2009). https://doi.org/10.1007/978-3-642-10366-7_36

TP17. Takagi, T., Peyrin, T. (eds.): ASIACRYPT 2017. LNCS, vol. 10625. Springer, Cham (2017). https://doi.org/10.1007/978-3-319-70697-9

TW21. Tibouchi, M., Wang, H. (eds.): ASIACRYPT 2021. LNCS, vol. 13093. Springer, Cham (2021). https://doi.org/10.1007/978-3-030-92068-5

ZFY23. Zhang, J., Feng, D., Yan, D.: NEV: faster and smaller NTRU encryption using vector decoding. In: Advances in Cryptology – ASIACRYPT 2023 (Singapore) (Jian Guo and Ron Steinfeld, eds.), Springer Nature Singapore, pp. 157–189 (2023). https://doi.org/10.1007/978-981-99-8739-9_6

Analyzing Pump and Jump BKZ Algorithm Using Dynamical Systems

Leizhang Wang$^{(\boxtimes)}$ (iD)

State Key Laboratory of Integrated Service Networks, Xidian University,
Xi'an, China
lzwang_2@stu.xidian.edu.cn

Abstract. The analysis of the reduction effort of the lattice reduction algorithm is important in estimating the hardness of lattice-based cryptography schemes. Recently many lattice challenge records have been cracked by using the Pnj-BKZ algorithm which is the default lattice reduction algorithm used in G6K, such as the TU Darmstadt LWE and SVP Challenges. However, the previous estimations of the Pnj-BKZ algorithm are simulator algorithms rather than theoretical upper bound analyses. In this work, we present the first dynamic analysis of Pnj-BKZ algorithm. More precisely, our analysis results show that let L is the lattice spanned by $(\mathbf{a}_i)_{i \leq d}$. The shortest vector $\mathbf{b}_1$ output by running $\Omega\left(\frac{2Jd^2}{\beta(\beta-J)}\left(\ln d + \ln\ln\max_i \frac{\|\mathbf{a}_i^*\|}{(\det L)^{1/d}}\right)\right)$ tours reduction of pnj-BKZ(β, J), $\mathbf{b}_1$ satisfied that $\|\mathbf{b}_1\| \leq \gamma_\beta^{\frac{d-1}{2(\beta-J)}+2} \cdot (\det L)^{\frac{1}{d}}$.

Keywords: Lattice Reduction · Pnj-BKZ · Dynamical Systems

1 Introduction

In recent years, with the development of quantum computers and quantum algorithms like Shor's algorithm [26], the current mainstream public key cryptography schemes (RSA, ECC) are threatened by quantum computing. Therefore, the National Institute of Standards and Technology (NIST) in the United States has called the cryptography schemes which can resist attacks from quantum computers (Post-Quantum Cryptography schemes). As one of the main parts of post-quantum cryptography, lattice-based cryptography recently attracted much interest, since it can construct numerous cryptographic primitives, and the security of lattice-based cryptography schemes is guaranteed by the hardness of lattice problems with worst-case which is considered to be quantum-resistant. In 2022, at the process of NIST's PQC standardization [1], three over four selected schemes as next-generation standard are lattice-based candidates (Kyber [5], Dilithium [9] and Falcon [24]). In the standardization process of lattice-based cryptography schemes, it is necessary to give an accurate estimation of the concrete hardness of lattice problems.

A lattice L is generated by a basis $\mathbf{B}$ which is a set of linearly independent vectors $\{\mathbf{b}_1, \mathbf{b}_2, \dots, \mathbf{b}_n\} \in \mathbb{R}^m$. In lattice-based cryptography, the approximated

M.-J. Saarinen and D. Smith-Tone (Eds.): PQCrypto 2024, LNCS 14771, pp. 406–432, 2024.
https://doi.org/10.1007/978-3-031-62743-9_14

shortest vector problem is a basic and central computational problem. The α-approximate Shortest Vector Problem (α-SVP): given an arbitrary basis $\mathbf{B}$ on lattice $L = L(\mathbf{B})$, find the shortest non-zero vector $\mathbf{v}$ s.t. $\|\mathbf{v}\| \le \alpha \cdot \lambda_1(L)$.

Over the past few decades, a series works of reduction algorithms were proposed to solve α-SVP. In 1982, Lenstra et al. proposed the first polynomial-time lattice reduction algorithm: LLL algorithm [18] which can solve α-SVP with an exponential approximate factor α. Then Schnorr and Euchner give a stronger lattice reduction algorithm *Block Korkin-Zolotarev reduction* (BKZ) [25] which combined the LLL algorithm and the enumeration algorithm to balance the algorithm's time cost and the quality of output (e.g., the approximation factor α) by adjusting a parameter β called blocksize. In the literature, many variants ([4, 7, 11, 12, 22]) of the original BKZ algorithm [25] are proposed. e.g. By using the extreme pruning technique [13] and early termination operation, BKZ 2.0 [7] speed up enumeration and improve the efficiency of the BKZ algorithm.

In 2019, Albrecht *et al.* [3] designed the *General Sieve Kernel* (G6K) which implemented a new version of BKZ named *Pump and jump BKZ* (Pnj-BKZ) which has two adjustable parameters: size of Pump (β) and size of jump (J). Unlike classical BKZ using an enumeration algorithm as its SVP oracle, Pnj-BKZ(β, J) adopts Pump to do the reduction in each block. The Pump used in G6K combined progressive sieving technology [17] and dimension-for-free (d4f) technique [8] can not only return one short vector but return a lattice basis which is almost HKZ reduced. Pump can selectively call the Gauss sieve [21], NV sieve [23], k-list sieve ([15,16]) or BGJ1 sieve [2] to solve α-SVP with very small approximate factor like $\alpha \in [1, 1.05]$. In 2021, Ducas *et al.* [10] improved the efficiency of G6K using GPU and implemented the fastest sieving algorithm BDGL16 [6] in both G6K and G6K-GPU-Tensor.

Another parameter the jump value J controls the jump stage of blocks in BKZ with each Pump, which can jump by more than one dimension. For instance, after $L_{[1:\beta]}$ is reduced by the first Pump, the next Pump will be used to do the reduction on $L_{[1+J:J+\beta]}$. However, unlike the Slide BKZ [11] which can be considered as BKZ with jump value equals β. The jump value J in Pnj-BKZ(β, J) is flexible to adjust witin $[1, \beta]$. So Pnj-BKZ(β, J) algorithm is different from Slide BKZ [11].

The Pnj-BKZ algorithm is efficient in solving α-SVP in practice. Recently many lattice challenge records are cracked by using Pnj-BKZ algorithm, such as the TU Darmstadt LWE Challenges:[1] $(n, \alpha) \in \{(40, 0.035), (90, 0.005), (50, 0.025), (55, 0.020), (40, 0.040)\}$, TU Darmstadt SVP Challenges[2] dimensions from 180 up to 186, and TU Darmstadt Ideal Challenges[3] 750-dimension approximate-SVP. Therefore, the study of the reduction effect of the Pnj-BKZ algorithm is crucial to accurately measure the concrete hardness of α-SVP which characterizes the security of the lattice cryptographic schemes.

To simulate the reduction effect of the Pnj-BKZ algorithm, the Pnj-BKZ simulator [28] and its optimized version [27] was proposed which is a polynomial time

---

[1] https://www.latticechallenge.org/lwe_challenge/challenge.php.
[2] https://www.latticechallenge.org/svp-challenge/halloffame.php.
[3] https://latticechallenge.org/ideallattice-challenge/index.php.

the simulator of pnj-BKZ can predict how the length of Gram-Schmidt lattice basis vectors change during the process of running each tour of Pnj-BKZ(β, J) without actually running Pnj-BKZ(β, J). Pnj-BKZ(β, J) is an exponential time algorithm with respect to blocksize β.

However, there is no theoretical analysis like the analysis in [14,19] to analyze the upper bound of the approximate factor that Pnj-BKZ(β, J) can achieve in solving α-SVP. More specifically to study lattice reduction algorithms like BKZ-β can solve α-SVP with how small the approximation factor α, many analyses are proposed. In 2011, Hanrot et al. [14] analyzed a certain variant BKZ' of BKZ by dynamic systems. Their results show that after a polynomial number of tours reduction of BKZ'-β, the shortest vector output from BKZ'-β has norm smaller than $2\gamma_\beta^{\frac{d-1}{2(\beta-1)}+\frac{3}{2}} \cdot (\det L)^{\frac{1}{d}}$. In 2020, Li and Nguyen [19] present the first rigorous dynamic analysis of BKZ rather than BKZ'. They proves that after at most $\Theta\left(\frac{d^2}{\beta^2}\log d\right)$ tours reduction of BKZ-β, the Euclidean norm of the first basis vector output from BKZ-β at most $\gamma_\beta^{\frac{d-1}{2(\beta-1)}+\frac{\beta(\beta-2)}{2d(\beta-1)}} \cdot (\det L)^{\frac{1}{d}}$. In 2022, Li and Walter [20] give a rigorous dynamic analysis of Slide BKZ [11]. Slide BKZ is similar to a BKZ with jump, but the jump value J equals the blocksize β in Slide BKZ.

1.1   Contribution

In this paper, we use the dynamical system to analyze the upper bound of the approximate factor in solving α-SVP by using how many tours reduction of Pnj-BKZ(β, J). Here the jump value $J \in [1, \beta]$ rather than $J = \beta$ as that of Slide BKZ [11]. Besides, we focus on a slightly modified ideal variant Pnj-BKZ'(β, J) instead original version of Pnj-BKZ(β, J) algorithm. We construct the dynamical system of Pnj-BKZ' by using the sandpile model and use it to give the first dynamical analysis of an ideal version of Pnj-BKZ'. Our results show that:

Set L be the lattice spanned by $(\mathbf{a}_i)_{i \leq d}$. The shortest vector $\mathbf{b}_1$ output by running $C\frac{2Jd^2}{\beta(\beta-J)}\left(\ln d + \ln\ln\max_i \frac{\|\mathbf{a}_i^*\|}{(\det L)^{1/d}}\right)$ tours reduction of Pnj-BKZ'(β, J), which satisfied that $\|\mathbf{b}_1\| \leq \gamma_\beta^{\frac{d-1}{2(\beta-J)}+2} \cdot (\det L)^{\frac{1}{d}}$. See Table 1 for the details about comparison with other works. From Table 1, we can see that with the same block size β, although the time cost of one tour of Pnj-BKZ(β, J) is only $1/J$ times the time cost of BKZ. However, with the same block size β, when J is greater than 1, the full reduction effect of Pnj-BKZ is not as good as that of BKZ or that of Slide reduction. Therefore, J can be regarded as a new trade-off parameter of the BKZ type lattice reduction algorithm in addition to the block size β, which balances the reduction quality of Pnj-BKZ reduction and the time cost of Pnj-BKZ.

Table 1. Comparison with other works

Technique	GN08 [11]	LW23 [20]
Algorithm	Slide reduction	Slide reduction
$\|\mathbf{b}_1\|/\lambda_1(L)$	$\leq ((1+\varepsilon)\gamma_\beta)^{(d-\beta)/(\beta-1)}$	$\leq (1+\varepsilon)\gamma_\beta^{\frac{d-1}{2(\beta-1)}}$
Convergence needed Tours	no	$O\left(\frac{d^3 \ln \frac{d}{\varepsilon}}{\beta^2}\right)$
Discrete dynamical systems	no	yes
Technique	HPS11 [14]	LN20 [19]
Algorithm	BKZ'	BKZ
$\|\mathbf{b}_1\|/\lambda_1(L)$	$\leq 2\gamma_\beta^{\frac{d-1}{2(\beta-1)}+\frac{3}{2}}$	$\leq \gamma_\beta^{\frac{d-1}{2(\beta-1)}+\frac{\beta(\beta-2)}{2d(\beta-1)}}$
Convergence needed Tours	$\Theta\left(\frac{d^3}{\beta^2}\left(\log d + \log\log\max_i \|\mathbf{b}_i\|\right)\right)$	$\Theta\left(\frac{d^2}{\beta^2}\log d\right)$
Discrete dynamical systems	yes	yes
Technique	Our	
Algorithm	Pnj-BKZ'	
$\|\mathbf{b}_1\|/\lambda_1(L)$	$\leq \gamma_\beta^{\frac{d-1}{2(\beta-J)}+2}$	
Convergence needed Tours	$\Theta\left(\frac{2Jd^2}{\beta(\beta-J)}\left(\ln d + \ln\ln\max_i \frac{\|\mathbf{a}_i^*\|}{(\det L)^{1/d}}\right)\right)$	
Discrete dynamical systems	yes	

2 Preliminaries

2.1 Notations and Basic Definitions

We use $\mathbf{J}_{i,j}$ to represent all-ones matrix where every entry is equal to 1 with i rows and j columns, $\mathbf{0}_{i,j}$ represent $i \times j$ zero matrix, $i, j \in \mathbb{N}^*$.

Definition 1 (Lattice). *A lattice L is generated by a basis $\mathbf{B}$ which is a set of linearly independent vectors $\{\mathbf{b}_1, \mathbf{b}_2, \ldots, \mathbf{b}_n\} \in \mathbb{R}^m$. We will refer to it as $L(\mathbf{b}_1, \mathbf{b}_2, \ldots, \mathbf{b}_n) = \{\sum_{i=1}^n z_i\mathbf{b}_i, z_i \in \mathbb{Z}\}$. In this paper the length of $\mathbf{v} \in \mathbb{R}^m$ is the Euclidean norm $\|\mathbf{v}\|_2$.*

A non-zero vector in a lattice L that has the minimum norm is called the shortest vector. We use $\lambda_1(L)$ to denote the norm of the shortest vector.

Definition 2. *(α-approximate Shortest Vector Problem(α-SVP)) Given an arbitrary basis $\mathbf{B}$ on lattice $\mathcal{L} = \mathcal{L}(\mathbf{B})$, find the shortest non-zero vector $\mathbf{v}$ s.t. $\|\mathbf{v}\| = \alpha \cdot \lambda_1(L)$.*

Definition 3 (Gram-Schmidt Basis and Projective Sublattice). *For a given lattice basis $\mathbf{B} = (\mathbf{b}_1, \mathbf{b}_2, \ldots, \mathbf{b}_n)$, we define its Gram-Schmidt orthogonal basis $\mathbf{B}^* := (\mathbf{b}_1^*, \mathbf{b}_2^*, \ldots, \mathbf{b}_n^*)$ by $\mathbf{b}_i^* = \mathbf{b}_i - \sum_{j=1}^{i-1} \mu_{ij}\mathbf{b}_j^*$ for $1 \leq j < i \leq n$, where $\mu_{ij} = \frac{\langle \mathbf{b}_i, \mathbf{b}_j^* \rangle}{\|\mathbf{b}_j^*\|^2}$ are the Gram-Schmidt coefficients (abbreviated as GS-coefficients). In this paper we use l_i to represent the value of $\log(\|\mathbf{b}_i^*\|)$. The lattice determinant is defined as $\det(L(\mathbf{B})) := \prod_{i=1}^n \|\mathbf{b}_i^*\|$ and it is equal to the volume*

$vol(L(\mathbf{B}))$ *of the fundamental parallelepiped. We denote the orthogonal projection by* $\pi_i : \mathbb{R}^m \to span(\mathbf{b}_1, \ldots, \mathbf{b}_{i-1})^\perp$ *for* $i \in \{1, 2, \ldots, n\}$. *We denote the local block of the projective sublattice* $L_{[i:j]} := L(\pi_i(\mathbf{b}_i), \pi_i(\mathbf{b}_{i+1}), \ldots, \pi_i(\mathbf{b}_j))$, *for* $j \in \{i, i+1, \ldots, n\}$.

The notion of the norm of the shortest vector is also defined for a projective sublattice as $\lambda_1(L_{[i:j]})$.

Heuristic 1 (Gaussian Heuristic). *Given an n-dimensional lattice L with determinant* $\det(L)$, *the Gaussian heuristic predicts that there are around* $vol(C)/\det(L)$ *many lattice points in a measurable subset C in* $\mathbb{R}^n$.

In addition, the length of the shortest vector can be approximated by the radius of a sphere whose volume is $\det(L)$. This is usually called the Gaussian heuristic of a lattice. Under Gaussian heuristic, it can be denoted as $\lambda_1(L) = \mathrm{GH}(L) = \det(L)^{1/n}/V_n(1)^{1/n}$, where $V_n(1)$ is the volume of unit ball of dimension n. Besides $\mathrm{GH}(L) = \det(L)^{1/n}/V_n(1)^{1/n}$ is usually approximated to $\sqrt{\frac{n}{2\pi e}}\det(L)^{1/n}$ by using Stirling's formula.

Definition 4 (Hermite-Korkine-Zolotarev (HKZ) Reduction). *A lattice basis is HKZ reduced, if it is size reduced and all Gram-Schmidt vectors satisfy* $\|\mathbf{b}_i^*\| = \lambda_1(L_{[i,d]})$, *where d is dimension of lattice.*

Heuristic 2 (Sandpile Model Assumption (SMA)[14]). *For any HKZ reduced basis* $(b_i)_{i \leq \beta}$, $x_i = \frac{1}{2}\ln\gamma_{\beta-i+1} + \frac{1}{\beta-i+1}\sum_{j=i}^{\beta} x_j$ *for all* $i \leq \beta$ *with* $(x_i = log\|\mathbf{b}_i^*\|)_{i \leq \beta}$.

Here γ_i in Heuristic 2 is the i-dimension Hermite's constant which equals to $\frac{\lambda_1(L)^2}{(\det L)^{\frac{2}{dim(L)}}}$. In this paper we use $\frac{dim(L)}{2\pi e}$ to approximate this $\gamma_{dim(L)}$.

Under SMA, once $\sum_i x_i$ (*i.e.,* $|\det(b_i)_i|$) is fixed, the $(x_i = log\|\mathbf{b}_i^*\|)_{i \leq \beta}$ of an HKZ-reduced basis is uniquely determined.

Definition 5 (Hermit factor). *A d-dimensional lattice with basis* $\mathbf{B}$, *the Hermite factor of* $L(\mathbf{B})$: $\mathrm{HF}(\mathbf{B}) = \|\mathbf{b}_1\|/\det(L)^{\frac{1}{d}}$ *is one of quality measurement for a lattice basis* $\mathbf{B}$ *which is reduced by lattice reduction algorithm. And the root Hermite factor (rhf) is defined as* $\mathrm{HF}(\mathbf{B})^{\frac{1}{d}}$.

Definition 6 (Characteristic Polynomial). *The characteristic polynomial* $\chi(\mathbf{A})$ *of a matirx* $\mathbf{A}$ *is the polynomial defined as:* $\det(\mathbf{A} - \lambda\mathbf{I})$, *where matirx* $\mathbf{A}$ *is a square matrix and* $\mathbf{I}$ *is the identity matrix of identical dimension.*

2.2 Pump and Jump BKZ Algorithm

Pnj-BKZ is a BKZ-type reduction algorithm that uses Pump as its SVP oracle. However, Pump can return not only one short vector but many short vectors and insert them at different positions to obtain an almost HKZ-reduced basis.

Specifically, inputting a projected sublattice basis $B_{\pi[\kappa,r]}$, after the reduction of Pump, the output $B_{\pi[\kappa,r]}$ by $\text{Pump}(B_{\pi[\kappa,r]}, \kappa, \beta, f)$ is an almost HKZ reduced basis. Here f is a dimension for free function related to block size β and the information about the dimension for free technology can be seen in [8]]. More detail about Pump can be found in Algorithm 1 or the description of Pump in Sect. 4.1 of G6K [3].

Algorithm 1. Pump

Input: B, $\kappa, \beta, ds = f, \text{stn} = 30$

Output: B

1: $r := \kappa + \beta; l := max\{\kappa + f + 1, r - \text{stn}\}; ilb := \kappa; L := \emptyset;$
2: $B_{\pi[\kappa,r]} := \text{LLL}\left(B_{\pi[\kappa,r]}\right);$
3: //Phase="init";
4: $L := \text{gauss sieve}\left(B_{\pi[l,r]}, L\right);$
5: //Phase="up";
6: **while** $l > \kappa + f$ **do**
7:     $L := \left\{\text{EL}\left(\mathbf{v}, 1\right) \big| \mathbf{v} \in L\right\}, l := l - 1;$
8:     $L := \text{sieve}\left(B_{\pi[l,r]}, L\right);$
9: **end while**
10: //Phase="down";
11: **while** $d > 1$ & $ilb < \kappa + ds$ **do**
12:     $BL := \text{best lifts}\,(L);$ //score all the vectors in best lifts list of L, and score each $\mathbf{v}_i$ with $score\,(\mathbf{v}_i) := \theta^{-i}\frac{\|\mathbf{v}_i\|}{\|\mathbf{b}_i^*\|};$
13:     **if** $BL \neq \emptyset$ **then**
14:         $ii := BL.\text{index}\,(\max\,(BL));$ //Find the best scoring position;
15:         Insert $\mathbf{v}_{ii}$ into the basis $B_{\pi[\kappa,r]};$
16:         $ilb := ii + 1;$
17:     **else**
18:         $L := \left\{\text{SL}\,(\mathbf{v}, 1) \big| \mathbf{v} \in L\right\};$
19:     **end if**
20:     $L := \text{sieve}\left(B_{\pi[l,r]}, L\right);$
21:     $l := l + 1;$
22: **end while**
23: **return B**

Besides unlike classical BKZ, Pnj-BKZ performs Pump with an adjustable jump which can be bigger than 1. Specifically, PnjBKZ runs each Pump with blocksize β and jump=J, after a certain block $B_{[i:i+\beta]}$ is reduced by Pump, the next Pump will be executed on the $B_{[i+J:i+\beta+J]}$ block with a jump count J rather than $B_{[i+1:i+\beta+1]}$. More detail can be seen in Algorithm 2. In addition, the jump value J in Pnj-BKZ(β, J) is within the range $[1, \beta]$. When $J = \beta$, it is similar to Slide BKZ [11]. However, when one uses Pnj-BKZ(β, J) to do the reduction of a d-dimension lattice basis in practice, usually there is the following relationship:

$J \ll \beta \le d$. Since the inserting area of each `Pump` is at most the value of dimension for free d4f(β) (Eq. (1)) according to entire block size β. To ensure the output lattice basis of each `Pump` is almost HKZ-reduced lattice basis, one needs $J \le$ d4f(β). Equation(1) shows the dimension for free value used in the implementation of G6K ([3,10]). In other words, to ensure the output lattice basis of each `Pump` is almost HKZ-reduced lattice basis, under the dimension for free value setting in G6K, $J \le 0.076\beta \ll \beta \le d$ when β is bigger enough.

$$d4f(\beta) = \begin{cases} 0, & \beta < 40 \\ \lfloor \frac{\beta-40}{2} \rfloor, & 40 \le \beta \le 75 \\ \lfloor 11.5 + 0.075\beta \rfloor, & \beta > 75. \end{cases} \quad (1)$$

Algorithm 2. Pump and jump BKZ

Input: B, β, f_{extra}, $jump = J$
Output: B$'$

1: $f := min \left\{ max \left\{ 0, \frac{\beta-40}{2} \right\}, \lfloor 11.5 + 0.075\beta \rfloor \right\} + f_{extra}$;
2: $ds := f + 3$; $\beta := \beta + f_{extra}$;
3: **B**=LLL (**B**);
4: **for** $i \in \left\{ 1, \ldots, \frac{d+2f-\beta}{jump} \right\}$ **do**
5:    **if** $1 \le i \le \frac{f+1}{jump}$ **then**
6:      $\kappa, \beta', f' := 1, \beta - f + jump \cdot i - 1, jump \cdot i - 1$
7:    **else if** $\frac{f+1}{jump} \le i \le \frac{d-\beta+f}{jump}$ **then**
8:      $j := jump \cdot i - f$
9:      $\kappa, \beta', f' := j, \beta, f$
10:   **else**
11:      $j := jump \cdot i - (d - \beta + f)$
12:      $\kappa, \beta', f' := d - \beta + j, \beta - j + 1, f - j + 1$
13:   **end if**
14:   $\mathbf{B}_{\pi[\kappa:\beta'+k-1]} \cdot \mathbf{v}_i =$ Pump $\left(\mathbf{B}_{\pi[\kappa:\beta'+k-1]}, \kappa, \beta', f', ds \right)$
15:   **B**=LLL (**B**)
16: **end for**
17: **B$'$** =Pump $\left(\mathbf{B}, d - \beta + f + 1, \beta, f \right)$
18: **return B$'$**

One can obtain an (almost) HKZ reduced basis, by turning on sieving during the Pump-down stage, which has actually already been the default operation in the implementation of G6K-GPU [10]. After turning on sieving during the Pump-down stage the output projected basis of pnj-BKZ(β, J) is very close to an HKZ reduction. More detail about the reduction effect of a `Pump` can be seen in the description of `Pump` in Sect. 4.1 of G6K [3].

3   Analysis of Pnj-BKZ' in the Sandpile Model

Although the output of a Pump is very close to the HKZ reduced basis, it is still not strictly equal to the HKZ reduced basis. In this paper, we will not analyze the original Pnj-BKZ algorithm used in practice, but we will focus on a slightly modified ideal variant instead. That is to say, when each Pump called by Pnj-BKZ algorithm, the input projected sublattice basis $B_{\pi[\kappa,\kappa+\beta]}$, after the reduction of $\text{Pump}(B_{\pi[\kappa,\kappa+\beta]}, \kappa, \beta, f)$ is strictly satisfied the property of HKZ reduced basis.

3.1   The Sandpile Model and Dynamical System in Pnj-BKZ'

Heuristic 3 (Ideal Pumpvariant: Pump') *A projected sublattice basis $B_{\pi[\kappa,\kappa+\beta]}$ after the reduction of Pump'$(B_{\pi[\kappa,\kappa+\beta]}, \kappa, \beta, f)$ strictly satisfied the property of HKZ reduced basis (Definition 4), for all $\kappa \in \{1, ..., d - \beta + 1\}$, dimension of entire lattice basis B is d.*

Then we call a Pnj-BKZ which replaces Pump by Pump' as Pnj-BKZ'. In this paper, we focus on the analysis of this slightly modified ideal variant of Pnj-BKZ instead.

Under Heuristic 3, the lattice basis $L_{[i:i+\beta-1]}$ reduced by a Pump' is a HKZ reduced lattice basis. Let $L'_{[i:i+\beta-(i-1 \bmod J)]}$ or $L'_{[i:d]}$ be the projected sub-lattice after l_j for all $j \in [1, i-1]$ have been replaced during the previous embedding.

Under Sandpile Model Assumption [14] (Heuristic 2), after one tour reduction of Pnj-BKZ'(β, J), new l'_i can be expressed as:

$$l'_i = \begin{cases} \ln \text{GH}\left(L'_{[i:i+\beta-(i-1 \bmod J)]}\right) &, i \in [1, d-\beta] \\ \ln \text{GH}\left(L'_{[i:d]}\right) &, i \in [d-\beta+1, d] \end{cases} \tag{2}$$

We set a_i as:

$$a_i = \begin{cases} \ln\left(\sqrt{\frac{\beta-(i-1 \bmod J)}{2\pi e}}\right) &, i \in [1, d-\beta] \\ \ln\left(\sqrt{\frac{d-i+1}{2\pi e}}\right) &, i \in [d-\beta+1, d] \end{cases} \tag{3}$$

Using Stirling's approximation, Eq. (2) can be written as:

$$l'_i \approx \begin{cases} a_i + \frac{1}{\beta-(i-1 \bmod J)} \ln\left(\text{vol}\left(L'_{[i:i+\beta-(i-1 \bmod J)]}\right)\right), & i \in [1, d-\beta] \\ a_i + \frac{1}{d-i+1} \ln\left(\text{vol}\left(L'_{[i:d]}\right)\right), & i \in [d-\beta+1, d] \end{cases} \tag{4}$$

Set $c_i = \ln\left(\sqrt{\frac{i}{2\pi e}}\right)$, $(l'_i)^{(k)}_i$ be the ln value of the length of Gram-Schmidt vectors after k-th Pump'$(\kappa = 1 + (\alpha - 1)J, \beta)$ reduction. $k \in \left[1, ..., \left\lceil\frac{d-\beta}{J}\right\rceil\right]$, based on Eq. (4), it gives that:

$$l_1'^{(1)} = c_\beta + \frac{1}{\beta}\sum_{i=1}^{\beta} l_i^{(0)} \tag{5}$$

Since after $l_1^{(0)}$ changed to $l_1^{'(1)}$, all $l_i^{(0)}$ for $i \in [2, d]$ will change to some $l_i^{\star(0)}$ and such change is hard to predicate. However the value of $\mathrm{vol}\left(L_{[1:\beta]}\right)$ will not change after $l_1^{(0)}$ changed to $l_1^{'(1)}$, so we can predict $l_2^{'(1)}$ by calculating $l_2^{'(1)} = c_{\beta-1} + \frac{1}{\beta-1}\sum_{i=2}^{\beta}l_i^{\star(0)}$ by $l_2^{'(1)} = c_{\beta-1} + \frac{1}{\beta-1}\left(\sum_{i=1}^{\beta}l_i^{(0)} - l_1^{'(1)}\right)$. Since $\ln\left(\mathrm{vol}\left(L_{[2:\beta]}'\right)\right) = \ln\left(\mathrm{vol}\left(L_{[1:\beta]}\right)\right) - l_1^{'(1)}$.

Combined with Eq. (5), $l_2^{'(1)}$ can be written as:

$$l_2^{'(1)} = c_{\beta-1} + \frac{1}{\beta-1}\left(\sum_{i=1}^{\beta}l_i^{(0)} - c_\beta - \frac{1}{\beta}\sum_{i=1}^{\beta}l_i^{(0)}\right) = c_{\beta-1} - \frac{1}{\beta-1}c_\beta + \frac{1}{\beta}\left(\sum_{i=1}^{\beta}l_i^{(0)}\right) \tag{6}$$

Lemma 1. *For* $j \in [2, ..., \beta-1]$, *Eq. (7) holds.*

$$l_j^{'(1)} = \frac{1}{\beta}\sum_{i=1}^{\beta}l_i^{(0)} + c_{\beta-j+1} - \sum_{k=1}^{j-1}\frac{1}{\beta-k}c_{\beta-k+1} \tag{7}$$

Proof. $l_2^{'(1)}$ already satisfied Eq. (7). Since $l_{j+1}^{'(1)} = c_{\beta-j} + \frac{1}{\beta-j}\left(\sum_{i=1}^{\beta}l_i^{(0)} - \sum_{k=1}^{j}l_k^{'(1)}\right)$, we obtain that:

$$l_{j+1}^{'(1)} = c_{\beta-j} + \frac{1}{\beta-j}\left[\sum_{i=1}^{\beta}l_i^{(0)} - \sum_{k=1}^{j}\left(\frac{1}{\beta}\sum_{i=1}^{\beta}l_i^{(0)} + c_{\beta-k+1} - \sum_{s=1}^{k-1}\frac{1}{\beta-s}c_{\beta-s+1}\right)\right]$$

$$l_{j+1}^{'(1)} = c_{\beta-j} + \frac{1}{\beta-j}\left[\frac{\beta-j}{\beta}\sum_{i=1}^{\beta}l_i^{(0)} - \sum_{k=1}^{j}\left(c_{\beta-k+1} - \sum_{s=1}^{k-1}\frac{1}{\beta-s}c_{\beta-s+1}\right)\right]$$

$$l_{j+1}^{'(1)} = \frac{1}{\beta}\sum_{i=1}^{\beta}l_i^{(0)} + c_{\beta-j} + \frac{1}{\beta-j}\left(-\sum_{k=1}^{j}c_{\beta-k+1} + \sum_{k=1}^{j}\sum_{s=1}^{k-1}\frac{1}{\beta-s}c_{\beta-s+1}\right)$$

$$l_{j+1}^{'(1)} = \frac{1}{\beta}\sum_{i=1}^{\beta}l_i^{(0)} + c_{\beta-j} + \frac{1}{\beta-j}\left(-\sum_{k=1}^{j}c_{\beta-k+1} + \sum_{k=1}^{j}\frac{j-k}{\beta-k}c_{\beta-k+1}\right)$$

$$l_{j+1}^{'(1)} = \frac{1}{\beta}\sum_{i=1}^{\beta}l_i^{(0)} + c_{\beta-j} - \sum_{k=1}^{j}\frac{1}{\beta-k}c_{\beta-k+1}$$

Therefore, Eq. (7) is held by induction proving. □

Besides, since β-dimensional $\text{Pump}'(\kappa = 1, \beta)$ only affect the GS values in $L_{[1:\beta]}$, for these rest of GS values we have the same conclusion as that in [14]:

$$j \in [1, d] \setminus [1, \beta], \; l_j^{'(1)} = l_j^{(0)} \tag{8}$$

Combining the Eqs. (7) and (8) together shows how these ln values of the length of Gram-Schmidt vectors change after one reduction of a β-dimensional $\text{Pump}'(\kappa = 1, \beta)$ on lattice basis $L_{[1:\beta]}$. Based on Eqs. (7) and (8), $\forall j \in [1 : d]$ we can give the estimation of how Gram-Schmidt lengths $l_j^{(original)}$ change to $l_j^{(new)}$ after the reduction of a β-dimensional $\text{Pump}'(\kappa, \beta)$ on any position $\kappa = i \in [1, d - \beta + 1]$.

$$l_j^{(new)} = \begin{cases} \frac{1}{\beta} \sum_{j=i}^{i+\beta-1} l_i^{(original)} + c_{\beta-j+1} - \sum_{k=1}^{j-1} \frac{1}{\beta-k} c_{\beta-k+1}, & j \in [i, i + \beta - 1] \\ l_j^{(original)}, & j \in [1, d] \setminus [i, i + \beta - 1] \end{cases} \tag{9}$$

Based on Eq. (9), we can give the discrete-time linear dynamical system of Pnj-BKZ'. During one tour reduction of a $\text{Pnj-BKZ}'$-(β, J), it will call $\left\lceil \frac{d-\beta}{J} \right\rceil$ time Pump' whose first index κ as $\kappa \in \left\{ 1, 1 + J, 1 + 2J, ..., 1 + \left\lfloor \frac{d-\beta}{J} \right\rfloor J \right\} \cup \{d - \beta + 1\}$.

Let $\mathbf{x} = (l_i)_i$, $(l_i)_i^{(\alpha)}$ be the ln value of the length of Gram-Schmidt vectors after α-th $\text{Pump}'(\kappa = 1 + (\alpha - 1)J, \beta)$ reduction, $\mathbf{x}^{(\alpha)} = (l_i)_i^{(\alpha)}$, $\alpha \in \left[1, 2, ..., \left\lceil \frac{d-\beta}{J} \right\rceil \right]$. Then we know that $\forall i \in \left\{ 1, 1 + J, 1 + 2J, ..., 1 + \left\lfloor \frac{d-\beta}{J} \right\rfloor J \right\} \cup \{d - \beta + 1\}$ and, $\mathbf{x}^{(1+\lfloor \frac{i}{J} \rfloor)} = \mathbf{A}^{(i)} \cdot \mathbf{x}^{(\lfloor \frac{i}{J} \rfloor)} + \mathbf{c}^{(i)}$ with:

$$\mathbf{A}^{(i)} = \begin{pmatrix} \ddots & & & & & \\ & 1 & & & & \\ & & \frac{1}{\beta} & \cdots & \frac{1}{\beta} & \\ & & \vdots & \ddots & \vdots & \\ & & \frac{1}{\beta} & \cdots & \frac{1}{\beta} & \\ & & & & 1 & \\ & & & & & \ddots \end{pmatrix} \begin{matrix} \\ \\ (i) \\ \\ \\ (i+\beta-1) \\ \\ \end{matrix}$$

and $\mathbf{c}_j^{(i)} = \begin{cases} 0, & j < i \\ c_{\beta-j} - \sum_{k=1}^{j-1} \frac{c_{\beta-k+1}}{\beta-k}, & j \in [i, i + \beta - 1]. \\ 0, & i + \beta \leq j \end{cases}$ It can be seen that the dynamic system of Pnj-BKZ' actually only has part of the matrix $\mathbf{A}^{(i)}$ that $i \equiv 1 \pmod{J}$ in the dynamic system of BKZ' [14].

The effect of Pnj-BKZ' tour on $\mathbf{x}$ is $\mathbf{A}\mathbf{x} + \mathbf{c}$ with $\mathbf{c} =$

$$\mathbf{c}^{(d-\beta+1)} + \mathbf{A}^{(d-\beta+1)} \left[\mathbf{c}^{\left(1+\lfloor \frac{d-\beta}{J} \rfloor \cdot J\right)} + \mathbf{A}^{\left(1+\lfloor \frac{d-\beta}{J} \rfloor \cdot J\right)} \left(\mathbf{c}^{\left(1+\lfloor \frac{d-\beta}{J} \rfloor \cdot J - J\right)} + \mathbf{A}^{\left(1+\lfloor \frac{d-\beta}{J} \rfloor \cdot J - J\right)} \cdot (\cdots) \right) \right]$$

and $\mathbf{A} = \mathbf{A}^{(d-\beta+1)} \cdot \mathbf{A}^{\left(1+\lfloor \frac{d-\beta}{J} \rfloor \cdot J\right)} \cdot ... \cdot \mathbf{A}^{(1+J)} \cdot \mathbf{A}^{(1)}$.

We use $\mathbf{J}_{i,j}$ to represent all-ones matrix where every entry is equal to 1 with i rows and j columns, $\mathbf{0}_{i,j}$ represent $i \times j$ zero matrix, and $\mathbf{I}_n$ represent n-dimensional identity matrix. It is easy to get that:

$$\mathbf{A}^{(1+J)} \cdot \mathbf{A}^{(1)} = \begin{pmatrix} \frac{1}{\beta}\mathbf{J}_{J,\beta} & \mathbf{0}_{J,J} & \mathbf{0}_{J,d-\beta-J} \\ \frac{\beta-J}{\beta^2}\mathbf{J}_{\beta,\beta} & \frac{1}{\beta}\mathbf{J}_{\beta,J} & \mathbf{0}_{\beta,d-\beta-J} \\ \mathbf{0}_{d-\beta-J,\beta} & \mathbf{0}_{d-\beta-J,J} & \mathbf{I}_{d-\beta-J,d-\beta-J} \end{pmatrix}, \quad \mathbf{A}^{(1+2J)} \cdot \mathbf{A}^{(1+J)} \cdot$$

$$\mathbf{A}^{(1)} = \begin{pmatrix} \frac{1}{\beta}\mathbf{J}_{J,\beta} & \mathbf{0}_{J,J} & \mathbf{0}_{J,J} & \mathbf{0}_{J,d-\beta-2J} \\ \frac{\beta-J}{\beta^2}\mathbf{J}_{J,\beta} & \frac{1}{\beta}\mathbf{J}_{J,J} & \mathbf{0}_{J,J} & \mathbf{0}_{\beta,d-\beta-2J} \\ \frac{(\beta-J)^2}{\beta^3}\mathbf{J}_{\beta,\beta} & \frac{\beta-J}{\beta^2}\mathbf{J}_{\beta,J} & \frac{1}{\beta}\mathbf{J}_{\beta,J} & \mathbf{0}_{\beta,d-\beta-2J} \\ \mathbf{0}_{d-\beta-2J,\beta} & \mathbf{0}_{d-\beta-2J,J} & \mathbf{0}_{d-\beta-2J,J} & \mathbf{I}_{d-\beta-2J,d-\beta-2J} \end{pmatrix},$$

We can set $\mathbf{A}^{(1+(k-1)J)} \cdot \ldots \cdot \mathbf{A}^{(1+2J)} \cdot \mathbf{A}^{(1+J)} \cdot \mathbf{A}^{(1)} =$

$$\begin{pmatrix} \frac{1}{\beta}\mathbf{J}_{J,\beta} & \mathbf{0}_{J,J} & \mathbf{0}_{J,J} & \cdots & \mathbf{0}_{J,J} & \mathbf{0}_{J,J} & \mathbf{0}_{J,d-\beta-(k-1)J} \\ \frac{\beta-J}{\beta^2}\mathbf{J}_{J,\beta} & \frac{1}{\beta}\mathbf{J}_{J,J} & \mathbf{0}_{J,J} & \cdots & \mathbf{0}_{J,J} & \mathbf{0}_{J,J} & \mathbf{0}_{J,d-\beta-(k-1)J} \\ \frac{(\beta-J)^2}{\beta^3}\mathbf{J}_{J,\beta} & \frac{\beta-J}{\beta^2}\mathbf{J}_{J,J} & \frac{1}{\beta}\mathbf{J}_{J,J} & \cdots & \mathbf{0}_{J,J} & \mathbf{0}_{J,J} & \mathbf{0}_{J,d-\beta-(k-1)J} \\ \vdots & \vdots & \vdots & \ddots & \vdots & \vdots & \vdots \\ \frac{(\beta-J)^{k-2}}{\beta^{k-1}}\mathbf{J}_{J,\beta} & \frac{(\beta-J)^{k-3}}{\beta^{k-2}}\mathbf{J}_{J,J} & \frac{(\beta-J)^{k-4}}{\beta^{k-3}}\mathbf{J}_{J,J} & \cdots & \frac{1}{\beta}\mathbf{J}_{J,J} & \mathbf{0}_{J,J} & \mathbf{0}_{J,d-\beta-(k-1)J} \\ \frac{(\beta-J)^{k-1}}{\beta^k}\mathbf{J}_{\beta,\beta} & \frac{(\beta-J)^{k-2}}{\beta^{k-1}}\mathbf{J}_{\beta,J} & \frac{(\beta-J)^{k-3}}{\beta^{k-2}}\mathbf{J}_{\beta,J} & \cdots & \frac{\beta-J}{\beta^2}\mathbf{J}_{\beta,J} & \frac{1}{\beta}\mathbf{J}_{\beta,J} & \mathbf{0}_{J,d-\beta-(k-1)J} \\ \mathbf{0}_{d-\beta-(k-1)J,\beta} & \mathbf{0}_{d-\beta-(k-1)J,J} & \mathbf{0}_{d-\beta-(k-1)J,J} & \cdots & \mathbf{0}_{d-\beta-(k-1)J,J} & \mathbf{0}_{d-\beta-(k-1)J,J} & \mathbf{I}_{d-\beta-(k-1)J,d-\beta-(k-1)J} \end{pmatrix}$$

It is hold for $k = 1, 2, 3$. Then $\mathbf{A}^{(1+kJ)} \cdot \mathbf{A}^{(1+(k-1)J)} \cdot \ldots \cdot \mathbf{A}^{(1+2J)} \cdot \mathbf{A}^{(1+J)} \cdot$

$$\mathbf{A}^{(1)} = \begin{pmatrix} \mathbf{I}_{kJ,kJ} & \mathbf{0}_{kJ,\beta} & \mathbf{0}_{kJ,d-\beta-kJ} \\ \mathbf{0}_{\beta,kJ} & \mathbf{J}_{\beta,\beta} & \mathbf{0}_{\beta,d-\beta-kJ} \\ \mathbf{0}_{d-\beta-kJ,kJ} & \mathbf{0}_{d-\beta-kJ,\beta} & \mathbf{I}_{d-\beta-kJ,d-\beta-kJ} \end{pmatrix} \cdot \mathbf{A}^{(1+(k-1)J)} \cdot \ldots \cdot \mathbf{A}^{(1+J)} \cdot$$

$\mathbf{A}^{(1)} =$

Finally, we have: $\mathbf{A}^{(1+kJ)} \cdot \mathbf{A}^{(1+(k-1)J)} \cdot \ldots \cdot \mathbf{A}^{(1+2J)} \cdot \mathbf{A}^{(1+J)} \cdot \mathbf{A}^{(1)} =$

$$\begin{pmatrix} \frac{1}{\beta}\mathbf{J}_{J,\beta} & \mathbf{0}_{J,J} & \mathbf{0}_{J,J} & \cdots & \mathbf{0}_{J,J} & \mathbf{0}_{J,J} & \mathbf{0}_{J,d-\beta-kJ} \\ \frac{\beta-J}{\beta^2}\mathbf{J}_{J,\beta} & \frac{1}{\beta}\mathbf{J}_{J,J} & \mathbf{0}_{J,J} & \cdots & \mathbf{0}_{J,J} & \mathbf{0}_{J,J} & \mathbf{0}_{J,d-\beta-kJ} \\ \frac{(\beta-J)^2}{\beta^3}\mathbf{J}_{J,\beta} & \frac{\beta-J}{\beta^2}\mathbf{J}_{J,J} & \frac{1}{\beta}\mathbf{J}_{J,J} & \cdots & \mathbf{0}_{J,J} & \mathbf{0}_{J,J} & \mathbf{0}_{J,d-\beta-kJ} \\ \vdots & \vdots & \vdots & \ddots & \vdots & \vdots & \vdots \\ \frac{(\beta-J)^{k-1}}{\beta^k}\mathbf{J}_{J,\beta} & \frac{(\beta-J)^{k-2}}{\beta^{k-1}}\mathbf{J}_{J,J} & \frac{(\beta-J)^{k-3}}{\beta^{k-2}}\mathbf{J}_{J,J} & \cdots & \frac{1}{\beta}\mathbf{J}_{J,J} & \mathbf{0}_{J,J} & \mathbf{0}_{J,d-\beta-kJ} \\ \frac{(\beta-J)^k}{\beta^{k+1}}\mathbf{J}_{\beta,\beta} & \frac{(\beta-J)^{k-1}}{\beta^k}\mathbf{J}_{\beta,J} & \frac{(\beta-J)^{k-2}}{\beta^{k-1}}\mathbf{J}_{\beta,J} & \cdots & \frac{\beta-J}{\beta^2}\mathbf{J}_{\beta,J} & \frac{1}{\beta}\mathbf{J}_{\beta,J} & \mathbf{0}_{\beta,d-\beta-kJ} \\ \mathbf{0}_{d-\beta-kJ,\beta} & \mathbf{0}_{d-\beta-kJ,J} & \mathbf{0}_{d-\beta-kJ,J} & \cdots & \mathbf{0}_{d-\beta-kJ,J} & \mathbf{0}_{d-\beta-kJ,J} & \mathbf{I}_{d-\beta-kJ,d-\beta-kJ} \end{pmatrix}$$

When $d - \beta \equiv 0 \pmod{J}$, set $k = \frac{d-\beta}{J}$, we have:

$$\mathbf{A} = \begin{pmatrix} \frac{1}{\beta}\mathbf{J}_{J,\beta} & \mathbf{0}_{J,J} & \mathbf{0}_{J,J} & \cdots & \mathbf{0}_{J,J} & \mathbf{0}_{J,J} \\ \frac{\beta-J}{\beta^2}\mathbf{J}_{J,\beta} & \frac{1}{\beta}\mathbf{J}_{J,J} & \mathbf{0}_{J,J} & \cdots & \mathbf{0}_{J,J} & \mathbf{0}_{J,J} \\ \frac{(\beta-J)^2}{\beta^3}\mathbf{J}_{J,\beta} & \frac{\beta-J}{\beta^2}\mathbf{J}_{J,J} & \frac{1}{\beta}\mathbf{J}_{J,J} & \cdots & \mathbf{0}_{J,J} & \mathbf{0}_{J,J} \\ \vdots & \vdots & \vdots & \ddots & \vdots & \vdots \\ \frac{(\beta-J)^{k-1}}{\beta^k}\mathbf{J}_{J,\beta} & \frac{(\beta-J)^{k-2}}{\beta^{k-1}}\mathbf{J}_{J,J} & \frac{(\beta-J)^{k-3}}{\beta^{k-2}}\mathbf{J}_{J,J} & \cdots & \frac{1}{\beta}\mathbf{J}_{J,J} & \mathbf{0}_{J,J} \\ \frac{(\beta-J)^k}{\beta^{k+1}}\mathbf{J}_{\beta,\beta} & \frac{(\beta-J)^{k-1}}{\beta^k}\mathbf{J}_{\beta,J} & \frac{(\beta-J)^{k-2}}{\beta^{k-1}}\mathbf{J}_{\beta,J} & \cdots & \frac{\beta-J}{\beta^2}\mathbf{J}_{\beta,J} & \frac{1}{\beta}\mathbf{J}_{\beta,J} \end{pmatrix} \tag{10}$$

When $d - \beta \neq 0 (mod\ J)$, set $k = \left\lfloor \frac{d-\beta}{J} \right\rfloor$, we also have $\mathbf{A} :=$

$$
\begin{pmatrix}
\frac{1}{\beta} J_{J,\beta} & \mathbf{0}_{J,J} & \cdots & \mathbf{0}_{J,J} & \mathbf{0}_{J,J} & \mathbf{0}_{J,d-kJ-\beta} \\
\frac{\beta-J}{\beta^2} J_{J,\beta} & \frac{1}{\beta} J_{J,J} & \cdots & \mathbf{0}_{J,J} & \mathbf{0}_{J,J} & \mathbf{0}_{J,d-kJ-\beta} \\
\frac{(\beta-J)^2}{\beta^3} J_{J,\beta} & \frac{\beta-J}{\beta^2} J_{J,J} & \cdots & \mathbf{0}_{J,J} & \mathbf{0}_{J,J} & \mathbf{0}_{J,d-kJ-\beta} \\
\vdots & \vdots & \ddots & \vdots & \vdots & \vdots \\
\frac{(\beta-J)^{k-1}}{\beta^k} J_{J,\beta} & \frac{(\beta-J)^{k-2}}{\beta^{k-1}} J_{J,J} & \cdots & \frac{1}{\beta} J_{J,J} & \mathbf{0}_{J,J} & \mathbf{0}_{J,d-kJ-\beta} \\
\frac{(\beta-J)^k}{\beta^{k+1}} J_{d-kJ-\beta,\beta} & \frac{(\beta-J)^{k-1}}{\beta^k} J_{d-kJ-\beta,J} & \cdots & \frac{\beta-J}{\beta^2} J_{d-kJ-\beta,J} & \frac{1}{\beta} J_{d-kJ-\beta,J} & \mathbf{0}_{d-kJ-\beta,d-kJ-\beta} \\
\frac{(\beta-J)^k \cdot (kJ+2\beta-d)}{\beta^{k+2}} J_{\beta,\beta} & \frac{(\beta-J)^{k-1}(kJ+2\beta-d)}{\beta^{k+1}} J_{\beta,J} & \cdots & \frac{(\beta-J)\cdot(kJ+2\beta-d)}{\beta^3} J_{\beta,J} & \frac{kJ+2\beta-d}{\beta^2} J_{\beta,J} & \frac{1}{\beta} J_{\beta,d-kJ\beta}
\end{pmatrix}
$$

$$(11)$$

3.2 Solutions of the Dynamical System of Pnj-BKZ'

Same proof as that in the Lemma 3 in [14], we know that if $\mathbf{A} \cdot \mathbf{x} = \mathbf{x}$ then $\mathbf{x} \in \text{span} (1, 1, \ldots, 1)^T$.

So it suffices to find one solution of $\mathbf{x} = \mathbf{A} \cdot \mathbf{x} + \mathbf{c}$ to obtain all the solutions. Set $\beta_i' = \beta - 1 - (i - 1\ mod\ J)$ we define $\bar{\mathbf{x}}$ as follows:

$$
\bar{l}_i = \begin{cases} a_i + \frac{1}{\beta_i'} \sum_{j=i}^{i+\beta_i'-1} \bar{l}_j, & i \in [1, \ldots, d-\beta] \\ a_i + \frac{1}{d-i} \sum_{j=i}^{d} \bar{l}_j, & i \in [d-\beta+1, \ldots, d] \end{cases}
$$

and we can get $\bar{\mathbf{x}} :=$

$$
\bar{l}_i = \begin{cases} \frac{\beta_i'}{\beta_i'-1} a_i + \frac{1}{\beta_i'-1} \sum_{j=i+1}^{i+\beta_i'-1} \bar{l}_j, & i \in [1, \ldots, d-\beta] \\ \frac{\beta_i'}{\beta_i'-1} a_i + \frac{1}{d-i-1} \sum_{j=i+1}^{d} \bar{l}_j, & i \in [d-\beta+1, \ldots, d] \end{cases}
$$

$$(12)$$

Lemma 2. *For $\bar{\mathbf{x}}$ as the form shown in Eq. (12), we have $\bar{\mathbf{x}} = \mathbf{A} \cdot \bar{\mathbf{x}} + \mathbf{c}$.*

Proof. Let $\bar{\mathbf{x}}$ as the length vector of initial input vector. After the reduction of first **Pump'**, $\bar{l}_1^{(1)} = a_1 + \frac{1}{\beta} \sum_{j=1}^{\beta} \bar{l}_j^{(0)}$. As the definition of $\bar{\mathbf{x}}$ Eq. (12), we know that $\bar{l}_1^{(1)} = a_1 + \frac{1}{\beta} \sum_{j=1}^{\beta} \bar{l}_j^{(0)} = \bar{l}_1^{(0)}$. Therefore $\bar{l}_1^{(1)} = \bar{l}_1^{(0)}$, there is no change in the value of $\bar{l}_1$ after the reduction of first **Pump'**. Set $\bar{l}_i^{(0)} = \bar{l}_i^{(1)}$, it already hold when $i = 1$. For the case $i + 1$, $\bar{l}_{i+1}^{(1)} = a_{i+1} + \frac{1}{\beta_{i+1}'} \sum_{j=i+1}^{i+\beta_{i+1}'} \bar{l}_j^{(0)'} = a_{i+1} + \frac{1}{\beta_{i+1}'} \left(\sum_{j=1}^{i+\beta_{i+1}'} \bar{l}_j^{(0)} - \sum_{j=1}^{i} \bar{l}_j^{(1)} \right) = a_{i+1} + \frac{1}{\beta_{i+1}'} \left(\sum_{j=1}^{i+\beta_{i+1}'} \bar{l}_j^{(0)} - \sum_{j=1}^{i} \bar{l}_j^{(0)} \right) = a_{i+1} + \frac{1}{\beta_{i+1}'} \left(\sum_{j=i+1}^{i+\beta_{i+1}'} \bar{l}_j^{(0)} \right)$. According to the definition of Eq. (12), we know that $\bar{l}_{i+1}^{(0)} = a_{i+1} + \frac{1}{\beta_{i+1}'} \left(\sum_{j=i+1}^{i+\beta_{i+1}'} \bar{l}_j^{(0)} \right)$. Therefore $\bar{l}_{i+1}^{(1)} = \bar{l}_{i+1}^{(0)}$. Then we inductive proved Lemma 2. $\square$

We now give the lower and upper bounds for the coordinates of the solution $\bar{\mathbf{x}}$.

Lemma 3. *For all* $i \leq d - \beta + 1$, *we have* $2 \cdot \left(\frac{d-i}{\beta-J} - \frac{3}{2}\right) c_{\beta-J+1} \leq \bar{l}_i - \bar{l}_{d-\beta+1} \leq 2 \cdot \frac{d-i}{\beta-J} c_\beta$.

Proof. We first consider the upper bound on $\bar{l}_i - \bar{l}_{d-\beta+1}$. Since $\bar{l}_{d-\beta+1} \geq \cdots \geq \bar{l}_d$, it indicates that:

$$\forall i > d - \beta, \; \bar{l}_i - \bar{l}_{d-\beta+1} \leq 0 \leq 2 \cdot \frac{d-i}{\beta-1} c_\beta$$

According to Eq. (12),

$$\bar{l}_i = \frac{\beta_i'}{\beta_i' - 1} a_i + \frac{1}{\beta_i' - 1} \sum_{j=i+1}^{i+\beta_i'-1} \bar{l}_j, \; i \in [1, \ldots, d - \beta]$$

$\frac{\beta_i'}{\beta_i' - 1}$ decreases monotonically with respect to β_i'. $\beta_i' \in [\beta - J + 1, \ldots, \beta]$. So we obtian that:

$$\bar{l}_i \leq \frac{\beta - J + 1}{\beta - J} c_\beta + \frac{1}{\beta_i' - 1} \sum_{j=i+1}^{i+\beta_i'-1} \bar{l}_j, \; i \in [1, \ldots, d - \beta]$$

The average value $\frac{1}{\beta_i'-1} \sum_{j=i+1}^{i+\beta_i'-1} \bar{l}_j$ is smaller than $\frac{1}{\beta-J} \sum_{j=i+1}^{i+\beta-J} \bar{l}_j$ since $\bar{l}_i$ decreases as the index i increasing and $\beta_i' - 1 \geq \beta - J$. It shows that:

$$\bar{l}_i \leq \frac{\beta - J + 1}{\beta - J} c_\beta + \frac{1}{\beta - J} \sum_{j=i+1}^{i+\beta-J} \bar{l}_j, \; i \in [1, \ldots, d - \beta]$$

Next, we will prove $\bar{l}_i \leq \bar{l}_{d-\beta+1} + 2 \cdot \frac{d-i}{\beta-J} c_\beta$, $\forall i \in [1, \ldots, d]$ by inductive proof. $\forall i \in [d - \beta + 1, \ldots, d]$, $\bar{l}_i \leq \bar{l}_{d-\beta+1} + 2 \cdot \frac{d-i}{\beta-J} c_\beta$ hold. Since $\bar{l}_i \leq \bar{l}_{d-\beta+1}$ and $\frac{d-i}{\beta-J} c_\beta \geq 0$. Then for the case $i = d - \beta$, from $\bar{l}_i \leq \frac{\beta-J+1}{\beta-J} c_\beta + \frac{1}{\beta-J} \sum_{j=i+1}^{i+\beta-J} \bar{l}_j$, we have:

$$\bar{l}_i \leq \frac{\beta - J + 1}{\beta - J} c_\beta + \frac{1}{\beta - J} \sum_{j=i+1}^{i+\beta-J} \left(\bar{l}_{d-\beta+1} + 2 \cdot \frac{d-j}{\beta-J} c_\beta\right)$$

$$\bar{l}_i \leq \frac{\beta - J + 1}{\beta - J} c_\beta + \bar{l}_{d-\beta+1} + 2 \cdot \frac{d - i - \frac{\beta-J+1}{2}}{\beta - J} c_\beta$$

$$\bar{l}_i \leq \bar{l}_{d-\beta+1} + 2 \cdot \frac{d-i}{\beta-J} c_\beta \tag{13}$$

By inductive prove, Eq. (13) hold for $\forall i \in [1, \ldots, d]$.
We now give the lower bound on $\bar{l}_i - \bar{l}_{d-\beta+1}$.
According to Eq. (12),

$$\bar{l}_i = \frac{\beta_i'}{\beta_i' - 1} a_i + \frac{1}{\beta_i' - 1} \sum_{j=i+1}^{i+\beta_i'-1} \bar{l}_j, \ i \in [1, \ldots, d - \beta]$$

As $\bar{l}_j$ is decreased when j is increasing. $\beta_i' \in [\beta - J + 1, \ldots, \beta]$, for $\forall i \in [d-2(\beta-1), \ldots, d-\beta]$, $i + \beta_i' \le i + \beta$, it means $\frac{1}{\beta_i'-1} \sum_{j=i+1}^{i+\beta_i'-1} \bar{l}_j \ge \frac{1}{\beta-1} \sum_{j=i+1}^{i+\beta-1} \bar{l}_j$ and we obtain:

$$\bar{l}_i \ge \frac{\beta}{\beta-1} c_{\beta-J+1} + \frac{1}{\beta-1} \left(\sum_{j=i+1}^{d-\beta} \bar{l}_j + \sum_{j=d-\beta+1}^{i+\beta-1} \bar{l}_j \right), \ i \in [1, \ldots, d-\beta] \quad (14)$$

Next, we will prove $\bar{l}_i \ge \bar{l}_{d-\beta+1} + 2 \cdot \left(\frac{d-i}{\beta-J} - \frac{3}{2} \right) c_{\beta-J+1}$, $\forall i \in [1, \ldots, d-\beta]$ by inductive proof. As $\bar{l}_j$ is decreased when j is increasing, for $\forall i \in [d-2(\beta-1), \ldots, d-\beta-J]$, we get:

$$\frac{1}{i+2\beta-d-1} \sum_{j=d-\beta+1}^{i+\beta-1} \bar{l}_j \ge \frac{1}{\beta-J+1} \sum_{j=d-\beta+1}^{d-J+2} \bar{l}_j$$

$\forall i \in [d-2(\beta-1), \ldots, d-\beta-J]$, since $\bar{l}_{d-\beta+1} = \mathrm{GH}\left(L_{[d-\beta+1:d]} \right) \le \frac{1}{\beta-J+1} \sum_{j=d-\beta+1}^{d-J+2} \bar{l}_j + c_{\beta-J+1} = \mathrm{GH}\left(L_{[d-\beta+1:d-J+2]} \right)$. $\forall i \in [d-2(\beta-1), \ldots, d-\beta-J]$, we also have:

$$\frac{1}{i+2\beta-d-1} \sum_{j=d-\beta+1}^{i+\beta-1} \bar{l}_j \ge \frac{1}{\beta-J+1} \sum_{j=d-\beta+1}^{d-J+2} \bar{l}_j \ge \bar{l}_{d-\beta+1} - c_{\beta-J+1},$$

Since $-1 \ge 2 \cdot \frac{1}{i+2\beta-d-1} \sum_{j=d-\beta+1}^{i+\beta-1} \left(\frac{d-j}{\beta-1} - \frac{3}{2} \right)$

$$\frac{1}{i+2\beta-d-1} \sum_{j=d-\beta+1}^{i+\beta-1} \bar{l}_j \ge \bar{l}_{d-\beta+1} + \frac{2 \cdot c_{\beta-J+1}}{i+2\beta-d-1} \sum_{j=d-\beta+1}^{i+\beta-1} \left(\frac{d-j}{\beta-1} - \frac{3}{2} \right)$$

(15)

$\forall i \in [d-\beta-J, \ldots, d-\beta]$, since $\frac{1}{i+2\beta-d-1} \sum_{j=d-\beta+1}^{i+\beta-1} \bar{l}_j \ge \frac{1}{\beta} \sum_{j=d-\beta+1}^{d} \bar{l}_j = \bar{l}_{d-\beta+1} - c_\beta$ and $\lim_{\beta \to \infty} c_{\beta-J+1} - c_\beta = 0$ $(\beta \gg J)$, it gives that:

$$\frac{1}{i+2\beta-d-1} \sum_{j=d-\beta+1}^{i+\beta-1} \bar{l}_j \ge \frac{1}{\beta} \sum_{j=d-\beta+1}^{d} \bar{l}_j \ge \bar{l}_{d-\beta+1} - c_{\beta-J+1},$$

Then Eq. (15) also hold when $\forall i \in [d-\beta-J, \ldots, d-\beta]$. Therefore, $\forall i \in [d-2(\beta-1), \ldots, d-\beta]$ Eq. (15) hold.

Besides, $\forall j \in [d-2(\beta-1),\ldots,d-\beta]$, $\bar{l}_j > \bar{l}_{d-\beta+1}$ and $\sum_{j=i+1}^{d-\beta}\left(\frac{d-j}{\beta-1}-\frac{3}{2}\right) \leq 0$, we have:

$$\frac{1}{d-\beta-i}\sum_{j=i+1}^{d-\beta}\bar{l}_j \geq \bar{l}_{d-\beta+1} + \frac{2\cdot c_{\beta-J+1}}{d-\beta-i}\sum_{j=i+1}^{d-\beta}\left(\frac{d-j}{\beta-1}-\frac{3}{2}\right) \quad (16)$$

Plugging Eqs. (15) and (16) into Eq. (14), it gives that:

$$\bar{l}_i \geq \frac{\beta}{\beta-1}c_{\beta-J+1} + \frac{1}{\beta-1}\left((\beta-1)\cdot\bar{l}_{d-\beta+1} + 2\cdot c_{\beta-J+1}\sum_{j=i+1}^{i+\beta-1}\left(\frac{d-j}{\beta-1}-\frac{3}{2}\right)\right)$$

$$\bar{l}_i \geq \frac{\beta}{\beta-1}c_{\beta-J+1} + 2\cdot\left(\frac{d-i-\frac{\beta}{2}}{\beta-1}-\frac{3}{2}\right)c_{\beta-J+1} + \bar{l}_{d-\beta+1}$$

$$\bar{l}_i \geq \bar{l}_{d-\beta+1} + 2\cdot\left(\frac{d-i}{\beta-1}-\frac{3}{2}\right)c_{\beta-J+1} \quad (17)$$

By inductive proving remain for $\forall i \in [1,\ldots,d-2(\beta-1)]$, we have $\forall i \in [1,\ldots,d-\beta]$, Eq. (17) hold. $\square$

Next in Lemma 4, we give the upper bound of Hermite factor of the Pnj-BKZ' fully reduced lattice basis: $\ln \mathrm{HF}\,(\mathbf{B}^\infty)$. Here we set $\mathbf{B}^\infty$ as the lattice basis which is fully reduced by Pnj-BKZ'(β, J).

Lemma 4. $\ln \mathrm{HF}\,(\mathbf{B}^\infty) \leq \left(\frac{d-1}{\beta-J}+4\right)c_\beta \lesssim \left(\frac{d-1}{\beta-J}+4\right)\ln\sqrt{\gamma_\beta}$

Proof.

$$\ln \mathrm{HF}\,(\mathbf{B}^\infty) = l_1^\infty - \frac{1}{d}\sum_{i=1}^{d}l_i^\infty = l_1^\infty - l_{d-\beta+1}^\infty + l_{d-\beta+1}^\infty - \frac{1}{d}\sum_{i=1}^{d}l_i^\infty$$

Based on Lemma 3 and $\sum_{i=d-\beta+1}^{d}l_i^\infty = \beta\left(l_{d-\beta+1}^\infty - c_\beta\right) \geq \beta l_{d-\beta+1}^\infty + 2\cdot c_\beta\sum_{i=d-\beta+1}^{d}\left(\frac{d-i}{\beta-1}-\frac{3}{2}\right)$. This implies that:

$$\ln \mathrm{HF}\,(\mathbf{B}^\infty) \leq 2\cdot\frac{d-1}{\beta-J}c_\beta - \frac{1}{d}\left(\sum_{i=1}^{d}(l_i^\infty - l_{d-\beta+1}^\infty)\right)$$

$$\ln \mathrm{HF}\,(\mathbf{B}^\infty) \leq 2\cdot\frac{d-1}{\beta-J}c_\beta - \frac{1}{d}\left(\sum_{i=1}^{d}\left(2\cdot\left(\frac{d-i}{\beta-J}-\frac{3}{2}\right)c_{\beta-J+1}\right)\right)$$

$$\ln \mathrm{HF}\,(\mathbf{B}^\infty) \leq 2\cdot\frac{d-1}{\beta-J}c_\beta - \left(\frac{d-1}{\beta-J}-3\right)c_{\beta-J+1}$$

Meanwhile $\beta >> J$, $c_\beta - c_{\beta - J + 1} = \frac{1}{2} \ln \frac{\beta}{\beta - J + 1} \leq 1$, and $d = O(\beta)$, we can further obtain:

$$\ln \mathrm{HF}\left(\mathbf{B}^\infty\right) \leq \left(\frac{d-1}{\beta - J} + 3\right) c_\beta + \frac{d-1}{\beta - J} \leq \left(\frac{d-1}{\beta - J} + 4\right) c_\beta$$

Besides, $c_\beta = \ln\left(\sqrt{\frac{\beta}{2\pi e}}\right) \lesssim \ln \sqrt{\gamma_\beta}$. Finally we get

$$\ln \mathrm{HF}\left(\mathbf{B}^\infty\right) \leq \left(\frac{d-1}{\beta - J} + 4\right) \ln \sqrt{\gamma_\beta} \tag{18}$$

□

We can see that when $J = 1$, Eq. (18) the upper bound of $\ln \mathrm{HF}\left(\mathbf{B}^\infty\right)$ degenerates to the form in [14].

4   Convergence Speed of the Pnj-BKZ' Dynamical System

In this section, we study the speed of convergence of the discrete-time dynamical system $\bar{\mathbf{x}}_{k+1} := \mathbf{A}\bar{\mathbf{x}}_k + \mathbf{c}$ (where $\mathbf{A}_d$ and $\mathbf{c}_d$ are the d-dimensional $\mathbf{A}$ and $\mathbf{c}$ respectively). According to the principle of the power iteration algorithm, the asymptotic speed of convergence of the sequence $(\mathbf{A}_d^{(k)} \bar{\mathbf{x}})_k$ is determined by the eigenvalue of $\mathbf{A}_d$. And we can bound $\left\| \mathbf{A}_d^{(k)} \bar{\mathbf{x}} \right\| \leq \left\| \mathbf{A}_d^{(k)} \right\| \|\bar{\mathbf{x}}\|$, so we mainly study largest eigenvalue of $\mathbf{A}_d^T \mathbf{A}_d$. In fact the largest eigenvalue of $\mathbf{A}_d^T \mathbf{A}_d$ is 1. In the following subsection we want to show that the second largest singular value is smaller than $1 - \frac{\beta(\beta - J)}{2Jd^2}$.

4.1   Upper Bound of the Second Largest Eigenvalue of $\mathbf{A}_d^T \mathbf{A}_d$

Set $\mathbf{M}\left[a : b, c : d\right]$ to represent the block matrix composed of elements at the intersection of the area from row a to row b of the matrix $\mathbf{M}$ and the area from columns c to column d. Firstly, based on Eq. (10), we give the form of $\mathbf{M}_d = \mathbf{A}_d^T \mathbf{A}_d$ is Eq. (19).

In fact, according to Eq. (10), we give the form of $\mathbf{M}_{\beta + (k+1)J}$ by Eq. (19) that for $k = 0, 1, \ldots, \left\lfloor \frac{d - \beta}{J} \right\rfloor$:

$$\mathbf{M}_{\beta + (k+1)J} = \mathbf{A}_{\beta + (k+1)J}^T \mathbf{A}_{\beta + (k+1)J} =$$

$$\begin{pmatrix} \frac{J}{\beta^2} \mathbf{J}_{\beta,\beta} + \frac{(\beta - J)^2}{\beta^2} \mathbf{M}_{\beta + kJ} \left[1 : \beta, \ 1 : \beta\right] & \frac{\beta - J}{\beta} \mathbf{M}_{\beta + kJ} \left[1 : \beta, \ (\beta - J) : (\beta + kJ)\right] \\ \frac{\beta - J}{\beta} \mathbf{M}_{\beta + kJ} \left[(\beta - J) : (\beta + kJ), \ 1 : \beta\right] & \mathbf{M}_{\beta + kJ} \left[(\beta - J) : (\beta + kJ), \ (\beta - J) : (\beta + kJ)\right] \end{pmatrix} \tag{19}$$

Here $\dim(\mathbf{M}_{\beta + kJ}) = \beta + kJ$.

Proof. To prove Eq. (19), one can compare the form of $\mathbf{M}_{\beta+kJ}$ and $\mathbf{M}_{\beta+(k-1)J}$. According to Eq. (10), the coefficient of the first $\beta \times \beta$ dimensional block in $\mathbf{M}_{\beta+kJ}$ is $\sum_{i=0}^{k-1} \frac{J}{\beta^2} \left(\frac{\beta-J}{\beta}\right)^{2i} + \frac{(\beta-J)^{2k}}{\beta^{2k+1}}$, while the coefficient of the first $\beta \times \beta$ dimensional block in $\mathbf{M}_{\beta+(k-1)J}$ is $\sum_{i=0}^{k-2} \frac{J}{\beta^2} \left(\frac{\beta-J}{\beta}\right)^{2i} + \frac{(\beta-J)^{2(k-1)}}{\beta^{2k-1}}$.

$$\frac{J}{\beta^2} + \left(\frac{\beta-J}{\beta}\right)^2 \left[\sum_{i=0}^{k-2} \frac{J}{\beta^2} \left(\frac{\beta-J}{\beta}\right)^{2i} + \frac{(\beta-J)^{2(k-1)}}{\beta^{2k-1}}\right] = \frac{J}{\beta^2} + \sum_{i=1}^{k-1} \frac{J}{\beta^2} \left(\frac{\beta-J}{\beta}\right)^{2i} +$$

$\frac{(\beta-J)^{2k}}{\beta^{2k+1}} = \sum_{i=0}^{k-1} \frac{J}{\beta^2} \left(\frac{\beta-J}{\beta}\right)^{2i} + \frac{(\beta-J)^{2k}}{\beta^{2k+1}}$. Therefore, the relationship shown in Eq. (19) holds for the first $\beta \times \beta$ dimensional block.

Meanwhile, Eq. (10) shows that

$$\mathbf{M}_{\beta+(k+1)J}\left[1:\beta,\ (\beta-J):(\beta+kJ)\right] = \frac{\beta-J}{\beta}\mathbf{M}_{\beta+kJ}\left[1:\beta,\ (\beta-J):(\beta+kJ)\right]$$

$$\mathbf{M}_{\beta+(k+1)J}\left[(\beta-J):(\beta+kJ),\ 1:\beta\right] = \frac{\beta-J}{\beta}\mathbf{M}_{\beta+kJ}\left[(\beta-J):(\beta+kJ),\ 1:\beta\right]$$

$\mathbf{M}_{\beta+(k+1)J}\left[(\beta-J):(\beta+kJ),\ (\beta-J):(\beta+kJ)\right] = \mathbf{M}_{\beta+kJ}[(\beta-J):(\beta+kJ),\ (\beta-J):(\beta+kJ)]$ □

To give a more intuitive representation of $\mathbf{M}_{\beta+kJ}$ in Eq. (19), following we give the cases of $k=1,2,3$ which are easy to calculate by using Eq. (10).

$$\mathbf{M}_{\beta+J} = \mathbf{A}_{\beta+J}^T \mathbf{A}_{\beta+J} = \begin{pmatrix} \left(\frac{J}{\beta^2} + \frac{(\beta-J)^2}{\beta^3}\right) \mathbf{J}_{\beta,\beta} & \frac{\beta-J}{\beta^2}\mathbf{J}_{\beta,J} \\ \frac{\beta-J}{\beta^2}\mathbf{J}_{J,\beta} & \frac{1}{\beta}\mathbf{J}_{J,J} \end{pmatrix},$$

$$\mathbf{M}_{\beta+2J} = \mathbf{A}_{\beta+2J}^T \mathbf{A}_{\beta+2J} =$$

$$\begin{pmatrix} \left(\frac{J}{\beta^2} + \frac{J(\beta-J)^2}{\beta^4} + \frac{(\beta-J)^4}{\beta^5}\right)\mathbf{J}_{\beta,\beta} & \left(\frac{J(\beta-J)}{\beta^3} + \frac{(\beta-J)^3}{\beta^4}\right)\mathbf{J}_{\beta,J} & \frac{(\beta-J)^2}{\beta^3}\mathbf{J}_{\beta,J} \\ \left(\frac{J(\beta-J)}{\beta^3} + \frac{(\beta-J)^3}{\beta^4}\right)\mathbf{J}_{J,\beta} & \left(\frac{J}{\beta^2} + \frac{(\beta-J)^2}{\beta^3}\right)\mathbf{J}_{J,J} & \frac{\beta-J}{\beta^2}\mathbf{J}_{J,J} \\ \frac{(\beta-J)^2}{\beta^3}\mathbf{J}_{J,\beta} & \frac{\beta-J}{\beta^2}\mathbf{J}_{J,J} & \frac{1}{\beta}\mathbf{J}_{J,J} \end{pmatrix}$$

$\mathbf{M}_{\beta+3J} = \mathbf{A}_{\beta+3J}^T \mathbf{A}_{\beta+3J} = (\mathbf{M}_{\beta+3J}[(1:\beta+3J),(1:\beta+J)],\ \mathbf{M}_{\beta+3J}[(1:\beta+3J),(\beta+J+1):(\beta+3J)])$
$\mathbf{M}_{\beta+3J}[(1:\beta+3J),(1:\beta+J)] =$

$$\begin{pmatrix} \left(\frac{J}{\beta^2} + \frac{J(\beta-J)^2}{\beta^4} + \frac{(\beta-J)^4}{\beta^6} + \frac{(\beta-J)^6}{\beta^7}\right)\mathbf{J}_{\beta,\beta} & \left(\frac{J(\beta-J)}{\beta^3} + \frac{J(\beta-J)^3}{\beta^5} + \frac{(\beta-J)^5}{\beta^6}\right)\mathbf{J}_{\beta,J} \\ \left(\frac{J(\beta-J)}{\beta^3} + \frac{J(\beta-J)^3}{\beta^5} + \frac{(\beta-J)^5}{\beta^6}\right)\mathbf{J}_{J,\beta} & \left(\frac{J}{\beta^2} + \frac{J(\beta-J)^2}{\beta^4} + \frac{(\beta-J)^4}{\beta^5}\right)\mathbf{J}_{J,J} \\ \left(\frac{J(\beta-J)^2}{\beta^4} + \frac{(\beta-J)^4}{\beta^5}\right)\mathbf{J}_{J,\beta} & \left(\frac{J(\beta-J)}{\beta^3} + \frac{(\beta-J)^3}{\beta^4}\right)\mathbf{J}_{J,J} \\ \frac{(\beta-J)^3}{\beta^4}\mathbf{J}_{J,\beta} & \frac{(\beta-J)^2}{\beta^3}\mathbf{J}_{J,J} \end{pmatrix}$$

$$\mathbf{M}_{\beta+3J}[(1:\beta+3J),(\beta+J+1):(\beta+3J)]=$$

$$\begin{pmatrix} \left(\frac{J(\beta-J)^2}{\beta^4}+\frac{(\beta-J)^4}{\beta^5}\right)\mathbf{J}_{\beta,J} & \frac{(\beta-J)^3}{\beta^4}\mathbf{J}_{\beta,J} \\ \left(\frac{J(\beta-J)}{\beta^3}+\frac{(\beta-J)^3}{\beta^4}\right)\mathbf{J}_{J,J} & \frac{(\beta-J)^2}{\beta^3}\mathbf{J}_{J,J} \\ \left(\frac{J}{\beta^2}+\frac{(\beta-J)^2}{\beta^3}\right)\mathbf{J}_{J,J} & \frac{\beta-J}{\beta^2}\mathbf{J}_{.J,J} \\ \frac{\beta-J}{\beta^2}\mathbf{J}_{J,J} & \frac{1}{\beta}\mathbf{J}_{J,J} \end{pmatrix}$$

Let $\chi\left(\mathbf{M}_{\beta+i}\right)(\lambda)=\chi_{\beta+i}(\lambda)$. Next, we give the characteristic polynomial χ_d of $\mathbf{A}_d^T\mathbf{A}_d$. For $i\geq 0$, $d=\beta+i$.

Lemma 5. *For $i\geq 2$, $d=i+\beta$, $\chi_{\beta+i}(\lambda)=$*

$$\begin{cases} 2\lambda\cdot\chi_{\beta+i-1}(\lambda)-\lambda^2\cdot\chi_{\beta+i-2}(\lambda), & i \bmod J\neq 1 \\ \left[\left(1+\left(\frac{\beta-J}{\beta}\right)^2\right)\lambda-\frac{J}{\beta^2}\right]\cdot\chi_{\beta+i-1}(\lambda)-\left(\frac{\beta-J}{\beta}\right)^2\lambda^2\cdot\chi_{\beta+i-2}(\lambda), & i \bmod J\equiv 1 \end{cases}$$

Proof. When $i \bmod J\neq 1$, according to Eq. (19), the form of $\mathbf{M}_{\beta+i}$ is:

$$\mathbf{M}_{\beta+i}=\begin{pmatrix} a\,a & \mathbf{a}^T \\ a\,a & \mathbf{a}^T \\ \mathbf{a}\,\mathbf{a} & \mathbf{M}_{\beta+i-2} \end{pmatrix}$$

Then

$$\chi_{\beta+i}(\lambda)=\begin{vmatrix} 2\lambda & -\lambda & \mathbf{0} \\ -\lambda & \lambda-a & -\mathbf{a}^T \\ \mathbf{0} & -\mathbf{a} & \mathbf{M}_{\beta+i-2}-\lambda\mathbf{I}_{\beta+i-2} \end{vmatrix}$$

$$\chi_{\beta+i}(\lambda)=2\lambda\cdot\chi_{\beta+i-1}(\lambda)-\lambda^2\cdot\chi_{\beta+i-2}(\lambda)$$

When $i \bmod J=1$, the form of $\mathbf{M}_{\beta+i}$ is:

$$\mathbf{M}_{\beta+i}=\begin{pmatrix} a & b & \mathbf{b}^T \\ b & c & \mathbf{b'}^T \\ \mathbf{b} & \mathbf{b'} & \mathbf{M}_{\beta+i-2} \end{pmatrix}$$

Here according to Eq. (19), $\mathbf{b}=\frac{\beta-J}{\beta}\mathbf{b'}$, $b=\frac{\beta-J}{\beta}c$, $a=\frac{J}{\beta^2}+\frac{\beta-J}{\beta}b$, so $a=\frac{J}{\beta^2}+\left(\frac{\beta-J}{\beta}\right)^2 c$. Then $\chi\left(\mathbf{M}_{\beta+i}\right)(\lambda)$ is:

$$\chi_{\beta+i}(\lambda)=\begin{vmatrix} \left[1+\left(\frac{\beta-J}{\beta}\right)^2\right]\lambda-\frac{J}{\beta^2} & -\frac{\beta-J}{\beta}\lambda & \mathbf{0} \\ -\frac{\beta-J}{\beta}\lambda & \lambda-c & -\mathbf{b'}^T \\ \mathbf{0} & -\mathbf{b'} & \mathbf{M}_{\beta+i-2}-\lambda\mathbf{I}_{\beta+i-2} \end{vmatrix}$$

$$\chi_{\beta+i}(\lambda)=\left[\left(1+\left(\frac{\beta-J}{\beta}\right)^2\right)\lambda-\frac{J}{\beta^2}\right]\cdot\chi_{\beta+i-1}(\lambda)-\left(\frac{\beta-J}{\beta}\right)^2\lambda^2\cdot\chi_{\beta+i-2}(\lambda)$$

□

Lemma 6. *For* $J \geq i \geq 0$, $\chi_{\beta+i}(\lambda) = \lambda^{\beta+i-2}(\lambda-1)\left(\lambda - \frac{i^2}{\beta^2}\right)$

Proof. $\mathbf{A}_\beta^T \mathbf{A}_\beta = \mathbf{A}_\beta$ and $\dim \ker(\mathbf{A}_\beta) = \beta - 1$, so $\lambda^{\beta-1} \mid \chi_\beta(\lambda)$. Besides, $\mathrm{Tr}(\mathbf{A}_\beta) = 1$ thus it implies that $\chi_\beta(\lambda) = \lambda^{\beta-1}(\lambda-1)$. Meanwhile, $\forall i \in \{1,2,...,J\}$,

$$\mathbf{A}_{\beta+i} = \begin{pmatrix} \frac{1}{\beta}\mathbf{J}_{i,\beta} & \mathbf{0}_{i,i} \\ \frac{\beta-i}{\beta^2}\mathbf{J}_{\beta,\beta} & \frac{1}{\beta}\mathbf{J}_{\beta,i} \end{pmatrix},$$

$$\mathbf{A}_{\beta+i}^T \mathbf{A}_{\beta+i} = \mathbf{M}_{\beta+i} = \begin{pmatrix} \left(\frac{i}{\beta^2} + \frac{(\beta-i)^2}{\beta^3}\right)\mathbf{J}_{\beta,\beta} & \frac{\beta-i}{\beta^2}\mathbf{J}_{\beta,i} \\ \frac{\beta-i}{\beta^2}\mathbf{J}_{i,\beta} & \frac{1}{\beta}\mathbf{J}_{i,i} \end{pmatrix},$$

We grt that $\mathrm{Tr}(\mathbf{M}_{\beta+i}) = \frac{i}{\beta} + \frac{(\beta-i)^2}{\beta^2} + \frac{i}{\beta} = 1 + \frac{i^2}{\beta^2}$ and $\dim \ker(\mathbf{A}_{\beta+i}) = \beta + i - 2$, so $\lambda^{\beta+i-2} \mid \chi_{\beta+i}(\lambda)$. Meanwhile, it always has that $\mathbf{A}_{\beta+i}^T \mathbf{A}_{\beta+i} \cdot (1,\cdots,1)^T = (1,\cdots,1)^T$. Therefore, we obtain that for $i \geq 0$, $\chi_{\beta+i}(\lambda) = \lambda^{\beta+i-2}(\lambda-1)\left(\lambda - \frac{i^2}{\beta^2}\right)$. □

Since $J \ll \beta$, $1 = \lim_{\beta\to\infty}\left(\frac{\beta-J}{\beta}\right)^2$ and $0 = \lim_{\beta\to\infty}\frac{J}{\beta^2}$, we give the following Heuristic 4.

Heuristic 4. *For* $i \geq 2$:

$$\chi_{\beta+i}(\lambda) = \left[\left(1 + \left(\frac{\beta-J}{\beta}\right)^2\right)\lambda - \frac{J}{\beta^2}\right]\cdot\chi_{\beta+i-1}(\lambda) - \left(\frac{\beta-J}{\beta}\right)^2\lambda^2\cdot\chi_{\beta+i-2}(\lambda).$$

When Heuristic 4 is hold, we can prove that Heuristic 4 satisfies a second order recurrence formula.

Lemma 7. *For* $d \geq \beta$, *the largest root of* $\chi_d(\lambda)$ *is within*

$$\left[\frac{1}{J + \frac{2\beta(\beta-J)\pi^2}{J(d-\beta)^2}}, 1 - \frac{\beta(\beta-J)}{2Jd^2}\right]$$

The proof of the following result relies on several changes of variables to link the polynomials $\chi_d(\lambda)$ to the Chebyshev polynomials of the second kind.

Proof. Let $\bar{\chi}_i(\lambda) = \lambda^i \chi_i\left(\frac{1}{\lambda}\right)$, we have: $\bar{\chi}(\mathbf{M}_{\beta+i})(\lambda) = \lambda^i \cdot \chi(\mathbf{M}_{\beta+i})\left(\frac{1}{\lambda}\right)$,

$$\bar{\chi}(\mathbf{M}_{\beta+i})(\lambda) = \lambda^i \cdot \left[\left(1 + \left(\frac{\beta-J}{\beta}\right)^2\right)\frac{1}{\lambda} - \frac{J}{\beta^2}\right]\cdot\chi(\mathbf{M}_{\beta+i-1})\left(\frac{1}{\lambda}\right) - \lambda^i \cdot$$

$$\left(\frac{\beta-J}{\beta}\right)^2\frac{1}{\lambda^2}\cdot\chi(\mathbf{M}_{\beta+i-2})\left(\frac{1}{\lambda}\right)$$

$$\bar{\chi}(\mathbf{M}_{\beta+i})(\lambda) = \lambda^{i-1}\cdot\left[1 + \left(\frac{\beta-J}{\beta}\right)^2 - \frac{J}{\beta^2}\lambda\right]\cdot\chi(\mathbf{M}_{\beta+i-1})\left(\frac{1}{\lambda}\right) - \left(\frac{\beta-J}{\beta}\right)^2\lambda^{i-2}\cdot$$

$$\chi(\mathbf{M}_{\beta+i-2})\left(\frac{1}{\lambda}\right)$$

$$\bar{\chi}(\mathbf{M}_{\beta+i})(\lambda) = \left[1 + \left(\frac{\beta-J}{\beta}\right)^2 - \frac{J}{\beta^2}\lambda\right]\cdot\bar{\chi}(\mathbf{M}_{\beta+i-1})(\lambda) - \left(\frac{\beta-J}{\beta}\right)^2\cdot\bar{\chi}(\mathbf{M}_{\beta+i-2})(\lambda)$$

Let $\tau\left(\lambda'\right) = \left(\frac{J}{\beta^2}\right)^{-1}\left[\left(2\lambda'\right)\cdot\frac{\beta-J}{\beta} - \left[1+\left(\frac{\beta-J}{\beta}\right)^2\right] + \frac{J}{\beta^2}\right]$, $\psi\left(\mathbf{M}_{\beta+i}\right)\left(\lambda'\right) =$ $\left(\frac{\beta}{\beta-J}\right)^i\frac{\bar{\chi}(\mathbf{M}_{\beta+i})\left[1-\tau(\lambda')\right]}{\tau(\lambda')}$, we obtain $\psi\left(\mathbf{M}_{\beta+i}\right)\left(\lambda'\right) =$

$$\left(\frac{\beta}{\beta-J}\right)^{i-1}\left(\frac{\beta}{\beta-J}\left\{\left[1+\left(\frac{\beta-J}{\beta}\right)^2 - \frac{J}{\beta^2}\left(1-\tau\left(\lambda'\right)\right)\right]\right\}\right)\frac{\bar{\chi}\left(\mathbf{M}_{\beta+i-1}\right)\left[1-\tau\left(\lambda'\right)\right]}{\tau\left(\lambda'\right)}$$

$$-\left(\frac{\beta}{\beta-J}\right)^{i-2}\frac{\bar{\chi}\left(\mathbf{M}_{\beta+i-2}\right)\left[1-\tau\left(\lambda'\right)\right]}{\tau\left(\lambda'\right)}$$

$$\psi\left(\mathbf{M}_{\beta+i}\right)\left(\lambda'\right) = 2\lambda'\cdot\psi\left(\mathbf{M}_{\beta+i-1}\right)\left(\lambda'\right) - \psi\left(\mathbf{M}_{\beta+i-2}\right)\left(\lambda'\right) \qquad (20)$$

Next we will give the initial two values of $\psi\left(\mathbf{M}_{\beta+i}\right)$: $\psi\left(\mathbf{M}_{\beta}\right)$ and $\psi\left(\mathbf{M}_{\beta+1}\right)$. Then we can use Eq. (20) to represent all characteristic polynomials of different dimensions-d of $\mathbf{M}_d$, $d = \beta + i$, for $i \geq 0$.

Based on Lemma 6, for $J \geq i \geq 0$, $\bar{\chi}_{\beta+i}\left(\lambda\right) = \lambda^{\beta+i}\cdot\frac{1}{\lambda^{\beta+i-2}}\left(\frac{1}{\lambda}-1\right)\left(\frac{1}{\lambda}-\frac{i^2}{\beta^2}\right)$.

$$J \geq i \geq 0, \quad \bar{\chi}_{\beta+i}\left(\lambda\right) = \left(1-\lambda\right)\left(1-\frac{i^2}{\beta^2}\lambda\right)$$

Specifically, $\bar{\chi}_{\beta}\left(\lambda\right) = 1 - \lambda$. Therefore, $\psi\left(\mathbf{M}_{\beta}\right)\left(\lambda'\right) = \left(\frac{\beta}{\beta-J}\right)^0\frac{\bar{\chi}_{\beta}\left[1-\tau(\lambda')\right]}{\tau(\lambda')}$ $= 1\cdot\frac{1-\left[1-\tau(\lambda')\right]}{\tau(\lambda')} = 1$.

Besides, since $\chi_{\beta+1}\left(\lambda\right) = \lambda^{\beta-1}\left(\lambda-1\right)\left(\lambda-\frac{1}{\beta^2}\right)$, $\frac{1}{\beta^2} \leq \frac{J}{\beta^2} < 1$, both matrix with eigenvalue $\lambda = \frac{1}{\beta^2}$ and matrix with eigenvalue $\lambda = \frac{J}{\beta^2}$ are Lyapunov asymptotically stable according to Lyapunov stability theory (First Method). Therefore, even if we set $\chi_{\beta+1}\left(\lambda\right) = \lambda^{\beta-1}\left(\lambda-1\right)\left(\lambda-\frac{J}{\beta^2}\right)$, it still asymptotically stable. Then we have $\bar{\chi}_{\beta+1}\left(\lambda\right) = 1 - \lambda$ and $\bar{\chi}_{\beta}\left(\lambda\right) = \left(1-\lambda\right)\left(1-\frac{J}{\beta^2}\lambda\right)$.

$$\psi\left(\mathbf{M}_{\beta+1}\right)\left(\lambda'\right) = \left(\frac{\beta}{\beta-J}\right)^1\frac{\bar{\chi}_{\beta+1}\left[1-\tau\left(\lambda'\right)\right]}{\tau\left(\lambda'\right)}$$

$$\psi\left(\mathbf{M}_{\beta+1}\right)\left(\lambda'\right) = \frac{\beta}{\beta-J}\cdot\frac{1-\left[1-\tau\left(\lambda'\right)\right]}{\tau\left(\lambda'\right)}\cdot\left[1-\frac{J}{\beta^2}\left(1-\tau\left(\lambda'\right)\right)\right]$$

$$\psi\left(\mathbf{M}_{\beta+1}\right)\left(\lambda'\right) = \frac{\beta}{\beta-J}\left[1-\frac{J}{\beta^2}+\frac{J}{\beta^2}\tau\left(\lambda'\right)\right]$$

$$\psi\left(\mathbf{M}_{\beta+1}\right)\left(\lambda'\right) = \frac{\beta}{\beta-J}\left\{1-\frac{J}{\beta^2}+\left(2\lambda'\right)\cdot\frac{\beta-J}{\beta}-\left[1+\left(\frac{\beta-J}{\beta}\right)^2\right]+\frac{J}{\beta^2}\right\}$$

$$\psi\left(\mathbf{M}_{\beta+1}\right)\left(\lambda'\right) = 2\lambda'-\frac{\beta-J}{\beta}$$

For $i \geq 0$, let U_i be the the sequence of Chebyshev polynomials of the second kind, $U_0 = 0$, $U_1 = 1$, $U_2 = 2\lambda'$, $i \geq 2$, $U_i = 2\lambda' U_{i-1} - U_{i-2}$. Meanwhile, we know that $\psi(\mathbf{M}_\beta)(\lambda') = 1$, $\psi(\mathbf{M}_{\beta+1})(\lambda') = 2\lambda' - \frac{\beta - J}{\beta}$.

Then for $i \geq 2$, based on Eq. (20), we obtain $\psi(\mathbf{M}_{\beta+i})(\lambda') = U_{i+1} - \frac{\beta - J}{\beta} U_i$. Finally, we get $\psi(\mathbf{M}_d)(\lambda') = U_{d-\beta+1} - \frac{\beta - J}{\beta} U_{d-\beta}$.

Chebyshev polynomials satisfying that:

$$\forall d \geq 0, \forall x \in \mathbb{R} \setminus \{2k\pi; kx \in \mathbb{Z}\}, U_d(\cos x) = \frac{\sin(nx)}{\sin x}.$$

Since $\psi(\mathbf{M}_d)\left(\cos \frac{\pi}{d-\beta}\right) = U_{d-\beta+1}(\cos \frac{\pi}{d-\beta}) - \frac{\beta - J}{\beta} U_{d-\beta}(\cos \frac{\pi}{d-\beta}) = \frac{\sin(\frac{\pi(d-\beta+1)}{d-\beta})}{\sin \frac{\pi}{d-\beta}} - 0$ and $\frac{\sin(\frac{\pi(d-\beta+1)}{d-\beta})}{\sin \frac{\pi}{d-\beta}} < 0$, we know $\psi(\mathbf{M}_d)\left(\cos \frac{\pi}{d-\beta}\right) < 0$.

$\psi(\mathbf{M}_d)\left(\cos \frac{\pi}{2(d-\beta+1)}\right) = U_{d-\beta+1}(\cos \frac{\pi}{2(d-\beta+1)}) - \frac{\beta - J}{\beta} U_{d-\beta}(\cos \frac{\pi}{2(d-\beta+1)}) = \frac{1}{\sin \frac{\pi}{2(d-\beta+1)}} - \frac{\beta - J}{\beta} \cdot \frac{\sin(\frac{\pi(d-\beta)}{2(d-\beta+1)})}{\sin \frac{\pi}{2(d-\beta+1)}}$ and $1 > \sin(\frac{\pi(d-\beta)}{2(d-\beta+1)})$, we get that:

$$\psi(\mathbf{M}_d)\left(\cos \frac{\pi}{2(d-\beta+1)}\right) > 0.$$

Then using intermediate value theorem, there exists $\lambda'_0 \in \left[\cos \frac{\pi}{d-\beta}, \cos \frac{\pi}{2(d-\beta+1)}\right]$ such that $\psi(\mathbf{M}_d)(\lambda'_0) = 0$, and $\psi(\mathbf{M}_d)(\lambda') > 0$ for all $\lambda' \in (\lambda'_0, 1)$. It indicates that

$$\bar{\chi}_d(1 - \tau(\lambda'_0)) = \left(\frac{\beta - J}{\beta}\right)^{d-\beta} \tau(\lambda'_0)\psi(\mathbf{M}_d)(\lambda'_0) = 0,$$

hence $\lambda_0 = (1 - \tau(\lambda'_0))^{-1}$ is a root of $\chi_d(\lambda)$. Since the image of $(\lambda'_0, 1)$ by $\lambda' \mapsto (1 - \tau(\lambda'))^{-1}$ is $(\lambda_0, 1)$, we obtain that λ_0 is the largest root of $\chi_d(\lambda)$ smaller than 1. Next we give the upper bound of λ_0.

$\cos \frac{\pi}{d-\beta} \leq \lambda'_0 \leq \cos \frac{\pi}{2(d-\beta+1)} \leq \cos \frac{\pi}{2d}, 1 - \frac{\pi^2}{(d-\beta)^2} \leq \lambda'_0 \leq 1 - \frac{2\pi^2}{17d^2}, 1 - \tau(\lambda') = (-2\lambda')\frac{\beta(\beta - J)}{J} + \frac{\beta^2}{J}\left[1 + \left(\frac{\beta - J}{\beta}\right)^2\right]$, it implies that:

$$1 - \tau(\lambda') \leq \left(\frac{\beta^2}{J}\right)\left[1 + \left(\frac{\beta - J}{\beta}\right)^2\right] - 2\frac{\beta(\beta - J)}{J}\left(1 - \frac{\pi^2}{(d-\beta)^2}\right)$$

Combining with $\left(\frac{\beta^2}{J}\right)\left[1 + \left(\frac{\beta - J}{\beta}\right)^2\right] - 2\frac{\beta(\beta - J)}{J} = J$, it gives

$$1 - \tau(\lambda') \leq J + \frac{2\beta(\beta - J)\pi^2}{J(d-\beta)^2} \tag{21}$$

$$\left(\frac{\beta^2}{J}\right)\left[1 + \left(\frac{\beta - J}{\beta}\right)^2\right] - 2\frac{\beta(\beta - J)}{J}\left(1 - \frac{2\pi^2}{17d^2}\right) \leq 1 - \tau(\lambda')$$

Since $1 \leq \left(\frac{\beta^2}{J}\right)\left[1 + \left(\frac{\beta - J}{\beta}\right)^2\right] - 2\frac{\beta(\beta - J)}{J} = J$, we have:

$$1 + \frac{\beta(\beta - J)}{J}\frac{2\pi^2}{17d^2} \leq 1 + 2\frac{\beta(\beta - J)}{J}\frac{2\pi^2}{17d^2} \leq 1 - \tau(\lambda')$$

Combining this with Eq. (21), we can obtain that

$$\frac{1}{J + \frac{2\beta(\beta - J)\pi^2}{J(d - \beta)^2}} \leq \frac{1}{1 - \tau(\lambda')} \leq \frac{1}{1 + \frac{\beta(\beta - J)}{J}\frac{2\pi^2}{17d^2}} \leq 1 - \frac{\beta(\beta - J)}{J}\frac{1}{2d^2}.$$

In addition, set $\varphi_d(\lambda) = \frac{\chi_d(\lambda)}{\lambda - 1}$, based on Heuristic 4, we have $\varphi_d(1) \neq 0$, for $d \geq \beta$, which means that 1 is never a multiple root of $\chi_d(\lambda)$. $\square$

5   Upper Bound of the Length of the Pnj-BKZ' Reduction Vector and Convergence Speed

In this section, we combined the conclusion in Lemma 4 and Lemma 7 to prove the following theorem which describes the upper bound of the length of fully Pnj-BKZ' reduced vector and the convergence speed of Pnj-BKZ' reduction.

Theorem 1. *Under SMA, there exists $C > 0$ such that the following holds for all d, β and J. Let $(\mathbf{a}_i)_{i \leq d}$ be the input of Pnj-BKZ'(β, J). Set L be the lattice spanned by $(\mathbf{a}_i)_{i \leq d}$. After $C\frac{2Jd^2}{\beta(\beta - J)}\left(\ln d + \ln \ln \max_i \frac{\|\mathbf{a}_i^*\|}{(\det L)^{1/d}}\right)$ tours reduction of Pnj-BKZ'(β, J), the output lattice basis $(\mathbf{b}_i)_{i \leq d}$ satisfies $\|\mathbf{x} - \mathbf{x}^\infty\|_2 \leq 1$, here $\mathbf{x} = (x_1, \ldots, x_d)^T$ and $x_i = \ln \frac{\|\mathbf{b}_i^*\|}{(\det L)^{1/d}}$ for all i and $\mathbf{x}^\infty$ is the unique solution of the equation $\mathbf{x}^\infty = \mathbf{A}\mathbf{x}^\infty + \mathbf{c}$. Specifically $\|\mathbf{b}_1\| \leq 2\gamma_\beta^{\frac{d-1}{2(\beta - J)} + 2} \cdot (\det L)^{\frac{1}{d}}$.*

Proof. Let $\left(\mathbf{b}_i^{(k)}\right)_{i \leq d}$ be the basis after k tours reduction of Pnj-BKZ'(β, J) and set $\mathbf{x}_i^{(k)} = \ln \frac{\|\mathbf{b}_i^{(k)*}\|}{(\det L)^{1/d}}$, we have $\mathbf{x}^{(k)} - \mathbf{x}^{(\infty)} = \mathbf{A}^k\left(\mathbf{x}^{(k)} - \mathbf{x}^{(\infty)}\right)$. Both $\mathbf{x}^{(0)}$ and $\mathbf{x}^{(\infty)} \in \mathrm{Span}\,(1, \ldots, 1)^\perp$. Using $\mathbf{A}_\varepsilon$ be the restriction of $\mathbf{A}$ to $\mathrm{Span}\,(1, \ldots, 1)^\perp$,

$$\left\|\mathbf{x}^{(k)} - \mathbf{x}^{(\infty)}\right\|_2 \leq \|\mathbf{A}_\varepsilon\|_2^k \left\|\mathbf{x}^{(0)} - \mathbf{x}^{(\infty)}\right\|_2 = \rho\left(\mathbf{A}_\varepsilon^T \mathbf{A}_\varepsilon\right)^{k/2} \left\|\mathbf{x}^{(0)} - \mathbf{x}^{(\infty)}\right\|_2$$

By Lemma 7 we know the largest eigenvalue $\mathbf{A}_\varepsilon$ is bounded in Lemma 7 by $1 - \frac{\beta(\beta - J)}{2Jd^2}$. Then we obtain that

$$\left\|\mathbf{x}^{(k)} - \mathbf{x}^{(\infty)}\right\|_2 \leq \left(1 - \frac{\beta(\beta - J)}{2Jd^2}\right)^{k/2} \left\|\mathbf{x}^{(0)} - \mathbf{x}^{(\infty)}\right\|_2$$

Meanwhile the tern $\left\|\mathbf{x}^{(0)} - \mathbf{x}^{(\infty)}\right\|_2$ can be bounded by $\left\|\mathbf{x}^{(0)}\right\|_2$ $+ \left\|\mathbf{x}^{(\infty)}\right\|_2 \leq \left(\ln \max_i \frac{\|\mathbf{a}_i^*\|}{(\det L)^{1/d}} d\right) + d^{O(1)}$, then $\ln \left\|\mathbf{x}^{(0)} - \mathbf{x}^{(\infty)}\right\|_2 = O$ $\left(\ln d + \ln \ln \max_i \frac{\|\mathbf{a}_i^*\|}{(\det L)^{1/d}}\right)$.

There exists constant number C to make $\left\|\mathbf{x}^{(k)} - \mathbf{x}^{(\infty)}\right\|_2 \leq 1$ when $k \geq$ $C \frac{2Jd^2}{\beta(\beta-J)} \left(\ln d + \ln \ln \max_i \frac{\|\mathbf{a}_i^*\|}{(\det L)^{1/d}}\right)$.

Next we give the uppper bound of $\left\|\mathbf{b}_1^{(k)}\right\|$. By Lemma 4, $\ln \mathrm{HF}\,(\mathbf{B}^\infty) \lesssim$ $\left(\frac{d-1}{\beta-J} + 4\right) \ln \sqrt{\gamma_\beta}$, i.e. $\mathbf{x}_1^{(\infty)} \lesssim \left(\frac{d-1}{\beta-J} + 4\right) \ln \sqrt{\gamma_\beta}$. Using the inequality $\mathbf{x}_1^{(k)} \leq$ $\mathbf{x}_1^{(\infty)} + 1$, we directly get the upper bound of $\left\|\mathbf{b}_1^{(k)}\right\| \leq \gamma_\beta^{\frac{d-1}{2(\beta-J)}+2} \cdot (\det L)^{\frac{1}{d}}$. $\square$

6 Verification Experiments

From Sect. 5, after running sufficient tours of Pnj-BKZ(β, J), the first vector $\mathbf{b}_1$ in lattice basis output from Pnj-BKZ(β, J): $\frac{\|\mathbf{b}_1\|}{(\det L)^{\frac{1}{d}}} \leq \gamma_\beta^{\frac{d-1}{2(\beta-J)}+2}$. In this part, we show that the actual the root Hermit factor of the Pnj-BKZ reduced lattice basis $\left(\frac{\|\mathbf{b}_1\|}{(\det L)^{\frac{1}{d}}}\right)^{\frac{1}{d}}$ is indeed smaller than the theoretical upper bound $\gamma_\beta^{\frac{d-1}{2(\beta-J)d}+\frac{2}{d}}$, which we give in Sect. 5. See Figs. 1 and 2 for more details.

The x-axis in Figs. 1 and 2 is the number of Pnj-BKZ(β, J) that have been run. The y-axis in Figs. 1 and 2 is the root of the Hermit factor. The red line in Figs. 1 and 2 is the theoretical upper bound $\gamma_\beta^{\frac{d-1}{2(\beta-J)d}+\frac{2}{d}}$ of the root of Hermit factor for a Pnj-BKZ(β, J) reduced lattice basis. The blue points in Figs. 1 and 2 are the root of the Hermit factor of lattice basis reduced by each tour of Pnj-BKZ(β, J).

From Figs. 1 and 2, we can see that the actual reduction effort of Pnj-BKZ is consistent with our theoretical estimation. Specifically, the root Hermite factor of the lattice basis reduced by each tour of Pnj-BKZ(β, J) will gradually decrease and finally is smaller than our theoretical upper bound of root Hermite factor $\gamma_\beta^{\frac{d-1}{2(\beta-J)d}+\frac{2}{d}}$. In addition, the theoretical upper bound is very close to the actual value for the small block size reduction testing. The test results of larger blocks show that the actual reduction effect is better than the theoretical upper bound. It may be caused by the contraction of our theoretical derivation, and we will give tighter theoretical upper bounds in the future.

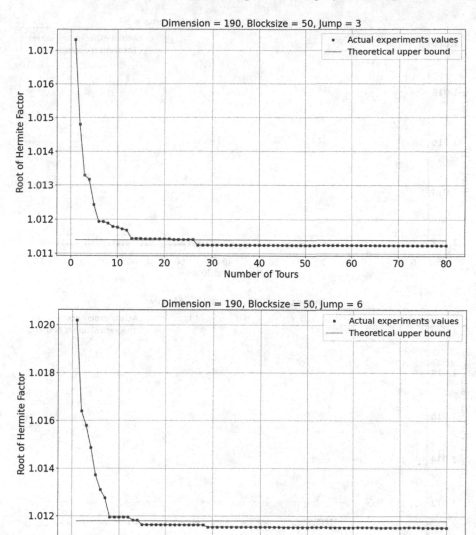

Fig. 1. Actual experiments value and theoretical upper bound of the root Hermit factor during Pnj-BKZ reduction for TU Darmstadt's SVP challenges (Dimensions 190). We test also 5 times for each reduction parameters.

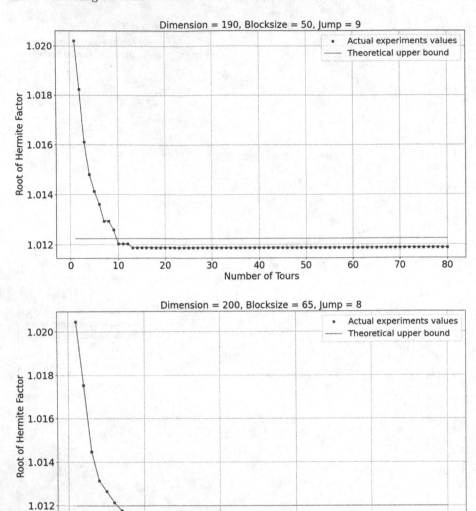

Fig. 2. Actual experiments value and theoretical upper bound of the root Hermit factor during Pnj-BKZ reduction for TU Darmstadt's SVP challenges (Dimensions 190-200). We test also 5 times for each reduction parameters.

References

1. PQC Standardization Process: Fourth Round Candidate Announcement (2022). https://csrc.nist.gov/News/2022/pqc-candidates-to-be-standardized-and-round-4
2. Becker, A., Gama, N., Joux, A: Speeding-up lattice sieving without increasing the memory, using sub-quadratic nearest neighbor search. In: IACR Cryptology ePrint, pp. 2015/522. IACR Cryptology ePrint Archive, (2015)
3. Albrecht, M.R., Ducas, L., Herold, G., Kirshanova, E., Postlethwaite, E.W., Stevens, M.: The general sieve kernel and new records in lattice reduction. In: Ishai, Y., Rijmen, V. (eds.) EUROCRYPT 2019. LNCS, vol. 11477, pp. 717–746. Springer, Cham (2019). https://doi.org/10.1007/978-3-030-17656-3_25
4. Aono, Y., Wang, Y., Hayashi, T., Takagi, T.: Improved progressive BKZ algorithms and their precise cost estimation by sharp simulator. In: Fischlin, M., Coron, J.-S. (eds.) EUROCRYPT 2016. LNCS, vol. 9665, pp. 789–819. Springer, Heidelberg (2016). https://doi.org/10.1007/978-3-662-49890-3_30
5. Avanzi, R., et al.: Kyber(Round 3), p. 42 (2020)
6. Becker, A., Ducas, L., Gama, N., Laarhoven, T.: New directions in nearest neighbor searching with applications to lattice sieving. In: Proceedings of the Twenty-Seventh Annual ACM-SIAM Symposium on Discrete Algorithms, SODA 2016, pp. 10–24. Society for Industrial and Applied Mathematics, USA (2016)
7. Chen, Y., Nguyen, P.Q.: BKZ 2.0: better lattice security estimates. In: Lee, D.H., Wang, X. (eds.) ASIACRYPT 2011. LNCS, vol. 7073, pp. 1–20. Springer, Heidelberg (2011). https://doi.org/10.1007/978-3-642-25385-0_1
8. Ducas, L.: Shortest vector from lattice sieving: a few dimensions for free. In: Nielsen, J.B., Rijmen, V. (eds.) EUROCRYPT 2018. LNCS, vol. 10820, pp. 125–145. Springer, Cham (2018). https://doi.org/10.1007/978-3-319-78381-9_5
9. Ducas, L., Eike Kiltz, T.L., Lyubashevsky, V., Schwabe, P., Seiler, G., Stehlé, D.: Dilithium(Round 3). NIST PQC probject (2020)
10. Ducas, L., Stevens, M., van Woerden, W.: Advanced lattice sieving on gpus, with tensor cores. In: Canteaut, A., Standaert, F.-X. (eds.) EUROCRYPT 2021. LNCS, vol. 12697, pp. 249–279. Springer, Cham (2021). https://doi.org/10.1007/978-3-030-77886-6_9
11. Gama, N., Nguyen, P.Q.: Finding short lattice vectors within mordell's inequality. In: Proceedings of the Fortieth Annual ACM Symposium on Theory of Computing, STOC 2008, pp. 207–216. Association for Computing Machinery, New York, NY, USA (2008)
12. Gama, N., Nguyen, P.Q., Regev, O.: Lattice enumeration using extreme pruning. In: Gilbert, H. (ed.) EUROCRYPT 2010. LNCS, vol. 6110, pp. 257–278. Springer, Heidelberg (2010). https://doi.org/10.1007/978-3-642-13190-5_13
13. Gama, N., Nguyen, P.Q., Regev, O.: Lattice enumeration using extreme pruning. In: Gilbert, H. (ed.) EUROCRYPT 2010. LNCS, vol. 6110, pp. 257–278. Springer, Heidelberg (2010). https://doi.org/10.1007/978-3-642-13190-5_13
14. Hanrot, G., Pujol, X., Stehlé, D.: Terminating bkz. In: IACR Cryptol. ePrint Arch, vol. 2011, p. 198 (2011)
15. Herold, G., Kirshanova, E.: Improved algorithms for the approximate k-list problem in euclidean norm. In: Fehr, S. (ed.) PKC 2017. LNCS, vol. 10174, pp. 16–40. Springer, Heidelberg (2017). https://doi.org/10.1007/978-3-662-54365-8_2

16. Herold, G., Kirshanova, E., Laarhoven, T.: Speed-ups and time–memory trade-offs for tuple lattice sieving. In: Abdalla, M., Dahab, R. (eds.) PKC 2018. LNCS, vol. 10769, pp. 407–436. Springer, Cham (2018). https://doi.org/10.1007/978-3-319-76578-5_14

17. Laarhoven, T., Mariano, A.: Progressive lattice sieving. In: Lange, T., Steinwandt, R. (eds.) PQCrypto 2018. LNCS, vol. 10786, pp. 292–311. Springer, Cham (2018). https://doi.org/10.1007/978-3-319-79063-3_14

18. Lenstra, A.K., Lenstra, H.W., Lovász, L.: Factoring polynomials with rational coefficients. Math. Ann. **261**(4), 515–534 (1982)

19. Li, J., Nguyen, P.Q.: A complete analysis of the BKZ lattice reduction algorithm. In: IACR Cryptol. ePrint Arch, vol. 2020, p. 1237 (2020)

20. Li, J., Walter, M.: Improving convergence and practicality of slide-type reductions. Inf. Comput. **291**, 105012 (2023)

21. Micciancio, D., Voulgaris, P.: Faster exponential time algorithms for the shortest vector problem. In: Proceedings of the Twenty-First Annual ACM-SIAM Symposium on Discrete Algorithms, SODA 2010, pp. 1468–1480. Society for Industrial and Applied Mathematics, USA (2010)

22. Micciancio, D., Walter, M.: Practical, predictable lattice basis reduction. In: Fischlin, M., Coron, J.-S. (eds.) EUROCRYPT 2016. LNCS, vol. 9665, pp. 820–849. Springer, Heidelberg (2016). https://doi.org/10.1007/978-3-662-49890-3_31

23. Nguyen, P.Q., Vidick, T.: Sieve algorithms for the shortest vector problem are practical. J. Math. Cryptol. **2**(2), 181–207 (2008)

24. Prest, T.,et al.: Falcon: Fast-Fourier Lattice-based Compact Signatures over NTRU, p. 67. falcon-sifn.info (2020)

25. Schnorr, C.P., Euchner, M.: Lattice basis reduction: improved practical algorithms and solving subset sum problems. In: Budach, L. (ed.) Fundamentals of Computation Theory. Lecture Notes in Computer Science, pp. 68–85. Springer, Berlin, Heidelberg (1991). https://doi.org/10.1007/BF01581144

26. Shor, P.W.: Polynomial-time algorithms for prime factorization and discrete logarithms on a quantum computer. SIAM J. Comput. **26**(5), 1484–1509 (1997)

27. Wang, L., Wang, Y., Wang, B.: A trade-off SVP-solving strategy based on a sharper pnj-BKZ simulator. In: Proceedings of the 2023 ACM Asia Conference on Computer and Communications Security, ASIA CCS 2023, pp. 664–677. Association for Computing Machinery, New York, NY, USA, (2023)

28. Xia, W., Wang, L., GengWang, Gu, D., Wang, B.: Improved progressive BKZ with lattice sieving and a two-step mode for solving USVP. Cryptology ePrint Archive, Paper 2022/1343 (2022). https://eprint.iacr.org/2022/1343

Author Index

M.-J. Saarinen and D. Smith-Tone (Eds.): PQCrypto 2024, LNCS 14771, pp. 433–434, 2024.
https://doi.org/10.1007/978-3-031-62743-9

Printed in the United States
by Baker & Taylor Publisher Services

Printed in the United States
by Baker & Taylor Publisher Services